THE SECOND EMPIRE

EMPEROR NAPOLEON III

From the Portrait by Flandrin

THE SECOND EMPIRE

BY
OCTAVE AUBRY

TRANSLATED BY
ARTHUR LIVINGSTON

27 ILLUSTRATIONS

J. B. LIPPINCOTT COMPANY
PHILADELPHIA   NEW YORK

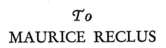

To
MAURICE RECLUS

CONTENTS

CONTENTS

ILLUSTRATIONS

THE SECOND EMPIRE

CHAPTER I

Oath of Office

It was late afternoon on a Wednesday, December 20, 1848. In awed silence the National Assembly watched a short little man make his way towards the speaker's platform. He was dressed in a black swallow-tail. The badge of the Légion d'honneur glittered on his chest. As he walked along he twirled the points of a brown mustache but not, apparently, in nervousness. Sideburns and a goatee suggested a retired officer of the Empire. He looked still young. His pale face gave an impression of gentleness. Reaching the top of the steps he turned and faced the Assembly, motionless, expectant, his blue eyes half-closed.

Armand Marrast, the chairman of the Assembly, rapped on his table with a paper-cutter and proceeded to read the oath of office of a president of the Second Republic:

"In the presence of God and of the French people here represented in its National Assembly I swear fidelity to the democratic Republic one and indivisible, and to fulfill all the duties laid upon me by the Constitution."

Just then a gun thundered at the Invalides. Louis Napoleon raised a white-gloved hand and answered:

"I swear."

Marrast was an adversary whom the Prince's victory at the polls had not disconcerted. In a threatening tone he commented:

"We have God and men as witnesses to the oath that has just been taken."

There were signs of restlessness on the Left, but Boulay de la Meurthe called out:

"He's an honest man. He will keep his oath."

It had been assumed that the Prince would at once return to his seat on the Floor. Instead he drew a folded sheet of paper from

11

a pocket and began to read, slowly, without gestures, and in a voice that had a heavy German accent:

"The ballots of the nation and the oath I have just taken are to control my future conduct. My duty is laid out for me. I shall do it as a man of honor. I shall regard as enemies of the country any persons who might be disposed to change by illegal means what France as a whole has decided. . . ." A number of promises followed, remarks about a progressive republic that would subordinate party prejudices to the general welfare—all pretty vague. Finally a last sentence: "God helping, we shall do good things if we are not able to do great things. . . ."

Jerome Bonaparte, the sometime king, and his daughter Mathilde, the Princess Demidoff, were sitting in the section reserved for ex-deputies. They listened to their respective nephew and cousin, stunned, disappointed. The hall was dark save for, here and there, splashes of yellow glow that seemed to hang about the great oil lamps. As Louis Napoleon ended his speech and folded up the sheet of paper, there was applause, not very enthusiastic. Then, instinctively, the representatives rose to their feet and gave a mighty cheer:

"Long live the Republic!"

It was a rather noble moment. The Assembly of 1848 was not the Convention. It was never to strike tragic or passionate attitudes; but apart from the leaders, who were looking out for themselves as a matter of habit or of political ambition, the representatives were almost all men of good faith, loyal to principles and devoted to their country. Republicans or liegemen of the former monarchies as they may have been, they were suspicious of this mushroom that had sprouted overnight from the mycelium of the Empire, this pretender, disguised as a plain man, whom universal suffrage had placed at the head of France for four years to come. Nevertheless many of them sighed with relief. Such an unimpressive individual, this president, so naïvely civilian, with such an uninteresting voice! And a number of them exchanged an old witticism of Thiers:

"An idiot! He can be steered!"

Calmly descending the steps again, Louis Napoleon walked to the Republican section. There sat General Cavaignac, the candidate of the Provisional Government who had been beaten at the polls the day before. The new president held out his hand. Haggard, unshaven, the general looked away, finding something to say to Marie the deputy at the next desk. (That same evening Louis Napoleon was to return to the charge, offering the general the grand cordon of the Légion d'honneur through a common friend, Heeckeren. Again Cavaignac was to refuse.) The Prince turned to Marrast and expressed his thanks in a few words. Then, escorted by dignitaries of the Assembly, he left the Chamber. Outside drums began to beat. The National Guard was drawn up in double file. The Prince walked down between the two lines of soldiers to the gate of the Palais Bourbon. There he entered a coach and with a guard of lancers and dragoons about him drove off along the dark wintry avenue to the Elysée.

That evening Louis Napoleon gave a private dinner at the presidential residence in the room painted by Carle Vernet. His closest intimates were there: his old teacher, Vieillard; the physician Conneau, a friend of his youth; confederates and accomplices of Strasbourg and Boulogne, Persigny, Laity, Vaudrey; recent friends, Edgar Ney, Fleury, Béville. Then the chandeliers in the great halls were lighted for a short general reception. Not a few campaign opponents came to offer congratulations. The Prince greeted them courteously, but with the proper reserve. At the Hôtel de Ville, meantime, jests were being thrown about at his expense. But Marrast, raising a rosy, baby-face in a head that was a mass of gray curls, gave them pause.

"Do not laugh, gentlemen! That man knows all the power that lurks in his name. He knows what he can do, and what he can do he will try to do. . . ."

CHAPTER II

The Man with a Name

LOUIS NAPOLEON'S PICTURE WAS TO BE SEEN IN ALL SHOP-WINDOWS in Paris. He had been born in that city just forty years before. It was commonly asserted that he was not the son of Louis Bonaparte, younger brother of the great Napoleon and former King of Holland. Gossip noted certain significant facts about the Prince's birth. Hortense de Beauharnais, like her mother, the attractive Josephine, had had numbers of amorous adventures. Figuring back from the day of Louis Napoleon's birth, April 20, 1808, one reached some such date as July 27, 1807. At that time Hortense was travelling in the Pyrenees to recuperate from the shock of her first son's death. She could not have seen her husband between July 6th, when he left her to begin a course of baths at Ussat, and August 12th, when he joined her again at Toulouse. In the meantime, she had been much with her equerry, Charles Van Bylandt, who, throughout the rest of her life, was to remain a close and devoted friend. Was Louis Napoleon the son of this Dutch courtier? For him to belong to Louis Bonaparte one would have to assume a prematurity of birth of some nineteen days—a thing by no means impossible. In fact, the child was very frail and for some days was kept in cotton soaked in wine. On the other hand, there is a strange inadvertence in the memoirs of the Queen of Holland (II, 1): "I had only eight more days to go. . . ." In that she would have been counting from a day eleven days before her reunion with her husband (a slip in arithmetic?). King Louis, for his part, long denied, and in the most brutal terms, that the child was his. He went so far as to write to Pope Gregory XVI: "I am married to a Messalina who breeds. . . ." (*"J'ai épousé une Messaline qui accouche. . . ."*) He took no interest in this doubtful scion, leaving him entirely to the mother. But then again, Louis Bonaparte was a man of a jealous, unhappy

14

disposition, ready to suspect the worst of others; and, eventually, when the child became his sole heir, he was to change tack, as came easy to him, and show the youth real marks of affection.

Gossip, of course, did not reason thus carefully. It gave the Napoleonic pretender impossible fathers—Admiral Van Huell, and then the Admiral's brother, Decazes, a diplomat. As for the first, the Admiral, he was at The Hague at the time of the Prince's conception. The second was an obese, grotesque individual, hardly the type to have caught the roving eye of Hortense. It is known that Decazes, at the critical period, was plunged in sincerest mourning for the very recent death of his young wife.

Hortense reared her child, first in the little castle at Arenenberg, on the Lake of Constance, where she had thought of settling after the fall of the Empire; then at Augsburg. The little Prince was slow, absent-minded, sensitive. His mother called him "Oui-oui" and "little darling-obstinate." At twelve he was given a tutor, Philippe Le Bas, an ingenuous, tiresome republican, son of the Conventionist. Le Bas helped him through grammar-school at Augsburg. So, with some important deficiencies, he managed to get an education, especially in the sciences and with a European rather than a French outlook. The French language he never mastered, always writing it without inspiration, thinking in German. He knew Italian and some little English. He could draw skillfully and was outstanding in physical amusements—swimming, dancing, fencing, riding. The youth was like the child—obstinate, dreamy, affectionate. He had inherited the engaging charm of his mother. All who came to know him liked him.

In the course of several trips to Italy he established contacts with the Bonaparte family at large; then, in the autumn of 1827, he became fast friends with the young Count Arese, an enthusiastic patriot. A number of first love affairs fall in this interval, for he was of a precociously passionate nature. Freed of the exacting Le Bas, he was sent to the military academy at Thun, in Switzerland, studying under the supervision of Vieillard, a retired artillery officer, who was a disciple of Auguste Comte. The Prince thought for a time of joining the Russian army in the war against Turkey. Louis, the ex-King, vetoed that proposal, so the young man drifted along, reading, making love and corresponding with his elder brother, who was in business in Florence. The two boys shared grand dreams of a future in politics. Secretly they joined the Carbonari and talked of freeing Italy, where the great Napoleon was still remembered with wistful longing as a first national king.

The crisis of 1830 kindled high hopes in the young conspirators, but they were disappointed. Louis Philippe, the Orleanist, walked away with the French crown, while Metternich tightened his clutch upon the Duke of Reichstadt, whom France seemed, early in August, about to call to the throne. But excitement in Italy reached a higher pitch and died down more slowly. Riots against Austrian rule broke out all over the peninsula. The Pope's police chased Louis Napoleon from Rome. The Bonaparte clan had definitely retired from glory and was looking to its ease. It was with general family disapproval that the two boys joined the insurrection in Romagna. Side by side they fired upon the Papal troops, and Louis Napoleon even seized the town of Civita Castellana. At his side fell a man who had served in the Grand Army and made the retreat from Moscow—one Andrea Orsini. Orsini's son was to appear at a later moment in the Prince's life. In February, 1831, the movement in Romagna seemed about to succeed. Then Gregory XVI called Austria to his aid. The Revolution recoiled before those white-coated regulars who had known real war. The two princes fled towards Forlì, leading a handful of men. During the retreat, the elder brother was shot through the heart either by a traitor or by a camp thief. To protect the mother it was reported that the boy had died of measles, which was epidemic in the region [1]—Louis himself came down with it. Hortense rushed to his aid, saved him, took him to Ancona and thence to Paris, boldly placing herself under the protection of Louis Philippe. Looking out from their windows on the 5th of May, mother and son could see the great pile of wreaths and emblems which the veterans of the Grand Army, unfailingly loyal to the Emperor, heaped about the pedestal of the Vendôme column still without its statue. Cordial at first, the King eventually grew nervous. Hortense and Louis were asked to make their stay in Paris as short as convenient. They journeyed on to England and thence returned to Arenenberg.

The brother's death promoted Louis Napoleon from his obscure

[1] The story has few defenders today. The Empress Eugénie, Arese and Dr. Conneau asserted that Hortense's eldest son had been assassinated. Valérie Mazuyer's Memoirs were first published in their complete form by M. Jean Bourguignon. They make out a good case for the theory of a Carbonaro vendetta.

position as a junior. A year later the fatal illness of the King of
Rome marked him as the obvious heir of the martyr of St. Helena.
The Emperor's brothers were passing into an inert old age. The
young man could feel the whole future of the Bonapartes weighing
upon his shoulders, a future that was uncertain but of limitless possibilities. He set out to prepare for them with a calm attentiveness
that was never to falter.

In his Swiss hermitage, perched high above the Lake of Constance, he reread Las Cases' *Mémorial,* learning long passages of it
by heart. He studied military history and crammed himself with
half-digested economic and social theories. He printed two pamphlets—"Political Reveries" and "Thoughts on Switzerland," then
an "Artilleryman's Handbook." He cultivated correspondence with
all liberal leaders, whether republican or Bonapartist, whom he
could reach. La Fayette liked him. He interested Chateaubriand.
About him now were his mother, who had mended her frivolous
ways and was showing herself a sober, intelligent, even superior
woman, patient and ambitious; then a number of forlorn hopes
of the imperial cause, Parquin, an old veteran, Mocquard, a young
lawyer and an enthusiast, Persigny—the perfect Friday for a Robin-
son Crusoe of history, who was perhaps closest of them all to the
Prince. In that company Louis Napoleon looked ever forward to a
day when he would be able to strike a chord in French emotion
by sounding his incomparable name. Sooner or later, he was sure,
the day would come. Slipping free from his tomb in the deep Atlantic the spirit of the great Napoleon was stalking the country.
In every peasant's cottage, in the lowliest hovels, chromos of the
"Battle of Austerlitz," of the "Farewell at Fontainebleau," flanked
the holy Easter sprays of box. A poignant mourning, a resolute
affection, was stirring in the hearts of the people, ennobling them.
Forgetting the hosts of dead and the heartaches of an older generation, the nation was now throbbing with memories of a glory that
was no more. In the eyes of France, and indeed of Europe, Napoleon had become an avenging, invincible idea, the idea of Revolution, of Freedom, of a nation's right which the kings had flouted.

Of what avail against such magic was the shrewdness of a government that had no idea except material prosperity, no ideal except
comfort in peace? For ten years Louis Philippe tottered on an ill-
won throne. Riots in Paris every spring, grumblings in Lyons, rest-

lessness in the Vendée! Secret societies dug under-ground in all directions—a good seventy of them have been listed, not counting the Freemasons: Friends of Truth, Friends of the People, societies of Progress, of Political Prisoners, of Families, of the Seasons, of Regenerate Franks, of Gauls. Plot followed on plot. Conspiracy was everywhere. Conspiracy, moreover, was something that Louis Napoleon had in his blood. Romantic, melodramatic, he liked schemes that involved secrecy and which promised silent achievement of catastrophic purposes. Danger had no terrors for him. In devoting his life to a glorious emprise he did not stop to ask whether the combat might require of him more intelligence and more resources than he possessed. Let the occasion offer, with its twin risk of victory or ruin, and he would be ready!

He was ready in the fall of 1836. With Parquin and Persigny and without his mother's knowledge, he made a sudden descent on Strasbourg, where he had already won the support of Colonel Vaudrey (a hero of Waterloo now in command of Napoleon's old regiment, the Fourth Artillery), a young lieutenant, Laity, and a number of other army officers. At daybreak on October 31st, wearing a captain's uniform, the Prince appeared before the cannoneers and addressed them, holding in hand a flag topped with an eagle. It was not a very stirring speech, but the soldiers answered: "Long live the Emperor!" However, the division commander, Voirol, was loyal to his duty and halted the mutiny. The infantry closed in about the artillerymen. There was a scuffle in which the eagle fell to the ground. Louis Napoleon ended under arrest and was led away to prison.

On learning of what had happened Hortense had visions of her boy standing in front of a firing squad. She rushed to Paris to beg mercy of Louis Philippe for her last remaining child. The King was kind and also diplomatic. He stopped at putting the pretender aboard ship for the New World.

The young man spent some months in the United States. Then he hurried back to Europe to be present at the deathbed of his mother. The French government shortly demanded his expulsion from Switzerland. That was a mistake as lending importance to the madcap of Strasbourg. Louis Napoleon went to London to lead a life of fashionable dissipation, a Byronian dandy well calculated to inspire Disraeli with a bad novel, *Endymion*. In three years' time he had run through Hortense's fortune. She had left him an income of about 120,000 francs. Mme. Salvage, Hortense's executrix, allowed him to see a letter which the dying ex-queen had written to Morny. That was the first knowledge the Prince had had of the existence of this half-brother. He expressed himself as grieved and shocked at the discovery.

But life in London was not all amusement. Louis Napoleon worked. His friends Vaudrey, Persigny and Conneau had joined him. With them he kept in touch with European opinion, corresponding meantime with the secret societies and trying to learn how to speak and write better French. He bought the support of two newspapers in Paris; the *Capitole* and the *Commerce*. In order "to prove" as he said, that he "was not just a soldier of fortune" (*un hussard aventureux*), he published, in 1839, a book that was to attract some attention, *Idées napoléoniennes*.

From the acts and alleged opinions of the Emperor, Louis Napoleon concocted a body of doctrine that was somewhat arbitrary, to tell the truth, but was not without its attractive sides. The Napoleonic spirit, he contended, was alone able to reconcile freedom for the peoples with orderly and efficient government. Peace in Europe could be based only on the liberation and regrouping of nationalities. Individual prosperity could be guaranteed by far-reaching economic reforms. Pauperism could be abolished by turning the working classes into property-holders—unused lands being handed over to them. The arbitrary powers of employers over labor should be more closely watched by the State. Free trade would provide an easy living for the consumer while increasing profits for the producer. Napoleon's ideas? Not at all! No one could seriously have imagined they were. They were the ideas of the great man's nephew, masquerading, as the nephew himself was, under an illustrious name. To his generation this factitious Napoleon was offering not the adventure of military conquest, but the adventure, perhaps even more hazardous, of social reform.

The ministers of Louis Philippe could shrug their shoulders all they pleased: this imperialist fire-raft had been launched at a moment of danger for the monarchy. Thiers had just obtained consent to the Return of the Ashes. Napoleon was to be rescued from St. Helena and laid to sleep in the Invalides. Many heads were heating at the thought of the triumph that awaited the great man, dead, indeed, but so very much alive. Sober thinkers saw only a political manoeuvre in the whole noisy business, but sober thinkers are the ones who are almost always wrong. Lunatic? Louis Napoleon might well be one; but give him time, and not such a very long time, and the lunatic would prove to have been the prophet.

With the idea of turning the public excitement to good account, the pretender tried a new surprise, but with inadequate preparation and with ridiculous support. On the 6th of August, 1840, he landed at Wimereux with a boatload of enthusiasts, among them Parquin, Ornano, Montholon, Conneau. Advancing on Boulogne he made his way into the barracks of the Forty-Second Infantry. There, as at Strasbourg, a cool-headed officer nipped the *pronunciamiento* in the bud. Shouldered out of the barracks, the Prince and his party tried to enter Upper Boulogne, but that attack also failed. A brigade of the Forty-Second and the local National Guard started in pursuit. The raiders dispersed and made for their boat on the shore. Louis Napoleon was for staging a dramatic death, since, in the course of considerable shooting, a number of his men had been hit. His comrades dragged him away. However, their boat capsized in the surf. They were picked up and brought ashore under arrest. The Prince was taken first to the Castle in Boulogne. Later he was transferred to the Conciergerie in Paris.

The Strasbourg raid had been more or less carefully planned and might have succeeded. The Boulogne affair was absurd from beginning to end. The press both in France and abroad referred to it contemptuously. Louis Philippe should have taken advantage of that state of opinion and released the buffoon who had made the imperial movement ridiculous. Ill-advised by Thiers and Guizot he decided, instead, to send the case to the Court of Peers. Nothing could have been more to the liking of the pretender than a trial in the full public gaze. It was a chance to take a stand before national opinion. Examined by the chancellor, Pasquier, he answered with self-possessed impertinence:

"Here before you, gentlemen, I represent a principle, a cause, a defeat. The principle is the sovereignty of the people; the cause is the cause of the Empire; the defeat is Waterloo. The principle you have recognized; the cause you have served; the defeat you are going to avenge. . . . I cannot recognize any political jurisdiction as the judge of my intentions and acts. Your forms deceive nobody. In the struggle that is opening there is one victor and one vanquished. If you are men of the victor I have no justice to ask of you, and your generosity I spurn."

If the speech angered the Peers it heightened the prince's stature in the eyes of the country. After all, people thought, the man had ideas and had not been afraid to risk his life for them. Despite the effort of his attorney, a Legitimist, Berryer, Louis Napoleon was condemned to imprisonment for life. As the clerk read the sentence the Prince smiled and replied:

"It has often been said, sir, that the word 'impossible' is not French. It is the same, you may be sure, with the words 'for life.'"

He divided what money he had among his friends and entered the fortress at Ham without a penny. On that very day the frigate *Belle Poule* arrived off Jamestown at St. Helena to bring the Emperor's body home to France.

CHAPTER III

1848

In company with Montholon and Conneau Louis Napoleon was to stay in his prison at Ham for six years. He was otherwise treated leniently. He was allowed to receive visits from anyone he pleased. Most of the time he spent reading, filling in many serious gaps in his education. Ham, as he was to say later on, was his university course. His interest in political economy and in the sciences increased and deepened. He annotated Saint-Simon, Proudhon and Fourier, and without abandoning his own principles opened correspondence with such democrats as Quinet, Michelet, Carnot. To George Sand he wrote (Jan. 24, 1845): "I want liberty and I want power too; but I would rather die in prison than owe my throne to a lie. I am not a republican, because in a monarchical Europe and in view of party divisions I think a republic is impossible today."

Frankness of that sort, one might remark, belongs to no vulgar spirit; and with the same straightforwardness he said to Louis Blanc, whom he had asked to come and see him: "My creed is the Empire. I am convinced that the country wants the Empire." In the field of science he peppered the rural magazines with articles—articles on "Electricity," on "Beet-sugar," on "The Nicaragua Canal." As the years dragged wearily along he seemed never to lose faith in his cause. To be sure he had moments of dejection, but he was young and he felt certain that the future would repay him for everything.

Meantime he could see the July Monarchy slowly rotting away in moral prostration, political scandals, abjectness before the foreigner. "France is bored!" exclaimed Lamartine. France was worse than bored. France was nauseated. The junior monarchy had sinned of the Spirit. Louis Philippe had much good sense, but he was far from having enough imagination. Those defects were to dethrone

22

him. A host of theorists and thinkers had been sapping the foundations of bourgeois society ever since 1830, and the crisis was nearing. Saint-Simon and Enfantin were dreamers, but their disciples
were to obtain far-reaching practical results when they ceased pursuing phantoms. Then there were Fourier, with his phalanstery,
Cabet with his Icaria, Proudhon with his vapory communism,
Leroux with his foggy humanitarianism, Louis Blanc with his
opiniated collectivism. The poets and writers came trooping to the
flag of revolt: Lamennais, a great soul disgusted with dogma;
Quinet, a philosopher• of history; the fiery, nervous Michelet;
George Sand the priestess of feminism and the propagandist of social regeneration. From all that activity a current of ideas and emotions issued which only the greatest political wisdom, seconded by
no little good luck, would have been able to attenuate and absorb.

Louis Napoleon could sense the upheaval from the depth of his
fortress. Was he to wait for it at Ham? Was he not in danger of
being forgotten? Was it not time for him to be recovering his freedom of action? He grew restless, impatient. Early in 1846 (January
14th) he petitioned the government to release him on the ground
that he needed to go to Florence to be present at the deathbed of
his father, the sometime King of Holland. The ministry expressed
its willingness to consent but only in exchange for a humiliating
avowal. The Prince refused:

"I shall leave Ham only for the cemetery or for the Tuileries."

Doubtless from this incident came the abiding aversion, indeed
hatred, that he had for the House of Orléans.

Thereupon his thoughts turned to escape and he made up his
mind to risk the effort. He had no money, but, by an operation that
had its questionable aspects, he managed to procure a loan of
150,000 francs from the Duke of Brunswick. On May 25, 1846, in
a workman's clothes, and with soiled face and hands, he slipped by
his guards, escaped from the fortress and reached first Brussels and
then London.

The death of the ex-King Louis had now provided him with an-
other fortune to squander. He resumed his life as a London dandy.
During these next two years which he spent in England he was to
be in intimate association with the Rowles family of Camden Place,
Chislehurst (the house to which he was to return in 1871). From the
Rowles' was to come some of the money with which he financed his

presidential campaign in France. He carried on a semi-serious flirtation with Emily Rowles, who was later on to marry the Marquis Campana. (The Campana art collections Napoleon III was to buy for the Louvre at the suggestion of Mme. Cornu.) Meantime his eyes were on Paris.

"Fortune has betrayed me twice," he said. "I shall be all the more certain to win next time."

And in that he was right.

Tocqueville declared the fall of the Orleanists imminent as early as January, 1848, and the young Renan wrote:

"This royal dotard, resting wearily on a bed of superannuated hopes, has now but one real concern—the interests of his dynasty."

The revolutionary virus, compounded of republican, Bonapartist and Masonic infections, was festering into sores on all hands. Disdainful, icy, Guizot forbade the holding of a banquet, and barricades began to sprout from the Paris pavements. Louis Philippe, refusing to grant inevitable reforms, blew the sand from one of his signatures and remarked to Horace Vernet:

"When I choose to, I will dispose of them like that."

Then suddenly panic! The King decided to restore power to Thiers, but the "insect-Mirabeau," as Mme. de Genlis called him, offered a devotion that was a matter of words. A mob of men in caps, blouses and overalls gathered in front of the Ministry of Foreign Affairs, singing the *Marseillaise* arm in arm, while Guizot, who had been dismissed, was packing his belongings. A designing trouble-maker fired a pistol at the guard. The answer was a volley. Fifty dead! The mob dispersed with cries of horror, then it reformed, raging, gathered up the dead. Sixteen bodies were piled into a cart, which moved off down the boulevard, spattering the pavement with revolting blotches of blood. A milling procession of torches followed in a whirlwind of fury.

"To arms! For our murdered brothers!"

The mob became a tidal wave. The workingmen of the Bastille district gathered, arms in hand, and chanted the chorus of the *Song of the Girondins*.

The King saw the danger but shrank from using force.

"Then Your Majesty is done for!" said Bugeaud.

At the July Column the mob was crying: "Long live the Republic!", and at the Vendôme Column, "Long live the Emperor!"

Louis Philippe had too keen a memory of the great Revolution. He pictured that 24th of February as the 10th of August. At the urging of the overbearing Emile de Girardin, and of his two sons, the Dukes of Nemours and Montpensier, and finding about him, furthermore, only cowardice or treachery, he finally signed his abdication. Then, with his aged queen, the only cool head in the lot, he climbed into a carriage and drove away, while the mob, bent on plunder, streamed into the Tuileries and the Palais Royal.

Never did a throne fall so uninspiringly. Never was a royal family, with a fairly good record for achievement, so basely deserted. Never was a revolution more grossly fraught with thoughtlessness and peril.

"Friends," called the aged King from his half-open carriage door, "France is yours!"

And into what hands, in truth, was he commending her! The next day the regency of the Duchess of Orléans was discarded, thanks to Ledru-Rollin and Lamartine. In the Hôtel de Ville a provisional government was made up from the veriest scum of the gutters. Pressure from the mobs, along with the influence of Louis Blanc, a diminutive prophet with a woman's face, gave the revolution a social aspect—proclamation of the right to work, workingmen's relief, national workshops, abolition of taxes. Red flags waved over the crowds. The red flag had been a national emblem in France since the time of Charles VII. Now it became the symbol of social extremism. Lamartine, with his pigtail standing out horizontal in the wind, drove it into hiding with an eloquent phrase and saved the day for the tricolor of Valmy and Austerlitz.

These mobs were made up of violent but honest people led by leaders who were almost all sincere but were living in the clouds of one utopian illusion after another. Of these leaders, Dupont de l'Eure was an aged dotard whom everyone respected and no one heeded; Lamartine was gallant, chivalrous, but too eager to please the masses; Garnier-Pagès was a bloodless individual with a lowering eye, who liked to gabble all the time. Ledru-Rollin, fat, ruddy, athletic, saw himself in the rôle of a Danton. Jules Favre was a witless lawyer always ready with a sobbing peroration. Marie was a tense, worried, bitter individual. Crémieux, apish, grimacing, was so uncertain of his views that he looked like a selfish opportunist to everyone. Albert was a naïve labor leader fresh from the factory. Raspail and Arago were scholars who had lost their way into the political clubs and seemed out of place there. Barbès was a high-minded creole who had been freed from the jails of Louis Philippe. Blanqui was a sort of ascetic corpse that seemed to stalk vampire-like from conspiracy to conspiracy.

In this romantic revolution sentiment was overwhelmingly to the fore. In other words, humanitarian enthusiasms, noble intentions and avowals, boundless hopes were expressed in fiery declamations. Anything suggesting rationality, consideration for public interest, a sense of sound politics, struck as it were a false, chilling note. Lamartine had foretold a revolution of contempt. What eventuated was a revolution of illusions of a motley democratic hue. Thiers wrote: "I will have none of the possible restorations. The day of kings has passed." Falloux declared that "the people of Paris had made their victory a sacred rite." The Duke of Mouchy "accepted the Republic with all its social implications." Rouher judged the clubs "indispensable" and exclaimed: "Everything for and by the people!" Ségur d'Aguesseau protested his "unalterable devotion to the Republic." Montalembert excitedly came out for "the divine right of nationalities." [1] Socialism, along the lines of Fourier, looked like a mystic promise held out to masses that had been too long and too unfairly distressed. Even the conservatives, along with the legitimists themselves, dared not resist the rising socialist tide. Clergy, bureaucracy, army, society, all climbed on the band wagon immediately, unanimously. All readily, nay eagerly, came to terms till such time as realities would blow the fogs away.

But brotherly love was not the only sentiment to be sweeping France. Disorder and hatred were in control in many districts. The anarchy spread to laboring centers. Factories were destroyed at Romilly, Rethel, Rheims. Rails were torn up on several railroad lines. Four bridges were blown up in the neighborhood of Paris (at Bezons, Nanterre, Chatou and Meulan). Convents were raided and plundered. State forests were felled in the Pyrenees and the wood carried off. Lands were seized and occupied by peasants in the Var and the Nièvre. Tax offices were raided and tax lists and records destroyed at Saint-Dizier, at Castres, in the Cher. In some cities the extremists managed to break up discipline in army garrisons.

Louis Napoleon concluded a little too soon that his hour had

[1] Bertaut, *1848 et la seconde République,* 178 f.

struck. He packed his bag in London and came hurrying to Vieil-lard's house in Paris "to enlist under the colors of the Republic." The Republic sent him back to England by return train, Lamartine warning Persigny privately that a warrant for an arrest was out.

A period of chaos followed. The eleven provisional dictators, from Ledru-Rollin to Arago, from Marrast to Crémieux, from Garnier-Pagès to Albert, began to snarl and tear at each other. Under the ever-present threat of the Paris mob—for the mud that had spurted from the sewers refused to drain back through the gutters—the coalition of one day became the ball of hissing snakes of the next. The business panic assumed catastrophic proportions. There was a moratorium on debts. Factories ceased operations. Trade negotiations halted. Money went into hiding. The govern-ment's measures were of little avail. Fiat money was made obliga-tory tender. In order to get a little cash into the treasury the direct tax was raised by half a franc. But public confidence was too far shaken. Mistrust and disorganization reigned everywhere. Already the provinces were quivering with alarm. The steadier portions of the public yearned wistfully for the authoritarianism that had gone into exile.

That frame of mind became apparent in the April elections (1848) which gave the National Assembly a majority of purely nominal republicans, men who knew little about public affairs but were resolved to rescue France from demagoguery. Louis Napoleon was not a candidate, but two of his cousins, Pierre Bonaparte, son of Lucien, and Napoleon, son of Jerome, ran on a Rightist platform and were elected, and so was Lucien Murat.

In June a second series of by-elections came. This time the Prince entered the lists and he was elected in four different depart-ments. Lamartine tried to prevent ratification of his election and placed Persigny and Laity under arrest (June 12th). However, Louis Blanc declaimed:

"Let the Emperor's nephew expose himself to the sunlight of our Republic, and he will evaporate in its rays."

Jules Favre also put in a word.

The Prince was seated. Unfortunately for him, however, his partisans made too much noise over their victory. They gathered in crowds at the gate of the Palais Bourbon, shouting *"Vive l'Empereur!"* The democrats stormed in answer and General

Cavaignac rattled the sword. Louis Napoleon therefore resigned, with a letter, which, by its haughty tone, enraged the republicans:

"My name is synonymous with order, nationality and glory. . . . If the people lays duties upon me I shall find a way to live up to them."

The episode raised his prestige in the eyes of the public, while the governing Commission, now made up of Lamartine, Arago, Marie, Garnier-Pagès and Ledru-Rollin, was rushed from one unsolvable difficulty into another. Barbès, Blanqui, Pujol and Esquiros, leaders of the extremist parties, made a move to seize power and replace the bourgeois republic with the proletarian republic. Their hooligans and provocateurs worked at the masses. As early as May 15th a mob made its way into the Assembly with cries of "Long live Poland!" The "socials" almost walked away with things that day. Later, on June 13th, Changarnier was called upon to handle a riot stirred up by Ledru-Rollin.

Abolition of the national workshops offered a new pretext for the agitators and a wide-spread insurrection broke out on June 23d. The slum districts "went down into the streets," Saint-Antoine, Saint-Marcel, Belleville, La Villette. There was nothing preconcerted about the movement. It had no known leaders. Barbès, Blanqui, Raspail and Albert had been under lock and key at Vincennes since the 15th of May. Louis Blanc stayed quietly indoors. Ledru-Rollin for once sided with the authorities. Thousands of men milled about the squares in midtown chanting "Bread or lead!" in hoarse, disquieting monotony. The Assembly took fright and entrusted full powers to Cavaignac. Thiers had proposed transferring the Assembly to Bourges (He was to think of the same thing twenty years later, in 1871). Cavaignac shouted in reply:

"If the gentleman continues to talk in that language I shall have him shot."

Thiers said no more, but his house in the Place Saint-George was virtually dismantled by a mob (as was also to happen twenty years later under the Commune).

Cavaignac was the son of a regicide of '93. A man of sturdy republican faith, but truculent, he was a soldier of the Plutarchian type. Offered the choice he would have preferred the Republic to his honor. Later on when Cavaignac was shown beaten in the elections of December (1848), one of his intimates, Bastide, came to him and proposed that he seize the dictatorship by force.

"No," the General replied, "I refuse to have anything to do with a *coup d'état,* and I never will have. Liberty cannot be established by despotic measures."

For three days Cavaignac battled fiercely with the riot and finally put it down. It was one of the most savage moments in French history. The "blouses" fought the "liners" tooth and nail, often led by female harpies who seemed to sprout from the gutters to harangue the mobs or even to shoulder guns. Mérimée reports the case of one of them who cut the throat of a captured officer with a kitchen-knife. Victor Hugo tells a story of two prostitutes who mounted a barricade, lifted their skirts and dared the soldiers to fire. They did fire, and the two bodies fell, to lie on top of the barricade till sundown, riddled by musket balls.

But fanaticism was equal on both sides. On July 1st Renan wrote to his sister, Henriette:

"You would not know Paris. The atrocities that have been committed by the victors make one shudder. Along the rues Saint-Martin and Saint-Antoine every house has been cannonaded. All the windows and steel window coverings have been riddled with musket balls."

A young Russian, Paul Annenkov, recounts as an eyewitness in his letters:

"The sand and litter on the streets turned to mire from the blood. . . . The cavalry was bivouacking in the open and the streets were filled with hay and straw. One could hardly breathe in the neighborhood of the Tuileries from the smell of the piles of dead. Fifteen hundred prisoners were locked up there in the cellars. The few who managed to make their way to freedom were hunted through the neighborhood like wild beasts." [1]

Trying to interpose with a call for peace between a platoon of soldiers and a mob General Bréa was treacherously seized by the soldiers, stood against a wall and shot at point blank range, his body being literally blown to pieces. Monsignor Affre, Archbishop of Paris, put on his violet robes and went, crucifix in hand, to the Faubourg Saint-Antoine to halt the massacre. He fell a martyr.

[1] *Istoritcheski Sbornik,* 1936.

"The Republic is lucky," muttered Louis Philippe in his refuge at Claremont. "It can use guns on the people."

In fact, it was easier for the Republic to kill than it had been for the monarchies, and it was not blamed so long or so bitterly for killing. The "days of June" drove the middle classes wild. Moderates were overawed and in fear for themselves said nothing. Fifteen thousand dead lay on the streets, not counting casualties among the soldiers. Twenty-three thousand arrests were made. About half of those detained were later released, but martial law was maintained and other suspects were taken into custody. Freedom of the press was abolished. There were mass convictions and deportations. Two riot leaders, Lahr and Daix, were condemned to death and guillotined. Others were sentenced to imprisonment for life, still others to long terms. More than four thousand people were sentenced to deportation overseas and about eleven hundred were actually shipped to the tropics.

The country on the whole approved the second White Terror. France was swept by a mighty wave of reaction. The upper and middle bourgeoisie, businessmen, manufacturers, the peasants, no small fraction of the factory hands themselves, were disgusted with disorders, riots, street fighting and pillaging. They drew apart from the "democrats," the "reds," the "bandits," mingling them all under one label as enemies of the social order. The Leftist leaders either went into hiding or fled abroad. Lamartine, heartbroken, could only weep over his lost illusions. Socialism was denounced from every platform. On the other hand, Cavaignac was a marked man. He had been swept, partly by events, partly by temperament, into a sort of red-handed dictatorship. Tightly buttoned in his long coat, pounding the speaker's desk with clenched fist, he overawed the Assembly by sheer threat and intimidation. The country obeyed him but did not love him. "He tracks blood," said the Parisians, pointing in their minds to the footprints that they saw his heavy stride leaving on the sanded pavements.

New by-elections came in September. It was a red-hot campaign. Louis Napoleon's agents bombarded the electorates with circulars, posters, letters. Persigny was in charge of things and committed many imprudences for which the Prince scolded him roundly, "not desiring that any question should be raised as to his devotion to the Republic." Louis Napoleon was elected to the Assembly by five departments. Announcement of the count let pandemonium loose in Paris. Regimental bands paraded the streets, playing the Napoleonic hymn, *Veillons au salut de l'Empire*. Promenaders on the boulevards greeted each other with *Vive Napoléon*. A torchlight procession spontaneously formed and went on a rampage at night. The Prince was cautious. He waited a week before appearing at the Assembly. Modest, unassuming, inconspicuous, he listened to the ratification of his election and then walked to a seat on the Left. Thence he muttered a declaration of loyalty to the Republic.

"The speech of a Swiss!" commented Montalembert.

The next morning's press was either ironical or hostile—it flayed him unmercifully. However, opinion was drifting his way in a mighty, rising tide. An active publicity represented him as a soldier who had risen against the social revolution in defense of order, and the idea sank in. Victor Hugo, to be sure, was shortly to change his tune, but at the moment he effused in the *Evénement:*

"He is not a prince, he is an idea. The man whom the people has just chosen is not the pretender of the fizzle at Boulogne. He is the hero who won at Jena. . . . His candidacy was announced at Austerlitz."

Inspired by Cavaignac, thrown together by Marrast, the Constitution was published on November 4th. It proclaimed the general principles of 1789 and established universal suffrage. As legislative organs there were to be, first, an Assembly of 750 members elected for three years, then a Council of State. In majestic isolation opposite the two houses, in other words against them, stood a president to be elected by popular vote for a period of four years and ineligible for a second term. He was to administer the executive power.

Young Grévy, a parliamentarian with a future, voiced the fear that a dangerous ambition might be free to influence such a president. He thought there should be a plain president of a Council of Ministers, named by the Assembly and removable at any time.

"That means permanent disorder," replied Lasteyrie, and Grévy's amendment was rejected.

Lamartine succeeded in maintaining universal suffrage.

"Let God and the people decide," he declaimed. "Something must be left to Providence!"

In the course of the long debate, the question of "Representative

Louis Bonaparte" was raised by a deputy, Anthony Thouret. The Prince could not make a speech *ex tempore*. He stammered through a few halting sentences that conveyed a protest against the word "pretender" that was constantly being thrown in his face. The Assembly stood aghast at his incompetence, and Ledru-Rollin thundered in his famous clarion voice:

"What an idiot! The man is sunk." (*Quel imbécile! Il est coulé.*)

France was a country where even the leaders of mobs had to be master orators. What was there to fear of a man who could make such a wretched spectacle of himself? Mistrust waned. There would be no trouble after that in keeping such a person in his place! Louis Napoleon's candidacy for the presidency took wing from that otherwise disastrous quarter of an hour!

Fixing his residence in the Rhine Hotel on the Place Vendôme, surrounded by friends old and new, unostentatiously, with his eyes for the most part lowered upon the ash-point of a cigarette, Louis Napoleon began to execute his plans. It was an adroit campaign based on cheerfulness. His platform promised prosperity, progress, peace, for the people.

Mlle. George, Napoleon's old mistress, called on the Prince at the Rhine Hotel. They talked of the Empire. Finally Louis Napoleon took the lady by the hand, led her to a window and pointed toward the Vendôme Column.

"I spend my whole day looking at that!" he said solemnly.

"It's pretty high!" the aged actress replied.

The pretender needed money badly, but money, after all, was available. His mistress, Miss Howard, his cousin, the Princess Mathilde, a banker, Fould, English friends, anonymous donors, supplied the few millions that were absolutely required. There was a Bonapartist organization in all the various departments. These groups intensified activities and doubled enthusiasms. Pamphlets, lithographs, placards, were distributed by the bundle to barracks, town halls, schools. The Prince himself did his utmost to disarm oppositions. The "Committee of the rue de Poitiers" counted among its members all the leaders of the Rightist factions from Odilon Barrot to Montalembert. It hesitated a moment between Louis Napoleon and Cavaignac. The General was inclined to too stiff a republicanism. Louis Napoleon, in contrast, promised everything that was asked of him. He would keep the peace, he would guarantee property rights, he would favor religion, he would rescue the Pope, who had been chased from Rome by his subjects. Good-humoredly he reminded Berryer of the speech he had made in his own defense at the trial in 1840. Bugeaud and Changarnier had thought for a moment of becoming candidates. He persuaded them to hold off. He paid court to Thiers. Seeing that he could have no hope of becoming president, Thiers struck a Warwick pose and offered to write the Prince's campaign platform.

The only real competitor was Cavaignac. The General was making a bitter fight. Backed by the resources of the government he too was playing every card, distributing money, favors, appointments, flooding the departments with laudatory pamphlets. But the odds were all against him. The factory workers did not like the slaughters of the days of June. The peasants bore a grudge for the extra half franc on the tax. The army mourned a glory that seemed to have gone sour in this republican direction. The secret societies, especially Freemasonry, were wholeheartedly for the Prince, viewing the triumph of the sometime Carbonaro as the reward of thirty years of underground intrigue. In the *Presse* Emile de Girardin conducted a violent and unremitting campaign against the General. But all that was nothing. Greater than all other adversaries combined, giving the watchword for the opposition, waving a flag above them, was the Great Ghost of '21, home at last in the Invalides and thence appealing to all Frenchmen for his heir and avenger. The republican General was beaten in advance. What weight would the resolutions of the bourgeois liberals have as against such a call from Caesar?

The other candidates hardly counted. Lamartine was a noble soul and could be said to belong to no party. He was ridiculed, ignored, "relegated to the Muses." Ledru-Rollin and Raspail were there to frighten everybody who was anxious to get away from the revolutionary tradition, and that meant the vast majority in the country.

The voting took place on December 10th in a gay holiday atmosphere. The main results became known on the 13th. Cavaignac received 1,434,226 votes; Ledru-Rollin, 370,119; Raspail, 36,920; Lamartine, 17,910. It was a landslide for Louis Napoleon, with five and a half million votes. Such the response of France to the "days of June" and the menace from the Left! Reaction always seems to rest on excesses in the field of social struggle. Frightened by the spectre of anarchy France had surrendered to the Emperor's nephew, less for what he was in himself than for the name he bore, and all that the name stood for in terms of prestige, authority and . . . Hope!

CHAPTER IV

The Presidency

BOULAY DE LA MEURTHE WAS RIGHT. THE OATH DID BIND THE MAN of honor. This dreamy Beauharnais was a thoroughgoing gentleman. Touched by the wondrous trust that the nation reposed in him, he resolved to live up to his promises. He had promised loyalty to the Republic and he did everything to keep his word. It was no great hardship for that matter. Anxious to fall in exactly with the stride of the first Bonaparte the Prince thought of his presidency as a pendant to the Consulate. The future could take care of itself. The clique about him was set on monarchy, but a return to the Empire still seemed a remote and hazy possibility to him. After all, a Napoleonic republic shaping itself pliantly to a progressing age and to democratic ideas might have even better prospects of succeeding and lasting than a personal régime.

But the compromise Louis Napoleon had in mind presupposed full accord between the executive and the legislative powers, and that was something that he was never to enjoy. For three years— and not seldom through fault of his own—he was to see himself opposed and threatened by Parliament. In the end, when things came to the breaking point, he was to drift under pressure of the people about him into a *coup d'état*.

He assumed power with a quite unusual inexperience. He had had no preparation whatever for the task of governing. His uncle had been schooled in Italy and Egypt. He, Louis Napoleon, had known prison life at Ham and a frivolous butterfly existence in London. He was still little more than a society Lothario and a writer of editorials that were accepted because of his name. However, he had a platform, and around him stood a group of men who had no great scruples and were bent on clothing him with a power which they intended to use for their own purposes.

35

He entered the Elysée with two main lines of policy in mind—order and prosperity at home and, abroad, a restoration of France to the leadership in Europe that she had lost in 1815. The immediate problem, of course, was to make sure of his hold on the government. His personal preference was for a ministry of republicans. However, Cavaignac and Cavaignac's friends shied off.

"It was a bad stroke of luck for me," Napoleon III was to remark later on to Falloux, "that I was unable to begin with a government of republicans and so was forced to put myself into the hands of the rue de Poitiers people." [1]

He turned to Lamartine, but that gentleman could not find the necessary cooperation. Thiers declined the premiership, suggesting a friend of his, Odilon Barrot. Barrot was a parliamentary wiseacre, good-natured, verbose, fatuous. The cabinet he managed to get together showed a strong coloring of Orleanist liberals: Drouyn de Lhuys in Foreign Affairs, Malleville in the Interior, Passy in Finance, Léon Foucher in Public Works. An outstanding Legitimist, the Comte de Falloux, was called to the portfolios of Education and Public Worship. These veteran war-horses of politics looked upon the Prince as a lucky adventurer. They mistrusted him and set out, with Odilon Barrot himself in the lead, to fetter and paralyze him. Deliberately ignored in all transactions of the cabinet, he turned the matter to jest for some days, saying among other things:

"They are trying to make me out the Prince Albert of the Republic."

Then suddenly he lost his temper. Malleville failed to show him current police reports, certain diplomatic correspondence, and the papers of the Boulogne and Strasbourg cases which he had asked for. He addressed a letter to the minister, and its caustic tone caused all the cabinet to resign.

That was going a little too fast and a little too far. Louis Napoleon drew back a step, having, as he was to say, no vanity in matters of state. Actually his position was somewhat precarious. The army at Lyons was in the hands of Marshal Bugeaud and the army in Paris in the hands of General Changarnier. Rebuffed by the moderate republicans and the radicals, the Prince could only come to terms with his ministers. He apologized all around and good-hu-

[1] Falloux, *Mémoires*, I, 522.

moredly. The cabinet came together again, having learned that the president could not be regarded as altogether a figurehead. Malleville, meantime, did not withdraw his resignation, and his friend Bixio went with him. The post in the Interior was assumed by a young deputy, Buffet, before whom a long and brilliant road in politics was opening.

Louis Napoleon set out, doggedly, intelligently, to use his mysterious charm upon the outstanding individuals in the various parties. In some cases the charm worked. Montalembert, for one, succumbed. Berryer held off, and an epigram in verse kept the drawing-rooms laughing over the president's discomfiture:

> En vain l'Empire met du fard:
> On baisse ses yeux et sa robe,
> Et Berryer-Joseph se dérobe
> A Napoléon-Putiphar. . . .[1]

Béranger had been gilding the Legend with sonorous imagery. The Prince called twice at his house at Passy. To the satisfaction of them both, on neither occasion was the poet at home.

The main attack, of course, was upon the army—a Bonaparte could be relied upon to think of that. The President was a frequent visitor at the military schools, the veterans' homes, the barracks, where he messed with the soldiers, talked to them, reviewed them— in the uniform of a general of the National Guard. He cut a majestic figure on horseback. His body was, on the whole, too long for his legs, but in the saddle that defect became an advantage. The Assembly took umbrage at all this parading, and the capital press likewise. Thiers still had illusions of seizing power as late as 1852. He voiced his disapproval of this military attitude upon which he would never himself have dared to venture. Display at the Elysée kept pace along the same lines: liveries, uniforms, coaches decorated with the Imperial escutcheon. Jerome, ex-king and uncle to the President, was named a marshal of France and made governor of the Invalides. On his induction into that office the veterans cried: "Long live the Emperor!" The deputies grumbled, and one of them, Froissart, even went so far as to ask what it all meant. Louis Napoleon smiled, indifferent.

Just then foreign affairs moved into the foreground of public

[1] Vainly the Empire rouges up. Eyes drop, skirts are lowered, and Berryer-Joseph gives the slip to Potiphar-Napoleon.

interest. The storm of 1848 had swept in waves over the whole of Europe, from the Baltic to the Dardanelles, from the Vistula to the Rhine. Bohemia, Hungary, the Austrian capital itself, blew up. For forty years Metternich had been the "coachman of Europe." He now dropped the reins and took to his heels, the Emperor Ferdinand abdicating in favor of his young nephew, Francis Joseph. Germany likewise reared and demanded a liberal government and national unity. The regional monarchs and the free cities feared the worst and granted constitutions to their subjects. Ludwig I of Bavaria had been completely discredited by his passion for a dancer, Lola Montes. He abdicated unconditionally. Barricades in Berlin forced the King of Prussia to send delegates to the Germanic Parliament which had been elected by universal suffrage and assembled at Frankfurt on May 18th.

French public opinion, and Louis Napoleon along with it, was more particularly stirred by events in Italy, a country that stood much closer than Germany to France because of a common Latin background, common historical memories and a common dislike of Austria viewed as an outpost and a stronghold of the Holy Alliance. What was to become of Italy? An instinct seemed to warn the French that the lot of Italy was, for a generation to come, to be the lot of France. French feeling in regard to Italy at the time of the movement of '48 was nobly and significantly expressed in the famous circular which Lamartine sent to French diplomatic agents abroad on behalf of the government:

"The treaties of 1815 have lapsed in law as well as in the eyes of the French government. If it should happen that the hour for reconstituting some oppressed nationality should strike, or that the independent states of Italy should be invaded, the French Republic would think it had a right to take up arms in defense of these legitimate movements of peoples aspiring to be born as nationalities."

So the revolution adopted as its own the policy of "interventionism" in behalf of the independence of nationalities that Napoleon III was to carry to partial triumph in 1859.

Mistress of Lombardo-Venetia Austria had been in full control in the peninsula since 1815. For thirty years the liberals had been grumbling and conspiring against Austrian despotism. Their defeat in 1830 did not discourage them. Secret societies had worked a close-meshed net all over the country. A new pope had just been hailed enthusiastically by the Romans. Metternich, contemptuous, judged the man "a warm heart but a feeble mind."

Actually Pius IX was a quite unusual person. Coming of an ancient family, he had had a youth of brilliant promise. Then an epileptic affliction had turned him from army to church. He crossed the ocean to Chile, and in his pastoral career there showed piety, kindheartedness, courage, three virtues that were basic in his character. Returning to Rome he was made an archbishop at thirty-nine and pope at fifty-four.

He ascended the throne of St. Peter with a mind that opened towards the future and with a sincere desire for reforms. He may have been one of the first to coddle the dream of uniting all Italy under a papal presidency. Unfortunately he was to fall victim to a backward environment which he was not strong enough to master and his efforts were to come to naught. At first a believer in freedom he was eventually to seek refuge in dogma and reject progress. Trials and persecutions were a tonic to his sturdiness. As the stormy seas of the new times broke upon him, he moored his white boat to the Cross. One faith was in his heart and one light before his eyes, so that when temporal possessions were taken from him, he was ready to fence in the highest spiritual authority in the world behind the walls of the Vatican.

He began by promising reforms, and all Italy looked to him as her saviour. News of the fall of Louis Philippe upset the hopes of the sober. The Italian stewpot had boiled too long. It now exploded from pent-up steam. All the reigning sovereigns were overrun. Milan revolted, Brescia rose in riot. Barricades and tricolored flags were everywhere. Marshal Radetzki found it wise to retreat upon the forts of the Quadrilateral. The Dukes of Parma and Modena went into exile. Venice in her turn expelled the *todeschi,* and the republic of the Doges came to life again with Daniele Manin. King in Piedmont was Charles Albert of Savoy, a wavering, inconclusive soul, compounded of a mixture of mysticism and ambition, a liberal in his views of other countries, a despot as regarded his own. He thought the moment had come for him to step forward as leader of the new Italy. He crossed the Ticino on March 29th, won a few preliminary skirmishes and captured the fortress of Peschiera. Milan, the duchies, even far away Sicily, offered their submission to him. *"L'Italia fara da sè,"* he declared haughtily in an historic phrase. Italy would look out for herself! But at the very start a back-wash of jealousies and petty rivalries undermined the leadership of the Italian awakening. Austria had been stunned by the first on-slaught and seemed to lose her head. She now took heart, resigned herself to any sacrifice and resolved to fight. Courage proved to be a better course for her than panic. The Italian nationalists were routed and dispersed on all fronts. Radetzki reoccupied Venetia. Beaten at Custozza Charles Albert evacuated Lombardy and signed a most humiliating truce.

As the democratic flood swept down upon Rome, Pius IX made a first effort to dyke it. He granted a constitution and selected lib-eral ministers, a writer, Terenzio Mamiani and a great lawyer, Rossi. It was all in vain. Mamiani was forced to resign and before long Rossi was assassinated on the steps of the Papal Chancellery. Anarchy reigned in Rome. The Pontiff fled in disguise to Gaeta, in the territory of Naples. A Roman Republic was set up with the hard-headed enthusiast Mazzini acting as chairman of a ruling tri-umvirate (February, 1849).

Louis Napoleon thought of intervening in Italy the very mo-ment of his election to the presidency. He preferred, however, not to come to a hasty decision. He was in an unsound position. His Carbonaro past, his sincere sympathy for the Italian liberals, were at war with his need of retaining the support of Catholics in France and therefore of supporting the Pope. The ministry was divided. Odilon Barrot and Drouyn de Lhuys were hostile to the demagogic government in Rome. They were certain that it would fall of its own weight. Falloux, on the other hand, was for immediate inter-vention. Unable to make up his mind, the Prince thought it best to weigh the various opinions and bide his time.

Events proceeded to clarify the situation. Beset by the revolu-tionaries in Rome and Florence Charles Albert thought he could save his tottering throne by a bold manoeuvre. He ended the truce with Austria and again took the field. But Radetzki crushed him at Novara (March 23d). Having sought vainly to die in the battle the King abdicated in favor of a young son, Victor Emmanuel, and dropped out of sight in Portugal. The White Coats overran the plains of the Po. Brescia fell. The dukes resumed their thrones in Modena and Parma, the Grand Duke in Tuscany. Victory in war was a new experience for Austria. She abused this one. Northern and Central Italy were drawn and quartered. Bologna was taken, and then the Imperials advanced on Rome.

Would they be allowed to settle there as masters? In that case all Italy would be at their mercy. Louis Napoleon had declared for war on the first news of the disaster in Piedmont, and Thiers had had a time of it in restraining him. But the occupation of Rome was too much. Louis Napoleon could not consent to it. Italy lay too close to his heart. Odilon Barrot persuaded the Assembly to authorize the dispatch of an armed force to Civita Vecchia under General Oudinot. Falloux remarked to Veuillot at the time:

"Don't be mistaken as to the Roman expedition. The President is acting against Austria, not for the papacy. In the matter of the Temporal Power he follows the family tradition and cherishes the sentiments of his youth." [1]

The republicans in Rome raised loud cries of treason, and called the adventurer Garibaldi to their aid from the Tyrol where he had been shooting it out with the Austrians. Garibaldi entered the city at the head of a troop of volunteers in red shirts and Catalonian berets. They welcomed Oudinot with solid shot (April 30th) and he had to retreat.

The setback raised a parliamentary storm in Paris. Jules Favre demanded Oudinot's removal from command and the resignation of the ministers.

"French blood," he shouted theatrically, "has been shed for absolutism."

Louis Napoleon shrugged his shoulders. The Assembly was on the point of disbanding, its term expiring within a matter of days. He promised Oudinot to send reenforcements:

"Our honor as soldiers is involved. I shall allow no stain to rest upon it."

Bearer of the letter to Oudinot was an adroit diplomat, Ferdinand de Lesseps, who was given the task of bringing the republicans to an understanding of the French point of view. Lesseps could do nothing with Mazzini. He was shortly called home.

By the time he reached Paris the political atmosphere had changed. A new chamber, the Legislative Assembly, was in session. Uncompromisingly hostile to the Roman Republic it insisted that Pius IX be restored to his throne.

[1] *Mémoires*, II, 129.

The elections of May 13th (1849) had in fact resulted in a land-slide for the parties of reaction. Fear of the "reds" had enabled the Legitimists and Orleanists to seat most of their candidates, so that a Rightist majority of 500 deputies faced 120 socialists, a mere handful of Bonapartists and some 70 moderate republicans. Lamartine, Marrast, Garnier-Pagès, Marie, Dupont de l'Eure, Carnot and Jules Favre, in a word most of the outstanding leaders of '48, had failed of election. The Assembly chose Dupin, an Orleanist, as its president. Dupin was an old political roué who never cared what company he kept. Commenting on the Rightist sweep Falloux was well able to jeer insolently at the Left: "France will have no more of people who have astounded her by their inexperience and incompetence. She wants neither men who can't do anything—nor men who can."

Louis Napoleon was disappointed. The elections seemed to call his own mandate in question. The combined monarchist groups were in a position to squeeze him as in a vise at any moment they chose. What should his policy towards such an Assembly be? Should he play to its factions and work for a split? Should he seek to turn the masses against the deputies while he gained more and more in popular favor? . . . He thought of luring Bugeaud into the premiership, but the marshal refused—a few days before coming down with the cholera. It seemed better, therefore, to halt at a "replastering," with Tocqueville in Foreign Affairs and Dufaure in the Interior, Barrot continuing to wield the gavel.

On the 3rd of June Oudinot carried Villa Pamphili and became virtual master of Rome. The socialists in the Assembly thought their chance had come for making a supreme bid for revolution. On the 11th Ledru-Rollin demanded the impeachment of the president and the ministers for attacking the Roman Republic.

"The Constitution has been violated," he thundered. "We shall defend it at all costs, even by force of arms."

The Assembly angrily defeated his motion, whereupon the Mountain openly set about rousing the mob. Jacobins everywhere came to life in the belief that their hour had struck again. The newspapers of the Left seethed with incendiary editorials. Louis Napoleon replied in tone of earnest admonition:

"It is time that the law-abiding had some of the fun and the trouble-makers some of the worries. The Republic has no enemies more implacable than men who are forever causing disorder, obliging us to keep France an armed camp. . . . This must stop."

The President's declaration made a deep impression. A cholera epidemic was raging. The city lay under a pall of nervous, feverish gloom. At noon on the 13th a procession of agitators and National Guardsmen began moving along the boulevards under the lead of Etienne Arago, shouting for the Roman Republic and the historic Mountain.

Changarnier had been commissioned to preserve the public peace. He planned his procedure down to the last detail. As the mob reached the end of the rue de la Paix he charged with dismounted chasseurs and cavalry. The "reds" were halted and then thrown back. Vainly they tried to impair discipline among the soldiers. "Would you fire on your brothers?" they shouted—but they shouted over their shoulders, in flight. Changarnier followed in pursuit. Aping the Convention a half-century out of season, Ledru-Rollin and some twenty deputies of the Mountain were in session in the Arts and Crafts Building. As the troops drew near they took to their heels, Ledru-Rollin making London and allowing the costs of his folly to be paid by men who were less able than he to look out for themselves.

For that matter the casualties were not serious—seven rioters killed, two soldiers wounded. Late in the afternoon Louis Napoleon appeared in the streets and received an ovation. There were some few disturbances in the provinces, especially at Lyons, where Magnan used cannon on the barricades with a count of 200 dead.

Administration and Assembly both stood ready to strike without mercy: martial law, suspension of the right of free assembly, a Draconian muzzling of the press, a vigorous prosecution of the rioters who had been arrested. Montalembert delivered a forceful speech on the occasion.

"When," he said, "we forget the great law of respect for others, we forget the very premise of freedom. . . . Liberty may be born of revolution, but it can endure only by killing its parent."

Even as he was speaking the Roman Republic breathed its last. After a month's siege Oudinot entered the city in the face of bitter resistance by Garibaldi and restored the sovereignty of the Pope (July 3rd). The French occupation was to last for many years. It tried to be liberal and it was at least considerate; but the pontiff was surrounded by the famous "cardinals in blinders" and followed a policy of stubborn, uncompromising reaction. While still at Gaeta, before entering his own territory, he restored absolutism throughout the Papal States.

Louis Napoleon was quite ready to rescue the Pope, but he feared the wrath of the Roman patriots. While the siege of Rome was in progress, he had a conference with M. de Courcelles, the French ambassador to the Holy See, who was returning to his post. The President suggested that he get in touch "with some of the men I used to know in Italy." Then he checked himself as though aghast at the recollection. Finally he added with a smile: "To be sure, my friends will probably all be on the wrong side!" In his dilemma he resorted to a bold stroke which was understandable enough in the light of his past, but which was hardly consistent with his status as head of a state. To a friend of his, Colonel Edgar Ney, he wrote in his own hand a letter which was designed to serve as a warning to the Roman Curia, but was also calculated to win back the support of the liberals in Italy and of the democrats at home:

"The French Republic has sent an army to Rome not to smother Italian freedom but to organize Italian freedom by saving it from its extravagances. . . . In the days when our armies were marching over all Europe, everywhere as mementoes of their passing they left an abolition of the abuses of feudalism and a sowing of the seed of liberty. It shall not be said that in our day a French army can have acted in any other intent or achieved results at all different."

Wholly at variance with conventional forms, this document is basic in the career of the Prince. It amounted to nothing more nor less than an assumption of personal power. It also brought Italy back to the forefront in French policy. All Europe pricked up its ears. London and Berlin were hostile to Catholicism. They approved. Vienna and St. Petersburg criticized with no mincing of words. In France the democrats applauded, but the Catholics complained. As for the ministry, Tocqueville seemed discouraged.

"This President," said he, "is uncontrollable."

The Pope for his part fell back in anger from Gaeta upon Portici. Resenting the Prince's apparently plain talk he nevertheless brought himself in the end to issuing a *motu proprio* that was designed to reorganize his states. However the reforms that he promulgated were wretchedly inadequate. To make matters worse, Venice had finally surrendered after a gallant resistance and Austria was again trampling Italy underfoot as in the days of Metternich. Dissatisfaction mounted in all French political groups with the sole exception of the blacker Catholics.

The question of paying the bills for the Roman expedition came up for debate in the Legislative Assembly. On that occasion the Odilon Barrot cabinet disavowed "the letter to Edgar Ney," admitting that it was "a trifle brisk." Those stodgy ministers, so unceremonious with the President personally, so contemptuous of the men about him, had often hurt his feelings. He now decided to be rid of them, and informed the Assembly to that effect in a haughty presidential message (October 31st):

"I have been entrusting the management of affairs to men of widely varying views, but that procedure has not achieved the happy results which I expected of it. France is worried because she can perceive no certain policy in all this confusion. She misses the directing hand and will of her choice of December 10th. It is apparent that she can feel that will only if there be complete oneness of thought, outlook and conviction between the President and his ministers. . . . A whole system triumphed on the 10th of December . . . for the name of Napoleon is by itself a platform and a policy. At home that policy means responsibility, authority, religion, prosperity for the people. Abroad it means national dignity. That policy received its mandate through my election, and I intend to carry it to triumph with the help of the Assembly and the people."

A definite breach with parliamentary tradition! A definite inception of personal government! The fact became evident in the choices of new ministers. They were all virtually unknown men: two generals, d'Hautpoul and La Hitte, for War and Foreign Affairs; a banker, Achille Fould, for Finance; a scientist, J. B. Dumas, for Agriculture; a young lawyer of Riom, Rouher, for Justice; a magistrate, Baroche, for the Interior. The Assembly at first looked askance at these upstarts, but the President's spokesmen soon allayed antagonisms with their unassuming ways. The Assembly majority was grimly conservative. The ministry set out to "clean up" in all departments of administration. Office-holders were enjoined to ferret out all revolutionary agents and to bear down upon public opinion in every possible way. The army was taken severely in hand. A tight-meshed net was drawn over all the country. Liberty poles were cut down everywhere. Celebrations of the 24th of February were strictly forbidden.

This ministry of unknowns went even further. The Assembly majority was solidly royalist but divided, some following the Comte de Chambord and others the House of Orleans. There was no agreement even among the majority leaders. Guizot wanted a royalist fusion. Thiers was against any such thing. Molé was satisfied with Louis Napoleon. All the same the majority still expected somehow to effect a compromise that would lead to a restoration of royalty, and the cabinet, for its part, acquiesced in reactionary measures that seemed to prelude such a development: the educational reform bill, and a move from universal to a limited suffrage. As things turned out, these changes were to have profound repercussions, and the Elysée was to manoeuvre with such skill that the responsibility for them, in the eyes of the people, would fall upon the deputies.

The law of the 15th of March (1850) on the freedom of education was drawn up by Falloux and it was to keep his name. It ended the monopoly in education that had been conferred upon the state by Napoleon I and which subsequent régimes had failed to interfere with. By a curious oversight the Restoration simply forgot to restore the right to teach to the clergy. Montalembert passionately voiced the demand under Louis Philippe, but at that time the matter dropped out of sight in a morass of pressing material concerns. Now in order to bar the way to revolution the leaders of the Right set out to reenforce the social influence of the Church by legalizing sectarian education. Montalembert and Father Dupanloup opened the campaign for this basic conservative interest.

Charles de Montalembert, a man of forty, had a mixed background. On his father's side he derived from the old nobility. His mother was English. Once a disciple of Lamennais, he later on offered his submission to the Church and with wholeness of heart. He showed a smooth ascetic face under a shock of long waving hair. Proud, self-assured in his beliefs, he had an eloquence that was warm, ironical, earnest, and at the same time gentle with a touch of bitterness. He was a chivalrous gentleman, a Christian and a patriot. More than that he was passionately fond of politics as a game. A pure reactionary with his eyes on the past, he lived in the light of the past and could see no other light. He thought he had a mission to rescue France from all manners and forms of democratic illusion. He wanted to shackle her in chains, but in chains that would save her soul and give her back her feeling and her respect for the old social rankings. He wanted to erase a century of pride and mockery in France and give the country back to God.

The Falloux Bill Montalembert regarded as a first and necessary stage.

"Society," said he, "is menaced by conspirators from the gutter, by repulsive, insignificant spellbinders. . . . I say that today, even for unbelievers, the priest represents order—moral order, political order, material order. . . . A demoralizing and anarchical army of school-teachers has to be met with an army of priests."

The image of the howling, raging demagoguery that had run riot in '48 was fresh in all those minds. Fear of it, hatred of it, won Montalembert most unexpected support. Thiers was indifferent in matters of faith, but he came out for the bill. Resistance, however, was stubborn on the Left. Victor Hugo had hoped to receive the portfolio of Education in the cabinet of October 31st. Disappointed he turned against the President and fought him through his newspaper, the *Evénement*. He answered Montalembert grandiloquently:

"Men of the clerical party, I will have neither your hand nor your influence upon the rising generations. . . . Your law masquerades as a quest for freedom but it is a design for enslaving. It is a confiscation which you label a gift. . . ."

Barthélemy Saint-Hilaire voiced the alarm of the University.

At that point Thiers intervened. Once the disciple of Talleyrand, the "little minister" of Louis Philippe, had only one love, love of his personal glory—or if glory seem too pretentious a word for such a small man, love of success. Pliant, adroit, sagacious, having already played an important rôle in public life, Thiers wanted to get hold of a still more important one at any price and by whatever means. He thought himself indispensable to France—in that lies his excuse. With a forelock almost white, with two piercing eyes glittering behind his spectacles, he raved on the speaker's platform and in the lobbies like a real devil from Provence. His mind never soared aloft, nor his heart either. But he knew a great deal and he had an uncanny sense of the moment. His high-pitched falsetto voice seemed to break down resistance by a sort of charm, the charm of clarity. He was a born debater, a type which is rare among the French, which one can admire or despise as one may choose, but which always acquires influence and does useful work in parliaments and assemblies.

Armed with a powerful dialectic, Thiers could embrace any cause. On this occasion he played false to his liberalism and pretended to see another Concordat in Falloux's bill.

"Yes," said he, "it is a compromise. . . . In the face of the dangers which threaten society today I extend my hand to men I once fought."

A voice on the Left rose:

"In behalf of a clique?"

The little man drew himself up:

"You say a clique? Society is a clique? The clique you mention, sir, is France!"

The law passed by a big majority. No more "study-certificates," no more state examinations for diplomas in primary schools! The French "baccalaureat" was opened to pupils in clerical seminaries and private schools. Anyone could offer courses in secondary education. All the same supervision by the State was, in a measure, safeguarded. The University was not, as has been claimed, made subject to the Church, but the latter did acquire a voice in University management. It was free to have as many friars' schools and religious private schools as it saw fit.

The suffrage question came next. The Rightists had been clamoring for restrictions on the ballot for a long time. They grew even more vociferous when returns came in from the elections of substitutes for the thirty deputies whom the High Court had barred from the Assembly for participation in the disorders of the 13th of June. In defiance of the conservatives, eighteen representatives of the Mountain were elected in rural France. In Paris, Carnot, Eugène Süe and Paul de Flotte, candidates of the Social Democratic Committee, ran up majorities of 130,000. A new wave of alarm! Public bonds dropped on Exchange.

The general uneasiness drew the Assembly and the Presidency close together. Thiers led "the Burgraves" (leaders of the Right) to the Elysée—Berryer, the Duc de Broglie, Molé, Montalembert,

Buffet, Daru. The President offered Thiers and Molé posts in the ministry, which he said he was determined to make "the stronghold of order." Scenting an Imperialist trap, the Burgraves held off, but, as a means for paralyzing the Mountain, both sides agreed to ask for a revision of the election law.

Baroche presented a bill on May 8th. His idea was to "moralize elections" by keeping from the polls not only men convicted of crimes, but citizens who could not prove three consecutive years of residence in one same district.

"That is violating the Constitution!" cried the deputies of the Left.

"No," sneered the salacious Dupin, "it's merely lifting her skirts a trifle high."

Michel de Bourges threatened the Rightists with civil war. Montalembert replied:

"We want legal war on socialism in order to avoid civil war. Our idea is to meet anarchy with a Roman expedition here at home."

In a carefully worded period Thiers flayed "the despicable mob of louts that had handed the freedom of Rome over to Caesar in exchange for bread and circuses."

The debate was a series of short, violent exchanges in which animosities clashed as steel on steel. But the Right was stubborn. Closure was voted and the law passed (May 31st).

That was the end of the Assembly in the eyes of the French people.

Louis Napoleon hoped that the concessions which his government kept making to the Burgraves would prompt them to greater good will in his regard. He was mistaken. That majority received and never gave. As early as June a sordid conflict spoiled the understanding between the Elysée and the Palais Bourbon. The President's emoluments had been fixed at 1,200,000 francs, but extravagant living, personal publicity expenses and also the needs of a hungry entourage drove Louis Napoleon to incredible financial expedients. Fould, the Finance minister, finally requested a hundred percent "raise" to 2,400,000 francs. The proposal went through, but at the cost of bitter and frankly insolent recriminations, and in the end only because of the acquiescence of Changarnier. Thereupon the Assembly returned to its reactionary haymaking, strengthening its defenses with a number of fat bastions: a political club law, a deportation law, a press law that reestablished stamp taxes and bonds for good behavior. By the end of the session the anti-republican arsenal was completely stocked.

The parliamentary adjournment by no means implied an adjournment of politics. One hope on the Right was still left unrealized—the restoration of monarchy, and the parties of reaction were to devote all the summer months to work on that task. The Legitimists set out for Wiesbaden to offer their homage to the Comte de Chambord, the Orleanists for Claremont, where Louis Philippe had just breathed his last (August 28th)—Changarnier ordered a memorial service in his honor at the Tuileries. There was talk of fusion between the two branches of the dynasty. Unfortunately too many obstacles still intervened. After much bitter wrangling, the partisans of "Henri V" and the partisans of the Comte de Paris dug in solidly in their respective positions and the "King's return" to France was indefinitely postponed.

Meanwhile, flanked by his most trusted supporters, Louis Napoleon was visiting the Eastern departments. In the East his friends were fewest. However, catcalls from the democrats in Burgundy did not disconcert him. He was better received at Lyons, and was able to deliver a carefully worded speech:

"I am not the representative of a party. I represent the two great national uprisings which, in 1804 and again in 1848, sought to save the great principles of the French Revolution by upholding public order."

He protested his loyalty to the Constitution:

"Talk of a *coup d'état* has doubtless reached your ears. You have refused to believe it and for that I thank you. Parties that have no following in the nation may dream of usurpations and seizures by force, but the man who has been elected by six million votes executes the will of the people and does not betray it."

That was straight talk, clear and crisp. At Besançon, the Prince was jostled by a hostile crowd. The municipal council at Strasbourg refused to receive him. He worked back towards Caen, where his speech quite pointedly hefted the future:

"If stormy days were to come again and the people saw fit to lay a new burden upon the head of the government, he on his side would be doing a great wrong were he to shirk such a lofty assignment."

In that his thought was a shade less transparent and he was equally indirect at Cherbourg, where he seemed to foresee and to desire a prolongation of his mandate. That was in responding to resolutions passed by fifty-two General Councils, calling for an extension of his term and for a change in the Constitution that would permit it.

All in all he was much better known in the provinces by the time he returned to Paris, and his contact with this real France, the France of the farms and the workshops, the France of the lower middle classes, had been of the greatest benefit to him. Technically he was the head of the Republic but already he had the look of a sort of sovereign. He gave dinners and balls at the Elysée, more or less mixed and haphazard affairs where things pretty much took care of themselves. Among the guests one noted great names that recalled the Empire; then a few lorgnettes from the Faubourg Saint-Germain (which, for that matter, became fewer and fewer as time went on); finally hosts of unknowns—and these people seemed to be the real people in the place. They were, so to say, campers on the building site of a new Empire.

This impression deepened as autumn wore on. The Society of the Tenth of December held rally after rally in the Bonapartist cause. The President's newspapers threw mud and then more mud at Parliament. The President himself held reviews of troops, the men first being put in good humor by extra rations of food and wine. At a ceremony for the distribution of arms to the cavalry at Satory in the presence of a great crowd, shouts of "Long live the Emperor!" rose again and again from the ranks.

Changarnier was attending the President on that occasion. He was seen to frown, and the Assembly's standing Committee for Military Affairs took notice of the incident. General d'Hautpoul, the Minister of War, hemmed and hawed in explanation. Changarnier lost his temper:

"That demonstration was not merely encouraged. It was staged, and in the face of my explicit warnings."

From then on it was open war between the Elysée and the military commander of Paris. Changarnier, an old soldier of Algeria, was a curious cross between a man and a mannekin. A Royalist, he despised both the Republic and its President. At first he had thought that he could keep the pretender in hand, and in a moment of disgust at all the demagoguery in the waning Constituent Assembly (Jan. 29, 1849), he had suggested to Louis Napoleon at the Elysée, in the presence of Thiers, Victor de Broglie and Molé, that the Prince "make an end of it" with a *coup d'état*. Thiers did not like the idea.

"What harm," he said, "does all this foolishness in the Assembly do, all this bickering and heckling, all this strong language? If it discredits the legislative power, it strengthens the executive power."

The Prince agreed with Thiers, and Changarnier remarked to the latter as they were leaving:

"Did you see the expression on the President's face? What a jackass (*jean foutre*)!" A little later he exclaimed at a meeting of his staff: "The President lost a fine chance today to go to the Tuileries!"

As time went on Changarnier's opinion of the Prince did not improve and he was forever plastering him with spicy witticisms, even going so far as to boast that if Louis Napoleon ever made a slip, he would "take him to Vincennes in the 'salad basket' " (the "Black Maria"). Changarnier was convinced that before very long he would be called upon to govern France, and against that day he began to take laughable pains with his personal toilet, bedecking his beadle's head with an auburn wig, overperfuming with musk, lining his figure with a corset. All that won him the nickname of "General Bergamotte"—General Blood-orange.

In the twin command of the National Guard and of the First Division Changarnier was in actual fact the master of Paris; and he was a member of parliament besides. The deputies humored him, thinking of him as "their General," but without as yet knowing for certain whether he was to serve as their sword or their buckler. On several occasions Louis Napoleon had sought to win him, but the General rebuffed him contemptuously. Not yet daring to remove him from his command, the Elysée thought he could be taught a lesson. They cashiered General Neumayer, his chief of staff.

If it was a fight they were looking for, Changarnier was the man to accommodate them. In an order of the day he reminded his troops that while they were on duty they should refrain from cheering anybody. The President champed at his bit. Evidently his moment had not yet come. Well, he knew how to wait! He had done plenty of waiting in his time—and he threw out ballast in a presidential message in which he professed all his respect for legality.

All the same, for the first time, frankly and squarely, he brought up the question of a change in the Constitution that would permit his reelection at the end of his term:

"Whatever measures the future may require, let us understand each other all along, that the fate of a great nation may never be determined by passion, surprise or violence."

This conciliatory language eased tension in the Chamber, which, for that matter, was pleased to note that Baroche had dissolved the Society of December Tenth.

But the truce was short-lived. A few weeks and the battle between the President and the General was on again. A skirmish between deputies at the Palais Bourbon once more made Changarnier an issue. The President decided to strike.

He gave notice of his intention to the principal Burgraves. They rose in vain to the defense of "their General." The Prince listened as a mere matter of form. The next morning (January 9th) he announced a remodeling of the cabinet that made room for Drouyn de Lhuys, Regnault de Saint-Jean d'Angély, Ducos and Magne. At the same time he relieved General Changarnier of his two commands, assigning General Baraguay d'Hilliers to the First Army and General Perrot to the National Guard.

Opinion in Paris seemed to approve of the President's action, but the Assembly declared war then and there. Baroche and Rouher were still novices. They were easily outplayed. The dramatic voice of Berryer rose in solemn warning to his colleagues:

"I do not know who your successors are to be. These walls, perhaps, may remain standing, but they will be peopled by legislators without tongues."

And Thiers said:

"If the Assembly weakens on this point, where there are now two powers there will be but one. One can say the words whenever one chooses; but the fact is, *the Empire is here.*"

That was uttering prophecy, and the little man was to foretell just as soundly on other occasions. His destiny, for twenty years, would be to play Cassandra to the Napoleonic régime.

The cabinet was defeated by a vote of 417 to 278. The President proceeded to replace it with a non-parliamentary ministry in which one notes names that were to become famous in the history of the

Second Empire: Schneider, de Royer, Vaïsse, General Randon. Magne retained his post.

When this new cabinet appeared before the Assembly, the latter did not dare to overthrow it. Angry, anxious, paralyzed by its abuse of words, the Assembly blindly sought revenge, and it thought it had found it in a stupid gesture. Overriding Montalembert it refused the President a new credit of 1,800,000 francs for expenses of official entertainment.

"We will grant Louis Bonaparte," the deputies grumbled, "neither one hour's extension nor one penny."

The Bonapartist press suggested opening a public subscription. Louis Napoleon refused. "The lion has turned poodle!" jeered Victor Hugo. The President dismissed a doorman or a butler here and there, sold some of his horses, borrowed right and left to meet his more pressing needs.

Was he to force a pitched battle? Not in the least! He was to side-step and draw back. Such was the conduct of the man at that time and such it was always to be. First a fairly vigorous onslaught, then a slowing down, a marking of time! He still had hopes of a change in the Constitution. That would net him a sort of Consulate which could be prolonged without any resort to force, and without any obligatory pushing on to monarchy—monarchy probably he disliked, at bottom, as a matter of taste and of principle.

For the moment he tried to patch things up with the Assembly. He sounded out Barrot as to an offer of the premiership. Thiers thwarted the manoeuvre. Thereupon the Prince fell back upon a cabinet of makeshifts, again with the inevitable Baroche, again with the inevitable Rouher.

To this cabinet the President expressly set the task of obtaining a "constitutional revision." The country seemed to be calling for one in no end of petitions which local authorities fomented and sponsored with a fairly transparent zeal. A million and a quarter signatures were so obtained. The Assembly reared, Orleanists and republicans alike. In his exasperation, and just as the debate in Parliament was about to open, Louis Napoleon made a false step. Speaking at Dijon on June 1st, he bitterly assailed the ill-will of the people in Parliament:

"Whenever I have tried to do good, to ameliorate the lot of the people, I have found in Parliament nothing but ineptness." And he went on to say that, since he was above and beyond political cliques, "France would not perish in his hands."

Changarnier saw in that a chance to get his revenge. With the Assembly in a tumult he mounted the speakers' platform.

"If we are to believe certain people," he said in his crackling voice, "the army stands ready to lay hands on the law of the country in an access of enthusiasm. But to ease your worries, probably, I should have only to ask—where would the army ever find a pretext for enthusiasm? . . ."

A crash of laughter greeted this thrust at the pretender. The General resumed:

"No one is going to force the soldiers to march against this Assembly. Not a battalion, not a company, not a squad, could be enticed down that fatal road. . . . Mandatories of France, deliberate in peace!"

And he returned to his seat amid thunderous applause.

But Tocqueville had been designated to report on the bill. He declared in favor of a change in the Constitution. His upright and earnest sense of his political responsibilities, his concern for the country's welfare, caused him to dread too sharp a conflict between a single Chamber which thought itself all-powerful, and a President, who was master of a very dangerous power in virtue of his election by the people. Falloux proposed a return to monarchy. Cavaignac contemptuously rejected any change whatever in the Constitution. Berryer, tall, imposing in his great blue swallow-tail, delivered an indictment of despotism for having, as he said, "adulterated glory."

"Woe unto the nation," he cried, "whose existence depends now on the changeable passions of the masses and now on the wisdom of one man. You have to have principles. I am a royalist because I am a patriot."

Revision did not obtain the majority required by the Constitution. Louis Napoleon had to become a private citizen again in May, 1852; or else, if he wished to retain power, he had to violate the law.

CHAPTER V

The Coup d'Etat

HIS WISH WAS TO REMAIN IN POWER, SO HE MADE READY FOR THE VIO-lation. To improve his chances of succeeding, he tried to intensify his popularity with the masses and to enhance still further his prestige with the army. A number of generals, Bedeau, Lamoricière, Cavaignac, Le Flô, to say nothing of Changarnier, were hostile to him. He would offset them with new leaders for the army.

First of all, Saint-Arnaud. Saint-Arnaud was a tall, thin, sharp-featured individual with a hard, silent face and a pair of piercing wolf's eyes under bushy eyebrows. Someone called him "a Richelieu turned cutthroat." His life had been one breath-taking and un-bridled gamble. Son of a sometime prefect of the Empire, youthful escapades long kept him marking time in the subaltern ranks. He fought for the Greeks and met Byron at Missolonghi. Jailer of the Duchess de Berry, at Blaye, he was dragged out of the rut by Bugeaud, who sent him to Algeria. There he fought with reckless valor and was a general by 1848. He hated the Republic tempera-mentally, instinctively, and stood ready to do anything to its hurt.

"I will never let myself be governed by the gutter," he wrote. "I would rather raise the standard of a bandit chief—and from that to becoming Caesar would not be an impossible jump."

Fleury sounded him out and informed Louis Napoleon that he could be counted on. He had met Fleury's hints and innuendoes with the words:

"My dear fellow, please assure the Prince that he can count on me this minute. Tell him to make me major-general as soon as he can. I will answer for the rest."

The Prince knew all the value of the acquisition. Such a man would quail at nothing. But no one knew him as yet. To bring him a little to the fore, he was entrusted with a command in Kabylia.

He distinguished himself on the expedition, and the Elysée newspapers featured his successes even beyond his deserts. He was called home to Paris a major-general as a prelude to a promotion to the portfolio of War. In that key position he would be just the rough-handed auxiliary required. Castellane and Baraguay d'Hilliers declined command of the Paris army, but General Magnan accepted with a gesture of delighted obedience. Fleury, Espinasse, Lourmel, stout soldiers of Africa all, were assigned to strategic positions. In all these men the Prince possessed a secret general staff that was ready to act at the first signal.

But that was by no means all. He was just as circumspect in organizing a civilian general staff. He could already count on Persigny and Mocquard, devoted followers of the dangerous years. He reenforced them with a hustling young prefect, Maupas, who had rushed to his standard with a spectacular display of Napoleonic devotion. Finally he struck a close alliance with a character who of all his associates was probably to exert the greatest influence upon his life—his half-brother, the "Count" de Morny.

Charles-Auguste de Morny was the child of the liaison of Hortense with Flahaut, who in turn was a bastard of Talleyrand. In his makeup he represented the perfect, the finished blend of the prince with the adventurer. Resigning a commission in the army, he had gained an entrée to industry and banking and made a fortune there. Thence, still young, he had turned to politics. He reached the Chamber under Louis Philippe and won notice for adroitness in a number of debates. Handsome, stylishly dressed, well-bred, this man of affairs and of pleasures, with an attractive mind, but cynical and amoral, may have lacked application and disliked hard work, and he may have thought of the world as an open gaming table where a man was free to risk not only his own fate but the fate of the nations as well; but he was endowed with a clear intelligence and a broad view, with cool courage and a limitless ambition.

At first Louis Napoleon had disliked him as a walking advertisement of his mother's shame. Morny, in fact, had blatantly taken for his coat-of-arms an eagle issuing from a hortensia bush, with the motto: *Tace sed memento*. Walewski, also a bastard, son of the great Napoleon and the "Polish woman," had brought them together. Prescient of the future, Morny gradually wrapped himself round the President, friendship and complicity soon replacing mistrust.

The Prince found in his half-brother the intelligent prop that he could never have found in, for instance, a hotheaded enthusiast like Persigny. From then on Morny was in regular attendance at conferences at the Elysée and also at the intimate evenings at Miss Howard's—Miss Howard being Louis Napoleon's blonde amour; and he was to push the Prince to extreme resorts, prepare him, as Morny said, "to take the plunge."

By the end of August, 1851, an armed stroke calculated to keep the President in power had been settled on in principle. Louis Napoleon had hesitated long. The thought of his oath tortured him, but his intimates insisted, arguing that in view of the hatreds in Parliament no other course was open to him. The question of procedure was discussed at Saint-Cloud. Carlier, the prefect of police, submitted a plan in the presence of Morny, Persigny and Rouher. The Assembly would be dissolved. Being in recess, it would not be able to reassemble in time for effective protest. The troops would have orders to suppress any signs of disturbance. Then the country would be deluged with placards and other publicity. This plan was adopted. But Saint-Arnaud was to be the mainspring of the whole enterprise. He suddenly thought of a flaw in the plan. The representatives, he argued, would be in their provinces and therefore out of reach. They might appeal to the army at one point or another throughout the country and so manage to start a civil war. His argument seemed sound. It was better to postpone everything and wait for the next session. Then a sudden arrest of the party leaders would decapitate the Assembly and frustrate any attempt at resistance in Paris.

Louis Napoleon had hit on an excellent idea for winning popular support. He would ask for a repeal of the law of May 31st, which had maimed suffrage and stricken the names of three million citizens from the voters' lists. To be sure he had lent his support to that bill, expecting that in exchange the Assembly would yield on the point of revision. His ministers did not dare to follow him in so startling a right-about. The President accepted their resignations in order to have a cabinet freer of embarrassing scruples. Saint-Arnaud took the portfolio of War, Maupas, the prefecture of police.

The army in Paris seemed won. Magnan led six hundred officers to the Elysée to assure the President of their loyalty. Louis Napoleon addressed them:

"If the hour of danger were ever to strike, I would not say to you: 'March, I follow you!' I would say: 'March, you follow me!' "

Audacious words, all the more since they were brazenly featured in the *Moniteur*. The Prince was surely burning his bridges behind him!

The moment the deputies were reassembled, Thorigny, the new secretary of the Interior, demanded a return to universal suffrage. As had been foreseen, the government bill lost, but only by a majority of seven. The parliamentary auditors, Le Flô, Baze and Panat, saw through the President's manoeuvre and realized all the danger that lurked in it. They tried to parry by introducing a bill that would give the chairmen of the Assembly the right to call on the army directly to defend national representation in case of threat to its independence (November 17th). The ministry of course opposed. Michel de Bourges, in a characteristic flight of oratory, denied the existence of any threat to the Assembly:

"An invisible sentinel stands guard over us and that sentinel is the people!"

Colonel Charras moved that the ministers be impeached. The Chamber blew up, everybody talking at once. At the height of the storm Saint-Arnaud slipped out, calling insolently back at Thorigny:

"There is too much noise in this place! I am going out to get a policeman. . . ."

In spite of all that Thiers could do the Chamber stupidly tabled the motion. The incident aroused great glee at the Elysée. Had the bill passed, they stood ready there to bring matters to a head, but under the circumstances a *coup d'état* would have been more than perilous. The ineptness of the Assembly now left the President a free hand and he was the man to profit by it. On the one side stood a Parliament, mistrustful, divided, narrow-mindedly conservative, entirely retrogressive in its points of view. On the other stood a man who wore a halo—and such a halo! He was supported by an army. But more than that he knew how to talk to the people in a language vibrant with high-sounding words—national honor, the future, progress. The match was far from equal. The scales had already tipped. Called upon to make a choice, the French chose Louis Napoleon by a landslide majority.

On the evening of December 1, 1851, the President of the Republic received at the Elysée, as he did every Monday evening. Calm and affable as usual, twirling his mustache, he moved from one drawing-room to another through the crowds of government officials, diplomats, distinguished foreigners, generals, ladies not so much of society as of Bonapartist society. There he was joking with Dr. Véron, director at the Opera and owner of the *Constitutionnel.* There he was shaking hands, smiling to right and left, chatting now with Haussmann, prefect of the Gironde, now with the Marquis of Douglas, now with the Comte de Flahaut, Morny's father, now with his cousin Mathilde and other ladies. Nothing in his demeanor, nothing in the glint of his eyes, betrayed any special worry or excitement.

Once he was seen to speak in inaudible tones to Colonel Vieyra (who had just been made chief of the general staff of the National Guard).

"Colonel," said he, "keep your feelings in hand. It is set for tonight. Can you promise me that tomorrow there will be no drums in the streets to call out the reserves?"

"I will kick in every drumhead in Paris," Vieyra answered.

"Good! Be at Headquarters at six in the morning."

The *coup d'état*, first planned by the presidential clique for November 25th, had been postponed to December 2nd, the twin anniversary of Napoleon's coronation and the battle of Austerlitz. Whatever rumors may have reached their ears, the outstanding leaders in Parliament were sitting tight in watchful security. During the preceding days and, to be sure, only after last and frantic efforts to reach an amicable settlement, a number of important men on the Right, among them Daru, Montalembert, and Falloux, had come out in favor of a resort to force by the President. Louis Napoleon let them talk and confer to their hearts' content. Financially Morny stood back to the wall as a result of unlucky exchange speculations. Persigny was rabid for action at any price. Saint-Arnaud was answering for the army, Maupas for the police. Under these pressures, and certainly after an inner struggle, the Prince had stifled his last scruples, and, once the question had been decided, his sole concern was to do a perfect job.

Two days before, at the Opera, he had dropped a word to his cousin Mathilde, a fiancée of his in the days of Arenenberg. Mathilde afterwards had stupidly gone off and married a Russian prince, Demidoff, and was now regretting the brilliant position that Louis Napoleon would have won for her. Opposite them sat Thiers and Roger du Nord. The conversation ran as follows:

"I haven't been able to take my eyes off those people. They are thinking of overthrowing me and tossing me into Vincennes. They may easily be in prison within two days themselves."

"So you are going to do something in earnest?"

"Yes, before long. All will be lost if I do not act."

He was sincere in that. The fight between him and the Assembly was a finish fight. For him, as he thought, it was conquer or perish. He knew from Flahaut that the Prince de Joinville and the Duc d'Aumale were packing their bags for a return to France. He had to get a start on them.

The public could sense that a great political change was in the offing, but was not yet certain what it was to be. Granier de Cassagnac, overtly an editorialist for the Elysée, had befuddled public opinion by a violent article in which he denounced alleged schemes for a dictatorship on the part of parliament, with either Changarnier or Cavaignac.

The Prince's intimates followed his example in affecting complete nonchalance. On that same evening, December 1st, Morny was parading up and down at the Opéra Comique, and when a friend of his, Madame Liadières, asked him what he intended to do "in case there were to be some sweeping," he answered, laughing:

"Try, of course, to be on the broom handle and not under the broom."

At the President's reception a deputy joked good-humoredly with Granier de Cassagnac:

"Well, when are you going to throw us out?"

"Before long, I hope, my dear fellow."

Shortly after ten o'clock, with the orchestra still playing, Louis Napoleon slipped into his private study, followed by Maupas. Mocquard, Morny, Persigny, Saint-Arnaud came in, then the orderly, Béville. The Prince opened a folder of papers on which he had scribbled in blue pencil a single word: *Rubicon*. He had his men read over the documents inside: a decree dissolving the Assembly, an address to the army, an appeal to the people. A brief discussion followed, in low tones, Louis Napoleon sitting expressionless and taking no part. He had sized up those men about him, each and all. Morny alone was level-headed and to be relied on in an emergency. He was the man to direct this "little police operation" that "might seem a trifle harsh," but which, as he, the Prince, had been assured, would cause no spilling of blood. At daybreak Morny would take possession at the Ministry of the Interior, replacing and ejecting the timorous Thorigny. Béville would take the proclamations to the national printing-plant and see to it that the type was set in the greatest secrecy. At daybreak Maupas would arrest sixteen members of the Assembly, the sixteen judged the most likely to build up an organized resistance: Thiers, Roger du Nord, the auditor, Baze, seven deputies of the Mountain, not very well known but men of vigor, finally General Changarnier, Generals Lamoricière, Cavaignac, Le Flô and Bedeau and Colonel Charras. Sixty-two other individuals, either newspaper men or members of secret societies, were also to be detained.

The Prince and Saint-Arnaud did not like so much arresting, but Morny declared it necessary if civil war were to be averted.

"You don't have to abuse a person in prison . . . ," he said. "To arrest a man under certain circumstances is to do him the greatest possible favor."

And he went on to quote remarks that Thiers and Changarnier had made two years before, in advocating a *coup d'état* by the Orleanists.

"Lamoricière," said Thiers, "certainly has to be arrested. He is an eccentric, brave and very dangerous. Cavaignac must not be arrested. He's too popular."

Changarnier objected:

"Lamoricière is a newsboy. I can attend to him. Cavaignac is the dangerous one. He is the man I want to make sure of."

Morny concluded that the wise course would be to compromise by arresting them all, Lamoricière and Cavaignac, Thiers and Changarnier.

Persigny had dreamed of himself as playing a very important rôle on this occasion to which he had looked forward for years. Now suddenly he found himself playing second fiddle to Colonel Espinasse, who had the task of occupying the Palais Bourbon. His fury knew no bounds, but Louis Napoleon consoled him with a friendly word:

"The essential thing is to prevent any gathering of the deputies."

The Prince opened a drawer and took out the last of the funds at his disposal—twenty thousand francs in gold, forty thousand in paper. He suggested dividing them around. Saint-Arnaud accepted ten thousand francs. It was agreed that Fleury would distribute the balance to the troops taking part.

Towards midnight the Prince rose and his friends took their leave. "Of course," said Morny, "we all understand that we are playing our hides!"

"Of course," answered Mocquard, laughing. "Mine unfortunately is worn so thin that I don't consider it much of an ante."

That language showed them to be what they all were, gamblers pure and simple. Down to then they had staked money, career, reputation. This time they were staking their lives. Beyond this great adventure, if they failed, they would find a scaffold awaiting them; yet not one of them seemed in the least perturbed. Louis Napoleon embraced them in turn.

"I am sure we're going to win," he said. "I always wear a ring my mother wore. Around the bezel runs a motto: H O P E."

"Whatever happens," Morny called back as he went out, "you'll have a sentry at your door tomorrow."

Alone, the Prince sat down and wrote some letters, then he stretched out on his bed without undressing. He had left a call for five o'clock.

Morny started off for the Jockey Club. Mocquard, an incurable man-about-town, ended up at a ball.

Maupas worked from two to four in the morning, interviewing separately at the prefecture the numerous policemen who were to make the arrests. All of them accepted the difficult errand entrusted to them by the prefect—all but one, and he was locked up till morning for safekeeping. Maupas instructed them to be firm. In case of need the municipal guard would be on hand to assist them. Other policemen were detailed to accompany the bill posters who were to have the manifestoes then in press on the walls of all public buildings by daybreak. The Mazas prison was ready to receive the statesmen who were to be detained.

With these preliminaries over, Maupas proceeded at once to the arrests.

Changarnier answered the knock at his door in person, an amusing sight in his shirt-tail, barefoot, wigless, a pistol in each hand.

"What are you thinking of, General?" said the policeman. "Nobody's going to hurt you."

The veteran of the African wars laid his artillery aside, while his butler helped him into his uniform.

On the way to Mazas he remarked indifferently:

"The President was going to be reelected anyway. He didn't need to stoop to a *coup d'état*."

Later he even added without show of resentment:

"When he gets into a foreign war, he will be glad I'm here to command an army for him. . . ."

Thiers was awakened suddenly from a sound sleep. He rolled his near-sighted eyes wildly about under his white cotton nightcap. Scared out of his wits he protested volubly: he was not a criminal—he had never done anything wrong in his life—and no conspiracies either. He was willing to give up politics and live abroad. . . .

The deferential attitude of the policeman gradually reassured him, whereupon he assumed a tone of importance:

"You are aware that I am a representative?"

"I can only obey orders."

He rose from bed and then, standing completely naked with his arms crossed, the little orator tried to intimidate his captor, a police commissary, Hubault:

"What you are doing may lead you to the scaffold!"

"Monsieur Thiers, I have a duty to perform."

"But, sir, what if I blew your brains out?"

"I believe you incapable of such an act, Monsieur Thiers. In any case, I have taken precautions and could easily prevent you."

He finally consented to dress, and a carriage whisked him off towards Mazas. On the way his self-possession deserted him again.

"You are going to shoot me," he moaned shamelessly. "I know that you are taking me to my death."

Inside the prison he regained his composure. Having taken the full measure of the man's character, Morny was to set him at liberty the following evening at the President's order.

General Bedeau offered physical resistance. He was collared and dragged off by main force, shouting: "Treason, help!" all the way to the cab, which drove off at a gallop. Le Flô and Lamoricière made vain efforts to intimidate the men detailed to arrest them. Cavaignac brought his fist down violently on his table, then at once turned frigid and dignified. The others submitted readily. By half-past six, and really with no great amount of noise, they were all under lock and key within the walls of Mazas. There Bedeau still kept fussing. He was finally ordered to be silent, but with the proper amount of consideration.

Catching sight of Thiers, Cavaignac remarked ironically:

"You wanted a strong government! Well, you have one!"

Colonel Espinasse marched on the Palais Bourbon with his regiment, the 42nd of the line. The 42nd had been detailed that week to guard the Assembly and one of its battalions was already waiting inside the palace. The other battalions entered at early dawn, as soon as the gate was opened for routine service. General Magnan had been warned during the night. He ordered the army of Paris to duty and called on the garrisons of Versailles and Saint-Germain. The soldiers left their barracks silently and took up positions at the Tuileries, in the Place de la Concorde, along the avenue Marigny and the Champs-Elysées, in front of the Hôtel de Ville. All the ministries were occupied. Thorigny was already at the Interior wondering what all this marching of troops could be about. At seven o'clock he received a call from Morny, who walked in cheerily, informed him that he was dismissed, and then proceeded to take possession of his office. The prefects were at once apprised of the changes in their superiors by telegraph.

Paris awoke to find its walls covered with white notices:

"In the name of the French people:

"The National Assembly is dissolved.

"Universal suffrage is re-established.

"The French people is summoned to its polls. . . ."

"Martial law is proclaimed throughout the First Military District. . . ."

Skillfully worded sentences served notice that the Republic had been reorganized somewhat along the lines of the Consulate. The President was to be elected for ten years. Louis Napoleon, nevertheless, declared that if the nation did not give him a majority of its votes, he would resign his office.

The appeal to the army was even more significant than this civil message. Louis Napoleon struck an attitude as a military dictator, as an upholder of imperial glory:

"Soldiers, be proud of your mission! You are to save your country!

. . . In 1831, and again in 1848, you were slighted as a vanquished army. . . . Today, at this solemn moment, it is my desire that you shall make your voice heard. . . . I need say nothing to you of the memories that my name recalls. . . . We share a common inheritance of glory and misfortune! . . ."

Louis Napoleon could well ask the support of that great body of soldiery, hurt in its feelings and silent. He could be sure that it would not fail him.

The people as a whole exhibited no emotion at first. Emile Ollivier relates that he was reading the announcements of the *coup d'état* on the Quai Voltaire when he found Proudhon at his side, also reading.

"So their worthies, the bourgeois, want a try at despotism!" said Proudhon. "Well, it will be a good lesson for them. Despotism is the most unstable thing in the world."

"What is the people going to do?" asked Ollivier.

"What will the people do? It will not stir." [1]

The people, in fact, realized that the long and irritating conflict between the legislative and the executive powers could be decided only by force. By its factions, its bootless wrangling, its too evident desire to restore monarchy, the Assembly had chilled public interest. The humbler people, the working-classes, laughed at the trick which the President had finally played on parliament. They had threatened him, he had boxed their ears! "It served them right," people said. "The 'twenty-five frankers' are out!"

The fact that the Republic was still functioning served to reassure public opinion. The return to universal suffrage was generally pleasing. Apprised of the favorable atmosphere, Louis Napoleon ventured forth from the Elysée towards ten o'clock to review the troops, riding a handsome English horse that Miss Howard had given him. Before him rode a platoon of cavalry with drawn pistols, behind, in full dress uniform, came Saint-Arnaud, Marshal Exelmans, Prince Murat, Edgar Ney, Fleury, Generals Magnan, Flahaut, Daumas, and many other army officers. At their head rode Jerome Bonaparte, though Napoleon Bonaparte, Jerome's son, was not in the party. Showered with favors by the President, Napoleon had joined the Mountain and sat in the Assembly on the benches of the opposition. In fact he had rushed to the Palais Bourbon to resist

[1] Emile Ollivier, *L'Empire libéral*, II, 465.

the *coup d'état,* hoping that his cousin would fail, but only that he or his father might be able to take advantage of the moment and seize the dictatorship.

In the Faubourg Saint-Honoré and along the rue Royale, curious onlookers craned their necks at windows or behind the rows of cavalry on the sidewalks. A few shouts of "Long live the Emperor!" were to be heard, but there were also cheers for the Republic. On the Place de la Concorde the President was greeted with an enthusiastic ovation from the Cotte brigade. The cavalcade then entered the gardens of the Tuileries which were held by Dulac's brigade. For a moment it looked as though the President were going to take possession of the royal residence; and he may even have thought of doing so just to have things over with once and for all. But, according to the story, a caution from his uncle held him in check.

"Louis," the ex-King is said to have whispered, "you are going too fast!"

Louis Napoleon therefore turned his horse towards the Pont Royal and slowly returned by the Quai d'Orsay and the Champs Elysées, followed by his staff.

While this bold promenade was in progress the parliamentarians made an effort to upset the *coup d'état.* Colonel Espinasse had overlooked and left unguarded a door of the Palais Bourbon on the rue de Bourgogne. Through it some three score deputies made their way into the palace, took their seats in the assembly hall and, angry, wild-eyed, vehement, prepared to open session.

But a detachment of mobile police entered the amphitheatre. The deputies leapt to their feet, shouted, "Long live the Republic!", and then sat down again. One of them, Monet, began reading in a loud voice—Articles 36 and 37 of the Constitution, which proclaimed the inviolability of deputies to arrest, and Article 68, which deposed the President in case of treason.

The officer in command unsheathed his sword and, in the language of Murat at the Orangerie, ordered their expulsion:

"Forward march! Chuck them all out, all of them! (*Foutez-les tous dehors!*)"

In a scuffle of flying fists and brandished gun-stocks the representatives were pushed out of the hall into the street and thence into the Place de Bourgogne. There several who still showed fight were placed under arrest. However one group succeeded in getting back into the palace where they went looking for their president, Dupin. Dupin had refused all along to call the Assembly to order and now had prudently shut himself up in his chambers. The deputies summoned him to place himself at their head and go back to the amphitheatre. Dupin refused:

"What do you expect? When force comes in the people loses its rights. Make the best of it! That's what I'm doing! Leave me alone!"

The sly old clown of the law courts was in fact to make so much the best of it that he was shortly to solicit and obtain of Napoleon III the position of Attorney-General to the Court of Appeals. At the moment the deputies put the chairman's scarf around his neck by main force and proceeded to drag him away towards the Chamber. But Espinasse had by now been notified and came in on the run. In the presence of that lean, tough-skinned soldier the chairman of the Assembly could find only a few stammering and shamefaced words to voice a routine, official protest:

"You have bayonettes. . . . I appeal to the law and take my departure. I have the honor, sir, to wish you a good day."

And he vanished, greatly relieved that Espinasse stationed two sentinels at his door to protect him from any chance assaults from his own conscience.

There were other meetings, one at the home of Yvan, another at Odilon Barrot's. The long-faced Daru got as many as a hundred representatives together in his drawing-room on the rue de Lille.[1]

There was a hasty discussion and a bill of impeachment against Louis Napoleon was drawn up. It was about to be put to vote when a battalion of infantry appeared on the scene. Daru was placed under arrest, but allowed to remain at home under guard.

Before the house was surrounded, the deputies reached the gardens and then the rue de l'Université. Thence they made their way to the quarters of the Tenth Arrondissement near the carrefour de la Croix-Rouge. By that time their numbers had swelled to nearly three hundred. Rightists and republicans mixed in together, they managed by eleven o'clock to open a tumultuous session, with Benoist d'Azy and Vitet both presiding. Berryer carried a bill of impeachment against Louis Napoleon and then measures calling

---

[1] The house was at no. 75. Victor Hugo describes this episode in detail in his *Histoire d'un Crime*, I, 79-90.

out the National Guard and mobilizing the army, with Oudinot as commander-in-chief.

Army officers and police sergeants vainly sought to disband the gathering. They were overawed and ejected. But on learning that the resistance was continuing, Saint-Arnaud and Maupas realized the danger. They sent General Forey to dissolve the session at whatever cost.

It was three o'clock when the troops forced an entrance to the building. Berryer, Vitet, Oudinot, frantically appealed for the respect due to the Assembly.

"You dare to arrest us, the representatives of the people?" cried Vatimesnil.

"Watch and see!" answered a "liner."

There was cursing and imprecating aplenty, but the soldiers shoved the deputies outside the hall. Two rows of bayonettes formed, and between them the representatives of the people filed in a long line to the Quai d'Orsay barracks where they were quartered under guard. Then a common impulse of fraternal gaiety came to tinge the picturesque disorder. The tragic, bitter note disappeared. The deputies began jibing at one another laughingly. Those on the Right took up the dramatic phrase of Michel de Bourges: "Here we have the invisible sentinel!" The republicans replied with the concluding sentence of Changarnier: "Mandatories of the people, deliberate in peace!"

Meanwhile the High Court, called for by the Constitution in case of an attack on the Assembly, convened by spontaneous accord at the Palais de Justice. Maupas, however, had only to show a company of the Republican Guard for the court to vanish as into thin air. The members of the High Court, however, were all judges of the Court of Appeals. They met that evening at the home of the chief justice and, faithful to the letter of their oaths and with a sort of mechanical valor, handed down a decision which established the fact of an attack on the Assembly with the use of armed force, and adjudged Louis Napoleon guilty of high treason. The next day the court adjourned *sine die,* "in view of unforeseen obstacles interfering with the exercise of its functions."

That was the end of the legal resistance. In the course of the afternoon there was more or less haphazard discussing by deputies of the Left. Victor Hugo, Michel de Bourges, Carnot, Arago and

Jules Favre organized a "Committee of Resistance." Troops were sent after them, without attracting any interest whatever on the part of the public. The outward aspect of the capital was not affected. A gentle rain was falling. The Stock Exchange, the shops, the cafés, the theatres, went about their business as usual. Here and there one heard a cheer for the Republic that was quickly hushed, or a few bars of the *Marseillaise*. A single shot, so far as known, was fired. It came from a window on the boulevard Saint-Denis as a column of cavalry was passing. The bullet grazed the head of General Fleury.

Hübner, the Austrian ambassador, observes as an eyewitness:

"Large bodies of troops everywhere, the soldiers gay and good-natured, conscious of being masters of the situation. The people on the streets, the public in general, were calm, indifferent. The streets were crowded with the curious—well-dressed people at first. As the day wore on workingmen in smocks and sinister-looking individuals from the slums replaced the bourgeois. Towards evening the streets emptied and deep calm succeeded the excitements of the day."

The Minister of Foreign Affairs, the insignificant Turgot, had the diplomatic corps for dinner that night. Louis Napoleon had been expected. He did not appear, sticking to the Elysée and receiving rare visitors—Morny, Persigny, the Princess Mathilde. His coolness astounded—it was "phlegm sublimated to genius," as Dr. Véron was later to say. As he figured up the day's accounts with his closest intimates, the Prince had every reason to congratulate himself without qualification. The *coup d'état* seemed to be accepted everywhere.

However, by the following morning, December 3rd, the atmosphere began to cloud, in spite of numerous arrests of deputies and of heads of political associations that had sprouted during the night. Hugo's Committee of Resistance succeeded in printing and posting appeals to the people declaring Louis Napoleon a traitor and an outlaw. In the Faubourg Saint-Antoine, the perennial powder-magazine of Paris, mobs formed around republican deputies who paraded the streets in their insignia of office, Esquiros, Madier de Montjau, Schoelcher, de Flotte, Baudin. . . .

At the crossing of the rue de Cotte and the rue Sainte-Marguerite, a barricade of overturned carts and omnibuses was hastily thrown up and behind it Baudin settled with a handful of sup-

PRINCESS MATHILDE

From the Portrait by Edouard Dubufe

porters. He called to some workingmen who happened to be in the neighborhood, asking them to bring up fresh materials.

"Bah!" jeered one of them in reply. "Do you think we are going to die to save your twenty-five francs?"

Baudin smiled mournfully and answered:

"Well, hang around, and you'll see how a fellow can die for twenty-five francs!"

A child suddenly shouted:

"The troops!"

It was true. The troops were coming. Two companies of "liners" were being rushed from the Bastille to demolish Baudin's barricade. As the soldiers appeared, seven deputies, with Schoelcher in the lead, advanced to meet them, ordering them, in the name of the law, to halt.

A captain, Petit by name, replied:

"You can see that you're alone. Not one of these people is listening to you. Withdraw, or I shall fire."

De Flotte bared his chest and cried:

"Fire!"

The deputies came forward and stood in line at his side, facing the muskets. The officer was touched. He changed his mind and ordered his men to cross bayonettes. The soldiers advanced at double quick, fell upon the deputies and hemmed them in, being careful not to hurt anybody. But at that moment a shot came from the barricade. It killed a soldier, a conscript, who was standing at Schoelcher's side. The troops replied with a volley. Baudin fell, with three bullets in his chest and, next to him, an unidentified youth. The barricade was stormed and its last defenders scattered. There were no arrests. The Faubourg seemed to look on indifferently.

In the course of the day disquieting movements occurred in the vicinity of the Temple. Deputies of the Left, among them Victor Hugo, had been canvassing the unswept streets; but it was more particularly the secret societies that gradually aroused the people. The heroic sacrifice of Baudin had caused a seep of sullen anger. Smocks from the faubourgs began to foregather towards the centers of Paris. Such crowds as formed were almost everywhere hostile to the Prince, jeering and spitting at his name and cheering for the

Republic. Platoons of cavalry dealt with groups that appeared on the boulevards.

At the Elysée itself, around Louis Napoleon's person, a definite vacillation of feeling took shape. Success was no longer deemed so certain. Many partisans of the Prince went into hiding. The drawing-rooms were empty. Louis Napoleon himself, though no coward, dared not go out into the streets. The prefect of police, Maupas, was so filled with consternation by rumors which kept pouring in that he sent Morny and Saint-Arnaud terrified dispatches, which they could answer only by shrugging their shoulders.[1]

Louis Napoleon had difficulty in forming a makeshift ministry. Many of those to whom he appealed refused outright. Morny and Saint-Arnaud consented to retain their posts. Rouher, Fould, Magne and Fortoul accepted the more important portfolios, but without enthusiasm. The day before the first two had written a joint letter to the Director of the National Press requesting him "to omit their signatures" from the proclamations relative to the *coup d'état* that were to be sent to the provinces.[2] Napoleon III got hold of the letter and kept it in a special folder till the end of the Empire. During the entire day of the third of December, Rouher was nowhere to be found.

In the evening fresh barricades rose on the rue Beaubourg, to be demolished by the troops after a spirited resistance. Such of the defenders as did not flee were shot. Driving a mob down the boulevard Montmartre the lancers added several more casualties to the count. The bodies were paraded through the streets by torch-light. Impressions of foreign observers at this moment were decidedly unfavorable. Hübner wrote: "The government is very much embarrassed by the lack of a real enemy to fight. . . . Its situation is critical. The faubourgs are preferring to wear the soldier down, trying to disgust him with his job by marches and counter-marches that come to nothing. It begins to look doubtful whether the *coup d'état* will succeed after all." [3]

During these anxious hours Morny alone retained a wholly clear head. He had ordered the prefects to keep him posted as to the impression produced by the *coup d'état* in their several departments. One of them telegraphed:

[1] Véron, *Souvenirs d'un bourgeois de Paris,* VI, 189-198.
[2] *Papiers des Tuileries,* I, 214.
[3] *Souvenirs,* I, 39.

"I have a dispatch that says that the Chamber is winning over the whole line."

He replied, graciously punning:

"No, the 'line' is winning over the whole Chamber."

Not for a moment did he forget his own interests. Stocks had crashed. He bought to his last franc, betting on a rise. Ever with an eye upon the Prince and upon his friends, keeping at Maupas from moment to moment, he had martial law proclaimed and decrees repressing riots without mercy.

A proclamation by Saint-Arnaud, drawn up on the evening of the 3rd, read:

"Any person found building or defending a barricade, or with arms in his possession, will be dealt with according to the extreme penalties of martial law."

Morny deleted the last phrase, replacing it with the words, "will be shot."

At this point Louis Napoleon lost his composure. The prospect of bloodshed frightened him. His half-brother had not a little difficulty in obtaining a free hand. With the approval of Saint-Arnaud and Magnan, but over objections from Maupas, he determined upon a bold plan of action, which, for that matter, was an imitation of Cavaignac's tactic in June, 1848. The troops were to return to their barracks, abandoning the town to the insurgents. During the night of the 3rd to the 4th, they would tear the paving-stones from the streets and build new barricades. The more serious the rebellion, the more rigorous could measures for dealing with it be, and the more lasting, therefore, results.

At dawn on December 4th Paris was, in fact, in the hands of the republicans. All the old streets in the center of the city were blocked by barricades of carriages, house furniture, mattresses. The city echoed with revolutionary songs, and the boulevards with cries of "Down with the praetorians!" The bourgeoisie ran to cover. The partisans of the coup d'état seemed lost. Maupas called for help. Morny chuckled:

"They've made the barricades for you and still you're not satisfied!"

So the forenoon passed, a damp, foggy morning. About noon the troops occupied the quarters of the Fifth Arrondissement, in the Faubourg Saint-Martin. Maupas pleaded with Morny:

"Reports are getting worse and worse. The situation calls for the noise of cannon and for cannon-balls; and they are called for at once."

Morny did not swerve from his plan by a single jot. Not until two o'clock did the order come from Magnan for his troops to march. By that time the men were thoroughly rested. They had had a good dinner with more wine than usual. Their spirits had been roused by gifts of money and by speeches from their officers. They were eager to wipe out the disgrace of the 24th of February, when they had allowed Louis Philippe to vanish without trace.

The Renaud division advanced along the Left Bank to hold the Latin Quarter. Levasseur slipped through the maze of dark muddy streets that twist and turn from the Saint-Martin and Saint-Denis gates to the Place de Grève. Carrelet swept the boulevards, beginning at the Madeleine. A few shots came from windows on the boulevard abreast of the Faubourg Poissonnière. The troops, "too quick tempered," to use the phrase of Magnan himself,[1] "replied by useless firing."

Useless, in fact, it was and horrible too! Strollers, idlers, customers in the cafés, tradesmen in their shops, women, children, all were struck down! An artillery officer lost his head and cannonaded the Sallandrouze mansion. General Canrobert, commanding one of the brigades, came up on the run, cane in hand, and beat at his men to induce them to stop firing. Someone took a shot at him from a window and his bugler was killed at his side. In spite of his well-intentioned efforts, the massacre continued for ten minutes, sprinkling the sidewalks with dead.

A huge barricade on the rue Saint-Denis was carried by a furious assault. The rue Rambuteau, the rue Aumaire, the rue du Petit-Carreau, Saint-Eustache corner, were swept clean with merciless energy.

Twenty-seven soldiers were slain, more than four hundred "rebels" and innocent by-standers (the *Moniteur,* evidently underestimating, reported the dead at 380). By evening all resistance had been quelled. Flooded with soldiers, Paris went into hiding and fell silent. Morny had sought to break down resistance in Paris; and resistance in Paris had been broken down. The *coup d'état* had triumphed, but the capital had paid dearly for it and would not for-

[1] Report of General Magnan to Saint-Arnaud, December 4th, 10 P.M.

get. Louis Napoleon became master of France. He was never to
become the real master of Paris.

There were a few more tremors of disorder during the night and
on the following morning, the work, doubtless, of agents provocateurs. Maupas's police went to extremes the more thoroughly to
repress them. However, traffic had soon returned to normal. Re-
pairs on the streets were begun, stores reopened, the city's life of
business and pleasure resumed its habitual course. Public debt
bonds rose five points, which was famously to the liking of Morny.
Meanwhile the police were "cleaning up." Houses were raided and
searched. Two thousand two hundred arrests were made—members
of secret societies, newspaper writers, lawyers, sometime deputies,
republicans all. The deputies who had been taken to Mazas on December 2nd were sifted out. Those judged more dangerous were
transferred to Vincennes or Mont Valérien. The generals—in irony,
perhaps?—were sent to Ham. The rest were freed, some of them
against their will. Thiers tried at first to walk the boulevards. He
was eventually recognized by some street urchins and catcalls drove
him to cover. Victor Hugo, Schoelcher and their colleagues on the
Committee of Resistance had already fled abroad.

With Paris gagged, what would the provinces have to say? Morny
urged vigorous measures on the prefects, and they joined in with
enthusiastic zeal. Republicans were hunted down everywhere. The
larger towns were overawed by their garrisons and kept silent.
Violent backwashes occurred in the Nièvre at Clamecy, in the Jura
at Poligny, in the Gers at Mirande and Lectoure, in the Hérault at
Béziers and Bédarieux, in the Drôme around Crest. In the Var a
veritable revolutionary army defied the regulars. In the Basses-
Alpes a whole department caught fire. An insurgent government
was set up at Digne while a modern Jacquerie spread terror through
the rural districts. But these movements had no real leaders. Un-
coordinated, they died down under the mailed fist after a few days.
Repression was merciless. Thirty-two departments were placed
under martial law. Suspects to the number of 26,642 were arrested.
Such victims were tried in the seats of the districts concerned by
"mixed commissions" made up of the prefects, of the commanding
generals and of the local State's attorneys. Sentences by such courts
were without appeal. A decree of the 8th of December, drawn up
by Morny, ordered the deportation "of any person whose presence

in the country seemed dangerous to public order." Such a text was unheard-of to begin with, but the proscribers went even beyond it. Republicans were treated like common outlaws. More than 5,000 were placed under "home surveillance"; 2,700 were compelled to take up residence in towns not their own; 1,545 were banished from France; 9,530 were transported to Algeria, most of them to military camps or fortresses; 240 went to faraway Guiana. These are mere figures, but they are eloquent. Exile rid the government of Thiers, of Rémusat, of Emile de Girardin, of Edgar Quinet, of Generals Changarnier, Lamoricière, Bedeau and Le Flô. Seventy-one republican deputies were driven from France. One of them, Miot, was even deported.[1]

The business classes in the towns, the propertied classes in the country, had long been trembling for their worldly goods, doubtless dearer to them than their lives. They applauded these rigorous measures. Many people of the working classes were proud to have their right to the ballot back again. They also approved. Morny congratulated his prefects. The Prince-President showered crosses and promotions upon the army. That was the least he could do— to the army he owed everything. Two obscure generals, Vaillant and Harispe, were made marshals. Magnan received the Grand Cross of the Legion d'honneur. Mass "bakes" of generals and colonels rewarded "upholders of public order."

The *coup d'état* was in itself a reprehensible act, but we shall see as we proceed that it was also a political blunder. Any notions of a return the princes of Orleans may have been cherishing presented no danger. As Changarnier said, as they were taking him to Mazas, "the President would have been re-elected anyway," in May, 1852. The Assembly was less of a menace to Louis Napoleon than he thought and less than his friends kept telling him. It might have taunted him, it might have intrigued or even legislated against him. It would never have put him in Vincennes. He could have remained in power by the prestige of his name alone, without violating his oath, without resorting to force. Certain of the support of the country, he could then have forced his will upon a remod-

---

[1] La Gorce: *Histoire du Second Empire*, I, 22 s. The work of P. de La Gorce in seven volumes, published between 1894 and 1904, is both the most important and the most complete of all the writings that have been devoted to the reign of Napoleon III. The author takes this occasion to express his appreciation of it.

elled parliament in which men of his party would beyond any doubt have far outnumbered his antagonists.

Granted as necessary, the *coup d'état* should have been managed differently. Morny as its head and Magnan as its arm bear an overwhelming responsibility in this regard. Morny was to admit as much later on when he said:

"The trouble with a *coup d'état* is that it amounts to a compromise with happiness."

Louis Napoleon was the first victim of these two men. The grandson of Talleyrand elected to achieve by terror, and that policy resulted first in atrocious slaughter, and then in a most brutal proscription. The new regime in consequence was to look like a military dictatorship from the start, and that blemish was to hamper it to the end. In the melancholy words of Empress Eugénie, "it would always be dragging that ball and chain on its foot."

CHAPTER VI

The New Consulate

HAVING ONCE SHEARED SO ROUGHLY IT WAS IMPERATIVE TO RESEW—not so much for a remissive France as for the alert foreigner abroad. A quick plebiscite, therefore, one that would approve and consolidate Louis Napoleon! His ministry first courted the Catholics: The Panthéon was restored to Christian worship and Lord's Day Observance was ordered for public shops and dockyards. In return for these gestures Montalembert and his friends conducted a warm campaign. The great Christian orator, usually more generous, added an assault on the defenders of legality.

"To vote for the Prince," he said, "is to give arms to power that it may subdue the army of crime, protect your churches, your homes, your wives, against men whose covetousness stops at nothing."

The vanquished could never have found a way to resist the fury of the victors. The press was meticulously muzzled. There was no opposition that dared to express itself. Nevertheless Morny was nervous. He at first prescribed a publicly registered vote for the plebiscite. At the suggestion of the ex-King Jerome, that device was abandoned: the balloting was to be secret. Now that his worries were over, Louis Napoleon, personally, had no doubts as to the result. He seemed more confident of ultimate success than the people about him. Did he not have the army on his side, then the masses and the wealthy classes, to say nothing of an overpowering remembrance?

On the 20th and 21st of December, France justified his fondest hopes: 7,439,216 votes—two million more than in 1848—against 646,737! That gave him all the authorization he needed to settle on a new Constitution as he saw fit. There was one fly in the ointment: the capital sulked. In Paris, in spite of official pressures, Louis

78

Napoleon got only 133,000 votes out of a recorded total of more than 300,000. The thorn pricked the conqueror to the quick. Thenceforth he would always mistrust Paris and always fear Paris.

A "Consulting Commission" was functioning as a feeble substitute for a legislative power. Chairman of it was Baroche, an ever eager fixer of ticklish business. He appeared before the Prince on December 31st to present him with the official figures of the plebiscite for a New Year's gift. In his presentation speech he counseled: "Re-establish the principle of authority in France! It has been too thoroughly dismantled during these past fifty years! Combat these anarchistic passions that are striking at the very foundations of society!"

Louis Napoleon replied in more liberal terms, even touching here and there an apologetic note:

"France has responded to my call. She has understood that I overstepped legal bounds only to return within them. . . . More than seven million votes *have just acquitted me*. . . . I hope to safeguard the future of France by founding institutions which will reflect both the democratic instincts of the nation and its universally expressed desire to be governed henceforward by a strong and respected power."

Democratic instincts, a strong power! He could hardly better have stated the dilemma that faced him. A long and latent struggle between liberty and authority makes up the very substance of the inner history of the Second Empire.

On January 1st a Te Deum was sung at Notre Dame, where the Prince-President was welcomed by the triumphal march that Lesueur had composed for Napoleon's coronation. After the ceremony he left the Elysée to take up residence in the Tuileries. French currency was being stamped with his portrait. He was already virtually a sovereign.

However, the decisive step had by no means yet been taken. What Louis Napoleon was resuscitating to his own advantage was not the Empire. He now desired a monarchy without a doubt, and the people closest about him wanted it even more. But he judged that the time still was not ripe. He wanted to draw a humble furrow parallel with the mighty trench that his uncle had dug in the history of Europe. He viewed his *coup d'état* as a replica of the 18th of Brumaire, and the period about to open as his own Consulate. Lasting or merely a necessary transition as the event might prove, the Constitution that Louis Napoleon proclaimed on the 14th of January reproduced the system of the Year VIII.

"The framework of our social edifice," he declared, "is the Emperor's creation. It has survived his fall and three revolutions. Why should political institutions deriving from the same source not have the same chances of lasting?"

That was forgetting that social institutions almost always run a different course from political institutions. At any rate, like the First Consul, the President of the Republic was to be elected for ten years. All prerogatives were vested in him. He was commander-in-chief of the armies. He could declare war and make peace. He made all appointments to public office. Cabinet ministers were responsible only to him and they could not be deputies in parliament. He alone could initiate legislation. Parliament functioned entirely at his pleasure. He could convene, adjourn, dissolve it, as he saw fit. He owed an accounting only to the French people. All of which was a way of saying that he was to be absolute master so long as luck was with him.

Again as in the Year VIII and using the same names, the Constitution set up three legislative organs: in order of ranking, a Senate, a State's Council, a Legislative Body. The Senate was to be made up of 150 men selected for life terms by the Head of the State—princes, high officials, prelates, military leaders, justices of the higher courts, distinguished talents of whatever sort—in theory at least. Its functions were to criticize laws before they were put into effect, to interpret the Constitution by resolution or senatus-consultum, in case the Legislative Body were not in session to vote emergency bills proposed by the President. Powers, in short, as comprehensive as they were vague. The Constitution was drawn up by Rouher and Troplong, more particularly the former. Working on short notice, they threw it together, catch as catch can. They mistrusted the Legislative Body that emanated from the country. They had no mistrust whatever of the Senate which emanated from the Chief. In it, one may be sure, they expected to figure importantly themselves.

The State Council was to draft legislation and appoint delegates from its own membership to move and defend the bills proposed before the Legislative Body.

The latter was rather small—261 deputies, elected for six years and bound by oath. It voted all laws and it also voted the budget. This last was the one effective weapon that the Chamber, in its complete prostration, still retained. No initiative whatever was left it. It could not question the ministers. They were never members of the Legislative Body, and it had no contacts whatever with them. Its labors, apart from a succinct minute, were not to be published.

Deputies to the Legislative Body worked without salary. State Councillors received salaries of 25,000 francs. The President reserved the right to grant dotations of 30,000 francs to certain senators of his choosing.

"No one will accept such a gift!" exclaimed Montalembert, when Louis Napoleon mentioned this arrangement to him.

"You think so?" answered the Prince, quietly.

And he was right. He was to suffer very few rebuffs.

All in all, the silent legislators foretold by Berryer a year earlier had come on the scene and with a vengeance. It was the 18th of Brumaire over again. France was tired of inner convulsing. She was surrendering to a leader. The great Napoleon in his day had rewarded her for her trust with a period of order and glory. His nephew set out to imitate him; but the nephew also meant to do something more. He shared in that stirring of lofty ideals that characterized the epoch, and he wanted to bestow a larger measure of well-being upon his country. In that lies his peculiar originality. Despot that he was, Louis Napoleon was to be the first socially minded sovereign in Europe.

While the new gearings were being fitted together, the Prince-President released a flood of decrees designed to insure his peaceful hold on power. Cooperative societies were dissolved, book-publishing was taken severely in hand, national guards were disbanded, political clubs were forbidden to reopen. Emblems of the Republic were obliterated from public buildings. The last Liberty Poles were felled. For another reminiscence of the Consulate and Empire, the Ministry of Police was reestablished—this as a plum for Maupas.

Outstanding in this mass of ordinances, which swelled the *Moniteur* of January, 1852, to double size, were two decrees confiscating the properties of the princes of Orleans. On becoming king Louis Philippe had, irregularly enough, bestowed all his personal properties upon his children. That gift was now annulled, the properties returning to the State, to which they should have gone in the first place. They were eventually to be sold, the proceeds being divided among public institutions of one sort or another, loan and credit societies, housing projects, the Légion d'honneur. At the bottom of this act of thievery lay Persigny. Louis Napoleon was led into it by his long-standing aversion to the House of Orleans and in disregard of the entreaties of his cousin, Mathilde.

It won a public disapprobation that was virtually unanimous. Hübner wrote:

"The confiscation has let loose a veritable tempest in society and in parliamentary circles."

In fact the salons began to buzz like beehives and in no little disparagement of the Prince.

"The first flight [theft] of the Eagle!" (*C'est le premier vol de l'aigle*), remarked Dupin, for a courageous pun, and the jest caught the public fancy.

Rouher, Magne and Fould resigned from the ministry. Morny was momentarily at outs with his half-brother for having tactlessly alluded at a public dinner to the secret ties that bound him to the dictator. He seized upon this convenient and creditable pretext to withdraw into his tents. Montalembert had so far gone along with the Prince-President. He now haughtily severed the alliance. The brand-new State Council itself balked, and two of its members were summarily dismissed.

The Orleanist scandal so created three vacancies in the cabinet. Louis Napoleon replaced Morny in the Interior with Persigny. Persigny really wanted Foreign Affairs, two missions to the King of Prussia in 1849 and 1850 in the Prince's behalf having stirred diplomatic ambitions in him. That portfolio was left with Turgot. Abbatucci, one of the Prince's closest friends, took Justice, and Bineau, Finance.

Another batch of decrees came along. They dealt with the disciplining of public officials, with the prerogatives of prefects and mayors, with election procedures. More particularly they set up a far-reaching control of the press. Newspapers were left even less freedom than they had enjoyed under the Restoration. Advance authorizations were required, bonds for good conduct, a stamp tax per copy. High postage rates finished the muzzling. If an article, or even a drawing, proved displeasing to the government, the Minister of the Interior could issue a warning or suspend publication outright. Any independent news-gathering was made an offense to be tried not by jury but before the Courts of Correction. In Paris hardly more than a half dozen newspapers stood the strain.

Working under such handicaps, however, newspaper writers—and there were plenty of good ones in those days, as the government was soon to discover—gained in ingenuity and in wit. Prévost-Paradol could well exclaim:

"Long live oppression, when it comes to giving full value to thought and developing all its resources! What an education in concentrating force, in drawing the subtle and shrewd nuance, in disciplining a terse, sharp-edged style! The general quiet is favorable to the man who has something to say. The old fogies are silenced. The mountebanks get off the streets. There is room, at last, for the artist!" [1]

Public office-holders were required, like the deputies in the Legislative Body, to swear an oath of fidelity to the President personally. Numbers of university men refused to take such an oath and resigned. Fortoul, as Minister of Education, bullied and ragged the Ecole Normale. Full-fledged professors were obliged to submit outlines of their courses for government approval. For an amusing extravagance, they were forbidden to wear beards, which were somehow felt to smack of sedition.

As personal representatives of the executive, the prefects soared aloft with him. Fatly salaried, invested with all powers and functions, they were masters absolute in their departments. The government appointed all mayors and deputy-mayors. In the great city, in the rural hamlet, they became fawning agents of the dictator.

Local organizations kept the masses well in hand. Closely watched also by the gendarmerie and the police, and daily blessed with an unending fall of manna in the shape of governmental contracts, they could well be allowed the privilege of universal suffrage, which it was hardly possible to deny them in view of the Prince's recent past and his pledges. Their use of the suffrage, however, was narrowly limited. The plebiscite which, it was hoped, would never again be necessary, was to be followed by a "consultation" every six years, and such elections could, naturally, be carefully supervised by the

[1] Letter to Gérard, March 17, 1853.

government. That, in literal truth, was taking the people's rights at their face value.

"I am quite willing to be baptized with the water of universal suffrage," said the Prince to Montalembert, "but I do not intend to live with my feet in a puddle."

He had no reason to fear. He was to live dry-shod.

Coming next to the problem of economic reorganization, Louis Napoleon was eager to open his rule with a group of improvements in the nation's plant: railroads in large numbers connecting Paris with Lyons, Strasbourg, the manufacturing centers of the North; a thick network of telegraph lines covering all the country; as a help to agriculture, a loan and mortgage bank; public pawn-shops and aid and loan societies to be overhauled and modernized.

Moving too precipitately in the field of finance the Prince-President ordered a conversion of 5 percent debt bonds into $4\frac{1}{2}$ percents. A panic on Exchange resulted, which only the support of the banks could halt. Finally he fixed by decree, with some slight increase, the current budget which had not been passed by the Assembly as late as December 2nd.

Four months of rigorous dictatorship thus prepared for the opening of a parliament that could be little more than servile. The elections of February 29, 1852, ground out by the prefects under the harsh driving of Persigny, resulted in a complete triumph, too complete a triumph, for the government's ticket. Of the 261 deputies only eight could be counted in opposition, five royalists and three republicans, Cavaignac, Carnot, and Hénon.

Apart from the array of cardinals, marshals and admirals that usually adorn appointive higher houses, the Prince named only 72 senators, most of them undistinguished men. The ex-King Jerome, now a marshal of France, was to manage the Senate, in name at least. Rouher and Magne had not lost favor because of their recent resignation from the ministry. They entered the State Council, of which Baroche was president, as section chiefs. A State Minister, Casabianca, was designated to represent the government before the Chambers, ordinary ministers being barred from those precincts.

On March 29, 1852, the President gathered the senators and deputies together at the Tuileries in the Hall of the Marshals, with a display that foresavored of a new Imperial court. He wrote his own speech and it was a skillful one. He justified the *coup d'état*, dissected the Constitution, and promised that, if things remained quiet in the country, liberties which had been curtailed in the interests of order might soon be extended. He made no bones of it in broaching the matter of a second Empire. "If the various factions accept the situation, nothing will be changed." If they persisted in their opposition—"if they continue forever compromising the future of the country with their attacks, *then, but only then,* may it seem reasonable to ask the people, in the name of peace for France, for a new title that will fix upon my head beyond recall the authority with which it has invested me." He ended, however, with the words:

"Let us not worry too much over contingencies that may in all probability never arise. Let us keep the Republic. It harms no one. It can be a comfort to everybody."

The Prince desired that Morny should take the chairmanship of the Legislative Body—for the Chamber did not have the right even to elect its own officials. Persigny and Maupas were bitter enemies of Morny. They did not like the idea. They thought that he had too many irons in the fire. He had not dismounted from his high horse in the President's regard, criticizing him at times in the most bitter language. They persuaded the Prince to accept Billault, a man whom Jerome was sponsoring. Billault had been a deputy in the time of Louis Philippe and was an orator of talent. Considered as a man, he had moved from the liberal to the imperial camp somewhat precipitately, but in the exercise of his new functions he was to show himself a man of real parts.

The session opened at the Palais Bourbon on the 30th of March. The deputies, for the most part, were newcomers, without political experience and henchmen from the start of the power that had made them. Without leaders, closely supervised by a number of State Councillors who directed legislative activities from above down, they were obliged—a very suggestive precaution—to speak from their desks: the tribune had been abolished.

The three republicans, Cavaignac, Carnot and Hénon, refused to take the oath of allegiance to Louis Napoleon and were forthwith declared unseated. A handful of royalists, and a number of individuals, also, who were devoted to the Prince but could not stomach such craven servility of intellect, alone maintained a certain semblance of self-respect in the face of two hundred and fifty factory owners and prosperous farmers who were content to bleat in unison.

A solitary figure in the assembly was Montalembert, who vainly sought to fertilize that desert with his courage and his eloquence. The question of the budget for 1853 came up, in disquieting circumstances, since the figures showed a current deficit of 40 millions on top of a floating debt of 750 millions. The Catholic orator voiced a bitter, however tempered, protest:

"You are condemned to vote this budget as a whole or else to reject it. You are presented with an alternative: all or nothing. . . . Now such an alternative I regard as absurd. It is revolting in a matter of finance. I regard it as a grievous wrong to abolish all criticism and to reduce to nothing the one elective body that exists in the French government. Sooner or later the country will find itself in serious difficulties on this account."

That was seeing clearly. A government that has no safety valve will some day crack or maybe explode.

Louis Napoleon was in attendance at the session. He listened to that sage warning in anger. Straightway, through a communication from State Minister Casabianca, he reminded the Legislative Body that it could either assent or decline to act. The Assembly assented. As the question of secret funds came up, the Ministry of Police, the brazen promotion of Espinasse to the rank of general in recognition of his services on December 2nd, only a few rapid comments were flashed, and such that the government could pretend not to have heard them. With its cut-and-dried agenda disposed of, the Assembly disbanded on the 28th of June, without the country's having been aware that it existed.

In this silence born of tyranny the bourgeoisie forgot the "red menace" and breathed freely and expansively. Many Legitimists, out of hatred for the Orleanists, rallied to a political system that bore such a close resemblance to monarchy, that rested on the clergy and was bent everywhere on reestablishing moral and social peace. The Church, of course, approved wholeheartedly. Some few clericals, Lacordaire, Monsignor Dupanloup, Father Ravignan, did not like the *coup d'état*. Other leaders of French Catholicism, Montalembert, Falloux, Veuillot, gave it their qualified approval. The farming masses had as yet acquired little sense of civic liberties. They clung to a hope of gradual and pacific improvements in wages. Factory hands in the towns were inclined to accept the accomplished fact—in many of their hearts traces of old Napoleonic idealism still lingered. They knew, moreover, that the Prince was interested in social questions and they relied on him for improvements in the lot of the working classes. Banking, manufacturing, business, construction, thought that a Golden Age was opening before them.

Society had soon returned to its normal rhythm of activity, with perhaps an accentuation in gaiety and animation. The Senate assigned the Prince a salary of twelve millions. He was no longer required to count his pennies: gorgeous receptions at the Tuileries, at the Military School, at Saint-Cloud. His power seemed to be so well established, he felt so sure of himself, that he readily mitigated his first asperities. Martial law was ended. Three Commissioners, Quentin-Beauchart, Canrobert and Espinasse, were sent to the departments to review sentences of the "Mixed Commissions" and recommend pardons. Quentin-Beauchart, a State Councillor with a tender heart and a lavish hand, granted 3,440 pardons. Canrobert was more timid. He stopped at 727. Espinasse was averse to any dilly-dallying whatever. He issued a bare 300. Nevertheless, after all this appeasement, 6,000 proscripts still remained under the government's ban.

Gradually, inevitably, the road to monarchy was opening. General and local councils, which had been elected under the eye of the prefects, began to petition in large numbers for a reestablishment of the Empire. Napoleonic emblems and mementoes began appearing on all hands. Eagles were distributed to the regiments. The 5th of May was observed by a solemn service in Notre Dame. The 15th of August was made a national holiday. The Civil Code was again referred to in public documents as the Napoleonic Code.

The Republic had ceased to exist as anything more than an inscription on the back-drop of the French political stage. The new regime was now a reality both in the fact and in the national state of mind. Six months were to pass before it became a reality as regarded legal forms. That postponement was necessary to make sure of a definite settling down in the country, to reenforce the already powerful position of the Prince-President, to accustom opinion in Europe to a Napoleonic restoration, finally and perhaps particularly, to overcome the last shreds of reluctance, the last lingering hesitations, of the man who was already master of everything in France but would not yet call himself Emperor.

On the 28th of July the Prince overhauled his cabinet. In the Ministry of State the adroit Fould succeeded Casabianca, who had proved inadequate to the many delicate manipulations that fell to that important office. Drouyn de Lhuys replaced Turgot in Foreign Affairs. Persigny, still in the Interior, remained the effective head of the government.

Success had in no sense changed the man. Brutal, erratic, moody, all of a piece, his head crammed with ideas, some sound, some fantastic, Persigny was part prophet and part the incorrigible child, at once indispensable and a nuisance. The *Mémorial* of Las Cases was his Gospel and Napoleon his God. He had devoted his life to the wondrous adventure. Now he thought the time had come to crown its achievement and he was ill-disposed to wait. With all his Napoleonic mysticism, with all his oaths, diatribes, rages, he pestered this friend of his youth whom he had followed in so many escapades and whom a dazzling reversal of fortunes had slipped into the cloak of the First Consul.

Louis Napoleon held out. Was it timidity, indolence, unwillingness to tempt Fortune too far? He knew perfectly well that he would someday be Emperor, but he did not feel quite ready to assume the crown. Persigny kept at him, nagged him as to his intentions, stormed at his spinelessness.

To Falloux he said one day:

"You know what's holding the Empire off? It's the Emperor himself, nothing more! His timidity is a disease! He is taking his ten years seriously. . . . We have not convinced him yet, but we still have hopes." [1]

As Minister of the Interior he held the immediate exercise of power in his own hands, and deliberately and wholeheartedly he set about compromising the Prince in public opinion, frankly boosting him to a throne that sat waiting and into which by now he had only to let himself fall.

To bring things to a head he arranged a trip for his master through the departments of the center and south. Louis Napoleon told his ministers that his idea was to feel out public temper in those districts. Some time previous Persigny had asked in open cabinet meeting what attitude he should order the prefects to assume when anyone cheered for the Emperor in their presence.

[1] Ollivier, *L'Empire libéral,* III, 36.

The inquiry had seemed grossly premature and the imprudent minister had almost been asked to resign. That was a lesson to Persigny. On this occasion he set about working up an ovation for the "Emperor" without any warning either to the President or to his colleagues in the cabinet. He sent a circular to the prefects who were to receive the Prince, ordering them to arrange demonstrations everywhere along his route with copious vivas for the Empire and the Emperor.

The Head of the State set out for Bourges on the 14th of September in company with Saint-Arnaud and Maupas. Prompted by their general the troops hailed him as Emperor. His reception at Nevers, at Moulins, at Saint-Etienne, was exactly the same.

The Prince was scheduled to unveil a statue of Napoleon at Lyons. He did so, amidst sincere outbursts of enthusiasm. But his speech on the occasion astounded and grievously disappointed the clique about him. There in public he examined his own conscience and with a touch of real nobility expressed his doubts:

"We have scarcely issued from critical moments when conceptions of right and wrong have lost their distinctness so that the best-intentioned minds often go astray. Patriotism, nay, ordinary wisdom, require that at such moments the nation should ponder deeply before deciding its ultimate destinies. . . . If the modest title of President should suffice for performing the mission that is entrusted to me and which I have not shirked, I, certainly, should never, out of considerations of personal interest, desire to change it for the title of Emperor."

Words, shall one say? They had the ring of sincerity. Louis Napoleon had not as yet made up his mind. On meeting Persigny again at Roanne he snubbed him flatly for having tried to force his hand. But there was no stopping that mad devotion. Persigny made short shrift of his master's fears and scruples. In the southern provinces the police were fearful of hostile demonstrations and therefore had doubled both precautions and preparations. Citizens known to have democratic tendencies were locked up for several days. City governments ordered flags by day and lamps by night for all houses, under pain of fines. That was overreaching needs. As a matter of fact, as he rode under embowered arches, or lettered flags that hailed him as Emperor or lauded the 2nd of December, Louis Napoleon met everywhere eager and enthusiastic crowds. At Grenoble, at Avignon, at Marseilles, Montpelier, Toulouse, it was one procession of flattering prefects, bishops, generals, to burn incense along his path. Could he have any further doubts that France wanted to go back to the Empire?

He noted the fact officially in the speech he delivered at Bordeaux, where a shrewd prefect, Haussmann, had arranged demonstrations without end. The speech answered in advance criticisms that the restoration of the Empire could be expected to attract from die-hards in the various oppositions:

"There are those who, in a spirit of mistrust, say to themselves that the Empire means war. I say to you, the Empire means peace. Peace, because France desires peace, and when France is satisfied the world is quiet. Glory can well be handed on as an inheritance. That is not the case with war."

He went on to outline the policy of his future reign, a policy that had political, religious and economic facets and so was designed to please everybody and in fact did so—immensely.

"I agree—I have, like the Emperor, many conquests to make. Like him I wish to win dissenting parties to friendliness. . . . I wish to win for religion, for morality and for prosperity that still so large part of our population which lives in a country of faith and piety and yet hardly knows the Commandments of Jesus, which dwells on the most fertile lands on earth and still hardly enjoys its products of prime necessity.

"We have waste lands of vast extent to bring under cultivation; we have roads to build, harbors to deepen, rivers to make navigable, canals to finish, a railroad system to complete. Across the sea in front of Marseilles we have a huge empire to assimilate to France. . . . Everywhere we have ruins to repair, false gods to overthrow, truths to bring to triumph.

"In such fashion would I conceive of the Empire, if the Empire is to be again. Such are the conquests that I am premeditating, and you here about me, you wish as I wish the welfare of our country, and you are my soldiers."

On his way back to Paris he stopped at Amboise and set Abd-el-Kader at liberty—the Arab hero who had been a prisoner since 1847.

The scene was a pretty one:

"You have been an enemy of France," the Prince began, "but in all justice I must recognize your courage, your integrity, your fortitude in misfortune. That is why I consider it an honor to put an end to your captivity, having absolute trust in your word."

Standing straight and erect in his white burnous, his beard prematurely grey, a string of beads in his small slender hands, more like an Oriental saint than a military chief, the blue-eyed emir gazed softly at the man in gold braid and epaulettes who was addressing him, who like himself had known life in prison, but whom prison had exalted to the pinnacles of power. He thanked him with noble graciousness:

"My bones are old. The rest of my body you have made young again by your kindness."

And that kindness Abd-el-Kader was to remember eight years later, at the time of the Syrian massacres.

Paris welcomed Louis Napoleon in triumph. Bells rang, cannon boomed, the police watched. There was but one cheer to greet him: "*Vive l'Empereur!*"

One evening, at the Comédie Française, Rachel appeared on the stage and declaimed some very wretched lines on a now classic theme, "The Empire means peace." Directly afterwards, as more than one wit laughingly remarked, the curtain rose on Musset's skit: "*You Can Never Be Sure*" (*Il ne faut jurer de rien*).

Meantime, the racing locomotive bowled along. The Senate met on November 4th to amend the Constitution. Upon a hurried report by Troplong, it adopted a resolution calling for the reestablishment of the imperial status for the benefit of Louis Napoleon and his descendants. There was one single "nay." It came from the republican Vieillard, the sometime friend and adviser of the Prince whom the latter had named senator in gratitude and despite their differences in political faith.

A plebiscite was taken on November 21st to ratify the Assembly's decision. There were diatribes from the exiled democrats. There was a vigorous protest from the Comte de Chambord. Two Legitimist deputies resigned, Kerdrel and Calvières. In spite of that no one had any doubt as to the outcome.

That evening, Louis Napoleon gave a little ball at Saint-Cloud, to celebrate, as Hübner expressed it, "the burial of the Republic." The burial certificate was countersigned by France to the tune of 7,824,000 votes against 253,000. However, large numbers of voters kept away from the polls—more than 2,000,000. This huge figure was due to the royalist provinces in the west and the republican cities of the south, but its size should have given pause to moderately prudent souls. Unfortunately, a sort of intoxication had laid hold on the Prince's entourage, and he himself, in that rosy sunrise of sovereign power, allowed himself to get out of hand. He had just bought the pretty château at Villeneuve-l'Etang. Forthwith he demolished the wall that separated its park from the domain of Saint-Cloud. Bacciochi, his factotum, remarked that later on that procedure might give rise to trouble with the State.

Louis Napoleon looked at him in astonishment.

"For me," he said, "there is to be no 'later on.' I shall live or I shall die, right here."

CHAPTER VII

Napoleon III

DURING THE NIGHT OF DECEMBER 1, 1852, SENATORS, COUNCILLORS of state, deputies, escorted by cavalry bearing torches, set out in a procession of carriages to hail the Emperor at Saint-Cloud. Billaut made a speech on the theme, "France places herself in your hands." Louis Napoleon replied with the decorum characteristic of his utterances at this period. He appealed to all parties and factions and voiced oneness of interest with the former dynasties. His one wish was to represent the country, and all the country.

"Help me, gentlemen," he pleaded, in a voice husky with emotion, "help me to set up a stable government which shall rest on piety, probity, justice, love for the suffering masses."

The next day was the triple anniversary of Austerlitz, of Napoleon's coronation and of Louis Napoleon's *coup d'état*. The Emperor entered Paris in all solemnity. He threaded the Arch at l'Etoile, riding between Saint-Arnaud and Persigny. The troops lining the Carrousel welcomed him with unrestrained huzzahs. After all the restoration of the Empire was in a very special way a triumph for the army too. In spite of successes in Algeria the soldiers were still under the depression of Waterloo. Now like horses whinnying at the sound of the trumpet, they raised their heads joyously towards the gleaming eagle, which, as of yore in the days of the Other One, tipped their new battle-flags.

Returning to the Tuileries the Emperor found a gold-braided crowd fawning in homage about him. Bees and crowned N's had reappeared everywhere, on walls, on upholstery, on rugs and tapestries. Twirling the points of his mustache which was sweeping broader and broader, he walked straight ahead, slowly, his eyes half-closed, his face brightened with just the suggestion of a smile.

He had taken the name of Napoleon III, the only one appropriate after all, since the King of Rome had regularly succeeded his father and been proclaimed Emperor in 1815 both by the Representatives and the Peers.

His first visit was to the Hôtel-Dieu. His first decree accorded a generous amnesty. His two confederates of December 2nd, Saint-Arnaud and Magnan, were named marshals, along with General de Castellane. Morny was given the Grand Cross of the Légion d'honneur, Walewski became Grand-Officer. The senators were awarded a uniform honorarium of 30,000 francs. In return they doubled the civil list of the Emperor to 25,000,000.

This came as a complete surprise to Napoleon III. He had been satisfied with his 12,000,000. Persigny, however, was eager to see a little real magnificence. He fooled Troplong by a clown's trick, altering the figures in the sketch of the Senate bill, and persuaded him that the Emperor's secret wish was to have a civil list of 25,-000,000. Troplong made haste to have the "raise" passed by the Senate. When Napoleon received the resolution, he was the picture of astonishment. He understood that Persigny had been up to something, but he said nothing. Not until ten years later did he allude to the matter. Then, complaining one day to Persigny about the burdens that were falling on his privy-purse, he exclaimed:

"Where would we be if you had not altered the figures for my civil list?"

Troplong succeeded Jerome as president of the Senate. The ex-king had shown himself incapable of performing any useful function in that office. The cabinet in power was not modified. Walewski went as ambassador to London, Castelbajac to St. Petersburg, Bourqueney to Vienna, Moustier to Berlin. Morny, half in disgrace, was left cooling his heels offstage. He busied himself there, however, working on a fifty-fifty basis with his pretty mistress, Mme. Le Hon, wife of the Minister from Belgium, arranging little deals which brought in money perhaps too easily. For that matter he was to return to favor before very long.

It is known that Morny's real wish on the occasion of his half-brother's accession would have been to be recognized as a prince of the blood. The matter was long on his mind. After his death a curious note that well reflects his state of mind was found among his papers:

"I am the last son of the Queen born during her marriage to the

EMPRESS EUGÉNIE

From the Portrait by Edouard Dubufe

King of Holland. Consequently, according to law, I am very regularly Prince Bonaparte, legitimate brother to the present Emperor and the victim of a crime—the crime of suppressing an individual's legal status. I have more than enough evidence to establish my rights, if I were the man to use it. Though I am, as a matter of principle, not at all inclined to use it, that is no reason for . . ."

His pen stopped at that point.[1]

While thus busy rewarding his friends and showing an indulgent disposition towards his adversaries, Napoleon III got the Senate to augment his powers still further. Henceforward he would have the right to modify commercial treaties at will and to order such public works as he should choose. He gained full control of the budget by virtue of a power to authorize transfers of credit from one account to another. That stripped the Legislative Body of the little influence it still retained; but the pill was sugared for the deputies by an award to all of them of an "indemnification" of 2,500 francs a month while in session. That was a favorite tactic of the regime: to distract attention from the absence of liberties by satisfactions of a practical nature.

The proclamation of the Empire came as no surprise to Europe. Louis Napoleon had sent a man of his confidence, Heeckeren, to sound out tempers in Vienna, Berlin, St. Petersburg. In Berlin the reception was courteous, cold. At St. Petersburg, Czar Nicholas was anxious to preserve the edifice of 1815. He showed himself resolutely hostile to any reestablishment of the Empire. In Vienna Chancellor Buol was encouraging. He said:

"Austria is an old power. You are a new government. Well, deal with us gently—treat us with consideration! In good society, remember, it's the wall-flowers that make the reputations of the young."

The rise of Louis Napoleon to the presidency had been viewed with favor by the sovereigns abroad. They regarded him as a bulwark against the revolutionary tide. France, ever idealistic, ever nervous, had shaken too many thrones in times past. The kings wanted nothing so much as to see a sound social order, a real stability, get a foothold in that country.

But an imperial restoration was another matter. It frightened them. It involved a grave question of principle, moreover. At the

---

[1] Frédéric Lollée, *La Comtesse Le Hon.*

Congress of Vienna, the Powers had engaged mutually never to allow the return of a Bonaparte to the throne of France. Europe at that time respected treaties. Would they recognize the new Emperor now, or would they not? Worse still, the three great monarchies, Russia, Prussia, and Austria, still stood united in the Holy Alliance. Their diplomatic policy had been fixed for a third of a century. Could they consent to such a signal repudiation of it?

The second line powers made up their minds soonest: the Two-Sicilies, Switzerland, Belgium, the German principalities. Spain followed before long.

With an eye to the future, Victor Emmanuel, King of Sardinia, was more expansive than any of the others. He sent an old friend of Louis Napoleon's, the Count Arese, to congratulate him on his accession. The Emperor received Arese affectionately, lodged him in quarters next to his own in the Tuileries, begged him to urge the King to come to Paris.

"Be sure to tell him," he exclaimed, "that he can count on my friendship."

Even England had no great difficulty in deciding. The *coup d'état* of the previous year aroused a storm of anger across the Channel. The spilling of so much blood shocked Queen Victoria. She ordered her ambassador, Lord Normanby, not to attend the service of thanksgiving that was celebrated at Notre Dame for the success of the *coup d'état*. The liberal press caught fire. Palmerston was old friends with the Prince-President. When, rashly, he applauded the fall of the Republic, he was forced to resign from the government. But the passage of time had weakened principles and soothed long-standing indignations. Napoleon III was personally attractive, if not to the English public at large, at least to London society. He had lived for long years in the English Mayfair. He passed for a gentleman and a progressive mind. His pacific pronouncements had pleased the British. As early as December 6th, the new head of the Foreign Office, Lord Malmesbury, also an old personal friend of the Emperor's, announced to Parliament that the Queen would recognize the French Empire.

"The new sovereign," said he, "has assumed the title of Napoleon III; but he derives his power not from a claim of imperial descent, which would be contrary to the declarations of the Congress of Vienna, but from the will of the nation."

The British Cabinet went further still. It exerted its influence to obtain the assent of the other European courts.

Frederick William, King of Prussia, remained overtly hostile. A mystical Lutheran, with an inflexible conscience, always trying to find an unattainable balance between his moral principles and his worldly ambitions, he feared France and hated the name of Bonaparte. The *coup d'état* gave him visions of a new upset in Europe. He thought that Belgium was in danger, and proposed a defensive alliance to England, Russia, and Austria, offering his own army as a nucleus.

Neither St. Petersburg nor Vienna took the erratic statesman seriously.

Czar Nicholas, as an autocrat, thoroughly approved of December 2nd in itself, but he could only view with displeasure the rise of another empire in Europe and especially a Napoleonic empire. He finally came around to recognizing Napoleon, but with bad grace. The credentials to Louis Napoleon with which he supplied his ambassador, Kisselev, began with the words, "Sire and good friend," instead of the words "Dear brother," that were usual among sovereigns. Drouyn de Lhuys, the French Minister of Foreign Affairs, called Kisselev's attention to the point.

"The court of St. Petersburg is rather young," he remarked, "to be breaking with tradition or trying to create new precedents."

Napoleon III, for his part, wittily pretended to like the Czar's originality.

"You must thank His Imperial Majesty warmly for his kindness," he said to Kisselev, "and especially for the words, 'good friend,' which he used. One has to put up with one's brothers. One chooses one's friends."

Kisselev enjoyed a good joke.

"There can be no doubt about it," he said on leaving the Tuileries. "That man is somebody."

Napoleon III had, nevertheless, felt the Czar's slight and he was to lay it aside for future reference.

Recognition of the imperial regime by Prussia and Austria soon came along in the routine forms and without incident.

CHAPTER VIII

Eugénie de Montijo

THE FIRST CONCERN OF A DYNASTY MUST BE THE TRANSMISSION OF its status by heredity. The Bonapartes were in the saddle again, but if the son of Hortense should become unavailable, who would succeed him? The Senate did not like the ex-King Jerome. He was known of old as a rake and was generally execrated. Jerome's son, Prince Napoleon, was known to be much too friendly with "reds" and demagogues. The Senate, therefore, left the succession unsettled.

On December 26, 1852, the Emperor ruled by decree in favor, *ad interim,* first of his uncle, then of his cousin, for he hoped soon to have direct heirs of his own.

He had decided that it was high time for him to marry—was he not forty-four? A few months previous he had asked the hand of the Princess Wasa, grand-daughter of his cousin, Stephanie of Baden. The Archduchess Sophie, mother of the young Emperor Francis Joseph, was the mistress of the Prince of Wasa and led him around by the nose. She foiled the projected match. She could not bring herself to seeing the son of Hortense occupying a place that should have belonged to the King of Rome, whom she had loved.

Shortly afterwards Morny opened negotiations with Prince Hohenlohe-Langenburg, a connection of the British royal family. The Prince's daughter, Adelaide, would have liked nothing better than to become an empress. Queen Victoria was sounded out by Walewski. She did not know. She was not sure the new regime would last. She had also heard that at that very moment Napoleon III was being very attentive to a Montijo woman, said to be a very beautiful Spanish girl.

Like his mother Hortense, and his grandmother Josephine, the new emperor was of an amorous disposition. He had had mistresses without number and from all classes in society, for he considered externals only and his heart was fickle. Already he could count three natural children at least, two born during his detention in the fortress at Ham of the beautiful "girl in sabots," Eleanore Vergeot; and another by Miss Howard, his "English tie." To Miss Howard he was linked by force of habit, and also by gratitude. He was anxious now to work their relation over into a bond of loyal friendship. For several months past he had been fascinated by Eugénie de Montijo, a lady of the high Spanish nobility, Countess of Teba, who was visiting the capitals and watering-places of Europe under the chaperonage of her mother and was having a great success in brilliant circles in Paris. Her beauty, her natural and easy grace, attracted, then infatuated him.

Eugénie was a girl of twenty-seven: red hair, a transparent complexion, a little head perched on a long, graceful neck; blue eyes, perhaps too close together, but with eyelids shaped like sea shells; a straight nose; fresh, rosy lips. She was made to infatuate: her sloping shoulders, her full breasts, showed her already the mature woman. Of narrow intelligence, she was proud, impulsively chivalrous, tenacious in her affections as in her prejudices, of which she had not a few. She was uncompromisingly Catholic though without bigotry. There were numerous and serious gaps in her education, but she had read, knowing four languages and speaking all of them vivaciously, not seldom brilliantly. Something of a flirt, dressing stylishly but perhaps too conspicuously at times, she was the finished woman of the world and had all the men about her. Male society was the society she preferred. The women gossiped and did not seek her company.

Just before the restoration of the Empire, the Countess de Montijo and her daughter were invited to a hunt which the Prince gave at Fontainebleau. More and more Eugénie was in his thoughts. The pleasure he at first found in seeing her now ripened into a besetting desire of which he was sure he could never free himself. Had he thought of marrying her already? That is not likely. His followers, his family, and his cousin Napoleon in particular, kept insisting that the Spanish girl would ask nothing better than to become another Pompadour. They were sadly mistaken. The young lady had family behind her and character, to say nothing of religious scruples. She would never have accepted an equivocal status.

During the sojourn at Fontainebleau the Prince lost his head completely and spoke his heart. Mlle. de Montijo replied evasively. Doubtless she had no very clear intentions herself.

Her mother had them for her. The Countess de Montijo had been a political figure in Madrid, and despite a number of reincarnations, she had outgrown neither intrigue nor ambition. Just the right move now and her daughter would be an empress! The señora played her cards with a masterly hand, though Eugénie disliked her game and Lesseps, her cousin, Mérimée, her friend, and the Duchess of Alba, her eldest daughter, were openly contrary.

Shortly after the proclamation of the Empire there was another hunt at Compiègne. Napoleon III pressed Eugénie still more ardently. They went for a walk and he so far forgot himself as to pluck a branch of ivy, shape it to the form of a crown and place it on her head.

"Till the other one comes!" he murmured.

He had reached this half-promise to the serious damage of the Hohenlohe project, which was still hanging fire; and he followed it up at a ball at the Tuileries on December 31st. Mlle. de Montijo was snubbed by Mme. Fortoul, wife of the Minister of Education. The Emperor patted her hand and assured her of his devotion. But the next day came a visit from the Ambassador to London. Walewski was greatly alarmed at the rumors that were flying about. He begged the Emperor not to compromise an alliance that might assure the new regime of England's friendship.

Caught off guard, a trifle sheepish, Napoleon III finally forced himself to reply:

"Well, I will sacrifice my own feelings. I will marry Princess Adelaide of Hohenlohe, if the decision we are awaiting from her involves marriage. If she refuses, I shall marry Mlle. de Montijo at once."

He was hoping for a refusal from Queen Victoria, and in fact, the Queen lectured her niece, painted the French Emperor as a flighty, unreliable person, convinced her that however brilliant the present with such a husband might be, there was no guarantee of either happiness or security in the future.

The British embassy gave the appropriate hint to Napoleon III as early as January 8th. He at once made his decision. Ministers such as Drouyn de Lhuys, Persigny and Fortoul, threatened to resign if he lowered himself to an unkingly marriage. He ignored their arguments, indifferent to the effects which such a union might have upon courts where the question of his recognition was still pending. On January 13th he sent the head of his cabinet, Mocquard, to present to Señora de Montijo his formal request for her daughter's hand.

He announced his betrothal at the next cabinet meeting:

"I am not asking your opinion, gentlemen. I am informing you of my resolve."

The rumbling storm immediately fell silent before the sovereign will. The ministers bowed. The imperial family swallowed its disappointment.

The impression in society was bad. The Faubourg Saint-Germain veiled its face in holy horror. Stocks dropped on Exchange. The salons quoted an in fact amusing thrust of Thiers:

"I always thought the Emperor was a man of wit. Today I see in him a man of foresight. By this marriage he makes sure of being at least a grandee of Spain."

The disastrous views in diplomatic circles were reflected by Hübner who wrote:

"When a man of forty-five, and an emperor to boot, decides on a sentimental whim to marry for love and metamorphose his wife into an empress at the risk of ruining himself in the opinion of his country and of Europe—such a man is a man one may well mistrust."

But the general public in France was inclined to a rather favorable judgment of the match, especially in Paris where the women liked this touch of romance.

On the 22nd of January, Napoleon III assembled the officers of the Senate, the Legislative Body and the Council of State at the Tuileries and announced his forthcoming marriage to them in a speech that might easily have seemed impertinent to courts abroad, but which was well calculated to reach the country's heart:

"When, in this old Europe of ours, one is lifted by the power of a new principle to the level of the ancient dynasties, one is not necessarily obliged to age one's coat of arms, or elbow one's way into some royal family, in order to be accepted. . . . The lady who has my preference is a lady of noble birth. French by her sentiments, by her training, by the memory of the blood which her father shed in the cause of the Empire, she has, as a Spaniard, the further advantage of not having any family in France to whom honors and dignities would be owing. . . . I come here, therefore, gentlemen, to say to France: I have preferred a woman whom I love and respect to a woman whom I would not have known and with whom marriage would have had advantages mixed with sacrifices. Shortly I shall go to Notre Dame to present the Empress to the people and the army."

This speech brought a frown from members of the old aristocracy, but it was the sort of speech the French public liked to hear. Mlle. de Montijo proceeded to win wide approval by refusing a gift of 600,000 francs which was set aside by the Municipal Council of Paris for the purchase of a diamond necklace. She asked that the sum be devoted to charities. So to charitable purposes she applied the dowry that Napoleon III settled upon her.

Eugénie de Montijo had not so much desired this fairy-tale marriage as accepted it under pressure from her mother and the Spaniards about her. Her pride finally vanquished her apprehensions. She did not love the Emperor. He was twenty years her senior and differed from her in many tastes and interests. She did feel a sincere friendship for him, and also a profound gratitude for the "knightly gesture," as she expressed it, whereby he had overthrown every obstacle in order to follow his heart's desire. She was especially grateful to him for the attitude he took towards religion in order to please her—for his promise to take communion with her on the morning of their marriage in the Elysée, which Napoleon III had placed at her disposal directly after official announcement of the betrothal.

On Sunday, January 30, 1853, under a beautiful sky, while cannon thundered and church bells pealed, Eugénie de Montijo seated herself beside Napoleon III in the golden coronation coach, and in the midst of a dazzling procession left the Tuileries for Notre Dame. She found the portal of the ancient church ablaze with the colors of cardboard decorations and flags. From the top of the podium, she made a charming gesture, which exhibited all her "caballero" grace and graciousness. She left the Emperor's arm, turned towards the square and to the huge crowd made a sweeping court curtsey, so low, and yet so lithe and supple, that for a moment she appeared to be kneeling. She rose, very pale, then entered the cathedral in rhythm with the march of the *Prophet,* to receive from Monsignor Sibour the benediction which was to make of her, a young foreign girl, the third Empress of the French.

Napoleon III had decided on this match, partly in spite at his failure to negotiate a more important one; partly because of his eagerness to make sure of direct descendants at an early moment; partly to satisfy the passionate whim of an aging man. But the marriage was to have a most direct and far-reaching influence upon his destinies, upon the destinies of the Second Empire, upon the destinies of France. There can be no doubt that had the son of Hortense married Carola Wasa or Adelaide Hohenlohe, less beautiful women, but closely connected with the houses that reigned in Europe, he would have followed a general policy far different from the one that he adopted, especially after 1860, when the Empress began to take an active part in affairs. Rarely has the influence of an individual's sentiments and private life upon historic events been more clearly measurable than in this case. The fact has too long been denied. Even in democratic systems history carries the burden of private impulses and motives. Whether they govern republics or monarchies the leaders of men are men, and their public acts are all too often inspired by personal passions or interests.

CHAPTER IX

The New Regime

FROM THIS MOMENT ON THE EMPIRE APPEARS IN ITS OLD FORMS. THE households of the sovereigns were fixed upon, the offices of the First Empire were reestablished; Grand Marshal of the Palace—Marshal Vaillant; Grand Master of Ceremonies—the Duke of Cambacérès; Grand Chamberlain—the Duke of Bassano; Grand Almoner—Monsignor Menjaud, Bishop of Nancy; Grand Equerry—Marshal Saint-Arnaud; Grand Master of the Hounds—Marshal Magnan; First Chamberlain—Count Bacciochi; First Equerry—Colonel Fleury. All of them were provided with fat stipends. Saint-Arnaud, 300,000 francs a year; Magnan, 200,000; the others in proportion. These salaries, however, were relatively small as compared with salaries and perquisites under the First Empire.

The plant at the Tuileries was radically remodelled. At the time when Napoleon III came to live there, the château was magnificent rather than comfortable. In order to accommodate the numerous family of Louis Philippe apartments had been cut by gloomy corridors and the various stories linked by spiral staircases lighted by kerosene lamps. The rooms fronting on the rue de Rivoli were very dark. There were no conveniences, not even those required by hygiene. Running water had never been installed in the chambers and toilets and every morning water carriers had to be relied on.

Important alterations were undertaken to restore the palace and give the sovereigns a background befitting them. The Emperor had his quarters on the ground floor. The Empress lived on the second, on a level with the great reception suites—the Salon of the First Consul and the Hall of the Marshals. Everything was done over, repainted, regilded, refurnished, heavily, without taste, and at enormous costs.

Napoleon III, like his uncle, was eager to surround his Empress

with women of the old aristocracy. In that he did not succeed. The
Faubourg Saint-Germain never brightened the expression of disdain
on its face. The new regime disgusted polite society both through
its origins and its brilliant display, which was found gaudy. Napoleon III, therefore, had to rest content with an Imperial personnel:
the Duchess of Bassano as Lady of Honor; the Princess of Essling
as Grand Mistress, Count Tascher de la Pagerie as Grand Master;
for Ladies of the Palace, Mesdames de la Tour-Maubourg, de
Montebello, de Lezay-Marnesia, de Pierres, de Las Marismas; later
on, Mesdames de la Bédoyère, de la Poëze, de Saulcy, de Rayneval,
de Parabère. Most of these were personal friends of the young
Empress.

As a background for the ceremonies a corps of picked men was
formed—the Hundred Guards, truly superb men dressed in dazzling
uniforms. A magnificent regiment of Guides, which was to form
the nucleus of the Imperial Guard, was reconstituted for the private
service of the master. All the military staffs received dress uniforms
which copied the picturesque uniforms of the Grand Army of old.

The almost complete aloofness of Legitimist and Orleanist society
obliged Napoleon to make up a court out of the notable families of
the First Empire, his diplomatic corps, his army heads and high officials, and a few friends, French or foreign. Court etiquette, stuffy
rather than not, was based largely on the rules followed at the Court
of Bavaria. Before very long the Emperor and his friends were appearing at receptions in knee breeches and laced coats. Lavish dinners, great balls, concerts without end, began to shake the ancient
frame of the palace of the Valois and the Bourbons. The search was
for magnificence. At first the new dignitaries seemed a little awkward, a little self-conscious, in their rôles. Ney, Fleury, gay men
about town, were at their ease from the start. Morny was distinction
in person when he deigned to appear. In the general opinion of
Paris, the only one at court who comported himself like a truly great
gentleman was the sovereign himself.

Her marriage never went to the Empress's head. She remained a
gay, easy-mannered young woman, much more concerned with her
gowns than with politics. She was aware roughly of what was going
on, but she took a personal interest only in sudden bursts. She liked
social life and received graciously, talking perhaps a little too freely,

especially with ambassadors, and according to the passion or the caprice of the moment.

Following the lead of the Tuileries, the Ministries, the embassies, some few semi-official salons threw their doors wide open and shone. Brilliancy returned to French social life. In the time of Louis Philippe society went dull in imitation of the court of the citizen-king, where Queen Marie-Amélie could be seen sitting under a carcel lamp with her knitting in her lap between a brace of wives of officers of the National Guard. The Second Empire broke with those modest ways. It wanted to make an impression of splendor on France and on Europe. Simple enough in their private life, Napoleon and Eugénie believed that pomp and display had their uses. Under their leadership, an atmosphere of gaiety, which may have been a little too shrill, brought Paris to life again.

Napoleon III did not forget his family in the generous moods of his accession. The ex-King Jerome, and his son, Napoleon, were installed in the Palais Royal and provided with splendid incomes. They played the rôle that the princes of Orleans had played under the old monarchy—younger sons always greedy, always discontented, always hostile to their reigning elders. Jerome retained only one post, a wholly decorative one, as Governor of the Invalides. He cut a showy figure on parade, imposing, evoking great memories. The only important thing was to keep his seamy side from showing.

The Emperor may well have gilded Jerome's old age so sumptuously out of consideration for his cousin, Mathilde. He retained a tender attachment for Jerome's daughter. She had left Prince Demidoff. Haughty and quick-tempered, both of them, they had not agreed very long. Czar Nicholas hastened their separation. Mathilde was cousin to the Czar on his mother's side. He had been displeased to see her marry one of his subjects whose nobility was hardly of imperial grade. Mathilde led an independent life in Paris, surrounded by artists and writers, so taking on the air of a Marguerite de Navarre. She often brought echoes of society to Napoleon, keeping him posted on feeling in Paris. She was, and would always remain, frankly devoted to him.

Her brother, Prince Napoleon—"Plonplon," as the Parisians called him, perpetuating an endearment of his babyhood—was not of a character to show much devotion for the Emperor or for anybody else. He had an inordinate desire to play a rôle in history,

and tried to, during the Republic, becoming a Montagnard, a socialist, an anti-clerical, as the chance seemed to require. The *coup d'état*
would have failed had he had his way. The Empire succeeding, he
donned very grudgingly the cloak of a royal highness, but only while
waiting for something better to turn up. He was a real Corsican, a
genuine nephew of the founder of the dynasty. In his eyes Napoleon
III was just a bastard Beauharnais. It was he, the son of Jerome,
for all of a German mother so like the Consul in his lustreless
Roman face, who should be occupying the spotlight on the stage.
He was prone to forget that, had it not been for the calculating
audacity, the visionary cool-headedness of Louis Napoleon, for the
risks of Strasbourg and Boulogne, for the six years in a fortress, for
the daring military coup that might have sent its authors to the
scaffold, the Empire would never have been restored.

Napoleon's bitter, jealous nature never softened. He had the
traits of a leader. Possessing no real education, he was intelligent and
not too scrupulous. He had strong views and no little eloquence. He
could make himself feared and also loved. He was far from having
only the face of a Caesar. He had the talent too. He might have
done great things, but fate stubbornly denied him the opportunity.
Prince Napoleon was to remain an abortive emperor, always held
in reserve, never rising to the first rank, always acting under orders
from others and therefore on a secondary plane. After a Prince
Imperial was born and the war in Italy had disappointed his hopes
of a throne, there was nothing left for him but to live on snarling
at his relatives and eating out his own heart.

His erratic excursions to the Left, his open hatred of the Church,
sometimes brought Prince Napoleon a reprimand from the Emperor.
For that matter, even before he became president, Louis Napoleon
passed rather severe judgments on his cousin.

"Sometimes," he once said, "he is frank, loyal, aboveboard, and
his heart seems to talk in terms of glory, to suffer, to leap with you,
for all that is great and generous. Then again it seems to express
little but hardness, knavery—just nothing." [1]

All the same Napoleon III always had a soft spot in his heart for
Mathilde's brother—ever since the days in Arenenberg when he had
given the boy lessons in mathematics. He never could bring himself

[1] Letter to Veuillot, December 10, 1846.

to dropping him completely. He was always thinking that somehow he could find a way to canalize the young man's talents to the profit of the regime. Now and again he would call him to the Tuileries to discuss policy, Italian policy especially. Prince Napoleon always took a position of fiery hostility to the little monarchies on the Peninsula. In private and in public he was an advocate of Italian unification.

Using first General de Cotte, then Monsignor de Bonnechose and Monsignor de Ségur as intermediaries, Napoleon III tried to get the Pope to come to Paris to crown him, as the first Emperor had done. Pius IX offered no objection, in principle, but he manifested no great enthusiasm either. At the very least he wanted to have the "Organic Articles" repealed as an advance bonus on such a tiring journey. Napoleon III was in doubt for a long time. He at first seemed willing to revise the amendments that Napoleon I had affixed to the Concordat. He even hinted that he was considering changes in the marriage articles of the Civil Code in order to bring them into line with church regulations. Everyone whom he consulted on the matter—Persigny, Billault, Delangle, Portalis—protested so violently that Napoleon finally, and with great reluctance, dropped the project in fear of too great a shock to public feelings. He therefore decided to get along without an Anointment as coming too high at the price asked.

The restorer of the Empire in no way resembled its founder, to whom he owed everything and whose trail he was forever trying to pick up and follow. He was a born leader, but he was not a soldier. He did not like war, regarding it as something absurd, monstrous.

"War," he wrote in all sincerity in his *Napoleonic Ideas,* "is the scourge of humanity. The era of conquests has passed, never to return."

He lacked the unbridled ambition of his uncle, and his insatiable thirst for domination. He had no *"coup d'œil,"* as the French say, no gift for off-hand but sound and clean-cut decisions. The great Corsican had a keen sense of realities. In the nephew the vision of facts as they were was clouded by fancies, ideals, dreams. He sparkled, but without warmth, without fire. Indolent, uncommunicative, persistent, he plodded on towards his goal without sharing his hopes or fears. Lord Malmesbury knew him well. He said of him:

"The outstanding trait in his character is stubbornness, which is supported by a cold calculation and therefore overcomes all difficulties."

Marshal de Castellane wrote:

"When he has decided on a course of action, nothing can turn him from it."

He did everything in an unfailing spirit of adventure, and that attitude he was to retain to the end. During the war in Italy Marshal Vaillant would call his attention to the dangers involved in a certain attack.

"If you are unwilling to run the chance of being defeated," he would answer, "you ought never to give battle."

Later on at a very critical juncture he said to Ollivier:

"Risk nothing and you have nothing."

He was an adventurer with a profound confidence in his destiny, which he sincerely believed to have been providentially foreordained. He kept as a sovereign the merits, the eccentricities and even the outward appearances of the conspirator, reigning as a crowned Carbonaro.

"Scratch the Emperor," said Guizot, "and you will find the political refugee."

Yearning for glory in a bastard age, he had no instinct for the old time grandeur that stiffened and exalted the celebrities of the Revolution and the Empire. The summits of history did not allure him. His intelligence, if not very keen, was at least comprehensive and tended preferably towards social problems, inventions, progress in industry. A mass of projects and dreams had been piling up in his head for twenty years and they made a most curious mixture: revolutionary principles, imperialistic doctrines, conservative tastes, pacifistic inclinations, a hankering for military renown. This hodge-podge exposed his thinking, as it did his governmental policies, to sharp reversals and incoherences. One basic trait took precedence over all others in him. By education, by experience in life, by contacts and friendships, he was a European. He remained a European upon the throne, and to such an extent that sometimes he would fail to see French interests clearly enough, deeply concerned as he was with them.

Neither experience nor the passing of the years caused him in any respect to repudiate the theories that he had propounded in his *Napoleonic Ideas.* Here he was now master of everything. He set out to put them into practice.

The "principle of nationality," for instance, or, if one will, the "theory of nationalities," seems to have been stated for the first time by Condorcet in a speech before the Legislative Assembly, April 20, 1792. In a note dictated at St. Helena Napoleon had argued for "the centralization of all geographical peoples which revolution or policy have dissolved or partitioned." Napoleon III, therefore, regarded the "principle of nationality" as a Napoleonic principle. As he and the men of his time understood it, the doctrine asserted the inalienable right of all clearly defined ethnic groups to obtain recognition of their individuality and to govern themselves as they saw fit.

Napoleon III accordingly desired to assist in freeing the various national groups that had been broken up by the Holy Alliance, and especially the two greatest of the martyred nations, Italy and Poland. He thought no differently in these regards from the majority of the outstanding men of his epoch, Thiers, for instance, or Lamennais, Lamartine or Victor Hugo, Emile Ollivier or Blanqui. All these men felt, all these men wrote, or else contended in parliament, that the first duty of France was to go to the rescue of oppressed peoples. More than any of the men mentioned Napoleon III was to promote the still hazy theory of nationality into an active and aggressive reality. With many halts and backslidings it was to be the main guiding idea of his reign. It was to impel him to generous acts but also to lead him into gross imprudences and dangers.

In his study on the ground floor in the Tuileries, he read, meditated and wrote a great deal. Like his uncle, like most of the Bonapartes, he was born and remained a publicist. His easy, prolix flow of language abounded in commonplaces. For immediate assistants he had three men who, one may say, never left him, who alone had his implicit confidence: Mocquard, Conneau and Pietri.

Mocquard, good-looking, dashing, had been a long-standing friend of Queen Hortense. Over sixty, he remained alert of mind, brimming with wit and a lusty gaiety. His conversation sparkled with jests. At the same time he was absolutely trustworthy. In his relations with others he showed himself ever obliging, ever unselfish. A brilliant man of letters, he had full control over the Emperor's correspondence and speeches, as well as over audiences, tours and changes of

PRINCE NAPOLEON

From the Portrait by Hebert

abode. Napoleon wrote nothing that did not pass under Mocquard's eyes.[1]

Dr. Conneau,[2] family physician to Napoleon III, was the Emperor's shadow. He helped him sift his numerous charities, acted at times as the Emperor's secret agent, and on journeys read the Emperor's telegrams to him aloud. He seemed to have had no other interest in life than the interests of his master—along with the enrichment of a collection of Bibles in all languages, which he was eventually forced to sell in order to live. For he was to be left poor, after seeing millions run through his fingers.

The young Corsican, Franceschini Pietri, was a plain assistant who finally became the Emperor's private secretary. Likable, discreet, Pietri devoted his whole life to the Emperor's service and stood faithful in the unhappy as in the happy days.

This privy cabinet, small as it was, was the fixed pivot around which imperial policy revolved. The ministers were in principle, especially at the beginning of the regime, only executive agents. Napoleon had no intention of governing by delegating power, like a sovereign of the old school. He thought that he had been invested by the people with a complete dictatorship and he insisted on carrying the full load. He assembled his ministers in council at the Tuileries two forenoons a week, but he permitted discussion, which for that matter was entirely free, only of matters which he himself brought before the meeting. He would listen to the opinions of his consultants, then, when the Council was dismissed, decide for himself. The actual work was done in his study in conferences with the ministers concerned. So Napoleon I had done in his time. Like his uncle the nephew claimed to "know all because he alone was responsible for all." Unfortunately his mind was too different from his model's for the same system, applied to the same country forty years later, to have the same happy effects. The first Napoleon's instinct, energy, physical endurance and capacity for close attention

1 [Trans. Note: As a young Negro scholar, W. B. Scott, has shown in a Columbia dissertation Mocquard also toyed with playwriting. His influence made a considerable reputation in the French theatre for a young American Negro from New Orleans, Henri Séjour, with whom Mocquard collaborated on several plays.]

2 Dr. Henri Conneau, a man of Corsican origin, was born in Milan (June 3, 1803). He had first been secretary to the ex-King Louis in Florence. Later on in Rome the Bonaparte family became the nucleus of his practice. He joined Louis Napoleon in the Romagna escapade and then settled at Arenenberg. Hortense, on her deathbed, had made Dr. Conneau promise never to desert her son. He kept his word. He was to remain in attendance on the Emperor down to the latter's death. Conneau was one of the soundest and most estimable characters of that era in French history.

to details, enabled him, along with his personal prestige, to have men of the stamp of Talleyrand and Fouché about him and still keep everything in his own hands. It means little to give orders unless one is ever on watch to see whether and how they are obeyed. Napoleon III was given to hesitation, and the failing grew worse as the years wore on. Sometimes he seemed to suffer an acute prostration of will. He might well govern France. He could not manage an office.

"To govern is all very well," he said one day, not without sadness. "Unfortunately you've got to be a manager too!"

The art of management, in its daily, unremitting, subtle and ever-shifting progression, was not among his gifts. He realized this failing, was distressed by it, and tried to offset it—sometimes by sending one of his officials to get direct information and report. But, as he confessed naïvely to Marshal Vaillant, all his agents were in league to keep things from him; and if ever he pointed to one of the thousand opportunities for improvement that were inevitable in the nature of things, the men he criticized conceived grudges against him instead of being grateful for his interest.

The government officials thus were left as the actual driving force of the great machine. The ministers met the demands of the Emperor with graduated opposition. "I have no influence," Napoleon III sometimes said. The tyrant experienced great difficulties in placing or advancing people whom he sponsored.

Like Napoleon, he was to keep about him during virtually his whole reign the men who were with him when he came into power. Those men profited by his accession. He showered them with titles and incomes. Their interests were tied up with his fortunes. Maupas, it is true, soon fell out with Saint-Arnaud and disappeared early from the scene (1853). The others continued to occupy all the key positions down to 1870. There were some changes in the uses made of them, to be sure, as they chanced to become inconvenient in their original posts or to meet some set-back.

Napoleon considered Morny necessary in spite of their frequent clashes. Morny received the presidency of the Legislative Body in 1854, replacing Billault. Except for a brief interruption occasioned by a diplomatic mission to Russia, he was to hold it to the time of his death in 1865. Persigny passed from the Ministry of the Interior to the embassy in London, returning thence to checkmate the prefects with his usual hard hitting. Rouher, an honest worker but talkative, was to be successively vice-president of the Council of State, Minister of Agriculture and of Commerce, Minister of State, Minister of Finance and president of the Senate. His rôle continuously expanded until it earned for him, towards the end of the reign, the surname of "vice-emperor." Named Minister of the Interior, in place of Persigny, Billault, who was a consummate lawyer, became minister without portfolio in 1860, in order to defend government bills before the Chamber. Baroche was also an expert tactician. With his long solemn face and his vast experience in matters of administration he was to keep the presidency of the Council of State down to 1869.[1] Pierre Magne, a high official, was a resourceful Perigordian. He directed Public Works or Finance throughout the reign. Fould, a wide-awake businessman, took the portfolio of Finance after serving ten years as Minister of State. Drouyn de Lhuys was a career diplomat and a good deal of a courtier, but when occasion required he could voice an honest opinion. He went back to the Quai d'Orsay on the establishment of the Kingdom of Italy, and did not retire till after Sadowa. Walewski was the son of Napoleon I and Marie Walewska. Leaving the army he took charge of publicity and propaganda, then became ambassador. He successively replaced Drouyn in Foreign Affairs, and Fould in the Ministry of State, eventually succeeding Morny in the presidency of the Legislative Body.

Prince Napoleon ridiculed the Emperor roundly for all this rotating in office:

"Your ministers are Jacks-of-all-trades; you dress them up now as coachmen, now as cooks, but no one is fooled!"

It was the same with the army. Vaillant, a veteran of Waterloo, served successively as Grand Marshal of the Palace, Minister of War, Major-General in the army, and finally Minister of the Emperor's Household. Marshal Pélissier, conqueror of Malakoff, became ambassador to London, then governor of Algeria. Marshal Magnan was first Grand Master of the Hounds, then commander of the army in Paris.

These tools of imperial government were not without talents.

---

[1] The author is indebted to the Marquise de Bérulle, a descendant of Baroche and of Billault, for her gracious kindness in making available to him important letters and notes which were of the greatest assistance in prosecuting this work. He seizes this opportunity to express all his thanks to her.

Many of them had education and traditions and sometimes even a flair for large affairs. On the whole, however, with the exception of Morny, a truly remarkable man, who alone in that empty era attained the stature of a statesman, most of the men in high position were errand-boys, patriotic Frenchmen, to be sure, but with no real knowledge, creatures of chance and of favoritism, too greatly worried over public opinion at home, which they strangled and feared, incapable of properly restraining sudden flights of the Emperor's fancy. They gave France a wholly partisan administration.

In foreign policy one or two rose to broad views, Thouvenel, for instance, who was called too late to affairs of state and disappeared too early. The others, for the most part, had definite notions and followed personal preferences. Their vanities, their convictions, their interests, were always clashing, always compromising, keeping French foreign policy forever in confusion. Friends of Austria like Drouyn de Lhuys, of England like Persigny, of Russia like Morny, caused diplomatic policy to swing back and forth between Pope and Italian unification, between a united Germany and a traditional Germany, between Polish liberation and an alliance with the Czar. So the possibilities of all systems were eventually exhausted since none of them was followed consistently, and all were abandoned before the fruits they might have yielded were harvested.

For that matter Napoleon III's henchmen had a good excuse in the conduct of the Emperor. He never took them into his confidence, he often misled them, settling with foreign ambassadors or sovereigns questions for which his ministers were nominally responsible. He had, for instance, a private code with which he could communicate with the King of Italy behind the backs of the Quai d'Orsay. Following the example of Louis XV, Napoleon III had a corps of secret agents working all over Europe. Conneau, Pietri, Arese, Pepoli, Prince Napoleon, later on Vimercati and General Türr, knew what he was about much better than Walewski and Drouyn de Lhuys, the titular heads of Foreign Affairs. Just when these latter thought they were beginning to understand his policy and the means of applying it, they would discover that he had fooled them completely.

At the Paris Conference General La Marmora inquired as to the limitations within which the delegates from Piedmont were to be admitted.

"They will be admitted to all discussions that concern Piedmont," answered Walewski.

"They will be admitted to all discussions," ruled the Emperor a few hours later.

Walewski also knew nothing of the undertakings the Emperor had assumed towards Cavour at Plombières, and of the treaty that embodied them. He ordered La Tour d'Auvergne, the French envoy at Turin, to protest against the rash policy that Piedmont was following as "contrary to the Emperor's intentions."

"Really?" answered Cavour ironically. "Here is a letter from the Tuileries that tells me just the opposite."

Charles of Hohenzollern, pretender to the throne of Roumania, sounded out Paris as to whether he would be at liberty to make a *coup d'état* in Bucharest. Drouyn de Lhuys replied:

"The Emperor will never recognize the accomplished fact."

Through Mme. Cornu Napoleon urged the Prince to go ahead. When the minister complained the Emperor feigned surprise and evaded an argument.

At the height of the great European crisis of 1866, Drouyn de Lhuys opposed the annexation of the duchies by Prussia. Napoleon favored it. What prestige could the cabinet heads possibly have, when they were stripped of such freedom of action as was left them by the Emperor who wanted everything to come from himself? To the Prussian ambassador, Von der Goltz, he said:

"A statement from one of my ministers would have no importance. I am the only one who knows what the policy of France is to be."

This system very properly surrounded French diplomacy with fear and suspicion. Napoleon gained a reputation for duplicity all over Europe, and created an ever-mounting antipathy towards himself which was to prove fatal in the hour of misfortune.

How could he—such a discerning, such a shrewd mind—persist in a course so disastrous? Probably because, at heart, he was a solitary soul and loved his solitude. Sceptical as to the moral stamina of human beings, he could not bring himself to trust anybody altogether. And then again, and perhaps most importantly, for all of his gentleness of heart, his considerateness, his kindness, he remained the most willful, the most imperious of men. To be sure there were influences about him during his whole reign, influences

that weighed heavily upon his decisions. A matter of atmosphere
rather than of words, they were the influences, indefinable but no
less powerful, of intimate friends such as Mocquard, or Arese, or
his goddaughter, Hortense Cornu. Still others, operating now in
succession now simultaneously, came from Persigny, erratic and
ardent; from Morny, who, once the *coup d'état* was safe and over,
turned instinctively to liberalism; from Rouher, a bureaucratic
despot; finally from the Empress—and her influence was to grow
with the years and have far-reaching consequences. But nobody was
ever really to dominate Napoleon III. His mysterious, evasive disposition saved him from encroachments, importunities, greeds. He
was narrowly jealous of his power, shielded it as he would his life,
refused to share it with anyone. He wielded it incessantly himself,
according now to his principles, now to his theories, now to his
hopes and fears, and by unexpected, however carefully considered,
resorts—by sudden shifts and reversals, by underground intrigues.
In the last years of his reign he was ill and was weakening in body
and mind. Not till then did he yield to a rising tide of adverse
forces and finally bring himself to abdicate from his long dictatorship, allowing the Empire too tardily to enter upon a liberal path,
along which—apart from a catastrophe so unthinkingly provoked—it
might have been revitalized.

CHAPTER X

The Crimea

NAPOLEON III DID NOT FEEL SUFFICIENTLY STRONG TO TEAR UP THE treaties of 1815 and liberate the oppressed peoples without the support of an alliance; and the only alliance he could regard as feasible, durable, and promising of results was an alliance with England. During the days of his imprisonment at Ham, and ever since, he had dreamed of making his future policy revolve around that alliance. England was a country of high civilization. She was faithful to tradition without being chained to the past. In his eyes, as compared with the absolute monarchies of the Holy Alliance, Russia, Prussia and Austria, England represented progress and liberty. The long and ruinous struggle of the First Empire should serve, he thought, as an example. Napoleon's basic error was to have thrown himself on the British colossus. His nephew would not fall into that mistake. The instructions dictated by the dying Emperor at St. Helena gave Louis Napoleon a piece of advice which he appreciated all the more from having found gracious refuge on English soil during the years of his exile, and because he had many friendships there and close ones. He was dazzled by the economic advances England was making, by the astounding increase in the number of her machines. Her principle of free trade coincided exactly with his personal outlook. It would be easy for him, he thought, to go along with England hand in hand.

He evinced this state of mind at the time of Wellington's funeral, to which he sent a representative.

"I want to forget the past," he said.

He did not add, "in order to build a sounder future"; but his words were understood in that sense across the Channel.

An opportunity presented itself early in 1853 in the regard of the Holy Lands. In that question the whole question of the Near East, really, was coming to the fore again. Basic in the problem was the decay of the Turkish Empire. The matter was first broached at Tilsitt between Napoleon and Alexander. In 1840 it almost involved France in a war against all Europe in defense of Mehemet-Ali, commander of the Turkish army in Egypt, who had revolted against the Sultan. For all of Thiers, who may have been a fine parlor strategist, Louis Philippe wisely avoided a too unequal struggle. Ten years later rivalry over the custodianship of the Christian sanctuaries broke out between the Orthodox Catholic Greeks, supported by Russia, and the Roman Catholics, supported by France. That issue brought on a new, but for the time being fairly mild, conflict. In our own time there have been most distressing sectarian struggles inside the Church of the Holy Sepulchre in Jerusalem. Those who have witnessed such things can readily imagine the bitterness with which, in an age of strong faith, the Orthodox popes fought the Roman Catholic monks for the possession of the cradle and tomb of Jesus. In May, 1850, Louis Napoleon lodged a protest against the encroachments of the Orthodox Greeks with the Sublime Porte. Czar Nicholas I, on the other side, rose to his full height and sent a warning to the Sultan. Caught between two fires, the Porte temporized. Diplomatic moves and counter-moves came by the hundreds. Towards the close of 1852 the matter seemed to have found an amicable adjustment, owing to the extreme eagerness manifested by France for conciliation.

The attitude of the French government was far from meeting unanimous approval in France. Proudhon, for instance, was close friends with Prince Napoleon. In a letter to the Prince written in January, 1853, he stormed:

"We have wasted thirteen months marking time, whereas a simple shifting of French troops would have been enough to bring the Holy Alliance to the Emperor's feet. Here we are buried again under the shame and the spinelessness of the Eighteen Years' Reign! And this abdication we owe, Heaven help us, to the name of the Emperor, to a Napoleon!"

The opposition as a whole shared these sentiments.

But the Czar had other views. He was an austere despot, with an Asiatic strain predominant in his character. Ruling by the knout, the gibbet and Siberia, he was as stern with himself as with others. He lived like a hermit in his palace, sleeping on a straw mattress on two boards, without sheets or pillows, a soldier's overcoat serving him as a blanket. Living that way, he died that way. Up at four in the morning he worked all day, ate sparingly, drank nothing but water. He permitted no expressions of opinion by his ministers. If one of them ventured a timid remark, he would order him from the room with the words:

"A subject does not discuss my orders."

Half tyrant, half saint, he set himself up in the midst of his enslaved peoples as a representative of God on earth, created with a mission to force an uncompromising social order upon all Europe. Everybody and everything was obliged to defer to his bitter pride. He had gone back to an old dream of Peter the Great, to plant the Cross once more on Saint Sophia.

Two-faced, he heaped amenities upon the French ambassador, Castelbajac, but meantime proposed to the English envoy, Sir Hamilton Seymour, an accord whereby Russia and England should divide Ottoman territories.

"We have a 'sick man' on our hands," he said to Seymour, "a very sick man. He may die at any moment. Would it not be wiser to prepare in advance against that emergency rather than expose ourselves to the chaos and confusion that will follow from it? If we two can come to an understanding, it will make little difference what others do."

He offered Egypt and Crete to England. The Roumanian principalities, Moldavia and Walachia, Serbia and Bulgaria, would become independent under the suzerainty of the Czar. As for Constantinople, if it became necessary for him to occupy that city, he would not settle there permanently. He would hold it "on deposit." [1]

England declined, but without anger, the Foreign Office explaining that it favored the *status quo*. The independence of the Ottoman Empire had been guaranteed by the five great powers in the treaty of 1841. If the succession of the "sick man" should ever come in question, it would be a matter for a European conference to settle.

Thus rebuffed, Nicholas went ahead on his own. He sent an ambassador extraordinary to Constantinople, his navy minister, Prince Menschikov. Pompous, insolent, extravagant in display, Menschikov

[1] Audiences of January 9, January 14, February 1, 1853.

demanded full satisfaction for Russia in the matter of the Holy Lands, and the recognition, by a treaty that was to remain secret, of what amounted to a protectorate by the Czar over all Orthodox Catholic subjects of the Sultan. This was nothing less than a diminution of Ottoman sovereignty.

Abdul-Medjid, intelligent, but of a weak character, too engrossed with his harem, took fright. He dismissed his grand vizier, Fuad, and replaced him with Rifaat pasha, a man somewhat better liked in Russia. He would perhaps have given in had not the British ambassador, Lord Stratford de Redcliffe, come to his aid. Very stiff, very dry, treacherous under his polish, Redcliffe was known in Constantinople as the "English sultan." He detested Russia. He spread Menschikov thick with honey, meantime pressing Rifaat to yield on the Holy Lands but to resist on the other points.

His advice was followed. A firman by the Sultan settled the religious controversy to the Czar's satisfaction; but Menschikov then proceeded to deliver an ultimatum calling upon the Sublime Porte to grant the protectorate over the Orthodox Greeks. Rifaat refused in conciliatory language. The Moscovite's rage knew no bounds. He broke off negotiations and left the Bosphorus for Odessa (May 22, 1853).

Europe stirred. In Vienna Buol commented severely on the Czar's attitude. There were hopes in Berlin, where servility towards Russia was more pronounced, that the Czar would disavow Menschikov's arrogant ultimatum. The press in Paris kept within bounds by government order, but French public opinion was very uneasy. As the crisis opened, Drouyn de Lhuys and the other ministers (with the exception of Persigny) were for temporizing. Napoleon III ignored them. He ordered the French fleet to leave Toulon and proceed to the Aegean Sea.

The Aberdeen cabinet in England was a coalition government and its policy was not very coherent. It hesitated, uncertain, and the very delay encouraged the Czar in his uncompromising attitude. The English masses were still rather hostile to France. Suddenly fear that Napoleon might act alone laid hold on St. James and it made overtures to the Tuileries. Clarendon declared before the Peers and Russell before the Commons that the Queen, acting in concert with the Emperor, would uphold the integrity of the Sultan's states. A fleet was stationed at Malta under Admiral Dundas. To point a formal protest to Russia, it set sail for the Dardanelles, where it was joined by the French squadron.

Nesselrode, the Russian chancellor, vainly sought to incline his master to a more circumspect course. Nicholas would not listen. He ordered and Nesselrode obeyed. He addressed a new and haughtily worded ultimatum to the Porte, and a note to the powers.

"I still feel the Sultan's five fingers upon my cheek," he said to one of his advisers.

On July 3, 1853, the Russian army that had mobilized in Bessarabia under the command of Prince Gortchakov invaded the Roumanian principalities.

Negotiations continued through July and August. Austria feared any change in the balance of power in Europe. She did her utmost to preserve peace. Outwardly, and playing a very shrewd game, Napoleon III seconded her efforts. He kept in the background, talked moderation, in order to avoid annoying England and at the same time to induce her to take a decisive step. He so neglected military preparations that Prince Albert lost his composure and wrote contemptuously to a friend, Stockmar (Sept. 21st):

"Louis Napoleon wants peace, happiness and—cheap wheat."

The French opposition was also disappointed and it raged. Victor Hugo gibed in the *Châtiments,* in the poem called *Retreat:*

> O soldats, quel réveil! L'Empire, c'est la fuite!
> Soldats, l'Empire, c'est la peur! [1]

And he went on, in the poem called *The End:*

> Tu frémis, effaré devant les Dardanelles . . .
> Malgré ta couardise, il faut combattre; allons! . . . [2]

Edgar Quinet wrote from Brussels (Jan. 8, 1854):

"France has never been more self-satisfied than in the midst of these disgraceful ignominies. She has found a government which fits her size to a tee: she lies, sells, surrenders, dances and titters."

A "Note from Vienna" suggested a compromise which would soothe Russian pride and maintain the substantial rights of the Sultan. St. Petersburg accepted it, but now it was Turkey's turn to refuse. She refused in the face of official remonstrances from

[1] "Oh, soldiers, what an awakening! The Empire means flight!
Soldiers, the Empire means fear!"
[2] "You shudder in dismay before the Dardanelles!
But cowards that we are, we have to fight!"

France and England—one has to say "official" for unofficially Red-cliffe was egging the Turks on. In Reschid pasha, Rifaat's successor, the soul of the ancient Turk seemed suddenly to come to life again. The holy war was already being preached in the mosques. On October 8th Turkey summoned Russia to evacuate the Roumanian principalities. Her best general, Omer pasha, massed his troops along the Danube opposite Gortchakov.

However, the diplomats talked on. France, England, Austria and Prussia came together in an effort to mediate. Could war be avoided? It could not. It not so much broke out as burst out, and very dramatically: The Turkish fleet was totally destroyed at Sinope on the south shore of the Black Sea. The squadron of Osman pasha had taken refuge in that port on November 30th. It was overwhelmed by the far superior forces of Admiral Nakhimov. A single Turkish ship, the steamer *Taïf*, escaped. Four thousand dead! Sinope in flames! The disaster was as complete as it was sudden.

Napoleon III now abandoned his fencing. He proposed to England that their two navies occupy the Black Sea. Feeling in London was running much higher than in Paris. The British jumped at the offer. In the Aberdeen government, Palmerston, the old friend of the Emperor, after a dramatic resignation, had just moved from a secondary to a key position. He insisted on the French alliance. He was for war.

Napoleon III wanted war although vaguely he feared it. He had a double grudge to settle with Russia, one personal: Nicholas I had treated him slightingly on his accession to the crown; the other dynastic: Russia was responsible for the first Napoleon's downfall. This fierce Czar, own brother to Alexander, was the main prop of the Holy Alliance, of the Europe that had been parcelled out at Vienna, of everything against which he, Napoleon III, had risen to power, and everything which he had been vowing since his boyhood to wipe out.

A victorious war against Russia would bring France and her sovereign back to the front rank in Europe—and could victory be doubted, once England went in on his side? The war, also, as he imagined, would be a short war, and not very expensive—something like a colonial expedition. Early in 1854 no one saw any farther ahead than that. Aid to Turkey offered the further advantage of strengthening the secular policy of France in her relations to the Sublime Porte.

There, meantime, stood the Emperor's earlier pacifism. "The Empire means peace," he had himself proclaimed. Did that cause him any embarrassment as far as the country was concerned? He was too intelligent a man not to realize that the Empire could not mean peace. The Empire was a regime based on force by force of circumstances. Its fundamental principle was popular support. In order to live and take root it was obliged not only to maintain its prestige abroad but to increase it, for the masses prize splendor much more highly than happiness in calm. A nephew of Napoleon could never halt at mere progress under peace. Could he triumph over Russia on this occasion, the Fourth Dynasty would have no more surprises to fear. It would have truly solid foundations.

In view of the religious pretext for the conflict the Emperor felt assured of the approbation of French Catholics. All the same—and the fact shows how subject he was to conflicting impulses and self-reversals—when the two fleets had entered the Black Sea and the diplomats were packing their trunks, he tried one last effort at conciliation. In a personal letter to Nicholas I he proposed a compromise that would be honorable to everyone: The English and French fleets would return to the Mediterranean, while, simultaneously, the Russian troops would evacuate the Roumanian provinces:

"If Your Majesty should refuse, then France and England would feel obliged to entrust to the issue of arms and the hazards of war things that might now be decided by justice and reason" (January 29, 1854).

The Czar refused haughtily.

"Russia," he answered, "will show herself to be in 1854 what she was in 1812."

1812! The year of Napoleon's retreat! A slap in the face!

Diplomatic relations were ended forthwith. At a banquet Palmerston proposed a toast "to the united navies of France and England." In France trained elements in the classes of 1849 and 1850 were called to the colors. Nicholas, on his side, armed to the teeth, and the popes of rural Russia began preaching a crusade against the Mohammedans.

On March 3rd, the Legislative Body opened session. In his speech from the throne, the Emperor declared:

"I have gone as far as honor allowed. . . . Europe well knows that France has no thought of aggrandizement. . . . The day of conquests by force is past, never to return. Not in extending the limits of its territory may a nation henceforward be honored and powerful. It must take the lead in behalf of noble ideals and bring the dominion of justice and righteousness everywhere to prevail."

The sentimental underpinning of Napoleon's foreign policy is all laid bare in those words.

The Chamber voted a credit of 250,000,000 without debate, and the loan was to be raised not from the banks but by a public subscription, which actually brought in 467,000,000.

The Russian ambassadors had already departed from London and Paris; Seymour and Castelbajac left St. Petersburg. On April 10, 1854, an alliance was concluded between Great Britain and France for the defense of the Ottoman Empire. Cannon would do the talking from then on.

How reach and shake the immense country, girt about by its solitudes, that had swallowed up Charles XII and after him the Grand Army? The naval superiority of the Allies suggested a war in the Baltic with an attack on Cronstadt threatening St. Petersburg. Were they afraid, perhaps, of worrying Prussia? At any rate, the people about Napoleon III wanted a war on land, a strictly military glory of which the French Army would garner the fruits. The Emperor was the first to think of the Crimea. Palmerston and the Duke of Newcastle, Minister of War, accepted the suggestion. It would be a good idea to destroy the great war port and arsenal at Sebastopol.

Leaders for the expedition were appointed, for England, Lord Raglan, former aide-de-camp to Wellington, who had lost an arm at Waterloo. He was an old gentleman of impressive bearing, exquisite manners and limited intelligence. For France, Saint-Arnaud, a great meat-eater whose heart was going back on him. The Emperor hesitated a long time before entrusting the command to such a sick man. Saint-Arnaud pleaded passionately.

"I prefer," said he to Trochu, a colonel attached to his division, "I prefer dying among my troops to dying in a bed."

The War Ministry was passed along to Marshal Vaillant, and Saint-Arnaud left for Marseilles where the troops were gathering.

At first it was a matter of one army corps of four divisions, allotted to Canrobert, Bosquet, Forey and Prince Napoleon—the

Prince was now a general in virtue of his name alone and because the Emperor was anxious to push him into the lime-light. The English were fitting out at Malta with a force smaller still—25,000 men. Eventually, in utter confusion, the two forces joined at Gallipoli on the sea of Marmora. The troops were destitute of everything essential, but they were in high spirits. French Zouaves and riflemen fraternized with Raglan's Scots and Irishmen. By the end of May, 1854, they were ready to be shipped to the Crimea.

The Allied command hesitated. The Russians had crossed the Danube and laid siege to Silistria. Omer pasha, a Croatian adventurer commanding the Turkish forces, persuaded Saint-Arnaud to take the offensive along the Danube in order to free Silistria. The French staff pointed out to the Marshal the imprudence of such a project when supplies and munitions were still at sea. Saint-Arnaud changed his mind, then a few weeks later went back to the idea of supporting the Turks. The whole Anglo-French army was therefore dispatched to Varna.

The Russians were not very much worried by this advance of the allied troop. They were worried by the enigmatic attitude of Austria, whom England and France were urging to join the alliance. They therefore raised the siege of Silistria and evacuated the principalities (Aug. 2nd). Saint-Arnaud exclaimed:

"Paskevitch is robbing me by thus running away."

Whither now should he direct his efforts? The decision came from England. The London press, the cabinet, Prince Albert himself, were calling for an occupation of the Crimea and an attack on Sebastopol. The enterprise was a daring one. On August 30th Count Benedetti, French chargé d'affaires at Constantinople, wrote to Thouvenel, second to Drouyn de Lhuys and already his rival in secret:

"The idea of throwing 90,000 men and 200 pieces upon an open coast, 1,400 miles from home and under the walls of a formidable fortress! That is plunging into the unknown! Nobody knows the terrain. Nobody knows the enemy's strength. . . . Everything is being left to chance and accident."

That far in Saint-Arnaud's life chance and accident had served him very well. Delighted with an opportunity to do something, he threw himself enthusiastically into the adventure. Orders were issued to prepare for the expedition.

Perhaps in order to occupy the minds of the soldiers while they were awaiting ship for the Crimea, perhaps to mislead the Russians by the bait of a campaign in another quarter, Saint-Arnaud committed the blunder of sending three divisions to make a drive to the north of Varna, in the fever-infested swamps of the Dobrudja. A cholera germ had been brought from Marseilles, and the plague developed in those warm damp lowlands. Men died by hundreds each day. General Canrobert wrote: [1]

"Horrible as it may seem, in the hurry that was shown during those fatal days to dispose of the dead as soon as possible some must certainly have been buried alive."

With no means of transporting supplies, with no ambulances, no hospital service, the army was obliged to go back. The absurd prank had cost the lives of more than 4,000 men. To make matters worse, Varna, a city of wooden houses, was virtually destroyed by fire and the sufferings of the troops were increased many-fold.

Bent double with pain, going about with a bottle of salts in his hand, Saint-Arnaud did his best to cope with the disaster.

"I shall get out of this," he wrote, "but it will probably cost me what life I have left."

His doctor urged him to resign the command.

"I cannot desert my men," he replied, "as long as I have breath in my body. I shall lead the army into the Crimea, and die there if need be."

There spoke the hot-headed veteran of the guerilla wars in Africa. The Crimea would give him his revenge. A short and brilliant campaign, such as the English foresaw, victory, and then peace by snow-fly!

Already the Franco-British navies were showing themselves masters of the Baltic. They had occupied the Aaland Islands, and General Niel had taken Bomarsund. Jealous of those successes, the Marshal hastened the sailing of the army. On September 14th, 64,000 men in all—30,204 French, 27,000 English, 7,000 Turks, debarked at the Old Fort, some twenty miles from Sebastopol.

The campaign that was about to open was very badly managed. The expedition ought to have been, and could easily have been, rapid, brilliant and economical. Through bad organization of services, through the rivalries and inadequacies of the leaders, it

[1] Germain Bapst, *Le Maréchal Canrobert*, II, 165.

was to become an extremely hard and murderous campaign, where victories were due exclusively to the valor of the troops. Most of the French soldiers had been under fire in Algeria. They were vigorous and adroit, hardened to fatigue and privations and with no end of endurance. The subaltern personnel was excellent. The generals, on the other hand, were mere lieutenants who had been pushed into the higher ranks. They were as brave as they were incompetent. They kept their men well in hand, lived with them, loved them and were loved by them. All the wars of the Second Empire were to show these same traits: slipshod organization, mediocrity in command, a marvelous spirit in the rank-and-file. The plain soldier with his bravery, his sharpness of wit, his high morale, was the one to save the honor of the flag in hours of extremity.

An unbelievable disorder featured the Crimean campaign down almost to the very end. The supply system was always inadequate, the hospital service almost non-existent. Saint-Arnaud wrote to the Emperor:

"I am pained to say so, but we are not organized for waging war. . . . You cannot fight a war without bread, without shoes, without camp-kettles, without canteens."

In a personal letter he scolded:

"Curses upon the stupid asses, upon the brainless routineers, without foresight and without knowledge of military affairs, who have thrown an army of 70,000 men to a distance of 1,600 miles from France with barely half the means and resources that are required in the way of men and materials!"

But, as Bellesort justly remarks,[1] Saint-Arnaud had been Minister of War ever since the *coup d'état*. He was himself as much responsible as anybody else.

The English army, too, had only its coolness and its doggedness to rely on at first. It was in no sense prepared for a real war. It was far and away the most backward army in Europe. It had changed nothing since Waterloo, keeping the same weapons and, for the most part, the same leaders. Very badly organized, also, without ambulances and supply trains, it was to suffer even greater hardships than the French. During the early weeks of the campaign, exposure and disease were virtually to decimate its ranks.

The ancient Tauric Chersonese had been wrested from the Turks

[1] *La Société française sous Napoléon III*, 130.

by Catherine the Great. In the north it was just a grassy steppe that sloped down towards the Sea of Azov to merge with the salt marshes along the shore. In the south the horizon was marked by a range of hills known as the Iaïla Dagh. There were green valleys threaded by fordable streams. A strange land of hills, savannahs, endless pastures, and peopled by a motley hodgepodge of races—Tartars, Armenians, Jews, Greeks, even Russians. Towns were rare. Sebastopol, a creation of Catherine, was the one large port. Ill protected on the land side, it had strong defenses on the Black Sea. Facing the delta of the Danube towards the west, it seemed to be the natural base for any enterprise against Constantinople. The arsenal was a strong one, but it also had a symbolic value. Russia had a sort of superstitious attachment to it, as the Allies did.

Menschikov was in command of the defense. The army on the Danube had now become useless, but, through some aberration on the Czar's part that is hard to understand, Menschikov had received only one army corps, a scant 40,000 men. He nevertheless boldly advanced to meet the Allies, halting his troops on the steep bluffs of the Alma, halfway between Eupatoria and Sebastopol.

On the evening of September 19th, the two armies bivouacked face to face. The battle began the next morning. Menschikov, in a very advantageous position, held the heights. The Bosquet division was to cross the Alma and fall upon the Russian left, while Canrobert, Prince Napoleon and the English attacked in the center. The English, however, were slow in coming into action and Bosquet was obliged to wait a long time. The signal was not given till one-thirty. The Zouaves charged. Descending the steep broken slopes in front of them, they reached the banks of the Alma, but in small detachments.

General de Martimprey was frightened by the scattering of the forces.

"Let them alone," said Saint-Arnaud. "It's going to be a battle of soldiers."

Indifferent, in fact, to the Russian fire, the whole army plunged into the river, the Zouaves in the lead, the others joining them in their joyous scamper. The Alma was rather shallow. The French were across it and up the opposite bank in a flash. Menschikov made the mistake of not throwing all his forces in in time. The British attacked on his right, and in spite of heavy losses also gained a foothold on the plateau. Now the divisions of Canrobert and Prince Napoleon charged in their turn, throwing themselves heads down, bayonets forward, upon the grey masses in the enemy's center. The English, on their side, battled furiously. By five o'clock, the flags of the Allies were floating over the Russian redoubts. Menschikov ordered a retreat. The Allies could make no pursuit. They had no cavalry, ammunition was running low, and the regiments were scattered. Saint-Arnaud pitched tents.

During the battle his physician, Dr. About, had not once left his side. In order to keep him conscious when he seemed to be fainting, the doctor applied a large magnet wrapped in a leather bag to the region about his heart. Saint-Arnaud kept to his horse in that manner for more than twelve hours. Now exhausted, half dead, he sat down to write his first bulletin of victory. He thought himself already before Sebastopol.

A dash should have been made at once. The fortress being as yet defenseless could not have held out. Menschikov was expecting the assault. To protect the city on the sea side he sank five old vessels and two frigates at the harbor entrance. Saint-Arnaud held a council of war. Lord Raglan and Admiral Lyons were for an immediate attack from the north. Burgoyne, the head of the English engineers, a timid, spiritless soul, objected. Saint-Arnaud was too sick to think straight. He adopted Burgoyne's suggestion of advancing on Sebastopol from the south. That was a fatal blunder. It was to determine the whole course of the campaign.

The army advanced from the Alma to Sebastopol in a disorder which the officers could not correct. The men marched in mobs with their coats unbuttoned and without caps. Pointing to them, Prince Napoleon exclaimed to Canrobert in disgust:

"So that's war? Not so very inspiring!"

Saint-Arnaud followed in a carriage, stretched out on a mattress. During those last days under the torture of angina pectoris he would sometimes throw himself moaning and writhing to the ground; then, the crisis past, he would get up, rouge his cheeks, strap himself into his tight-fitting coat and pretend vigor and gaiety, though with glassy eyes. Now he came down with the cholera, and on the 26th of September, just before reaching the Tchernaia, he resigned the command to Canrobert. He was carried by sailors on a stretcher past his troops. He smiled at them in farewell. They saluted in silence. He was set aboard the *Berthollet,* with a flag draped over him and a priest at his side. He died before the coast of the Crimea had dropped below the horizon.

Napoleon granted him the honor of burial in the Invalides, a distinction he would in no way have deserved had he not managed to die a hero.

Canrobert, Saint-Arnaud's successor, was like him a soldier of the African campaigns. A Gascon still young, undersized, ruddy of complexion, with a mane of black hair and a curling mustache, he was dash itself. He was kind towards his subordinates and full of concern for his troops. Though very vain he was open-hearted and altogether unselfish as regarded his personal advantage. At the time of the *coup d'état* he almost resigned. He was utterly distressed over the shooting on the Boulevard Montmartre, which had been done without orders from him, and for the moment refused a promotion to the rank of brigadier-general. That, under the circumstances, took courage. He had had, and was always to have, a great gift for inspiring men on attack. But with all that he was really nothing more than a subaltern. He could carry out orders to perfection. The command of a great army was quite beyond him. He was afraid of taking responsibility and dared not make a decision himself. The men called him "Cap'n Anxious." He was not at all the leader they needed.

Rounding the city to the east, the English settled at Balaklava, the French on the Chersonese plateau, which was cut by deep ravines and swept by the wind from the Euxine. That whole countryside was to be devastated during the operations connected with the siege, but on the morning of the army's arrival before Sebastopol (September 27, 1854) it seemed to offer a beautiful, attractive prospect. The plateau was one great meadow dotted with autumn flowers. The city spread out vast and bright in a deep basin behind the hillocks. The coppered church domes shone in the sun. The port was alive with shipping. A number of monuments were visible, stretching along with colonnades like ancient temples. At the right, on a piece of high ground in front of an outlying spur of the city, towered a heavy mass of white stone: the Malakoff Tower, built with donations from the merchants of Sebastopol when war was declared. To the left, bristling with guns, lay the Fort at Quarantine, Fort Alexander, Fort Constantine. Trenches flanked with earthworks zigzagged down to the sea. A whole population of men in beards, women in skirts of varied colors, children, were still busily at work on them.

Those improvised diggers were to save the fortress. It could not have held out against a determined attack, even from the south where it was strongest. The garrison left by Menschikov on his retreat inland did not exceed 16,000 men. But those Russians, digging under the enflaming exhortation of their popes and the encouragement of Admiral Kornilov, were tireless movers of earth. They were to complete their defenses in a matter of hours, under the guidance of a young lieutenant-colonel whose name, Todleben, was to become better known thereafter. Sailors, soldiers, workingmen, businessmen, even prisoners in the jails, dug day and night. From their hands came a continuous, unbroken system of trenches, reinforced by powerful redoubts: the Quarantine Bastion, the Central Bastion, the South Bastion, the Big and the Little Salients, the Barracks Battery, the Point Battery. The Malakoff Tower, which was being made stronger and stronger, served as the pivot of the whole defense.

Canrobert and Raglan allowed the enemy thus to strengthen himself for fear of a defeat if they attacked at once. They rested content with digging trenches some two miles to the south and began a bombardment. The defenses were well armed with heavy naval guns landed from the ships. They replied with marked advantage. The English, however, succeeded in silencing the Great Salient and in opening a breach in its earthworks. Failing to receive support in time they did not dare to throw their infantry forward (Oct. 17th). Their success so came to naught.

Three days of cannonading followed. Two thousand Russians were killed, among them being Kornilov, who was hit by a cannonball at the Malakoff Tower. Dying, he said to those about him:

"Save Sebastopol! Never give it up!"

The Allied command now perceived the truth: Sebastopol was not to be taken without a long siege. The English were to be the first to admit it. As for the Russians, more spirited than ever, they expected their deliverance from a counter-offensive by Menschikov.

Menschikov, in fact, was in the open territory to the north. He kept receiving reinforcements till he had 100,000 men. On October 25th he attacked the Anglo-Turkish redoubts at Balaklava.

The Cossack cavalry swept the Turks before them but broke on the wall of Highlanders who awaited them with sighted muskets and squealing bagpipes. They were forced to turn back, pursued by great waves of cavalry in red and brown uniforms, the Scottish Grays and the Dragoons.

The engagement should have ended there. An order, misunderstood, threw Lord Cardigan's Light Brigade upon the Russians in a marvelous but useless charge.

"That's superb," exclaimed Bosquet, "but it's not war."

The Light Brigade, driving forward at a mad gallop, was cut to pieces by the Russian guns. Canrobert sent the African Chasseurs to support the attack and the Brigade was rescued, but with heavy losses. Most of the English officers were killed or wounded. The Russians withdrew in good order and the day ended without a decision.

Still wishing to profit by his superiority in numbers, Menschikov launched another attack on November 5th. At break of day, in a thick fog, he fell upon the British on the Inkermann plateau. The English were taken by surprise and fell back. Then they rallied and their accurate gunnery drove the Russians to cover in Cartroad Gully, so-called. A second attack, on the so-called Sand-bag Battery, was met by the Coldstream Guards. It ended in a desperate hand-to-hand. In spite of their heroism, the English were in a tight fix.

Canrobert was standing at Lord Raglan's side at the height of the battle. As cool as he was at Waterloo, the Englishman remarked to him at the critical moment in French:

"*Nous sommes f——s!*"

"I hope not, Milord," answered Canrobert. "Listen! That's *La Casquette!*" (*La Casquette*, "The Cap," was a soldiers' song of the Algerian campaigns.) [1]

In fact Bosquet was coming in with his light infantry, his Zouaves and sharpshooters. The bugles that the two generals could hear came from Bourbaki, who was arriving with his first battalions. The Russians were unable to hold. They gave ground and finally took refuge inside the town.

The bitterly fought battle of Inkermann cost the English three

[1] [As-tu vu la casquette, la casquette?
     As-tu vu la casquett' du pèr' Bugeaud?

The song recalled an incident in which General—in the song, "old man"—Bugeaud, surprised by an Arab attack, forgot to put on his helmet and fought the battle in his night-cap.—A. L.]

thousand men, the French eight hundred, the Russians more than ten thousand. Victory rested with the Allies, but it was a barren victory, merely emphasizing to them that the game on which they had entered was a risky one indeed. Winter fighting had not been foreseen. The troops were shivering in their summer uniforms, drenched by rain and stiff with the cold. Their wretched tents were swept by an unremitting winter wind. The trenches dug in the clay plateau were mere drains of icy mud. The commissariat had never been adequate. It now became unspeakable. The navy alone on more than one occasion saved the army from perishing of hunger.

Thouvenel was ambassador to Constantinople, at the time. A well-balanced individual, he said later on:

"I could name commissaries who deserved to be hanged, and I would have been glad enough to attend their hangings. . . . The food was wretched and even unhealthy: salt pork, and never any fresh meat—whence the scurvy epidemic that took off twenty thousand men; worm-eaten biscuit, and rarely any regulation bread. . . . The state failed to provide even a standard equipment. From four in the evening until eight in the morning the camps were in darkness." [1]

Under these frightful conditions the ingenuity of the French soldier stood him in good stead. He built huts and cabins lined with grass. He dug underground shelters. He uprooted stumps of trees for firewood, broiled his horsemeat and laughed at his wretchedness. The English were accustomed to more substantial rations and were not in training to begin with. Their officers took little interest in their comfort. They were in a much sadder plight than the French. The Highlander of the Coldstream Guard could often depend in his misery on the bantering and comradely encouragement of the French Zouave or chasseur. But as the cold increased the numbers of sick grew. They were sent away to Constantinople, which became virtually one great hospital.

In the end the English remedied the food shortage a great deal more effectively than the French, and they also succeeded in reorganizing their hospital service. Mortality among the English soldiers from disease was to fall to an insignificant figure—two percent of the men engaged during the last six months of the siege. The French army was sorely tried by typhus, scurvy, and lung diseases

[1] G. Bapst, *op. cit.*, II, 383.

till the very end, the figure reaching twenty-two percent of the effectives during the same period. All in all the expedition took a toll
of 105,000 lives in the Allied armies, only 10,000 actually falling
in the field.

Military operations came to an end: an occasional cannonshot;
here and there a new trench, the French and Russians striving to
keep parallel with each other. The soldiers may well have found
this "mole's war" tedious, but their spirits were kept high by their
commanders, Canrobert, Bosquet, Bizot, and they met the situation
in good humour. Bosquet wrote:

"One sees more laughing faces than frozen noses."

Reinforcements arrived—three new divisions under General
Pélissier, a hard and daring war-dog, who was replacing Forey.

Prince Napoleon had distinguished himself at the Alma, but he
had no patience with this "camping in the bush." Military life
held no attractions for him. He criticized everything, found time
hanging heavy on his hands, and to cap the climax fell ill of dysentery. He asked to be called home. The Emperor refused at first,
allowing him merely a furlough in Constantinople. But the Prince
was stubborn and soon found his way back to France. From that day
on and for the duration of the Second Empire he was snubbed
by the army, by staff and rank-and-file alike. Canrobert, for his part,
was delighted to see the last of a harsh and sometimes insolent critic.

"It wasn't fear of the bullets that drove him away," he said.
"There wasn't a braver man in the army. What he couldn't stand
was the mud, the rough life, the sleeping on the hard ground, the
filth, the lice—yes, the lice. We were covered with them, and there
seemed to be nothing one could do about it." [1]

Disappointment in France was bitter. Paris had been imagining
that Sebastopol would fall at the first sound of French bugles. The
press was muzzled but public opinion got the bad news through
the letters that the soldiers sent home. Little by little uneasiness
grew. The government called out 140,000 men of the class of 1854
and opened a new loan of 500,000,000. Official circles feigned optimism. The *Moniteur,* indeed, speaking of the winter season in the
Crimea, went a little too far when it reported that "the mild tem-
perature reminded one of the climate in Italy." Men were dying of
cold there every night.

[1] Bapst, *op. cit.,* II, 365.

The opposition exulted. Victor Hugo wrote:

"The Empire is back again at 1812. The French army is in its death throes, the English army is dead"; and in *Pendant l'Exil,* forgetting that he had himself called aloud for war, he entered for November 20, 1854:

"Widows weep and mothers wring their hands because M. Bonaparte, the murderer of Paris, has taken it into his head to have himself blessed and crowned by M. Mastaï, the strangler of Rome."

Some slight fluctuation in political opinion may perhaps be allowed to a poet.

Quinet sent word to Arago:

"Even foreigners are thinking that this wonderful house of cards that Franconi has built cannot endure."

Only one of the republican leaders hoped for victory. That was Barbès, a prisoner at Belle-Isle. Napoleon discovered the fact from a letter of Barbès that was intercepted by the police and referred to him. It contained the lines:

"A success would in no wise strengthen this man [Napoleon III] if the people are against him. Defeats may kill us—France, I mean; and our dear country must live and be great and strong for the good of the world."

On reading the letter, Napoleon III wrote to the Minister of the Interior:

"A prisoner who retains such patriotic sentiments in spite of much suffering cannot remain in prison while I am governing the country. Set him free at once and unconditionally."

The conservatives grumbled, but the public at large was touched.

Napoleon vainly sought to make a show of confidence by ordering a season of brilliance and festive gaiety at his court. He was worried. The sufferings of the army distressed him deeply. Looking over the maps at long range he concluded that the siege was being badly conducted, and he was inclined to blame his generals. He sent a number of officers of his trust to the Crimea to look over the army and report on their impressions—first Montebello, and later Niel, who was to remain before Sebastopol as his official representative. In England the public was openly denouncing the Ministry of War and the Commons were demanding an inquiry. Despite the efforts of Gladstone, the Aberdeen cabinet fell. Queen Victoria personally mistrusted Palmerston, and her dislike was increased by an unfortunate gesture by Napoleon III in his behalf. However, she overcame her prejudices and invited Palmerston to form a government. As soon as he was in power he took energetic steps to strengthen the English force in the Crimea and provide it with suitable equipment and an abundance of supplies that was shortly to be the envy of the French.

Meantime complex diplomatic manoeuvres were in progress, in which Frederick William IV of Prussia revealed the full extent of his muddled mind, and Bismarck, his minister at the Frankfort Diet, won his first laurels by dissuading the German princes from allying with Austria against Russia. Prussia and the Confederation declared their neutrality. However mistrustful and jealous they may have been of Prussia, the South German States were from that time on primarily anti-French. Bismarck stated the situation exactly when he wrote from Frankfort, March 31, 1854:

"The cabinets of Munich, Stuttgart, Dresden, Cassel and Karlsruhe are more likely to come out against France than against Russia."

On the other hand, in Vienna, the young Emperor Francis Joseph was concerned to maintain a balance of forces in the East. He took a determined stand at first. He massed an army in Transylvania, floated a loan and made a treaty with the Sultan. On August 8, 1854, he accepted the "Four Points" in the note presented by France and England: 1. The Russian protectorate over the Danubian principalities to be replaced by a collective guaranty by the powers. 2. Unrestricted navigation on the Danube. 3. A revision of the system controlling the Bosporus and the Dardanelles. 4. Protection of the Christian subjects of the Sultan without prejudice to the latter's prerogatives. On December 2nd, at the instance of Buol, Francis Joseph concluded an alliance with the western powers.

France and England were entangled in a war which was something altogether different from the one on which they thought they were embarking. They therefore set great store on the alliance with Austria, and especially France. Drouyn de Lhuys did not take his eyes off Vienna, and so too the Empress, though her influence was as yet not very great. If Austria should finally join forces with the Allies, the Holy Alliance would have seen its last days and Russia would not be able to hold out very long. To be sure the Austrian Empire was not the mighty state that Metternich had ruled in the period following 1815. The shock of 1848 had shaken it seriously. But extending from the Ticino to Galicia, from Bohemia to the Sava, possessing an excellent army of trained veterans, it was still a first-rate power, serving as the cornerstone of the Europe of old. Austria, moreover, shared boundaries with Russia and was so in a position to threaten her at points far more vulnerable than the coasts of the Black Sea.

The Czar was well aware of all that and avoided any rupture of relations, temporizing, trying to manoeuvre. Interests and conceptions of foreign policy were far from unanimous in Vienna, and so, after a first decisive step, Austria halted and marked time. That was the chance that Cavour seized for Piedmont. Cavour was eager to capture the sympathies of France and England with a view to the future aggrandizement of his country. He pushed Piedmont into the part that Austria was hesitating to accept. Napoleon III encouraging, Cavour joined the alliance. He was to send 15,000 men to the Crimea as a first installment (January 10, 1855).

Austria took offense despite the fact that, with a view to quieting her alarm, Napoleon III stated in the *Moniteur* of February 22nd that "if her armies joined the French and English, Austria's possession of her Italian provinces would be guaranteed for the duration of the war."

Austrian policy became more and more uncertain and all the more so because of the Czar's disappearance from the scene. His defeats in the Crimea had deeply hurt Nicholas in his pride—pride was the very life of that autocrat, so stiff and inflexible in his hard shell. Death was about all that remained for him, and on March 2, 1855, he died. Seriously ill, he insisted on reviewing a regiment that was leaving for the Crimea. His doctor tried to restrain him.

"You are doing your duty in trying to keep me indoors," Nicholas replied, "but I am doing mine when I do as I please. I am the Czar."

An icy wind was blowing across the parade ground. On the Czar's return he took to his bed. A week later the doctors gave him up. His last moments were calm. He dictated a circular to all his governors informing them that "the Emperor was dying." His last words were addressed to the members of his family: "After Russia you are the ones I have loved best."

There was some hope in the west that the Czar's son, Alexander, would be more inclined to listen to reason. Napoleon III made a chivalrous gesture and sent him official condolences on his father's death. Nesselrode replied:

"There is war between France and Russia but no hostility. We can have peace as soon as the Emperor Napoleon desires."

Napoleon III desired peace, but the decision did not rest with him alone. A conference met at Vienna. The Russian ambassador, Gortchakov, agreed to the "Four Points" in the Franco-British note, but rejected Austria's proposal for a limitation of naval forces in the Black Sea. Drouyn de Lhuys represented France at Vienna. He supported the Austrian proposal, of which London only half-heartedly approved.

Negotiations dragging along, Napoleon III conceived the notion of going to the Crimea and taking charge of operations in person. His idea was to mass a reserve army at Constantinople and suddenly hurl it upon Menschikov's rear in the upper Crimea for a battle that would end the war. Queen Victoria's ministers sought to discourage him. They feared he would prove incompetent, or at best, that the English army would be relegated to a secondary position. In France, too, sentiment was resolutely opposed to the plan. Drouyn de Lhuys complained. Fleury asserted that the Emperor "would not even be well received by the troops, since they would regard him as a civilian." Persigny overstepped all bounds in saying to Malmesbury:

"The Emperor must be prevented from going to the Crimea at all costs. If he ever gets there, the army will be lost and there will be a revolution."

Napoleon III and the Empress accepted an invitation to Windsor, where they were graciously received by the Queen and Prince Albert (April 16, 1855). The visit strengthened the alliance. From the standpoint of the French sovereigns it had the even more considerable advantage of socially recognizing their accession. At last they had been genuinely admitted to the society of monarchs. London had long been host to Louis Napoleon and the city now welcomed the sometime exile enthusiastically—reviews, theatrical performances, balls, a banquet at the Guildhall. London held many memories for the Emperor. Smilingly he pointed out to Eugénie the house in King Street where he had lodged after his escape from Ham.

The sovereigns of the two countries formed a real friendship. Queen Victoria bestowed upon Napoleon the Order of the Garter. She seems really to have been won by the Emperor's personal charm. She admired his self-composure, his chivalry, his gentle simplicity. "It is surprising," she wrote, "how one becomes attached to the Emperor. . . . I felt safe in his presence. . . . In spite of all the prejudices one might have there is something fascinating about him, a sadness that draws one to him. . . ." "That he *is* a very *extraordinary* man, with great qualities there can be *no* doubt," she wrote again. "He is evidently possessed of *indomitable* courage, unflinching firmness of purpose, self reliance, perseverance and great secrecy."

She was astonished at his competence in public affairs despite his few years' experience, and she noted in her diary:

"We are almost the only people in *his* own position . . . to whom he can talk easily and unreservedly . . . I . . . think that it is in our power to *keep* him in the right course and to protect him against the extreme flightiness, changeableness, and to a certain extent want of honesty of his own servants and nation."

Victoria also liked the Empress Eugénie for her deference and lack of pretentiousness, and took her under her wing. She urged her in particular to take a greater interest in politics. She believed in government by royal couples and set the example. The advice made a great impression on Eugénie. When she got back to France she ordered herself a uniform of the Imperial Guard and a little Spahi outfit, to wear at reviews.

Naïvely Napoleon III confided some of his dreams as to the future of Europe to Prince Albert. He wanted to free Lombardy of Austrian rule. He wanted to free and reunite Poland, starting with the Warsaw district as a nucleus. He wanted a union of German states, leaving out Prussia and Austria. The union would serve as a counterbalance to those two troublesome powers.

The Prince did not agree. He was, and was ever to remain, incurably German. His manners were perfect but his distrust of France was unshakable.

The four talked over the war together. The Emperor did not hide his intention of going to the Crimea.

"I should very much like to go out there," he said. "I'm afraid our generals are not showing initiative enough."

The Queen argued: It was too far away and the dangers were great!

"Oh," replied Napoleon III, "there's danger everywhere."

Marshal Vaillant implored Queen Victoria to dissuade Napoleon from the project.

"I must speak plainly," said he in his blunt soldier's manner. "If the Emperor should meet with a reverse, there would be reason to fear the consequences."

The Queen doubled her entreaties, but when the time came for Napoleon to bid her farewell, he had not yet changed his mind.

Shortly after his return to Paris, however, while Napoleon III was riding along the Champs Elysées, a young Italian named Pianori fired at him twice with pistols. Questioned, Pianori refused to say anything except that he had sought to avenge his country which had been "ruined by the Roman campaign." He was condemned to death and executed.

Napoleon III displayed his usual imperturbability on the occasion, but the attempt on his life gave him food for thought. He realized that his absence might encourage the revolutionists and endanger his throne. Without definitely abandoning his trip abroad he postponed it. The question never came up again.

The Conference at Vienna could find no way out of the impasse into which it had drifted. In spite of French and British pressure, Francis Joseph could not make up his mind to march against Russia. Schwarzenberg had said in 1849:

"Austria will astonish the world by her ingratitude"—ingratitude towards the Czar who had saved her the year before.

What astonished the world now was Austrian apathy. The alliance she had concluded with the western powers remained a dead letter. Napoleon III was dissatisfied with Drouyn de Lhuys, who had allowed himself to be duped by Buol. He recalled him from Vienna, deprived him of the portfolio of Foreign Affairs, and transferred the latter to Walewski, who was more docile to the Emperor's wishes. Persigny took Walewski's post in London. More and more Napoleon III was becoming engrossed with the one concern to please England. He treated the British ambassador, Cowley, as an intimate friend, taking him into his full confidence. Cowley's Austrian colleague, Hübner, noted that "the Emperor now sees only through Cowley's eyes." Whether in fear or in pique Vienna drew farther and farther away from the Allies.

The weather in the Crimea grew milder towards the end of February (1855) and operations were resumed. The army now numbered 130,000 men, 80,000 of them French. They had relieved the exhausted English at the Malakoff Tower, with Bosquet in command. Sebastopol was surrounded by a network of trenches, but the city's defenses, in compensation, had become formidable. Indefatigably circling the battle area by the back roads on his little black horse, Todleben guessed that the next attack would fall on the Karabelnaya district. He seized the Green Hill, so-called, and fortified it under the very noses of the Allies. Canrobert wanted to get even. At dawn on the 9th of April, in a downpour of rain, he began bombarding the town with all his five hundred guns. The Russians answered measure for measure. The duel lasted for ten days in a fog of rain and fire. The Russian fortifications were battered to pieces and an assault would have carried them. But the Allied command could not profit by any lesson. It dared not venture an infantry offensive. The Russians lost six thousand men in that futile storm of solid shot, the French and British together almost two thousand. General Bizot was among the slain, the finest brain on the Allied general staff.

Napoleon III was grievously disappointed. With too limited an understanding of the difficulties of the war, he tried to force his plans from the Tuileries. He envisaged nothing less than a total investment of the Russian stronghold, supplemented by a campaign in the interior of the Crimea. That would have involved far heavier forces than were available. The English turned a deaf ear. The Emperor insisted, relying on advices from Niel. His dispatches crossed orders with counter-orders. The completion of a submarine cable between France and Sebastopol only served to make matters worse.

Niel replaced the fallen Bizot at the head of the latter's army corps. Niel was an officer of the engineers and a good organizer. He had never commanded troops in the field. Tall, handsome, with wavy hair, of a melancholy disposition, he had a fine education, talked well and worked hard. His positive, vigorous personality set him off against Canrobert, who was too lacking in perspective as a strategist and never achieved a comprehensive view of what was going on.

Canrobert had gone on a naval expedition against the Russian fortress and storehouses at Kertch. A telegram from the Tuileries called the enterprise off. Canrobert's patience gave way under the unending interference of the Emperor, the lectures by Niel, the steady opposition of Bosquet. On his return he resigned his command in favor of Pélissier and requested to be transferred to a subordinate position. He wrote on May 16, 1855:

"I implore the Emperor to assign me to a fighting post at the head of a simple division."

That was a wise decision. Canrobert was not the man to unsnarl a situation that was far too much for him. He felt so discredited by the conditions under which he had to work that one day he offered to hand the post of commander-in-chief over to Lord Raglan. The latter consented but only on altogether unacceptable terms. Canrobert's despondency knew no bounds. He tried to commit suicide by leaping out of a trench into the Russian fire. He was seized by his coat-straps and forcefully pulled down behind the parapet.

When Pélissier became commander-in-chief Canrobert was assigned to Pélissier's corps. He conducted himself gallantly in that command, but his constant criticizing annoyed his successor. Napoleon III recalled him on July 24th in the face of his protests, Niel taking command of the corps.

The soldiers were never overfond of Pélissier, but they sensed that in him they had a leader, and they were right. A heavy man, sixty years old, with white hair and black eyebrows, and a sharp, commanding, facial expression he had an exquisite cultivation and a fine native intelligence. His jokes, which he delivered with an amusing nasal twang, were famous. In his character, probably, there was more than a trace of cruelty. Even his critics granted him a flair for large scale warfare.

Pélissier had a plan, a simple one, and he went ahead to carry it out, allowing nothing to distract him from it. He rejected Niel's suggestions and ignored orders from the Emperor. He would have nothing to do with the campaign in the interior of the Crimea. A total investment of Sebastopol seemed to him absurd—what were they to do with it? His idea was to prosecute the siege but with vigor. He would carry the fortifications and defenses to the south of the town one by one: first the Green Hill, then the White Works,

MARSHAL PÉLISSIER

1794-1864

then the whole position commanded by the Malakoff Tower. When that had been done, Sebastopol would fall.

"It's going to be a tough job," Pélissier wrote to Bosquet, "but I have made up my mind to do it, and I am going ahead."

Ignoring Napoleon's prohibition he returned, in agreement with Lord Raglan, to the entirely reasonable expedition against Kertch. The fleet destroyed all the supplies that were intended for Sebastopol. The Emperor was not convinced by the success. He intended that his orders should be obeyed. Pélissier had other views.

"I am confident," he wrote to Paris, "that my shoulders are strong enough for the burden laid upon me, but I shall bear it all the better if I am conscious of a certain freedom of conduct."

Napoleon stiffened and on June 11th wrote through Vaillant:

"I order you positively to do nothing about the siege until you have invested the fortress."

Pélissier paid no attention. He went doggedly ahead with his plan to attack the Russian positions.

The engineering corps was directed by General Forey. By June 6th Forey's sappers had prepared the ground by their numberless tunnels. The bombardment began. Great breaches were opened in the Green Hill and the White Works. The Allies advanced to the attack on the evening of the 7th, and in half an hour were in control of the two positions. They were carried away by their enthusiasm, however. Going on to attack the Malakoff Tower, they were repulsed with such heavy losses that they retired in great disorder. For a moment the Green Hill was taken by the Russians, but Bosquet snatched it back again by throwing in his reserves.

The army was heartened by this partial success and on June 14th the Emperor congratulated Pélissier, but with a bit of a lecture:

"A pitched battle deciding the fate of all the Crimea would not have cost you more men." And he reissued his order to drop the war of position for an open campaign.

Pélissier replied stiffly. If he were not to be allowed entire freedom of action, he would resign.

"It is impossible," he wrote the Emperor, "to carry out your orders of June 14th in full. You force me either to break discipline or to accept a humiliation. I have never yet been guilty of the one. I should not care to submit to the other."

Without awaiting further comment from Paris, he ordered another assault. On June 18th the English attacked the Big Salient, the French the Little Salient and the Malakoff. The attack had insufficient preparation and despite the gallantry of the troops the Russians held fast. Pélissier ordered a retreat. Casualties were so numerous that a day's armistice was concluded in order to bury the dead.

A shiver of anguish swept over France when news of this bloody defeat arrived. Public opinion veered against a futile war where the end was not in sight and which would require even more grievous sacrifices. Napoleon convoked the Legislative Body and on July 2nd it enthusiastically voted a new levy of 140,000 men, a loan of 750 millions, and a diversion of a tenth part of income from taxes to military purposes. But the Emperor's calm was to some extent impaired by the growing danger. He relieved Pélissier of his command with a letter that was unusually harsh:

"My patience is at an end. I can no longer allow soldiers to be profitlessly wasted, and the truth to be either misstated in dispatches or held in abeyance by silence."

And he concluded:

"You will do nothing further without having my consent in advance. Otherwise hand over the command to General Niel."

Vaillant, with Fleury's connivance, held up the letter for sufficient time to allow its interception at Marseilles. On this occasion Vaillant acted with courage and tact.

Pélissier was well aware of the growing distrust of the English and of the disapprobation that was mounting about him from subordinates such as Niel, Bosquet and Regnault de Saint-Jean d'Angély. He held out against them all. He gave Niel a sizzling rebuke:

"There is no Emperor's aide-de-camp here, no repository of his ideas and plans. What there is here is one commander-in-chief, then there are subordinates. You have but one job: to obey. If I hear anything more from you, I shall arrest you and ship you home." [1]

Cholera was raging again. The terrible exertions of the campaign had tired the army out. Lord Raglan himself died on June 28th and was replaced by the aged General Simpson. That left Pélissier more elbowroom than ever. The French command kept the minds

[1] G. Bapst, *op. cit.*, II, 470.

of the troops off their troubles by setting them to work digging new trenches towards Malakoff and the Great Salient.

Luckily things were not any better on the other side. Resistance from within Sebastopol was gradually losing its vigor from the heavy casualties in battle, from disease and all sorts of privations, and especially from the loss of the two main sources of inspiration to the defenders: Todleben had been wounded, Nakhimov killed. Vainly the Czar sent reinforcements to re-man the pile of ruins that the city had become. They merely added to the wretchedness and confusion.

General Gortchakov replaced Menschikov. Like Pélissier he was endlessly tormented by advisers and critics. On August 16th he decided to throw in his reserve army, which was encamped on Mackenzie plateau. The attack failed after a furious engagement on the Tchernaïa. The Piedmontese army, facing the Russian left, made a brilliant showing under the lead of General La Marmora.

Gortchakov lost heart. He wrote to St. Petersburg a week later: "Everyone here thinks it sheer madness to continue the defence."

From his ambulance bed Todleben prevented the evacuation of the southern section of Sebastopol. But the Russians were at the end of their rope. Pélissier sensed the fact and telegraphed the Emperor, exultant:

"Everything is going well. We are getting ahead."

Napoleon calmed down on this news, and also because Queen Victoria and Prince Albert had come to Saint-Cloud to repay his call. The visit created a profound sensation among the European cabinets. Magnificent entertainments were offered them. Impulsive as ever, and always loving a parade, Paris acclaimed the English sovereigns. The Queen visited the exposition at the Industry Building—the first World's Fair to be held in France. She went to the Invalides. The coffin containing the remains of the great Napoleon had been brought back to France fourteen years earlier, but was still awaiting its final interment. While torches flickered and a thunder-storm crashed outside, the granddaughter of George III paused solemnly before the catafalque, gazed reverently upon it, and finally took the Prince of Wales, the future Edward VII, by the hand, and made the slender, fair-haired boy kneel in his amusing Scotch kilties before the remains of the man whom the English had defeated at Waterloo.

Intimate talks between the sovereigns strengthened their now long-standing friendliness. Queen Victoria again declared that she was "fascinated" by Napoleon III, but she wondered what the morrow was going to be:

"Everything is so lovely here! There is so much prosperity! The Emperor seems to be just the man for the position he occupies. Yet how uncertain one feels about his future!"

So thought the willful little lady of the beautiful complexion, the ugly mouth, the soft intelligent eyes, as she took her departure in a hat trimmed in marabout. She was an ally of Napoleon III in view of a common interest, but she did not judge him a sound proposition. That impression was to have its influence on their future relations, for she prized sound people above all else.

Everyone thought the end of the war near at hand. Pélissier was determined to bring things to a finish by October. It would be hard to coax the army along through a second Crimean winter. He had carried his trenches to within twenty-five yards of Malakoff, to within forty of the Little Salient and two hundred of the Great Salient.

The assault was fixed on for September 8th. A hellish preparatory bombardment opened. It shattered the Russian fortifications and overwhelmed the defenders. Fires started everywhere. Many of the powder magazines exploded. On the evening of the 7th Pélissier assigned the generals their respective tasks and said to them:

"Well, gentlemen, good night. Quite a number of us will show smashed faces tomorrow, but Sebastopol will be ours."

The 8th dawned with a wind blowing furiously under a lowering sky. The Allied troops left their trenches at noon on a signal from Bosquet. With their bands playing a gay march and with shouts of "Vive l'Empereur!", MacMahon's Zouaves gallantly scaled the terraces of the Malakoff. A brief but fiery hand-to-hand, and the Russian batteries were carried. The tricolor was run up over the Tower. The Little Salient was taken at the same time. Raked by a hail of grape the English were unable to reach the Great Salient and had to fall back. Fortunes seemed to turn at that moment. Levaillant's division failed before the Central Bastion. Dulac had to evacuate the Little Salient. The men on both sides were displaying fierce heroism in the face of frightful carnage. Generals Courtois, Trochu, Bosquet and Bourbaki were wounded. Pélissier took his stand on the Green Hill and held on. MacMahon at Malakoff fought off desperate counter-attacks by the Russians one after another.

"What do you propose to do?" asked Simpson by messenger.

"Here I am and here I stay," answered MacMahon.

Gortchakov finally decided that the battle was lost. He drew his troops back and prepared to abandon Sebastopol during the night. Endless lines of wagons began leaving the city in the early evening. Everything that might be of use to the Allies was destroyed. Powder magazines were blown up, guns were thrown into the sea, the last remaining warships were scuttled in the harbor. Sebastopol burned all night. The Russians, from the north of the fortress, the Allies from the tops of the trench embankments, looked down on one enormous furnace that turned the sky red with its glare. Pélissier entered the town amid a respectful silence the next day but one, September 10th.

The Emperor named him Marshal of France that morning.

Cannon thundered at the Invalides, cannon thundered at Hyde Park, to announce to the capitals of England and France that Sebastopol had fallen. Jubilation ran high in both countries—but was there going to be peace? Napoleon III was not so very sure. He sent Canrobert to Stockholm to arrange an alliance. He urged Pélissier to complete his victory by a campaign in the Crimea, where Gortchakov was awaiting him in good order. But the army was too tired. A few minor operations showed that its fighting spirit could not be sustained much longer. Pélissier was impassive to repeated entreaties of the Emperor, declaring the latter's plans impracticable.

Napoleon was eager to profit by the Russian defeat to make a start, at least, towards a restoration of Poland. He broached the matter to London. Clarendon had always been opposed to the idea. He refused again. Walewski met with no better success at Vienna. Disappointed, the Emperor from then on thought only of hastening the end of hostilities.

Opinion in France was calling for peace. The masses knew what blood the war had cost. The bourgeoisie complained of the prolonged interference with business. The banks were in a bad way. What advantage, even in a moral sense, could one expect to gain from a prolongation of the conflict?

On November 15, 1855, at the exercises for the closing of the Exposition, Napoleon made an appeal for peace.

"France," he said, "hates nobody."

Confidential negotiations began in Paris between the minister of Saxony and Walewski. The English did not participate. They were worried about their future in Asia and were disposed to crush the giant of the north. They had not had a satisfactory share in the victory. Their set-back at the Great Salient was still on their minds. The whole British press objected to a settlement as premature.

In private letters to Queen Victoria Napoleon strove to bring her around to a more moderate attitude; but just at that moment Victor Emmanuel arrived in Paris in company with Cavour. Thirty-four years old, with a shaggy head, bulging eyes, and a wide-spreading mustache, the King of Piedmont made a strange and at the same time impressive figure. He was a bit of a rogue, given to drinking, roughing the girls—and fighting like a hero; but under the rogue was a fine fellow, affectionate with his family and kind to the poor. He was very much the realist and bore for his motto, "Be, rather than seem." He was ever proud of his origins and family background, his arrogance in this regard often bordering on insolence. Speaking of Napoleon III one day with La Tour d'Auvergne, French Minister to Turin, he had the audacity to say:

"Who is that bastard, anyway? The newest comer among the kings, an intruder among us!"

When need required, on the other hand, he could evince an exquisite humility. During the war in Italy he placed himself at the Emperor's command like an ordinary officer, and stood at attention in the Emperor's presence. Since the death of his queen he had lived by preference at La Mandria, in a château-farmhouse, with the daughter of a soldier in his bodyguard, Rosina by name, by whom he had had three children.

His loose manners and language caused loud laughter at the Paris court, where he was extremely popular. Thouvenel vouches for the fact that he said to the Empress:

"You cause me the tortures of Tantalus."

One evening at the Opéra a young danseuse caught his eye.

"How much do you suppose that little one would cost?" he asked the Emperor.

"I have no idea," Napoleon replied. "Ask Bacciochi."

The King put the question to the First Chamberlain and Bacciochi replied:

"Sire, for Your Majesty it might be a matter of five thousand."

"The devil you say! That's a lot of money!"

"You can charge it to me!" said the Emperor to Bacciochi, laughing.

One evening at Compiègne Napoleon said to Cavour:

"Write confidentially to Walewski and tell him what you think I might do for Italy and Piedmont."

At that moment Austria had again come on the scene. She feared the war might be ended without her or perhaps against her. Buol formulated a set of proposals as a basis for peace talks: acceptance of the "Four Points" of the Franco-British note of 1853, plus some rectification of boundaries in Bessarabia and a few matters of detail. The young Czar, Alexander II, was weary of the war. He hesitated. His army had taken a Turkish stronghold in the Caucasus, the fortress at Kars. This had somewhat retrieved his military prestige. He was in a better position for talking peace, but was disinclined to cede any territory.

Frederick William of Prussia used his good offices with Alexander. On the 16th of January, 1856, yielding to the entreaties of the King of Prussia but also with a thought to worries at home, the Czar accepted the conditions formulated by Austria. Debt bonds leapt up five points. Paris broke out in flags. England grudgingly signed the preliminary agreement at Vienna. The treaty of peace would be drawn up at a conference in Paris. This was a striking satisfaction accorded to Napoleon III and France. They could very properly see in it a counter to the Congress of Vienna.

Meetings began on the 25th of February, 1856. At England's request Prussia was not represented. Clarendon, Orloff, Buol, Ali Pasha, Cavour, were the leading plenipotentiaries. The first step was to arrange an armistice between the belligerents.

Walewski, the French Foreign Minister, was elected president of the Congress. Actually he was to do nothing save at express orders from Napoleon. The latter arranged everything of importance in private conferences in his study.

Walewski patiently submitted to this complete eclipse. A man of his pleasures, affable of approach, indolent, vain, ignorant, mouthing empty phrases, he had a round, smooth face that bore witness to a glorious descent which he did his best to disclaim, though to it and to nothing else he owed his fortune and position in the world. A liaison between the Emperor and his wife resulted in an increase in the fortune and in its consolidation; but it gave Walewski no influence over his master and no prestige in Europe. That was a pity, on the whole. Though not possessed of great understanding, Walewski was no fool. He had moderation and good taste and the policies he favored ran towards conciliation and balance.

Napoleon III's design was to profit by the occasion in order to get the treaties of 1815 formally annulled. The British government was opposed to this and also refused to allow the Polish and Italian questions to come up. An agreement was quite easily reached on the neutralization of the Black Sea. No riparian state was to maintain a navy in its waters, or build an arsenal on its shores. The status of Christians in the Turkish Empire was determined and guaranteed by a *hatti-humayoun,* or personal edict, of the Sultan. Freedom of navigation on the Danube also offered no serious difficulties. A commission of representatives of the powers was to act as its custodian. Discussion of the question of the Roumanian principalities opened a thornier road. Russia was willing to surrender her protectorate. Napoleon III proposed that Wallachia and Moldavia be united into a single independent state. Turkey and Austria would have none of that. The two principalities were finally allowed to go their separate ways, under an all-European guaranty. Russia ceded the mouths of the Danube to Moldavia. They had hitherto belonged to Bessarabia.

As the labors of the conference proceeded, fringed with a gay round of receptions and banquets, the outlines of a Franco-Russian rapprochement were quite plainly discernible. Napoleon's utter charm captured the Czar's envoys and Alexander for his part was eager to please Napoleon in every way. France was no less devoted to the British alliance, but London began to doubt her loyalty and to manifest some vexation.

On the 16th of March a great happiness fell to the Emperor's lot. After three years of marriage and several disappointments, an heir was born to him.

The night had passed in the greatest anxiety. In the morning Doctor Conneau rushed into Napoleon's presence:

"Sire, it's a boy!"

Smiling, trembling, with tears streaming down his cheeks, the Emperor knelt at Eugénie's bedside, then made his way through the palace halls that were crowded with dignitaries and attendants.

"A son, a son!" he cried. "How happy I am!"

In his joy he kissed five or six people at random. Then, recovering his dignity, he said in a voice that carried through all the rooms:

"I cannot embrace you all but I thank you for this demonstration of your interest."

Two days later at dessert at a dinner in the Tuileries, the Emperor signalled that he desired to offer a toast. As the table fell silent he lifted his glass of champagne and said:

"To my good friends, Marshal Canrobert and Marshal Bosquet!"

And he shook hands with the two new dignitaries, who had been the artisans of his triumph.

The birth of the Prince Imperial was received with great happiness in France as a whole. This young child, it was felt, would serve the twin purpose of consolidating the Empire and of withholding it from dangerous adventures. The dynasty could take root at last.

Prince Napoleon, however, was not with the majority and behaved most ungraciously. The happy event in the Emperor's household deprived him of his status as heir to the throne. He refused for a long time to sign the official certificate, and in spite of his sister's entreaties. In the end a sharp letter from his father, the ex-King Jerome, was required to put an end to his insulting obstinacy.

Napoleon III's head was not turned by his great good fortune. At that radiant hour he was host in Paris to representatives of the monarchies which, forty years before, had banished the Bonaparte family from European society. To the congratulations of the Chamber he replied with a speech that was sane and almost disillusioned:

"The acclamations that surround the cradle of my son only prompt me to reflection on the destinies of those who have been born in the same place and under similar circumstances. . . . History teaches lessons which I shall not forget. History tells me that one must never abuse the favors of Fortune, that a dynasty has a chance of enduring only as it remains loyal to its origins."

Prophetic words, which he was to have occasion to remember!

The conference had adjourned for the festivities. It resumed its sittings on March 18th. Its membership was now increased by the admission of a representative from Prussia, Manteuffel, who had finally been seated at Napoleon III's express and repeated request. King Frederick William had been terribly hurt by his exclusion from the conference and had begged the Emperor to move heaven and earth to overcome British opposition.

The Paris Congress therefore began to look like a real senate of Europe. In that capacity it solemnly guaranteed the integrity of the Ottoman Empire, and on March 30th the treaty of peace was signed with a quill taken from one of the eagles at the Zoo.

This peace finally brought a hazardous enterprise to a close, but it not so much settled as quieted the Near Eastern question—quieted it, that is, for a matter of twenty years. When France seemed to be eliminated by the disaster of 1870, Russia resumed her inexorable pressure upon Constantinople. The Black Sea became her sea. The autonomous principalities were to wrest their complete independence from Turkey; and not to be left out in the cold, England was to lay hands on Egypt and Cyprus. With her keen sense of realities, she was also to take part in curing "the sick man" whom she had tried to protect in 1854 at the cost of most exhausting sacrifices.

The peace of 1856 was by no means profitless, however. For one thing it stands by itself as not planting any particular seeds of new discords. It recognized no victor and no vanquished. The Czar, perhaps, may have had some grounds for being hurt for a time because of a secret agreement whereby France, England, and Austria combined to supervise the execution of the treaty—Napoleon III, with no great propriety, thought it only fair to inform the Czar of this ex-parte convention. Actually, France and Russia had taken each other's measure in a heroic struggle, and a sincere mutual respect had been born of it. Morny was as much set on a Russian alliance as Persigny, his rival, was on the British alliance. Through Morny's influence France and Russia were to come closer and closer together. Had Napoleon been shrewd enough to exploit the possibilities of this accord to the full and had he not spoiled it later on, it might have been the effective check to Prussian ambitions and so have changed the destinies of all Europe.

In any event, France derived one important advantage from this treaty, not a material but a moral advantage. The valor of her soldiers set her again in the forefront among the nations of Europe. The humiliation of 1815, the Holy Alliance, now became mere ashes of history. In the words of Hübner, "The great result for France was to have shattered the European league which the first Revolution had forged against her and which had lasted for sixty years."

Through it, in addition, the personal position of Napoleon III gained a relief which no European sovereign had achieved since the fall of the Empire. The old dynasties could no longer treat him as a lucky upstart. The English noted this change in his situation with some vexation. The two governments continued to maintain the friendliest relations but the *entente* was henceforward to be less and less *cordiale*.

Standing out more and more positively as the arbiter of Europe, Napoleon III persuaded the Congress not to dissolve till it had settled in the general interest a question which had long been awaiting adjustment: the matter of rights at sea. The plenipotentiaries arrived at an agreement on four fundamental principles: that privateering should be abolished; that a neutral flag protected enemy goods, with the exception of contraband of war; that neutral goods were to remain neutral even under an enemy flag; that a blockade had to be actual and effective in order to be recognized.

With that much accomplished, Walewski, acting on orders from the Emperor, gradually and by indirection lured the Conference down a new path which led towards nothing less than a reorganization of Europe. He did not venture to speak too overtly of Poland. That would have lost him the Czar. He did ask that the Greek ports be freed. Then he broached the Roman question, proposing that the Papal States be evacuated by French and Austrian troops alike.

That was tossing an apple of discord out upon the greensward of the conference. Clarendon, haughty, handsome, bitterly criticized the government of the Pope. That brought Buol to his feet in protest. There were abuses in the Papal States under the Papal government—the fact could not be denied. Lamoricière, who was to become commander-in-chief of the pontifical army, said:

"Nothing good will ever be achieved in Rome, until four monsignors have been strung up at the four corners of the city." [1]

Next came the turn of the King of Naples, whose administration

[1] Bellesort, *op. cit.,* 153.

was openly assailed by France and England, the Russian, Turkish and Prussian representatives maintaining an attitude of cautious reserve. But Cavour now had his chance to produce a memorandum on the necessary revision of the status of Italy. So, over the head of Austria and in the face of her manifest ill will, the most serious question of the time was deliberately formulated and with Napoleon III's consent.

"Let's do something for Italy," he kept repeating.

The final protocol, cleverly worded by Benedetti, stopped at a mere voicing of hopes; but the conference of Paris that had met to end one war adjourned when it had cleared the ground for another. Only three years were to elapse before the war broke out.

CHAPTER XI

France and the Dictatorship

THE PERIOD THAT BEGAN IN 1852 AND WAS TO END IN 1860 HAS BEEN called the period of the "authoritarian Empire." During that period Napoleon III enjoyed a virtually unlimited power in France. IIis sovereign authority governed the nation absolutely, subject to no supervision or restraint. With a Senate named by the ruler and a Chamber issuing from official candidatures, all political activity in the domestic field necessarily lapsed. The Emperor counted on that development, for in opening the session of 1853 he remarked unostentatiously and in a language that curiously parallels Renan's:

"Freedom has never made any contribution to the establishment of an abiding political structure. Freedom crowns the edifice when time has firmly settled it on its foundations."

"Freedom crowns the edifice." The words contained a promise that was vague, but perhaps sincerely intended. Certainly they were to force themselves upon Napoleon's mind in after days. In the dawn of his reign they were hardly more than a gracious turn of phrase. That was an era of unmitigated, uncompromising dictatorship. Bills of prospective laws were prepared by the Council of State under the guidance of Baroche. They were moved before the Legislative Body during its three months' session in such numbers that the deputies had to pass them wholesale without ever knowing what they were about.

All the same the Assembly sometimes balked. Budgets grew heavier year by year. They were often the subject of fairly sharp debates, echoes of which reached the public, three days stale, in the faint murmur of an inspired summary that the newspapers printed on the page of official advertisements. That semblance of an opposition, nevertheless, was enough to compel the government to withdraw its bill for reductions in the tariff, which the Emperor was eager to try out as a feeler towards a free trade policy. The members of the Legislative Body were protectionists and arrogantly conservative. In the majority they were of an Orleanist coloring, standing by the regime only in fear of the new revolution that would come if it should chance to fall. They were devoted to the public welfare, and showed their devotion in a tremendous concern to evince some shred of intellectual integrity in the face of a power that was altogether too strong.

When Morny replaced Billault in the chairmanship, relations between the Chamber and the sovereign became more cordial. The Emperor's half-brother managed to avoid all manner of clashes by his instinctive tact. He checked the assembly when it was minded to try to glide down some perilous slope; but at the same time, without seeming to, he gave it back some of its vitality. Interpellations were forbidden by the rules, but he found a way—Montalembert was the first one to profit by it—to authorize "observations" which were presented tactfully, loyally, and in good will. The period between recesses was made gradually longer. In five years' time the Legislative Body enacted just about a thousand laws.

The Senate was vassalized to begin with and complete servility was asked of it; but it, too, raised its head from time to time. Its main function was to make sure that the texts of bills presented for enactment conformed with the language of the Constitution. Boldly, sometimes, it went on to discuss the merits of the bills themselves. The government rudely rebuffed such efforts. On January 11, 1856, an article in the *Moniteur* reminded the Senate that "it would be wasting its time in a bootless and illegal activity if it were to debate any bill which it had no power to change."

The senators took the rebuke ungraciously and Drouyn de Lhuys went so far as to resign. Soon after he presented himself as a candidate for the Institute. He was elected all the more easily in that he was regarded as an open opponent of the regime. Before long he confessed his sins and Napoleon III restored him to his place in the Senate. The incident was in no wise to damage his ministerial career.

The Senate rejected a sumptuary tax on carriages in Paris as unconstitutional. Finally, after the birth of the Prince Imperial, a debate flared up on a resolution conferring the Regency upon the Empress in event of the Emperor's death. La Valette asked that in the oath which the Empress would be required to take a phrase should be inserted binding her "to respect the laws of the Concordat and liberty of worship."

This was obviously a thrust at the "ultramontaine" views of the Empress. The amendment was rejected, but by such a slender majority that the allusion gained very considerably in force. To avoid making matters worse, the Emperor thought it the wiser part to overlook the incident.

Public opinion was controlled much more severely under the Second than under the First Empire. The press was reduced to a small number of publications with editors-in-chief to the liking of the government. If a publication raised an independent voice, it received an immediate warning. If a paper did not heed the warning, it was suspended. That spelled ruin for both editors and owners. The wiser policy therefore was to submit.

The provinces had nothing, one might say, except official newspapers. In Paris, *Le Constitutionnel, Le Pays, La Patrie,* were governmental; *La Gazette de France, L'Union, L'Assemblée Nationale,* Legitimist; *L'Univers,* Catholic-Imperial; the *Journal des Débats,* Orleanist; *Le Siècle* cautiously republican.

Emile de Girardin edited *La Presse* in accord with his views and interests at the given moment. He had reopened that paper on his return to Paris soon after the *coup d'état.* Later on he sold it to the banker Millaud. In 1866 he bought *La Liberté* and raised it to a position of great prominence.

The private conversation, like the written word, was under police surveillance. When the war in the Near East broke out Persigny called the presidents of the three more important clubs to the Ministry of the Interior and enjoined on them to hold off on politics. Once in a café the actor Grassot thought he was being served too slowly. He was so imprudent as to say:

"Things here are the way they are at Sebastopol: No one ever gets anywhere!"

The sally cost him his freedom.

Jules Simon criticized the government in a private conversation in his own home. He was warned to be more discreet in the future. The police were everywhere.

"All resistance is dead," wrote Victor Cousin. "No one in the provinces dares to speak, no one in Paris dares to write. The aristocracy has been destroyed. The middle classes are thinking only of making money."

An Englishman was questioning Lavergne about the state of mind in France. The famous economist replied sadly:

"How could I tell you anything? No one talks to us except the government, and we do not believe what it says."

Nevertheless, in spite of these restraints, opposition to the imperial regime was still watchful and awake. In a letter to Reeve (December 25, 1851), Guizot had written some prophetic lines:

"The higher classes who take an interest in politics, Legitimists, Orleanists, or republican as they may be, will offer no opposition at the present time. They are afraid of socialism or a Jacquerie. But they will eventually change. Then memory of all the insults they have endured, their stolen liberties, ill will, contempt, the factional spirit—everything, in a word, that makes the educated classes ungovernable, will come back again. For a longer or shorter period of time they will tolerate the government of Louis Napoleon. I doubt whether they will ever support it."

The royalists continued to be divided by the rivalry of the Comte de Chambord and the Comte de Paris, and they were paralyzed by the flocking of the clergy *en masse* to Napoleon III's standard. The Legitimists were reduced to sulking haughtily in their retirement. The Comte de Chambord—"Henry V of France"—was surrounded by aging partisans. He knew nothing about the new France. Though he had remarkable native qualities—intelligence, a strong will, shrewdness, he gradually sank into pietism and a sort of royalist do-nothingism. He ordered his adherents to create a vacuum around the usurper, not to accept any post or commission from the Empire. He was obeyed. A banquet here and there on Saint Henry's day; here and there a white flag or a portrait of the "King," which the police drove to cover on the outbreak of war in the Crimea; some few inept eulogies of the Czar as the prop of counter-revolution in Europe—such were the manifestations of royalism. They caused the government no very great annoyance and Napoleon III did not deal severely with them.

A number of Legitimist leaders, such as La Rochejaquelin or Fortoul, rallied to the Empire in sheer desperation, as a way of escaping from the state of gross depression to which their prince reduced them. Others such as Berryer and Falloux remained faith-

THE TUILERIES

Residence of all the French 19th Century Monarchs, it was set afire by Communists in 1871 and almost totally destroyed

ful to their cause, but vainly protested to Froshdorff against the "policy of folded arms." They won no following and the party fizzled out. A few Legitimist centers sputtered in Languedoc, in Provence, and in the West, but the passing years were to sprinkle them as with a powdery ash, under which it seemed that no spark could ever again glow.

The Orleanist leaders, on the other hand, were active and aggressive. The Empire feared them and kept an eye on them. Most of the Orleanists—landlords, manufacturers, merchants—were interested primarily in order and profits, and they soon accepted a ruler who guaranteed just those things. A number of men who had been in parliament under the July Monarchy accepted portfolios or important posts in the new government and became most trustworthy agents of it.

For a moment Thiers himself was tempted to strike his bargain. In his preface to the twelfth volume of the *History of the Empire* he paid homage to the victors at Sebastopol.

"The greatest consolation one can have," he wrote, "for being nothing in one's country, is to see that country holding the position it ought to hold in the world."

A lumbering style, a creditable thought! The Emperor recognized the tribute by officially greeting Thiers as "our illustrious and patriotic historian." Maupas had been in storage in the Senate since his fall from grace. He tried to be of service by arranging things with Thiers, using a mutual friend, Lady Holland, as intermediary. Thiers laid down his conditions: If he were to serve the Emperor he must be offered the Presidency of the Council and the portfolio of Foreign Affairs. Walewski, speaking for Napoleon, offered just a post at the Quai d'Orsay, and two or three ministries for Thiers's friends. The bargain fell through.

The other Orleanist leaders, Guizot, the Duc de Broglie, Molé, Duchâtel, Barante, not to mention Lamoricière and Changarnier, who withdrew to Belgium, stubbornly held out, uncompromising, fearless. Having no platform available in the assemblies or in the press, they waged a warfare of epigrams in the salons and of letters to newspapers abroad, stinging the government, the imperial couple and their court, with merciless darts.

At home the *Journal des Débats* worked with a caution that limited but was far from crippling the free play of wit. It became the recognized organ for this implacable Orleanist raillery. Saint-Marc-Girardin, Samuel de Sacy and before long Prévost-Paradol, gave evidence in the columns of that paper of talents that seemed only to be whetted by their need of expressing themselves by allusions, omissions, ironies.

The French Academy became the refuge of independent thought during this eclipse of freedom. It elected the representative men of the time and gave them an opportunity to censure absolutism in orations that not seldom touched the peaks of style. Guizot, for instance, delivered the reception address for Montalembert. Salvandy did the same for Berryer—and Berryer proceeded to excuse the Head of the State from according him the traditional audience. Mocquard turned a deft and elegant rejoinder to Berryer, on this hostile gesture:

"The Emperor regrets that political motives have weighed more urgently upon M. Berryer than his duties as an academician. Otherwise, in the lofty position which he occupies, His Majesty would have seen in the choice of the Academy only the orator and the writer, and in the adversary of today only the defender of a day gone by."

Samuel de Sacy owed his quiet reputation to the *Journal des Débats*. He seasoned with Attic salt his address on the abuse of muzzles. The Duc de Broglie succeeded Sainte-Aulaire. He paid his respects to the "reconstructive achievements of the Consulate," and then went on to deliver a courageous eulogy of Louis Philippe, whose friend he had been and whom he had served as minister. Fearlessly he referred to "the sanctuary of the law besieged and invaded by armed force," to "cities laid waste by civil war," to "prominent men" who had been "persecuted, proscribed and sent into exile." In a disdainful period he condemned "this indifference to principles, this alacrity to burn the idols of yesterday, this zeal for conversion, these new greeds, this thirst for gold, ostentation, indolence. . . ."

His peroration struck a melancholy note:

"The Emperor Severus, faced with sudden death, saw a centurion advancing to ask him what the password was to be. He drew himself up on his couch and said in an unshaking voice, '*Laboremus.*' Those were his last words. Let them be ours as well so long as the blessing of life is left to us, and the strength to raise a voice that will be heard by our countrymen. Let us labor!"

The Duc de Broglie was a favorite with all parties. Forty years before he had risen courageously in the Chamber of Peers to attack the death sentence pronounced against Marshal Ney. When Napoleon III received him he pretended to know nothing of the sarcasms the Duc had been hurling at the imperial government. Smilingly he said:

"I hope, sir, that your grandson will also be a member of the Academy, and that he will praise the 2nd of December the way you have praised the 18th of Brumaire."

The Duc was too polite to reply that the 18th of Brumaire had shed no blood.

Activities of this sort in the Academy echoed far in waves that were invisible but deep. Finally, in 1857, Falloux succeeded to the chair of Molé.

"Since I am quite resolved to vote for him," said Guizot, "I'd rather not read his books."

This election was the occasion for a new rumble of repressed hostility against the regime. Indignation waxed hot in the Emperor's entourage. There was a proposal to suppress the Academy, or at the very least to set up a rival institution. Napoleon III was wiser than his favorites and refused. Like his uncle he thought that having strangled the Republic he might at least allow some little breath of life to "the republic of letters." He knew that the intellectual élite was and would remain powerless in the realm of practical affairs. Under his control he had hand-picked staffs, a loyal army, the clergy, the peasantry. Why be concerned about the play of words at the Institute and in the salons? If they did create an annoying buzz about his throne, they fell harmless before the stern reality of power and the onward march of institutions.

Fortoul, nevertheless, executed a decree of April 14, 1855, which established a new section in the Academy of Moral Sciences. It contained ten members nominated by the Emperor. The French Academy, at the time under the presidency of the Duc de Noailles, protested in vain.

A danger as yet unvocal, but which was real and constant, came from the republican opposition. Exile had not disarmed the leaders of the Mountain. Victor Hugo was at Jersey, Emile Deschanel,

Challemel-Lacour, Edgar Quinet, were in Brussels, Louis Blanc, Schoelcher and Ledru-Rollin in London. Tirelessly they published articles and pamphlets such as *Napoleon the Little* and, later on, *Les Châtiments,* which reached France in peddlers' packs or in the pockets of obliging tourists. Associations of exiles such as "The Revolutionary Commune" and "Revolution" multiplied in England for the purpose of organizing or assisting the victims of the regime. In such societies the wretched exiles tore each other to shreds. Their poverty, unsystematically relieved, lifted some to flights of irrational fanaticism and reduced others to secret compromises with the governments: a pathetic turmoil of ideas and convictions, family interests and affections, and especially of homesickness for the country they had lost. For a Frenchman loss of country is a hurt that nothing can ever heal; and unless he is sustained by pride of birth, loftiness of character, or some fierce hope of revenge, he can only succumb. The government worked to sap the more steadfast hearts by frequent distributions of favors, amnesties and pardons, especially after the birth of the Prince Imperial.

Ledru-Rollin frankly advised exiles to return to France, though he himself had been condemned *in absentia* and was unable to do so.

"Every republican," he said, "who gets back to France without loss of character is, in spite of everything, a beacon that radiates light and a warrior for the coming day."

Proudhon, Emile Deschanel, Challemel-Lacour and many others followed Ledru-Rollin's advice after the amnesty of 1859. Soon only stubborn and strong-willed intransigents remained abroad, with Hugo for their mouthpiece:

Et s'il n'en reste qu'un je serai celui-là.[1]

Edgar Quinet, Barbès, Charras, Schoelcher and Louis Blanc behaved in the same spirit. Ledru-Rollin did not reappear on the French scene till 1870.

Le Siècle seemed ostensibly to serve as an organ for democratic and republican ideas. Actually it was a mere safety valve for their pent-up energies. The editor, Havin, was primarily concerned with keeping his post and offered hardly any resistance to suggestions from the government. He affected an anti-clerical tone that pleased

---

[1] And should but one be left, that one will be I!

a Voltarian element in the middle classes and gave him a great success in the cafés. Of Havin, Ludovic Halévy said in his witty *Notebook (Carnets*, I, 37):

"The government has its police and its prefects; M. Havin has his wine-sellers, whom he respectfully styles 'Messrs. the Dispensers of Liquids.' "

Veuillot was altogether right when he wrote:

"*Le Siècle* is under police protection."

In the whole history of the French press there are few examples of so long-lived and lucrative a betrayal.

In Paris the working classes remained republican. A few small-fry agitators of Leftist tendencies kept up their spirit of resistance by disturbances at funerals—the funerals of Armand Marrast, then of Arago, finally of Lamennais.

Perhaps the loftiest and saddest figure of the era, the hermit of La Chesnaye died in utter destitution, without ever becoming reconciled with the Church. Monsignor Sibour, the archbishop of Paris, generously besought him to do so, but he died without flinching, contemptuous of the proffered forgiveness. He died not of poverty, but of his soul, which was too vibrant with life, too hotly aglow with humane tenderness, too seething also, it may be, with a yearning for glory. Lamennais's life was just one heart-tearing struggle with himself. Like an imprisoned eagle he flung himself from one barrier to the other in his cage. A priest, he became a prophet; but rearing against faith, his heart never ceased to bleed from the divine struggle. He went out to the masses in quest of a love that would compensate and console, but there too he found only disappointment and tears.

Dying in his glorious poverty, he asked for the pauper's grave. A silent struggle took place between the police and the humble friends of the dead man as the hearse raced to the potter's field in the fog of that Ash Wednesday afternoon. Had the crowds that strove to accompany his body thither succeeded in uniting they would have formed a dangerous throng. A few shouts were heard, a few blows were struck; but the wintry air was too fraught with reverence. When the rebellious ascetic had been laid in his grave the only sounds about him were a few bars from the *Marseillaise*, whispered rather than sung, that nothing might disturb his slumber.

Students read Victor Hugo, Michelet, Proudhon, and were kept at fever heat by their writings. They organized tin-pan demonstrations against Sainte-Beuve at the College de France or against Nisard at the Sorbonne. Nisard had advanced a two-morality theory, one system of ethics to serve for the guidance of governments, another to serve for individuals. He was alleged, baselessly, to have devised that scheme to justify crimes of state.

These surface movements overlay subterranean stirrings that expressed themselves in a whole series of conspiracies against the life of the Emperor: the attempt at the Opéra Comique, a silly, childish affair (July, 1853); the bomb at Perenchies (September, 1854); the pistol attack by Pianori; another by Bellemare, a wretched lunatic who was to end up at Bicêtre. In the same year (1854) a sort of insurrection broke out at the slate quarries at Trélazé. All of these attacks failed owing to the untiring vigilance of the police. But Napoleon III felt himself too seriously menaced to think of attenuating his dictatorship by any jot.

Only Catholics were exempt from the constraints which he laid upon all France. To the Catholics in large part he owed his capture of power, and he still needed their help. He was not, strictly speaking, a devout man. He accepted forms rather than principles in matters of faith. Fundamentally the Church interested him only as an adjunct to his policies. With a softer note, which went with the general toning down from the model which the age required, he felt towards religion as his uncle had felt. But he needed the Church more than Napoleon I had needed it. The Church was more important in his day than it had been immediately after the Revolution. It was less dependent on him than it had been on the man of Brumaire. If, therefore, he was shy on warmth of regard or eagerness of faith, he made up for the defect by granting the Church lavish privileges.

He allowed the Organic Articles to fall asleep and did not oppose the introduction of the Roman liturgy in a large number of dioceses. He tolerated provincial councils which the old monarchy had forbidden. The budget for religion was increased. Stipends of bishops were raised and the list of state-paid curates extended. Numbers of organizations of teaching nuns were recognized and many Catholic secondary schools were opened. Work was suspended in public shops, and dockyards and wine-shops were closed during service hours on Sunday. The police confiscated anti-religious books. Generous subsidies from the state allowed the erection or completion of new churches all over France. Government employees were required to attend Mass, and soldiers took part in religious processions.

All the same a number of difficulties arose with the Church. The government refused to give legal recognition to Lord's Day Observance or to the precedence of religious over civil marriage. Prince Napoleon, Persigny and Pietri, the prefect of police, all sworn enemies of ultramontanism, and jurists such as Delangle and Portalis, were ever pressing the Emperor to limit his concessions to the clergy. The Falloux Law was retouched slightly, to the great displeasure of the Catholics. Sixteen university rectors were appointed, each assisted by a council of professors. As a result the French University acquired new vigor and became more independent of bishops and prefects alike.

The alliance between throne and Church seemed to be in no way affected by these measures. Throughout the early years of the Empire they were in tacit but profound accord.

Napoleon III had not succeeded in getting a coronation by the Pope. He got something almost as good: Pius IX agreed to stand godfather to his child. The Emperor deftly surrounded the baptism with ostentation and pageantry in a hope, which was very largely realized, that the country would be taken in by it.

"Quite as good as a coronation!" he remarked to the Empress on their way home from Notre Dame.

It was the most brilliant ceremony of Napoleon III's reign, and the one that aroused greatest enthusiasm in Paris.

During his six long years of imprisonment at Ham Napoleon III had dreamed of an economic reorganization of France. He belonged to the generation of men that are now known as "the men of '48." It was characteristic of those men to lose themselves in a fog of theories, a snarl of formulas, but at bottom they were noble souls, and they were sincere in their desire to improve the lot of the working classes and to achieve the progress of nations by up-to-date administrations of their resources and by coordinating national wealth with national needs. When Napoleon III found himself invested with a power more absolute than the kings of France had ever had, his first thought—and in that he deserves unstinted praise —was to essay a basic reorganization of the French social system.

One or two special laws were passed as a sort of prelude. First a national pension fund was set up for government employees. Next the recruiting system for the army was reformed on the basis of exemption from service on payment of a fixed sum.

Today such a thing would seem a monstrous injustice. For its period it represented a great step in advance over a system ·where substitutes were "sold" by "man-dealers." From that time on French soldiers received a fixed wage and became entitled to pensions if they reenlisted. The military code was recast. Though it did grant certain guarantees to the accused, it still remained very severe, since it provided for none of the extenuating circumstances that are recognized in civil law.

Political economy in France was at the time under the dominion of admirers of Saint-Simon—Father Enfantin, the Pereire brothers, Michel Chevalier, Guéroult. In an active enterprising spirit they propounded free trade, the expansion of wealth by credit, a gradual extension of well-being to all social classes—all ideas that found a ready response in the private hopes of the Emperor and the men about him.

In a few years the Crédit Foncier (Mortgage Bank) became an important institution in France. It made loans to towns, corporations and individuals, to facilitate the construction of all sorts of buildings. The Pereire Brothers established the Crédit Mobilier (Bank of Finance) for the purpose of making credits available to manufacturing and commercial enterprises. In a very short time it created far-reaching interests for its founders, especially mines, municipal gas plants and railroads.

In 1852 France had a scant 3,000 kilometers of railway and they were in the hands of twenty-four lifeless and disappointed companies, almost all of them on their last legs financially, with their shares going begging. Morny, as Hübner said, "always had an eye on the Bourse." Taking care to look out for himself, he persuaded the Emperor to combine the railroads into six great systems covering the whole country, and to provide for state guarantee of dividends. The man who engineered this necessary reorganization was Franqueville, director of the Ministry of Public Works, a talented businessman and an excellent public servant.

Thereafter railway construction took on new life. Lines were surveyed on all hands. By 1858, 18,000 kilometers of railroad were open to traffic, drawing the population together, increasing the availability and consumption of commodities, levelling prices. This progress also entailed one baneful consequence: a slow but accelerating shift of population from country to city.

Telegraph lines expanded at the same time paralleling the railroads. Hitherto reserved for official communications, the telegraph now became available to the public at large.

Navigation had been neglected by earlier regimes. It became one of the Empire's special cares. Three steamship lines subsidized by the state were organized to connect France with North and South America and the West Indies.

A remodelling of Paris began towards the end of 1852. The capital at that time remained very much as the First Empire had left it. It was still primarily a city of the Middle Ages and the Renaissance: a motley accumulation of palaces, residences, churches, convents, hotels, and slums for the working classes. A labyrinth of narrow winding streets lent itself readily to insurrections, as was demonstrated in June, 1848, and in December, 1851, when hundreds of barricades sprang up within the space of a night. Primarily for reasons of strategy, but also with a view to cleansing and beautifying the city and leaving visible upon it abiding marks of his reign, Napoleon III decided to open wide avenues which would bring out monuments to better advantage, flood the laboring districts with air and light and facilitate movements of troops and guns in case of disturbances.

In executing these designs the Emperor had run foul of the fears and hesitations of Berger, the prefect of the Seine. He made up his mind to get someone else. Persigny recommended Haussmann, at the time prefect of the Gironde. Haussmann was a sort of ogre, tall, with a ruddy complexion, a brisk tongue, a zest for work, and no end of perseverance, cunning, self-confidence. His ancestors came from the Rhine territory. He was the son of a newspaperman and the grandson of a member of the Convention. He hated parliamentarians and, next after parliamentarians, newspaper writers. In the words of Ollivier, he had "the impudent manner of a flunkey in an important house."

The Emperor made Haussmann prefect of the Seine and found in him a trustworthy aid. For sixteen years Haussmann enjoyed a real dictatorship over everything relating to city-planning. Arbitrary and dictatorial by nature, nothing could stop him. He ignored the Municipal Council and the ministers of state, who were often against him. As for money, he caused it to gush forth in loan after loan till obstacles and adversaries were drowned in its successive floods. Paris became one immense construction yard. Haussmann tore open the proletarian slums, the old nurseries of revolution, Saint-Antoine, Saint-Martin, Saint-Merri, Saint-Denis, the Cité. Drawing a great cross from the Gare de L'Est to the Observatoire and from the Trône toll-gate away along to the Place de l'Etoile, he levelled to the ground thousands of houses, at once squalid and enchanting. Tall middle-class buildings in uniform style replaced them, dull commonplace structures in which one might well suppose revolution would never gain a foothold. The Petite Pologne slum disappeared in a cutting for the Boulevard Malesherbes. Vistas and perspectives were planned. Docks were built along the river, bridges, sewers, barracks. The Louvre was completed in accord with the original plan of Pierre Lescot, two long wings connecting it with the Tuileries. The Hôtel-Dieu, the Market, the Industry Building went up, and new churches—ugly ones: Saint-Augustin and La Trinité. Garnier was soon to begin work on the Opéra. The Hôtel de Ville and Notre Dame were disentangled and opened to the sunlight, though the change stripped them of all the humanity that the centuries had deposited on their stone courses and welded to them.

That was the end of the picturesque in Paris.

"Why, it's Philadelphia, it's St. Petersburg," grumbled Théophile Gautier. "Paris has ceased to be."

Haussmann was in truth no artist. His hand was heavy and his taste poor.

Veuillot cried:

"The Amphion of this city must be a corporal."

But the protest had no echo. Public opinion approved in one unanimous voice. Louis Blanc himself wrote:

"Away with our unhealthy streets! Let us have broad, spacious thoroughfares! Make way for a little sunlight in our dark dingy quarters! Paris needs lungs in places where she can hardly breathe. All this is necessary. Hygiene requires it, progress commands it."

In 1860 the city of Paris doubled in size through the incorporation of the metropolitan area from Auteuil to Batignolles, from

Grenelle to Bercy. It now stretched away to the very fortifications. As in London—and on this point there can be only approval—public gardens opened in the inner sections of the city, and large parks in the outskirts—at Montsouris, at Buttes-Chaumont, on the Monceau flats. The Bois de Boulogne and the Bois de Vincennes were carefully landscaped.

The water supply had been inadequate, so the Dhuys and the Vanne were harnessed and an abundance became available to the whole population. Illuminating gas had been uncommon. It now came into general use. Street lighting improved with the disappearance of the old Argand lamps. Electricity was still a definite novelty, indeed a curiosity. It existed, but was used only on great occasions.

The first Napoleon had had a presentiment rather than a conception of this enormous program of public works. Only an absolutist regime of long duration could possibly have carried it through. It made Paris the paragon of capitals in the eyes of the world.

The big provincial cities, Lille, Le Havre, Marseilles, tried to follow suit. In the eminent prefect Vaïsse, Lyons found a sort of Haussmann, but one who worked more tastefully and with far less bombast. There was a debauch of building all over French territory, and the face of ancient France was everywhere renewed.

So many improvements could not be made apart from prodigious outlays that quite upset municipal budgets, and also, one must add, apart from large amounts of frankly indecent speculation, especially in Paris. Under pressure from Haussmann's henchmen and from those in favor at the Tuileries the condemnation awards which were granted by the juries overstepped all bounds. The Emperor knew that perfectly well. He knew that a frenzied graft regularly worked a piece of ground before the picks of the excavators ever got near it. But he thought that extravagance meant prosperity, and results seemed to bear him out. Never had money flowed so rapidly or in such torrents from the Treasury into the pockets of private citizens and thence back again into government loans—a merry-go-round that swelled the banks with business and brought joy to middlemen and brokers.

It was an artificial prosperity, however. The wealth was all on paper, and during those early years of the Empire France experienced a severe attack of hard times which the government, accustomed as it was to singing its own praises, could hardly dissemble. The wheat harvests failed. Pests attacked the grape, the potato and the silk crops. Floods ravaged the Garonne and the Rhône valleys. In the three years between 1853 and 1855 cholera carried off two hundred thousand people in France. On top of all those troubles came the losses in the Crimea. The government purchased grain abroad. It rained subsidies and relief, especially upon the rural population. But these remedies did not avail. In many districts it became necessary to ration bread. Externally the Empire had a brilliant look, but, underneath, the nation was sick and languishing.

Peace came in the nick of time and then it seemed as though one stroke of good fortune brought others in its trail. Everything began to mend, to succeed, to blossom out. The Emperor regarded the World's Fair of 1855 almost as an enterprise of his own. After a faltering start it ended in a blaze of glory. Five million visitors, among them the kings of Portugal and Sardinia, Queen Victoria and Prince Albert, most of the Kings and princes of Germany! For the first time the achievements of human civilization as a whole were made visible to the eye in ingenious compendium—products of agriculture, works of art, finally the marvels of an inventive machine age that was just emerging from infancy. A new era with all its wonders and possibilities was brilliantly displayed before the eyes of the throngs. Steel was king. Applications of it, as of electricity and chemistry, were henceforward to multiply by leaps and bounds.

The year 1855 in this respect is a most significant date. That year marked a definite launching forth of the world upon a new adventure, the adventure of intensive industrialism. At that time no one could imagine that in "progress" any perils lurked. Quite to the contrary, adorned with fanciful dreams of the economists, it seemed to hold out to humanity a promise of greater and greater happiness. Matter in its infinitely varied workings had hitherto been held in balance by spirit. Henceforward it was to rule the masses, multiplying their wants the better to enslave them. Life was to become greedy and cruel, the winged Ariel taking flight before an inventive Caliban.

The first elections for the Legislative Body were scheduled for June, 1857. Had opinion been somewhat free that would have been a fine chance to see whether the country agreed with the policies the regime had followed, and were still attached to the institutions born of the 2d of December.

Unfortunately the Minister of the Interior informed his prefects in a circular:

"Just as the government reserves the right to propose bills to the deputies, so it reserves the right to nominate candidates for the voters and the latter will make their choices."

For that matter, the deputies whose terms were expiring were all renominated and the opposition was stripped of all means of opposing those official candidacies. Campaign committees, meetings, publications of platforms, were prohibited. Prefects and under-prefects conducted an enthusiastic campaign of panegyrics with one end in view: to get out the vote. The prefect of the Dordogne went so far as to proclaim:

"The government wants its candidates to win the way God wants the good to win, leaving everybody free to choose the wrong."

In the departments it was a difficult matter to offer any effective resistance to the pressure of power. Only two republicans and three independent Catholics were elected in all provincial France. The republicans were Hénon at Lyons and Curé at Bordeaux. Unable to compromise, Montalembert went down to defeat.

In Paris, it was a different story. The press was gagged, surveillance was ever so close, yet the opposition managed to organize. A committee got together, made up of veterans of the Republic such as Cavaignac, Garnier-Pagès, Carnot, Goudchaux, Bastide, supported by numbers of young lawyers and newspapermen—Ernest Picard, Jules Simon, Emile Ollivier, Nefftzer, Darimon. Two tendencies, born of the difference in generations, clashed in this group. The doctrinaires of '48 saw their "ingenuousness" made the butt of ridicule from the newcomers, who were bent on fighting the Empire from inside its institutions. After long and stormy conferences, held in secret, the two wings of the opposition were unable to agree on common candidates. They were obliged to come forward with two lists with all the handicap of a divided vote. Billault and Haussmann attacked them fiercely, but five republicans were nevertheless elected: Carnot, Goudchaux, Cavaignac, Ollivier, and Darimon. The five remaining districts were carried by the official candidates, but the set-back was no less painful to the government.

Publicly, to be sure, Napoleon III could count the election a landslide, but taking France as a whole, the opposition had managed to win 665,000 votes against 5,471,000 for the government. Since the country had been completely muzzled under five years of absolutism, the results showed that the republican party had most tenacious powers of resistance. Napoleon III was at Plombières at the time. He confided his disappointment to Fould. The Empire still held its enormous majority, but it had been able to do nothing with its opponents. They were still on their feet, numerous, active, though constrained to caution.

Béranger died on July 16th. The episode had every likelihood of supplying a pretext for a demonstration by the opposition, but by a deft manoeuvre the government ordered a state funeral and a great military parade for that songster, who had tried only half successfully to play the part of the plain Frenchman, but who had found a way to turn the glory of the Empire into solid cash.

Béranger was hardly cold in his grave when he was completely forgotten in the excitements attending the discovery of a new plot by the police. Three Italians were arrested: Tibaldi, an oculist, and two conspirators of his. They had been preparing to assassinate Napoleon III at the instigation of Mazzini. So went the story, though proofs were weak. Their trial was rapid. Tibaldi was deported and his accomplices were sentenced to imprisonment for fifteen years.

The Emperor affected, all through this case, an indifference he was far from feeling. Brave as he was personally, what would happen to his wife and child if he were killed? To turn the matter off he multiplied official trade exhibitions, held a great review at Châlons after army manoeuvres, opened the remodeled Louvre with a brilliant ceremony, dedicated at Vincennes a home for "disabled soldiers of industry," awarded a "Medal of St. Helena" to surviving veterans of the major wars. Last of all and best of all he went to Osborne with the Empress for another call on Queen Victoria.

As far as public appearances went, the Anglo-French alliance had been sealed by comradeship in the Crimea and remained as sound as ever; but, with all his ideas of a rearrangement in Italy, Napoleon III had of late been making advances to Russia and so interestedly that the Court of St. James took umbrage. The Emperor's idea was to woo both London and St. Petersburg in order to have a freer hand. This policy was the resultant of the two rival influences of Morny and Persigny. The former was now ambassador extraordinary to Alexander and kept preaching the Russian alliance. Persigny was for strengthening the bonds between France and England. Under the two pressures the Emperor began to play a see-saw game that was not a little underhanded and fraught with danger.

His scheme for arranging a triple entente was altogether impracticable. Any expression of sympathy for the Czar annoyed the ministers of Queen Victoria in the extreme. Napoleon III sent a New Year's card to Alexander, extending his best wishes for the year 1857 but also voicing the hope that "if contingencies of great importance should arise in Europe, the interests of the two countries would allow them to fight on the same side." The Russian chancellor replied in vague enough terms; but then the Grand Duke Constantine came to Paris and had private talks with the Emperor. London grew alarmed. Napoleon tried to smooth things out by a private letter to the Queen, while Persigny, deploring the "utopias" of his master, proposed to Clarendon that the sovereigns meet to clear up the situation.

The reunion that took place on August 6, 1857, was something infinitely colder than the French had expected. Conversations between Napoleon and Prince Albert lacked nothing in politeness, but they showed traces of mistrust and reproachfulness. Roumanian affairs came up in the first place—they were endangering peace in the Near East. The Congress of Paris had decided, at the request of France, that the peoples of Moldavia and Wallachia were to be consulted in the matter of any final disposition of the principalities. They wanted union under a single ruler, and that was what Napoleon III wanted. The constitution of a Roumanian nationality seemed to him an excellent stepping-stone to a liberation of Italy. In the negotiations that had taken place on the subject between the great powers, Piedmont and Russia had sided with France, followed reluctantly by Prussia. Turkey and Austria were opposed. The Sultan, as suzerain over the two great provinces, was minded to keep them under his control. Austria feared the rise of another Piedmont on her southern borders. In spite of her liberal tradition England stood with Turkey and Austria out of enmity for Russia.

The Roumanians could count serious adversaries even among French statesmen. Persigny, as a vassal of the Court of St. James, was afraid of losing the friendship of Britain "over such a trifling matter."

"The Emperor," he said, "should not be drawn into disputes with no real object in view. What the present dynasty needs is not more glory, but more time. For time there is no substitute" (July 20, 1857).

Unfortunately Persigny did not confine himself to arguing in memoranda to the Emperor or Walewski. He made the great blunder of openly attacking the policy of France before his colleagues in the diplomatic corps and even before the British ministers.

Thouvenel, the ambassador at Constantinople, was just as opposed to Roumanian unity. Shrewdly he suspected the Emperor of desiring "to settle on the Po questions that were merely asked on the Danube." Napoleon III held his ground. Embarrassed in his manoeuvres by these impediments, he ordered the hesitant Walewski to send imperative instructions to Thouvenel: Plebiscites should be held at once in the principalities, and they should be honest plebiscites.

That was asking a great deal of the Near East. The representatives of the Sublime Porte, Ghika in Wallachia, and Vogórides in Moldavia, loaded the dice now by trickery, now by violence. The elections not so much expressed as suppressed the will of the Roumanian people, especially in Moldavia. Thouvenel demanded that the elections be annulled and, to the great rage of the English, threatened to leave Constantinople if he did not receive satisfaction.

Despite this momentary clash of outlooks a partial compromise was effected at Osborne. Prince Albert was strong for maintaining the integrity of the Ottoman Empire. For what else had the Crimean War been fought? And there was the Czar with all his ambition, trying to pulverize Turkey into a dust of small states! What England wanted was the preservation of the *status quo*.

Napoleon III confessed that he had scant interest in Turkey really. His complaint was against Austria—and there he was back to his main point: a revision of the treaties of 1815; and he threw out a hint that Mussulman territories in the Mediterranean might be redistributed, Spain taking Morocco, Piedmont Tripoli, England Egypt.

Albert replied evasively; but meantime Walewski, Palmerston and Clarendon succeeded in working out a compromise on the Roumanian issue: London agreed to support Paris in the demand that the elections be cancelled. France, in exchange, gave up the idea of having a single ruler for the principalities.

As matters were to work out, Napoleon III was to score a success by this arrangement and secure a first application of his principle of nationalities; for, as regards the question of a single ruler, the Roumanians proceeded to get around difficulties by electing one same person, Colonel Couza, as hospodar in each of the principalities. Turkey and Austria at once objected. A conference, therefore, met in Paris (May 22-August 19, 1858). By that time France and Russia were working together. Those two countries, followed by Prussia and in the end by England, came to an agreement that Couza should be recognized in his twin powers, and the new hospodar went to Constantinople in September, 1859, to pay his homage to the Sultan.

When the Emperor and Prince Albert separated at Osborne they were on better terms than when they had met, but in spirit they were still far apart; and Napoleon's trip to Stuttgart to meet Czar Alexander two months later (September 25-27, 1857) was not calculated to improve matters. On this occasion, in order to avoid meeting "Mlle. de Montijo," the Czarina excused herself from accompanying her husband. Napoleon III pretended not to notice the subtle thrust.

As he had done at Osborne, he brought Walewski with him to negotiate detailed texts with Gortchakov while he and the Czar were exchanging views on the more general questions. The meetings led to an entente, in principle: France and Russia were to act in concert on any matter affecting the status of Eastern Europe. They would not take definite positions on any question of importance without informing and consulting each other.

Such an agreement hardly consorted with Franco-British friendship. At Stuttgart Napoleon III succeeded only in weakening the accord between England and France without asking in compensation any formal alliance of Russia. So the dilemma, which he had himself created, became more and more serious. He still regarded the British alliance as indispensable; but he had made up his mind to tear up the Vienna treaties and also "to do something for Italy." Neither of those policies could be carried out under the alliance with England, which depended on maintaining the *status quo* on the continent. To prosecute them in the face of the alliance was to reduce the latter to a discreditable game in double-dealing. But failing to conserve the English alliance. Napoleon III also failed to provide himself with any support on the continent. From this time on, therefore, his foreign policy became evidently topheavy and lay at the mercy of an incident, a whim. Persigny or Morny could not both be right. One had to choose between them.

The English alliance, on the one hand, promised a long and fruitful peace. It guaranteed the security of Napoleon III's Empire so long as he followed policies of peace and sought the grandeur he desired in achieving economic and social progress for his country. But in this case he would have to forget all about reorganizing Europe and freeing no end of oppressed nationalities.

The Russian entente, on the other hand, would hold Germany in check and give him a free hand in encompassing the liberation, say, of Italy.

In a word both alliances had their strong points, but a choice had to be made between them; and then the consequences of the choice had to be followed out resolutely and energetically. In all this matter Napoleon III gave his measure as a statesman. He refused to make the choice, and the refusal was based on his belief that by deft manipulations he could play both ends against the middle. Morny saw things much more clearly than he. From St. Petersburg he warned (September 15, 1856):

"Let us fight shy of a policy of sentiment. Let us stick to a policy that is based on the best interests of France. Otherwise within two years' time we shall have ceased to stand well with England and be standing badly with Russia."

Cavaignac died. His wife, grief-stricken, Spartan, bore his body to Paris by post-chaise, wrapped in a water-proof cloak, for an unostentatious burial. That high-minded soldier of the Republic, so stern yet at bottom so tender, ever disinterested, ever impartial, when his ideals and his country were not concerned, had fought on single-handed against the hate and the fear the masses had for him, and against the greed of ambitious self-seekers over whom he towered, morally and spiritually, as a giant. In the end the strain had proved too great for his heart.

Cavaignac never recovered from "the days of June," 1848, when he ordered a bloody repression in an effort to save the nation and the social order. The Emperor's triumph crushed him, leaving him a despondent misanthrope. He was elected to the Legislative Body in 1857, but never attended any of the sessions. How could he swear fealty to a lucky adventurer who had overthrown the law and the Republic? Far better for him to drop out of sight, escape from a life that he would have found dragging uselessly on his hands. Cavaignac was by no means a great mind. He lacked adaptability, versatility and at times, perhaps, even balance. But he was the most scrupulous of men. An honest man, a courageous man, enamoured of liberty, enamoured of justice, a stranger to intrigue and falsehood, utterly lacking in greed, he stands out as one of the figures most entitled to respect that that second-rate age produced.

The Legislative Body convened on November 28th to examine credentials and seat its members. Two of the republicans, Carnot and Goudchaux, refused to take the oath, automatically unseating themselves by that act. Left facing the vast conformist majority was an opposition of just three practically unknown men, Hénon, Darimon, and Emile Ollivier, a youth of thirty-two. The elections held to fill vacancies were to reenforce these with Jules Favre and Ernest Picard. In future the group was to be known as "the Five." It was a small group but, in view of the ideas it represented, an important one. In those days of an Empire bloated with successes, it was to remain the "toothing-ring" of the republican party, not to say the party's forlorn hope.

Three of the Five were hardly to count. Darimon was just a well-educated man, an economist. Ernest Picard was nothing more than a glib lawyer. Hénon was small timber to begin with and never counted for more than his vote. The other two were to shine—Jules Favre, a veteran of '48 and, more especially, Emile Ollivier.

Ollivier was a typical Marseillais with a lively, facile flow of words and a light touch. He had a democratic background, his father having sat in the Constituent Assembly and gone into exile on December 2nd. He himself, after getting to be prefect of the Rhône, had settled in Paris as a practicing lawyer. Tall, slim, cold, unassuming, with his dark-complexioned face, side-whiskers, spectacles, the strong lips of the born orator, hair always badly trimmed and already growing thin, he made, all in all, an interesting figure. He was an honest man, generous, patriotic, and withal engrossingly ambitious. He had the gift of thoroughly mastering political problems, and that competence, combined with his utter self-assurance, attracted the attention of the fighting wing on the Left. There was a general feeling, which he himself shared, that he was destined to go far, that he was to be a sort of democratic Thiers, a Thiers with more style and especially more heart.

CHAPTER XII

Italian Enchantment

So far, in spite of mistakes that were seemingly offset by its success as a whole, the Second Empire had followed the lines that its leader had laid down for it on his ascent to the throne. Now it was to depart from them, abandoning two of its essential bases, the friendship with England and the alliance with the Catholics. The responsibility here lies beyond any doubt with Napoleon III. Considering his past and his temperament, it may have been unavoidable, but at a time when France was asking for nothing but stability and peace, the Emperor turned again to adventure. His memories, his dreams, his fears, were to drag him into intervention in Italy.

After the great overboiling of 1848, the Peninsula had fallen back into a state of apparent torpor. Only two states of any considerable size were still independent: the House of Savoy reigned over Piedmont, Savoy, Nice, Genoa and Sardinia; the House of Bourbon over Naples and Sicily. The Church domain that lay between them was occupied in the north by the Austrians, in the south, including Rome, by the French. With garrisons of White Coats about them, the Grand Duke of Tuscany and the Dukes of Parma and Modena were mere vassals, not to say mere employees, of Austria; and Austria, besides, had her hands on the wealthiest and most wide-awake portion of Italy, the district that stretches from Milan to Venice, governing it under a name with an unmistakably Teutonic ring, the Kingdom of Lombardo-Venetia. From that vantage point Austria had a finger and a say in everything that went on anywhere in the country.

Patriotic Italians found Austrian domination insufferable. They had been beaten, punished and dispersed in 1830 and again in 1848. But now they had gradually formed new groups under resolute leaders and were merely awaiting the signal to rise in revolt a second time. The heir of the first king of Italy, now the Emperor of the French, had grievously disappointed them by his considerate attitude towards the Church, but he was still their great hope. He belonged to them, they felt, through his past as a Carbonaro. They had no doubt whatever of his sympathy or of his eagerness to give them their freedom. At Lyons, in 1851, during the barn-storming tour of the departments that had led to the restoration of the Empire, Louis Napoleon had had a talk with General La Marmora, whom Victor Emmanuel had sent to him as the bearer of his greetings. To the General he had remarked that "at the time he had to work to build up the prestige of France," but that "if he succeeded in that, he was resolved to do something for Italy, a country that he loved as his second country." [1] In 1852, in a talk with the Sardinian minister, Collegno, he had gone even farther:

"The day will come when our two countries will fight side by side for the Italian cause."

An Italian patriot, Count Arese, a chivalrous Milanese, was a boyhood friend of the Emperor and was always in touch with him. Napoleon III, moreover, had invited Piedmont to take part in the Crimean War. He had procured the admission of that kingdom to the Congress of Paris on a footing of equality with the great powers, and during those historic sessions he had treated Cavour, the Sardinian prime minister, as a friend and a confidant. The Italian patriots looked upon Cavour as the man most capable of "regenerating" their country.

Unquestionably, at that moment, Count Camillo di Cavour was the most remarkable statesman in Europe. Endowed with an eager, fiery imagination, he had a shrewd sense of the possible. He always knew just what he could do, but he was also able to refrain from doing it in deference to the broader view of the future. By family he was to a certain extent French, and his education was primarily French and English. The creator of Italian unity was never to master the purest Italian language nor was he ever to set eyes either on Rome or Venice. He knew nothing whatever of art, philosophy, or literature. He knew mathematics and political economy, and extremely well. After serving for a time as an officer in the army, he traveled abroad and came to know members of parliament, bankers, businessmen, society, in London and Paris. These contacts opened

[1] Ollivier, *op. cit.*, III, 191.

his eyes to the ways of the world and gave him the sense of large affairs. Home again in Piedmont he became first a farmer, then a manufacturer and exchange speculator, amassing a fortune. Turning at last to politics, he organized groups of liberals under comfortable, conservative names and founded a newspaper, *Il Risorgimento*. Though not holding any official position he had become an important man before the age of forty, respected and even feared. He entered the Chamber at Turin in 1848 and, after Charles Albert's disaster, the cabinet. In the one capacity he proved himself a keen and spirited orator, in the other a skillful executive. His superiority to his colleagues, along with a touchy, despotic temperament, caused the collapse of the D'Azeglio ministry. After some months in retirement, however, he was recalled to public life by the young king, Victor Emmanuel II, and made prime minister of Piedmont (November 4, 1852).

This undersized, pudgy, bespectacled, awkward man, was a man of utter good sense and clear-thinking energy. He had an unparalleled gift for hard work and was sustained especially by a force that no great modern leader can be without—the force of an unimpeachable love of country. Within a few years Cavour was to give body to the hopes of the Italian patriots and transform their dreams into workable plans. Like Talleyrand before him and Bismarck after him, he was to exemplify the influence that a dominant personality can have on events, guiding and changing history. Through him Italy was to gain half a century, perhaps a whole century. To the realization of his great plan to unite all Italy, starting with Piedmont as a center, he was to devote himself down to his very last breath. To it he was to sacrifice everything, his interests, his comfort, his health, his life. Success is certain when the resolve beforehand is great and inflexible. Cavour was to succeed.

He felt that it would be impossible for Italy to act alone. The formula *Italia farà da sè* had died at Novara. The young Sardinian army could not hold against the seasoned troops of the Hapsburgs. Cavour saw that he would have to have the support of a first-rate power to free Lombardo-Venetia, first of all, from the Austrian yoke. After that one would see.

Such a power could only be France. An entente with Prussia later on? Cavour may already have been considering that; but at best it was something for a remoter future. By her inclinations, by the family relations of her then reigning sovereign—more than that, through the antipathy which the majority of the French cherished for Austria, France alone could and should aid in the work of Italian liberation.

The name of Italy had, in fact, exercised a sort of magic spell over Frenchmen in every age, but the charm was especially potent over the French of those days, for whom the campaigns of Bonaparte were still recent history. The idea that a people so closely related to the French should, in the full midst of the nineteenth century, be enslaved by pandoors aroused in most Frenchmen of that generation, whether imperialist or republican in coloring, only anger and a feeling akin to remorse.

Cavour bided his time for several years. The King recognized his abilities and left him free to act in all confidence, much as Louis XIII had done with Richelieu. To be sure, at important moments Victor Emmanuel was concerned to show that he was still master.

He said to Della Rocca, his aide-de-camp, one day:

"Cavour must not get it into his head that I do everything he wants. It's all right when we agree. When we don't agree, he has to do what I want."

With this support behind him, Cavour reorganized the monarchy, gave it a sound administration, recast the army, built railroads and steamship lines, negotiated commercial treaties. He offered asylum in Piedmont to all Italians who had participated in the recent disturbances and had therefore been driven from Rome, Naples, Florence, Milan. He gave them positions, made them servants of his cause and turned them into mouthpieces of liberalism and modern ideas. So at home, in France, in England, he built up about his name one great cloud of approval and sympathy, which would precipitate a rain of precious assistance when the occasion presented itself.

It presented itself with the outbreak of war in the Crimea—and the Piedmontese flag floated over the Tchernaia. At the peace congress that followed the war, Cavour wooed Napoleon III dexterously and made friends among the people about him, often without regard to means—of means in general Cavour asked only that they serve his purposes. With peace reestablished in Europe, Cavour sent the Countess Castiglione, a cousin of his, to France "to flirt with the Emperor, seduce him if need be," but at any rate, to rouse him to greater interest in the Italian cause.

It was no very great task for that matter. Now nearing his fifties Napoleon III was still very much the philanderer. The Countess Castiglione was admitted to court at the Tuileries in spite of the Empress's aversion, and she at once attracted the Emperor's attention. She was a beautiful woman and as greedy as she was extravagant. She got the jewels and the money; but when—in the little house in Passy which the Emperor had set up for their meetings—she ventured into the domain of public policy, he turned a deaf ear. The Countess Castiglione had never been cut out by nature for the rôle of an Egeria.

But really, Napoleon did not need any Countess Castiglione to lure him to the quest of an emancipated Italy. The Prisoner of the Kings had said at St. Helena:

"In the midst of the great scramble the first sovereign to embrace the cause of the peoples in good faith will find himself at the head of Europe and be able to do anything he chooses."

That heroic counsel ever haunted Napoleon III, but he had to be cautious and adapt himself to circumstances. To have undertaken an enterprise in Italy directly on ascending the throne would have roused the Holy Alliance against him—for the Holy Alliance was ill intact. The war in the Near East had enabled him to embroil etime allies with each other, so the time for action was now drawing near. The recent attempts on his life were a warning that the revolutionaries were growing impatient. He had better do something to calm them. To restore the Peninsula to its own rule, to make of it, if not a single united country—he did not go that far as yet, realizing the danger for France that lay in a powerful united Italy—at least a federation of free states under the honorary presidency of the Pope and the actual leadership of Piedmont—that was still his plan. To judge by appearances, it seemed a fairly simple plan to carry out.

At that moment he was at the peak of his career. He had won the war in the Crimea. He had a son and heir. Save for some few nests of hostility France had come over to him heart and soul. The eyes of every chancellery on the Continent were turned towards Paris. Still the nominal ally of England, he was good friends with Russia. Austria and Prussia were treating him with deference.

Against the stuffy backdrop of a Tuileries that blazed dazzlingly as the center of a remodeled capital, brilliant, luxurious, merry, he moved as the first Alexander of Russia had moved in the day of the fallen Napoleon, as a European Agamemnon, "king of kings."

However Napoleon III was not so blind of eye as not to see that he was far less free in his policies and conduct abroad than many of the people about him imagined. Annex northern Italy to Piedmont? That meant war, and an easy war no doubt. From its troubled waters there was nothing to prevent France from fishing substantial profits for herself. But with that much gained, would there be any stopping of the Italian patriots for any length of time? They would go mad after such a victory! In the mix-up the Pope would probably lose his States. Well, what of it? Napoleon III had no slightest interest in the pontiff's temporal sovereignty. He had nothing but contempt for the government at Rome which, in truth, deserved the severest censure. But could he throw the Holy See overboard? Deprived of the support of the Catholics at home the imperial government would run into serious domestic difficulties.

Intimate, personal influences, besides, were working upon him. The Empress was as yet playing no great rôle in public affairs, but she could not hear reference to a change in Italy without flying into a rage. Her Castillian devoutness and her loyalty to the Holy See had deepened with the Pope's consent to be godfather to her son— and then he had gone on and awarded her the decoration of the Golden Rose. She took his part stubbornly, violently indeed.

"This job of being a redeemer is a fool's job," she wrote to Arese, with no beating about the bush.

A Legitimist at heart she leaned towards a conservative alliance with Austria. She had a keen personal liking for the young Emperor, Francis Joseph. The idea of an eventual rupture with the Vatican horrified her. Who could say? Excommunication, perhaps! Then there was the Castiglione woman! She was jealous of her, as much through pride as anything else, and therefore she hated Cavour, well knowing that the Florentine girl was acting as his agent.

Walewski, Morny and Persigny were altogether hostile to the Italian adventure—Walewski as Minister of Foreign Affairs; Persigny, who often came home from London and was always in close touch with the Emperor; Morny, who was back from his mission in Russia and had resumed the presidency of the Legislative Body, whence he was in a position to exert a direct influence on the government—in Russia Morny had married a mere chit of a girl, the ravishing Princess Sophie Troubetskoy. All three agreed and vehemently declared that an upset in Italy would mean another upset in Europe, which might result in a collapse of the Empire in France. They accused Cavour, and on very good grounds, of pursuing an irritating and aggressive policy towards Austria and the Italian princes. He was giving wide publicity to their reactionary views, to the inefficiency and the partiality of their governments, to the ill-treatment and injustices to which the Italian patriots were being subjected. At the same time he was fomenting the spread of secret societies throughout Italy and facilitating, instead of suppressing, their propaganda.

Working upon the Emperor in the other direction were his cousins, Prince Napoleon and Mathilde. Prince Napoleon was mere window-dressing for the intrigues of the imperialist Left; but he hoped to fish some princely establishment or other out of a re-shuffling of territories and was therefore urging the Emperor to immediate action. Mathilde chimed in out of a natural devotion to her brother's interests. Still with Napoleon III also were two friends of his boyhood, both comrades of the Romagna escapade: Conneau and Arese. Not for a moment since Louis Napoleon's accession to the throne had either of them doubted that as Emperor of the French he would sooner or later keep his oath as an insurrectionist of '31.

In the small, stuffy, gaudily decorated rooms of his apartment in the Tuileries Napoleon III would sit and watch through the smoke of his cigarette the infinite play of combinations about him. They would form, dissolve, then form again. He was well aware of the many dangers. He could not really make up his mind, any more than he could really abandon his dream. So he played the game. He encouraged high hopes in Cavour. He told Europe, his ministers, the Empress, not to worry. He would even drop a word now and then that betrayed his real intentions. He thought he could play the game. Circumstances had always been with him so far and luck would probably be with him again. He would rely on his destiny, on time, on chance, on the unexpected, which swoops down on states and countries the way it does on individual men.

COUNTESS DE CASTIGLIONE

CHAPTER XIII

Felice Orsini

On Thursday, the 14th of January, 1858, the Emperor and the Empress were scheduled to attend the farewell performance of the baritone Massol at the Opera. By eight o'clock the streets about the theatre were filled with crowds waiting to see the imperial pair. The auditorium inside presented a dazzling scene: uniforms, evening coats, light-tinted gowns cut low over the breast to follow the fashion set by the Empress. All the beauties of the day were to be seen in the grand-tier boxes, all of them from Mme. de Persigny to "*la* Castiglione."

The performance began with the second act from *Wilhelm Tell*. At half-past eight a troop of Lancers of the Guard rode up on the rue Le Peletier. They were clearing the way for the landau of the sovereigns. The crowd cheered; but just as the carriage turned in to the curb of the peristyle there were three violent detonations, so close together as to count almost as one.

The gas jets that lighted the Opera façade were blown out. There was a great crashing of glass as the roof of the marquis caved in and the windows in buildings nearby. When the smoke cleared a little, the imperial carriage could be seen, lying without wheels on the sidewalk, its sides broken in and torn to shreds and tatters by bullets and bits of flying glass. The horses lay dead on the pavement. The crowd was in flight, panic-stricken. Screams of terror mingled with moans of agony from Lancers, policemen, bystanders, who lay scattered on the ground. The officers in the escort ran to the carriage. As torch-lights flickered upon faces that were hollow and white, Napoleon III emerged from the wreck. His hat had holes in it. His nose was cut and bleeding. For the rest he was perfectly cool. He offered a hand to the Empress. She leapt lightly to the sidewalk, her white gown and opera cloak spattered with blood. General Roguet was with them. He had a wound in the neck. People came running and pressed about.

Eugénie cried impatiently:

"Never mind about us—these are the risks of the trade! Help those who are hurt!"

Those who were hurt! They numbered one hundred and fifty-six and eight of them, in the end, died! Napoleon III, in the crisis, was a human being and nothing else. He ordered the victims nearby to be picked up, then, forgetting himself and his rank, started to go with them to a drug store on the corner where they could be treated. A police sergeant, Lanet, had a perfectly cool head. He made bold to remind the Emperor that the people inside the Opera-house had heard the bombs. If he did not appear in his box at once they would think he had been seriously hurt, or perhaps killed.

"Such a mistake," he went on to explain, "might have serious consequences for the public peace."

"You are perfectly right," answered the Emperor. "I'll go in, but I'll be back shortly to see how those poor people are getting on."

He offered an arm to Eugénie, then, followed by the Princess Mathilde, the couple entered the imperial box. The people in the audience were all on their feet. They cheered thunderously. The orchestra struck up the insipid song written by Queen Hortense: *Partant pour la Syrie*. Since the *Marseillaise* had been hushed it had become unofficially, in fact, almost officially, the national anthem.

Véron, the manager of the Opera, was awaiting the Emperor's command.

"Go on with the performance," directed the Emperor. "Don't change anything."

Morny, Fould, Walewski, other ministers, generals, officials, crowded into the imperial box to congratulate the Emperor. He received them with his normal affability. Grasping Senator Heeck-eren's hand he cried:

"Well, I escaped—by a miracle! King Louis Philippe had ten attempts on his life. This is only my fourth. I still have something to look forward to."

However, he could not resist a fling at Billault, of the Interior:

"Your police is being broken in famously!"

At the first intermission the sovereigns started back for the Tui-leries. Paris had lighted up. As the imperial cortège moved along at a walk towards the palace, it was acclaimed with never-ending cheers. The drawing-rooms were packed with ministers, ambassadors, dignitaries. After a few words of appreciation the Emperor fell silent.

Eugénie, seated on a sofa, was not doing so well. She addressed a bitter rebuke to Pietri, the prefect of police.

"You know, sir? You are responsible to me for the Emperor's life!"

Her imagination was running away with her. She saw Napoleon seriously wounded, killed, the dynasty overthrown, herself and her son in the shoes of Marie Antoinette and the little dauphin . . . the scaffold. . . .

It was a long, hectic evening, with crested surges of rage, fright, vows of vengeance and repression. Before the minds of all those people, Frenchmen and foreigners alike, the imposing imperial structure towered as something that had suddenly turned fragile and unsafe.

Pietri's police were not so green after all. Before morning the perpetrators of the outrage were under arrest—Felice Orsini, and his chief confederates.

Orsini was a man forty years old, dark-complexioned, with a wavy beard and sparkling eyes, handsome. His father, in the old days, had fallen at Louis Napoleon's side during the retreat on Forlì. He himself had plotted from childhood for the emancipation of his country. He had wallowed in the filth of Metternich's prisons and rowed on the galleys of the Pope. Released by the amnesty of '48, he became a member of the Roman Constituent Assembly in '49. He raised the Marches against the Austrians, was caught and shut up in Mantua. Making his escape, he became a refugee in London. He was the perfect type of the political adventurer, sincere, unstable, enthusiastic, honest, a bit of a poseur but never vulgar, never small. Orsini had long believed in Napoleon III. Then he had seen him strike an alliance with the conservatives and the clericals, hunt down the liberals in France, strangle the Roman revolution beyond the Alps. So the Emperor became the obstacle, the enemy. He should die, therefore, that the Republic might take the reins in France again and bring on the republic in Italy.

Orsini set out to recruit a conspiracy to assassinate the Emperor and he gathered in a number of second-rate accomplices. Simon

Bernard, a doctor gone wrong, furnished him with the gunpowder. Then came Pieri, a professional crook, and two young men of good family, Gomez and Rudio, who were ready to do anything because they had no sources of income and had nothing to lose. Orsini reached Paris on false passports by way of Belgium, using the name of Allsop, the French customs passing his baggage, which contained the materials for the bombs, without examination. Pieri, Gomez and Rudio joined him a month later.

Their plans were complete by January 14th and, save for Pieri's awkwardness, they carried them out to the last detail. They made four bombs and three of them were thrown. The would-be assassins made good their escape in the general disorder. Pieri, however, was picked up by a policeman on suspicion and, losing his head, made a clean breast of everything. His disclosures led to the prompt arrest of the other three. At once Orsini not so much confessed as claimed the responsibility for everything.

While the case was being investigated the Empire passed through a double crisis, one at home, the other abroad. The seriousness of the moment has never yet been fully realized by historians. High officials of the Empire, Napoleon's closest advisers, were scared, terribly scared—far too much so for statesmen. Well aware that if the Emperor were murdered the dictatorship of which they were the main beneficiaries would collapse, they set out to discourage assassins by a mass of repressive measures that were exceptionally harsh. Napoleon III declared for extreme severity. He asked for the papers in the case of the bomb in the rue Saint-Nicaise in Napoleon's day, and again following the example of the founder of his line, sought to produce the atmosphere of terror that the First Consul had produced in 1800. In all that he was failing to realize that times had changed and how greatly.

The executive staffs of the government departments met for a reception at the Tuileries on January 16th. He listened, pale and stern, to the addresses of the presidents of the Senate and the Legislative Body. Troplong denounced in emphatic language a "revolutionary spirit" that had been driven from France, found asylum abroad and become "cosmopolitan." Morny followed, and for once dropping his courteous manner, stormed indignantly:

"The people are alarmed at a clemency on your part which is patterned too closely upon the kindness of your heart. They are wondering why governments who are our neighbors and presumably our friends are powerless to destroy real laboratories of murder."

This was a thrust straight from the shoulder at Belgium, Piedmont, and especially England; for England, especially, was offering asylum to all sorts of political refugees and allowing them to hatch their plots at will within her borders.

Undoubtedly Morny thought he had found a chance to weaken the accord with England and replace it with a Franco-Russian entente. Napoleon III was not inclined to follow him in such an emphatic reversal. The next day, January 17th, he sent a private letter to Queen Victoria:

"In the excitements of the moment, the French are seeing accomplices everywhere, and I am put to it to resist the extravagant measures to which they would constrain me. But this episode will not cause me to deviate from my habitual calm and, though I shall do my best to strengthen my government, I shall not stoop to any injustice."

That was throwing out ballast, but the Emperor was overreached. In this case, as on December 2nd, Morny proved to be the real conductor of the orchestra, Walewski playing second by protesting to Brussels, Turin and London, and in the last case in language altogether unsuited to England's status as an ally:

"Does the right of asylum cover systematic murder? Is hospitality owing to assassins? Should England's laws shelter their designs and their manoeuvres?"

Palmerston made no reply. He merely had the Foreign Office inform the British ambassador "that the British Parliament would never vote a law barring refugees from the country. That would be tantamount to suggesting that England should be annexed to France." To give Paris a reasonable amount of consideration the cabinet did take under advisement a law that would punish plots hatched against foreign sovereigns on English soil as high crimes and no longer as misdemeanors.

Piedmont was handed an even stiffer rebuke: Walewski demanded the suppression of Mazzini's paper, *L'Italia del Popolo,* and penal guarantees. Cavour sidestepped the first request and applied himself somewhat laxly to satisfying the second. His sovereign, Victor Emmanuel, sent Della Rocca, his aide-de-camp, to Paris bearing a haughty but cleverly worded message that was well calculated to touch Napoleon in a sensitive spot:

"Tell the Emperor of the French that I have never submitted to an act of personal violence, that I follow the path of honor and for that honor am answerable only to God and my people. For eight hundred and fifty years we have carried our heads high. No one will make me bow mine. Tell him, further, that with all that I have no greater desire than to be his friend."

Napoleon III was the man to appreciate the tone of such a reply.

"Your king is a fine fellow," he said to Della Rocca.

However, for some little time the Paris and Turin cabinets were to remain on decidedly chilly terms.

In a speech from the throne on January 18th, the Emperor informed the representatives of the domestic policy he intended to pursue from then on:

"Power must be strong. . . . Unlimited freedom is impossible. Danger lies not in excessive prerogatives of power but in the absence of repressive laws."

Active steps followed in short order: two newspapers were suppressed, the *Spectateur,* royalist, the *Revue de Paris,* republican. Domestic passport regulations were tightened. The territory was divided into five military commands, Paris, Lyons, Nancy, Toulouse and Tours, each in charge of a marshal. In the hour of danger the regime turned instinctively to the army as the basic instrument of governing.

A general public safety law was next brought up before the Legislative Body. It laid heavy penalties not only on provocation to bodily attempts on the sovereign but on "any encouragement of hatred or contempt of the government." The administration was empowered to banish from the country or intern in France or Algeria any individual who had ever been convicted of conspiracy, rebellion, unlawful assembly, unlawful possession of firearms, or disparagement of the Emperor's person. The law might also be applied to persons implicated or suspected of being implicated in the disturbances of June, 1848, June, 1849, and December, 1851, "and whom facts of moment have again marked as dangerous to public safety."

Such a law was Draconian indeed. Its brutality terrified the country and antagonized even a Chamber that stood ready to vote anything. Morny was president of the Legislative Body, but he procured for himself the assignment of reporting on the bill. He luffed and tacked to appease anxieties and mistrusts. When the bill came up for debate, Emile Ollivier for the first time moved into public notice. With an impressiveness that astounded in a man of his years, he protested against a law which gave the Minister of the Interior the right to impose harsh penalties without guarantees of any sort for the accused.

"This bill must be voted down," he concluded, "not in a spirit of petty carping, but in deference to sheer wisdom, and in all loyalty to the sovereign, as a way of pointing out the sound direction in which the policy of the future must move."

Baroche, as official spokesman for the Council of State, replied with strict observance of courteous forms but with an impudence that had its savor, coming from a lawyer such as he.

"The Empire," he made bold to say, "repudiates the exaggerated respect for legalistic niceties that led to the revolutions of '30 and '48."

A crude avowal that the Empire was based on force and held on solely by force!

The bill passed the Legislative Body by a vote of 227 to 24. In the Senate it was rushed through in a single session, despite the honorable, indeed courageous, opposition of MacMahon (February 19, 1858).

The weapon had been forged. Who, now, was to use it? Not Billault. The Tuileries thought him soft and he had the Catholics and imperialists of the Right against him. He resigned and on February 17th was replaced by General Espinasse, who was given the significant title of Minister of the Interior and Public Safety.

Espinasse had been the policeman of December 2nd. He was ready to set to work again, and at once. Repeating the Prince-President's phrase of June, 1849, "It is time for the law-abiding to have some of the comforts and the trouble-makers some of the worries," he called a conference of prefects and urged them to proceed with arrests, he himself designating the numbers—ten in some departments, eight in others, four hundred in all. The victims selected were, in the majority, earlier victims of '48 and '51—lawyers, physicians, factory foremen. Sometimes, to fill out the specified number, names were picked haphazard. Almost all those arrested were transported to Algeria.

From then on a preliminary oath of loyalty to the Emperor was demanded in writing of all candidates at elections. Finally, in order to safeguard the throne against any mischance, the Emperor appointed a privy council, composed of the ex-King Jerome, Prince Napoleon and the chief dignitaries. It was to stand by the Empress in case of the sovereign's death and uphold her in her rights as Regent.

At the direct instance of Morny, the colonels of all the regiments sent declarations of loyalty to the Emperor. These documents were conceived in the most extravagant terms, flaying the "demagogic" spirit and insulting England as "an iniquitous refuge which had to be destroyed."

Losing their heads completely, the ministers allowed the letters to be printed in the *Moniteur*.

Effects in London were immediate—and they were deplorable. A violent press campaign started on both sides of the Channel. The Palmerston bill for the punishment of conspiracies had passed a first reading in the House of Commons by a majority of two hundred. It came up for second reading shortly after the publication of the letters of the colonels in France. Parliament refused to consider the bill, declaring that the government had "been lacking in dignity" with regard to French demands. Palmerston fell. Lord Derby replaced him with Malmesbury in the Foreign Office and Disraeli in the Exchequer.

Persigny quite forgot himself in his position as ambassador. He appeared at the Foreign Office in full dress uniform, and, with his hand on his sword, shouted:

"This means war! This means war!"

Not only did the alliance seem lost. Peace itself was threatened. However, Napoleon returned forthwith to a saner view of things. Violence was not in his character and he was afraid of finding himself isolated in Europe. He ordered Walewski to backwater:

"My dispatch of January 20th was designed solely to call attention to a state of things that we consider regrettable. Since our friendly intentions have been misconstrued, we shall abstain from any further discussion that might affect good feeling between our two nations. We pin our faith to the English people's sense of fairness."

Persigny resigned and was replaced by Marshal Pélissier. Pélissier may have had no faintest conception of diplomacy, but he wore the halo of the Crimea and stood as a living witness to the comradeship of France and England in arms. He was given a wonderful welcome in London, where reception after reception was held in his honor. The bluff soldier carried all his characteristic manners to the English court.

"At his first dinner with the Queen," wrote Prince Albert, "he spoke frankly of conditions in France and of the Emperor's measures, of which he heartily disapproved."

With Pélissier and the Emperor's backdown, the atmosphere cleared. The two presses changed their tone. Soon the Emperor was to find his relations with England sufficiently improved to permit his inviting the Queen to visit France. The entente was reestablished—a checkmate for Morny, but a profound satisfaction to Napoleon III. Still considering changes in Europe, he hoped he could keep the entente with England as the cornerstone of his foreign policy. Unfortunately its best days were over. It was never really to recover from the great shock it had received and was destined to founder at the first jolt.

The trial of Orsini and his accomplices opened on February 25th before the Court of Criminal Sessions of the Seine. It was a curious affair. The defense and the state were in entire agreement. Pietri, the prefect of police, got a pledge from Orsini that no mention of Carbonarism would be made during the trial. While his accomplices were arguing, quibbling, throwing the blame on him, the defendant-in-chief maintained an attitude of manly courage. He did not excuse himself: Napoleon III was opposed to the freeing of his country. He had tried to do away with him. The state's prosecutor, Chaix d'Est-Ange, became entangled in his long sentences during his plea. Jules Favre then spoke for Orsini.

Jules Favre was a Southerner, with a grim, shaggy head on which the hair seemed to eat up the flesh. Always a wretched politician, he was a marvelous lawyer, with a flair for the romantic, rioting in the pathetic, drawing tears and shedding them himself. His tactic was not to save Orsini from the guillotine but to ennoble his act, make him out the patriot and the martyr, pleading less for the man than for his ideas. Orsini disappeared behind the portrait of an enslaved and desolate Italy. Summing up, Jules Favre read in a hollow tone *and with the Emperor's permission,* an appeal that the defendant had addressed to Napoleon III:

"I solemnly beg Your Majesty to restore to Italy the independence which her children lost in '49, and through fault of the French. Your Majesty must not forget that Italians, and among them my father, poured out their blood joyfully for Napoleon the Great, wherever he wished to lead them. May Your Majesty not forget that they stood loyal to the day of his downfall. May Your Majesty remember that as long as Italy is not free any peace for Europe and for Your Majesty will be mere illusion. May Your Majesty give ear to the supreme prayer of a patriot standing on the steps of the scaffold and free my country, that the blessings of twenty-five million citizens may go down with you to posterity."

The courtroom sat in stunned silence and there was all but a burst of applause. That eloquent plea—it was published in the *Moniteur* at Napoleon III's express direction—upset and conquered everyone. Orsini and two of his accomplices, Pieri and Rudio, were sentenced to death, but Paris forgot the crime, seeing only the self-sacrifice of the criminal. On his transference to La Roquette to await his doom, Orsini became even more the hero by addressing a petition to the Emperor, disavowing his belief in political assassination, interceding for his accomplices, but refusing all clemency for himself:

"I go to my death calmly and I wish no stain to rest on my memory. For the victims of January 14th I offer my blood, and I pray that one day when Italians have become free and independent they will make amends to all who have suffered."

Napoleon III was deeply stirred and the Empress with him. She asked for a pardon for the condemned man and went so far as to say:

"Orsini is not a common murderer like Pianori. He is a man and has my respect."

She wanted to visit him in his prison to help him find his peace with God. Napoleon forbade that melodramatic gesture as beneath the Empress's dignity. However he was impelled by a natural generosity, and also, perhaps, by a thought for his safety in the future, to pardon Orsini.

The ministers and the Privy Council were set on the execution of the sentence.

"Don't forget, sire," said Fould, "that French blood was shed in the rue Le Peletier."

Alas! The Emperor had escaped, but too many innocent people had perished. Even the archbishop of Paris, Monsignor Morlot, declared in favor of expiation. Napoleon yielded. He pardoned Rudio. Orsini and Pieri went to the guillotine on March 13th. Pieri sang the hymn of the Girondins. Orsini watched him die in silence, but as he placed himself in the executioner's hands he shouted in his loudest voice to the great crowd:

"Vive l'Italie! Vive la France!"

Few cries in history have echoed so long and so far!

CHAPTER XIV

The Campaign in Italy

MORE THAN THE ATTEMPT ON HIS LIFE IN ITSELF, THE CIRCUMSTANCES of the trial, the veritable thrill that had coursed through France during those dramatic weeks, tied Napoleon III to his Italian dream. In dismissing Della Rocca he told him clearly that in case of trouble with Austria Piedmont would find him at her side, and he charged him to ask Cavour to begin direct correspondence with him (February 20, 1858).

Orsini's death caused an outburst of excitement through all Italy, somewhat contained in the center and south, uncontrollable in the north. Chromos of the conspirator were to be seen everywhere. The official gazette in Turin published his letters with the express approval of the Emperor.

"You had better take care!" Cavour had written to Napoleon III. "To publish them would be an attack on Austria not by Piedmont only, but by France."

"Go ahead and publish!" replied the Emperor.

With that encouragement Cavour manoeuvred to bring the two courts closer together still. He had his Parliament vote the law against conspiracies which the Tuileries demanded. The Emperor, in his turn, expressed his satisfaction to the Sardinian envoy, Villamarina, asking further a significant question:

"How far along are the forts at Casale? And at Alexandria?"

"Sire," replied the Ambassador, "we are constantly preparing for the great day."

By that time Napoleon had made up his mind. Secluding himself in his study, he kept poring over the maps of the Milanese. On them, one may guess, he noted many a golden name—Arcole, Rivoli, Marengo. Must they not have touched in him that yearning for personal glory that had been with him ever since the days at

Arenenberg? What was an emperor, especially in France, unless victory had crowned him?

Early in May he commissioned General MacMahon, whose honest judgment he respected, to visit Italy as an ordinary tourist and inspect works at the chief Cisalpine fortresses between Milan and Pola. A little later he sent for Dr. Conneau and asked him to advise Cavour semi-officially that he would soon be visiting Plombières to take a treatment. Cavour took the hint and replied that he was himself thinking of a trip to Switzerland and would be happy to call on the Emperor and extend him his greetings in person.

On July 21st Cavour appeared at Plombières under the name of Giuseppe Benso and was ushered into the unpretentious reception room where Napoleon III awaited him. Had the eyes behind his glasses not been so bright and sparkling, one would have taken him for some plain, good-natured country lawyer.

The Emperor's first words announced that "he was disposed, on certain conditions, to march with Piedmont against Austria."

What were the conditions?

First of all there had to be a plausible reason for the war, in order not to alienate European opinion.

So close to seeing his great hope realized Cavour was disconcerted by such a frank overture. He racked his brain for the plausible reason and could not find it. Finally, after going over the maps, the sovereign and the minister agreed on a fairly wretched pretext. An insurrection would start at Massa-Carrara. The Duke of Modena would ask help of Austria, the inhabitants of Piedmont would rise— and the war would be on.

But the Emperor thought it was going to be a localized war, localized in Europe as well as in Italy. England, Russia and Prussia would all keep out, all for different reasons, he thought. He was counting on a rapid, brilliant campaign. Once the Austrians were out of Milan and Venice, the Peninsula would get a new constitution.

From that point on, the discussion came more down to detail. The two conspirators finally agreed that Victor Emmanuel would fatten by the Cisalpine kingdom of Napoleon I: Lombardy, Venetia, Emilia, Romagna. Tuscany and Umbria would be made into a kingdom, which could be offered to the Duchess of Parma—the Duchess of Parma had seemed of late to be pulling away from

Austria; Napoleon III was in friendly correspondence with her through his cousin, the Duchess of Hamilton.

Napoleon insisted on handling the Pope with gloves. The pontiff would retain Rome and the original patrimony of St. Peter and be given, in addition, the title of "President of the Italian Confederation." Naples would be left to the Bourbons, in order not to lose the sympathy of Russia, who was sponsoring the family. However, the Bourbons would have to modernize their ramshackle government. If their subjects should ever rebel, Napoleon III and Cavour would have a chance to decide what their final attitude was to be. In his report to Victor Emmanuel, Cavour wrote:

"As for Naples, the Emperor would be glad to see Murat seated on his father's throne."

A terribly delicate question was still left to be settled. Napoleon's day-dreaming did not cloud his realistic outlook. France would be making sacrifices in men and money. Piedmont, meantime, would be increasing her territory enormously and becoming a great State. Why not transfer Savoy and Nice to France? That, moreover, would supply the Empire with a dowry to give the nation.

Cavour expostulated, less on account of Savoy, the cradle of his dynasty, than of Nice, where so many Italians lived. How give Nice to France without betraying the principle of nationality?

The point was left unsettled.

"It's a minor matter," said the Emperor, sharpening the points of his mustache. "We can go into it later."

The interview lasted four hours. The Emperor dismissed Cavour, inviting him for a drive later on in the afternoon. He himself held the reins. The phaeton left Plombières and made the wooded valleys of the Vosges.

In this second interview he confided to the Sardinian minister his keen desire to see the political entente with Piedmont reinforced by a family alliance; and in the name of his cousin, Prince Napoleon, he asked for the hand of the Princess Clothilde, eldest daughter of Victor Emmanuel.

Cavour was terribly embarrassed and thought of a number of objections: Clothilde was a mere child, the Prince not a very reliable sort of person.

The Emperor pleaded his cousin's cause:

"He is better than his reputation makes him out. . . . He has caused me some embarrassment at times, I admit . . . always likes to be on the opposite side, in a scoffing spirit. But he's intelligent and a good fellow at heart."

Napoleon III, however, did not insist on the marriage as a basic condition of the military alliance.

Cavour's opposition lessened by degrees. He was too eager for French support to worry very much about the outcome of a mere marriage. By the time the sovereign and the minister were back at Plombières again he declared himself convinced, subject only to the final decision of his King. Of that decision Cavour could be certain. Much as Victor Emmanuel loved his daughter, he was not the man to recoil before such a profitable sacrifice.

Napoleon III grasped the hand of the nimble Piedmontese.

"Have confidence in me," he said to him in farewell, "the way I have in you."

In that he was going wrong. Cavour was pretending to accept the Emperor's principle of a free, but not a united Italy. Actually he was bent only on an Italy united under the sceptre of his sovereign. Emile Ollivier was to write very soundly:

"To free Italy from Austria was really to hand her over, lock, stock and barrel, to the house of Savoy. It meant destroying the temporal power of the Pope, the kingdom of Naples and the duchies, regardless of stipulations that might be made to prevent just those consequences. If there was any unwillingness to accept the inevitable unity of Italy, the Italian question should never have been raised." [1]

Cavour, for his part, was looking far ahead. He was altogether certain that once Victor Emmanuel found himself master of the Po valley he would see all the regions of the Peninsula coming to him one by one, in a series of revolutions. He stated as much in a report which he sent the King two days later from Baden. And Victor Emmanuel shared his conviction. He would give his daughter to Prince Napoleon and risk the adventure.

"Next year," he said, "I will be King of Italy or plain M. de Savoie."

It was too good a game, and the chance too exceptional.

"All the same," he warned Cavour, "let's not get messed up in diplomacy. What we need, to get somewhere, is cannon. . . ."

[1] Ollivier, *L'Empire Libéral,* IV, 498.

Back again in Paris Napoleon III took pains to hide his moves from the sharp eyes of his ministers. Walewski, a man of good sense, hazarded a number of remarks on "this bath-resort diplomacy," of which he had somehow got wind and which a brief dispatch of the Havas Agency finally reported. The Emperor misled him with the greatest of ease. Walewski, he knew, was hostile to the Italian adventure and he seems to have considered replacing him in Foreign Affairs, a step which his own liaison at the moment with the Countess Walewski prevented.

To turn liberal opinion in his favor again, Napoleon III relaxed, at least in appearances, the grip of authority. Espinasse had already left the Ministry of the Interior, Delangle, the judge who had presided over the Orsini trial, replacing him. Delangle was an out-and-out anti-clerical. Prince Napoleon was made minister of Algeria and the Colonies. The *Siècle* and the *Presse* were not slow in launching a campaign against Austrian oppression in Lombardy. In the *Moniteur* itself Edmond About published a series of brisk, lively articles on the dyspeptic administration of the Papal States. The Empress was displeased but the Emperor enjoyed About's Voltairian thrusts. The Mortara affair came on—a case of abduction by pontifical order of a Jewish child at Bologna who had been baptized without the knowledge of its parents. The case provoked a sharp polemic in the press, Veuillot, in the *Univers,* alone defending the Curia, and with more talent than fairness.

At the same time Napoleon III planned a move in diplomatic seduction. On August 4th Queen Victoria and Prince Albert landed at Cherbourg to celebrate the opening of the new harbor there. Cordial toasts were exchanged, but really the spell had been broken. The sometime allies were just a grumbling, sulking, middle-aged couple. Victoria was worried by the rebirth of the French fleet, to which a bit too much advertisement was given. On her return to England she ordered an increase in her own navy.

In a speech he made at Cherbourg during just those days at the unveiling of a statue of Napoleon, the Emperor once more glorified peace. But his words had a ring of insincerity:

"A government that depends on the will of the masses is the slave of no party. It makes war only when it is forced to do so in defense of national honor or of the great interests of the peoples."

QUEEN VICTORIA
From the Portrait by Winterhalter

From Cherbourg he made a pilgrimage to Saint-Anne d'Auray to humor his Catholics.

Meantime he asked Walewski to ease the worries of Hübner, the Austrian ambassador:

"An impression is being spread abroad that I have hostile intentions towards Austria. . . . To be sure my sympathies are with Piedmont; to be sure I love Italy and shall always give the Italians every evidence of my affection—but all within certain limits."

"In other words," added Walewski, of his own brew, "without endangering peace!"

The Emperor sent word to Prince Napoleon to meet him at Biarritz, and the morning after his own arrival he went in person to waken the Prince, who was still in bed, and took him for a walk on the beach. There, where no one could hear them, he told him of the talks with Cavour and of the plans he had in view.

"Keep all this secret, with no exceptions," he said. "The Empress suspects nothing, neither does Walewski who is here, and even less Fould, who will be here tomorrow. Don't say anything to any of them."

Behind his ministers' backs he sent the Prince off to Warsaw, ostensibly to deliver his greetings to the Czar, but really to propose an alliance. Russia should send an army to the Galician border and do nothing about the rebellion in Hungary. On her side France would drop the clause in the treaty of 1856 that neutralized the Black Sea.

Alexander II nibbled at the bait but did not swallow it. He was not ready for a war and would go no farther than a promise of friendly neutrality.

That was in itself a great deal. Cavour wrote to Prince Napoleon (October 25, 1858):

"Even if the Czar should confine himself to preventing Germany from interfering in our affairs, his support would, in my opinion, assure our success in the war. By procuring this collaboration Your Imperial Highness has rendered our cause the greatest of services."

Still proceeding in secret Napoleon III got word to the Prince Regent of Prussia that the latter might annex Hanover and Holstein while Austria was held powerless in Italy. This was a most imprudent move. Napoleon III was quite overestimating the gratitude that Prussia might have felt for him for extricating her from an embarrassing predicament in the Neufchâtel affair.

Neufchâtel had at one time been a possession of the Hohenzollern family but had become part of Switzerland again in 1848. In September, 1856, the nobles of Neufchâtel rose in rebellion in an effort to reestablish Prussian sovereignty. The movement failed and the rebels were put in prison. Frederick William asked Napoleon to use his good offices to obtain their release. The Emperor took the matter up with the Swiss authorities and the rebels were set free, while the status of the canton of Neufchâtel was definitely settled at a conference.

King Frederick William, for his own part, was grateful enough for Napoleon III's help, but he suffered a stroke of apoplexy in October, 1857, and his brother, Prince William, was declared regent (he was to become King in 1861). Hostile to France, he dismissed his brother's minister, Manteuffel, the moment he came into power, as too favorable to France and Russia, replacing him with his cousin, Prince Anton von Hohenzollern, who was also anti-French, though under friendly externals.

Prince William curtly declined the Emperor's suggestion about Hanover and Holstein—it was in truth a strange one—and reported the whole matter to Queen Victoria.

What would England do in case of war? That riddle was well calculated to worry the Emperor. His court had moved to Compiègne for the hunting season. Thither the Emperor invited Palmerston and Clarendon, the two leaders of the Whig Opposition, and sounded them out in a number of conversations. His desire, he explained, had always been to liberate Poland and Italy. As to Poland he was willing to give up his idea, for the time being at least, in order to retain the Czar's support. As for Italy, it seemed to be a simple matter and the moment looked favorable. Clarendon, in great alarm, expostulated with a flood of objections which the Emperor did not rebutt. Shortly afterwards, Lord Cowley advised him "to come to an understanding with Austria instead of starting a quarrel, and to obtain with her help a thoroughgoing reorganization of the pontifical government." Queen Victoria, for her part, wrote a private letter to Napoleon, warning him that he could cease to count on her friendship the moment he set out to turn Europe upside down. On December 9th the Queen wrote more emphatically still, in a letter to Malmesbury:

"The Emperor will not listen to reason. He considers only what he wants himself. If he makes war in Italy, that war will probably lead to a war with Germany and thence on to a war with Belgium. We shall be dragged into the conflict through our treaty of guarantees, and France may find that she has all Europe against her as she did in 1814 and 1815." [1]

The Emperor paid no attention. At just that moment he was discussing texts for the treaty of alliance, with Prince Napoleon and Cavour; but when the *Patrie* and the *Presse* came out with open allusions to "military operations that were near at hand," he ordered a denial in the *Moniteur*.

Cavour, meantime, had by no means wasted the four months. With his sovereign's approval he applied himself with alacrity to setting the machinery in motion for the revolution that was to supply the pretext for opening hostilities. In accord with the leading patriots and agitators of the day, La Farina, Garibaldi, Pallavicino, Minghetti, Pasolini, he spurred the "Italian National Society" to action, and it organized committees and laid plans for insurrection through all Italy. With a view to creating a diversion in Hungary, he got in touch with General Klapka, a comrade of Kossuth. Well seconded by La Marmora, his Minister of War, he strengthened and reequipped the Piedmontese army. Come what may, he would be ready.

In his bounding joyous hope he probably talked too much. Quite apart from the underhanded and very cautious manoeuvres of Napoleon III, Europe could have had no doubt that war was shortly to break out. Austria in particular had no illusions whatever left. Apponyi, her ambassador to London, said to Malmesbury:

"France will tear up the treaties of 1815 and create complications that will give Lombardy to Piedmont and Naples to Murat. She herself will take Savoy."

Cavour sent Nigra, a young but very adequate man, to Paris to establish the various articles in the treaty. Nigra did his best to stand in the Emperor's good graces, but he by no means neglected the Empress. Eugénie fought shy of Italians, as a rule, but she came to like Nigra.

[1] Retranslated.

The Plombières talks supplied the basis for the accord. France pledged herself to send 200,000 men to Italy "if Austria should commit any act of aggression," and to sign a peace only after "the total expulsion of the Austrians." Piedmont was to receive the kingdom of Lombardo-Venetia, the duchies, and a part of the Papal States. Savoy and Nice would be ceded to France. Full agreement was reached on December 10, 1858 (the treaty itself was formally signed six weeks later, January 26, 1859). Not until then did Napoleon take his Minister of Foreign Affairs into the secret.

Walewski was stunned.

"Sire," he protested, "you are headed in a fatal direction!"

Outraged that the Emperor should have worked to that extent behind his back, he submitted his resignation. Napoleon refused to accept it and, without at all rewinning Walewski, wheedled him sufficiently to induce him to swallow his resentment.

A diplomatic reception was held on New Year's evening, 1859. The Emperor walked past the papal nuncio without a word, approached the Austrian ambassador and said slowly, with his eyes half-closed:

"I am sorry our relations are not as good as I wish they were, but I hope you will write Vienna that my personal feelings for the Emperor are still the same."

He had worked up the scene and timed it, to the last detail. Effects were tremendous. All Europe stirred. Napoleon III, indeed, was afraid that he might have shown his hand too soon and tried to backwater. He showed special attentiveness to Hübner during the days following and basted Walewski with all sorts of explanations. A note in the *Moniteur* declared that "nothing in the diplomatic field justified any alarm whatever."

Then Victor Emmanuel stepped to the front of the stage. On January 10th, at the opening of the Piedmontese parliament, he delivered a warlike speech. It came as no surprise to Napoleon III. He had inspected the text in advance, revising it and even making it stronger in places.

"The horizon is dark . . ." said the King, in substance. "While we respect the treaties we have made we are not insensible to the cry of anguish that reaches our ears from all Italy."

General Niel set out at once for Turin, to confer with La Marmora and formulate a military agreement to supplement the diplo-

matic accord of December 10th. It was signed on the evening of
January 18th and, pen in hand, the King remarked to Niel:

"I am looking forward with joy to the war of freedom."

"We must wait, sire," Niel replied.

"I have been waiting—for ten years!" said the King.

Prince Napoleon left Paris in Niel's company. His engagement
to Princess Clothilde of Savoy had so far been known semi-
officially. It was now announced in the *Moniteur*. A second Marie-
Louise, the Princess Clothilde was not a beautiful woman but she
had character. In a spirit of nobility sustained by religious faith
she was sacrificing herself to necessities of state. She desired a postponement of the wedding, but the Prince was eager—not, surely, out
of passion. He saw himself, once he was grafted on the oldest reigning dynasty in Europe, sitting on the throne of Central Italy. But
that was just for a start. He was ambitious to play a far more important rôle in history than that. Caesar in reserve, all he asked of
the Caesar actually on the scene, whom he envied at bottom and
to an extent despised, was the cue that would call him to the spotlight. Disliked by royal family, court and public, he rushed matters
along, stooping, for all of his vociferous atheism, to go through the
farce of a confession.

On January 30th, in the Royal Chapel at Turin, the wholly
political marriage was celebrated, and the young couple, attended
by Victor Emmanuel, proceeded at once to Genoa to take ship for
Marseilles. A crowd gathered at the pier shouting, "Down with
Austria!" and cheering for war. The reception in Paris was altogether cold. In spite of the clamors in the semi-official press the
public seemed more and more to dread the coming conflict.

Towards that conflict Cavour was racing with all his art, concentrating all his resources upon it as his single goal. He had his
parliament vote a loan of 50 millions to match military precautions
that Austria was taking in the Milanese.

"An attack upon us is in preparation," he declared before the
Chamber. "Piedmont must be ready to meet it, and without delay."

Simultaneously with this speech by Cavour, and as it were in echo
to it, an anonymous pamphlet appeared in the French capital. It
came from the platitudinous pen of La Gueronnière, the councillor
of state, but the Emperor had revised it in his own hand and had
himself gone over the proofs. It was entitled *Napoleon III and Italy*

and boldly set forth his views and intentions. Unsparingly it stigmatized the princes who owed allegiance to Austria, the Duke of Modena, the Duchess of Parma, the Grand Duke of Tuscany, "who was held aloof from his people by Austrian bayonets," the King of Naples, "contemptuous of all reforms and isolated by his own fault in Europe," finally the Pope himself, who, however, was criticized with some show of deference. The pamphlet sang a hymn to the theory of nationalities and concluded with a toast to a "federated Italy from which all foreign influence would be banished." The concept of a "united Italy" was explicitly rejected.

"Shall Italy become one single kingdom?" it asked. "History as well as nature itself stands opposed to any such solution. The goal must be not absolute union, but federated union."

Everyone ascribed the pamphlet to its actual inspirer. It created a profound sensation. Business came to a standstill, stocks wavered on the Exchange, money went into hiding, there was an epidemic of business failures. Disapprobation was general in the Emperor's personal environment. On February 7, 1859, at the opening session of the Legislative Body he came out with a cryptic speech that was anything but reassuring. Complaints poured in from all sides. Persigny wrote the Emperor bluntly:

"Europe and France have been accepting you for nine years because they trusted your promise to respect treaties. Cease respecting them and you will lose that trust."

And Walewski:

"The effects of the pamphlet have been deplorable. . . . If it were an official document Europe would stand allied, not tomorrow but today, and not against France but against the Emperor personally. I repeat, sire: In the state of mind that prevails in France and abroad at this moment war is impossible!"

The ministers chimed in on the same note. Fould and Delangle would not listen to talk of war. Rouher was above all else anxious to please: he hemmed and hawed. Thiers had written not so long before that "the territorial emancipation of Italy was conformable to sound policy," but at Mérimée's request he formulated his objections to an Italian adventure in a memorandum for the Emperor. The Emperor glanced over it and said:

"Well, there is some truth in it, but on the whole Thiers is just a bourgeois."

The Emperor in his turn drew up and read in Council a letter to Walewski in which he massed all the arguments he could think of in favor of intervention.

"The Empire is still young," he jested. "It is entitled to a few wild oats. . . . The war in the Near East was not enough since none of the changes in territory that had been expected of it resulted. . . . If France drives the Austrians out of Italy, safeguards the Pope's temporal power, refrains from going too far and declares she will make no conquests apart from Savoy and Nice, she will have Europe on her side and win powerful allies in Italy, allies who will owe everything to her and live only through her life."

He figured that hostilities could be localized:

"England is terribly afraid of war. . . . Germany will not move . . . !"

Marshal Vaillant commented on the document in his private diary (January 22nd):

"The Emperor read us a big affair of his own on the reasons that justify his going to war. It was all pretty weak. The real reason is that he wants war."

Morny was a sterner soul than any of these. Moreover he had built the throne plank by plank and saw far ahead into the future. He declared in very frank terms before the Legislative Body that the Empire had to remain loyal to its policies of peace.

"The blood of the peoples," he said, "can no longer be lightly spilled. . . . Few the difficulties today that cannot be ironed out by diplomacy or settled by arbitration. . . . All governments now have to reckon with a new power: public opinion."

The Catholics were specially influential in the provinces and their reprobation was loud. They could sense all the danger that the Emperor's whim spelled for the Papacy. Cardinal de Bonnechose, a personal friend of the Emperor, implored him "not to break with his old policy, which had so far been so Christian." And he went on to say:

"Once the protector of the Holy See, France has now become the right hand of its enemies. This is sheer madness!"

To gain greater freedom in his private life Napoleon had been giving the Empress a larger share in public affairs. She was now talking with ministers and ambassadors, disconnectedly, as a rule, leaping from topic to topic, and impulsively, according to her likes and dislikes of the moment. On this occasion she spat fire, predicting the worst catastrophes. The military from Pélissier to Castellane, from Vaillant to Niel and Fleury, protested that the army had hardly recovered from its losses in the Crimea and was in no condition to undertake an enterprise which in all probability would prove difficult and costly. The bankers had been going in for gigantic investments and could think of no way of extricating themselves. They saw only ruin ahead. At a court ball James de Rothschild gave an amusing twist to the Prince-President's famous slogan:

"The Empire means peace? Well then, no peace, no Empire!"

Everybody in financial circles called for the abandonment of a personal policy which would lead no one could say whither, and a return to a policy based strictly on the visible interests of the country.

With the Emperor stood Prince Napoleon, Mocquart, Conneau, Pietri. They were his only defenders in the court circle. But he had other support—and what embarrassing support! The support of the republicans! Europe abroad repudiated his policy in virtual unanimity. He flattered himself that he had won Russia, but all he had of her was a promise of friendly neutrality. Prussia was openly and entirely hostile, and behind her the princes of the Confederation were stirring and plotting. England kept repeating her warnings in a crescendo of shrillness. A Coburg through and through, Prince Albert could see in Napoleon III only a reckless adventurer who was about to set fire to the continent in pursuance of dark designs of his own. Victoria wrote again at the Prince-Consort's instance, demanding the preservation of peace (February 4, 1859):

"If anything could increase the pain I should feel at the outbreak of another war, it would be to see Your Majesty embark on a path where I should find it impossible to follow." [1]

King Leopold of Belgium, uncle to both Victoria and Prince Albert, was very naturally eager for peace and made himself the heart and soul of the Continental opposition. [2]

To all this royal admonition Napoleon III replied protesting his good intentions. At that moment, in fact, worried by such general and such vigorous opposition, he was again hesitating. Malmesbury took advantage of his mood to make a move for mediation. Austria

1 Retranslated.
2 Dispatch of Bismarck, January 17, 1859.

was favorably disposed. She had concentrated troops on the Pied-montese frontier but was short of men and guns. She did not think war could be avoided but she might at least gain time to complete her preparations. Lord Cowley went to Vienna and obtained very substantial concessions. The Papal States would be evacuated by the Austrian troops. There would be reforms in the Italian govern-ments, a guarantee of peace to Piedmont, new agreements with the duchies.

The idea of an Italian confederacy was not abandoned at the Tuileries, but the wind veered towards conciliation. On March 5th the *Moniteur* gave the lie to rumors of war: The Emperor had promised to defend the King of Sardinia against any aggressive act on the part of Austria. He had promised nothing but that. Stocks and bonds at once reacted, and before long Prince Napoleon will-ingly or unwillingly retired from the Algerian Bureau. The public scented promise of a change of policy in that move.

At the Congress of 1856 Napoleon III had had the stature of an arbiter of Europe and memories of the experience so thrilled him that he enjoyed the thought of settling the Italian business with another European conference. At his request the Russian chancel-lor, Prince Gortchakov, brought the suggestion before the great powers. England accepted half-heartedly. Prince Albert had a copy of a letter in which Thiers had said:

"The congress will necessarily delay war, but I believe that delay is all that Napoleon wants, his adversary being ready while he is not. Delay would serve his purpose admirably—to wear Austria down by a process of disintegration, prolonging a critical and irritating state of affairs that will finally exhaust her." [1]

Prussia followed England. Napoleon III had been deeply im-pressed by German hostility, and to help things along drew up a note which appeared anonymously in the *Moniteur*:

"On mere presumptions that are wholly unjustified and are in fact belied by the plainest facts, a sort of crusade has been launched against France. . . . Germany need fear no threat to her inde-pendence on the part of France. We have a right to expect her to manifest a fairness in her judgment of our intentions as great as the sympathy we have manifested for her nationality."

[1] J. Martin, *Vie du prince Albert*, II, 343.

Austria came in with Prussia, but stipulating that Piedmont should first disarm.

So the diplomatic horizon was again cleared. But Cavour and his King wanted war and they wanted it badly. They tried to blackmail Napoleon III, threatening to publish his secret pledges. They mobilized the Piedmontese army and shouted at the top of their voices that if France deserted them they would attack Austria all by themselves and unchain the revolution in Italy. The prospect of a conference was not calculated to calm Cavour. He hurried to Paris and was received by Napoleon III on March 26th.

It was a painful, stormy interview. The wily Piedmontese alternated denunciation with entreaty. Napoleon tried to calm him:

"I am biding my time. Do as I am doing. This is a difficult moment, but we have to pass it. In the end the delay will be no greater." [1]

The Emperor was so upset by the interview that he kept to his bedroom for two days. Another meeting took place, this time with Walewski present. Then Cavour started back for Turin.

Victor Emmanuel received him angrily.

"That dog of an Emperor!" he cried. "He is making jackasses of us! . . ."

Cavour tried to reason with him. He had not obtained any definite promises, but he had tightened his grip on the Emperor. He was convinced now that he could lead him any way he wished; and he showed a letter from Napoleon III which he had received on his return. It was almost apologetic:

"All this talk of war has lost me public opinion all over Europe. If war were declared today, I should be obliged to send my army not to Italy but to the Rhine. My interest and my duty, if I am to prove useful to the cause which the King of Piedmont represents, oblige me, therefore, to reassure Germany and England as to my intentions and to prove to them, without disowning my sympathy for Italy, that I am in a conciliatory frame of mind. . . . I am sorry you do not seem wholly to understand the difficulties of my situation."

England, meantime, redoubled her efforts for peace. She proposed a general disarmament in advance of the conference. Austria agreed under English pressure, and an imperative telegram from

[1] Cavour to Buoncompagni, April 22, 1859.

Walewski on April 19th left Cavour no other alternative. He yielded, sick at heart. He burnt his papers and even toyed with thoughts of suicide.

"There is nothing left for me," he cried to a friend, Castelli, who was trying to comfort him, "but to blow out my brains."

Only a miracle could save him but the miracle happened: Austria had shown no end of patience. Now, suddenly, her patience gave out. She was short of money. She either had to demobilize her troops or use them. The personality of the young emperor, Francis Joseph, also figured in the matter. Inexperienced and, it must be added, of no great brains, narrow-minded, cold, vacillating, treacherous, he could not stand out against counsels of violence.

On April 20th his chancellor, Buol, sent an ultimatum to Turin ordering Piedmont to disarm within three days.

It was a supreme blunder. It put Austria in the wrong, discouraged England and Prussia, her best friends, dispelled Napoleon III's scruples and fears, exasperated the Italian public—and drove Cavour wild with joy.

"We have held the last session of the Piedmontese Chamber," he cried. "Our next will be a session of the parliament of Italy."

This time the die was in truth cast, and events were to develop with clocklike regularity. Cavour rejected the ultimatum and appealed to France. On April 24th, an Easter Sunday, in the midst of cheering crowds, the regiments in Paris were marching across the Faubourg Saint Antoine to entrain for Italy at the Gare de Lyon.

Old Jomini, a relic of the First Empire, was still alive with his mind still clear. That Easter morning Napoleon III sent a messenger to his home on the outskirts of Passy asking him for a plan of campaign. The veteran of the great wars did not realize that railroads existed or that armaments had improved immensely since the old days. He suggested attacking the Austrians on the left, crossing the Ticino at Magenta or Turbigo. An old-fashioned, thoroughly Napoleonic plan, but a fairly good one at that, since it was a question of beating just Austrians.

Curiously enough, the Emperor, through Walewski, put the same question of strategy to Thiers. The historian, in reply, suggested building up an army on the Rhine simultaneously with the army for Italy. That too would have been a good idea had there been troops enough. It would have ended the Prussian menace and, as the event proved, made the too precipitate truce of Villafranca unnecessary.

The Legislative Body voted a loan of 500 millions and a bill raising the next levy of troops to 140,000 men. Cheerful in the face of what he thought a disaster Morny made a patriotic speech on the occasion:

"There must be no looking backwards now: the flag of France waves ahead!"

That he disapproved of the Emperor's policy, and that all the leading men of the regime shared the same disapproval, there can be no doubt. A number of deputies even went so far as to protest that the Assembly had been kept in the dark down to the very last moment. Some very embarrassing questions were asked by Plichon, a representative from the North.

Jules Favre, on the other hand, speaking for the republicans, came out in favor of the war and hailed the emancipation of Italy.

"France," he cried in his deep, melodious voice, "cannot sheathe her sword without dishonor so long as one German is to be found south of the Alps."

The Five, however, abstained from voting on the credit bill.

As if to justify himself to the country and with his Catholics particularly in mind, Napoleon III issued a proclamation on May 3rd:

"Austria violates treaties, she outrages justice, she threatens our frontiers. . . . She has brought matters to such a pass that either her sway must be extended to the Alps or Italy must be free as far as the Adriatic. . . . We are not going to Italy to foment disorder. We are not going to shatter the power of the Holy Father. We are going to rescue him from foreign oppression."

When this text came up before the Council of Ministers, Walewski insisted upon the suppression of the phrase relating to the Adriatic. He thought it pledged too much. On the Emperor's insistence it was retained. Victor Emmanuel issued a war manifesto at the same time. It appealed to Italy as a whole:

"Taking up arms to defend my throne, the freedom of my peoples, the honor of the Italian name, I fight for the right of the whole nation."

A week later the Emperor arranged for a regency by the Empress during his absence. The ex-King Jerome was to act as president of the Council of Ministers. Pélissier, to his great regret, was recalled from the embassy in London to take command of an observation corps along the Rhine. Arrighi, Duke of Padua, a very devout man, took Delangle's place in the Ministry of the Interior.

With the home stage thus framed Napoleon III set out for the army, of which he was to assume supreme command. He set out filled with apprehension for the safety of his wife and child whom he was leaving behind. When he appeared in his field uniform on the threshold at the Tuileries, many of the people about him burst into tears; but the crowds that lined the sidewalks on the way to the Gare de Lyon sang and cheered. Their acclamations comforted him. Again like the Great Napoleon, he was going off to a campaign in Italy. By what grace no one could say—by grace of his happiness perhaps—he fancied himself a great military leader; though according to Du Barail, who had watched him at manoeuvres, whenever he tried to direct a movement, even one that he had studied out in advance, he mixed everything up.

"If the men had followed his orders," said Du Barail, "they would have gone over a precipice or to the bottom of a river."

But was he not a Bonaparte? The name had to have its magic, and its magic in truth it had. The indolent artillery student of Thun, ever a schoolboy among the strategists, could never fool the generals about him. But Luck had always been with him and Fate had not yet wearied of serving him. He was to fool all France, and Europe into the bargain.

CHAPTER XV

Magenta

THE FRENCH ARMY WAS NOT READY. THE CRIMEA LESSON HAD GONE for nothing. No special preparation had been ordered, for fear of alarming Europe too soon. During the weeks preceding a number of divisions had been massed in the southeast, mostly from troops recalled from Algeria, but they were short in provisions and in equipment of all sorts. Baggage trains and medical corps were wretched. New rifled cannon of more rapid and accurate fire had been ordered by the Emperor the year before, but not more than sixty were as yet in use. The Austrian smooth-bores were definitely inferior to these French rifles. On the other hand, the Lorenz musket of the Austrians had an adjustable sight. It could be aimed more accurately and had a greater range than the old French large-bore musket which had not kept pace with improvements in the years between 1842 and 1858. Ammunition was extremely scarce. There was not a trace of bridge equipment for a terrain that was cut by dozens of rivers. There was no siege artillery, though there was every prospect of an attack on the fortresses of the Quadrilateral. There was a shortage of ten thousand horses.

As he was crossing the frontier Bourbaki complained:

"The troops in my division have no blankets, and it's cold. We have no tents, no canteens, no camp equipment, not even cartridges."

And Canrobert chimed in at the same moment (April 26th):

"My army corps is also without a few things: it is without general staffs, commissariats, and police and ambulance services. It is without artillery and without engineers!"

Vaillant replied:

"I am sorry to note that your troops are not organized for war. You will attend to the matter."

214

In extenuation for the half-witted minister it could be said that the Emperor did not order him to prepare for war till January 2, 1859, and even then cautioned him to keep everything extremely quiet. But that excuse did not lessen the indignation of soldiers and generals. Vaillant had to resign.

"The army has it in for you," Napoleon III wrote, "because of everything we have failed to do. . . . We are in a critical situation. A few months hence we may have all Germany about our ears."

Marshal Randon succeeded Vaillant in the portfolio of war, the retiring minister moving on to a major-generalship in the Army of Italy. That was another absurdity. Vaillant was sixty-nine. He had never been able to direct a sham battle and had not mounted a horse for years. He was a sceptical soul, who hid a gift for flattery under a brusque exterior. He was intelligent and well educated, but he was a man of no real force and risked endangering everything by his slackness. However, as Castellane noted, Napoleon III found him convenient, and at times useful. He had grown attached to the man and did not like to hurt his feelings.

Giulay, the Austrian field-marshal, had one hundred and ten thousand men at his disposal and they were ready for action. He could have taken advantage of the unpreparedness of the allies and of their poor communications to fall on the Piedmontese and crush them before the French came up. Had he marched boldly on Turin he would have found it practically undefended. His officers were so sure of that that many of them had their letters forwarded to Turin addresses. But Giulay was slow and he was stubborn. A series of misunderstandings further misled him. He thought that Austria's major effort would be thrown against the Rhine, while he played a mainly defensive rôle, pivoting on the Quadrilateral. Informed too late, he wasted still more time and did not cross the Ticino till April 29th, advancing on Turin at a rate of four miles a day. Then at two days' march from the Piedmontese capital, he halted and shortly fell back on Mortara.

It was marvelous luck for Napoleon III! When he got to Genoa, he found Arese waiting for him and he remarked, laughingly:

"You owe the Madonna a good fat candle. If she had not driven the Austrians across the Ticino, I would not be here."

A little later, while driving with Arese, he suddenly turned pale and murmured, half to himself, words that revealed what was going on deep down in him:

"Just think: twenty-five years ago my brother died in my arms for the sake of Italy and my mother snatched me from the claws of the Austrians." [1]

The French were advancing in two divisions by way of Susa and Genoa. Giulay's error allowed them to reconcentrate at Alexandria. There the Piedmontese joined them. One hundred and fifty thousand men in all. But the Emperor was horrified at their poor equipment.

"We send an army to Italy," he wrote to Randon, "before assembling any provisions there! The War Office has been very remiss. There are whole army corps that haven't even a camp-kettle."

Fortunately the spirits of the troops could not have been higher. Evenings the men would light fires near their stacked muskets to cook their suppers, and the Emperor would hear songs drifting up to him, all the men joining in:

> Il nous faut de la graine d'oignons
> Pour les canons du roi de Sardaigne.
> Il nous faut de la graine d'oignons
> Pour les canons du roi de Piémont.[2]

Tuscany rose in revolt against the Grand Duke and a provisional government was set up in Florence. Prince Napoleon was dispatched thither with a small force of troops. Leopold of Tuscany left his capital in broad daylight and in perfect dignity. As he crossed the city limits, he turned back and shouted:

"Till we meet again!"

"In Heaven!" answered a wag in the crowd, and the people laughed.

The army moved down along the Po towards Piacenza. Giulay could not get the thought of the first Bonaparte out of his head. He believed the French were going to cross the river and turn his flank. He pushed a reconnaissance to the south of Pavia and suffered a defeat at Montebello (May 20th).

Napoleon III then decided to follow Jomini's plan. He strung his troops out on a flank march to the north to fall on the Austrian

---

[1] Bapst, *Canrobert*, II, 265.
[2] "We need onion seeds for the King of Sardinia's guns! We need onion seeds for the King of Piedmont's guns."

right. On the way Palestro was taken by the Piedmontese and held against counter-attacks by the French Zouaves, who named Victor Emmanuel a "corporal" in their corps that evening (May 30th) amid great acclaim. With his waggish bravery the King had, in fact, been the hero of the day.

Giulay fell back behind the Ticino to block the road to Milan. The French followed. MacMahon crossed the river at Turbigo, where his Algerian riflemen, the "Turcos," fought magnificently. Thence he advanced, fighting all the way, upon Magenta. Espinasse seized the San Martino bridge, but farther along was stopped by a deep canal, the "big Naviglio." For that matter the whole region was one great swamp, planted with acacias, willows, mulberry trees, grapevines and tall maize. On such ground visibility was closely limited and one could get about only on narrow, slippery causeways. It was an awkward terrain to lead an army into.

On the evening of June 3rd the French billeted in a triangle marked by Turbigo, Trecate and Novara. That was stringing their line too thinly. They had no idea where the Austrians were. Not till day broke did the general staff discover that they were bivouacking around Magenta.

Napoleon III had established headquarters in an inn at San Martino. He intended to wait before attacking, till MacMahon, following orders, had reached Magenta. It was just noon before the Emperor heard MacMahon's guns in the direction of Buffalora. He thereupon ordered the guard to cross the Naviglio. The "New Bridge" offered the only road and it was defended by a terrific fire. Cler's Zouaves finally managed to take it with a series of doggedly sustained attacks. So the way was open for the Guard to advance on Magenta. The Austrians, however, rallied in full force. It was four regiments already depleted and tired against the avalanche of a whole army. Cler was killed. The French fell back, foot by foot. An unexplainable miscarriage of plans—where was MacMahon? His artillery had fallen silent.

Actually there had been a blunder by Espinasse which resulted in a scattering of MacMahon's troops. Worried by the disarray, the general lost several hours reuniting his regiments. So the battle got off to a very bad start (June 4th).

Régnault de Saint-Jean d'Angély, in command of the Guard,

asked the Emperor for reenforcements. Napoleon III stared at him blankly:

"I have nothing to send you! Hold your ground."

The Grenadiers and the Zouaves faced the furious onslaught as best they could. Their defense was the feat of the day. Finally, about half-past three, a brigade of light infantry and "liners" arrived and rescued them from their plight—and it was high time. A counter-attack drove the Austrians back. Just then MacMahon's artillery began to be heard from again. He had finally reached the outskirts of Magenta.

Giulay tried a bold move. He pushed Schwarzenberg with four brigades between the Ticino and the canal with the idea of cutting the French army in halves. Canrobert and Vinoy, fighting with mad bravado, halted the manoeuvre at the village of Ponte-Vecchio. It was a desperate battle with heavy losses on both sides.

The decision, however, was to come from another section of the field—from Magenta. MacMahon attacked the town about six in the evening, throwing forward the divisions of Espinasse and La Motterouge. The Austrians were entrenched in the houses and fought desperately. Espinasse was mortally wounded. Gradually the Zouaves wore the enemy's resistance down, and finally took the little town at the point of the bayonet. That episode settled the fortunes of the whole battle. The Austrians drew back from their position at Ponte-Vecchio and retreated to the East under the fire of Auger's guns.

The Emperor had been all the while at San Martino. He did not learn of the victory till dark. Having no certain news he thought that he had been defeated.

"It's going badly, badly," he kept murmuring, at his wits' end. When Frossard brought word of success he would not believe it. Not till MacMahon's report came in did he recover confidence, find his tongue and enough life to light his first cigarette in hours and then sit down to scribble a telegram to the Empress with a piece of pencil. His joy was great, though the rambling disconnected battle had settled nothing and chance had played a large part in the victory. There had been no strategy nor even tactic. Orders had been given haphazard, producing a chaos of marching columns and stalled baggage trains. On that difficult terrain neither army had been able to use half of its effectives.

Whether from caution or from irritation at being under orders from a French general, Victor Emmanuel had held his troops ready but inactive.

The next day (June 5th), Napoleon III rode over the field. The rich plain was ploughed by cannon-balls and strewn with red and white patches—the still unburied dead. The Austrians had lost 10,200, the French, 4,530. The Emperor was overwhelmed. So much blood! So much blood!

The body of Espinasse passed in review before him, lying side by side with the body of his aide-de-camp in a closed wagon. The Emperor bared his head.

"Poor Espinasse!" he groaned.

To the victors he distributed rewards with a lavishness that corresponded with the fright he had experienced. MacMahon was made Marshal of France and Duke of Magenta. The aged Régnault de Saint-Jean d'Angély had really been the more deserving of the two, but he got his bâton second to MacMahon. Promotions, crosses, citations rained in torrents all around.

On receiving Victor Emmanuel at headquarters Napoleon III rebuked the King for his inactivity. It had thrown the whole effort on the French and, for a time, endangered the outcome of the battle.

"Sire," he said, "when one has to effect a junction in the enemy face, orders have to be strictly obeyed. One has to live up to one's task. I regret that Your Majesty did not do so yesterday."

In spite of his exuberant good nature, the King was much abashed. He apologized and promised to do better next time.

"Sire," he said, "in the next brush I insist that you place me with the advance guard."

The Emperor was mollified and invited him to luncheon.

CHAPTER XVI

Solferino

GIULAY HAD THOUGHT HIMSELF VICTORIOUS AT FIRST AND HAD SENT a dispatch to Francis Joseph announcing that "not a Frenchman was left on Lombard soil." For two days Central Europe assumed that the French had been defeated. Vienna lighted up and so did all Germany.

The Austrians, actually, continued withdrawing to the East, leaving Milan uncovered. The oldest inhabitants in the capital of Lombardy still remembered the dazzling entry of Bonaparte, and French and Italian banners appeared on all houses. Napoleon III made his entry on June 8th, side by side with Victor Emmanuel, and established headquarters at the Villa Bonaparte. Milan gave them a fair ▓▓▓▓e, but to arouse enthusiasms to higher pitch the Emperor ▓▓▓ered an address "to the Italians," which was exceedingly imprudent:

"My army will confine itself to holding your enemies in check and to maintaining order. It will in no way interfere with manifestations of your legitimate desires. Rally to the flag of King Victor Emmanuel! Be soldiers today one and all, and tomorrow you will be free citizens of a great country!"

Such language was only too well calculated to fire a people already overwrought. Napoleon III was soon to perceive the consequences of his words. Tuscany had already passed under Piedmontese rule. Parma, Modena and Romagna were hatching insurrections. Forgetting his promises Cavour was driving an Italy in tumult towards unification rather than towards liberty. The Emperor must have foreseen that as soon as the Austrians evacuated Bologna and Ravenna the flag of the Pope would be lowered. At Plombières, to be sure, he had consented to the mutilation of the Papal States, but now he was beginning to see how much unrest was being created in France by even a partial spoliation of the pontiff.

The Catholics were crying treason and business was fearing political repercussions. The ministers had been kept in perfect ignorance of what the Emperor was doing. The Empress lacked the experience required for her office as Regent and was frightened by her responsibilities. All Paris was hoping for an early peace. Irritation and ill-will could be seen rising in Europe. Queen Victoria was openly accusing the Emperor, wondering whether "he were not trying to make himself master of the continent." [1] Germany was on the alert. The King of Prussia was proposing armed intervention and had mobilized four army corps. Russia objected to the idea of a revolution in Hungary that Napoleon III and Kossuth were working on, in hopes of taking Austria in the rear and paralyzing her. Dangers everywhere! Napoleon III was only too sensible of them. What he had already seen of the war disgusted him and he too began to wish it were over. His aide-de-camp, Fleury, confessed as much in a private letter:

"The practical difficulties of the war have already worn the Emperor out and brought him back a long way from his idea of commanding a great army. . . . He is well aware that the same telegraph wire that told you of the victory at Magenta barely missed announcing a most terrible defeat."

On June 23rd the Emperor and Victor Emmanuel were taking a pleasure ride along the shore of the Lake of Garda, inspecting incidentally the allied positions. Stopping on a hilltop Napoleon III drew a letter from his pocket and read it to the King. It was from the Empress. It warned that the Prussian army was concentrating at Cologne and Coblenz and begged the Emperor to treat for peace or else send part of the army back to France. The King listened in silence, and then they rode down into the valley, gloomily, side by side.

Unfortunately the victory at Magenta had not been decisive enough to induce Austria to lay down her arms. The White Coats had evacuated Lombardy and Romagna and concentrated along the Mincio in front of the Quadrilateral on the borders of Venetia. That was a formidable position. They had received reenforcements

[1] Retranslated.

so that the Austrian army now numbered 180,000 men, with Emperor Francis Joseph in personal command.

The Austrian supply service was far superior to that of the French, who had pursued the enemy indifferently, through the heat and the dust, by way of Brescia. Napoleon III's men were without biscuits and without coffee. The region supplied corn meal in abundance for polenta. But the French soldiers had no appetite for the famous Italian dish and emptied the pots that were filled with it into the ditches on the roadsides. Four million bandages for wounds had been sent from France in sealed cases. They went astray in transit and were not found again until after the war. Wounded French soldiers had their wounds dressed with strips torn from their shirts. The Emperor donated his own linen, even down to his handkerchiefs. It was cut into bandages, and sent to the field-hospitals.

The first outpost skirmishes occurred on that same day, June 23rd. Little attention was paid to them. The Austrians recrossed the Mincio and took solid hold of a strong position to the south of the Lake of Garda on a group of steep-bluffed hills near the village of Solferino. The French, hardly four miles distant, did not suspect this movement, nor did anyone foresee the battle that was to result the next day from the collision of two armies that were marching in opposite directions.

French and Piedmontese had about 150,000 men, divided into six army corps. Niel had imprudently gone too far ahead. He carried Medole and was thenceforward outflanked on both sides. MacMahon had started out from Castiglione. He halted before the Cavriana spur, which was strongly held by the enemy. Baraguay d'Hilliers, on MacMahon's left, was the only allied general to have shown a little foresight. He attacked the hills which rise one behind the other in front of Solferino. Further to the north, near Pozzolegno, the Piedmontese were halted by Benedeck's vigorous defense. So four separate battles started simultaneously on an eight-mile front.

Napoleon III climbed the bell-tower of the church in Castiglione and studied them through his field glass, trying to think of a way to tie them together. Finally, with the idea of cutting the enemy's line in two, he ordered the main effort to be aimed at the tower of Solferino, the famous "Spia of Italy," that rose red and square from

NAPOLEON III AT SOLFERINO

In this battle, France and Sardinia defeated Austria, June 24, 1859

Painting by Meissonier

the summit of a rocky cliff. Nearby a white cemetery glistened, framed with a procession of black cypress trees.

The struggle continued for hours under a smothering sky that hung low with imminent storm. The Austrians had the advantage on either flank. The Piedmontese were beaten on the left by Benedeck. On the right, Niel was in great danger near Medole through Canrobert's failure to support him in time. But in the center, after a bitter fight, the steep heights of Solferino, the cemetery, the Spia, were captured. MacMahon then marched on Cavriana where Francis Joseph had fixed his headquarters. He took Monte Fontana, the key to the position, suffering heavy losses. A counter-attack drove him out, then back he came, only to be ejected a second time.

It was a critical moment and Fleury saw the danger. The Emperor was looking on as in a daze, giving no orders.

"Sire," cried Fleury, "this is taking a long time. . . . We must not lose that hill. Don't do what your uncle did at the Moskowa! Send your Guard in! There's no time to lose."

The Emperor turned to Régnault de Saint-Jean d'Angély and ordered in the last division of the Guard, the grenadiers and Mellinct's Zouaves. They attacked like men possessed and the enemy finally had to give way. Little by little the French reached the top of all the heights, and then shortly MacMahon and the Guard entered Cavriana.

So the Emperor's simple but sound strategy was justified. The Austrian line was cut in two. A furious storm of hail and rain broke, coming from the direction of the lake. It put any continuance of the fighting out of the question. Francis Joseph feared that his flank would be turned. He took advantage of the lull to order a retreat. Napoleon III was for starting in pursuit, and very soundly: There was a chance to annihilate the Austrian army. MacMahon dissuaded him on the ground that the French troops were too tired and hungry. The enemy was therefore allowed quietly to withdraw to the other bank of the Mincio. The French had lost 12,000 men, the Piedmontese 5,600, the Austrians more than 22,000, with thirty guns.

That evening Napoleon III occupied the headquarters of Francis Joseph at Cavriana and ate his dinner there. He dictated the day's bulletin and sent a brief dispatch to the Empress:

"A great battle, a great victory."

And he made Niel a marshal.

The next morning the Emperor again toured the battlefield, and his horror at the carnage was even more terrible than it had been at Montebello or Magenta. There lay a glorious landscape dotted with smiling villages, ennobled with myrtle and cypress, crowned with the white coronet of Alps; yet the roads, the ravines, the hills, the meadows, the rice-fields, were littered with dead bodies, most of which had already been robbed by prowlers, or else with wounded men who were still writhing or groaning. The weather was hot and muggy. Many of the dead faces had already blackened. Some lay with open mouths and seemed to laugh. Flies were swarming everywhere in clouds.

Napoleon III entered a field-hospital that had been improvised in a barn half ruined by cannon balls. He gazed at the scene with a pale face and clenched teeth: a frightful stench, cries of pain, gasping, dying men; surgeons, dripping with blood and perspiration—they cut into quivering flesh and tossed bits of arms and legs aside, this way and that, indifferently. The Emperor broke into a cold sweat and all but fainted. Mastering himself with great effort he managed to utter a few encouraging words, then, with tears streaming down his face, wearily mounted his horse. He rode back to Cavriana with his eyes closed.

CHAPTER XVII

Villafranca

THE AUSTRIANS RETREATED BEYOND THE ADIGE. INSTEAD OF HURRY-
ing after them the armies of France and Piedmont lay inactive for a
week. Typhus was raging—though of this the public heard not a
word. The sick were more numerous than the wounded. A fourth
of all the effectives crowded the public buildings of Brescia and
Milan. Food was completely lacking. The people in Brescia lived
on fruits and vegetables, setting all bread aside for the hospitals.

Though a more clean-cut victory had been won at Solferino than
at Magenta, the army showed much less enthusiasm. The men were
worn out. Disorderly, breaking discipline, they cursed the generals
because no decisive engagement had yet been fought. Ahead of
them now lay the necessity of taking the forts of the Quadrilateral,
by siege probably, and the Adige would have to be crossed. The
enemy remained intact, and as he drew back nearer to his bases he
would be more and more strongly reinforced. There was a plan to
take Venice by sea, and the squadron of Admiral Romain-Desfossés
entered the Adriatic and seized the island of Lossini. But from the
general staff down to the humblest infantryman it was clearly realized that now the war was entering upon a long and difficult phase.

"As I see it," Fleury wrote, "this victory should open the way
rather to diplomacy. The longer we wait the more lives will be lost.
War is a grand thing to look at at a distance; it nets profits for the
generals-in-chief and glory, perhaps, for the nation that needs glory.
But all that is at the cost of many tears."

And that frank and wideawake soldier concluded:

"Butcheries of this sort are not in the spirit of our times."

The uneasiness that was general throughout the army was a mere
orchestration of the Emperor's personal uneasiness. Not only did
the spectacle of war rend his heart. He was more and more afraid

that Cavour would overstep the treaty, raise all Italy and annex it to Piedmont. The dukes of Parma and Modena had been obliged to flee. Bologna had driven out the Papal legate. In all these districts agents of Victor Emmanuel were exercising power in his name. There was a still graver and more pressing danger: Prussia was hastening mobilization. Czar Alexander had sent Schouvalov, his aide-de-camp, to the Empress to tell her:

"Make peace at once! Otherwise you are going to be attacked on the Rhine."

Then Schouvalov had gone on from Paris to Italy, meeting Napoleon III on July 4th at his headquarters at Valeggio.

The Czar's good offices, meantime, stopped at that warning. The new Palmerston-Russell cabinet in England was much more favorable to Italy than the Derby ministry had been; but English aid could not be counted on in the event of war with Prussia. At that moment, moreover, British opinion was violently hostile to France because a number of propagandists were accusing her of preparing an invasion of the United Kingdom.

Walewski and Randon were even more thoroughly frightened than the Empress. France could muster no more than five divisions, composed largely of conscripts, to defend its Eastern border. Ex-King Jerome and the majority of the ministers proposed mobilizing 300,000 National Guards to resist an eventual attack on the Rhine. The Empress refused to "sign before all Europe such a confession of military impotence."

Jerome rose in the full midst of the Council and said:

"My dear niece, you are ruining France. You are laying us open to invasion."

"In any case," she replied, "I shall not do what Marie-Louise did. Even if you were to advise me to, I should never flee before the enemy."

That was to be the last appearance in politics of the sometime King of Westphalia. He was to die the following year.

Each day brought Napoleon III new and increasingly urgent dispatches from Paris:

"Treat! We have got to treat with Austria!"

These pleas corresponded with his secret wishes and he was encouraged in the same direction by Prince Napoleon. The latter

could not stand the heat in Italy and kept saying that prolonging
the campaign might lead to some defeat.

But what of the Emperor's promise to liberate Italy as far as the
Adriatic? He was now aware of what a great blunder his first proc-
lamation had been. Persigny had returned to London to replace
Pélissier. Napoleon III asked him to request Palmerston to mediate
—on the basis of a cession of Lombardy to Victor Emmanuel, while
Venetia and Modena would be given to an archduke.

England held off. Palmerston, the Emperor's friend of a day gone
by, had now conceived a keen dislike for a man who could think
of nothing but remodelling the world, and who was always walking
a tightrope strung between absolutism and revolution.

"Napoleon's mind," he said contemptuously, "is a rabbit warren.
It has a litter of new ideas every other day."

Disappointed again in that direction the Emperor decided to
communicate directly with his antagonist, Francis Joseph. That
would be betraying Cavour and it would exasperate the patriots in
Italy; but his first duty was towards France.

On the evening of July 6th he called Fleury and ordered him to
go to Verona and deliver a letter to the Emperor of Austria. The
letter proposed an armistice which "would provide time for diplomatic negotiation of conditions of peace."

The move might have seemed chivalrous. In actual fact it was
merely irregular and quite obviously manifested the Emperor's
eagerness to treat. Luckily Francis Joseph was as bad a diplomat as
he was a general.

At Verona Fleury was received by a tall young man, slender, fair-
haired, with a bright face framed in side whiskers. The tall young
man was in uniform—a blue tunic and grey linen trousers.

Napoleon III's proposal astonished the Austrian Emperor. He
asked for time to think it over. Fleury bowed, but found a way to
intimate that a prompt reply would be necessary. The French fleet
had captured Lossini and was about to open the attack on Venice.

The next morning Francis Joseph handed him a letter. He was
accepting the armistice.

"Good news!" cried the aide-de-camp, entering Napoleon III's
study—and he caught a look of great relief that flitted across the
Emperor's face.

The armistice was signed on July 9th and it was agreed that the two Emperors would meet the next day at Villafranca, a town lying between Verona and Valeggio.

Leaving his mounted escort to wait on a dusty road that was lined with mulberry trees, Napoleon III rode chivalrously on beyond Villafranca to meet the young Emperor. They shook hands and stepped into a house by the roadside where they were left alone together.

The conversation was cordiality itself. They exchanged expressions of regard and compliments on the bravery of their respective troops. Napoleon III was considerate, obliging. He formulated not so much conditions as hopes. Francis Joseph seemed captivated. He bore France no ill-will. His grudge was against Piedmont. He gave frank answers in the matter of terms. He accepted all of Napoleon III's proposals—at least almost all.

"I have lost Lombardy," he said, "and I am willing to give it up. But I won't cede it to Piedmont. I will give it to France to do with as she sees fit."

He intended to keep Venetia. He would make reforms in the government there that would leave the country "not merely satisfied, but happy." Yes, he agreed, Parma could go to Piedmont, but Modena and Florence should be returned to their princes. There would be no difficulty about an Italian Confederation under the presidency of the Pope; and of course, a European conference could arrange any matters which were found to have been left unsettled.

In his faith in the constructive possibilities of European conferences Napoleon III was more than half a century ahead of his time.

The two rulers were mutually charmed with each other by the time they came to separate. That very evening Prince Napoleon delivered the preliminary articles to Francis Joseph for his signature.

Victor Emmanuel knew about the offer of an armistice. The Emperor had not consulted him on the matter of terms. When Napoleon III revealed them to him, he flew into a rage of disappointment.

"Poor Italy!" he cried. "You mean to say—we are not to have Venetia, Mantua, Peschiera, Modena? What a disaster!" [1]

He seemed about to create a scene, then suddenly mastered him-

---

[1] Maurice Paléologue, *Cavour*, 244-45.

self; and quite as much out of political tactic as of concern for his personal dignity, he assured Napoleon III that, in spite of his distress, he would not forget the service that the Emperor had rendered the cause of Italy. The Emperor could rely on his faithful friendship.

Returning to his headquarters at Monzambano Victor Emmanuel told Cavour the news. Cavour was not the man to be brow-beaten. The evening before he had made a scene at the mere news of the armistice, even going so far as to call his master names. Now he started to tear to shreds the agreement that Victor Emmanuel was bringing him:

"You are not going to sign such a paper! Why, it's disgraceful! You must go on with the struggle, even without France. If you are beaten—well—you can abdicate!"

The King had grown accustomed to familiarity on Cavour's part, though often it was carried too far. He now drew himself up and bade his minister be silent:

"I shall not allow you to repeat your insolences of last evening."

"Then I beg Your Majesty to accept my resignation."

"I accept it. You may go."

When Cavour had left the room, the King, still fuming, said to La Marmora:

"Cavour is a bully. He has been out of his head for a long time now. Since he is going of his own choice, I am not in the least sorry to be rid of him." [1]

After vainly trying to see Napoleon III, Cavour set out for Turin to await the designation of his successor. He delivered himself of torrents of complaint and abuse of Napoleon III, and public opinion was with him. Flags were flown from windows at half mast. In deliberate insult to the French sovereign shops again exhibited chromos of Orsini. Some Italians, however, manifested more understanding, seeing the real cause for the Emperor's hasty peace in the attitude of Germany. Della Rocca said:

"Napoleon knows what he is doing. He would not do this if he were not obliged to."

And Garibaldi, no less, in a proclamation to his Red Shirts urged:

"Do not forget the gratitude we owe to Napoleon III and to the

[1] Ollivier, *op. cit.,* IV, 249.

French army, so many of whose brave boys have been killed or wounded in the Italian cause."

On his way back to France Napoleon III touched Milan and then Turin. In the capital of Piedmont he received a dramatically cold welcome in all but deserted streets. At that moment it all came home to him. Vainly had he caused so much French blood to be shed, vainly had he estranged his friends in Europe. Italy would never forgive him for his betrayal of her hopes.

Cavour refused to attend the farewell banquet. Napoleon III sent for him and in a long conversation tried to justify himself to the man to whom he was bound in a complicity grounded on too many written and spoken words:

"I cannot think of our separating in a quarrel. I simply could not continue the campaign. It would have required 300,000 men. I did not have them."

He promised Cavour that at his European Conference he would plead the cause of the Italian provinces that had been restored to their princes; and he added that, since Piedmont had not received all the increase in territories provided for, he would give up the idea of annexing Nice and Savoy.

He left Italy by way of Susa and the Mount Cenis, dissatisfied with himself and leaving no regrets behind him.

"Ouf!" said Victor Emmanuel. "He's gone!"

At home in France he found an atmosphere of surprise and tension. No one understood his abrupt right-about. His victories had been noisily advertised. To have abandoned Venice in the face of them looked like a gross backdown. Napoleon III avoided Paris, therefore, and went directly to Saint-Cloud, where he could be sure of receiving an official ovation.

Morny and Baroche praised his moderation and wisdom. Troplong ventured to compare him with Scipio Africanus, who had refused to destroy Carthage after winning at Zama. The Emperor answered them with an avowal that sounded strange indeed on the lips of the head of a state:

"After a glorious campaign of two months the struggle was about to change radically in character. . . . I was called upon to make a frontal attack on an enemy entrenched behind great fortresses. I faced a Europe in arms. I would have had to accept battle on the Rhine as well as on the Adige. Speaking quite frankly, I should have found myself obliged to seek the support of the revolution everywhere. I halted, not through fatigue, not from faltering in loyalty to the noble cause that I was serving, but because there was something that spoke more imperatively in my heart—the interests of France."

The interests of France! But why had he not thought of those interests—the real interests—of France in the first place? Such the question that a less fawning audience might have put to him. But then the Emperor added apologetically:

"I made war against the will of Europe in order to serve the cause of Italian independence. When the destinies of my country were imperilled I made peace."

A strange situation, that of a ruler who claims to be victorious but feels obliged so insistently to justify himself! And in that one is faced with all the mysteriousness of that complicated personality, in which sentiment was always catching reason off guard.

All the same, the address was well received. The country saw some comfort in it and sighed with relief, happy to see its boys come home.

The returning troops paraded the boulevards on August 14th with the Emperor at their head. Eugénie and the members of the imperial household were crowded together with the ministers and the dignitaries on a platform in the Place Vendôme. Arriving in front of them Napoleon III halted and saluted with his sword. At a signal from the Emperor Fleury picked up the Prince Imperial and handed him to the Emperor, who seated him on his saddle in front of him. Together they reviewed the passing regiments. The child, three years old, wore the red and blue uniform of the Grenadiers of the Guard. He had the fair hair and the blue eyes of his mother, but the Emperor's good-natured mouth.

As the city shook with cheers, infantrymen, Turcos, artillerymen, marched by at the double-quick, following battle flags that were soiled with gunpowder and shredded by bullets. The crowds called the generals by name as they went by—Canrobert, MacMahon, Baraguay d'Hilliers. They acknowledged, happily. The Emperor was radiant with joy. The child whom he held pressed against his chest clapped his hands ecstatically.

The Zouaves got a tremendous ovation. They had been the heroes of the campaign. Their dash and doggedness had brought both victory and peace. A mere rag bleached by sun and rain was all the standard they had left. Canvas breeches torn and patched and faded jackets were their only uniform. But their eyes sparkled and they carried their heads high. They marched proudly, each with a flower in the muzzle of his gun, their ranks thinned out to leave the places of fallen comrades unfilled. There is a certain frenzy of enthusiasm of which Paris alone in the world is capable. It roared in the ears of the Zouaves that day. The little Prince caught fire from the emotion about him. He took off his Legion of Honor ribbon and threw it to the Zouaves. One of them snatched it up and it passed from hand to hand among the marching men till the colonel, finally, without stopping, pinned it to their battle flag.

That moment of happiness and glory marked the peak of the whole extraordinary adventure. It wiped out everything—the mistakes of yesterday, the worries of the morrow. At that moment the Empire seemed unshakable for generations to come. A certitude of grandeur seemed to descend in the bright sunlight from the Corsican standing on his column upon the lovely child whom the crowds adored.

With his cup of happiness thus overflowing the Emperor, in all sincerity but also with an eye to his advantage, moved to efface all memories of civil strife. The next day was his birthday. He marked it by a general amnesty valid for all exiles. Some of them were too proud, or too shrewd, to accept pardon of Napoleon the Little, but most of them returned. At the same time the *Moniteur* announced a reduction in the standing army—a gesture that emphasized an intent of peace on the part of the government that seemed at last to echo a more and more eager yearning on the part of the country.

CHAPTER XVIII

The Hornet's Nest

JOY MAY DISTRACT FROM A DISCOMFORT. IT DOES NOT REMOVE ITS cause. That brilliant campaign, so soon over, brought a serious problem to France and to all Europe. The Italian hornet's nest had been rashly stirred. It now buzzed and hummed frenziedly.

Cavour was replaced by La Marmora and Victor Emmanuel recalled his agents from Bologna, Florence, Modena, and Parma; but the peoples of those districts would not hear of any restoration of their princes. They peppered Paris with delegations, imploring the Emperor to allow them to unite with Piedmont. Walewski received them coldly, distantly, but the Emperor's demeanor encouraged them in their hopes. Arese appeared in his turn at Saint-Cloud and worked upon Napoleon III with all the weight of their common memories. The Emperor was at first resolved to oppose any modification of status in central Italy, but finally came around to admitting that Parma might go to Victor Emmanuel. He still held out on the other points. But Tuscany voted the house of Lorraine out of office. Then Bologna, Modena, and Florence demanded annexation to Piedmont. Worn out, bored with the whole business, the Emperor felt himself caught in a tangle that it seemed impossible to unravel. He finally yielded to pestering by Arese and remonstrances from Prince Napoleon, Conneau and Pietri, and in a letter to Victor Emmanuel, which was made public, promised that "he would support the aspirations of central Italy at the forthcoming conference."

But those aspirations became more and more comprehensive with each passing day. The Italian patriots thought they would be able to force the hand of Napoleon III and the hand of Victor Emmanuel too. For their better defense the four states in question formed a military league and the man really at the head of it was Garibaldi.

They set up a common government and offered its presidency to the Prince of Carignano, a cousin of the King. When Napoleon expressed his disapproval of this arrangement, the Prince simply handed his powers over to Buoncompagni, the former commissioner. That was a mere change in names. Under the outward form lurked an actual annexation.

What at bottom disturbed the Emperor most was not the establishment of Piedmont in the duchies, or in Tuscany where he reasonably hoped to see his cousin Napoleon made king. It was the seizure of Romagna. No district in Italy counted for so much in his memory—his brother had died at Forlì. At his farewell banquet in Turin Napoleon III could not help replying to Pepoli, his cousin, that a vote by the people of Romagna would be respected.

But that was the same as saying that the Legations would be separated from the patrimony of Saint Peter. From the standpoint of the French Catholics the agreement they had made with the Emperor was thus being violated in its very essence. Monsignor Dupanloup, the Bishop of Orleans, protested. Monsignor Pie, bishop of Poitiers and adviser to the Comte de Chambord, a bold and spirited standard-bearer of ultramontanism, launched a first fire-raft in the form of a pastoral letter. His example was followed by many prelates. Veuillot published their complaints in *L'Univers*. The police told him to stop printing them or else they would close his paper.

On a trip home to Paris from Biarritz, Napoleon III passed through Bordeaux, where Cardinal Donnet sermonized him vigorously:

"Sire, stand faithful to a Christian policy which has brought blessings upon your name and may well be the secret of the prosperity of your reign."

The Emperor replied in some embarrassment that the temporal power of the Pope could easily be reconciled with freedom for Italy. Did he really think so? He had such a capacity for self-deception! He thought, and in all sincerity it would seem, that his famous European conference would bring some order out of the chaos in which Italy was writhing.

But no one cared a fig for his European conference. The final treaties were signed at Zurich. They contained financial provisions which had been adopted in principle only, at Villafranca: Piedmont would pay forty million florins to Austria as an indemnity for the territory seized and sixty millions to France as a contribution to French expenses. But as soon as that matter was out of the way, the powers who were approached on the subject of the conference evaded one by one. England was annoyed that a treaty should have been concluded without consulting her. She disapproved of the peace as she had of the war. Lord John Russell, head of the Foreign Office, was the preponderant influence in the Palmerston cabinet. He came out clearly in favor of Italian unification, partly through aversion to the Pope, partly to spite France.

Austria continued to plead for the impossible—she wanted her Italian henchmen restored. Even Russia was irritated by Napoleon III's enterprising spirit. "If the man isn't stopped," said the Czar, "he will end by turning Europe inside out"—and St. Petersburg moved over closer to Austria. As for Prussia, Prussia said nothing. So France found herself more and more alone. With a general satisfaction in Europe that nobody was at any pains to conceal she was left to stew in her own juice.

Just then (December 22, 1859) the Emperor was impelled by his usual mania for pamphleteering to publish a brochure which he had virtually dictated to La Guéronnière: *Le Pape et le Congrès*. Its very anonymity was a sort of declaration of authorship. Napoleon III once more thought that he was on the threshold of a new era in his reign, and for a sort of preface to it, he decided to impart to the European public at large his views on the Roman question.

Deferential in tone, audacious in substance, the pamphlet declared that the temporal power of the Pope could not be brought in question. It was necessary. It had to be retained. On the other hand, it could be considered safe from attack only as it was limited in extent. Sovereignty over Rome and the immediate environs was enough to guarantee the pontiff's freedom. How could he need courts, an army, a governmental bureaucracy? His status as a petty Italian Prince had never brought him anything but annoyances, while it had unquestionably diminished his incomparable prestige as the spiritual ruler of mankind. Henceforth no concerns of a worldly nature should impair his moral authority. It would be the function of the forthcoming conference to give formal recognition to this great reform.

The sensation was tremendous—but what was the use of a conference now? "Napoleon had had his conference all by himself," said the English. And, in fact, gropingly at first, then brusquely, the Emperor had found his way out of the dilemma that had been gripping him. As between the traditional spirit and the modern spirit he had made his choice following the logic of his origins. Events had caught him off guard? Very well—he would double on his tracks and adapt his policy to events. At bottom it had always been that way with him, and it would ever be. He was less inclined to planning out of his own head than was generally supposed. Not infrequently he let himself be guided by "the needs of the moment." His own life had shown him with plenty to spare that a trend in events was uncontrollable.

Meantime his conflict with the Catholics grew more and more venomous. Grumblings, recriminations, insults, came flooding in from all hands. Monsignor Dupanloup published a brilliant and forceful refutation of La Guéronnière. L'Univers thought of a scheme to publish a series of petitions and "allocutions" to the Pope. It received a new and more pointed warning. Napoleon III was angered by this opposition and wrote in his own hand to the Pope, urging him "to resign himself to sacrificing the provinces that had revolted from him" and to "entrust" them to Victor Emmanuel.

The better to emphasize this change in outlook, Napoleon III recast his ministry. Walewski had all along been opposed to the enterprise in Italy and his heckling had been a good deal of a nuisance. Finally he lost his patience entirely and went so far as to write to his master:

"A sovereign cannot do without ministers to act as his agents and representatives. When he deals directly with members of the diplomatic corps or with agents official or unofficial, he paralyzes the development of his own policy. . . . The Times says that the doorkeeper at the Ministry knows as much as I do about the policies of Your Majesty."

These criticisms were only too well founded and they add stature to Walewski as a man.

Napoleon replaced him with Thouvenel, the ambassador at Constantinople, a good diplomat, who drew up reports in a fine literary style. Billault came back to the Ministry of the Interior, succeeding the Duke of Padua, who was considered a shade too ultramontane. By those choices the Emperor intended to indicate to the Catholics that if they were thinking of a fight, he would find ways to attend to them.

As was to be expected the Pope made a stiff reply to Napoleon's suggestion. He had already called the Emperor's pamphlet "a remarkable specimen of hypocrisy." He was to go farther and say, publicly losing his temper, that the Emperor Napoleon was just a liar and a knave:

"I have ceased to believe in the word he gives. What can he do to the Pope? Nothing whatever! To the man Mastaï? Everything, perhaps. But in that case I shall flee to the tomb of the Apostles. There he may have me seized in my pontifical robes, but he will learn to his cost what it means to lay hand to those vestments. The hour of judgment has sounded for him. The sword of the Almighty is drawn to smite him by the hands of men!"

As Pius IX viewed the matter, Charlemagne had turned Nebuchadnezzar.

On the 19th of January the Pope issued an encyclical ordering the bishops to rouse their faithful for the struggle of maintaining the integrity of the patrimony of Saint Peter. L'Univers courageously published it, thereby signing its own death warrant. Thouvenel protested vigorously against the encyclical in a circular letter to the prefects, but the Catholics were not frightened and continued their agitation. A number of prelates made an effort to patch things up, Monsignor de Bonnechose, archbishop of Rouen, Monsignor Morlot, archbishop of Paris, Monsignor Régnier, archbishop of Cambrai; but all they got from the Emperor was a courteous reception. The majority of the bishops had come out squarely for the Papal cause, following the lead of the Pies and the Dupanloups. Their hostility was the more dangerous in that a number of important laymen stood by them, Falloux, Cochin, the Duc de Broglie, Thiers, Guizot, Saint-Marc Girardin, Villemain.

The wealthy bourgeoisie did not like the Emperor's policy, and the Academy pointed its disagreement by electing to its membership a distinguished monk, Lacordaire. When Falloux, the director of the Academy, went, according to custom, to ask for the Emperor's approval of Father Lacordaire's election, Napoleon III spoke his mind with the utmost freedom. He complained of the attacks of the clergy:

"They take no account of the difficulties I have to deal with.

Just as though I could do exactly as I please in all these complicated matters! I have always been bound to the cause of Italy. I cannot turn my guns on her."

Falloux dropped a word about religious persecution. The Emperor retorted vigorously:

"There is no religious persecution whatever, nor will there be while I am on the throne."

With one of its natural props thus cut from under it, the imperial government was obliged to move closer to the liberals, and it inspired periodicals of an anti-clerical or republican hue—*Le Siècle, La Presse, L'Opinion nationale*—to attack the Pope.

Napoleon III was always extremely sensitive to expressions of public opinion. That, perhaps, was why he always tried, somewhat naïvely, to control it. In a conversation one day with Prokesch, the friend of the King of Rome, he dropped a remark that illumines one whole side of his policy.

"I am not the least interested in finding out whether public opinion is right or wrong on one or another of the big questions of the day. What I want to know is whether there is an opinion. On that point I must make no mistake and harbor no misapprehension. Otherwise I am lost." [1]

A most damaging admission on the part of a ruling sovereign!

So Napoleon III had now come to depend on his sometime opponents, and in making that tactical move he was probably not aware that the road on which he was entering was destined to lead him step by step away from his dictatorial system of government. The force that threw the inner structure of the regime off balance was the Roman question.

Was it a mere coincidence? The day after Pius IX touched off the powder magazine with his encyclical, Victor Emmanuel recalled Cavour.

During his six months in retirement Cavour had continued as the leader and guiding spirit of the unification movement in Italy. His King restored him to power less by personal inclination than of necessity. Victor Emmanuel too had to bow to the march of events. If he were to become King of Italy he had to place himself under the ferrule of the master, obtaining, at the very most, a solemn

---

[1] E. Denis, *La fondation de l'Empire allemand.*

pledge on Cavour's part that he would meddle no further in the King's private life.

Cavour took the two basic portfolios, Foreign Affairs and the Interior, and at once proclaimed aloud the right of the peoples of Italy to determine their own destinies—so giving the full measure of the consequences resulting from Napoleon III's new attitude. Cavour ordered his agents in Romagna, Tuscany, and the duchies to "rush demonstrations" in favor of union with Piedmont. "Take a menacing attitude," he said. "Before long I shall have to seem to have lost control of the situation."

With the powerful backing of Lord John Russell, Cavour then set out to force Napoleon III's hand. He sent Arese to the Emperor and the cunning Nigra, who was thenceforward to represent Piedmont in Paris. Napoleon III was caught between the driving force of Cavour, the bitterness of England and the veiled contempt of Austria. He wriggled about in a confusion which he sought vainly to disguise. He wanted all sorts of things: He wanted to get Tuscany out of the clutches of Piedmont. He wanted a reconciliation with the Pope, and through the Pope, with the French Catholics; finally, if there were going to be annexations in spite of everything, he wanted back the old "tip" that had evaporated in his very hands— Nice and Savoy. Vainly he sought to frighten Cavour with a sort of ultimatum that was really a pat on the cheek. Cavour replied by making preparations for a plebiscite, of the results of which he could be altogether certain beforehand.

Three months of confusion followed, three months of intriguing, bargaining, trading, double-crossing. Thouvenel played a clever hand in all this. To the contrary of Walewski he was in favor of aggrandizement for Piedmont provided France were to get some tangible consideration in return for her support of Cavour. Not conceiving that his country could have two different policies at the same time, his own and the Emperor's, Thouvenel tried to circumscribe and express Napoleon III's thought. "He was ready," as Ollivier said, "to retire if he felt at any point that he could not conscientiously adhere to it."

Thouvenel was a man of native good taste and fine education. He had a deep sense of duty. Physical ailments gave him in early youth an appearance of advanced age; but he performed great services for the state and it is to be regretted that Napoleon III did not retain him longer. He was the best foreign minister that the Second Empire produced, and the only one who had not merely opinions but firmness of character.

Finally the ambiguous situation cleared: the two cronies of Plombières got together again. Cavour was to have Tuscany, Napoleon III Savoy and Nice. But England very properly felt that she had been deceived by Napoleon III's repeated assurances of disinterestedness. She was greatly provoked. The proposed increase in French territory was very slight and in its favor it had considerations of race and history and the desires of the inhabitants involved. But to England it looked like a threat. The great surge of wrath that swept London was strong enough to make one think one was back in the days of Pitt. Influenced by English opinion the little countries nearby thought they were endangered too, or at least pretended to think so. Switzerland protested at great length. Belgium looked to her defenses and strengthened ties with Holland.

Napoleon III strained every nerve to recapture the good will of Europe. As far as the British Cabinet was concerned, he failed. He had completely lost countenance in English eyes. He went to Baden for a talk with the Regent of Prussia but succeeded in appeasing him in appearances only. The basic sentiment in Germany was definitely against him. Austria and Russia manifested either indifference or superciliousness.

On March 22, 1860, Modena, Parma, Tuscany, and the Legations were incorporated with Piedmont. At the end of April, Savoy and Nice became French following an almost unanimous plebiscite. So Napoleon III had at last obtained a visible success for his regime, but he had paid for it by a loss in personal esteem. Knowing neither the art of giving nor of refusing, unable either to keep a promise or resist a threat, he had lost much of the dazzling prestige he had acquired during the first years of his reign. A champion of Italian independence, he had abandoned Italy. A mainstay of religion, he was helping to despoil his pontiff—and losing the support of the Church he was about to discover that he would be obliged to change the nature of his government. The guardian of French security, he had set up on the very flank of France a new and powerful state which was already replacing gratitude with greed. All of Europe had come to regard him as a menace. The alliance with England had been the hub of his foreign policy. It was now virtually broken and was never to be resoldered. During the summer of that year, 1860, in a conversation with his old friend, Lord Clarendon, Napoleon III asked:

"Why has England lost her confidence in me?"

"Because all the declarations Your Majesty has made to us have been repudiated the day following. Your tactics of sudden reversals create universal uneasiness. Every morning when one wakes up, one wonders what new surprises you have cooked up for the world during the night."

"Well then . . . what? All I could do would be to crawl into my shell and take no interest in anything?"

"That would be a very wise policy indeed, and if Your Majesty were to follow it ever so little, our trust would come back to you in very short order." [1]

Napoleon III was not the man to follow any such advice. One can hardly help thinking, in this connection, of an association that was first made by Mérimée, one of the habitual guests at dinners at the Tuileries. Napoleon III reminded Mérimée of the sorcerer's apprentice in Herodotus, who could, by using the magical rigmaroles he had learned, set blind and dark-working forces in motion but afterwards had no means of controlling them. Napoleon III, too, uttered words of dark and terrible magic—emancipations of peoples, rights of nationality—and the world trembled, crevices opened in the social structure, torrents of events came rushing down the mill-race of history; and he could do nothing to halt the surge. For all of his efforts the irresistible flood swept him aside, washed him up on the shore, whence sorrowfully he was to be allowed to gaze on the gradual unfolding of the catastrophic consequences which, unbeknown to him, had been implicit in his initial miracle. After Villafranca only the most resolute will could have muzzled Piedmont and struck a proper balance between Italian aspirations and the legitimate interests of the Church. Napoleon III had never possessed a will so steadfast and never would develop one. His mind was a stewpot of contradictory impulses and ideals. May he, perhaps, have been a little too human? Men who presume to lead the peoples must stand on guard against feelings in which the rest of mankind are free to indulge.

[1] Paléologue, *Cavour*, 286-87.

CHAPTER XIX

The "Syrian Massacres"

NAPOLEON III THOUGHT HE HAD HIT UPON A GOOD PLAN FOR HUMOR-
ing England and bringing her back to her former friendship for
him. He would negotiate a new commercial treaty.

It was no ordinary undertaking. Nothing less than a complete
revolution in French tariff policy was involved. That policy had
been protectionist ever since the days of Colbert, and during its
first eight years the Second Empire had succeeded in making only a
few minor breaches in the tariff wall. To be sure, a tendency towards a more generous, less stuffy system was in evidence among
French economists as far back as 1848, but they had been able to
obtain reductions merely in the duties on wheat, cattle, coal, iron
and iron derivatives. The Emperor had all along desired a more
thoroughgoing, a more basic reform.

The impelling force here was supplied by his frequent conversations with Michel Chevalier, a sometime Saint-Simonian who was
functioning as an apostle of free trade in his chair at the Collège
de France. Napoleon III had a real friendship for the man. He
made him first a Councillor of State, then a senator. Chevalier had
attended the Bradford Convention and met there the famous Richard Cobden, leader of the Manchester School and oecumenical
pontiff of the free trade religion. He persuaded Cobden to come to
Paris and galvanize Napoleon III with the confidence he required
to start an operation on a grand scale. With the approval of the
British Cabinet Cobden went to Saint-Cloud and was received secretly and as a comrade in faith by the Emperor and Rouher—
Rouher was then Minister of Public Works and Commerce. No
word of these talks was made public, but late in the year 1859 they
took on an official character. Mixed up in the business at this stage
were Baroche, acting Minister of Foreign Affairs, Persigny, the am-

bassador to London, and Fould, Minister of State. Everything was
kept from Magne, the then Minister of Finance, who was an obstinate protectionist, and from the Legislative Body, which was packed
with manufacturers and business magnates. Luckily the Senate's
resolution of 1852 gave the Emperor power to conclude commercial
treaties without laying them before parliament. So a general agreement with England, valid for ten years, was reached. It eliminated
all prohibitive tariffs, replacing them with moderate *ad valorem*
duties for revenue only. The duty on coal was cut in half. The
French market was opened wide to English industry. In exchange
France received very substantial concessions with respect to silks,
fashion products, wines and liquors.

The treaty was to be signed on January 30th (1860). Early in
the month the publics in the two countries got wind from the press
of what was going on, and on January 15th a letter from the Emperor to Fould appeared in the *Moniteur*.

In this letter Napoleon III set forth his whole doctrine on economic reorganization. Media of exchange had to be increased in
number. Competition was a healthful thing for any sort of production. The national wealth had to be increased "in order to spread
the benefits of prosperity among the working classes." Though industry was no longer to be protected by prohibitive tariffs, it would
be encouraged by the abolition of all duties on raw materials, by
freer credit, and cheaper freights.

This system was certainly very bold for its time. Errors and omissions are readily detectable in it, but on the whole it was sound,
broadminded, fertile in possibilities, and deserving of unbounded
respect for its aim to achieve material progress as a means to greater
social justice.

Napoleon III liked theatrical procedures. He thought that his
letter to Fould would cause a reversal in French public opinion,
which down to that time had been very much in favor of the strictest
protectionism. He might have succeeded had mere theories been
involved. Unfortunately it was largely a matter of practical interests.
In all the industrial centers employers and working classes alike
foresaw only ruin, and they were disinclined to accept it in silence.
Four hundred factory owners gathered in Paris and asked for an
interview with the Emperor. They were obliged to go home without having had an opportunity to present their case. Thiers fared

no better. He never missed an opportunity for getting into public notice and thought this a good one. He asked to have a talk with the Emperor in order to dissuade him from going through with the proposed treaty. Napoleon III refused to grant the audience.

This highhanded attitude on the Emperor's part gave rise to bitter feelings which were to rankle for a long time. They found expression in the Legislative Body when the bill abolishing duties on wools and cottons came up for voting. The report on the bill was made by Pouyer-Quertier, a chubby, shrewd, plain-spoken man from Rouen, thoroughly versed in anything pertaining to business. As a parliamentarian he was henceforward to play an important rôle in all debates touching on economic questions. Pouyer-Quertier delivered a criticism of the new tariff plan which in places was exceptionally well informed. And it was bitter in tone. At one point, Pouyer even accused Rouher of falsifying figures in order to mislead the Emperor. Other speakers followed, representing many different sectors of public opinion. Some deplored the fact that the Emperor should have settled a matter of such capital importance in such haste and secretly. Without protection, others claimed, no competition with England would be possible. Numbers of factories would have to shut down entirely, others would have to lower wages.

Baroche answered with his usual skill and carried the vote, which, to be sure, in a body so servile had never been in doubt. But repercussions after the treaty had gone into effect were far-reaching. The new duties on textiles and on metal products were undoubtedly too low. They certainly had the effect of placing French industry in a position of inferiority to foreign manufactures. In Normandy and Flanders especially, manufacturers and workers both were to blame the Emperor for a depression into which they were thrown by a tariff policy that was promising in principle but too rigid, and too lacking in shadings and graduations to work smoothly in practice.

While public attention in France was thus concentrated on the respective merits of free trade and protectionist theories, General Cousin-Montauban, an old cavalryman who had won his stars in Algeria, set sail for China with a corps of 8,000 volunteers. The Emperor had at first intended to confer this command upon Trochu whom he had seen at work in Italy, but Trochu held out for diplomatic as well as military powers. Fleury then proposed Cousin-Montauban, under whom he had fought in Africa.

This enterprise far abroad attracted hardly any notice in Europe. In France it amused rather than interested the public and the future that it opened to Western commerce seems not to have been noticed by anyone. The French had confused and childish notions of China, thinking of it now as a romantic, now as a monstrous, country. The Chinese looked to them like a great swarm of cruel dolls. "How sorry I am that I invented gunpowder!" cried a fat Chinaman in a drawing that appeared in *Charivari*.

In 1844, after five years of war with the English, who were eager to soak China in opium at a considerable profit to themselves, the Chinese Empire had ceded Hongkong to Britain and opened to European trade in addition to Canton four ports including Shanghai. But the sly yellow man set out to get his revenge. He massacred missionaries, he pirated ships, he destroyed factories. French interests in China were insignificant as compared with those of the English who had settlements all along the Southern coast. Napoleon III, however, decided to intervene in concert with the British. After bombarding Canton the united fleets sailed up the Gulf of Pechili and broke through the defenses of Taku on the Pei-ho river below Tientsin. The Chinese Government was entirely paralyzed by the revolt of the Taipings, who had risen against the Manchu dynasty and had occupied Nanking and the Southern provinces. It yielded almost immediately to the Allies, signing four treaties with England, France, the United States, and Russia.

In June, 1858, all of the demands formulated by the Franco-British diplomats were accepted; but when it came to performance the Chinese held off. The European plenipotentiaries who had come on to ratify the treaties were halted on the Pei-ho by a bloody resistance, and the allied gunboats had to withdraw.

This set-back angered England, and when the war in Italy was over she proposed to the Tuileries cabinet that common action be taken "to punish China." Napoleon III accepted with alacrity. The two expeditionary forces met late in July on the shores of the Gulf of Pechili at the mouth of the Pei-ho. They scattered the Tartar cavalry and bombarded the forts, which were taken in a few hours. Armed with bows and arrows, pikes, staves and old match-lock muskets, the Chinese were unable to offer any effective resistance. Tientsin soon fell. Negotiations were opened, but a party of some forty French and English soldiers were ambushed at Tungchow.

Talks were broken off and the allies resumed their march on Peking.

On September 21st, a force of some 40,000 Chinese cavalry tried to stop the French, 800 in number, at Palikao. The Chinese were dispersed. Negotiations began again, and again came to nothing. The expedition then headed for the Summer Palace which was located a few miles to the north of Peking. For centuries the Summer Palace had been the repository of the Crown treasure and of the tributes from the provinces. An effort was made to effect a rough classification of the precious objects, but the soldiery forced entrance to the palace and made off with the priceless riches under the too indulgent eyes of their generals.

The Europeans entered Peking by the north gate on October 13th. Lord Elgin, the English ambassador, who was the son of the Elgin who plundered the Parthenon, ordered the Summer Palace burned, in reprisal for the torturing and killing of the hostages taken at Tung-Chow. With that barbarous act, at least, the French had nothing to do. The Chinese now decided to negotiate in earnest. On October 25th, 1860, Prince Kong, the Emperor's brother, accepted all the stipulations of the allies: an indemnity of 120 millions; the opening of Tientsin and six additional ports to Western commerce; immunity vis-à-vis of Chinese law of subjects or citizens of the two powers; commercial guarantees; freedom of Christian worship in all China. The ancient cathedral at Peking, which had been built by the Portuguese, was hastily repaired and a solemn mass was celebrated in it.

The Franco-British troops left the great city on November 1st, trampling through a blanket of dust on which the north wind had already begun to blow. In spite of Lord Elgin's pleading, Baron Gros and General Montauban, the French representative, insisted on avoiding a dangerous wintering in China. The expedition, all things considered, had been well organized, and it was brought to a close without very serious losses or expenditures. In appreciation the Emperor named Montauban Count of Palikao, with a seat in the Senate.

This first trip of the tricolor to the ends of the earth seemed to be a mere trifle after the wars in the Crimea and in Italy. The French were interested in Europe and especially in themselves. Far in arrears of their government they had not yet opened their eyes to realities in the great world.

So they all but overlooked the important acquisition of Cochin China which was made about this time. No great credit, to be sure, attaches to Napoleon III's government on this score. Events, rather than any design of its own, led the Empire into this adventure.

It began with a naval demonstration which was made to oblige the Emperor of Annam to permit Christian worship in his territories. The port of Tourane was occupied, but then the rainy season came on and the French landing party was decimated by heat-prostration and fever. It was unable to reach Hué, the capital. The fleet, therefore, dropped down to the mouth of the Mekong and took possession of Saigon. There the French marines entrenched, but with the idea merely of forcing the Annamites to negotiate.

The Chinese war called all French vessels in the Orient to northern waters. The marines at Saigon, however, held on against a siege which lasted till the fall of Peking. Then the French fleet came back and rescued them. Admiral Bonnard occupied the three provinces on the delta and set up an administration with a native personnel. The experiment was not a success and military government was restored. On June 5, 1862, the Emperor of Annam ceded the three provinces to the Admiral, in other words, all lower Cochin China, along with a protectorate over Cambodia.

The protectorate went into effect only after prolonged and tortuous negotiations with Siam. In the end King Norodom became in every sense a vassal of France. A few years later an Annamite rebellion broke out. Its suppression left all of Cochin China in French hands. Napoleon III thought of the dependency as a mere center for exerting possible French influence in the Far East. The Third Republic was to make of it the nucleus of an Asiatic Empire.

In 1856 the Sultan of Turkey had issued an edict granting equal rights to Christians and Mussulmans in his territories. In many parts of the Turkish Empire this edict had only served to increase hostility rather than concord between the rival populations. This was the case especially in Syria. The Maronites in the mountains of Lebanon were Catholic farmers traditionally under the protection of France. The Druses were a tribe of warlike shepherds more or less attached to Mohammedanism and regarded with a friendly eye by English missionaries and consuls. The two peoples lived side by side on the same soil but in a mutual hatred that flared up into slaughter and pillage at the slightest provocation. The whole region was a powder magazine at all times ready to explode. It did explode in the spring of 1860. Some Maronites burned a number of Drusian villages and the Druses killed some Maronites by way of reprisal, Kourchid, the Pasha of Beirut, helping with bands of Bashi-Bazouks and meanwhile throwing the responsibility for the trouble upon the Christians. So the famous "Syrian Massacres" began.

The Maronites were sabred by Turkish horsemen, their villages destroyed, their convents burned. At Saida and Hasbeya, and with the connivance of the Mussulman authorities, Catholics were slaughtered by the hundreds. The English and French consuls protested. A horrible butchery at Deir-El-Kamar was the only reply—women, children, the aged, all were put to the sword. Constantinople hypocritically saw nothing. The powers held languid conferences. Thereupon Damascus, the capital of Syria, blew up. Mobs of fanatics howled through the streets, setting buildings on fire, shooting in all directions. Five thousand Christians were killed in three days' time. Achmet, the Ottoman governor, did not interfere.

A sometime enemy of France, the Algerian Abd-el-Kader, was passing his retirement in Damascus. He came to the assistance of the French consul and the French who had sought refuge in the consulate. Organizing a small band of armed men he scoured the riotous districts for Christians and gathered them into his palace— the Lazarite monks, the Sisters of St. Vincent of Paul and the children in their schools. In the end his house was so crowded with refugees that they stood elbow to elbow in packed masses from the yard to the balconies. Mobs of cutthroats gathered around. Abd-el-Kader raised the French tricolor and withstood a siege for five days. Finally the mobs tired of killing and the massacre began to abate. Abd-el-Kader then spread word about the town that for every Christian brought to him unhurt he would give fifty piasters. He made the payments in person, seated on a carpet in front of the door of his house, with his pistols within reach. In this manner, between July 8 and 11, 1860, he ransomed nine or ten thousand Christians.

The "Syrian Massacres" stirred France deeply. A war in rescue of Turkey had been fought only four years before. Here now were massacres only too obviously inspired by the Turks. How could they be tolerated?

Nevertheless the Emperor hesitated to interfere. To go to the defense of the Catholics in the Near East might be a way of regaining the support of the Catholics at home. But there were the English, who were always worrying lest some day they might find the French astride their route to India. The commercial treaty may have pleased the City, but the Queen and her cabinet had lost none of their mistrust of Napoleon III. In May, 1860, Victoria wrote:

"There is no need for France to upset the whole world and do harm and spread discord everywhere. Some day all this is going to end in a crusade against this disturber of the general peace."

In order to be free to intervene in Syria the Emperor had to use all of his diplomatic cunning, meantime giving London express assurances that France would be acting only as a mandatory and policeman of the powers.

On July 27th Napoleon III wrote in a letter to Persigny, which was made public:

"I should be very happy not to be obliged to make the Syrian expedition and, in any event, not to make it alone; first because of the great expense, but then because I am afraid that any such intervention may open the whole question of the Near East again. On the other hand I do not see how I can resist public opinion in my own country. The French people will never be persuaded that these massacres of Christians can be left unpunished, not to mention burnings of our consulates, insults to our flag and the pillaging of monasteries that are under French protection."

An agreement was reached and signed on September 5, 1860. The expedition was to last not more than six months and the number of soldiers would be kept low, 7,000 men. They had arrived at Beirut under the command of General de Beaufort d'Hautpoul towards the end of August.

In order to forestall intervention from Europe the Sultan had hurriedly sent Fuad as commissioner extraordinary to Damascus, with full powers to punish the guilty and restore order. After a travesty of a trial Fuad hanged or shot some sixty poor devils. Four hundred others were banished or sent to the galleys. There was no indication that the Turkish Commissioner made any effort to punish the real instigators of the massacres. Governor Achmet was allegedly shot at dawn, but in such secrecy that there were doubts as to his having been executed at all. Fuad awarded Abd-el-Kader the ribbon of the Medjidie for his bravery and humanity, following Napoleon III, who had given him the Grand Cross of the Legion of Honor.

Fuad then went on to Beirut, again to play at meting out justice. A few Drusians were condemned to death but most of them escaped from prison. Kourchid too was imprisoned till the chance came for escaping in his turn.

General d'Hautpoul was not satisfied with this make-believe, which, on the other hand, the English thought answered the purposes quite adequately. His men were in poor condition from the muggy heat on the coast but he marched them towards Lebanon. There they were able to see with their own eyes all the destruction that the Druses had wrought. The Turks, however, kept the more important incendiaries and assassins carefully out of reach. Finally a commission of the great powers met at Beirut, and later at Damascus, and obliged Fouad to take more active measures of punishment. Some seven hundred Druses were arrested and transported to Tripolitania. Indemnities were awarded the Maronites; but after months of negotiations that called all the arts of Near Eastern manoeuvring into play, the only relief they got was the contributions sent from France and England, and especially France. In France the Committee for the Eastern Schools alone raised three million francs, which were distributed by Cardinal Lavigerie.

The British Cabinet meantime grew impatient at the protraction of the occupation. They insisted that the French expedition be recalled. Thouvenel was forced to argue point by point. To evacuate Syria so soon, leaving the country without organization or means of defense, would be to hand it over again to brigandage. Russell, head of the Foreign Office, replied insolently that he would not allow France to establish herself in Syria the way she had done in Rome. The conference of ambassadors meeting in Paris had the utmost difficulty in getting a postponement of the date of evacuation till June 5, 1861.

A special constitution was worked out for Lebanon on the basis of a plan suggested by Prussia: The country was divided into districts and placed under a Christian governor named by the Sultan and responsible directly to him. The police and the courts were to have a mixed personnel. This system brought order to the country for the next half-century.

The French soldiers embarked on the date agreed upon. All things considered, it had been a generous and a successful enterprise. It restored peace to a land divided against itself and increased French prestige in the Near East. In everything connected with it Napoleon III displayed tact, restraint and firmness of resolve. *The Saturday Review* vainly accused him of a design to stay in Syria. The Emperor could not have entertained such a thought. Any acquisition by France in the Near East would, under England's lead, have roused all Europe against Napoleon III at a time when Italy was creating new difficulties for him.

With the Milanese, Romagna, Florence and the duchies annexed to Piedmont Cavour was by no means satisfied. He wanted to achieve his full dream, take Venice, Rome and Naples, melt all Italy down and fuse it into a single body. He was not entirely to succeed but, in the space of the few months before his death, he was to carry out the essential parts of his vast program, thanks to a strange combination of circumstances with no little luck—the tactlessness of the Pontifical government, the stupidity of the court of Naples, the connivance of England, the indecision, not to say the duplicity, of Napoleon III and, finally, the impetuous dash of Garibaldi.

The French force that had been sent to Italy by the Prince-President in 1849 was still in Rome, but now that the Austrian troops had been withdrawn behind the Adige its presence there had no apparent justification. It could only seem to be an insulting precaution against moves by the Italian patriots. Thouvenel was not an ardent Papist. He kept urging that it be called home and the Duc de Gramont, the French ambassador to the Holy See, gave the same advice.

"The presence of a French garrison," he wrote, "gives the Vatican a sense of overweening security that paralyzes all political and diplomatic initiative."

Down to that time the Pope's policy had been entirely controlled by his Secretary of State, Cardinal Antonelli, a clever, perhaps too clever, individual whose one idea was to temporize. Antonelli's influence now began to wane in favor of the influence of a Belgian prelate who had once been an army officer in Algeria, Monsignor de Mérode. In contrast with Antonelli, Mérode was of an outspoken

turn of mind, always ready for a fight. When France seemed likely
to recall her soldiers, he set out to reorganize the pontifical army in
order to meet any possible surprise from the Piedmontese. He appointed a Frenchman as his general-in-chief, Lamoricière, a man
whom he had met years before in Africa, who had been proscribed
in 1851 and had remained stubbornly hostile to the Empire. Such
a choice was an affront to Napoleon III.

Lamoricière called for volunteers in France and hosts of them
responded, mainly from the deeply religious provinces in the West.
Money was plentiful. The "Peter's pence" device had just been hit
on and it was draining large amounts from Catholic Europe to
Rome.

With the Pope now truly so well protected the cabinet at the
Tuileries had no reason left for maintaining its regiments in Rome,
especially since Cavour had given a promise not to move against
the Pope. So in May, 1860, Gramont arranged with Antonelli for
a gradual evacuation of the Papal States: the last French soldiers
would be back in France by August. Napoleon III hoped by that
move to reassure Great Britain, regain the confidence of Europe,
and settle for good and all this Roman question that had entered
the very body of French foreign policy like a deadly parasite and
was sapping its life.

But all that was taking too little account of the feverish state of
mind in Italy, and no account of Garibaldi whatever.

Insurrectionary movements broke out in Palermo in April. They
were put down. Francis II, the young King of Naples, had just
ascended his throne. He hesitated to reestablish the constitution of
1848. Garibaldi, an astonishing free-lance of patriotism, then
hatched a scheme to descend upon Sicily with a mere handful of
volunteers. He made preparations in secret at Genoa, but Cavour
had a meeting with him there. Cavour was loath to encourage "this
buffalo-headed lunatic"—he was afraid of the man's caprices and
of his republican enthusiasms. Victor Emmanuel, however, was in
favor of the expedition. He liked the firebrand Garibaldi and had
faith in him. This strange Prince with all his dynastic pride had a
strain of the revolutionist in his makeup. Cavour yielded, allowing
Garibaldi to recruit a thousand men, arm them and put them
aboard ship. On the morning of the 6th of May "the Thousand"
set out for the South.

They landed at Marsala on the 11th. Reenforced by a number of local rebel bands they defeated the royal troops, got control of Palermo, which was wretchedly defended, and in a month's time were masters of Sicily.

The young king begged Napoleon III to intervene. The Emperor answered advising reforms and an understanding with Piedmont:

"I do not want to see Southern Italy annexed to Piedmont, but neither can I undo what I have created nor renounce my principle of non-intervention. Cavour is a sensible man. He understands the dangers of revolution and is sure to proceed in a constructive direction. Come to an understanding with him."

Francis II tried to follow the advice. He called a liberal minister, to power and tried to get in touch with Cavour. Cavour evaded a meeting in order to make it plain that he demanded the surrender of Sicily. The King of Naples refused. Then his troops were defeated by Garibaldi at Milazzo and his situation grew hourly worse. At this point Thouvenel proposed to England that the havoc be limited by prohibiting Garibaldi from crossing the straits into Calabria. Lord John Russell declined.

"Peoples have a right to overthrow tyrannical governments," he said.

Despising the Bourbons of Naples cordially Russell showed himself more and more clearly committed to the cause of Italian unification. Only the Czar favored intervention, on condition that France should join him.

France, however, did not move. To upset Cavour's risky game a vigorous veto from Napoleon III would have been more than enough. Then the Emperor could have gone on and created that division of forces in Italy which he himself considered "necessary":

"A kingdom in the North and a kingdom in the South, with a sovereign Papacy in between."

At that critical moment Napoleon III was unable to make up his mind.

"What I want," he wrote to Persigny (July 27, 1860), "is pacification in Italy *on any terms,* but without intervention from abroad. I want our troops out of Rome but without prejudice to the Pope's security."

A Pontius Pilate policy! Such policies almost never succeed.

Cavour replied to French representations by repudiating Garibaldi, though at the very time he was sending agents to Sicily to arrange for the annexation. But he was himself afraid that Garibaldi would go too far and grow too powerful; so he sent Admiral Persano's fleet to Naples to capture for Piedmont the revolution that was in the offing there.

The revolution, in fact, had been well prepared and it soon broke out. Garibaldi crossed the Straits. Betrayed by his family and his ministers, deserted by his army and his navy, Francis II embarked for the fortress of Gaeta on September 6th and Garibaldi entered Naples the following morning.

So all the South of Italy, a third of the whole peninsula, fell into the hands of the Savoy dynasty; but that was not enough for the leader of the Thousand. He wanted to march on Rome. Sir Henry Elliot, the English ambassador at Naples, reminded him that Rome was still occupied by a French garrison.

"What difference does that make?" answered Garibaldi. "Rome is an Italian city. . . . If the French resist, I shall drive them out. . . . When I have proclaimed Victor Emmanuel King of Italy, I shall go North, attack Austria and deliver Venice."

There again, with his cautiously working genius, Cavour was the first arrival on the field. As early as mid-August his agents were busy in Umbria and the Marches; and on pretense of protecting the Papal States from Garibaldi he made ready to occupy them. However, in all his boldest strokes Cavour retained a sense of prudence. He sent two friends of his to Chambéry, Farini and General Cialdini, to convey his greetings to Napoleon III. The latter had left Paris with the Empress on August 23, 1860, for a visit to Corsica, Algeria and the two provinces which had been regained, the Prince Imperial, meantime, being left in charge of Marshal Vaillant—the ex-King Jerome had died on June 24th. At the time of the visit of Farini and Cialdini Napoleon III was touring Savoy.

Choosing their words carefully the two envoys informed the Emperor of Cavour's intentions. What did he say in reply? The two Italians said that he said:

"Fate, ma fate presto!" (Do so, but do so at once.)

Incredible as it may seem it may well have been true. Napoleon III would have enjoyed seeing Lamoricière beaten. The old insurgent of the days in Romagna was a standoff to the Catholic sovereign in him. Arese also called on him at Thonon and very properly

THE RECEPTION OF THE SIAMESE AMBASSADOR AT FONTAINEBLEAU BY NAPOLEON III

From the Painting by Gérôme

left with the conviction that Napoleon III would give the people in Italy a free hand.

One man only sought to block Cavour's advance and conserve the real interest of France, which was to see the Papal States left intact. That was Thouvenel. Down to that point Thouvenel had been submissive, perhaps too submissive, to the Emperor's will; but he was a man of foresight and a man of integrity, and in his sense of patriotic duty he found the strength to insist that France should not become party to the plot hatched in Turin. Napoleon stopped at writing to Victor Emmanuel:

"If, as M. Farini has assured me, your troops are to enter the Papal States only in case of insurrection and to reestablish order, I have nothing to say; but if you attack the territory of the Church while my soldiers are in Rome, I shall be obliged to withdraw my minister from Turin and take the position of an antagonist."

Such language was neither clear nor resolute. Cavour saw plainly that he had nothing to fear and addressed an insolent ultimatum to the Pope:

"Unless the Holy See dismisses its foreign soldiery at once the army of Sardinia will enter Umbria and the Marches."

By "foreign soldiery" Cavour meant the force of Lamoricière. Thouvenel was indignant. The Emperor was then on his way to Algeria. Thouvenel proposed warning Cavour that diplomatic relations would be broken off if the Papal troops were attacked. Napoleon III again watered and diluted the threat contained in a dispatch he sent to the King on September 9th. Cavour waited no longer. On September 11th the Piedmontese army invaded the provinces of the Pope. Lamoricière strove vainly to halt the northerners. He was beaten by Cialdini at Castelfidardo on the 18th. He made a dash for Ancona with a handful of men, but there, in spite of all his courage, was soon obliged to capitulate (September 29th).

Three days after Castelfidardo (September 22, 1860), Cavour wrote to Nigra in one of those bursts of frankness that he often indulged in among the twists and turns of his tortuous policy:

"Do not try to justify our conduct by captious arguments. Let us face the fact that we are altogether in the wrong. What excuses us is the necessity we are under of saving the Italian cause from the extravagances of the Revolution."

So the patrimony of St. Peter had shrunk to Rome and the

Roman campagna. The French army of occupation had not stirred. Baron de Talleyrand, the French ambassador at Turin, was recalled, but a *chargé d'affaires*, Reyneval, took his place.

On his return from Algeria the Emperor had to face onslaughts from his ministers, from Randon, and Magne especially—Magne was an honest, hard-working assistant who was not at all afraid of incurring the displeasure of his master. Thouvenel seemed to be less positive. He did not regard intervention as any longer possible.

"Undoubtedly," he wrote, "one's moral sense is shocked by the conduct of Piedmont, but no one thinks it wise for us to offer any effective resistance. As pontiff the Pope is still revered. As a ruler he has lost all popularity."

A rebuke was forwarded to Turin and the French army in Rome was reenforced. But that was all; and Cavour wrote to Farini on November 2, 1860:

"The Emperor is having his newspapers 'hem!' at us, but his cannons are loaded with blanks, and the first Napoleon is surely applauding us."

For a moment, it seems, the Pope was minded to flee, but Gramont restrained him, so prolonging the wretched Roman question for ten years. Had the Piedmontese entered the *urbs* the question would have been settled painfully, but it would have been settled at least. Through the errors that Napoleon III and his agents piled on errors it was to continue to embarrass both the domestic and the foreign policy of France, and in the hour of panic in 1870, there it was still dogging the country!

Europe did not lose any sleep over the collapse of the Pope's temporal power. Austria expressed "her pained sympathy." Prussia protested half-heartedly. Russia manifested real anger at the fall of her protégés, the Bourbons of Naples, and broke off diplomatic relations with Italy. England, on the other hand, approved of all that had been done, and Russell even went so far as to congratulate Cavour. Napoleon III, for his part, wrote to Pius IX on January 8th (1861):

"I have done everything in my power to uphold the authority of the Pope so far as I could do so without damage to the interests of France. I am told that I did not do enough. That may be, but I answer: 'In spite of my veneration for the head of the Church, my troops will never be used as tools for oppressing foreign peoples.' "

Victor Emmanuel was excommunicated by the Pope but, believer that he was, the King seemed to take the curse rather lightly. He marched on Naples at the head of his army. He met Garibaldi near Capua on October 26th and the dictator hailed him as King of Italy. Victor Emmanuel tried to shower the conqueror with rewards and honors. but Garibaldi refused everything—the Order of the Annuziata, a château, a title, an income. He knew that he was a nuisance to the King and the King's minister and that they were trying to be rid of him. He bowed his head with dignified bitterness.

"You know," he said to Admiral Persano, "what people do with an orange? They squeeze out the last drop of juice, then toss it into a corner."

He set sail for his little rocky island of Capraia, unattended, there to busy his fertile mind devising schemes for giving Rome to Italy. Gaeta, the last refuge of Francis II, held out for four months, but Sicily, the Napolitano, the Marches and Umbria voted enthusiastically for annexation to Piedmont. Victor Emmanuel dropped his historic title as King of Sardinia and became King of Italy. Negotiating with Antonelli, Cavour tried to induce the Pope to surrender all claim to civil sovereignty. Pius IX indignantly refused and he also refused to annul his excommunication of Victor Emmanuel and the Italian government. When the Italian Parliament met for the first time in Turin, February 14, 1861, Cavour proclaimed just as emphatically before it that Rome "rightfully was and would become the capital of the new nation." Thouvenel then had the idea of forcing a settlement upon the Pope: the French force would be recalled and Italy would promise to respect Rome. That would have been a way of getting France out of a hole. Unfortunately Napoleon III could not see how he could leave the Pope without any protection whatever, and the project fell through.

Cavour died suddenly on June 6, 1861, less of swamp-fever than of the exhaustion brought on by years and years of unremitting labor and anxiety. He had undoubtedly been the most finished political genius of his time. The place he left vacant in the European world was soon to be filled by a personality of quite a different sort, by a man who came from the North and was no less shrewd in working to achieve his ends, but was far more brutal. Cavour used a skillful touch, Bismarck struck forcefully. The two men supplemented and completed each other in regard to Napoleon III. Cavour first applied the pick to the foundations of the Second Empire. Bismarck was to bring the whole edifice crashing down.

Following the logical consequences of his first mistake Napoleon III recognized the Kingdom of Italy when Cavour was hardly cold in his grave. He recognized the Kingdom of Italy, knowing well that he was to wound millions of Catholics in France in their tenderest hearts. England had set the example with a haste that worried him. Suddenly and without warning, as was his wont, at a meeting of the Council of Ministers on June 27, 1861, he had Thouvenel read a note which marked the end of the Italian adventure.

Ever since her brief regency, the Empress had been regularly attending these sessions. Napoleon had asked Thouvenel to have the note ready in his portfolio at every meeting of the Council. On the morning in question the Emperor simply requested him to read it. Unable to control her emotion, the Empress rose and left the room. She thought it was all Thouvenel's doing and never forgave him.

The recognition was not unconditional, however. It voiced no approval of all that had taken place, and it specified that France was to maintain her troops in Rome "so long as no adequate guarantees protected the interests that had called them thither."

Only one man could have given such guarantees and that man was Cavour. He had seemed at one time in favor of giving them but he had vanished from the scene. Rome was to fall into the hands of Italy on a day when France would need the last one of her soldiers at home.

CHAPTER XX

Morny and the Liberal Empire

THE COUNT DE MORNY WAS ABOUT TO BECOME A DUKE. OF LATE
he had been acquiring greater and greater influence over the Emperor's domestic policy. As President of the Legislative Body he was
in a key position which he utilized in such a way as to become a
sort of arbiter between the various factions. Not a mixer by nature,
even contemptuous of people when he did not watch himself, infinitely charming when he chose to be, he had a balance, a restraint
and a considerateness that won for him personally a general popularity. He had the art of giving a speaker the chance he wanted,
whether the man belonged to the majority or not. He could relax
a tense situation with a smiling jest and attenuate animosities by the
deft word of personal appreciation. He was not merely the chairman, he was the comrade. When a debate interested him he would
leave the chair to take part himself, always with talent. Jules Favre
did not like him but on one occasion said:

"I would be pleased if M. le comte de Morny would participate
more frequently in our debates, but on condition that he be brief
and resume the chair very promptly."

All in all Morny gave the Chamber the illusion that it was playing an important part in the government. That perhaps may have
been the real reason for its attachment to him.

For that matter Morny sincerely hoped that the day would come
when Parliament would recover its rôle of importance and hold it.
He had begun his political career in the assemblies of the July
Monarchy and the experience had left its mark on him. He did not
like to see the sovereign dictating to the elected representatives of
the country too highhandedly. The sometime gambler had now become a statesman with a sense for political realities and was tending
more and more to a liberalism that was basic in him. He regarded

259

freedom as the best guarantee for the continuance of the imperial system.

"Dictatorship," he said over and over again, "has just its moment."

Once it had been accepted, it had to loosen up, become flexible and comfortable for everybody.

Early in the month of March, 1860, Morny had a talk witȟ Darimon and asked him to use his influence to soften the opposition of the Five, at least on the surface, and he threw out a hint that a first step towards reform might be near.

"I assure you," he said, "that I am doing all I can to increase the prerogatives of the Chamber. I hope your friends will make my task easier by holding themselves in hand."

On November 24, 1860, and at Morny's suggestion, the Emperor published in the *Moniteur* a decree that tended to "give the great organs of the state a more direct participation in the government." The two Chambers would be allowed to vote an "Address" in reply to the Speech from the Throne which opened each session. The Legislative Body recovered the right to discuss bills in secret committee. Bills would be defended by ministers without portfolio. Finally, since 1852, the public had had no knowledge of debates in the two houses except in the form of brief digests. Henceforward they were to be published *in extenso* in the *Journal Officiel*.

These were very superficial changes. They in no way altered the framework of the dictatorial system. Napoleon III wanted to move towards liberty. He did not want to lose any of his power. In his eyes, as Maupas said, "ministerial responsibility, the distinctive trait of representative systems, was the very negation of the Empire: it meant abdication."

The reform was nevertheless an important one. Public opinion was at first taken quite by surprise. Then the various factions began to praise or blame, according to the outlook they represented. The imperialists of the Right denounced "this dangerous weakening of power." Orleanists like Guizot opined, without any heat at all, that "a door had been left ajar for the liberals" and that "through it the revolution would some day make its way." The Center and the Left approved.

"Well, are you satisfied?" Morny asked Emile Ollivier after the publication of the decree.

"If that is all, you are lost," answered the young liberal. "If it is just a beginning, you are on the right track."

He was sure it was just a beginning, that ambitious young attorney, whose republicanism was trying to find a compromise with a keen personal liking for the Emperor. There could be no doubt of it: Ollivier was drifting towards active cooperation with the regime. On the publication of the edict Ollivier entered in his diary:

"Yesterday's decree fills me with joy."

Morny was no less convinced than Ollivier.

"The Emperor is a good fellow," he said to Ollivier. "The trouble is no one knows who his successor is going to be. You have to build institutions."

They were right. The decree of November 24th may be regarded as the germ from which the Liberal Empire was to burgeon.

In the sovereign's immediate entourage the reform did not receive unanimous support.

"These new concessions to liberalism," Mérimée wrote to Panizzi on November 27th, "seem to me exceedingly strange. I believe they will be something to worry about hereafter."

The extreme Bonapartists called the decree "the crime of November 24th."

Napoleon III lost no time in reshaping his cabinet. Fould had shown himself firm and judicious in the Ministry of State but he was hostile to the parliamentary reform. In accepting his resignation the Emperor suggested that he take Finance. Fould refused.

"I am going to make you a duke," said Napoleon III.

"That would be ridiculous," Fould replied, and he stuck to his retirement.

Walewski took the Ministry of State, and a general utility man, Forcade la Roquette, half-brother to Saint-Arnaud, the Treasury. Chasseloup-Laubat received the Navy. Persigny went back to the Interior in spite of Morny's opposition. Delangle kept Justice, Thouvenel Foreign Affairs, Randon War. Vaillant, the Grand-Marshal of the Palace, was given the Emperor's Household, a department subtracted from the Ministry of State. At Vaillant's own request the incumbent of the new post had title as minister. Haussmann wanted to become head of a Ministry of Paris. What he won was the right to sit in at Council meetings on matters concerning his own work. Three ministers without portfolio were named—

Baroche, Magne and Billault. They, of course, sat in the Council.

Immediately on returning to active work in the government, Persigny underlined the change in outlook by a circular to the prefects enjoining them to "pay all possible regard to honorable and distinguished men of former governments." He relieved a number of newspapers of the restrictions they had incurred and allowed a new opposition paper to be started—*Le Temps*. The paper was to achieve an outstanding position in the French press.

The Legislative session opened on February 4th (1861). The two Chambers at once set to work on the "Address," discussion of which now afforded opportunity for debating foreign and domestic policy as a whole.

In the Senate the Roman question was brought up by numbers of orators of the Right who protested against the spoliation of the Papacy. That was a chance for Prince Napoleon to put in a word. Squaring his massive shoulders and throwing his Caesarian head far back, speaking in a harsh rapid-fire of sentences, he condemned divine right as opposed to popular sovereignty, attacked the temporal power and advised the Pope to give up Rome as necessary to Italian unification:

"Italian unity must be accepted fearlessly, without reserves, and with the necessary premise of Rome as the capital. . . . The Pope will have all the independence he needs if he is left walled in within the Leonine City on the right bank of the Tiber. Catholicism will supply him with a budget and a garrison."

The Emperor congratulated the Prince "though not agreeing with him on all points."

Persigny made haste to have the speech published in the *Moniteur des Communes*. The Prince had also attacked the Bourbons in that paper and now saw himself the victim of a sharp rejoinder from the Duc d'Aumale in the form of a "Letter on the History of France." The number of the *Moniteur des Communes* containing the letter was confiscated—but not till the article had made a great stir. The government then proceeded to get its revenge on the editor, who was condemned to a year in prison.

The Cardinals sitting in the Senate proposed a Catholic amendment to the "Address":

"France shall maintain the temporal sovereignty of the Holy See in Rome on which the independence of its spiritual authority rests."

That was a thrust at the Prince, not to say at the Emperor. The amendment was voted down by a bare majority of 18 votes.

Delighted and at the same time self conscious over its new lease on life the Legislative Body prolonged the debate on the "Address." Keller, a young Catholic orator hitherto unknown, delivered a bitter attack on Napoleon III's policy in Italy:

"Are you revolutionaries or are you conservatives? You have given ground step by step before Garibaldi. Declaring yourselves his greatest enemy, you have supplied Piedmont with rifled cannon and the King of Naples with cotton batting. With one hand you have upheld the Holy See, with the other you have led the attack upon it."

That orator of a day's renown, attaining through his strength of conviction an eloquence to which he was never again to rise, branded to the quick the incoherence and the unending shiftiness of the Emperor's outlook.

"The Revolution incarnate in Orsini," he concluded, "that was what caused the backdown of France."

The effect on the Chamber was such that Billault felt obliged to reply. Napoleon III, he said, was not afraid of the revolution. He was not afraid of assassination. The abolition of Austrian supremacy in Italy was in itself a great achievement.

The members listened. They applauded. But the assembly was grateful to Keller all the same. He had freed them of their fears and lifted them to a higher level of mental integrity.

During the days following crowds flocked to the galleries and the debate continued, with eager public attention. In a speech by Jules Favre the Five demanded the repeal of the public safety law and other laws of an emergency character. On March 14th Emile Ollivier delivered a carefully worded extemporization that was to have wide repercussions. After demanding more freedom for the press he made a personal appeal to the Emperor:

"Sire! When a man is acclaimed by thirty-five million people, when he is the most powerful among sovereigns, when Fortune has lavished all her favors on him, there is one unspeakable joy that he still may know—the joy of thrusting timorous advisers aside and becoming the courageous and voluntary leader of a great people to freedom. . . . I can answer for it: on the day when that call is sounded, there may still be men in this country who will be loyal to memories of the past or absorbed in hopes of the future: but the majority will eagerly approve. As for myself, I am a republican: but I would admire, I would support, and my support would be all the more effective in that it would be altogether disinterested."

That was a way of announcing in indirect, skillful terms that Ollivier was going over to the Empire. The Five repudiated him but he had attracted the attention of men in power. From that moment on he was regarded as a person whom the government might some day be able to fall back on.

A few days later Jules Favre vainly demanded the recall of the troops protecting Rome. On that occasion he delivered an impassioned defense of the principle of nationalities:

"Even should great national groupings form, even if there were the united Italy and the united Germany which you view with terror, if those peoples are inspired by the same political faith, they will prefer the way of peace that unites them to war which divides them."

On the Papal question the Catholics mustered a strong minority against the government (91 votes). Persigny went into a tantrum.

"We will be back at elections!" he cried, menacing.

That was the opening of a struggle between the Interior and the Catholics: Catholic orders were dissolved; country curates were deprived of their salaries because they had risen against imperial policy; lists of "dangerous individuals" were drawn up, men subject to arrest on the slightest provocation. The Duc de Broglie wrote a pamphlet called "Views on the French Government." It was seized at the printer's. The work, however, had not been intended for the public. The Duke was lithographing some fifty copies for circulating privately among his friends. The police highhandedly confiscated them. The Duke brought suit against the prefect of police. Worried by this vigorous counter-offensive the government backed down and the seized copies were returned.

Victor de Laprade lost his chair in the faculty at Lyons for a skit on "State Muses." In a letter of instructions to his curates, Monsignor Pie, the bishop of Poitiers, accused Napoleon of "betraying the Church the way Pilate betrayed Jesus."

"Wash thy hands, O Pilate! Posterity spurns thy justification!"

From that day on Napoleon was mentioned by Catholics only as Pilate or Tiberius.

The Bishop of Poitiers was called for trial before the Council of State for this act of lèse majesté and the Council ruled that he had abused his prerogatives.

Persigny enjoyed irony, and now he had the fun of persecuting both the Society of St. Vincent of Paul and the anti-clerical Freemasons. The Masons yielded, accepting a Grand Master of the Emperor's choice—Marshal Magnan. The central committee of St. Vincent of Paul showed fight and it was dissolved.

For another parallel with the First Empire, Fate, or at least Napoleon III's mistakes, led him, as his uncle had done, to exacerbate the quarrel with the Church and with its principles and agents in France. He should better have remembered what just such a conflict had cost the great Emperor in terms of moral prestige. But the possession of unlimited power fits strange blinders on a man! With Persigny's voice dinning in his ears Napoleon III never had any doubts about his prestige.

Morny and Billault were the men to see to it that none of these difficulties came up in the Legislative Body; but for all that they could do the session grew longer and longer till it had lasted five months.

The budget was voted after much talk. The government pretended not to notice, but France was in a period of depression. There was a shortage of cotton, due to the Civil War in the United States. Industry had slumped, the wheat harvest was poor, money went into hiding, the banks were shaky. The Bank of France was forced to raise discount rates to 6 percent. There was complaining on all hands. In measured language, to be sure, the *Revue des Deux Mondes* criticized the expenditure the government was making in city improvements—they were, in fact, of doubtful wisdom at times, and otherwise found fault with the fits and starts in the government's economic policy. Persigny sent the *Revue* a reprimand but, as his anger cooled, the Emperor began to think. He called in Achille Fould, who had stayed on as his private financial adviser. Fould agreed with the complaints of the business world, not hesitating to recommend a return to a regular budget without supplementary credits, which the Legislative Body would pass section by section.

"In that way," he said, "the Emperor and his government will be working in perfect harmony."

Napoleon recalled him to the ministry on November 12th to put the reform he advocated into operation. On December 31, 1861, it became law by a senatus-consultum. Transfers between accounts still held on, but the Legislative Body recovered its right of audit, which is basic to parliamentary practice.

Financial dictatorship, however, had not said its final word. A decree was soon to hand back to the government a right to "rectify the budget"—in other words, to plunge again into supplementary expenditures. That threw things back again into the morass of over-drawings, deficits and loans.

Few governments, truly, have had such chaotic finances as the Second Empire. It far surpassed the vagaries of the old monarchy and, in this respect, Napoleon III had no excuse whatever. He carried arbitrary whim in finance altogether too far.

Devoted to the Emperor, but even more devoted to his country, Thouvenel was still obsessed by the idea—for that matter a sound one, that the Roman Question not only sapped the domestic props of the government but paralyzed its whole influence abroad. He was always racking his brain to find a solution for an insolvable problem. Trying, further, to realize the twin hope of the Emperor to save what temporal independence the Pope had left and at the same time to help the new kingdom of Italy get a firm foothold, he kept manoeuvring this way and that without getting anywhere at all.

Napoleon III had sketched out a plan of his own, an altogether impracticable plan. The Marches and Umbria would be restored to the Pope, but the Papal States would be governed by the same laws as Italy. Roman deputies would sit in the Turin parliament and the Pope's soldiers would be incorporated into the Italian army.

The Emperor gave up this scheme in favor of another which Thouvenel submitted to the Holy See on May 31, 1862. According to this plan the powers would guarantee the Pope the territory he was then holding. He would receive a civil list, with France contributing to the tune of three millions. Some way would be found to fund his debt. He would grant liberal reforms to his subjects.

Speaking for Pius IX, Cardinal Antonelli scornfully rejected the proposal and, unfavorably disposed by the almost aggressive tone which the court of Rome adopted, Napoleon III began to lean more and more towards evacuation.

A sensational turn of events changed the whole outlook. Garibaldi slipped away from Capraia to Sicily, recruited a legion of forlorn hopes and, with the slogan "Rome or Death," landed in Calabria (August 25th). Garibaldi had a superstitious regard for holy images and paid public worship to them. He had no use for the Pope and said so. At this moment he was displaying an insolent contempt for Napoleon III:

"We owe the man no gratitude whatever! He has been well paid by the Nice and Savoy that we stuffed down his gullet!"

Garibaldi was figuring that an uprising by the Romans would hand the city over to him without his firing a shot. Ratazzi was prime minister in Italy at the time. He saw the danger to which the fanatic Garibaldi was exposing his policy. He sent troops to halt him and they cornered him at Aspromonte. Garibaldi was wounded, taken prisoner and sent to La Spezzia for safe-keeping, though an amnesty soon set him free.

Ratazzi took advantage of the episode once more to push his claim to Rome in an official circular to the powers:

"The whole nation demands its capital."

Napoleon III was annoyed and reversed his attitude. He recalled Benedetti and La Valette, his two ambassadors, from Turin and Rome, considering them too friendly to the plans of the Italians and, at Biarritz, he made up his mind to dismiss Thouvenel. That was under pressure from the Empress who regularly addressed Thouvenel in such ungracious language that the Minister of Foreign Affairs went so far as to say to her one day:

"Madame, if the Emperor had ever said to me half of what I have just heard from Your Majesty, I would long since have handed in my resignation."

Eugénie's lack of restraint in this whole affair really overstepped all bounds.

Back again in Paris Napoleon requested the resignations of all his ministers and set out to form a cabinet around Walewski. This move raised a storm of opposition. Persigny said to him:

"You let yourself be bossed by your wife, and so do I. But all I risk is my fortune. You are sacrificing your son and your country."

Morny also had his say. He was just as positive. Fould, Baroche and Rouher declared that they would resign.

In the end Napoleon gave in, halting at a substitution of Drouyn de Lhuys for Thouvenel. Drouyn had been sacrificed to England during the Crimean War. Always deferential to the claims of the papacy he continually advocated an entente, if not an actual alliance, with Austria.

Thouvenel took his departure with great dignity and carried the respect of almost the whole country with him. He had no money of his own. Rouher had him appointed then and there to the presidency of the Board of Directors of the State Railways.

The moment he assumed power the new minister answered Ratazzi's circular (October 26, 1862):

"The Italian government has taken its stand on grounds where the permanent interests of France forbid us to follow."

This change in direction on the part of France was categorical. Ratazzi had gone too far; and he was to pay the penalty for his mistake. Not choosing to compromise his fortune by too great haste Victor Emmanuel dismissed him very soon, and once more the Roman Question hung fire. For the time being at least Napoleon gave up all idea of settling it according to his own views. He hoped for some change in circumstances that would give him back his freedom of action. Meanwhile, as a sop to French public opinion which had grown alarmed at so much bustle, he made a definite turn towards a conservative policy.

Interest in public life had been greatly stimulated by the decree of November 24th and it continued to increase during the two years that followed down to the elections of 1863. The activities of the Legislative Body were closely watched by the public and at times it strove manfully to assert its independence, so making the liberals crow with delight while the dictatorship made wry faces.

The Emperor promoted a bill to grant General Montauban a 50,000 franc yearly dotation for his services in China. The deputies balked. The plundering of the Summer Palace was still too fresh in the public mind. The examining committee reported for rejection, and Napoleon III was obliged to withdraw his bill with the caustic comment (March 4, 1862):

"Only degenerate nations haggle over expressions of their gratitude."

Debates on the "Address" at the session of '62 gave occasion for some lively exchanges. The Five again demanded "an honest return to freedom" and they put Billault in a hole on the Roman Question. In 1863 they protested loudly against the slavery of the press and comment on the manoeuvres of the administration at elections rang loud and clear. A number of Catholic deputies joined in. The government pretended to belittle an opposition that was so weak in numbers, but it was evincing less resoluteness, less self-confidence in its procedures.

After a moment of apparent weariness the republicans came to life again. Victor Hugo's *Châtiments* and the writings of Edgar Quinet and Louis Blanc circulated everywhere despite the strict watch on book peddling kept by the police. Corrosive satires on the Emperor, the Empress and the court inflamed a generation of combative young liberals who had already detached themselves from the Five as too lukewarm for their taste. These young men made fun of the "gray beards of '48," who, they thought, were now in their second childhood. The "government of crooks" deserved no concession, no compromise. Crush the Empire! Avenge the *coup d'état!* Such the warcry of these newcomers of implacable energy! Struggle was the air they breathed. The human, generous, sincerely social side of Napoleon III's character, they regarded as mere pretense, mere sham. No matter what the Empire might do, no matter what pledges it might pay, they would never be grateful to it, they would never forgive it.

Government and opposition, legitimists and revolutionaries, Catholics and advocates of the evacuation of Rome, all waited impatiently, nay anxiously, for the elections of May, 1863. That expression of public opinion would show whether the country were demanding a more marked advance towards liberal forms of government. There had been twelve years of absolutism and two great wars. On the one side one could count on at least apparent prosperity, and some recovery of prestige abroad; but there had also been mistakes which would certainly leave their mark on the future. The vote was to be one of the most significant that the nation had been called upon to give since 1789. But it had to be an honest vote. Could there be such a thing in the face of the shameless pressure that an administration led in full cry by the barking bulldog Persigny would be sure to exert?

The struggle in any event was a bitter one, especially in Paris. The opposition, of course, again failed to fuse. There were too many party rivalries, too many rivalries of persons. There were also difficulties with principles. The Comte de Chambord stuck to his order of a boycott, but that did not prevent Berryer and Falloux from running as clerical candidates—Berryer making up his mind only after days of "moral torture" and under the encouragement of Father Ravignan. The Orleanists were divided. Among the democrats, Garnier-Pagès, Marie, Carnot, had to compete with enthusiastic and greedy newcomers, Floquet, Jules Ferry, Léon Gambetta. In Paris, finally, after many bitter fights a single opposition list of nine candidates was arrived at: Jules Favre, Emile Ollivier, Picard, Darimon, Havin, Guéroult, Jules Simon, Pelletan, and Thiers. At an Orleanist meeting at the Duc de Broglie's, Thiers had come out plainly for action and with his usual dialectic.

"One must never emigrate," he said, "either abroad or at home. The Constitution being revisable opposition is not incompatible with the oath."

The papers of the Left, the *Siècle* and the *Temps,* conducted a skillful and caustic campaign. A number of bishops came out openly for the "independents."

Persigny ordered the prefects to back the official candidates with all available resources.

"In order to be free," he wrote, without cracking a smile, "the voters need to be enlightened by their prefects."

Jobs, crosses, pensions, favors of all sorts! And not seldom threats: departments voting the wrong way could expect a very small share in the manna falling from on high. Officials, mayors, tobacconists, wine dealers, of whose soundness there was any doubt at all, lost their commissions. Pressure on the voter had never been so bold or so blatant. The administration had the posters of opposition candidates torn down, arrested their printers and destroyed broadsides of their campaign platforms and their leaflets.

Both parties hurled their whole souls and all their resources into the battle. The government's artillery, it must be admitted, was the heavier, and the country's response was adulterated at the outset by the play of too many irrelevant interests. All the same, though the Empire scored a mass success through the rural vote, it sustained a manifest defeat in the large cities; and that result had a far-reaching significance. In the Seine nine opposition candidates were elected by 153,000 votes, to 22,000 for the government. Opponents of the Empire triumphed at Lyons, Marseilles, Bordeaux, Lille, Nancy, Nantes, Toulouse, Le Havre, Saint-Etienne, Mulhouse, Toulon,

DUC DE MORNY

1811-1865

Limoges. They polled 1,300,000 more votes than in the elections of 1857.

The Emperor weighed the figures thoughtfully. On the advice of Morny and Billault he judged it expedient to give further guarantees to liberalism. Persigny left the ministry. He was made a duke and would remain a member of the Privy Council, but would no longer have any direct part in affairs.

"His policy is dead, dead as a doornail," Mérimée wrote to Victor Cousin.

Persigny was sore and blamed the Empress for ruining the Paris campaign by her meddling. His idea had been to hush the hostile newspapers by making their representatives official candidates.

"At the last moment," he wrote,[1] "the Empress vetoed everything that had been decided on and was under way, and forced the dropping of this plan, in the interests of a number of people whom I could mention."

The cabinet was recast. Walewski was dropped on Morny's insistence, Billault becoming sole Minister of State, with Rouher assisting him as Presiding Minister of the Council of State. The Orleanist Behic, a businessman of genius, replaced Rouher in Public Works. Baroche was considered to have been overdoing and was sent to recuperate as Keeper of the Seals. The historian Duruy became Minister of Education (June 23, 1863).

Morny was disposed to go farther than that. Aware of the many blunders that had been committed in foreign policy, conscious of the dangers to which the Emperor's shifting dreams and secret diplomatic moves might expose France at any moment, he thought the Empire should shed its dictatorial character once and for all and become frankly constitutional. On that condition only could the regime survive Napoleon III, the revolution be avoided and the Prince Imperial, a frail child of seven, come to sit on the throne. Morny sent the Emperor a strong and lucid note on the subject demanding "if not complete political freedom at once, then civil freedom at least," and a study of social problems. Morny's tone was truly bold.

"The elections," he declared, "have left just two forces facing each other—the Emperor and democracy. Democracy will grow stronger and stronger. It is imperative to satisfy it if one does not

[1] *Mémoires,* 397.

care to be overwhelmed by it. Could it be dealt with by a *coup d'état?* That would not be impossible from the mere standpoint of actual power. But how about afterwards? How could we keep going?"

He read the letter to Emile Ollivier, in whom he saw the statesman of the future who might lead the Empire to new triumphs. But Napoleon III was still in love with power, though he often appeared to be disgusted with it. He refused to "take the plunge."

Billault was to exercise the preponderant influence which his status as spokesman before the Assemblies gave him in the cabinet for only a few months. He died October 13, 1863. In him, with his insinuating voice and his mature and perceptive mind, the Empire lost one of its strongest supports.

To replace him the Emperor chose Rouher. Rouher had already rendered countless services in important posts, but never with any brilliancy. Here he was now, thrust forward into the full glare of the limelight. A man of no general culture, bombastic, rarely noble, never warm in utterance but a great worker, a crafty lawyer with an eye only for the name on the letter of recommendation, with no interest whatever in doctrines or ideas, a deep believer in government from above down though ready to take in sail at signs of a squall, the sturdy Auvergnat was to absorb power and hold it with a strong hand during this second period of the reign.

Down to 1863 Napoleon III had virtually ruled all by himself. Now he was to rule only through go-betweens. Rouher planned everything, directed everything, controlled everything. As Maupas, who detested him, was neatly to say, it was now "the Empire by delegation." The Emperor was run down by his bladder trouble and his general physical decline was day by day more evident. On a man in that condition, a counselor ever present, ever ready to be of service, never causing any trouble, could exercise an influence that a Morny or a Persigny had never had in the old days. Before long, by imperceptible gradations, Rouher moved from his status of a makeshift to the status of the old-fashioned prime minister. The Empire and France were to have reason to regret it.

Morny's speech at the opening of the new legislative session (November 3, 1863) was an appeal for national conciliation and good will. Deferentially he hailed Berryer and Thiers, "parliamentary glories of a day gone by" whom the votes of the people had returned to the assembly. The check-up on credentials revealed so many illegalities in the voting that an atmosphere of uneasiness prevailed in spite of all Morny could do.

Almost immediately the financial situation came up. The government had just borrowed 300 millions. Now at once it wanted 93 millions in supplementary credits to cover the Mexican adventure. Berryer opened fire with a detailed survey of imperial finance. Since 1852 drawings on the nation's savings had followed one another in accelerated rhythm.

"You have been able to make ends meet," he declared, "only by borrowing three billions in one form or another and by abandoning amortization."

Summing up he solemnly besought the Empire to return to economy and "to keep France at peace among the other European nations."

Thiers came next. This, really, was his first appearance on the speaker's platform after twelve years of silence. To be strictly exact he had taken the floor some days before on the question of the total of debt bonds outstanding, but that appearance had had no great significance and created no stir.

His speech was designed to strike a key-note for the debate on the "Address." It was a studied effort that was to be long remembered under the title, *"On Necessary Liberties"* (January 11, 1864). It voiced a demand and made an offer of collaboration. Thiers thought that five freedoms were indispensable to the smooth running of a modern state: freedom for the individual, freedom for the press, freedom for the voter, freedom for the elected candidate, freedom for parliament. That was a way of demanding the repeal of the law of public safety, a return to an independent press, the suppression of official candidacies, the right of interpellation for the members of both houses, in a word for ministerial responsibility to the nation's elected representatives.

After shedding a tear over the House of Orleans, his benefactors and his masters, their sometime minister declared:

"If we are given this necessary freedom I, for one, shall accept it and be in a position to be counted as one of the obedient and grateful citizens of the Empire!"

In a silence that emphasized his words and lent them impressiveness the old statesman added:

"One should beware: This country, at present so brilliant, is today barely awakening. We are still in time to ask favors for it in a most deferential tone; but the day will come when it will demand them."

The moment signalized by Thiers' speech is well worth a glance. Elections had just been held and their results were such as to give the Emperor food for thought. Heeding the thin, needle-like voice of Thiers, Napoleon III could head his government in a new direction and open a future of limitless possibilities to his Empire. With Thiers coming over to his standard, others would be sure to follow, among the first Ollivier and many of the latter's republican friends. That would be the real reconciliation within the nation that Morny was advocating. Still strong and vigorous the Empire would, of its own free will, be handing back some of the exorbitant powers it had usurped to a France to which it had brought order and prosperity. Such an act on its part could not have been interpreted as weakness or fatigue. Meantime it would be abandoning the path of adventures, losing its personal character and becoming incontestably one with the country.

To this course it was later to come, but of necessity and therefore too late, since by that time it would have made too many mistakes and its prestige at home as well as in Europe would be worn thin. In 1864 the Emperor was not ready to accept the transformation. Rouher rejected the offer in his name:

"The Emperor did not revive the throne for the purpose of not governing—just to hand the power back again to the unhealthy passions of the parliamentary system. . . . He will not allow himself to be stripped of this right in the light of antiquated notions of constitutionality."

To which Thiers answered:

"The only antiquated notion here is despotism."

And Thiers was right, Rouher wrong. So a magnificent opportunity was wasted. The histories of the nations are full of just such things—and the fact explains almost all of their misfortunes.

In the Speech from the Throne the Emperor announced early changes in the law on labor unions. Morny and Emile Ollivier came to an agreement, in conversations held after the elections, on the need of modernizing labor laws. Napoleon III needed no urging in that direction. He had intended from the very beginning to signalize his reign by an appreciable raise in standards of living for the working classes. He considered the prevailing system outworn, as he had dramatically shown the year before by granting immediate pardons to some typesetters, who had been sentenced to prison for organizing a strike to obtain better wages. By the winter of 1863-64 he seemed resolved on a comprehensive reform.

Such a change was in truth unavoidable. The French Revolution had suppressed all sorts of guilds and labor corporations. That reform had certainly freed the workingman of most oppressive bonds; but it had invented a so-called "crime of coalition," which made any form of grouping or association whether of employees or laborers illegal. That had left the wage-earner without any protection at all. As long as industries remained virtually family enterprises, the evils of the system were not so striking. When machines came into use and factories took the place of home workrooms, a group of employers interested chiefly in profits, and capable of concerted action through their chambers of commerce, granges and stock exchanges, stood over against the workingman, whose isolation, weakness and moral as well as material poverty, as compared with the employer, began to give serious concern to the statesmen interested in social peace. Prince Napoleon conceived the idea of rallying to the Empire a class of citizens who were hostile to the bourgeois parties that had slaughtered them in June, 1848, and whose natural protector seemed to be the Emperor. In 1861 he called a meeting of typesetters in the Palais Royal, and one of them drew up an appeal to the sovereign, protesting against "laws, customs and mechanical routines" which condemned workingmen to wretched, helpless lives. A delegation of workingmen chosen by their fellow-workers went to the World's Fair in London in 1862 and had conferences with workingmen in England. They discovered that English labor was better paid for less work, that English factories were healthy and well ventilated, that employees had formed "unions" in every branch of industry to look after their interests.

The comparison gave rise to a series of "claims" which at times were contradictory but which, in the essential respects, were to find their balance: the trade-unions for workingmen, mixed commissions to arbitrate disputed points, control of apprenticeships. For a decided novelty, in the elections of 1863 the wage-earners of Paris ran a candidate of their own, Blanc, against the republican, Havin. Blanc, to be sure, polled very few votes.

In accord with Morny and despite Rouher's objection, Napoleon III had a bill relating to strikes brought before the Legislative Body. The opposition thought that was a good war-horse and demanded the abolition pure and simple of the law forbidding indusrial "coalitions." Morny worked Ollivier into the position of reporting on the bill. Ollivier foresaw that the many manufacturers and businessmen in the Chamber would oppose the bill and modified its text somewhat. Associations of employers or employees would no longer be illegal, while any "attack by fraudulent manoeuvres or violence on freedom to work" was made a crime. Severe criticisms came both from Left and Right. In reply the brilliant orator marked his shift to the Empire a little more pointedly.

"It is a bad way of acting," he said, "to reject a step in advance on the ground that it does not go all the way. I am not a pessimist. I accept a thing that is good, whatever the hand that offers it: today the law permitting coalitions, tomorrow the law permitting unions."

Jules Favre was Ollivier's elder, bitter, therefore, and a little jealous of his younger colleague. He was saddened in particular by Ollivier's desertion and answered with some harsh words:

"The school of expedients never founded anything."

He, for his part, stood loyal to the school of principles. And he took Ollivier to task for his change of front:

"It would be interesting to hear how a man can abandon long held convictions by proposing absolutely contradictory things today."

Ollivier replied in some embarrassment and afterwards refused to shake hands. From that time on there was war between them, less personal than political as yet, and it was the end of the little group that had become famous as "the Five." In the eyes of the republican party Ollivier and his colleague Darimon were thereafter mere renegades.

While voting was in progress on the Coalition Bill, supplementary elections in Paris reopened the Chamber to two old-time republicans, Carnot and Garnier-Pagès (March 14, 1864). Their opponents had been workingmen, the first candidates to come out as representatives of a class. They published on this occasion a manifesto which was reprinted in Prince Napoleon's paper, *L'Opinion nationale*. It was signed by sixty workers, most of them from the building, printing or art-objects' trades, and contained a full-fledged platform of demands, social and political.

The "Manifesto of the Sixty" is of great interest from the standpoint of the doctrinal history of socialism. It owed nothing to the proletarian philosophers. Proudhon did not know of it till after its publication; but he was so struck by it that he sat down and wrote his last work under its inspiration, the essay "On the Political Capabilities of the Working Classes."

The manifesto first of all demanded "social emancipation":

"Equality stands written in the law, but it does not exist in manners and customs and it is far from being realized in facts."

Capital, it continued, was oppressing labor. What the working classes wanted above all else was to win the same freedom of action that the middle classes enjoyed:

"Let no one accuse us of dreaming of agrarian laws, divisions of property, maximum programs, tax exemptions and so on. Freedom to work, credit, solidarity, oneness of spirit—those are our dreams. We look forward to a day when there will be no more bourgeois, no more proletarians, no more working classes, but just citizens all equal in rights." And later on came a truly touching note:

"We do not want to be dependents or objects of charity. We want to be equals. We reject alms. We demand justice. We do not hate men. We want to change things." Urgently demanding a Chamber of Labor, corresponding to a Chamber of Commerce, the Sixty protested that they were not truly represented in the Legislative Body. Nothing substantial, they said, distinguished them from the "democratic bourgeoisie." Like the latter they wanted "universal suffrage freed from all shackles, a free press, freedom of assembly, complete separation of Church and State, a balanced budget, municipal autonomies." More insistently than the bourgeoisie "because more directly interested" they asked for free and obligatory elementary schools and freedom to work.

The Manifesto appeared on the 17th of February, 1864. Its demands were in themselves reasonable. They were free of any note of animosity or violence, keeping within the bounds of the French instinct for moderation from which they sprang. They were soon to be overpassed, however, by international doctrines, especially by

Marxism, and swallowed up in them. The last exponents of a socialism genuinely native to France were to perish with the Commune of '71.

That was to be a great loss for France. The country could have adjusted itself to many principles of such a socialism, which was substantially altogether assimilable. It could never withstand the assaults of German socialism apart from a disastrous scattering of forces.

The dawn of internationalism was in fact at hand. Six months later, in September, 1864, the International Association of Workers came into being in London. This group aimed to destroy capitalism and, with capitalism, the whole framework of modern society. The founders were mostly Englishmen, but a Frenchman, the engraver Tolain, who had been a candidate for a seat in the Legislative Body at the preceding elections, and Karl Marx, a German refugee, author of the Communist Manifesto of '48, were to play the major rôles.

The platform of the First International was drawn up by Marx and contained many of his personal ideas. The purpose of the union, it stated, was "the emancipation of the workers by the workers themselves." Party members were reminded that if there were no duties without rights, there were likewise no rights without duties, while truth, justice and morality were recognized as the basis of their conduct.[1] The First International subordinated political action to economic conquest. It was a class movement, regarding questions of form of government as incidental and secondary. This was a great disappointment and a cause of bitter anger to the French republicans.

The first branch of the International was opened in Paris in the rue des Gravillers in July, 1865. These headquarters were just an ill-furnished room where a handful of workingmen aflame with faith gathered around Tolain and a few friends of the latter. The subscription was two sous a week. A few "bourgeois" were admitted, notably Jules Simon and Henri Martin. This section had a rather Proudhonian and mutualist coloring and kept strictly aloof from politics. It was to hang on down to the Congresses of Geneva (1866) and Lausanne (1867), when the International was to change

[1] Translator's note: [This talk about rights and duties and the moral bases of conduct was inserted in the platform at the last moment, as a concession to Mazzini. Marx regarded such things as irrevelant to the class struggle. A. L.]

in spirit and in outlook, becoming demagogic and libertarian and dropping from an idealistic to a class struggle plane. From then on social hate began to bear its fruits and the membership increased. By 1868 the Paris branch counted several thousand "comrades."

Immediately after the elections of 1863 the Emperor called a new man, a man of distinguished intellect and independent character to the Ministry of Education—Victor Duruy. Napoleon III had made Duruy's acquaintance some years before when he had besought his advice in connection with his *Life of Julius Caesar,* a work in which he was deeply absorbed.

Son of a Gobelin artist, Duruy was a graduate of the Ecole Normale and an *agrégé* in history. At the *Lycée Henri IV* he had been teacher to the Duc d'Aumale and the Duc de Montpensier. His studies on Roman history had won international prestige. Ollivier said of him:

"He was extraordinarily well read. Of his life one can say that it was just one long day of close application." [1]

Napoleon III had benefited by Duruy's collaboration and grown accustomed to relying on his pen. He liked the man because of his frank, simple ways and shortly made him Inspector General in the schools. Duruy was at Moulins on an inspection tour when he received the dispatch that made him a minister.

So, for a miracle, a university man came to be placed at the head of the University. Duruy well knew all its defects and shortcomings and, active, hard-working himself, he set out to remedy them. In a very short time he had outlined a scheme of complete reorganization, which may have been open to criticism here and there, but which, on the whole, was most happy.

His reform was of a markedly liberal inspiration and in a number of respects was extremely modern. Duruy showed himself a real innovator when he created secondary courses for girls and established a special system of education for business. Higher education had fallen to very low levels. He restored standards, revived courses in philosophy that had been suppressed, and founded new chairs in law, science and medicine in huge numbers. He gave a marked impetus to the study of modern languages and organized scientific laboratories provided with suitable equipment. His work was even more significant and productive in primary education. To the

1 *Empire Libéral,* II, 602.

great scandal of the conservatives he declared himself, in a famous report that was published in the *Moniteur,* a firm believer in free, obligatory education. Disapproved by the Council of Ministers and too feebly backed by the Emperor, he was unable to carry this reform through. But he at least improved teaching methods, filled the teachers with enthusiasm and developed courses for adults which, according to Jules Simon, who could never be suspected of tenderness for the imperial government, came to count 800,000 pupils by the end of the Empire.

Attacked by partisans of an extreme dictatorship, such as Parieu, by Orleanists like Guizot and especially by the Catholics, Duruy was backed by the opposition press. The moment he came into power he made no bones of declaring his intention to limit application of the Falloux Law—he may perhaps have considered abrogating it. At one of the sessions of the Higher Council on Education, a prelate, Monsignor Parisis, grew worried at so many innovations and asked:

"What are your intentions? What are you driving at?"

Duruy replied sharply:

"You ask what I want, Monsignor! I want the opposite of all that you have been doing. What am I headed for? For public enlightenment!"

There was soon to be open war between him and the bishops. Duruy was avowedly an anti-clerical and certainly a free-thinker. He was not anti-religious. But the warmth of his convictions sometimes led him to do petty and unjust things. On the whole he has to be regarded as one of the most creditable servants of the Second Empire. A trifle sharp and over-direct, but devoted, persevering, disinterested, Duruy was the great popularizer of education in France and the restorer of the University.

The Catholics were shortly to find other pretexts for aversion to the imperial government and on matters far more serious than Duruy's innovations on mere problems of teaching. In the course of the year 1864 Napoleon III once more undertook to raise the Roman mortgage on his policy. Pius IX was seriously ill with erysipelas and, it was believed, dangerously. If he died there was every likelihood of an uprising in Rome. As things stood, the Minghetti cabinet seemed inclined to conciliation. It was proposing to transfer the Italian capital from Turin to Florence, and that gesture could be interpreted as an implicit abandonment of claims to Rome. Unbeknown to the Empress and even to Victor Emmanuel, long negotiations took place between Nigra and Pepoli, Rouher and Drouyn de Lhuys, Drouyn finally arriving at an arrangement which at bottom was an exact duplicate of the plan that had caused Thouvenel's downfall.

"Why, the man has picked my pocket!" exclaimed Thouvenel.

Rouher was not on good terms with Drouyn de Lhuys and was hoping to get Thouvenel back into Foreign Affairs. He had expected that Drouyn would never consent to an agreement that was so contrary to his personal views. But Drouyn was concerned above all else to stay in office and offered no resistance. Disappointed, Rouher was obliged to swallow his rage. According to the covenant of September 15, 1864, Italy agreed to respect Church property and to defend it in case of foreign aggression. She would move her government to Florence. France would gradually withdraw her troops from Rome in the course of two years, the time required for a proper reorganization of the Pope's forces (September 15, 1864).

This bargain was distasteful to Italy and Pope alike. The Minghetti cabinet fell before an angered public opinion, whereupon difficulties at once arose with France over interpretations of the agreement, and the two sometime allies began plastering each other with recriminations and demands. Pius IX allowed one complaint to escape his lips:

"They are treating me like a minor—or like a convict."

Then he lapsed into disdainful silence.

The Curia, however, made the mistake of addressing an encyclical, *Quanta cura,* and the *Syllabus* directly to the French bishops. The *Syllabus* hurled the anathema at various "errors of the present day": freedom of conscience, freedom of the press, popular sovereignty, the supremacy of the civil law, civil marriage, lay education and national-church or Gallican doctrines. Such thoroughgoing archaism set all the various elements in French public opinion by the ears and at each others' throats. The Gallicans could still count numerous representatives in high officialdom and they angrily called attention to the violation of the Concordat. Liberal Catholics feared a complete rupture with Rome. Montalembert, for instance, was profoundly saddened. He wrote to Falloux:

"I am off to Morvan to bury my grief—or rather, as I must confess, my shame in solitude."

Baroche forbade the bishops to publish the *Syllabus*. Many disobeyed and the conflict between the government and the defenders of the Holy See grew venomous. Duruy's predecessor in Education, Rouland, was a Gallican. He delivered an eloquent indictment of ultramontanism in the Senate during the debate on the "Address" of 1865. Cardinal de Bonnechose replied that there was no such thing as a French church or a French ritual, that Catholics in all countries followed the guidance of the Roman pontiff. Monsignor Darboy, archbishop of Paris, urged wisdom and conciliation. It was all a flash in the pan, but sullen angers lingered in many minds because of it.

Napoleon III's personal prestige was still very great in Europe.

"He holds us all in the hollow of his hand," said the King of Sweden, and Palmerston, though suspicious of the man, confessed:

"We feel his ascendancy ourselves. We dare not begin anything or even pass an opinion until we know the Emperor's views and aims. And to think the man lived for years in London and not one of us even dreamed that there was anything to him!" [1]

But behind this resplendent window-dressing of the Empire many signs of decadence were beginning to appear. The small towns, the rural districts and a fairly large majority of the working classes the Emperor still had with him. But the business classes felt threatened in their interests and the Catholics were disappointed. They both now moved away to swell the republican opposition, which had heretofore been a small minority. Paris might well applaud the reviews, the processions, the ostentatious and brilliant spectacles which it loved and with which the Empire lavishly provided it; but at heart the city was hostile. The young people in the schools were predominantly democratic and anti-clerical. The suspension of Renan's course at the Collège de France seemed to them an unendurable insult. Prosecution was instituted against members of republican committees who had campaigned in the elections of 1863, and the "Case of the Thirteen" brought out new leaders to replace the "gray-beards of '48" and the discredited Five: Hérold, Jules Ferry, Gambetta. Small newspapers, run on nothing and sometimes written out in long hand, were edited by such men as Méline,

[1] Pasolini, *Mémoires,* 376.

Clémenceau, Tridon, Vermorel, Longuet, Peyrot. They were so many focuses of discussion, bringing up the great moral and social problems of the day, glorifying the French Revolution in its very excesses, attacking religion and demanding that religious and war budgets be abolished. From his prison at Sainte-Pélagie Blanqui directed a group of fanatics that had one idea only, rebellion. Through its organ, *Candide*, it sounded echoes of the Terror.

The opposition slowly gained headway in the Legislative Body. Before ballots on the "Address" or on the budget the Empire's financial and foreign policies came in for stinging criticisms by Thiers, Berryer, Buffet or Jules Favre. Those men were tireless in their demands for reform. A group independent of the republicans formed under the name of the "Third Party." It comprised Catholics, conservatives and malcontents of every sort. Not very large during its early years it was gradually to grow, with Emile Ollivier, finally, as its leader.

The Third Party first took shape on the issue of the "Address" of March, 1866. A minority "Address" was put forward in the form of an amendment and it obtained forty-four signatures, notably those of Chevandier de Valdrome, Talhouët, Kolb-Bernard, Maurice Richard, Chambrun and Wendel. The text was drawn up by Emile Ollivier and said, among other things:

"Stability is by no means incompatible with wise progressiveness in institutions. France is strongly attached to the dynasty, which is her guarantee of order; but she is no less devoted to liberty, which she considers indispensable to the fulfillment of her destinies."

Buffet defended the amendment in a sober but very forceful speech. Rouher replied, relegating the Legislative Body to its pristine nonentity. Ollivier replied brilliantly in his turn. As was to be foreseen, the amendment was rejected, but the Third Party had come into being.

Morny was the only man of foresight among the statesmen of that era in France. He kept urging Napoleon to satisfy wishes that were voiced not only by members of the opposition but by large numbers of reasonable imperialists also, and liberalize the government. Prince Napoleon was hostile to Morny but he threw his weight in the same direction.

The Emperor hesitated under pressure from the Empress, who protested that to accede to the demands would be to vitiate the very essence of imperial rule, which was an affair for one ruler and could not be divided. Ollivier hoped to be given the task of working out the transition from the dictatorship to a constitutional system.

Early in 1865 liberalism won the day in the Emperor's mind. He seemed to have decided to try the experiment. Unfortunately Morny fell ill and after several weeks of suffering succumbed (March 10, 1865).

The Emperor and the Empress went to see him on the 9th at six o'clock in the evening. Morny was half conscious and did not recognize them at first. Finally, emerging from his coma, he murmured:

"The Emperor knows how devoted I am to him."

Napoleon III was deeply moved and stammered words of encouragement. As he left the room he whispered softly:

"*Au revoir,* Morny!"

The dying man smiled:

"No, it's goodbye. *Au revoir*—somewhere else!"

And he fell back on his pillows.[1]

Sitting somewhat slumped down in his chair but always supremely distinguished, with eyes too bright above hollowed cheeks, with a heart overstrained by so many shocks, fears and joys and working at best only on arsenic, that superior dilettante had dominated the parliament of the Empire down to his very last breath. The Chamber was a ferment of many leavens, but he had given it a surface calm, a charm of atmosphere, that may have deceived public opinion but at any rate gained time. His influence had grown with the years. The Empress, the dignitaries, the ministers feared him and treated him considerately. Fully alive to political realities he might have avoided the fatal mistakes and guided the government's bark to some haven of refuge where it could have recaulked its seams, repainted its planking and lived a long time. Unfortunately he died.

Morny's death dismayed Paris. For the Emperor it was a real disaster. Just a few months before (December 9, 1864), Napoleon III had lost his private secretary and life-long friend—Mocquard, the long-suffering, the discreet, the wise Mocquard. Mocquard, too, was a man who could not be replaced. The Emperor chose State Councillor Conti to succeed him. Conti was surely a man of parts, but he

---

[1] No description of Morny's death can equal Alphonse Daudet's admirable stories in *Le Nabab* and *La Doulou.*

Braun & Cie

EMILE OLLIVIER

1825-1913

EUGENE ROUHER

1814-1884

lacked Mocquard's experience and never managed to acquire the influence over Napoleon III that Mocquard had had. Morny's death pushed the Emperor back towards absolutism, for now Rouher, backed by his friend La Valette, whom he had worked into the Ministry of the Interior, had no counterbalance left.

Napoleon III had the final quarrel with Prince Napoleon because of an opposition speech the Prince delivered at the unveiling of the statue of Napoleon I at Ajaccio. The real political doctrine of the Emperor, the Prince claimed, was to be found in the Act Additional of 1815, which events alone had withheld from application. He defended the theory of nationalities, came out against any alliance with Austria and violently attacked the Holy See.

"Rome in the Pope's hands," he said, "is a breeding-nest of reaction against France, against Italy, against modern society."

He came out emphatically against dictatorship:

"I love freedom under all its forms, but I prefer what I call the freedom of all, in other words, universal suffrage honestly practiced, complete freedom of the press and free assembly. . . . Yes, I prefer freedom and a policy influenced by public opinion to ministers not seldom chosen from a parliamentary coterie that forces its will upon the sovereign."

Jules Favre could not have done better.

Napoleon III learned of the speech in Algiers. He replied by a stern letter that was published in the *Moniteur:*

"The political program which you place under the aegis of the Emperor can only be of use to the enemies of my government. To judgments with which I cannot sympathize you add sentiments of hatred and rancor that are out of place in the age in which we are living. Before one can apply the Emperor's ideas to present day problems one must have passed through the harsh tests of power and come to understand its responsibilities."

Before the Emperor's return from Algiers the Prince encountered the Empress and said insolently:

"Well, Madame, are you going to send me to Vincennes?"

"I should certainly do so," Eugénie replied, "if the Emperor had left orders. I await his decision."

And she turned her back on him.

Actually the Prince resigned his seat in the Privy Council and the presidency of the World's Fair of 1867 at that time in preparation.

Retiring to his estate at Prangins he affected ever after a complete lack of interest in public affairs.

By a very understandable reaction the Emperor became more stubborn still in his resolve "to stay put." The concessions he had made would have to suffice. He made the declaration expressly in a note in the *Moniteur,* which he had himself dictated:

"The newspapers have for some time been noisily predicting a change in the personnel and the policies of the government. We are authorized to state that such rumors are unfounded inventions of sheer malice" (September 13, 1865).

Ollivier personally was the object of gracious attentions from the Tuileries. He had an interview with the Emperor and the latter's charm completed its work. They talked of Thiers and the Emperor said: "Thiers always wants to have his way and he is dangerous."

After a rather brisk discussion on press reform Ollivier concluded:

"Your government is strong enough to take courageous risks!"

The next day the Emperor spoke glowingly of his impressions:

"M. Emile Ollivier is not an ambitious man as people have tried to make me believe. One has only to see him for a moment to be sure that he is an honest man, sincere in his beliefs. Morny was right."

But there was no question of calling him to the government as Morny had advised. The liberal Empire had still several years to wait—the years that were to seal Napoleon III's doom.

CHAPTER XXI

Mexico: First Phase

DURING THE EARLY PERIOD OF THE EMPRESS'S ATTENDANCE AT SESsions of the Council of Ministers she had played a very inconspicuous rôle. She did not always appear, she listened a great deal and spoke rarely. Beginning with 1865 she was regular in attendance and her part became increasingly important.

Daughter of a politician mother and with a taste for public affairs herself, she had grown interested more and more in public life through her talks with ambassadors and high officials, who had sought to use her influence even before it was very great. In the end she acquired a passionate interest in both domestic and foreign problems. Exercise of power helped, moreover, to take her mind off her husband's neglect and other family sorrows. (The death of her sister, the Duchess of Alba, in 1860, had been a great blow to her.) She could see that the Emperor was often ill and there was reason to fear that he might die before his time. The better to safeguard the crown for her son she resolved to take a hand in the details of governing. Napoleon III let her have her way, in order, as he put it, "to have a little peace at home." She therefore asserted herself more and more and assumed a growing authority.

Her ideas were clear-cut, courageous and sound. She showed good sense, energy and a great concern for the prestige of France. Unfortunately her imagination, coupled with a stubborn disposition, inclined her to extravagant views and dangerous enterprises.

The Emperor was well aware of these weaknesses.

"You never get an idea, Eugénie," he sometimes twitted. "The idea gets you!"

He mistrusted her, but in fear of her temper—for she could make a tremendous scene—he deferred more and more to her wishes. A clique that was virtually a party grew up about her in the higher regions of power—Vaillant, Walewski, Drouyn de Lhuys, at intervals, Rouher. First she helped to get Fould out of office and then intrigued to get him back again. She had a bitter hatred for Persigny. After the elections of 1863 she charged that "his brutalities were making more and more enemies for the government" and he was eliminated from public life, this time for good. She fought Thouvenel's policies untiringly and was the cause of his downfall. She thought the principle of nationalities a fatuous and dangerous thing. She was tenaciously bent on keeping the Pope in Rome and desired an understanding with Austria. She disliked and despised Prussia. At home her sympathies lay with the conservatives. She was afraid of freedom. Still very Spanish at heart, and despite a sincere interest in the welfare of her new country, she mistrusted Paris and feared the ever-flexible, ever-changing spirit of the French.

To the Empress's influence was in large part due the enterprise in Mexico, an enterprise that was to develop in ways no one foresaw at first and was eventually to undermine not only public confidence in France but the self-confidence of the government itself.

Mexico had broken away from Spain in 1821. First an Empire under Iturbide, then a republic, the country had been floundering about for almost a half century in the most violent upheavals. The United States had taken advantage of that situation to dismember the nation and snatch away three-fifths of its territory—Texas, New Mexico, California.

In 1858 disorder in Mexico reached a new peak in a furious struggle that broke out between so-called "conservative" elements, whose real leader was a twenty-five-year-old general, Miramon, and so-called Federal-Democrats under Benito Juarez.

Juarez was not, as has been said, a savage. He was a simple soul but profound. He was a man of Indian stock, coming from the Zapoteca tribe which had fled to the mountains to avoid falling under the Spanish yoke. First a shepherd Juarez eventually became house-man to a bookbinder in the city of Oaxaca. The man was struck by his intelligence and found a way to send him to school. Juarez acquitted himself brilliantly in law and history and soon became a representative in Congress in Mexico City, then governor of the State of Oaxaca. The dictator Santa Anna threw him into prison. He escaped to the United States, then returned under Alvarez, who made him head of the department of Justice. From that

post he moved on to the secretaryship of the Interior and then became chief justice of the Supreme Court. When President Comonfort came to terms with a conservative revolution backed by the
army, Juarez as leader of the so-called liberals, proclaimed himself
president in Comonfort's place. Headstrong and fiery, cruel less by
instinct than by policy and necessity, he was passionately devoted
to the independence of his country.

Miramon's conservatives were a party largely of great landowners.
They were said to want a monarchy, or at least a dictatorship that
would support the Church and protect their possessions. The Fed-
eral-Democratic platform provided for a republic along the lines of
the United States and for nationalization of Church properties,
which were enormous.

Late in the year 1860 Juarez overwhelmed Miramon and the latter fled to Havana. The Mexican treasury was empty and Juarez
had to suspend payments to foreign creditors, French, English and
Spanish, who were numerous. The creditors appealed to their respective governments, and Paris, London and Madrid began three-
cornered negotiations. France suggested that the three powers send
an army to Mexico to hold the republic to its pledges. England accepted on condition that the purposes of the enterprise be strictly
limited. She wanted to be paid and nothing else. She would take no
interest in questions of Mexican politics (London Agreement, October 31, 1861). Spain's sympathies lay with the Mexican conservatives. She wanted to help them back into the government.

Napoleon III had aims that were far vaster and also more definite.
While still a prisoner at Ham he had pondered on the future of
Central America. Now that the Civil War in the United States had
split that great country in halves, his mind often dwelt on the mani-
fold advantages that France would sometime gain if she could set
up a Catholic and Latin monarchy that would halt the Protestant
and Anglo-Saxon republic on the south. Puritan America Napoleon
III disliked, foreseeing and fearing a prodigious expansion on its
part. He could make the Archduke Maximilian, a brother of Francis Joseph, sovereign of this new empire and the gesture would
bring him back completely into the good graces of Vienna. Perhaps
in compensation for the throne he would be giving a Hapsburg
he could get Venetia and hand that province over to his beloved

Italy.[1] So he would be keeping his original promise to Victor Emmanuel and the Italian patriots and find himself in a position to refuse them Rome.

Before his death Morny had urged the expedition without seeming to; but his motives, as contrasted with the Emperor's, were altogether personal. He had a third interest in the money owing in Mexico to a shifty Swiss banker, one Jecker, who had lent several millions to Miramon and had been vainly trying to collect them from Juarez. He was now putting his claims at seventy-five millions and he wanted them sauced with interest at usury rates.

The Empress threw herself into the scheme with all her usual impetuousness. Mexico had revolted against the Spanish domination and had fallen into anarchy. She would save the country and bring it back to civilization and the Faith. This dream of an America Reconquered was fanned in her by General Almonte, an agent of Miramon in Paris; while a friend of her youth, one José Hidalgo, made the dream of a Reconquest seem all the more real in that the secession of the South had paralyzed any possible resistance from the United States. She unbosomed herself even too freely with Metternich, the Austrian ambassador and his young wife, and her talk with those friends ended by raising her hopes to fever heat.

That, really, was the whole story of Mexico: a variety of diplomatic considerations, plus an assortment of romantic ideas, plus a considerable body of cash interests! The Emperor was dreaming his old dream of a Nicaragua canal. The Spanish girl was seeing herself as a modern Isabella. The army chiefs were thinking of promotions, raises in salaries, pretty Mexican girls succumbing to waxed mustaches. The men in business were thinking of loans and high interest rates, gold mines, fabulous sub-soils that would gush fortunes forth. The Mexican émigrés gave their word that the moment the French troops set foot on the Mexican shore they would be welcomed as saviours by a grateful population and live in wealth and plenty ever after. Everyone in France believed them—forgetting a suspicious Europe, a hostile United States, the difficulties and dangers of a distant land for the most part still unknown. Dubois de

[1] "The ghost of Venice is stalking the halls of the Tuileries," wrote Nigra to Ricasoli. And Vimercati wrote to Castelli (February 6, 1862): "The offer of the Mexican throne to Maximilian of Austria is a concession which His Majesty hopes to balance, at the proper time, against a proposal that the Austrian cabinet cede Venetia."

Saligny was French minister to Mexico. He should have set French opinion right; but he was too much the slave of Morny and he had himself been a heavy buyer of "Jecker stock." He was, therefore, the untiring advocate of the inexcusable adventure and its "evil genius," to use the phrase of General Du Barail.

Rouher could well repeat before the Legislative Body that the Mexican expedition was "the greatest thought of the reign." Any sensible mind could hardly have failed to see in 1862 that the expedition had no real chance of succeeding. France was taken to Mexico by a party that had been beaten at the polls by the majority of the Mexican population. The United States was busy with its civil war and might at first be obliged to let things in Mexico take their course. Sooner or later, however, the French could be sure of finding the American republic against them. Napoleon III, in fact, joined England in according belligerent rights to the seceding South, and when the North won the war he was to pay a pretty sum for that backing of the wrong horse. Austria, for her part, could be certain to set little store on a crown offered to an archduke and that asset certainly would count for little in smoothing out Italian difficulties. Mexico was to be to the Second Empire what Spain had been to the First. Vast expanse of dangerous desert land, now freezing cold, now steaming hot, it would be hard and costly to conquer, impossible to hold for any length of time.

Napoleon III and Eugénie had had definite warnings. The trouble was, they paid no attention to them, Eugénie, in this respect, being especially blinded by her devout zeal. Just before committing himself the Emperor had one last touch of caution. He sent a squadron to Vera Cruz as England and Spain had done. The French force numbered a scant 2,500 men commanded by Admiral Jurien de la Gravière. Vera Cruz fell and an ultimatum was dispatched to Juarez. The Spanish General Prim was commander-in-chief of the allied army. He had a Mexican wife and may have been cherishing ambitions of his own. At any rate he took it upon himself to sign the Soledad Convention (February 19, 1862) with representatives of Juarez. That agreement authorized the European soldiers to camp on plateaus in the interior, in order to escape the dysentery and the fevers that were endemic in the coastal regions. Meanwhile negotiations for a final settlement of the debt question would be opened at Orizaba.

London and especially Paris were inclined to censure Prim. Sensible as his move had been it had recognized the independence of the Mexican Republic. Napoleon at once dispatched a reenforcement of 4,500 men under General de Lorencez. More than that, he sent Almonte along. Almonte quarreled with Prim the moment he stepped on shore, while Spaniards and English alike cried aloud at this "collusion" between France and "a conspirator and a rebel."

The breach between the Allies widened rapidly. Prim had no slightest desire to fight a war for the purpose of conquering a throne for Maximilian. He had sent a prophetic letter to Napoleon III away back in March, 1862 (March 17th):

"It will be a simple matter for Your Majesty to get Prince Maximilian to the capital and crown him king. . . . As a monarch he will have no support whatever left the moment French backing is withdrawn."

On the other hand Dubois de Saligny wanted war and its profits. He refused to ratify the Soledad Convention. By the end of April the concert of the three powers was at an end and the Spanish and English forces sailed for home, leaving a tiny French army to conquer a new Eldorado, where so far it had found only swamps and rocks, pestilence and famine.

Lorencez led the French to Orizaba. A difficult march over a mountainous country was enlivened by a number of skirmishes in the passes with poorly armed Indians. Finally the French arrived in front of the Cerro de Guadalupe, a hill that commanded Puebla on the road to Mexico. Overconfident of his superiority Lorencez ordered an attack on the position. A battalion of Zouaves and four companies of light infantry rushed gallantly forward, but the Mexicans met them with grape at point-blank range. Losses were heavy and on May 5th Lorencez was obliged to fall back.

It was a minor set-back but it was to have far-reaching consequences. All Europe stirred. The honor of the tricolor seemed to have been compromised. So far France had hardly been aware that she was intervening in Mexico. For ten years the country had known only successes in the field. The defeat at Puebla roused public opinion. A hot debate took place in the Legislative Body. Speaking on June 26th with a restraint that sent a shiver through the government, Jules Favre told the story of the whole shady origin of the enterprise, and he rarely attained such heights of inspiration:

"In this affair it would seem as if every possible mistake has been made. . . . To go on with the war would be to involve ourselves in the most unjust, the most reprehensible of adventures. The worst thing that could happen to us in this enterprise would be to win, for with victory would come responsibility. . . . Having set up a government we would have to maintain it."

Billault defended the Emperor's policy eloquently, adroitly; but he was careful to say nothing of the plan to set Maximilian on the Mexican throne.

New loans were voted and Napoleon III set actively to work preparing his revenge. Harassed by Juarez's guerillas Lorencez had great difficulty in getting back from Puebla to Orizaba and then in holding on at the latter place. His eyes had opened at last and he now denounced Saligny's lies and intrigues to the Emperor:

"We have no one on our side here. The liberal party does not exist. The reactionary party amounts to nothing and is despicable to begin with. I have not met a single soul who wants a monarchy."

The Emperor would not listen to reason and replaced Lorencez with General Forey. Forey was a huge fellow, rude and crude and unpopular with the soldiers, but he had made a good showing in Italy and was known to be a loyal imperialist.

At the time of Forey's departure Napoleon III explained his outlook in a letter to the general (July 3, 1862). His chief concern seemed to be to prevent any exclusive preponderance of the United States in the Americas:

"It is to our interests that the republic of the United States should be powerful and prosperous, but it is in no sense to our interests that she take possession of the whole Gulf of Mexico and become sole custodian of the resources of the New World. . . . If Mexico preserves her independence and maintains the integrity of her territory, if a stable government is set up there with the help of France, we shall have restored power and prestige to the white race overseas and have guaranteed the security of our colonies and the colonies of Spain in the West Indies. We shall have reestablished our beneficent influence in Central America and that influence will create vast outlets for our commerce and supply us with indispensable raw materials for our industries."

A force of 23,000 men embarked for Vera Cruz between July and September. Many were stricken with malaria or yellow fever the moment they set foot on those arid, pest-ridden sands. Effectives melted away like wax in the sun. Forey had grown fat of body and slow of mind. His main idea was to avoid a defeat. He proceeded very slowly to organize two divisions, one under Bazaine, the other under Douay. Though Paris kept calling for action he spent the whole winter at Orizaba, not taking the road towards Puebla till early in March (1863).

Not counting Mexican auxiliaries, which were few in numbers and untrustworthy, Forey had 28,000 men and 56 cannon at his disposal. Ortega, the Mexican general, had fortified Puebla with formidable redoubts. Every block of houses bristled with barricades and guns. All the streets were mined. It was another Saragossa for the French to take. Forey conducted a siege for two months. At one moment, at Saligny's suggestion, he thought of letting Puebla go and pushing on towards Mexico City. Luckily he did not make that mistake. It would have driven all parties into Juarez's camp and placed the army in a grave predicament. He resigned himself to carrying the blocks of houses one by one.

It was a long and murderous task! The troops grew restless. A Mexican relief army with supplies was approaching Puebla under General Comonfort. Bazaine suggested destroying it, then attacking the forts at Totimehuacán overlooking Puebla. Forey took the advice and Bazaine succeeded. On May 8th (1863) he attacked Comonfort at San Lorenzo and dispersed the rescuing army. That left the besieged garrison without food and ammunition. On May 16th the French artillery destroyed the forts at Carmen and Totimehuacán and General Ortega surrendered "arrogant Puebla" the following morning.

Saligny wanted the garrison deported overseas. Forey, much to his credit, refused. Officers would be sent to France. The rank-and-file could either enlist in the auxiliary unit or go to work with pick and shovel in the trenches. Ortega solved the problem as regarded himself by escaping with many of his soldiers.

The French had expected to be welcomed enthusiastically into Puebla by a devout and conservative populace that had long been oppressed by Juarez and his henchmen. Actually the reception chilled them to the bone. They entered a town that was to all appearances dead.

"We marched," wrote Du Barail, "through a waste in a mournful, gripping silence."

The road to Mexico City lay open. Juarez first thought of defending his capital, but he was short of men and supplies. Thinking that his end was near the conservatives came to life. Reluctantly, therefore, he decided to evacuate. He left the capital on May 31st, taking arms, baggage and government archives, and reached San Luís Potosí.

The French found two white, phantomlike peaks blotting out the horizon before them, Popocatepetl and Istaccihuatl, 15,000 and 12,000 feet high, with a high ridge between them. They crossed the ridge without a fight. At Buena Vista Mexico City came into view, a motley expanse of roof-tops, gardens, clock and bell-towers, spreading out among five lakes that sparkled in the harsh glare of the sun. On June 7th, with Bazaine in the lead, the French occupied the city. Forey made a solemn entry three days later, riding over a carpet of flowers while bells pealed. The clergy had rounded up the populace to acclaim the conquerors and Forey, naïvely joyous, reported to the Emperor:

"The soldiers of France have been literally buried under wreaths and bouquets."

He made haste to set up a government. Disdaining universal suffrage, and with Saligny's help, he appointed a junta of notables. These in turn elected a provisional Regency made up of General Almonte, General Sales, and the Archbishop of Mexico—the "three caciques" the army called them. The Junta was forthwith promoted to the status of a Constituent Assembly and reestablished the Empire in favor of Maximilian of Austria. The Regency, for its part, took advantage of its momentary omnipotence to annul sales of national properties and give the clergy back their domains. It carried partisan zeal to such lengths that Forey wrote, discouraged:

"There are only two parties here, demagogues and reactionaries. The one sees in power only a means of oppressing the other."

Paris gradually recovered from its hallucination. The ministers, especially Marshal Randon, began to think of ways to limit the intervention and abbreviate its duration. Drouyn de Lhuys advised Forey to treat with any power or individual who could furnish suitable guarantees. As in the Crimea, Napoleon III had his personal sources of information in Mexico, men who kept him informed and enabled him to check up on the veracity of official reports. Chief among these were General Douay and Captain Galliffet. Awakened at last by their letters to Saligny's responsibilities the Emperor called him home. Forey, he also learned, had gone far beyond his orders. He made him a marshal and recalled him too to France, Bazaine becoming commander-in-chief while the troops acclaimed.

A heavy, swarthy man, with small intelligent eyes set deep in a fat, jealous face, Bazaine was considered the most energetic field leader in the army. A sometime grocer's boy, he had fought for eight years in Spain in the Carlist war, serving in the Foreign Legion. Thence he had gone on to the Algerian campaign, quickly winning his stripes. He was almost beaten at Solferino, losing many men in front of the famous cemetery, but blood did not count in his eyes. They were fixed solely on his personal advancement. His training had been colored largely by the Algerian experience. He knew nothing about manoeuvre, nothing about tactic. There was something Oriental about him—a surface charm, a deep-lying roguery, a cold courage. He had no morals of any kind, no trace of religious or political conviction. He lied in season and out. Always hard up, never with a sou in his pocket, he surrounded himself with people to his taste—gamblers, sharpers, questionable men and questionable women. With all that he was not unpopular. He had the army's confidence.

Napoleon III directed Bazaine to check arbitrary procedures on the part of the Three Caciques and to see that Maximilian's election was ratified "by the greatest possible number of Mexicans, his hasty nomination having had the defect of not convincing Europe as a legitimate expression of the country's wishes."

That was a real scruple with the Emperor, but Bazaine set to work to lull it to sleep or at least to get around it.

He declared sales of national properties valid and at once he had the clergy about his ears. The conflict was undisguised and bitter. The general had the habit of going scrupulously to Mass every Sunday. When Monsignor Labastide, Archbishop at Mexico, threatened to have the doors of the Cathedral shut in his face, he answered:

"If you do, I will shoot them open with my cannon."

Elections, to tell the truth, would have been impossible in a country so disorderly. Instead of them Bazaine accepted "adhesions," which were more or less required of the inhabitants. So six million "votes" were "foraged" in favor of Maximilian. Napoleon III looked on at the yellow plebiscite with grave mistrust, but he had to put up with it. The guerilla bands were chased. French columns over-ran the country. Guadalajara was taken and San Luís Potosí. Juarez had fled to Monterey on the Texan border where the United States obtrusively supported him.

The opposition in France continued to criticize the Mexican expedition. From Guernsey Victor Hugo sent a proclamation to the Mexicans:

"I am with you. Here we stand both of us against the Empire, you on your side, I on mine, you in your country, I in exile. Fight on, struggle on, be terrible! If you think my name is of any use to you, make use of it. Aim at the man's head and let the cannonball be freedom."

Thiers, Jules Favre, Berryer, stressed the dangers of the venture in a debate before the Legislative Body, January 26, 1864. Thiers advised treating with Juarez. But Rouher brushed fears and cautions aside disdainfully. In this case as often he affected a grandiloquent optimism and spoke of the genius of an Emperor who had had "the courage to open sources of new prosperity to the nation."

The Assembly refused to listen to a reply from Jules Favre. Thiers then shouted:

"You do not want the truth!"

The voting showed only 47 in opposition, but at least three-quarters of the representatives were beginning at heart to disapprove of the expedition.

Bazaine's successes before long began to make Rouher look right. Napoleon regained his confidence and urged Maximilian to hasten his departure.

The tall, blond archduke, thirty-two, characterless, gentle, sensuous, had ended by accepting the crown of Mexico. His decision had required protracted negotiations and pressure from his wife, Charlotte of Belgium, granddaughter to Louis Philippe, an ambitious woman born to sit on a throne.

The royal couple made a preliminary tour of the northern capitals. In London they were coldly received. In Brussels the aged Queen Marie-Amélie tried to dissuade Maximilian from going to America.

"They will assassinate you!" she cried.

In Paris the Tuileries outdid itself in splendor, and Maximilian signed an agreement which settled his future relations with France. Napoleon III pledged himself to maintain 25,000 men in Mexico until 1867. The Foreign Legion would stay there till 1873. Maximilian was to assume all costs of the adventure as well as the original French debts. That was a big bill to pay and the future emperor shouldered the responsibility in total ignorance as to the resources he would have at his disposal in his new state. However, he was in the hands of France. How could he argue? Not only that: at the demand of his brother, Francis Joseph, he was obliged to renounce any rights he might thereafter have to the throne of Austria.

Brimming with hopes Maximilian and Charlotte bade farewell to their castle at Miramar and sailed for Vera Cruz. The carefree spirit in which the whole enterprise was regarded in imperial circles in France stands out in a letter of Mérimée's (April 21, 1863):

"The Archduke Maximilian has sent the Emperor an eight page letter expressing his thanks. . . . We are assured that things are going very well in Mexico. Colonel Dupin has been ordered to pursue the Juarist guerillas with African Spahis and Mexican counter-guerillas. He began at the start, as one must with that rabble, by shooting every one of them that he could catch. People out that way all approve. . . . It is thought that a few months more of it will make the country entirely safe."

Maximilian was very well received on his arrival. Everything, he thought, was coming his way. Mexico seemed submissive and he tried to govern in a liberal spirit. But European liberalism had no place in that feverish, violently contested country. What would have been tact anywhere else was sheer blunder there. Acting always with the best of intentions Maximilian managed in a few months to arouse hostility and anger on all sides. He needed the support of the clergy desperately, yet he quarreled with them by trying to force a concordat through and by declaring old sales of Church properties irrevocable. He antagonized the army by regulations that hurt the Mexican officers in their pride. He worried the great landowners, the hacenderos, and discouraged moderate elements which at first might readily have struck a bargain for their submission.

The penury of the Mexican treasury was distressing. Taxes failed to come in while expenses increased by leaps and bounds. A first loan of eight million pounds was negotiated in London, but half of it vanished in the bonuses charged by bankers and in the various commissions of go-betweens. A second loan, issued in France in April, 1865, bore a face value of two hundred and fifty million francs. Scarcely the half of that sum was made actually available and at a scandalously usurious interest. It passed the Legislative Body only through a trick by the government.

The military situation at least was still good. Bazaine had been made a marshal of France on August 30th, partly as a reward for his successes, partly to increase his prestige in his dealings with Maximilian. In the north French columns drove Juarez's bands to the Texas border. In the south, in the state of Oaxaca, his chief lieutenant, Porfirio Diaz, was captured (February 9, 1865). To discourage guerilla raids the government issued a decree fixing the penalty of death for the possession of arms (October 3, 1865). In pursuance of it a fair number of Mexican officers and soldiers were shot. That was a terrible precedent! In two years' time Juarez was to take his cue from it.

CHAPTER XXII

The Emperor of the Arabs

WHILE THIS DISASTROUS DRAMA WAS UNFOLDING, ANOTHER ENTER-
prise, essential, fruitful, truly national, was going forward less conspicuously overseas. Here Napoleon III made mistakes and suffered
setbacks—they may have been unavoidable—but on the whole he set
out to increase French colonial possessions and put them in running
order with a knowledge of actual facts and with the conscious purpose of enhancing French prestige throughout the world.

At the time the Empire took possession of Algeria that country
was a half-pacified country at best. The usual inveterate conflict
between military authorities and pioneer colonials had left it mud-
dling along in great disorder, without any economic life of its own.
In 1846 there were approximately 109,000 European settlers in
Algeria, 47,000 of them French. The Second Republic had taken
praiseworthy steps towards improvements. At an expense of some
27 millions in 1849 it sent out more than 21,000 working people
and supplied them with provisions, farming implements and seed.
About half of these were shortly to desert, but new centers of coloni-
zation had been established.

The Republic may have made a mistake in bringing the three
provinces too soon into the departmental system of the home country. That mixed them up in French domestic politics. The Empire,
at any rate, did not hesitate to take a step backward in this respect.
It placed Algeria under army rule again. From that moment the
French hold on the country was strengthened and expanded. Desert
oases at Laghouat, Ourgla and Touggourt came under French control in the years 1852-1854 and the tricolor was planted on the edge
of the Sahara. Upper Kabylia was still in a state of open revolt.
Kabylia was a great rich territory stretching along the sea and
peopled by a race of courageous Arabs. General Randon, the gov-

ernor-general, took the region in hand after careful preparation, gradually broke down the resistance of the tribes and finally conquered the entire plateau (1857). This time the conquest became an undisputed fact. Algeria was French. To speak more exactly, a new France came into being, facing the old France across the sea, a magnificent parallel such as no people in Europe since the days of ancient Rome had dared dream of achieving.

The government founded a hundred or more new villages. It granted liberal concessions to farmers who could show certain resources of their own. In 1851 Algerian products were admitted free of duty to the mother country and a boom in prosperity began. By 1854, 750,000 hectares of land were producing grains. Seven years later the figure exceeded two million. Vines were brought in about that time and in many regions replaced olive growing. Extensive public works were started, highways, reclamations of swamp lands, irrigation systems, forestations. Health conditions were at first very poor. As hygiene improved mortality dropped off. The European population, moreover, adapted itself readily to the Algerian climate. By 1861 it exceeded two hundred thousand.

The Emperor now in his turn thought that Algeria could be brought under the French civil system. He attached it to the French Interior under a special bureau headed by Prince Napoleon. The office of governor-general was abolished, prefects having full control over civil districts, with a general council for each department to assist them. An independent Algerian budget was created. A court of appeals was instituted in Algiers along with a normal school and a high school.

The experiment was abandoned after two years (1860). Prince Napoleon did not take his job seriously. The prefects had no influence over the Arab population. Napoleon III decided to go back to a governor-general again. A trip to Algeria with the Empress revealed to him a new land of extraordinary possibilities, but he returned convinced that a civil system would never go well there and he handed the leading rôle back to the army. Marshal Pélissier was put in charge.

During the years following the Emperor gave much thought to the situation of the Arabs. The problem, he concluded, was to protect them from two great enemies: officialdom and the colonists. On February 6th (1863), he published, according to his custom, a letter to Pélissier in which he declared his intention of pursuing a liberal policy towards the natives in Algeria.

"Algeria," he said, "is not properly speaking a colony; it is an Arab kingdom. The natives have the same right to my protection as European colonists. I am Emperor of the Arabs the way I am Emperor of the French."

A senatus-consultum of April 22, 1863, marked boundaries for tribal lands in Algeria, dividing them off into douars, the douar being the aggregate of families living in one same encampment. Individual property was virtually non-existent among the Arabs. The douar, therefore, would own "the lands to which it had permanent and traditional title."

A census of population and registration of properties for purposes of taxation were necessary but went forward slowly. Local officials and colonists both did their best to make things difficult. Pélissier was slow-moving, half asleep, jealous of power without ever actually having any. He let everything go its way. A vague feeling of unrest developed in the colony and in 1864 a serious insurrection broke out in Southern Oran. Colonel Beauprêtre and some hundred men were attacked and massacred near Géryville by Si Sliman, "aga" of the Ouled-Sidi-Cheiks. Even the Tell, the coastal lowlands, revolted. Reenforcements had to be sent from France and the army in Africa rose to a total of 85,000 men. More than a year was required to put the rebellion down. Pélissier died of pneumonia in 1864 (May 22nd) and MacMahon was appointed to succeed him.

In May, 1865, Napoleon decided to make another trip to Algeria and study the situation at first hand. For the second time he set up a regency for the Empress, placing her in the chair at meetings both of the Council of Ministers and the Privy Council.

On this occasion Napoleon III drew up the only will that was ever found among his papers on his death in 1873. It was dated April 24, 1865. It left the whole of the Emperor's private fortune to the Empress and declared that he died in the Catholic and Roman faith. Certain passages in all their simplicity of form were significant. He exhorted his son to steep himself in the acts and writings of the "prisoner of St. Helena." Then he added:

"Power is a heavy burden. You cannot always do the good you would like to do and your contemporaries are seldom fair. A man, therefore, must do his work and have faith in himself and a sense of his duty."

The moment he reached Africa Napoleon III issued two proclamations, the one urging colonists to come to closer and friendlier understanding with the natives, the other assuring the Arabs of his interest in them.

"It is my wish," he said, "that you should have a greater and greater share in the administration of your country as well as in the benefits of civilization."

He went in as far as Biskra, receiving ovations from the Europeans at Algiers, and from the Arabs in the Oran, in Kabylia, and in the southern sections of the department of Constantine. He issued pardons to the tribes that had last revolted, exempted them from war contributions and sent their hostages home. These acts raised a veritable storm of acclaim. The Arabs gave him the surname of El Kerim, "the generous," and they also said, "His spur is green," meaning that wherever he went he brought happiness and spread it abroad. Dazzling fantasias were given in his honor and sumptuous "diffas." He returned to France a conquering hero, escorted by a French and an Italian squadron.

He published a new letter directly on his return. It was addressed to Marshal MacMahon and set forth the chief items in a program that his visit had inspired: to win the friendship of the Arabs by tangible benefits, attract new immigrants, utilize to the full the natural resources of Africa and its man-power, and so gradually lessen the military and administrative expense to France. The natives were gradually to be admitted to status as French citizens. Their taxes were to be reduced and more soundly distributed. A hundred millions should be spent on public improvements. The prerogatives of the Arab bureaus were extended; they would watch movements in the tribes and make every effort to bring the leading native families over to the French side. The religious orders were very active and generally hostile to France. The same "bureaus" would keep an eye on them.

With the homages of great chiefs, the joyous cheers of an impulsive people, still ringing in his ears, Napoleon III dreamed of bringing that warlike race of men, that nation of simple chivalrous emotions, into close association with the sophisticated society of

France. That concept of the Arab Empire was far shrewder policy than was believed at the time, but years were to pass before it could be worked out in practical forms. Scourge followed on scourge in Algeria, first locusts, then cholera, then drought, then crop failures (in '66 and '67). Such things were to halt Algeria's climb to prosperity. For a time the native population fell off. French administration deteriorated and came to a standstill. The Emperor himself grew discouraged. By the end of the reign the "experiment" was so definitely regarded as a failure in Paris that after an investigation by the Legislative Body a return to civil government was recommended.

Algeria was not to come into her own till after Napoleon III's time. She none the less owed to him a very considerable increase in security and wealth—he was her true benefactor. For long years, to be sure, this second France in the making was to be torn by the never-ending conflict of races.

The Senegal was originally a tiny trading-post of the old monarchy. Seized by the English it was afterwards restored, to be neglected by the Restoration and Louis Philippe. At the beginning of the Empire it was still just a scattering of trading-posts paying blackmail to Moors and Toucouleurs and under constant menace from them.

A young captain of the Engineers, Faidherbe, had been appointed governor by Napoleon III. He held the place for ten years, taking the first steps towards really organizing the territory between 1855 and 1858. He raised a siege of Saint-Louis that had been laid by the Moors, drove the Toucouleurs away and compelled all the troublemakers to call it quits.

"We are here to stay," he could soundly declare in a speech he made in 1860 before his "school of hostages," an academy that he had started to educate the sons of native chiefs. "Africa's hour has struck."

He recruited and trained a strong force of Senegalese riflemen, the first of the battalions that were to render such signal service in the French army in after years. With them he made a series of expeditions and at the cost of few lives conquered both banks of the Senegal for the whole length of the river and built a great colony out of nothing. Meantime Faidherbe's eyes were already set on the Niger. He established relations with the Mussulman notables of that region, concluded commercial treaties and treaties of amity with them and so laid the foundations of what in our day was to become French West Africa.

Napoleon III took the most eager interest in all the details of this great achievement. So in two distinct domains, French expansion overseas and social economy at home, he gazed through his half-closed eyes into a future still far distant.

CHAPTER XXIII

Society Under the Second Empire

As THE YEARS ROLLED BY NAPOLEON III BECAME A SLOW-WALKING, slow-moving man whose health was evidently declining. He suffered from gout and renal troubles, attacks of this latter recurring at lessening intervals and leaving him each time more depressed. He was treated with drugs containing opium and they made him more sluggish still. His head with its puffy face drooped over his right shoulder. He dyed his hair. Otherwise it would have been snow-white.

Still kindly, still courteous, offhand and affable—too much so perhaps—with his intimates, he had a tendency to melancholia. He no longer manifested the old confidence in life and in his star. He had lost his last illusion regarding people. So many of his dreams had been disappointed, so many of his plans had miscarried, that he became more and more hesitant in his decisions and policies. The Empress, Rouher, Persigny, all tugged at the cart, pulling it now this way, now that.

"I am being quartered," the Emperor would sometimes say with a laugh, though he had jested on the same point years before:

"I hear the complaint that things never go straight in my government. How could they? The Empress is a legitimist. Morny is an Orleanist, I am a republican. There is only one Bonapartist. That's Persigny—and he is crazy!"

He needed only to lift his eyes to remind them that he was master. That gesture he could never bring himself to make. He withdrew, instead, into a silent distraction which might deceive outsiders but did not hide from intimates a weakening in his will-power.

His carelessness in money matters reminded one of the prodigality of his grandmother, Josephine. On himself he spent hardly anything.

"Charity," he said, "is the safety valve of pride."

And he helped everyone who asked for help out of his privy purse, disregarding party and opinion. He paid the debts of young army officers who were in danger otherwise of losing their epaulettes. He subsidized numberless charities and relieved many cases of distress that were known only to him and Dr. Conneau—Conneau was his adviser in such matters. His kindheartedness became a weakness, and people took advantage of it. He simply could not punish a rogue, rid himself of a nuisance, dismiss an incompetent.

One morning at Compiègne the Prince Imperial's big hound, Nero, came and stretched out behind the Emperor in his armchair. To give the dog more room Napoleon III huddled together as far as he could. Finally the dog went to sleep and pushed out with his paws. The Emperor got up. Pietri made a move to drive the dog away but the Emperor restrained him:

"No, don't disturb him. He's having such a good sleep."

The man and the monarch are drawn to the life in that remark.

Prince Napoleon was always out of step, coming out more and more as the leader of a dynastic opposition, flirting with republicans, passing caustic remarks on the dynasty even in the Tuileries itself. The Emperor always swallowed such things indulgently. In an argument one day the Prince brought in Napoleon I and went so far as to say:

"The Emperor? Why, you have nothing that he had!"

"You are wrong, my boy," Napoleon III replied, twisting the points of his mustache. "I have the family he had."

He was too fond of women and that failing wore him down in the end.

"He runs after every alley cat he sees," said his cousin Mathilde.

Neither age nor failing health seemed to make any difference with him in that respect. He succumbed to every temptation and temptations were one of the things that his court produced in greatest abundance. Social station did not figure in his tastes for women. He formed very varied attachments, sometimes such as to fill Hyrvoix, the chief of his secret bodyguard, with consternation. Marguerite Bellanger held his interest for a long time. With her the crowned grayhead cavorted like a schoolboy.

The Empress never suspected half his fancies, but the half she did suspect was enough to give her the keenest unhappiness. The time came when the royal couple were more friends and partners than husband and wife. Even then her wounded pride would break into violent scenes. In sheer exasperation she would flee the court, set out suddenly for Scotland—in November, perhaps, or go incognito to Schwalbach on pretext of taking the waters, calling herself the "Countess de Pierrefonds."

She was eighteen years younger than the Emperor—was in her prime, in other words, as he began to age. Her figure eventually filled out, her complexion developed blotches, but in her state robes she was still marvelous in the full glare of the lights. She acquired an assurance, a commanding air, that she had not worn in the earlier years. Her gaiety lost its glow. She seemed worried, and when matters of state went against her she would have sudden attacks of depression. Many people did not like her for a certain dryness or bruskness, an apparent lack of a sense for the other person. She took an active interest in charities, visited kindergartens, sewing schools, hospitals, but still was not popular. On her travels with the Emperor she would see him acclaimed by soldiers, workingmen, farmhands, with enthusiastic and sincere huzzahs. For that she envied him. She, the Empress, was never acclaimed in spite of all her efforts to win people. Paris especially never liked her. She knew it and suffered from it.

"If Paris would only accept me," she confided one day to Mérimée, "I would give ten years of my life."

Paris did not like her because she was a foreigner. Try as they may, the French are and will always remain provincial. They called her "the Spanish woman" just as in days long past they had called Marie Antoinette "the Austrian."

The opposition press always did its best to exaggerate breaks of tact on her part or altogether venial shortcomings. She was blamed for playing politics too much in favor of the Pope and the bigots. Harsh measures of government that actually were ideas of Rouher were ascribed to her influence. The styles she promoted brought money into Paris pockets, but she was criticized for the court's extravagance.

On the throne Eugénie remained the society woman—she was never quite recognized as the sovereign. The Emperor's nearest relatives, Princess Mathilde and Prince Napoleon, made her conscious of the fact, the Prince especially never sparing her an embar-

EMPRESS EUGÉNIE AND HER LADIES OF HONOUR

From the Painting by Winterhalter

rassment or a slight. He accused the Empress to her face of driving the regime to ruin by her bigotry and retrogressive notions. He would never drink in public to her health or, perhaps, on occasion, he would lift his glass and call out insolently:

"Madame, I drink to your forty years!"

Eugénie detested him and with good reason. She despised him for his loose morals and his irreligion and for the way he ignored and neglected his wife, the good, the devout Princess Clothilde.

"The Emperor lets him do anything!" she cried one day; and again, hurt to the quick, she mused regretfully:

"Unfortunately we are not living in the Middle Ages. The days have passed when one can do away with one's cousins!"

At times her boiling aversion would carry her too far and involve her in a duel of witticisms, in which he always came off best. Poking fun one day at his father-in-law, Victor Emmanuel, she dropped an ironical allusion to the Italian rout at Custozza. The Prince turned on her crushingly:

"I prefer a defeat like Custozza that wins a province to victories like Mexico that cost an empire."

The Empress could only bite her lips and leave the room.

Outwardly Princess Mathilde was more decent to her, but she could never forget that as a girl she had been the Emperor's fiancée and that, with a little more patience, a little more real love, she would have reigned as empress in place of the Spanish woman. She even wore the little ring that the son of Hortense had given her at Arenenberg. Massive, majestic, truly imperial, proud of her descent on her mother's side from St. Louis and Mary Stuart, proud of her right to call all kings in Europe cousins, proud especially of being the niece of the first Napoleon whose very footprints she worshipped, she could not help viewing the Montijo woman as an intruder.

At first Eugénie made an effort to win her with an attentiveness and a graciousness that did not come naturally to her and cost her dear. Continued rebuffs discouraged her in the end. The two women really had nothing in common, whether in temperament, in education, in beliefs, or in habits. They met often, to be sure—they had to meet; but apart from the necessary contacts they went their separate ways, the one to her historic palace and her great castles to be courted by officials and the officially great; the other to her cozy houses in the rue de Courcelles or her castle of Saint-Gratien, where painters, literary men, even men of state, scandal-mongered and lampooned. But Mathilde kept Napoleon III's friendship and confidence all along. Eugénie did not try to interfere on that score. She was loyal even in her hates.

Disappointed in her marital affections the Empress concentrated all her passion upon her son. He, she seemed to feel, was the tie that bound her to her husband and to France. He took after his mother, with a somewhat darker complexion. He had been a robust baby. He grew up frail and ailing. His health was Eugénie's incessant worry, but she resolved to rear him not like an invalid but like a man. With that in mind she often objected in ways that some considered harsh, but which were merely farsighted, to the Emperor's excessive spoiling and his inclination to overlook all the boy's faults. She feared the effects that adulation by courtiers would have on him. She made him work and stick to his work.

When he got to be seven she selected General Frossard, aide-de-camp to the Emperor, as his governor, having by chance heard the General reprimand the child one day. Frossard was in fact a strict soldier, but cultivated. Renan knew him in Rome in 1850 and described him as "truly exceptional in point of intelligence." Frossard was indeed remarkable as an engineer—more so, alas, than as a general! The Prince Imperial did his grammar school course under Augustin Filon, a talented Normalien whom Eugénie also discovered. Both these choices, in fact, were excellent. The "little Prince," as everyone affectionately called him, worked listlessly at his studies and with no very unusual results. He rode horseback well, evinced a taste for military affairs, was an instinctive draughtsman. Naturally open-hearted and affectionate, he grew up merry, simple, charming.

The court was still more or less boycotted by the old nobility. It was, nevertheless, the largest and the most brilliant that France had seen since the days of the old monarchy. But there was something unsettled, something superficial, about it—it was a sort of "gilded Bohemia," someone said. That came in part from the earlier lives of Napoleon and Eugénie. When not on official exhibition they acted and felt like private individuals. It came also from the large numbers of foreigners, not always friendly foreigners, whom they took into their intimacy. At times at court the French seemed to be lost souls among a throng of Englishmen, Spaniards, Italians, Germans—diplomats on special mission, transient guests, personal acquaintances of the two sovereigns. It was less a court of France than a court of Europe. Most of the continental princes were to be seen there at one time or another: Victor Emmanuel, Frederick William of Prussia, the kings of Belgium, Bavaria and Württemberg, Queen Sophie of Holland, Maria-Christina, the dowager-queen of Spain, the Grand Duke Constantine of Russia, the various archdukes of Austria, the princes of Coburg, Hesse, Baden and Brunswick.

The sovereigns spent the winter at the Tuileries, which the Empress redecorated and refurnished a second time in 1860, with the architect Lefuel in charge. Napoleon III and Eugénie took luncheon as a rule alone together in the Louis XIV Room. At dinner the Prince Imperial appeared, now that he was quite a boy.

Dinner was laid most often with twelve or fifteen places. It was rarely announced before eight o'clock—the Emperor being often late and making it his rule to call for the Empress at her apartments before they joined their guests. These, usually, were the aide-de-camp, the Chamberlain, the equerry on duty for the day, the orderly officers, the Prefect of the Palace, two or three of Eugénie's ladies-in-waiting, sometimes a personal friend. The men were in evening clothes or in uniform, the women in evening gowns—cut very low in the "Eugénie style."

The table was decorated with a large center-piece of flowers and Sèvres bowls. Dishes were of plated silver stamped with the imperial coat-of-arms. Early in the reign Napoleon III procured an estimate on a complete solid silver service. He found that it would cost between five and six millions. He winced at the expense and the imperial household resigned itself to eating off electroplate.

The Emperor and the Prince Imperial had a liveried footman each behind them, the Empress a handsome Negro in Turkish costume—Skander, a Nubian. This detail Eugénie borrowed from the *grandes dames* of the Louis XV era. The fare was bountiful but not very choice.

"Good secondrate boardinghouse fare," said the Princess Metternich, ever trying to belittle.

As a mattter of fact neither Eugénie nor the Emperor cared much about what they ate.

Coffee was served after dinner in the Apollo Room and the general party began. Napoleon III would half sit on a table and start doing a puzzle, or else would chat with some of his guests, always amiable, always charming and with a gentleness and naturalness that captivated all who came near him. The Empress would flit from group to group chattering tirelessly. True child of Madrid she long retained her love of dancing. Soon she would ask an army officer, or even the Emperor, to wind up a mechanical piano they owned and from it would stream polkas, mazurkas, waltzes, or else a lancer's quadrille—and they would laugh gaily as they got mixed up in its complicated interchanges that were still new. By the '60's Eugénie danced more rarely, paying more attention to her guests and keeping the best of the evening for talks with her ambassador friends— Metternich, Nigra, Prince Reuss, Lord Cowley. At times when a question really interested her, she would let herself go and talk carelessly, unguardedly, and the Emperor would try to check her by a word or a sign. She would obey, only to begin again where she left off as soon as his back was turned.

At eleven tea would be served in Queen Hortense's gold-lined set and the Emperor would shortly after withdraw. That was the moment for Eugénie to make her celebrated bow—a curtsy that took in the whole circle and bade them all good night.

On Monday evenings all members of the Bonaparte family who were in Paris gathered for dinner at the Tuileries—most often Prince Napoleon and the Princess Clothilde, Princess Mathilde, Prince Charles Bonaparte and his wife, the Marquise Roccagiovine, the Countess Primoli and the Princess Gabrielli and their three husbands. Ministers, Grand Officers of the Crown, diplomats, dined at the Tuileries twice a month.

Following the first Monday dinner after Easter Eugénie gave a ball in the First Consul's Room to a company of select guests. These evenings came to be known as the Empress's "little Mondays." The grand balls, three or four in number before the Lenten season began, were given in January. To them came members of the Senate and Legislative Body, ambassadors, ministers, admirals, generals, high officials, writers, artists, newspapermen, private individuals who had been presented at court. They were magnificent spectacles: diplomatic coats glittering with gold, embroidered court dress for officers of the imperial household, military uniforms, the burnouses of Algerian caïds, silken hoops or crinolines gay with flowers and blazing with gems. At nine o'clock came the grand march for the entrance of the Emperor and Empress—Napoleon III in a general's tunic overspread with orders and crosses, breeches of casimir-satin-ette, white silk stockings; Eugénie in her court gown—now satin, now moiré, now velvet, and in one of her favorite colors, either blue, or white or mauve, and wearing the Crown diamonds. In virtue of her carriage, her wondrous throat, her magnificent shoulders, she was the envy of all the women—and yet never had so many exquisite beauties or better-gowned beauties foregathered in that age-old palace.

The sovereigns brought the masked ball back into fashion. Napoleon III started not a few of his little love intrigues behind the convenient shelter of the domino, and many court flirtations took shape under the glistening paneled ceilings of the Tuileries. The Empress doubted the wisdom of so much incognito, but she too came to enjoy the fun. She would embarrass the men by piquant questions or allusions to things which indiscretions had revealed to her, or tease the women, frighten them, then vanish, laughing.

At the carnival of 1863 the guests at the Tuileries were treated to a surprise in the form of a "Ballet of the Bees," directed by the ingenious Countess Tascher de la Pagerie. Footmen dressed as gardeners brought four tall gilded beehives into the Diana Room. From them emerged twelve young women dressed as bees—tight-fitting striped corselets, translucent wings, quivering antennae. They went through a number of steps and figures—and the ball began.

Eugénie's accession was the accession also of blondes. Whether by nature or by grace of the coiffeur's art most of the beauties outstanding in those days in the public eye displayed light hair.

The Countess Walewska was a Florentine noblewoman. She was a mere girl when she married the son of Napoleon I and the Polish woman—that was after Walewski's rupture with the actress Rachel. The Countess was the delight of any eye for the beauty of her features and the impeccable taste and splendor of her gowns. She was great friends with the Empress in spite of a number of quarrels, and even more so with the Emperor. As her husband advanced in years he neglected her quite, and no one blamed the Countess for amusing herself. She was popular in the diplomatic world and, adroit, flexible, tactful, rendered more than one service to Napoleon III's policies.

The Countess de Pourtalès appeared in imperial society shortly after the Italian war. She caught the Empress's eye while riding in the Bois one day. Eugénie promptly invited her to receptions at the Tuileries. Shortly she was a member of the most intimate circle. The Countess de Pourtalès was, undoubtedly, the most attractive figure of the era: slender lines, light of carriage, a sweet face with deep blue eyes and laughing lips, a native charm and distinction, intelligent. She was a guest at all parties at the Tuileries and accompanied the court on all its country holidays.

The Duchess de Morny, born Princess Troubetskoy, had received her dowry from the Czar, with whom she was closely connected. Very slender, frail rather than not, with a rose-and-marble face brightened by large black eyes, she was full of originality and caprice, virtually lived in her hothouse and doted on monkeys and birds. She seldom appeared at the receptions that Morny gave so lavishly during his presidency of the Legislative Body and she was often on pouting terms with the Tuileries. Her husband deceived her endlessly but she worshipped him. When he died she cut off her hair, laid the curls in his coffin and otherwise evinced a wild desperate sorrow. Later on she recovered from her mourning and married the Duc de Sesto, whom the Empress as a young girl had nearly fallen in love with, when he was still just Alcanizes.

Mme. de Persigny was ravishing rather than beautiful. Eccentric, more or less insane perhaps, she displayed a looseness of language and morals that no consideration of her position could bridle. Her faux pas in London, while her husband was ambassador there, were to be counted by the score rather than the dozen—famous the time when she kept Queen Victoria waiting for dinner on the excuse that she wanted to see the boa constrictor fed at the Zoo. She was a constant headache to her husband whom she twisted around her little finger, trying his patience, ridiculing him, beating him. On many an occasion Persigny appeared at official receptions with scratches from his wife's fingernails on his face. She made no attempt to hide her fancy for the young Duc de Grammont-Caderousse. Of many other affairs Persigny knew nothing or else he forgave them. She was mad over everything English and in comment Paris called her "Lady Persington."

The Marquise de Contades, daughter to Marshal de Castellane, was an intrepid rider at the hunts. She had a gift for witty and malicious sallies which people thought she inherited from her father. She was one of the earliest partisans of the Prince-President and stood with the Princess Mathilde beside him at receptions at the Elysée. She was also one of the first to pronounce for Mlle. de Montijo. The favor she enjoyed at court was, one may therefore say, something that she had deserved. Napoleon III made his usual pass at her. She let him know that he was wasting his time.

Shortly after the Crimean War the Empress brought a young cousin of hers to court, Sophie de la Paniega, an orphan girl without a fortune. The Empress hoped to find a good husband for her. Unfortunately candidates were not numerous. Finally her eye lit on the aging Marshal Pélissier. He was sixty-five but Eugénie persuaded him that if he proposed to the young girl he would probably be accepted. Mlle. de la Paniega let herself be led to the altar, but with a manifest lack of enthusiasm, and as a Marshaless she ever paraded a wistful, disappointed beauty at imperial receptions.

The Duchess de Mouchy was, in plain language, Anna Murat. She was undoubtedly Eugénie's closest friend and confidante. She had a beautiful skin, sparkling eyes, a very average intelligence; but the Empress was never to forget that in the hectic days before her marriage Anna Murat had always stood by her, thoughtful, loyal, understanding.

Countess de Castiglione was related to Mme. Walewska. Conceited, selfish, not a little stupid, without visible charm, she long advertised and publicly exploited her affair with the Emperor, even going to the length of appearing at a masked ball as "Queen of Hearts." The Empress raged but could do nothing. "La Castiglione" forced her presence on the court for several years. Eventually the Emperor tired of her and moved on to other thoughts. That was a chance for Eugénie to have the lady escorted to her carriage one night when she appeared at a party at the Tuileries without an invitation.

One woman in the imperial circle eclipsed all others. She was to play an important rôle in the Second Empire as undevoted friend and adviser of doubtful loyalty to the Empress. None the less, all by itself, the name of the Princess Metternich symbolizes all the spangled lustre of the era. Prince Metternich replaced Hübner as ambassador from Austria immediately after the Italian war. The Princess was welcomed and made much of from the moment of her arrival. Ugly, with a dark-complexioned, pug-dog face, but with eyes that sparkled under heavy, bristling eyebrows, she was able to suggest one caustic description as "a cross between a monkey and a weasel." She had, however, an aristocratic bearing that no one ever missed. Offhand, easy of manner, noisy, loose of speech and of conduct, ever delivering herself of impertinences that as a rule showed more breeziness than good-nature, she soon became the arbiter of feminine fashion, made war on crinoline, discovered Worth and forced his "creations" on the Empress and on society. For ten years this foreigner reigned as queen of Parisian taste.

Her husband was a better pianist than diplomat. To help him she did her best to make her way into the intimate circle of the sovereigns. She plied the little Prince with toys, came mornings to talk fashions with the Empress, went with her on her drives in the Bois, tried to enliven the often tiresome evenings at the Tuileries with her fertile, nay unbridled, imagination. Her influence on Eugénie grew with time. The Empress forgave her everything, even snubs of a disconcerting insolence. The Metternichs encouraged the Empress in her invasion of French power, thought to profit by it and did so. The Metternichs were basically responsible for the war in Mexico. The Empress trusted them unreservedly. Through her they knew everything that was going on in the French government. Napoleon III urged her to be less expansive.

"We are surrounded by spies," he kept repeating.

It was all in vain.

In return for this trust and kindness the Princess Metternich rendered Eugénie only a perfunctory deference. Speaking one day with Mme. de Pourtalès, she said:

"My empress, the Empress Elisabeth, is a real empress. The Empress Eugénie is just Mlle. de Montijo."

She led the court into a whirlwind of receptions, parties, entertainments, that kept the society news columns filled and placed a powerful weapon in the hands of the opposition.

In strange contrast with this trouble-making couple two sound, two disinterested characters stand out in the immediate circle of the sovereigns: Prosper Mérimée and Hortense Cornu.

Mérimée was the Empress's oldest friend. The scholarly, sensitive, ironical writer, a dandy in dress and in turn of mind, knew the Montijos first in 1830 in Madrid where he had trotted little Eugénie on his knee. Later on, when she came to Paris with her mother, he gave her lessons in English, corrected her exercises, took her shopping or on walks along the Champs Elysées. He proved an ingenious and patient sponsor in introducing her to society. It was Mérimée, no less, who revised and sometimes actually dictated the letters that Mlle. de Montijo wrote to the Emperor at the height of his courtship. It was he who drew up the marriage contract, fortifying it with a formidable pile of deeds, titles and certificates. At all times he was the tried and ever affectionate adviser.

Eugénie never forgot services rendered. She was deeply grateful to Mérimée for his. He might be an unbeliever and a lukewarm supporter of the Empire—she did not hold those defects against him. Once married she forced him upon the Emperor, who did not like him, and tried to attach him to her household. The writer refused, preferring to retain his freedom. Very well—she would make him a senator, and if he did not accept this time there would be a quarrel in earnest! Mérimée yielded. He was too fond of Eugénie really to hurt her. To the attachment he was to sacrifice his career as an artist. All through the reign he was to be the real confidant, the "secretary of secrets." He was to stand by Eugénie in the bitter moments with all his aging heart, and when the unhappy woman was driven from France, it took the old sceptic just two weeks to crawl into his hole and die.

Hortense Lacroix, god-daughter to Napoleon III and a playmate of his childhood, was somewhat more than half a hunchback, with eyes popping out of her head. She had a quick wit and an incisive tongue. She had married an untalented artist named Cornu. Hortense was a republican and an out-and-out democrat. She had acted as unpaid secretary to Louis Napoleon during his imprisonment at Ham, supplying him with books and documents for his studies. The coup d'état spoiled everything. She broke in horror from the Emperor and even subscribed to a fund for Orsini's children. The intervention in Italy won her back part way. She resumed contacts by writing him a letter after Solferino. Shortly after that Mme. Walewska took her to the Tuileries. The Emperor welcomed her joyously and the Empress, too, was eagerly attentive. Thereafter Mme. Cornu was a frequent visitor, coming preferably mornings for chats with Napoleon III. Thinking of the old days the latter asked her to help him on the research for his Life of Julius Caesar. That was the beginning of Mme. Cornu's genuine influence upon him.

Not only did she help him on the research. She suggested new collaborators. Never asking anything for herself, she was assiduous in furthering the interests of her friends: scholars, writers, artists, seeking posts and commissions for them. She got Renan his chair at the Collège de France. She had a hand in Duruy's appointment to the Ministry of Education.

The first two volumes of the *Life of Julius Caesar* were to appear in 1865 and 1866. In that work Napoleon III intended to illustrate his theory of dictatorship and show, with Hegel and Carlyle, that the right man regularly appears on the historical scene when he is most needed. Hortense Cornu provided the Emperor with his principal and most constant collaborator, Albert Maury, a member of the *Académie des Inscriptions*. Maury was politically hostile to the Empire but enjoyed the Emperor personally. Hortense had him appointed librarian at the Tuileries, where there was no library, at a small salary. Maury did the research on the *Life* and prepared a first copy which Napoleon III redictated to Mocquard, Mocquard then making grammatical corrections and polishing the Emperor's somewhat slovenly style. Eventually Maury introduced Duruy to Napoleon III and brought him into the work.

At a later date Hortense Cornu induced the Emperor to buy the Campana collection for the Louvre and to found the *Ecole pratique des Hautes Etudes*. She was a skillful lobbyist, playing a dexterous political rôle backstage. She was a vigorous supporter of the cause of Poland, of oppressed Hungary, of dismembered Italy. An ardent anti-clerical, she was the leading spirit in a little camarilla that advocated the desertion of the Pope. It was Hortense Cornu who won Napoleon III over to the idea of letting Charles of Hohenzollern, a friend of hers, seize the throne of Roumania.

The Emperor had a real affection for Hortense Cornu. Some time after their reconciliation he said to her:

"The fact that I have been able to keep friends like you and Conneau gives me some respect for myself."

Death only was to end the friendship.

The court left the Tuileries in May or June, according to the weather, and settled at Saint-Cloud in the old palace of Monsieur, brother to Louis XIV. There Napoleon I, Charles X and Louis Philippe had each resided in their turn. The Empress, really, did not like that residence. It was too near the Paris which she feared and ever mistrusted. To be there, nevertheless, was a certain relaxa-

CHÂTEAU DE COMPIÈGNE

TYPICAL FASHIONS OF THE SECOND EMPIRE

Lithograph by Gustave Doré, from *Menagerie Parisienne*

tion for her, as a respite from formal court life. And it was good for the Prince Imperial, for at Saint-Cloud he could play on the lawns with boys of his own age, Fleury, Ney, La Bédoyère, his cousins the Alba girls, and especially with Louis Conneau, the doctor's son, the inseparable and brother-like companion of his studies and his games.

At Saint-Cloud court life was much simplified under a system of petty etiquette. Ministers attending the Council stayed for luncheon and conversations afterwards displayed the talents of such good talkers as Duruy, Marshal Vaillant, Drouyn de Lhuys, Persigny, Chasseloup-Laubat and the indispensable Mérimée. There were few if any receptions or parties. The Emperor seized this time for his historical writings, for work on plans for improving Paris, for following new inventions, in which he always took an interest. The Empress would drive a good deal in *wurst* or buggy with Anna de Mouchy or Sophie de Malakoff. Sometimes she would picnic with the children at a little dairy-farm she had started in imitation of the one at the Trianon.

Very different were the stays at Fontainebleau, where the imperial couple went in July, or especially at Compiègne, where they went in November at the beginning of the hunting season. At these palaces it was a question of week-long house-parties which, in the course of eighteen years, took in virtually the whole list of important foreign aristocrats as well as leading personalities in politics, letters, science and the arts. Certain intimates, the Metternichs, Count and Countess de Pourtalès, the two Walewskis, were regular guests.

There was a hunt at Compiègne once a week, and at these the Emperor of Austria, the Kings of Italy, Sweden, Prussia, the Netherlands and Portugal, were in at some fine deaths. Hunting costumes followed, for the most part, styles of the Louis XV era. While the hounds barked, the whippers-in shouted, the horns blew, the imperial charabancs would speed down avenues carpeted with fallen leaves. Galloping at the head would be the Prince of the Moskowa, Master of the Imperial Hounds. Meets were fixed for the King's Well, where the pack was assembled in charge of grooms in red livery and carriages from neighboring châteaux were parked.

On cold days a punch would be served in a clearing, the Emperor himself often deigning to light the brandy and serve his guests with his own hands. Then the hunt would be off again, to return to Compiègne by torchlight.

The Empress arranged the program of entertainments every morning. On days when no hunt was scheduled she took her guests on archeological excursions to Mont Berny, or to the château of Pierrefonds which Viollet-le-Duc was restoring at the expense of the privy-purse. Those who did not care for such amusements were free to do as they pleased—keep to their rooms, visit each other, read, play billiards. On sunny afternoons Eugénie, always on the go, would often suggest a walk. Her guests would usually accept as a matter of duty, but few of them really liked these long-protracted and half-athletic outings.

People on a select list were invited, each in turn, by the Empress to tea in the music room. With its great Coromandel cabinets and its Gobelins telling the story of Esther, this was the most agreeable room in all the palace. There artists and scholars took the spotlight, Arsène Houssaye and the younger Dumas talking on literature and the stage, the astronomer Leverrier on the world we live in, Pasteur, already famous, on the diseases of wines and silkworms. Gounod would sit at the piano and sing English love songs or Andalusian airs in his charming voice.

When the weather was really bad the imperial circle would turn to games such as "the miller," where a ring was hidden in a bowl of flour and the problem was to pick it out with one's teeth without getting flour on one's nose. At spelling bees Mérimée was master of ceremonies. His "Compiègne dictations" were famous. Adjusting his glasses to his nose he would sit back and dictate now to the Emperor, now to the Empress, and then on to a dozen or so more good-natured souls, an extravagant text of his own composition which contained all the pitfalls of French grammar and orthography that he could think of.

Evenings at Compiègne were extravagantly brilliant, the women outdoing one another in clothes. The train that ran from Paris to Compiègne required two baggage cars for the trunks of Mme. de Metternich and Mme. de Pourtalès alone. Ordinarily there were charades, then dancing to the modest offerings of a mechanical piano. Often the actors from the Opera, the Comédie-Française, or the Gymnase would come out and give performances in a little theatre that Louis Philippe had built. But the advent of the Princess Metternich brought society comedies into fashion. From her time the chief amusement was the rehearsing and staging of plays, skits in verse and music, "living pictures." This was great fun for everybody. The Marquis de Massa and Mme. de Metternich were the two stars in the troupe, though the Empress herself took part on a number of occasions, notably in the "Portrait of the Marquise," a mediocre sketch in which she played a give-and-take with the Comte d'Andlau. She won loud applause but was not convinced that she had deserved it.

"I was terrible, wasn't I?" she said to Mérimée.

"Dear me!" he answered. "One might have done worse."

"Thanks for the frankness," said the Empress, laughing. "I too had an idea that my future was not on the stage."

The imperial couple had their real vacations at Biarritz. Eugénie had built an ugly villa on that Basque shore so close to her native Spain, and she and the Emperor spent Septembers there, living as private individuals with none but their closest friends about them. There would be excursions to San Sebastian or Loyola, climbs up the Rhune, drives along the sea, spiritualist seances, informal evenings where the Emperor would sing in French, "Tell me, soldier boy, do you remember?" and "The Two Grenadiers" in German, while Edgar Ney would accompany on the piano, where Mme. de Metternich, with more skill, would recite in a nasal tone imitating Thérésa, "Nothing is sacred to a sapper."

All these entertainments had the informality, the not very distinguished atmosphere of an ordinary bourgeois home, though the pamphleteers talked of "orgies at Biarritz" and compared Compiègne to Sodom. Napoleon III and Eugénie might well laugh, but French public opinion was influenced by such talk in spite of everything. What the French most disliked was the too worldly and too cosmopolitan character of imperial life on vacation. The sovereigns were graciousness itself to all their guests; but "their immediate circle set up an invisible barrier between them and the rest of French society. . . . It was a strictly closed circle, opening only on rare occasion to new members, in its jealous exclusiveness preferring foreigners, however unimportant, to Frenchmen who might have embarrassed the company perhaps by brilliancy of talents." [1]

That was true. The Emperor, and the Empress even more so, were responsive to foreign influences. They were sometimes to prove too forgetful that they were not just wealthy inhabitants of a social

[1] Du Barail, *Mes Souvenirs*, II, 207.

Mayfair but sovereigns who governed a state and impersonated a country.

Turned upside down, enlarged, rebuilt, by Haussmann, Paris lost much of its picturesqueness under the Second Empire. Napoleon III and his relentless prefect made it the most modern city in Europe. Not only did Paris change in appearance. It changed in character and in its daily habits. Railroads, World's Fairs, easy money, brought foreigners and provincials in swarms to the capital. If the "boulevard" lost homogeneousness in the course of the change it gained in splendor.

Tortoni's flights of stairs had been the center of Parisian life under Louis Philippe. Now he saw his glory pale. Many artists and writers retained their seats at the banquet, however: Gustave Doré, Alfred Stevens, Arsène Houssaye, Henry Mürger, Tony Révillon. The Café de Paris had closed, but the Café Anglais had risen to become the rendezvous of "fashionables" and men about town. Leader of them all was the Duc de Grammont-Caderousse, who did a thousand crazy doings, some of them extremely funny, only to die of phthisis as a resigned Christian.

Almost opposite the Café Anglais were the Maison d'Or, a high-class restaurant, and the Café Riche, a very old establishment that had taken on a second and exuberant youth. At its round table or in its cozy little booths Victorien Sardou, Paul de Saint-Victor, Offenbach, the Goncourts, Roger de Beauvoir, Nadar, gathered every afternoon. Sometimes Théodore de Banville came, or Baudelaire; more frequently Gambetta and Jules Ferry, both all but unknown as yet. Other cafés sprouted or resprouted: the Café des Variétés, the Café de Suède, the Café des Princes, the Café du Helder. One lunched at Bignon's or Brébant's; one dined at the Palais-Royal, at Véry's, or at the Frères Provençaux's.

The boulevard was no longer the property of the gilded youth, the dandies, the "lions," of the previous generation. Now it belonged to newspapermen. Gagged as it was by the government, journalism learned its rules and took its leading place in the nation under the Empire. Was not Napoleon after all the most notable publicist of his day? To the press, official and semi-official, he sent articles—always anonymous—and suggestions for articles. His writings were not always to the liking of the ministry. One day Véron, at the *Constitutionnel*, received a summons for an article by Granier de Cassagnac which the Emperor had proof-read. Having made this point respectfully in answer to the summons, Véron was given a second summons at once—and prudently he dismissed Cassagnac!

That was the period of printed wit. Reporters were kings of public opinion. Their predecessor and dean was Emile de Girardin. That impudent Figaro had tried his hand at all professions, with his convictions following the more immediate interest. He manifested one moral quality only—a capacity for work. Nevertheless, in *La Presse,* he created the modern French newspaper. Now flattering the government, now teasing it, he always kept an eye on influence and on money.

Louis Veuillot began to edit the *Univers* in 1851. He was the exact opposite of Girardin the self-seeker, of the icy, smooth-shaven face. After a very profane novitiate he embraced the Church so tightly as almost to smother her. His ardor made him the bête noire of anti-clericals and sensible Catholics almost alike. Pailleron called him "a run-down slanderer, a bigot fit for the asylum." Augier attacked him on the stage in the *Fils de Giboyer.* The great Montalembert thundered against "that slanderer, that traitor, that madman." Actually Veuillot was just a vulgar, big-hearted plebeian, heavy-set, with a pockmarked face. He had educated himself, and in consequence there were incoherences and gaps in his education. But he had a combative temperament and an overweening cocksureness, writing in a bitter, scornful language twice heated by faith and by contempt for others. His special marks were the atheists, but he hated liberal Catholics even more, Monsignor Dupanloup especially. In his nature the ultramontane overshadowed the believer. He could not see God for the Pope.

Jean-Jacques Weiss wrote political analyses in the *Journal des Débats.* Later he was to found the *Journal de Paris* with Ranc, Spuller and Victor Noir around him. Weiss was of the lineage of Voltaire, polishing off a paradox or pointing a thrust in a direct, caustic style that killed and delighted. Being great friends with Emile Ollivier he was to become a state councillor in 1870 and secretary-general of the Ministry of Fine Arts.

One of the most gifted men of the era was Prévost-Paradol. A former *Normalien,* very well educated, he too wrote for the *Débats,* where his articles were more noteworthy for taste than for wit. He attacked the government skillfully for a time, but he was not the sort of man to remain in an opposition forever. To an aristocratic mind like his not so much republican ideas as republican manners were bound in the long run to prove distasteful. Towards the end of the reign he was to go over to the Empire, or at least to the Emperor, and become Minister to the United States. Shortly after the outbreak of the war with Prussia he committed suicide in a fit of depression.

Around these outstanding leaders who beat time for the unending ballet of controversy, there gathered, especially in the opposition, a throng of performers who almost all could write with wit and launch a pretty dart. Nestor Roqueplan, a sublimated Parisian, went from copydesk to the management of the Opera and then, in virtue of a too splendorous management, back to copydesk again. Xavier Aubryet made a point of imitating Joseph Prudhomme's flowery style, till in the end he could express himself only in a sort of pretentious drollery. Aurélien Scholl was the arbiter of elegances along the boulevard, but was otherwise an inventor of far-fetched improprieties. Villemessant, a man of talent, founded the *Figaro* and ran it like a jovial tyrant till it became the leading literary paper in Europe. But the list is long, very, very long: Henry de Pène, haughty, as sharp as steel, utterly charming; Havin, conceited, dense, editor of the *Siècle,* and eating a priest for breakfast every morning; Sylvestre de Sacy, editor-in-chief of the *Débats,* who played Jansenist to live up to his name; Granier de Cassagnac, an aggressive but compromising henchman of the Tuileries; Dr. Véron, for a time a man to whom all Paris went to school but whose star set; Saint-Marc-Girardin, more a literary man than a controversialist; Charles and François Victor-Hugo; Vacquerie and Paul Meurice, blind, deaf and dumb as instruments of the poet's vengeance; Nefftzer, the creator of the *Temps;* finally, a tall, thin, yellow-skinned young man with a Kalmuck's head topped with a frizzled tuft: with his *Lanterne* he was suddenly to become famous towards the end of the Empire—Henri Rochefort.[1] Truly a surfeit of talents —the French press had never boasted so many. They were the salt and the life of Paris and of Europe under the Second Empire.

[1] The list, really, should be longer still, for among the men who made France the land par excellence of wit would be: John Lemoinne, Edouard Hervé, Vitet, Cuvillier-Fleury, Alphonse Karr, Robert Mitchell, Philibert Audebrand, Monselet, Léo Lespès, Albert Wolff. [Translator's note: Take Karr, for instance: arriving thirteenth at a dinner he remarked to the circle of glum faces: "Don't worry: we are only twelve and a quarter (*douze et Karr*)."]

The little theatres lent an unending gaiety to the era, a light foam that drew foreigners to Paris and astounded them. A famous song in an operetta by Meilhac and Halévy called *La Vie Parisienne* preserves a record of the extraordinary fad:

> Nous venons
> De tous les pays du monde
> Italiens,
> Brésiliens,
> Japonais,
> Hollandais,
> Espagnols,
> Romagnols. . . .
> La vapeur nous amène:
> Nous allons envahir
> La cité souveraine,
> Le séjour du plaisir . . .
> Oh, mon Dieu! nous allons tous
> Nous amuser comme des fous. [1]

It all made up what was known as the "Imperial Carnival." For the better part of the reign Offenbach seemed to be orchestra leader, but he was not the originator of the opéra-bouffe. Hervé was there before him. The most amusing of Hervé's many light operas was the *Compositeur toqué* (The Dippy Typesetter). His career ran parallel to Offenbach with less brilliant successes—*L'Oeil crevé, Chilperic, Petit Faust, Mam'zelle Nitouche*. Offenbach's work was to set the type of the opéra-bouffe, and he gave it a sort of smartness that not seldom survives more substantial title to fame.

Jacques Offenbach came to Paris from Cologne when he was fifteen years old. His father had been a cantor in the Cologne synagogue. Offenbach was already a good violinist when he entered the Conservatory. Soon he was playing in concerts and at drawingroom entertainments, and began to compose. He was a big, hairy fellow, always quivering, with a thin face that seemed to all intents and purposes to be devoured by his sideburns and whiskers. Eyeglasses always set askew filled out the decoration. His first success was a bright sketch, "The Two Blind Men," which the Emperor and the

[1] "We come from every country in the world: Italians, Brazilians, Japanese, Hollanders, Spanish, Romagnoles. By steam we come to invade the sovereign city . . . the abode of pleasure . . . and we are going—aren't we though?—to have the time of our lives!"

Empress asked to see at the Tuileries. *Orphée aux Enfers* was pilloried into fame by the panning given it by Jules Janin.

"Music hall piffle," he pontificated. "Music in rags and tatters!"

Its gay, imaginative quality, its dash, won the heart of Paris, and Paris thumbed its nose at Janin. Morny himself supplied Offenbach with the libretto for a sketch: "Mr. Cauliflower Will Stay at Home."

The musician then moved from the small theatre of the *Bouffes-Parisiens* and settled at the *Variétés*. There Henri Meilhac and Ludovic Halévy were his regular collaborators, the fat and red-haired Hortense Schneider his leading interpreter. His best works began coming with a bewildering and ever-growing vogue: *La Belle Hélène, Barbe-Bleue, La Vie Parisienne, La Grande-Duchesse de Gerolstein, La Périchole, Les Brigands.* A winged mockery of the gods of Olympus, of the heroes of story, of the chivalry of the Middle Ages; a merry satire on the little German principalities, all set to tunes that were often tender and poetic as contrasted with the quips in the librettos! Nothing respectable, nothing sacred, nothing serious—just laughter, just nonsense! By this time the jest had ceased to be enough. People were too gay, too noisy. They wanted something more obvious, more vulgar—nonsense, in fact! The little blue auditorium at the *Variétés* was packed to the bursting point each night with hoops and dress-coats. The World's Fair of '67 yielded Offenbach an orchestra of kings more imposing than Talma had had at Erfurt.

Meantime, in its frenzied quest for pleasure, Paris threw itself for better or for worse upon dancing. Everybody danced—to the languorous somewhat insipid tunes of Strauss or Métra. Everybody danced everywhere—in the drawingrooms of the ministers, at the embassies, at the Opera, in the residences of the Faubourgs Saint-Germain and Saint-Honoré, then in the numberless public dancehalls that kept opening—chief among these, Mabille's, the *Château des Fleurs* and "The Lilac Field" (*La Closerie des Lilas*). Mabille's was a garden roofed over on one side to make a hall, on the avenue Montaigne. The *Château des Fleurs* was larger. It stood on the clearing once occupied by the Quartier Marbeuf. The *Closerie des Lilas* was a favorite resort of students. There one often met Gambetta, Floquet, Courbet, Barbey d'Aurévilly. Later on it took the name of a new proprietor and became Bullier's.

The masked ball fad started at the Tuileries. Masked balls supplied pretexts for historical fancies, picturesque quadrilles, ballets, marches. Receptions at the Marquis de Chasseloup-Laubat's showed a memorable march of the "Four Parts of the World," and a series of Venetian gambling evenings arranged by Arsène Houssaye—very free affairs at which Thiers and Marshal Canrobert in masks did not hesitate to hobnob with women such as Musard and Païva. Michelet gave a "Ball of Oppressed Nationalities" in which the Goncourts thought they saw "a dance of the future revolutions of Europe." [1] At the Opera a motley crowd of pierrots, marquises, longshoremen, sultanas and gutter dandies stepped on each other's toes.

To have a good time in any event, on any pretext, was the obsession of the era. There was a good deal of gambling: cards and roulette were much in evidence not only in clandestine resorts in the neighborhood of the Palais-Royal but in the great "circles" that arose in imitation of England's clubs. The smartest and most exclusive of these was the Jockey Club, a name that was short for "The Society for the Encouragement of Better Horse Breeding in France." It was founded in 1833 by a group comprising Lord Seymour, Prince Demidoff, Charles Laffitte, Rieussec and Edgar Ney. At its initiative races were started, and they enjoyed a wholly unforeseen popularity. The club built the Longchamps race-course on the site of the ancient abbey of the nuns of St. Clara, which went back to the days of St. Louis. At Morny's suggestion the Emperor lent his patronage to the enterprise, and Morny, in turn, established the Grand Prix de Paris, which was first contested in 1863. Bookmakers came on from England and betting rose to alarming proportions. The masses, at least, had no great share in it, save on the one day of the Grand Prix. To that event all Paris flocked, from the imperial couple down to dandies in yellow gloves, cocottes in frills and furbelows, students and street women. For that matter racing actually did render real service to horse-breeding in France. French horses began very soon to compete to advantage with English breeds—these latter so far had had no rivals. The sensational victories of *Vermouth* in 1864 and *Gladiator* in 1865 were hailed as national glories. In 1866 came the horse show, with backing from the Emperor and with active promotion by General Fleury.

Drawingrooms gradually lost much of the influence they had ex-

[1] Bellesort, *La Société française sous Napoléon III*, 183.

ercised early in the reign; but even though they no longer ruled society they still clung to their rôle as centers of social information and comment. Evenings at the mansions of the legitimist and Orleanist aristocracy were less brilliant than distinguished—the salons, for instance, of the Comte de Montesquiou, the Duc de Maillé, the Comte de Flavigny, the Marquis de Talhouët, the Countess de Béhague, the Baroness de Schickler, the Countess d'Haussonville. A narrowly circumscribed world, standing as it were on reserve, where friends of the government were admitted only under very exceptional circumstances and the government was spared neither criticisms nor impertinences.

Meantime other houses had opened, where writers and artists were welcomed as choice guests. Having missed a throne in the political sense Princess Mathilde was determined to reign as queen over the arts and letters of her day. Within a few years' time she succeeded in building up the most important salon in Paris. Her mansion in the rue de Courcelles was decorated and furnished in the stifling taste of the era, heavily hung with draperies, that is, and littered with bric-a-brac. There she welcomed and sought to hold all the celebrities of the day whether they stood with the Empire or against it. All she considered was intelligence and talent. The Princess was inclined to be overbearing, but she had a clear brain and a sound judgment. Opinions met and clashed in her drawingroom on a plane of courtesy and good nature. One could even ridicule emperors on condition that no fault were ever found with the genius loci, Napoleon the First.

Among the writers who attended the Princess Mathilde's dinners and the evenings that followed them were Renan, Littré, the two Dumases, Flaubert, François Coppée, Jules Sandeau, Taine; among the scientists, Claude Bernard and Pasteur; among men in politics, Darimon, Prévost-Paradol and Emile Ollivier; among the artists, Carpeaux, Hébert, Gérome and Gavarni. One could hardly mention in this last group the very indifferent sculptor, Nieuwerkerque, whose long affair with the Princess Mathilde netted him the Directorship in Fine Arts. That cynical cad was to take to his heels in 1870, deserting without a word the woman to whom he owed everything he had ever been or had.

Conversations at the Princess Mathilde's were spirited and daring. The Princess prided herself on her painting and actually painted to no great purpose; but she had an active, animated mind that often expressed itself in jests of the strong variety. She was devoted to the men who belonged to her circle, defended them, helped them on to the Institut or other official recognition, obtained crosses or commissions for them. She made Théophile Gautier her librarian, heaped favors and gifts on Sainte-Beuve, nursed him in his illnesses, finally made him a senator. The critic's ingratitude during the bad days was to hurt her cruelly. She forgave him only on her deathbed.

On the rue Saint-Guillaume a very old salon still held on, one that had seen Chateaubriand in his glory and offered Casimir Delavigne an audience, the salon of Mme. Ancelot. It was filled with canaries. Mme. Ancelot was, herself, a little wrinkled old lady, as pink as an apple, dressing always in white like Mme. Récamier. She received a rather heterogenous assortment of people—Alfred de Vigny, stoical with his cancer, ceremonious, his cheeks rouged under long hair that was turning white; the fable writer, Viennet; Lachaud the lawyer, as fat and sleek-cheeked as a Roman Senator; the poets Anaïs Segalas and Emmanuel des Essarts; the song writer, Gustave Nadaud, short, heavy-set, always playing *The Two Gendarmes* on the piano; then a handsome young man who was so far only secretary to the Duc de Morny but would some day be Alphonse Daudet.

Mélanie Waldor, a writer of poems and insipid novels, had a rival salon in the rue du Cherche-Midi. That sombre Muse, ever garbed in black, was always trying to lure Mme. Ancelot's lions away, though Mme. Ancelot had been her sponsor before society at first.

The Countess d'Agoult, in letters Daniel Stern, was a gifted lady who had been banished from her real social world by her too celebrated romance with Liszt. An aristocrat, besides, she wrote history like a republican. She presided over an "advanced" salon in the rue de Presbourg. There her son-in-law, Emile Ollivier, was unobtrusively to prepare for fame. Wagner came at times, "biting and witty, then suddenly vulgar and overbearing," to quote Mme. Adam. He played selections from his early operas on the piano.

Thiers, too, had a salon in the Place Saint-Georges. The aged statesman had never felt so young. Before a coterie of Orleanists and republicans he threw mud at the government, argued, handed down judgment from on high. But the real salon of the opposition, during the last years of the Empire, was Mme. Adam's, on the rue de Rivoli. That pretty, intelligent, cultivated, ardently patriotic young lady graciously entertained democrats of every shade and description, along with a number of writers. Young Gambetta made his first contacts with society at Mme. Adam's. Socially he was not a great success. The milieu to which he was really adapted was the café.

Amateur play-production became a fad not only at court but in town as well. Comedies were given under the paneled ceilings of the palaces and in bourgeois apartments in the Marais. Count Jules de Castellane built a theatre of four hundred seats in his garden on the rue Saint Honoré. There operas, comedies, "proverbs," were given almost all the time. The Duc de Mouchy staged reviews with the flower of the fashionable in the various rôles. As a benefit for the "Friends of Childhood" the Comte de Bethune gave "Henry III and His Court," a regular five-act play; while the Princess de Beauvau, a practiced tragedienne, produced the *Enfants d'Edouard* and *Le Sicilien* with amateur casts at the Conservatory. In his mansion on the rue Marbeuf Emile de Girardin gave the première of the elder Dumas's *Invitation to Waltz.* The Countess Tascher de la Pagerie organized a series of "living pictures" at the Mayendorff House. "La Castiglione" appeared in one as a nun and was hissed. In 1860 Prince Napoleon had had the architect Normand build him a Pompeian house on the avenue Montaigne. At the house warming he gave the première of Emile Augier's *Flute Player.*

The artists and authors fell in line with the fad, with less expensive settings but with much more talent and imagination. At Offenbach's there were gay performances of the *Little Troubadour* and *The Fall of Castelnaudary.* Gustave Courbet gave a number of "realistic" evenings in his studio. At a production of his *Pierrot posthume* in his little house at Neuilly, for which Puvis de Chavannes painted the settings, Gautier himself gave a spirited rendering of his character, Dr. Pantalon, while everybody who counted in letters and the arts in Paris thunderously applauded. Of that evening Théodore de Banville noted in his diary in verse:

> La littérature y comptait,
> La vieille aussi bien que la neuve,
> Si bien que Dumas fils était
> Assis auprès de Sainte-Beuve.[1]

[1] "Literature was the main thing there—the old as well as the new. So much so that Dumas the younger was seated beside Sainte-Beuve."

Maurice Sand gave marvelous puppet shows in his mother's house at Nohant, the mannekins gravely executing hilarious extravaganzas such as *Alonzi Alonzo le bâtard,* or *Le brigand des Sierras.*

The sovereigns and their court had no influence at all on the artistic and literary movement of their time. Neither the Emperor nor the Empress had any personal taste or any particular education. Mérimée tried to interest them in letters, the Princess Mathilde pleaded the cause of the artists. They took no interest and listened only so far as needs of state required. The Emperor liked science and history but knew nothing outside those fields, modestly admitting as much. The Empress never went out of her way to be gracious to writers. She had a poor opinion of them and treated them like cattle. All of a piece, too much so, she followed likes or dislikes that were often entirely unreasonable. At Compiègne Napoleon III asked her to present the cross of the Légion d'honneur to Sardou—he had just succeeded with *Les Ganaches.*

"I do that?" she cried. "Never!"

She had somehow got the notion that Sardou had poked fun at one of her charities, and she was not to forgive him for a long time.

Almost all the men who wrote for a living lived in Paris. Apart from the great celebrities, society paid little attention to them. They made up a real literary proletariat. Many men of talent were condemned to a haphazard existence in the "Bohemia" over which Mürger laid a glow of youth and love.

The government looked upon men of letters as a half-starved and very dangerous lot. Unable to destroy them it stopped at persecuting them. The press had hardly a breath of life. The stamp tax smothered it and after three warnings a newspaper was suppressed. The book trade was subject to a system of "peddling," *colportage,* which required the prefect's stamp on every copy sold. All works suspected of not conforming with official points of view were forbidden. A "licencing commission" arbitrarily rejected writings that were deemed "offensive to morals," "harmful to religion and its respectworthy ministers," "misleading as regards history." That meant dictatorship in the field of the mind as well as in more material fields—though, in such cases, the mind always wins out. Even after authorization not a few books were prosecuted as "offensive to public morals." The Goncourts in 1854, Flaubert in 1857, were brought before the Court of Misdemeanors on such grounds. Baudelaire got a sentence of three months in prison, Proudhon a sentence of three years.

Romanticism reached its peak in the storm of '48. Thereafter it was in evident decline. A number of its leading writers remained still active and famous, but their popularity was now more a matter of sentiment than of aesthetic conviction. The bankruptcy of humanitarian mysticism and of the socialistic utopias of the Second Republic turned younger generations towards a materialistic attitude which found superficial expressions in sensual living, political agnosticism and class exclusivisms. In art under the various forms it produced a genre called "realism" that was directly contrary to the romantic tendencies earlier prevailing.

Champfleury, a novelist of no great talent, had his hour of fame with *Les Bourgeois de Molinchart*. Realism he defined as "the greatest amount of reality possible in a story, in the adventures of its characters, in the language they speak. . . . To my mind, the novel, a work of the imagination, should appear as real as an indictment in a criminal court."

Realism was not, as has sometimes been said, "sincerity in art." Classicists and romanticists were altogether sincere in their way. The realists sought "truth," truth as contrasted with imagination. The writer was slave to his subject. It was his duty to remain as impersonal, as methodical, as exact, as the scientist. He was no longer free to exploit his own emotions. He should avoid poetic flights and picturesqueness in style. His aim should be to paint society as it was, and by a natural reaction to old idealisms now despised, he did his best to stress the tedium, the vulgarity, the unhappiness, the ugliness, that lurked under the social surface.

Gustave Flaubert was a romanticist by temperament and culture, but in *Madame Bovary* he forced himself to write the masterpiece of realism. As his subject he chose the life of a middle-class country woman obsessed with romantic ideas. In construction the book was strong and earnest, in atmosphere, pessimistic. Those traits all complied with the rules of the new art, though for a true realist Flaubert was too much concerned with perfection of style, seeking aptness and precision of diction, along with sonorousness and music in his sentence rhythms. He was to relapse into romanticism in *Salammbô* (1862), a book that took Paris by storm with its pictorial splendor.

In 1864 Edmond and Jules de Goncourt published *Renée Mauperin,* a novel dealing with the "modern" girl who is "emancipated" or seems to be. Its sharp, dry criticisms of society, its light, flitting touch in matters of style, passed almost unobserved. *Germaine Lacerteux,* the story of a vicious but loyal servant girl, appeared in 1865. It was probably their most important work. The Goncourts were forerunners of an impressionistic literature which, after the fall of the Empire, was to produce one of the greatest writers of France, Alphonse Daudet.

Mérimée was wholly absorbed in court life. He wrote nothing now but trifles or articles of no great scope. George Sand wrote indefatigably—love stories, adventure, history, scenes of rural life—*Les Maîtres Sonneurs, Jean de la Roche, Le Marquis de Villemer.* Giving up socialism, she retired to château life in her native region, Berry, where the intoxications of her youth mellowed into simple kindheartedness.

Théophile Gautier published *Le Capitaine Fracasse* in 1863, but journalism diluted and scattered his talents. Lamartine lived on as a prisoner to his vast debts. He became just a literary galley slave chained to his desk. The elegist of the *Méditations,* the lyrical historian of the *Girondins,* the statesman of 1848, wrote anything, everything, on order—short stories, biographies, memoirs, pamphlets, book reviews, textbooks on literature. At more than seventy he was working fourteen hours a day without ever making ends meet. He said to Emile Ollivier one day:

"Do you want to see the unhappiest man in the world? Look at me! The days I can still stand, but the nights—oh! the nights! Had I not believed in God I would have killed myself long ago!"

Insensitive as she was, the Empress took pity on him, but too late. At her request the government passed a grant which assured the poet a life-time pension of 25,000 francs. The gift was made in the form of a reward for services to the nation—and the form was important. Several years earlier Napoleon III had offered Lamartine two millions, but the poet proudly refused them. He would owe nothing except to the nation which, as he thought, did owe him something. The city of Paris gave him a pleasant house in Passy to live in. There, crushed by so much glory and so much despondency, the singer of "The Lake" was to drag out the days, till finally he should die with Elvire's crucifix clasped to his heart.

Sitting in his glass fortress at Guernsey Victor Hugo completed *Les Miserables,* a monstrous serial, naïve, magnificent. It was a farewell bouquet tossed to romanticism. It produced a tremendous sensation. *Napoleon the Little* was just a fireraft, weak in thought, weak in style, which he set afloat clandestinely. *Toilers of the Sea* was an eloquent banality.

Realism had a great influence on the artists of the period. It did not win any great popular favor. Whether or not he is conscious of his spiritual or bodily wretchedness, the human being will always prefer pleasant dreams to glum reflections of his misery. For the very reason that physical satisfactions meant so much to them, the people who lived under the Second Empire were to remain devoted to romantic idealism. Their real favorite was Victor Cherbuliez, pleasant, colourless, or Eugène Fromentin, author of one fine book, *Dominique.*

But the typical writer of the age was Octave Feuillet. Delicate, shaded, a trifle effeminate, Feuillet came into public notice in 1858 with the *Roman d'un jeune homme pauvre.* A fashionable world, noble sentiments, a happy, very moral ending! That delighted enormous numbers of readers. With that book Octave Feuillet became the favorite reading of the leisured classes. He was appointed librarian at Fontainebleau and almost matched Mérimée's prestige at court. Next he published *Sybille,* a novel in the same vein. Then, suddenly, as if he had become another person, he wrote a genuine masterpiece, *Monsieur de Camors* (1867). It showed a forceful style that no one expected of him. The hero's character was complex and original, the plot pathetic. As might have been foreseen *Monsieur de Camors* shocked many feelings and did not have the success of Feuillet's earlier books. All the same *Monsieur de Camors* remains one of the models among French novels.

Barbey d'Aurévilly was a first-class writer disguised as a dandy. With *Une vieille maîtresse, Le Chevalier des Touches, Le Prêtre marié* (1865) he set out on a great career as a novelist and, in spite of many affectations and artificialities, he would have gone far had he not suddenly turned to journalism and book reviewing. In both these fields he was to write some beautiful pages but they failed to utilize the greatest of his gifts.

Alexandre Dumas was a brilliant inventor of plots and a born entertainer. With the aid of numerous hacks he continued all

FURNITURE OF THE SECOND EMPIRE

A room in the Château at Compiègne

through the reign to pour forth a torrential flood of historical novels that were devoured by a whole nation of readers.

Edmond About was a grand-nephew of Voltaire's. He could polish off a pleasant story in a lively, florid language: *Le roi des montagnes, La Grèce contemporaine, Tolla, Les Mariages de Paris.* His *Trente-et-Quarante* was published serially. The Empress grew so interested in it that, on being called away before the last installment appeared, she asked Napoleon III to telegraph and tell her how it came out. The Emperor did so:

"Captain Bitterlin died."

Literary criticism was liberally represented under the Second Empire in Nisard, Saint-Marc-Girardin, Villemain, Jules Janin, dissertators, patronizers all, lesser gods in an Olympus where Sainte-Beuve was Zeus—a not very loud-thundering Zeus, but goodnatured, treacherous, with an intelligence, a keenness and at times an unfairness that were altogether remarkable.

A poet and a novelist gone astray, Sainte-Beuve threw himself, perhaps in spite, certainly by instinct, into the tanglewood of knowledge. He was one of the most interesting minds of the era. He had no moral loftiness, but his erudition was astonishing in variety and in range. Taken together his articles in the *Moniteur,* the *Constitutionnel,* and later on the *Temps,* yield a comprehensive picture of French, indeed European, thought during the era.

Sainte-Beuve aimed not so much at appraising books as at explaining their authors by analyzing their environments, their developments, their physical and mental traits. In all this he was the immediate predecessor of Taine. Away back in 1828 he had written in an article on Corneille:

"The general state of literature at the time this author began to write, the peculiar education he received and the peculiar temperament (*la génie propre*) that nature bestowed on him, are three influences that it is important to keep distinct."

Taine was to say hardly more or better than that.

Sainte-Beuve wrote under the influence of realism and therefore pretended to be doing something scientific.

"Criticism in our hands," he said, "is anatomical dissection with a light touch."

His studies were so many "positive" researches designed to establish the outlines of a "natural history of human minds." In view of his thoroughgoing scepticism Veuillot facetiously dubbed him a "camp-follower of atheism."

Paul de Saint-Victor occupied a place apart as a representative of formal artistic criticism. His *Men and Gods* are models of eloquence and humanistic culture. The style he manipulated was one of the richest of the era.

There was a serried phalanx of historians. Tocqueville wrote *The Old Regime and the Revolution* and then lost his way into political theory. Thiers went ahead with his monstrous *History of the Consulate and the Empire,* a work lacking in all grace of form but valuable for its learning, for its source materials, which often preserve the oral testimony of eyewitnesses, and for its conscientious quest of the actual facts in every situation. Thiers was clear and intelligent. He had no sense whatever of literary art.

Guizot finished his *English Revolution,* a compact, trustworthy history. Edgar Quinet, in exile, published his *Philosophy of the History of France* and his *History of the Campaign of 1815.* Louis Blanc, also abroad, wrote his *French Revolution,* a work replete with illuminating remarks and with strong, well-written pages. Mignet studied Maria Stuart and Charles V, Victor Cousin two beautiful amazons of the days of the *Fronde,* Mme. de Chevreuse and Mme. de Longueville. Duvergier de Hauranne and Barante published important works on the Restoration. Sainte-Beuve's *Port Royal* was a masterpiece which would have made him famous all by itself.

Michelet had a warm faith in humanity, in progress, in the rights of the peoples, and those sentiments were carried to fever heat by the events of '48. His *French Revolution* and later on his *History of France* became two gigantic frescoes prodigious for their color, life and fire. His condensed staccato style, flashing, poetic, full of feverish imagery, is without parallel in French historical writing. Michelet is the great romanticist among the historians. He can be reproached for lack of critical insight, for partiality, exaggeration, and even hysteria. His imagination often runs away with him and his feelings not seldom get the upper hand. He gives too much importance to instincts and mass movements in the history of a country and too little to initiative and character in individual leaders. All the same he was a historian of genius and one of the most admirable among French writers.

Henri Martin was in a sense the Joseph Prudhomme of history. An honest fool, stubbornly industrious but without a trace of talent, he turned out some fifteen volumes on the history of France, elementary affairs that won him a great reputation through the support of his friends among the democrats. Martin was the born sectarian. "He always has to have a fixed idea," said Sainte-Beuve, whose discriminating mind could only despise the sort of thing that Martin wrote. "And it has to be a big idea, a very big idea."

Fustel de Coulanges wrote his *Ancient City* in 1860, when he was thirty-four. It gave a comprehensive view of Graeco-Roman civilization, explaining the forms of ancient society by religious beliefs. Fustel then went on to study the *History of Political Institutions in Ancient France,* the first volume of which was ready in 1874. His incisive method, his scholarly integrity, his independence of systems and parties, along with a very considerable literary art, give him a place apart in French historical literature. His main interest was in the human being considered as a political animal and he follows man down through the ages to discover general laws in the needs and interests that have always prompted human conduct.

Proudhon was a self-educated scholar. He is far too prolix on the whole, but at moments he rises almost to the plane of genius. His principal work, *On Justice in the Revolution and in the Church,* appeared in 1858. It was prosecuted by the Empire and won him three years in prison without the usual reductions. Napoleon III had known Proudhon well and admired some of his ideas. He was certainly ungenerous in Proudhon's regard, an attitude that stands out all the more in contrast with the remission of a sentence of three months which Montalembert had received for an article in the *Correspondant.* Proudhon still had time to publish his *Federative Principle* (1863) two years before his death. He exerted a considerable influence upon his era, and echoes of the same influence are still heard today. An instinctive independent though nominally a socialist—his famous apothegm, "Property is theft," goes back to 1840—Proudhon was definitely opposed to the various forms of "statism" or state socialism. He was a severe critic of Fourier. At the same time he violently attacked the competitive system and the growing prominence of the machine in modern life. He advocated social revolution but he wanted his revolution to end in a reconciliation of classes and in harmonious cooperation between them.

Marx despised Proudhon, calling him "that petty-bourgeois French-man." He had, nevertheless, a powerful and penetrating mind. Some of his ideas, notably those on loan and easy credit systems, were far in advance of his day.

Meantime a taste for learning and a respect for it, along with scientific method as epitomized in Auguste Comte's positivism, had taken a firm hold in the higher regions of French thought—literary realism was really just one facet of this development. Three men, especially, men who were scholars but also writers, were to exert a widespread influence on French manners of thinking—Littré, Renan and Taine.

Littré was a laborious ascetic. In the course of a long life in pov-erty he was to amass an incredible amount of information in many fields—in philology, ancient and modern, in literature, in philos-ophy, and even in medicine. He was a modern Aristotle with a bent towards languages, studying these with a very personal method. He could hardly be called a literary artist. His aim was not to entertain but to know and impart.

"Littré," said Renan, "had such a great love of truth that he was perhaps the one man of his time who could confess an error without loss of prestige."

The first volume of the *Dictionary of the French Language* ap-peared in 1863. That work stands as a monument all by itself and it will never be surpassed. Patiently, conscientiously, with untiring resolve, Littré studied the French language in its history, quoting for examples not arbitrarily coined phrases but sentences culled from French writers back to the earliest times. Littré was a disciple of Auguste Comte and on the latter's death became leader of the Comtian movement. His absolute rationality held him aloof from religions and he was not liked in official circles, but he went on with his labors in silence, ever tolerant, ever kindly, a real saint of science.

Ernest Renan is probably the most exquisite product of French scepticism. Born in Brittany he was educated for the Church, lost his faith and then turned to religious history. He always kept the unctiousness of the clergyman, combining it with great personal charm and emotional warmth in a keenly agile mind. Renan, too, was a great worker, publishing one after the other, *Studies in Philol-ogy and Religious History, Averroës and Averroism* and a *General*

History of the Semitic Languages. These works made him one of the world's leading orientalists and the world's leading exponent of the "higher criticism."

In his earlier phase Renan was soaked through and through with German philosophy. Hegel he regarded as his master and he had a profound admiration for Goethe. He thought of Germany as the great teacher of modern civilization. An old friend, Hortense Cornu, called him to Napoleon III's attention. The Emperor liked him and in 1860 sent him on an archeological expedition to Pheonicia. At that time the Syrian campaign was at its height. The officers and soldiers of the French army lent Renan every possible assistance and he made a number of interesting discoveries. What more than anything else he gained was his sense of the magical beauty, the divine simplicity, that linger about the ancient lands of the Near East. Renan left for Palestine an epigrapher. He came back a poet, a story-teller, a first-class writer.

He began writing his *Life of Jesus* at Amschit in a little white cabin that had a trellis of grapevines around it. He worked at first with the help of his sister Henriette. A "fever sleep" descended upon them and he woke up alone. On his return to France Napoleon III gave him the chair in Hebrew at the Collège de France. His course was a sensation, delighting liberals and angering believers. The storm broke out at his first lecture as he stated his conception of a strictly human Christ:

"An incomparable man, a man so great that, though he has to be judged from the positive standpoint of science, I should not care to gainsay those who were struck by the exceptional character of his work and called him God, the founder of the eternal religion of humanity, the religion of the spirit."

As Renan finished the sentence there was a burst of mingled applause and of shocked outcries. He completed his series of lectures in spite of the tumult, though he was suspended immediately afterwards, retaining the title and the salary that went with his chair for two years.

The *Life of Jesus* appeared soon afterwards (1863). In that work Renan's interpretation of the Gospels is doubtful and his criticism untrustworthy. He very evidently rests content with mere plausibility and aims at emotional edification rather than at truth. But the book is a masterpiece of literary art. For suavity, flexibility, naturalness, purity of diction, a certain caressing charm, the style could hardly be equalled. In the story of Jesus' preaching, Renan recovers the very atmosphere of the Gospels. A chorus of mingled applause and insults greeted the work. The imperial censorship took no official action, a fact that prompted Aurélien Scholl to the quip that "Jesus is the only one who can be attacked with impunity nowadays." Renan paid no attention to the hubbub and went on with his studies, the *Origins of Christianity* appearing in 1866, *The Apostles,* also in 1866, and *Saint Paul* in 1869.

Renan had been a democrat in his younger days. Gradually he lost interest in popular government, in "Pambeotia" as he said. If he did not go over to the Empire he at least came to like the Emperor, lauding the latter's social outlook and his kindness of heart. He kept in close personal touch with Prince Napoleon. The war of 1870 was a rude blow to his dream of a brotherhood of the peoples. His disappointment was as bitter as Michelet's. Michelet was to die of the hurt. Renan was younger and farther removed from the world. He lived on, but a trace of uneasiness was ever after to be noted in his preaching in favor of civilization. It never recovered the old fervor.

For his doctoral thesis at the Ecole Normale Hippolyte Taine wrote on the subject of *La Fontaine and His Fables* (1853). That book already states one of Taine's favorite theories, that the work of art is the product of race, environment, the historical moment. Taine was first of all a philosopher. He regarded psychology as the basis of history and history as a science. He thought that history "like the organic world had an anatomy and a physiology."

The University nagged and ragged him. He fled to the Salpétrière in Paris to study mental pathology. At that moment he was an out-and-out materialist.

"Vice and virtue," he wrote, "are products, the way sugar or vitriol are products."

His frail health stood the strain of so much effort badly, but he was emerging from the throng. His essay on Livy, *Tite-Live,* and his *Journey to the Pyrenees* attracted attention. He laid the foundations of his basic work *On Intelligence*—it was not to appear till 1870; and soon a tour through Belgium, Holland, the Rhineland, England, was to furnish the elements required for his *Philosophy of Art* and the *History of English Literature.*

In Taine's eyes, to study a painter or a writer meant to discover a people's ways of feeling and thinking. He was looking for "the laws of human vegetation." He was to publish his great work on the *Origins of Contemporary France* after the fall of the Empire. He would then put forward new views of the Revolution based on an analysis of the French "psychosis" of 1789.

Taine reasons closely and forcefully, exaggerating logic, perhaps. His method oversimplifies the deeper motives of human conduct. He thinks he can explain the world of the mind the way the physical world is explained. He abolishes free will. The individual does not count in his eyes. That earnest, upstanding scholar did not dislike the frivolities of society. He was much invited for his sharp and sparkling wit. At one moment he sought diversion from more serious things by describing life in society, with more enthusiasm than depth, in *The Life and Opinions of Thomas Graindorge*. Like Renan and Littré, Taine was hated by the Catholics—Monsignor Dupanloup called him "a public poisoner." He thought the Empire "a necessary evil" though he had no personal reason to complain of it. First an examiner at the Polytechnique he afterwards became professor at the Beaux-Arts.

In form Taine was brilliant and picturesque, with less emotionality than intellect. He did color like a geometrician. Not an artist by instinct he yearned to be one, and managed to become a great master of French prose. More of a sceptic than Renan, too sceptical, perhaps, he was to come into his own, the moment the Empire fell, as the chief inspirer of French thinking. Naturalism was to find its philosopher and its predecessor in him.

French poetry did not escape the new influences under the Second Empire. Some of the great romantics—Vigny and Musset—were dead. Lamartine had become a talkative, shallow newspaper writer. Victor Hugo alone was still on the scene. He was a voluntary exile in Guernesey and profited by that status. For all of his paucity of ideas and his excessive verbalisms, he still remained, in virtue of his lyrical dash, his forceful imagery, his vigorous virtuosity in matters of form, the leading poet in Europe. In the *Châtiments* (1856), the *Contemplations* (1856), the *Legend of the Ages* (1859), he was not so much a true romantic as a seer, a "mage," dwelling preferably on the ever-varying world scene, on the changes in times and eras, on the hopes and sorrows of human life, with aspirations for progress and a passion for civic virtue.

Théophile Gautier published his last volume of verse in 1857. It was *Emaux et Camées,* poems so perfect in form that they were to serve as models for the Parnassians. This latter school stressed aloofness from emotion rather than emotion. It dropped the melody and the picture and banished loose, natural forms of expression in favor of a perhaps too studied verse technique. Prince of the Parnassians was Leconte de Lisle. His *Poèmes antiques* and *Poèmes barbares* (1859) are beautiful things in their nobility of line and their splendor of color. Their icy grandeur rests on a sort of haughty nihilism and delivers what has been called a "challenge to nothingness."

The real poetic novelty in the period was Baudelaire. Deriving originally from realism, Baudelaire, in actual fact, stands entirely by himself—he is altogether original. An artist to his fingertips, he feigned insensitiveness, but in him more than in anyone else one glimpses behind deep carefully wrought verses, an anguished sense of life and a horror of death. Matter never quite manages to hide the human soul from him. His *Fleurs du Mal* (1858) seemed to be an ingenious effort to scandalize the safe and sane middle classes in France by a choice of unhealthy, revolting subjects; but in a vague sort of way they still cling to a Christian's hopes. Rejected or else ignored in Baudelaire's lifetime, his work had to wait some fifty years to achieve the glory that it deserved.

One or two other poets might seem to deserve mention. In his *Odes funambuleuses* Théodore de Banville spoiled a charming talent by clownish acrobatics. Victor de Laprade expressed some altogether impeccable sentiments in a studied sort of verse. In his *Mireio, Calendau* and the *Trésor du Felibrige* the great Frédéric Mistral virtually created, or recreated, the language of the French South, Provençal.

The theatre enjoyed exceptional favor during this era. It too saw romanticism bow to realism. The historical drama had fallen into complete discredit, its place being triumphantly seized by the prose comedy of manners.

This form was an invention of Alexandre Dumas, the younger, and Emile Augier. The former made his debut in 1852 with a dramatization of a novel he had written, *La Dame aux Camélias,* known in England and America as *Camille.* It dealt with an old theme—the rehabilitation of the lost woman; but the play had an intensity of sentiment that has kept it, almost alone of its class, from growing old. Continuing to choose subjects from the life about him, the younger Dumas followed with greater and greater successes: *Diane de Lys, Le Demi-monde, La Question d'Argent, Le Fils naturel, Un Père prodigue, L'Ami des femmes, Les Idées de Madame Aubray, La Femme de Claude.* He had the outlook of improving morals in society by exposing its errors and vices—the ever-recurring, ever-praiseworthy and ever futile effort of those who write for the stage! These plays with a purpose are unfortunately marred by mortally tiresome lectures—there is a moralizer and a sermonizer in all of them; but otherwise they show skillful craftsmanship and a bold lively dialogue. Drawing with a firm hand the younger Dumas executed many portraits, at times conventional, often sound and always varied, of the modern woman, a woman who exercised a power and who held a place in society that no other had ever filled.

Emile Augier had much the same defects as the younger Dumas and he wrote with a heavier touch and more vulgarly: *Le Mariage d'Olympe, Les Lionnes pauvres, Les Effrontés, Le Gendre de M. Poirier* (in collaboration with Jules Sandeau), *Maître Guerin, Le Fils de Giboyer.* These plays pretended to chastise the demoralization of an era in which business, speculation, display, the quest for pleasure, tended to overshadow deeper values. Whether in prose or in verse Augier's plays lack imagination and they lack art. Their author followed an honored and lucrative career, while Musset's comedies—which are models of freedom and taste, and an adornment to the French language—were produced reluctantly before audiences that sat virtually unmoved by their poetic charm and their inner force of exuberant youth.

Edouard Pailleron was still very young when he won a first great success with his *Faux Ménages* (1869). That play gave promise of very substantial dramatic talents. In between two of their operettas Henri Meilhac and Ludovic Halévy presented *Froufrou,* a play noteworthy for its wit and bitter pathos. The Goncourts suffered a deserved setback with *Henriette Maréchal,* a hackneyed plot where the staleness was only emphasized by a spuriously up-to-date dialogue. Victorien Sardou, a tried and tested craftsman, superficial but gifted with a rare feeling for dramatic action, drew all Paris to his comedies. The Sardou play mirrored with cruel gaiety the blemishes, perversities and eccentricities of contemporary life: *La Famille Benoiton, Nos intimes, Nos bon villageois, Séraphine, Rabagas.*

Censorship of the stage was ever on the alert and often required the most incredible cuts and alterations in the texts of plays, which could not be produced without its approval. The *Tour de Nesle* was banned in the interests of public morals and of due respect to crowned heads. In *Les doigts de fée* by Scribe and Legouvé one character was described as "sister to a cabinet minister." The censor objected to that. Fortunately his zeal was often tempered by interference from higher up in the government.

The French farce took on new life with Labiche, a writer born to that type of play and who could utilize to the full all that by-product of the French talent for wit that is represented by caricature, punning and verbal clowning. Labiche was one of the great entertainers of the Second Empire.

The actors of the era make up one of the most brilliant troupes that the history of the theatre has known. In tragedy Mlle. George, the onetime friend of Napoleon I but now old and fat, still held sadly on at the Odéon. Rachel herself, the admirable Rachel, was also in her declining years. After a disappointing tour in America, she fell ill of consumption and the disease weakened her voice. She retired to the South of France (January, 1858) to die at last with magnificent courage and enable Prince Napoleon, a Caesar without laurels, and Mlle. George, a star past its zenith, to head her funeral procession.

Resplendent at the Comédie-Française were Augustine and Madeleine Brohan, daughters of the exquisite Suzanne—all three of them famous for their wit. In 1862 a young, red-haired girl, with a thin, wan face and a voice of extraordinary beauty, made her debut—Sarah Bernhardt. The following year the imposing Agar did *Andromaque.* The two appeared together in *Le Passant* at the Odéon in 1869 and together laid the foundations of François Coppée's fortune. Delaunay and Got were already artists of established reputations. Constant Coquelin and his brother, Coquelin the younger, began their careers around 1860. Mounet-Sully attracted attention at the Odéon by his accent and carriage in tragic parts. Two charming women divided honors at the Gymnase—Rose Chéri and Aimée Desclée. In the cheaper theatres Frédéric Lemaître reigned supreme as king of melodrama, and Virginie Dejazet, invincibly young, managed a theatre of her own with enthusiasm and success.

The period that stretches from 1850 to 1870 will probably be regarded as a great age for the opera. The old music represented by Auber, Rossini and Meyerbeer gradually made way for a new style in which Wagner, Berlioz and Gounod were to distinguish themselves.

Auber, a gay old man dating from 1782, was managing the Conservatory and directing musical programs in the Imperial Chapel. He was still holding an important place with second-line novelties such as *Manon Lescaut* or *La Fiancée du roi de Garbe*. His light, empty music had always been somewhat lacking in inspiration, but he remained the wit among the composers, exhaling a decided flavor of the eighteenth century.

Rossini had stopped working, well realizing that the symphony was destined to crowd out melody. Italian music was still popular, but its vogue was on the wane. So Rossini lived on as an agreeable epicurean in his Passy villa, always refusing invitations to court.

"I have seen so many kings!" he said.

He died in 1868.

Meyerbeer reigned virtually unrivalled at the Opera. He had created a genre, the historical opera, in which his color and his sonorousness, the richness of his themes, his skill in orchestration, his pathos, his gift for stage-setting, earned him real triumphs with *Les Huguenots* and *Le Prophète* (1849). He was not prolific, doing only three plays under the Empire: *L'Etoile du nord, Le pardon de Ploermel,* and *L'Africaine.* He hated Wagner—the man's name "struck him like a discord," he said—and the author of *Tannhäuser* owed nothing to him in finally managing to get a production at the Opera. That success was due to the all-powerful patronage of the Princess Metternich.

Wagner was a real genius. He quite upset musical tradition with *The Flying Dutchman* and *Lohengrin.* He was already at work on the *Ring* sequence though without having as yet completely won the German public. He came in quest of recognition to Paris, the undisputed center of artistic Europe. He began with three big concerts in the Ventadour Hall. The musical specialists were dazzled by his power and originality but they regarded his work as something for the few. Pauline Metternich was herself a good musician.

She took it into her head to launch Wagner the way she had launched her favorite fashions in gowns. Walewski was Minister of State at that moment. She worked on him until finally *Tannhäuser* was given a most expensive production at the Opera, with the tenor Niemann, the baritone Morelli, and the powerful soprano, Marie Sasse, in the leading rôles. The press created a great stir about the opening performance. Scalpers made big money on seats. The Princess Metternich rounded up all her friends at court and in society. Even so she was not able to fill the house, and such house as there was was hostile from the opening act. The audience turned their lorgnettes on the box where the Ambassadress of Austria swaggered impertinently with the music score spread out before her eyes. It was an affront to French customs that a foreigner should try to force applause for a foreign work. The subscribers laughed, jested, poked fun. The Princess rose to her feet and tried to fight back. This provoked an outburst of frank hoots and whistles, while the Princess angrily beat with her fan till she broke it. The evening closed before a booing, mocking audience (March 13, 1861).

The Ambassadress persuaded the Emperor and the Empress to attend the second performance. The tumult was only twice as great and at certain moments it almost seemed as though the jeering were aimed at the sovereigns. The third performance was broken off halfway through when the German tenor, Niemann, stopped singing and shook his fist at the audience.

Wagner left Paris in despair and he was never to recover from the grudge. For that matter the Princess Metternich's presumptuousness served him badly, for she was to desert his cause before very long, even going so far as to have a parody of *Tannhäuser,* composed by Baron Beyens, the minister from Belgium, performed in her house. Learning of his sponsor's rather cowardly betrayal, Wagner was to get his revenge in Germany, where Ludwig II, King of Bavaria, became infatuated with Wagnerian music and carried it to its final triumph.

Hector Berlioz was a Frenchman through and through, but he was to suffer quite as many disappointments as the German Wagner without ever enjoying the latter's triumphs. His haughty, bellicose temperament, his contempt for general opinion, as well as caustic articles he wrote for the *Journal des Débats,* won him abiding hatreds that were never to be exorcised. *Roméo et Juliette* met with indifference and contempt. The audience of the Second Empire was doubtless ill-prepared to understand the novelty, strength and spiciness that Berlioz brought into his music. His erratic, stormy genius, sometimes unconventional, always colorful, always vibrant, was irritating to a public that adored light melodies with repeating choruses. His admirable *Childhood of Jesus* was better received, perhaps because he tricked his critics by presenting it as the work of an unknown composer of the sixteenth century. In 1863 Carvalho put on *Les Troyens* at the Théâtre Lyrique. The critics fell upon it with one accord and the work failed. Berlioz was already a sick man. His irritability and despondency deepened. No more of his scores were played in France. His qualities were appreciated only abroad. For six years he dragged out a disappointed life, without a ray of happiness to brighten it. Death released him in 1869.

Gounod was more fortunate. Agreeable, cultivated, adaptable, he was sought after both at court and in town society. His simpler, more comprehensible art delighted French ears. Even at that his *Faust* (1859) was not very well received at first, though *Mireille,* an opera based on Mistral's poem, and *Roméo et Juliette* were recognized at once as masterpieces. His symphonies, oratorios and songs enjoyed sensational successes. Gounod's happy career was to continue long after the fall of the Empire. Towards the end of the century his music fell into complete discredit, then in our day admirers again appeared in large numbers.

It would be unfair not to mention Ambroise Thomas, who half failed with a number of things and finally won permanent status at the Opéra Comique (1866) with *Mignon,* with Mme. Miolan-Carvalho in the leading rôle. Though Bizet did not produce his masterpieces under the Second Empire he was already giving *Les pêcheurs de perles* in 1863 and *La jolie fille de Perth* in 1867.

The Second Empire knew many great singers—Roger, Meyerbeer's favorite interpreter, Massol, Capoul, Lablache, Faure—Faure was as good an actor as he was a musician. Among the women there were Giulia Grisi and Christine Nilsson. Mme. Alboni had a voice that astonished for its range and its precision of tone; she was very fat—Emile de Girardin called her "an elephant that had swallowed a nightingale." Adelina Patti was the first to win the gold-plated stamp of American approval, with a pure and altogether sensational voice.

In the domain of the plastic arts the Second Empire witnessed a violent reaction of realism against the cold, conventional classical tradition that was forced upon the nation by the faculty at the Beaux Arts. Early in the reign a galaxy of grand old men were still left. Horace Vernet, past sixty, was still brushing out a number of military paintings with a rapid hand that was losing vigor but could still impart a feeling for the picturesque which had made his great canvases on the conquest of Algeria famous. During the Crimean War he was to be seen cavorting in front of the troops in the brilliant uniform of a Colonel of the National Guard, spattered all over with decorations.

Vernet died in 1863 and the same year noted the passing of Delacroix. That noble artist, as great a thinker as he was a painter, did not lay down his brush till the very end, managing to complete the murals in the Chapel of the Angels at Saint-Sulpice. Late in life he went back to the East that had fascinated him as a youth, painting "Botzaris Surprising the Turkish Camp" and "An Arab Tax-Collection." Delacroix's intensity of expression and his dynamic coloring lifted his haughty genius to the plane of the ancient masters, though today his work is much discussed and arouses not a little opposition. His glory did not reach its peak till after his death.

Ingres, a stubborn adversary of Delacroix, survived him four years and never flinched in his antagonism. He made a secret visit to Saint-Sulpice to see Delacroix's murals in the Chapel of the Angels. He stood in silence before them for a long time, then, grasping the priest who was showing him about by the arm, he said:

"Well now, you're sure there's a hell, aren't you?"

Napoleon III made Ingres a senator, but the artist rarely appeared at the sessions. In his eighties he was still drawing faultlessly. Always rough and brusk, intolerant, sweeping, dogmatic, he professed to despise color, which he declared "good for drunkards." He kept very much to himself, dividing his off time between his wife and his violin. Long after his death people still referred to him as "Monsieur Ingres," partly in irony but in larger part still in awe.

Decamps devoted himself to large-scale paintings to which he was not at all adapted. He was at work on "Lot's Wife" when he died in 1860 of a fall from his horse.

The men just mentioned were relics from the past. The real painters of the Second Empire fall into two groups: on the one hand, a number of more or less official artists, successful but without any great originality; then a pleiad of "independents" who were to steer French painting—and that means European painting, for all Europe followed France in those days—towards a new era.

Among the former one might mention Winterhalter, a native of Baden, but who had lived in Paris forty years. Winterhalter painted, in his sleek, accurate, saccharine style, all the beauties of the day. Still famous is his canvas called "The Empress With her Ladies-in-waiting." Ricard, too, was a portraitist of talent with a delicate sense of color, though he never quite measured up to his real capabilities. Dubufe was too eager to flatter the people who sat for him. He had a great but ephemeral vogue. Chaplin, another darling of the Parisian world of fashion, was a *petit maître* come to life again from the eighteenth century, but bringing none of the wit of that age with him. Yvan was a good draughtsman and won many commissions to paint the wars in the Crimea and Italy. Meissonnier was an imitator of the Dutch school, devoting painstaking research to his settings and costumes. His canvases on subjects from the Napoleonic period won him a reputation he did not altogether deserve. Posterity has assigned him to a more rightful place as an adroit imagist of no great significance.

Hippolyte Flandrin was a melancholy soul, talented and conscientious but lacking the warmth and dash that makes the great artist. He also kept too strictly within the limits of the ideas of Ingres. As a fine decorator of churches he came very close to attaining real fame. The murals at Saint-Germain-des-Près say all there is to say about him. Chasseriau, a faultless draughtsman and a powerful colorist, died in 1856 at the age of thirty-seven. That gave him a life too short to realize his full promise. As a pupil of Ingres touched by the quivering dramatic sensitiveness of Delacroix, he stood at the point where the two arts represented by those two masters happily blended. Eugène Fromentin, writer and painter in one, specialized in Eastern themes—scenes of the Sahel and the Sahara. He was, on the whole, a second-rate artist, but two of his paintings rank as masterpieces for their sound taste and harmonious coloring, the "Arab Bivouac at Sunrise" and the "Arab Falconer."

Many of the artists of the other group are associated with what has been known as "the Barbizon school," a school of design that was started by Theodore Rousseau on the edge of the Fontainebleau

Forest. There, living in cabins or at "Old Man Ganne's," an inn, a dozen or more painters struggled to catch open air effects, forest lights and shadings, the poetry of land and sky and of labor in the fields. The best example of the school would be François Millet, one of the real saints of art. Millet first made a reputation for himself in "genre" subjects and could have earned a comfortable living in that field. Nevertheless he turned away from it to apply himself to the study of nature in the spirit of the Barbizons. In that renunciation an instinct probably figured, for Millet was the son of a farm-hand and had himself worked as a shepherd. Always living in poverty, which he accepted in sublime resignation, working at an easel that was tattered and torn, he painted his toilers, his old women with their bundles of faggots, his gleaners, finally his "Angelus." No painter was ever more sincere, more realistic and at the same time more vibrant with the ideal. His rough and sometimes heavy execution often expresses an exquisite delicacy of feeling. Sustained by religious faith alone Millet waited all his life long for recognition. Not till 1868 did the imperial government get around to thinking of him as a fit subject for the Légion d'honneur.

Rousseau himself was long the bugbear of the critics, and they kept him out of the Salon year after year. He worked patiently on, never satisfied with himself, never discouraged, painting his beloved forest and nothing but his forest. Finally he caught the eye of Nieuwerkerque, the friend of the Princess Mathilde, then director at the Beaux Arts, and Nieuwerkerque forced him on the Salon of '52. From that time on Rousseau began to make a little money, though he proceeded to use it to help his friends, notably Millet.

Born of Spanish parentage Diaz de la Peña was French by adoption. He was an exuberant artist, mad for color. His paintings of nymphs, cupids, bathing girls, are striking canvases devoid of any real composition. He found his best moments when he worked in Rousseau's manner, brushing out the tumultuous landscape of the Lower Bréau or of Apremont.

The roll of the "Barbizon school" ends with Jules Dupré, Ziem, Troyon, Charles Jacque and Gérome—the few other names that appear on it hardly count. Corot, however, often visited the group, who ever welcomed him joyously as the illustrious and beloved master. Corot, a man with a shrewd, ruddy face, was a gay soul. Always dressing like a farm hand, he was fond of eating, of small

LOUIS PASTEUR IN HIS LABORATORY

From the Portrait by Edelfelt

theatres, of pretty girls. Beyond any doubt he was the most poetic painter that French art ever produced. A letter he wrote to Jules Dupré shows him as he was:

"You get up early, before sunrise, about three in the morning, say. You go out and sit down under a tree, you look about and you wait. You don't see anything in particular at first. Nature is just a whitish canvas with at most the outlines of a mass showing here or there. But everything is fragrant, everything is quivering under the cooled breath of dawn. . . . The fogs of the night are still crawling along over frigid green grass like rolls of silvered cotton. . . . A first sunbeam! . . . You see nothing else—it's all in the sunbeam. . . . Now the landscape lies wholly behind the transparent gauze of fog, though the fog is lifting, lifting, sucked up by the sun, and as it lifts it reveals the river—a silver thread, the meadows, the trees, the cottages, the fleeting distance. . . . And there you have my picture done!" [1]

It was at Ville-d'Avray, rather than Barbizon, that Corot painted his transparent skies, his vapory ponds, his twilight and dawn effects, his airy nymph-dances. A man of noble unselfishness he bought the cabin at Valmondois from which Daumier had been ejected and gave it to him. Living joyously he died ecstatically. In his delirium he lifted his aged, wrinkled hand as though to seize the brush and whispered:

"How beautiful it all is! I have never seen such landscapes!"

Daumier's life was far less happy than Corot's. In fact art was perhaps his one consolation. He was one of the mirrors of his age and his age failed to recognize him. He came from the cartoon to painting but made himself a master in oil, producing canvases that are noted for their vigor, their vitality, their keen sturdy irony.

Gustave Courbet kept aloof from all groups and schools. A powerful realist he was a victim of the juries at first, though he managed finally to turn their flank and vanquish public indifference by sensational private exhibitions. He had known successes as early as 1849. "Burial at Ornans" carried off the honors in the Salon of 1850. Everything attracted him—landscapes, the sea, farm life, tramps, wrestlers, girls in bathing-suits, night life. Painting with extraordinary dash and speed, a little vulgar perhaps but with no end of talent, that magnificent artist was to waste his later years

[1] Fleury and Sonolet, *La société du Second Empire*, 316.

straying off into politics. Courbet nevertheless remains one of the guiding forces in painting in the nineteenth century, exerting an influence that was beneficent and far-reaching—in a way he foretells Manet.

Manet's significant work belongs to the generation of the '70's, though canvases such as "Picnicking in the Grass" or "Olympia" were attracting the attention of the connoisseurs under the late Empire. They caused a scandal in their day, now French museums point to them as ornaments.

The Second Empire developed a veritable phalanx of first-class landscape painters to rival their comrades of the Barbizon school—Français, for instance, for Bougival and Clisson, Daubigny for Auvers-sur-Oise, Harpignies for the north of France, Jules Breton for the Artois district, Lepine for the Seine valley. Nor should one fail to mention Constantin Guys, whose drawings and engravings supply perhaps the most vivid record we possess of the customs, fashions and for that matter vices, of the Second Empire.

As for the sculptors, Rude and David d'Angers passed from the scene in 1855 and 1856, leaving only two successors to hand on names to posterity—Carpeaux and Barye. Carpeaux was an out-and-out Frenchman of the lineage of the Houdons, the Pugets, the Jean Goujons. He combined grace with strength. The group he designed for the new Opera called "The Dance" is a marvel of movement, elegance, youth. His alto-relievos on the Flora Pavillon are very modern in spirit though in atmosphere and influence they tie up rather with the Renaissance tradition. Carpeaux also died too young, but he left works in goodly number, "Ugolino and his Children" and "The Prince Imperial and his Dog, Nero" remaining the best known. Napoleon III liked Carpeaux, showered him with orders and often invited him to Compiègne. Fortunately Carpeaux's native sincerity was left unspoiled by the court atmosphere. To the end he remained himself, with all his exuberance and freedom of temperament.

Barye was the best French *"animalier"*—a romantic with a classically sound background. "Theseus," the "Battle of Centaurs and Lapithi," his lions, his bears and his monkeys are inimitable and mark peaks in an art in which Barye had no earlier rivals.

A host of architects divided the profits of the virtual remodelling of France that Napoleon III essayed; but in that army three names stand out, though for widely differing talents: Hector Lefuel, Charles Garnier and Viollet-le-Duc. Lefuel not seldom lacks taste. He loved the theatrical and was inclined to overload his surfaces with ornament. All the same he managed to complete the new Louvre with a sound sense of monumental grandeur. Garnier was still unknown when he won the competition for the Opera in 1861. The façade was six years in building and the structure itself was not to be finished till 1875. Garnier's Opera has been universally admired and much copied. Modern architects still see that its technique is remarkable. Its proportions are, in fact, good but heavy; and as a whole, staggering under its burden of middle-class "magnificence," it strikes people today as typical "Napoleon III."

Viollet-le-Duc was infatuated with the Middle Ages and restored no end of monuments and churches with a strange mixture of piety and vandalism. He completed half-built towers and stripped magnificent Gothic portals of their statuary, replacing it with dreary modern "hand-mades." He remodeled the City at Carcassonne, he ruined Vezelay, he cleaned up and spoiled Notre Dame, Saint-Denis and the cathedral of Amiens. He restored the fortress at Pierrefonds on "historical" designs that he manufactured out of whole cloth. Napoleon III took an eager and early interest in Viollet's studies, and withheld neither favor nor money from him. On the Emperor's generosity, in fact, Viollet's exceptional and largely undeserved fortune for the most part rests, and he was to display a most degrading ingratitude to his benefactor after the fall of the regime. Had it not been for Viollet-le-Duc many ancient French monuments would have perished; but wherever he went by, and he ran up and down over the whole of France, his passage left its traces in more or less disfigured relics of an admirable age which he revered without ever grasping its spirit.

Napoleon III's generosity to Viollet-le-Duc emphasizes the fact that in spite of his extravagantly liberal disposition he did not do all he might have done in the regard of writers and scientists. One notes that secretly he provided Leconte de Lisle with a pension of 3,600 francs out of his personal resources, that he gave 10,000 francs to Foucault for his experiment with the pendulum, and 30,000 francs to Renan for his expedition to Syria. It is also known that he financed Taine's chair at the Beaux Arts. Apart from a few other gifts his interest in such people stopped at that.

Science like art produced a number of first-calibre men under the Second Empire. One thinks first of all of Pasteur. Though Pasteur was not a physician he has to be counted one of the greatest of healers. To agriculture and industry the world over he rendered services which will never be forgotten. Napoleon III came to his aid on many different occasions and so smoothed the ground for his very considerable career. The Emperor very properly saw in him one of the most useful and most representative glories of his reign. Not only that: he liked Pasteur personally, took an interest in his work and treated him with the greatest deference. Pasteur, for his part, remained grateful to the Emperor in good fortune and bad.

From the time Pasteur left the Ecole Normale, where he met Taine, he did not miss a day from his work. Early researches in crystallization led him to study fermentations and germ cultures, whence he went on to changes in wines and diseases in silkworms, finding remedies and saving the silk industry in France, which was threatened with extinction. Pasteur handed out no end of blessings to mankind with absolute unselfishness, but one of his highest titles to the world's gratitude lies in his work on charcoal and rabies. He generalized the use of vaccines, discovered methods of sterilization, antisepsis and asepsis and so was to save millions of human lives.

Claude Bernard, one might say, created modern physiology. He held chairs at the Collège de France, the Sorbonne and the Museum and won official honors as well, Napoleon III even naming him to the Senate. That was all very proper. Bernard's work almost equals Pasteur's in importance. His studies on sugar production in the liver, on the sympathetic nerve and vaso-motor nervous systems and on anaesthesia carried medicine and surgery forward in great strides. Bernard wrote a large number of books. Some of them have become classics, notably his *Lectures on Experimental Physiology,* his *Physiology and Pathology of the Nervous System* and his *Introduction to Experimental Medicine.* He was an incomparable teacher and expositor. In the field of ideas, where he was a determinist and a neo-vitalist, and in scientific method, he exercised a world-wide influence during the last decade of the nineteenth century.

Léon Foucault counts as one of the most original physicists. He measured the speed of light, demonstrated the rotation of the earth by the famous pendulum experiment—an experiment that was first performed under the cupola of the Pantheon—and perfected the telescope.

The scientific career of the great chemist Jean Baptiste Dumas probably suffered from the numerous public duties which were thrust upon him and which he accepted. He took his seat in the Senate seriously and became actively interested in problems of public health and water supply in Paris. He found time, nevertheless, for basic studies on fusel oil, indigo, albuminoids and fertilizers and on the phylloxera. His discovery of the "law of substitutions" revolutionized organic chemistry. In collaboration with Boussingault he published one important work: the *Essay on Chemical Equilibrium in Organic Bodies*. He also gave a famous course on the "philosophy of chemistry" at the Collège de France. Marcellin Berthelot, highly cultivated, incredibly versatile, touched on practically every phase of science in the course of a long life. His labors centered in the main, however, around two ideas, the synthetic production of organic bodies from elements and thermo-chemistry—thermo-chemistry became a new science through the work of Berthelot. Among his varied and voluminous writings are his *Chemical Synthesis* and his *Origins of Alchemy*, both published after the fall of the Empire. Henri Sainte-Claire-Deville conducted researches in essential oils, resins, silicon, sodium aluminium and platinum. He discovered a new method for analyzing minerals. His ingenious theory of "dissociation" has proved to be of very great utility. The astronomer Leverrier won immortal fame for his discovery of the planet Neptune. Unfortunately his character as a man did not measure up to his scientific talent. Napoleon III made him a senator and then director of the Observatory. In this post his vexatious disposition made him unable to get along with his colleagues, and he was eventually removed. He was the most fawning of courtiers during the good days of the Emperor and Empress. In their hour of misfortune he turned against them.

CHAPTER XXIV

The French Community

WITH BETWEEN THIRTY-SEVEN AND THIRTY-EIGHT MILLIONS OF PEOPLE France was still one of the largest nations in Europe. Germany had a population of about the same size. Austria was somewhat smaller. Italy had twenty-six millions, Spain eighteen. All the same, average density of population in France was rather low—about ninety-three persons to the square mile. The birth rate was declining, the excess of births over deaths having dropped from 30 per 1,000 in 1830 to as low as 25 per 1,000 in 1860. The year 1855 for some reason had shown a sudden rebound to 28, but that was a momentary fluctuation. Immediately afterwards the population curve began to go down again. The phenomenon was due to a complex of causes: the wars in the Crimea and Italy, the cholera epidemics, a number of poor harvests in succession. The major factor, however, seemed to be the general increase in prosperity. That correlation seemed surprising at the time. It has since been verified by social science.

France was a country of small towns and villages, a farming country especially. More than three-quarters of the total population lived by agriculture. Large cities were still few. Paris had a population of a little over a million. Marseilles, Lyons, Bordeaux and Rouen ran from one to two hundred thousand. Nantes, Lille and Toulouse did not reach a hundred thousand. Toulon, Brest, Saint-Etienne and Amiens were towns of between fifty and sixty thousand people.

A drift to the cities was already becoming noticeable. Population was visibly increasing only in urban and manufacturing centers. Districts in the hill-country such as the Franche-Comté, the South East, the Central Plateau, the Pyrenees, were in decline. Even in Normandie farmlands were more and more being turned into pasture. For all of that the era of the "tentacular city" was still far

356

away. The farms could find plenty of hands, though the labor supply was badly distributed.

The various classes of the French community were all equal before the law, but they were sharply distinguished one from the other by manners of living, by the food they ate, the clothes they wore, the language they spoke. In spite of such differences they seemed to be bound together in the national fabric by reciprocal goodwill, by a sense of spiritual solidarity. The peasant in blouse and sabots respected the owner of the rural château or the city mansion. The worker in his cap might jest at the "dude" in the fur-collared coat and top hat. He did not hate him.

Each social level had its particular amusements. The masses went to cabarets and public dance halls. The wealthier classes went to cafés, clubs and salons. The wealthy, too, were the only ones to travel—and very little at that. Few people in France had ever gone to Paris. Many of them had never seen the sea. Education was very unequally distributed. There was a cultivated élite, few in numbers but extremely well educated, made up of magistrates, writers, university and lyceum professors, a few society people. The bourgeoisie read newspapers, books and magazines, more commonly in public reading rooms. Workingmen and farmhands as a rule did not know how to read or write. Those who did had little within their reach save wretchedly printed pamphlets or almanacs, which were for the most part sold by peddlers.

The nobility and the upper middle-classes, who were more and more blending with the nobility, spent the winters in their city mansions and the summers—long summers—in their country châteaux. On their rural estates they still led fairly patriarchal lives, overseeing the farming, giving garden parties, dinners, hunts. Contacts with the laboring population were still close.

Boys of the aristocracy were ordinarily educated in Catholic schools and looked forward to careers in army, navy or diplomacy. Many, to be sure, remained "gentlemen" pure and simple, preparing for no profession at all. Nobles of Orleanist families were likely to be prominent in local politics. Strict Legitimists were careful to have no dealings whatever with representatives of the Usurper.

The middle bourgeoisie gave its children a more substantial and practical education. That class supplied the active elements in the country—magistrates, public officials, professors, lawyers, physicians, engineers, financiers and, in increasing numbers, army and navy officers. Bourgeois life was earnest, simple, parsimonious. The French bourgeois was inclined to disparage artists and writers. He had been deeply, too deeply, interested in money ever since the Restoration. The defect was deep-seated though in a measure offset by real worth and sound morals. While the nobility and the upper bourgeoisie thought sanely and safely and stood loyal to religious beliefs and practices, the man of the middle class proper not seldom held liberal and to an extent Voltarian views. The republican opposition was largely recruited from middle-class ranks.

The clergy enjoyed a select position in French society, finding itself better off than it had been even under the Old Regime. The Concordat protected priests and guaranteed them a minimum livelihood. Curates of village parishes received annual salaries of about fifteen hundred francs, then "casuals" and gifts in kind from their parishioners. They were under the absolute power of their bishops —only the district priests enjoying life tenures. The Church was considered a very desirable career and the priesthood was much sought after. The seminaries, big and little, were crowded with pupils deriving more especially from the rural masses. Not many of the religious orders were legally recognized but they all enjoyed lavish toleration. Strictly speaking the Jesuits and the Dominicans had no right to teach, but they could nevertheless point to prosperous and rapidly expanding educational institutions. The influence of the secular clergy was very considerable in all parts of the country, but it was especially marked in the mountainous east and in the north and northwest. The village curate lived the same life as the workers of the soil among whom he labored. He advised them and helped them. They in return loved and respected him, very properly regarding him as the natural protector of their families. Even workingmen of the revolutionary parties retained their reverence for the priest. Had he not blessed the Liberty poles of '48? The clergy was an important force to reckon with at election time, and in spite of the difficulties laid in its way by the Roman Question the government resorted to every conceivable device to win clerical support. It increased the "worship" budgets, awarded seminary scholarships in large numbers and shut its eyes to illegal encroachments by the church schools in the field of education. All in all, many bishops or other prelates may have been hostile to the Empire. The middle and lower clergy stood loyal.

France was not yet the nation of small property owners that she became towards the end of the century. Agricultural reports for the year 1862 show 1,745,000 farmers working their own lands, 648,000 employed hired labor also, 380,000 worked rented farms. There were 400,000 share-croppers and 2,000,000 farmhands, while 1,450,000 persons earned wages by unclassified farm services. Whatever their source of income very few farm workers were without a little house and garden and a bit of ground that enabled them to raise vegetables and fruit. Farm wages were very low—1 franc 50 to 2 francs per day for the occasional job, 300 to 400 francs a year for the steady male hand. As prosperity mounted towards the end of the Empire those figures rose by at least a third. This "boom," it might be noted, seems to have been soundly correlated with the drop in gold prices resulting from the discovery of new gold fields in California and Australia. It was the outstanding economic phenomenon of the Second Empire.

Farmers worked hard in the summer months. The enforced leisure of the winters they devoted to mending their farm tools, to little trades such as wood turning or shoemaking practised at home or, in the East more especially, to home work for the manufacturers, such as the making of watch springs. The women spun wool and knitted yarns. Religious ceremonies, saints' festivals, market days, fairs, weddings, supplied the main diversions, along with home parties where each guest sang ancient folk songs in turn. Farming methods had changed very little in the course of the centuries. There were few if any machines, and no fertilizer save the traditional manure pile. Sowing was done by hand, harvesting by scythe or sickle. Threshing still depended on the flail. Yields from worn-out lands too vast in extent were exceedingly low. Rich soil could still be found in the North. There a few people managed to practise intensive farming and obtain somewhat better results.

The chief crop was wheat, with a yield of about 300 million bushels. Vineyards totaled four million acres and French wines had no rivals in the world. French market produce was also the finest in Europe. Breeding was improving, but farm animals on the whole were badly cared for. Cows were underfed and gave very little milk. Sheep were too numerous for a country so rich—25 millions. They were undersized and grew too coarse a wool. The government started a sheep farm at Rambouillet, which produced new crossings with merinos.

This venture was quite in line with the interest which the Emperor and his ministers took in agriculture. As early as 1848 the Republic had established agricultural schools and district granges. Napoleon III hoped that a Loan Bank would eventually rid the peasant of the ruinous farm mortgage. As matters worked out the resources of that institution stimulated housing developments and real estate speculations in the towns.

Prices for farm produce had for ages been very low. With the Empire came a feeling of security that was country wide and prices rose rapidly. Districts such as Beauce and Normandie that were rich in grains and cattle enjoyed a phenomenal boom. Napoleon III was personally interested in land reclamation projects, and a law of 1854 smoothed his path in that regard. He forested many of the coastal moors, and control over the shifting dunes yielded huge profits for a number of years. Railroad developments made a better distribution of commodities possible and famine became just a painful memory of the Old Regime. There was an acute food shortage in France in 1855. Then famine vanished from the country—one may hope, forever.

France was primarily a land of farmers, but it was also a land of crafts and trades. Almost four million artisans earned their livings in their own homes. Towards the end of the Empire there were hardly more than two million factory hands in France. Paris itself remained as under the kings a city of small "shops" where a few hand workers toiled in company.

The factory, in the modern sense of the term, began appearing more especially in the East and North, where cotton and wool centers formed for the manufacture of sheeting and broadcloths. At Lyons and Saint-Etienne silks and ribbons flourished and prospered.

French mines employed some forty thousand miners, hardly more than the French quarries and salt works. Less than fifty thousand men were employed in foundries and steel works. Cutlery, edged tools and locksmithery were still home industries. Flour milling clung to the ancient methods—water mills, wind mills. Olive oil and alcohol were still farm products. At Marseilles, at Nantes, and in Alsace one could note a few factories for sugar, soap or chemical products.

Artisans lived very much as they had lived for centuries. They were townsmen of very modest means, learning their trades by long apprenticeships and continuing them from father to son.

The situation of factory workers was altogether different. Whether they were employed or unemployed depended entirely on the employer's convenience. They worked crowded together in unhygienic factories ten or twelve hours a day with no sort of guarantee for the future. Wages were wretched. Levasseur [1] computes for the year 1853 an average daily wage of 3 fr. 81 for men in Paris, of 2 fr. 06 for men in country districts. Women averaged 2 fr. 12 a day in Paris, 1 fr. 07 in country districts. Those figures, probably, are a trifle low. Working people lived in small tenements, unimproved and often unsanitary. In the North the members of a workingman's family were often scattered about among a number of mills and lived lives that were wretched indeed. Tuberculosis took a dreadful toll of human life in those regions. Conditions were somewhat better in the South. There the factory hand earned less money but he worked fewer hours and had time for air and sunlight.

The men in a number of trades, the stone cutters, the carpenters, the cabinetmakers, a distant posterity of the men who built the medieval cathedrals, had an organization, of obscure origins, called the "Comrades of the French Circuit" (*Compagnons du Tour de France*). It was a secret society with secret rules and passwords. Before members could become masters in their trades they were obliged to have served a long apprenticeship moving from town to town all over France. They could find work, shelter and comradeship everywhere.

Mutual aid societies came into being under the July Monarchy and gradually spread. They usually stopped at helping the sick and finding work for the unemployed. Credit, consumers' and producers' cooperatives were started under the Second Republic. Virtually all of them were badly managed and ultimately came to grief in politics. The Empire should have reorganized and supervised them. Actually it dissolved them, though it did lend some support to charitable and relief organizations among the working classes.

After the panic of 1852 wages in industry rose, but only in ratio

[1] *La population française.*

with the cost of living. All through the Second Empire living conditions for the working classes left much to be desired.

Business, however, had never been better. Profits were enormous and gigantic forward strides were made in all branches of activity in industry and commerce. New enterprises in banking, in mining, in smelting, in gas and water supply, in all departments of manufacturing, started every day. The whole country was torn up for one public improvement or another until it looked like one immense building project. Money flowed freely into these activities and provoked a new orgy of speculation and manipulation that took one back to the heyday of John Law. The Stock Exchange was swamped with traders and listed securities decupled in numbers. The number of stock brokers doubled during the Second Empire. Stocks and bonds leapt upwards in "dazzling" spurts (*mirobolant* was the word of the day) and they fell back in "catastrophic" drops ("catastrophic" is a word of all times and places). The Emperor raged at these manipulations but could do little to restrain them—for one thing too many "insiders" in his own entourage fattened on them. Sensational failures, such as that of the *Société Immobilière* (1867), which carried no end of enterprises sound and profitable along with it, finally brought the frenzy to an end; but its moral consequences were to prove far-reaching. The French bourgeoisie had all along possessed deep-seated traits of earnestness and responsibility. These were seriously shaken by the spectacle of great fortunes easily made in a few days of wild speculation, and French national prestige was damaged. The peoples abroad had gazed with jealous eyes upon the prosperous, luxurious living in France, of which in fact they only perceived surfaces. Too frequently they came to the conclusion that the country was inhabited by a reckless race of gamblers. Not till later on did the world come to see how sound, how substantial, how hard-working French society had remained at bottom. The French of the Second Empire were long judged on those hasty impressions. There could hardly have been a judgment that took less account of realities.

CHAPTER XXV

Sadowa

OTTO VON BISMARCK-SCHÖNHAUSEN WAS A PRUSSIAN JUNKER. HE studied at the University of Göttingen, then served in the army for a time as an officer. Finally he settled down on his estates in Pomerania and for six or seven years led the simple altogether rural life of a gentleman-farmer. In 1846 he was elected to the Prussian Diet and at once distinguished himself as an influential Conservative, extremely hostile to France. From that moment Bismarck dedicated his life to the service of authority. He was an authoritarian to the marrow of his bones.

The power of the princes in Germany was seriously shaken by the disturbances of 1848. Bismarck turned at that time to diplomacy, represented Prussia in the federal assembly at Frankfurt and there came forward as an enemy of Austria—"an old worm-eaten three-decker." [1]

That tall, redfaced, tough-speaking rustic with hard blue eyes under black bushy brows, was altogether up-to-date in his wit. He minced no words in ridiculing the backward courts of a Germany that was still loosely sprawling about inside a flabby belt of federation. He spent three years as ambassador at St. Petersburg. In June, 1862, he was accredited to the court of Napoleon III.

That summer, now at Fontainebleau, now at Compiègne, Bismarck charmed Napoleon III with his sparkling intelligence, his lively manners, his bursts of bluff good humor; and the Emperor even thought that he could find in the "big, good-natured ogre" a collaborator in his plans for the remaking of Europe. Just as Italy had crystallized around Piedmont, Germany, he thought, might crystallize around an uncouth, somewhat round-shouldered, but very vigorous Prussia. At that moment Napoleon III seemed more

---

[1] Bismarck to Manteuffel, February 13, 1854.

than ever set on his policy of nationalities. He was talking of "Iberian unity" and of "Scandinavian unity"—to the sole purport of angering England.

"Before very long," Queen Victoria wrote, "that man will have the continent at his feet and be in control in the Mediterranean and in the Baltic."

The nationality system was not altogether to the interests of France. That country would have been wiser not to foment the rise of powerful states on her borders; and, in fact, the Emperor was inclined to favor a united Germany only on condition that he should gain substantial profits in return—the left bank of the Rhine, for instance, though, of course, after a plebiscite. That had been an old scheme of his dating as far back as 1850, when, as Prince-President, he had sent Persigny to Berlin to offer an alliance to the King of Prussia with the object of establishing German unity to Prussian profit. Like most Frenchmen of his day Napoleon III had always had a penchant for Germany, and all the more so, doubtless, in that he had grown up in Bavaria. Austria, on the other hand, he mistrusted both by instinct and by family tradition, thinking of her as a reactionary power that had persecuted Italy far too long. His fondness for Prussia was outspoken. In spite of the diplomatic difficulties resulting, he had sponsored Prussia and served her interests. He had procured the admission of Prussia to the Congress of Paris in 1856. In 1857 he had arbitrated the Neufchatel quarrel with Switzerland. A threat of Prussian mobilization had forced him to conclude a too hasty peace after Solferino, but he had maintained the best personal relations with King William and, in 1861, shortly after the King's coronation, entertained him with special hospitality at Compiègne. He thought of Prussia as a Piedmont of the North which was seeking a normal expansion and trying to get balanced on its feet. He was quite willing to cooperate with her in such a praiseworthy endeavor.

For the moment he made no definite proposals to Bismarck. Things had not gone as far as that. Both men were feeling their way, sounding each other out by sequences of confidential unbosomings. They were batting the balls back and forth in practice for the opening of the real game. The question of a diplomatic entente had come up. Bismarck pretended to fall in line, flattering the Emperor and his ministers but judging them from above down. In

September, after three months in France, he was called back to
Berlin to head the King's Cabinet. His impressions of his stay in
France he summed up in a single caustic sentence:

"I met two amusing women there—and not a man."

Bismarck was forty-eight years old when he took charge of things
in Germany. No one in Europe was anywhere near his match in
diplomatic and statesmanly talents. He could foresee things far in
advance and make a decision on the spot when the occasion offered.
He was patient, tenacious, courageous, industrious, when necessary
adaptable, and, when necessary, brutal. In that sturdy, well-balanced
nature vices were few if any. Bismarck had no trace of vanity or
personal pride. He led a simple life with no tiring amusements.
He may have been over hearty at table, evincing a greediness for
food and wine that betrayed the savage deep down in him. Indeed,
in the polished and often amiable diplomat, the savage was never
very deeply buried. Bismarck was ever to show himself shrewd and
vindictive, scornful of all generosity, capable of the vilest betrayals.
Actually he despised the rest of mankind—he despised men profoundly.

"There is nothing on this earth but juggling and hypocrisy," he
once said. "In politics, no one ever does anything for anybody—
there is always some axe to grind."

Those were basic convictions with Bismarck. He had, however,
one controlling principle: service of his king. Bismarck was and
wished to be purely and simply his king's man, though he stood
ready, when the time came, to browbeat his prince in the interests
of the country. Very late in his life the aged Bismarck uttered one
melancholy reflection that fills out his character in a most striking
and unexpected way:

"I have made a great nation happy, yes, but how many, many
people unhappy! Had it not been for me three great wars would
not have been fought. Eighty thousand men would not have died
and their fathers, mothers, sisters, would not now be mourning
them. . . . Well, that is an account I have to settle with God." [1]

Eighty thousand men! Characteristically Bismarck was counting
only Germans!

The sovereign with whom Bismarck was to work closely from
that time on had ascended the throne in 1861, after ruling as regent

[1] Busch: *Unser Reichskanzler.*

for four years in the name of his insane brother. William I was the second son of Queen Louise, the beautiful and unfortunate enemy of Napoleon I. He himself had fought against the latter in 1813 and in 1814, nor had he changed by a jot since those faraway days: He hated the Revolution and he disliked the Bonapartes. He was a gentleman, all in all, scrupulous and sensitive. He had charming manners. But underneath such exteriors he was a feudal lord enamoured of force. At the time of his coronation he dropped a remark that was weighted down with significance:

"It is not Prussia's destiny to live satisfied with what she has."

Those words throw a world of light on his alliance with Bismarck. Bismarck was not a European as were most of the ministers in the other countries in Europe. He was just a Prussian, first and last a Prussian, and his one dream was to win primacy on the continent for his nation.

In London, in the summer of 1862, Bismarck had not hesitated to lay the outlines of his future policy before Disraeli.

"When our army is strong enough, I will seize the first opportunity to settle accounts with Austria, dissolve the Germanic Federation and bring Germany to national unity under the leadership of Prussia." [1]

"We must look out for that man," Disraeli whispered to the gentleman who was entertaining him and Bismarck. "He means what he is saying."

The bond between William I and Bismarck tightened as a matter of course on the part of them both and in spite of the minister's outbursts of temper and the King's not infrequent sulkings. It was never to be severed. They were guided by a common will that lifted them far above ordinary human vicissitudes. They would rid the German Federation of the time-honored suzerainty of Austria and make of Prussia, with her population of eighteen millions, a first-rate power absolutely dominating the Germanic world.

In order to succeed in such a gigantic project they needed, as they must have realized, a very strong army and some alliance or other. The army they already had and it was a good one, though in their eyes it was just a beginning. The Prussian Landtag was balky in granting credits to increase effectives and armaments. Once set-

[1] Jacques Bardoux, *Le Temps*, April 4, 1936.

tled in his new duties Bismarck taunted the representatives contemptuously.

"The Prussian dynasty has not fulfilled its mission. It refuses to be just an ornament in the parliamentary edifice which you seem inclined to erect."

The Chamber was dissolved. Chafing under the new taxes the country returned the same men. Bismarck ignored them. In the Chamber, in fact, he let fall a prophetic remark.

"The great questions of our time will be decided not by majority votes but by iron and blood."

As good as his word he went ahead with Roon, his Minister of War, and Moltke, his Chief of Staff, to reorganize and expand the army till he had the one he wanted, an army that would be ready from one day to the next to support and enforce his policies.

The other problem of the moment was to make sure of the good will of the Czar. Ever since 1815 St. Petersburg and Berlin had been held together by political and family ties. But of late, and largely owing to the work of Morny, Russia had drawn perceptibly closer to France. That was not at all the way Bismarck wanted things, and luck played into his hands very much as it had served Napoleon III ten years before. The Polish question suddenly came up, and he seized that opportunity to upset the chessboard and start a new game.

After a brief renaissance in the first Napoleon's day, Poland had risen in insurrection in 1830, only to be punished in a most thoroughgoing fashion by Nicholas I. That truculent autocrat made bold to say to the Municipality of Warsaw in 1835:

"I have built a fortress here and I serve you notice that at the slightest sign of disobedience I will have the city blown to bits. Once I have destroyed Warsaw I shall not be the man to build it up again."

For a time after his accession to the throne Alexander II seemed disposed to relax his strangle hold on the unfortunate people of Poland. Michel Gortchakov, the defender of Sebastopol, was appointed Viceroy and started to work out reforms with the support of a loyalist millionaire, Wielopolski. The Poles, however, were too sore from their past hurts and would not forgive. In February, 1861, violent public demonstrations featured the anniversary of the Polish victory at Grochow and open insurrection soon broke out.

It was smothered in blood—Gortchakov dying of grief because of the failure of his reform policy. What would France do? France was as far away as ever, but she seemed to be such a powerful country! She had freed Italy and the provinces on the Danube. The Polish patriots could be altogether certain of French sympathy. Paris of yore had applauded the heroic resistance of Warsaw. Montalembert said:

"Ever since Europe allowed Poland to be torn to pieces she has been in a state of mortal sin!"

Those words had sent a tremor through all the classes then ruling in France. Again in 1848 the mobs led by Barbès had demanded of the National Assembly that it declare war on Russia.

Napoleon III had all along been the advocate and champion of the rights of the peoples. He should have glowed like a burning coal in behalf of Polish aspirations. Unfortunately he had to consider the Czar's feelings. Alexander had done him a number of good turns during the war in Italy, and in a near future he might be needed as a husky ally to take the place of a lukewarm England. Napoleon III therefore deported himself more cautiously than usual. The French Press, almost without exception, came out on the side of Poland. The Emperor halted at a rather vague expression of sympathy in a letter to the *Moniteur,* declaring "his reluctance to encourage hopes which he would be unable to satisfy" (April 23, 1861). Repressions followed disturbances in Poland all through the year 1862; then finally, in January, 1863, a new insurrection broke out. Regiments of Polish conscripts in the Russian army mutinied and, armed with clubs and scythes, bands of peasants overran the country.

Emissaries of the Polish rebels began agitating in Prussia. That was the pretext that Bismarck seized. He approached the Russian government with a suggestion that they make a treaty of mutual assistance against the rebels. Gortchakov, the Russian chancellor, signed the document—without any great enthusiasm. Napoleon III manifested his disapproval. Public opinion in France raged. Drouyn de Lhuys sent a number of protests to Bismarck. The latter brushed them aside.

Drouyn de Lhuys favored intervention in favor of Poland as a stepping stone to a rapprochement with Austria and to winning Catholic sympathies in France back to the Empire. He even dreamed of combining Russia's Polish provinces with Galicia, in an independent Poland that would be governed by an archduke,. At such a price Austria would yield Venetia to Victor Emmanuel. With that in view he had several conversations with Metternich. In March, 1863, the Emperor came around to the same policy and ordered Metternich to make a definite proposition to Francis Joseph. The Austrian Emperor rejected the manoeuvre. England, for her part, suggested a joint move of the European powers at St. Petersburg, thinking in that way to nip any Franco-Russian alliance in the bud. Napoleon III saw through the English game and addressed a personal letter to the Czar, begging him to grant an amnesty. Alexander replied that he would not consider clemency until the insurrection had come to an end.

Sympathy for Poland rose to fever heat in France. Subscriptions were opened on all hands. Petitions came in by the thousands to the Senate. All circles, all parties—conservatives, republicans, legitimists, liberals, Catholics, anticlericals—stood united in a common pity, a common anger. As Emile Ollivier drolly remarked:

"Dupanloup and Quinet were bitterly disputing possession of an exclusive right to being pro-Polish." [1]

A great debate opened in the Senate on March 17th. Prince Napoleon led off with a diatribe against Russia.

"I do not want war," he cried, "but I don't want peace either."

That was not a very illuminating position, as Billault proceeded to point out. The Emperor had vainly besought his cousin (February 22nd) to put a damper on his warlike enthusiasms:

"I am counting on you to help me instead of embarrassing me. I implore you not to move out of tempo with the violins."

After the speech in the Senate, the Emperor very soundly reproached him "for flouting all proprieties," adding:

"I shall never admit that a man can talk in the Senate as freely as he can at his club, insulting everybody right and left."

And he gave the Prince the choice between keeping in line with the government and withdrawing from the imperial family. Prince Napoleon gave in. He made a trip to Egypt "for his health" and was received cordially by the Emperor on his return.

Though the Emperor saw the soundness of Billault's moderate policy he realized that he could not stem the tide of public opinion

[1] *Op. cit.*, VI, 99.

and the influences, for once combined, of the Empress and Prince
Napoleon. He yielded. In concert with England and Austria he sent
a note to St. Petersburg, emphasizing the seriousness of the complications that might result from a prolongation of chaos in Poland
(April 17, 1863).

Prussia had been careful not to associate herself with these moves.
On the contrary, she assured Russia of her wholehearted support in
case of a conflict. That accord between St. Petersburg and Berlin
was very close indeed. For that matter the two sovereigns were near
relatives—William was Alexander's uncle. Their letters to each
other at the time show a tone of complete mutual trust.

Encouraged by the attitude of Berlin the Czar made bold to reject
suggestions from the Western Powers which envisaged some sort of
autonomy for Poland within the framework of the Russian Empire.
In a moment of anger, indeed, he even proposed to the King of
Prussia that they declare war on Austria and France. Bismarck mod-
erated such a premature outburst. The Western Powers returned
to the attack but again obtained nothing. Meantime the Polish revolt was crushed to earth under the might of Russia's hordes. The
leaders were shot or hanged. Thirty thousand suspects were deported to Siberia. Bruised, bleeding, smothered, Poland fell silent
as she had done thirty years before.

At the November opening of the Legislative Body Napoleon III
once more put forward his proposal of a European conference. He
wanted to thresh out the Polish question and, on the same occasion,
procure the annulment of the treaties of 1815, "which had become
obsolete," having been "ignored, modified, misconstrued or threatened till nothing was left of them."

Speaking for England Lord Russell refused with impudent flat-
ness, declaring that "the principal stipulations of the treaties of 1815
were still in full force." That was a direct personal thrust at Napoleon III. The Emperor then developed his project with greater
amplitude. His idea was to call the attention of the powers not only
to the status of Poland but to all the problems that were endangering peace in Europe: the differences between Germany and Denmark, the Roumanian question, the unfriendly relations between
Austria and Italy, finally the French occupation of Rome. He even
thought a general limitation of armaments was remotely possible.

Russell again contemptuously rejected the proposal. The Em-

peror's program may in fact have been too comprehensive. It was
certainly high-minded. The other countries either sent half-hearted
acceptances or requested a more detailed proposition. That enabled
Drouyn de Lhuys barely to save his face by a concluding circular
breathing a spirit of hopeful patience.

The Polish business was a definite defeat for the French, and the
seriousness of its consequences was not slow in manifesting itself.
The Emperor had failed to hold French public opinion well enough
in hand and that had cost him the friendship of Russia. Meantime
Bismarck, talking straight politics, had won a virtual alliance with
the Czar. Having thus made sure of his rear, he could now feel
quite free to begin the realization of his larger ambitions.

Frederick VII of Denmark died on November 15, 1863. That
event reopened the "question of the duchies" at the very height of
the tension over Poland. The problem of Schleswig-Holstein was
particularly knotty. Frederick VII was Duke of Schleswig, a country
of Danish population, and Duke of Holstein, a German country. At
the instigation of Prussia the Germanic Federation laid claim to
suzerainty over Schleswig and, on the same grounds, to suzerainty
over Holstein. While the new king, Christian IX, was being proclaimed in Copenhagen, a distant relative of his from a side branch
of the family, the Duke of Augustenburg, was recognized by the
Federal Diet as Duke of Schleswig-Holstein. The Duke of Augustenburg was a genial rogue. In reply to a comment that "his rights
were not worth very much," he answered:

"The proof that my rights are worth a good deal is that from
father to son we have sold them three times already."

Recognition of the Duke of Augustenburg meant dismemberment for the Danish crown. A word from Paris could have prevented it. That word did not come. England was all for action, but
the Tuileries did not dare to follow. Napoleon III sent General
Fleury to Copenhagen to warn Christian that France could not
support him. He, the Emperor, was disappointed at the collapse of
his plan for a European Conference and preferred to avoid any new
complications. He failed to see, as Drouyn de Lhuys failed to see,
how unwise and how shocking it would prove for France to desert
Denmark, a loyal ally of the First Empire.

Fleury went on from Copenhagen to Berlin. Bismarck talked to
him of Germany's Polish interests and with admirable candor.

"We would rather die," he said, "than have any question raised as to our possessions in Posen. I would far rather cede our Rhenish provinces."

Fleury pricked up his ears and telegraphed to Paris:

"The Rhine frontier! The word has been pronounced. Shall I underscore it?"

The opening did not seem so surprising to Napoleon III. He replied:

"Don't mention the Rhine. Tone down on Posen."

He intended to bring up the Rhine question again—but later on.

Feeling a full breeze astern Bismarck decided on nothing less than the annexation of the Danish duchies. Troops from Saxony and Hanover were already occupying Holstein. Prussia prepared to invade Schleswig. Fearing that Prussia was outdistancing her in Germany, Austria joined in and on January 16th the two great powers called on little Denmark to hand Schleswig over. Denmark refused. On February 1, 1864, 60,000 Austro-Prussians crossed the frontier. The Danes dug in in Jutland and held out courageously, first at Düppel, then at Fredericia. But the attacking armies were too strong. Jutland was taken, leaving Christian IX in possession of islands only—Seeland and Fionia (July 14th). During the campaign England again suggested joint intervention to France: A fleet would be sent to Copenhagen to act or not act as the case might require. Drouyn de Lhuys refused. He was afraid of an attack on the Rhine. He was then offered his conference. Lord Clarendon, Napoleon III's old friend, came to Paris to make arrangements with him. The Emperor refused to assume any definite undertakings.

"We took a sound slap in the face from Russia in the matter of Poland," he confided to Clarendon with an absence of restraint which, secretive as he was, he sometimes manifested. "We could hardly risk another from Germany on account of Denmark without taking some notice of it. You see, I am not ready for a war." [1]

The Conference met in London all the same. It was just one long discussion of possible solutions for the question of the duchies. Arbitration and mediation being rejected, the plenipotentiaries went home altogether satisfied at having done completely nothing. With the Austro-Germans about to invade the islands of the Sund and with no hope of succor visible from any quarter, Christian resigned

[1] *Life of Lord John Russell*, I, 2, 404.

himself to asking for an armistice. The preliminaries were signed on August 1st. The duchies of Schleswig, Holstein and Lauenburg were ceded to Austria and Prussia jointly. The question as to what rights the Duke of Augustenburg may have had was entirely ignored.

So France lost an opportunity to resume her traditional rôle in Europe as a protector of small states. Napoleon III had first allowed Poland to be strangled. Then he had abandoned the Danes of Schleswig to the German yoke. Rothan has appraised the rôle of France in the Germano-Danish conflict in not at all unfair terms:

"All the governments more or less played Prussia's game, Russia by her premeditated reserve, Austria by her incoherences, the German courts by their fatuousness, Denmark by her stubbornness. But, compromising with its principle of nationalities, the French government was the one most deliberately to ignore its vital interests and to contribute most lavishly to the dismemberment of the Danish monarchy." [1]

Bismarck, for his part, had won his game twice over. Strong now with Russian support, and with an army that was growing steadily larger and was now practised in war, Prussia had in actual truth become the leading power in Germany. The one task still remaining was to eliminate Austria from influence in the German world. Bismarck was soon to succeed in that, and thanks to a series of new mistakes on the part of Napoleon III, the most serious mistakes he ever made and the ones that were to lead straight to his downfall.

The Emperor harbored no resentment against Prussia or against Bismarck because of these disappointments. Quite to the contrary, now that England and Russia had failed him, he was more than ever inclined towards a Prussian entente. French opinion was on the whole favourable to such a move and Prussia seemed ready for it too. Roon, the Prussian Minister of War, came to attend manoeuvres at the Châlons camp. William I commissioned him "to express to the Emperor his desire to see their relations become increasingly cordial." Carrying attentiveness a step too far, perhaps, the Emperor awarded Roon the grand cross of the Légion d'honneur, which was bestowed on him by the young Prince Imperial. At that same moment, chancing to meet the French ambassador, the Duc de Gramont, in Vienna, Bismarck repeated to him confidentially a re-

---

[1] *La politique française en 1866*, 17.

mark which he had shortly before addressed to the English envoy, Sir Andrew Buchanan:

"What, at the most, you can offer Napoleon III is permission to start a war to get the Rhine provinces away from us. . . . The only person who can give them to France is the man who owns them now. If the day ever comes when the game has to be played, we are the ones who can play it best on the side of France, because we can begin not by promising her but by giving her some wage for her help."

Gramont reported the "feeler" to Paris at once. It gave Drouyn de Lhuys and the Emperor considerable food for thought. Ambassador from Prussia at the time, succeeding the Prince of Reuss, was von der Goltz, a small-sized Bismarck, shrewd under an outward appearance of thickheadedness. On arriving in Paris von der Goltz had begun by feigning a personal admiration for the Empress in order to gain her favor, and in that, as a matter of fact, he seems to have succeeded. Von der Goltz was for going ahead with the arrangement with France. Bismarck hesitated. He had gone to Vienna with his sovereign in order to obtain Francis Joseph's authorization to annex Schleswig-Holstein, an as yet undivided loot. The two Prussians encountered only bad will in Austria and talks came to an end without any conclusive results. Bismarck was not at all satisfied but he did not care to hurry matters.

In the autumn of 1864 he went to Paris, saw many people and tried to be generally agreeable. Thence he went on to Biarritz for a talk with the Emperor. What did they say to each other? Bismarck, it seems, made no allusion to the Rhine, but talked rather of Belgium and Luxembourg, in case France should require some compensation as the price of her eventual cooperation.

"Everything he offered me did not belong to him," said Napoleon III.

The Emperor maintained a noncommittal attitude. Bismarck departed in no little disappointment, as an insolent sally on his part bore witness:

"The Emperor is a great incompetence that is grossly underestimated."

The matter of the alliance dragged along. Serious opposition came to light in Napoleon III's entourage. Drouyn de Lhuys, Walewski, the Empress, were in favor of a conservative entente with

Austria. They had never liked the Italian adventure. Here now was a Prussian adventure in the offing. Bismarck, on his side, was afraid of being dragged in farther than he liked. When von der Goltz pressed for a decision he wrote (February 20, 1865):

"Might not this arrangement involve more disadvantages than advantages?" The accord was to be clandestine. If France betrayed the secret would not Prussia lose face before all Europe? "After all France does not owe us anything. She would have every right to look to her own interests." If Austria could be brought around to accepting the annexation of the Danish duchies in one form or another, Prussia could very well get along without France. If Austria held stubborn, why then, but only then, would Prussia need the support or at least the friendly neutrality of Napoleon III.

Austria, as the event proved, held stubborn. Under pressure from Vienna the Duke of Augustenburg was recognized by the Federal Diet and for a moment war seemed about to break out. Bismarck and Moltke both advised King William to declare war, and a crushing ultimatum was actually drawn up (July 21, 1865). The two sovereigns, however, seemed to be equally afraid of casting the die and instead of breaking off relations continued bickering. The result was the lame "Agreement of Gastein," which gave administrative control of Schleswig to Prussia and control of Holstein to Austria, while Francis Joseph sold the little duchy of Lauenburg to William I for 14,500,000 francs.

Napoleon III was disagreeably impressed by this arrangement and at his order Drouyn de Lhuys protested it, in a diplomatic circular, as based on force and "offensive to justice, to the principle of nationalities, and to the will of the peoples."

That was an attitude that Bismarck had to deal with, and he set out for Biarritz to find out once and for all just what price Napoleon III would charge for seconding Prussia's aspirations. Bismarck was disposed to pay a real price. If the Emperor had talked business and asked for a rectification of frontiers to balance Prussian expansion, Bismarck, it is altogether probable, would have agreed, and with full authorization from his master. He was to remark confidentially to Persigny, in 1867, that "he had felt himself capable of the boldest course of action and had been eager to come to an agreement with the Emperor on all points." He seems actually to have offered Belgium, in indirect language at least, and perhaps

French Switzerland also. The Emperor, at any rate, turned a deaf ear. All the testimony agrees on this point. Napoleon III was not ready to talk business. He played a strong, sly hand against an adversary who was infinitely stronger and slyer than he. He had formed a mistaken opinion of Bismarck and was to cling to it for a long time. King William's minister was not the diplomat of outspoken aims with whom frank and honest agreements could be easily arrived at. He was the German par excellence, the harsh and hard-headed Prussian, who thought and acted in terms of brute force, who recognized no moral obligation except success, and who, moreover, envied the dominant position of France and was bent on weakening her by any means that should be required. In the claws of this kite of the cold eyes, the terror of the barnyards, what else but a pitiable pouter was this poor Emperor of the French, who was slipping into his dotage in a stew of dreams about balances of power in Europe and European happiness?

Long talks took place in the gardens of the Villa Eugenia and along the beach at Biarritz. Napoleon III came to the matter of the Gastein accord and asked whether, at that time, Bismarck had guaranteed Austria's possession of Venetia. Bismarck denied any such guarantee and he was in fact astounded: Was the Emperor really more interested in Italy than in France? Napoleon III went on to inquire as to Prussia's intentions with regard to Holstein.

"Why, we're going to pocket Holstein!" said Bismarck bluntly.

The Emperor was charmed. Since he did not bat an eyelash at the quip, Bismarck went gaily on and set forth the general outlines of the problem:

"The annexation of the duchies is just a beginning. We have a national mission to fulfill and the Tuileries cabinet has every interest in concurring in that mission. A strong Prussia must naturally come closer to France. As a weakling Prussia would be obliged to seek allies against France."

The Emperor did not contradict. In fact he seemed even to acquiesce.

Yet that was the moment he should have grasped. One word from him and Bismarck would have sheathed his eloquence and his sword and resigned himself to peace. Napoleon III did not seize the moment, he did not say the word. He smiled, twirled his heavy mustache, half closed his eyes, kept silent—the silence that almost spoke assent.

Other interviews were to follow, but not on the big questions, on irrelevant matters, such as the illness of the King of the Belgians, the death of Lamoricière, the cholera epidemic that had broken out in the South again. The weather was ghastly. The host and hostess at Villa Eugenia were entertaining the Prussian Chancellor intimately, leading a simple life quite apart from pomp and etiquette. Amusements came down to parlor frolics, even crude ones at times, as when Mérimée hid a mannikin made to look like Bismarck in the bed of one of the ladies-in-waiting. The Prussian Prime Minister was making a very favorable impression. Mérimée wrote:

"Bismarck has conquered everybody. This tall, very polished German is not in the least naïve. He has no trace whatever of *Gemüth*, but he is extremely witty. He won me completely."

Bismarck for his part reported to his king:

"I consider sentiment at the imperial court at the present moment singularly favorable to us."

At last they got back to business again. Napoleon III brought up the question of the Danubian principalities. Might they not be given to Austria in exchange for a transfer of Venetia to Italy? Italy again! Bismarck said neither yes nor no. What he wanted was *carte blanche* for Prussia. The Emperor was evasive but apparently well-disposed.

"Let's not cross that bridge until we come to it. We shall have to adapt policies to circumstances."

Did the conversation at any moment turn on the question of compensation for France on the Rhine? Persigny quotes a confidential declaration by Bismarck to the effect that Napoleon III said that "France wanted a frontier on the Rhine," but that those provinces were "so energetically refused by Germany and would, for that matter, be so hard for the French to govern, that such a transfer could hardly be considered seriously."

It is highly improbable that Napoleon III could have used any such language. What is certain is that when Bismarck took his leave nothing definite had been discussed and no promises had been exchanged. Doubtless the Emperor considered it unwise to reveal his intentions at that stage, preferring to wait for an offer instead of making a demand.

That was a mistake, a bad mistake. At that precise moment he had a choice between three policies. He could work for peace and a balance of power in Europe, and along that line he would have had England with him. He could go with Austria and by that alliance he could have won Venetia and satisfied Italian aspirations. Finally he could have accepted the Prussian alliance on profitable terms which he would have been at liberty to fix himself. Any one of those three policies, provided it were frankly adopted and resolutely pursued, would have left him diplomatic master of Europe. Instead Napoleon III was the man he was, with all his deficiencies of character. He did not adopt any of them.

His attitude therefore remained so obscure, so enigmatic, that, as Bismarck thought the matter over, he took fright. Could France really be disinterested? No one was ever disinterested. Napoleon III must be hoping for war between Austria and Prussia, with the further hope that Prussia would be beaten. Then he could intervene as master and collect any prize he chose. As time wore on Bismarck's anxiety lessened. One of his spies informed him that the French army did not seem to be in any condition to move. That led him to the conclusion that Napoleon III would not be able to interfere and that, if Italian unity was achieved by the cession of Venice, he would not be very exacting as to compensation for France.

Bismarck had been in touch with Italy as early as August, when he had asked La Marmora, Victor Emmanuel's minister, what attitude his country would take in case of war between Prussia and Austria. The Gastein dicker caused a delay in the reply, Italy turning to Austria and proposing that the latter sell Venetia for 400 million florins. Vienna refused. Bismarck resumed conversations with Florence on his return from Biarritz. At almost the same time his ambassador, von der Goltz, brought Napoleon III a letter from King William, which hinted that North Germany was about to unite around Prussia. That was a decisive step towards German unity—the Emperor was in no sense deceived by it. However, he made no objection, observing merely that in order to satisfy public opinion in France he would have to ask for some compensation. Just what compensation? In answer he alluded to Rhenish Bavaria, then to the frontiers of 1814, which would restore Landau and Sarrelouis to France.

"Really," he concluded, "I could not specify the exact character of the compensation. I can only assure you of my friendly neutrality. I will take the matter up with your king later on."

Von der Goltz could get no more than that out of him.

A crisis in Roumania came just then to complicate negotiations that were already intricate enough. Prince Alexander Couza had angered the *boyars* by abolishing slavery and he had involved himself in unsolvable financial difficulties. He was now arrested in his palace and forced to abdicate. The Roumanian leaders wanted a prince from abroad as sovereign. Why not an archduke? Florence and Paris agreed in thinking that in that move Austria would gain enough to justify a surrender of Venetia. England, however, made a wry face and Napoleon III finally proposed—at Mme. Cornu's suggestion—a young cousin of his, Prince Karl Hohenzollern-Sigmaringen, as ruler in Bucharest. Prince Karl, a young man of twenty-seven, was at the time a lieutenant of the Prussian Guards, serving with the Second Regiment garrisoned in Berlin.

This choice was agreeable to Prussia. It was highly displeasing to Russia and to the Sultan. Bismarck suddenly ended the matter by dispatching Prince Karl to Bucharest. The Roumanians welcomed him and set him on the throne. The Sultan threatened but vainly, the powers all holding him in leash. Thanks to Napoleon III and also to Bismarck, Karl of Hohenzollern was to remain "Prince of Roumania" as a preface to becoming the first King Carol of that land.

Pourparlers between Berlin, Florence and Paris were long protracted; but finally, on April 8, 1866, a treaty of offensive and defensive alliance was signed between Prussia and Italy. The agreement envisaged a campaign against Austria and was to hold for three months. Drouyn de Lhuys was eager to preserve peace and had refused any sort of advice to Italy. Unbeknown to him, however, Napoleon III urged Italy to join hands with Prussia. Not only did he encourage Nigra, whom he saw almost daily, but to Arese, who had come to get information, he said:

"Sign the treaty! I give you the advice as a friend."

And he sent Prince Napoleon to assure Victor Emmanuel of his support in case Prussia should go back on her promises.

As time went on these blunders were to loom to capital proportions. Whatever may be said in extenuation of them, there can be no doubt that Napoleon III was the real artisan of the Italo-Prussian alliance. As he saw the future, that alliance was to be the prelude to a triple alliance of Prussia, Italy and France, with the French playing the preponderant rôle. War he urged all the more readily in that he did not intend to take part in it. He had long thought such a war indispensable if the map of Europe was to be recast according to his views. As early as 1865 he had said to Walewski, when the latter expressed concern at the imminence of hostilities:

"Believe me, a war between Austria and Prussia would be one of those things one never dares hope for and which seem destined never to happen. It is not for us to interfere with bellicose inclinations in other people which will result in more than one advantage to our policy."

He thought he could win on both heads and tails. If Austria were beaten she would have to cede Venetia to Italy, and that would rescue the Pope.[1] If Austria won he could offer his good offices to Prussia. In any event he would be in a position to dictate the peace. That had been the reason all along for his refusal to stipulate in advance for France: he preferred to have his hands free in order to act according to outcomes.

Prussia and Italy began to mobilize. Austria protested, then followed suit. The nations round about began to grow uneasy. The French public in particular seemed instinctively to view the approaching conflict with foreboding. A significant debate opened in the Legislative Body on May 3rd, when the temporary budget came up for approval. Already on March 2nd Jules Favre had raised his voice against the dickering in territories of which everybody in Europe was talking.

"France," he said, "should put an end once and for all to the unfair mistrust which Germany seems to have conceived against her. But if she is to do that she must declare with honest loftiness that she will make no more conquests, that freedom must utterly lay the ghost of the left bank of the Rhine which is always being conjured up as an obstacle between France and Germany."

Speaking for the Emperor on May 3rd, Rouher declared that France intended to remain neutral but conserving entire freedom

---

[1] Rothan, *op. cit.*, 58: "He thought that the only means of settling affairs in Italy, rescuing the country from the social revolution and at the same time saving the Papacy, was to obtain the surrender of Venice. Venice, in his eyes, was to be the saving of Rome."

of action, and his banal eloquence won mild applause. Thiers rose
in reply and at once raised the discussion to a far different level.
Might, he said, was flouting and oppressing right. Small nations had
lost all security in Europe. Denmark had been mutilated and no
one went to her defense. She had been robbed of her duchies simply
because Prussia coveted their fertile soil and their harbors. Now, in
order to remain sole mistress of them, Prussia was considering an
attack on Austria. If she won, she would rule all Germany and be
in a position through her alliance with Italy to restore the empire
of Charles V.

As the Chamber listened in awe-inspired silence, the aged statesman inveighed against any idea of compensation, as a mere wage
of iniquity unworthy of France; and he besought the government
to act in such a way as to prevent a war either by threatening to
support Austria against Prussia, or by preventing Florence from
supporting Berlin. Left to herself Prussia would come to her senses.
Peace would be preserved and Europe would find her way back to a
rule of law.[1] Thiers' speech made a deep impression on Paris. It
was in truth an amazing effort. Perfect in tone and in earnestness
and sincerity, with no trace of rhetoric or studied brilliancy, it pene-
trated by sheer force of the aged statesman's logic and enlighten
ment.

"You have saved the honor of political life in France," Guizot,
Thiers' rival of other days, wrote to him.

Unfortunately the debate was not to receive governmental sanc-
tion. The previous question was moved and the budget voted.

Far from opening Napoleon III's eyes, far from dissuading him
from his imprudent policy, Thiers' interference threw him into one
of those sudden rages which at times broke through his mask of reserve and led him into impulsive language. Three days later in
awarding prizes at a country fair at Auxerre, he digressed into an
almost warlike speech in which he declared that he "detested the
treaties of 1815, which some people were inclined to regard as the
sole pivot of French foreign policy."

---

[1] "If we would preserve peace," Thiers said, "we must talk not to Austria but to
Prussia. We might speak a language of force and say to her: 'It is you who are
threatening peace, not Austria. Well, we will not allow it.' We might speak a softer
language that would express a clear and curt refusal of assistance. We might, finally,
take a mere attitude, which also would be sufficient, an attitude that would halt
Italy on her course of alliance with Prussia. Seeing Italy escaping from her hands
Prussia would lose all hope of having France for her accomplice and she would hesitate to go forward with her plans."

The speech made a very bad impression. Thiers was heard to say: "I forced a speech from a man who never says anything, and I made him make a blunder."

Thiers was not alone in that opinion.

Drouyn de Lhuys thought he could save peace by a European conference, and once more Napoleon III succumbed to the tempting thought of acting the rôle of an Agamemnon with Europe as an audience. Again chancelleries began crisscrossing notes, comments, proposals, refusals, "acceptances with reservations." Bismarck, perplexed, asked the French ambassador, Benedetti, just what France wanted for herself. Benedetti, personally, was a liberal, hostile to Austria, favorable to Italy. Aside from that there was nothing very definite that he could say. Drouyn de Lhuys did not like him because his appointment to Berlin had been forced upon the Foreign Office by Rouher. Benedetti really knew nothing of Paris's intentions. Von der Goltz, on his side, insisted. Drouyn de Lhuys replied that "it was for the state that was expanding to declare its aspirations." Queen Victoria, who was mother-in-law to the Prussian Crown Prince, took advantage of that status to make a noble effort to forestall the struggle that she could see developing.

"In the name of all you hold sacred," she wrote to King William, "I implore you to give up this terrible thought of a war. It is in your power to avoid one. Such a fratricidal conflict would be ghastly." [1]

Napoleon III maintained his sphinxlike attitude. He had just received a new proposal from Metternich, who had passed it to Persigny at the Longchamps races: Austria would cede Venetia to Italy. In case of an Austro-Prussian war the French and Italian governments would remain neutral. If Austria won she would annex Silesia and wink at anything that France might do on the Rhine.

Napoleon III was cold to the proposal. As he was accompanying Persigny to the door, his sometime companion in adventure remarked in comment on the rebuff:

"I must congratulate you. If this Austrian offer is not entirely to Your Majesty's liking, Your Majesty must have some very pretty cards up your sleeve."

The Emperor thought he had all possible cards up his sleeve. Nevertheless he passed the Viennese suggestion on to Italy, and

[1] Kurt Jagow, *La Reine Victoria, lettres inédites,* 1936. Retranslated.

Victor Emmanuel and his minister La Marmora were sorely tempted. Unfortunately they were bound to Prussia by the treaty until July 8th. Couldn't Napoleon III play for time? So there they were back at the idea of the European Conference. England and Russia had already accepted, but Austria, the everlasting muddler, qualified her acceptance with so many conditions as to make it tantamount to a refusal.

That rushed things to a climax. The Emperor called his councils together and they showed a stew of opinions and counter-opinions. Duruy was for annexing the Rhineland. Persigny suggested "favoring Prussia's ambition to the extent of allowing her to expand in North Germany, but on condition that she find compensation on the left bank of the Rhine for the princes she would be dispossessing on the right bank, and in such a way as to be left with no possessions of her own on the French side of the Rhine." This, he thought, would be a way for France later on to recover her natural frontiers pacifically.

Napoleon III decided in the end that France would remain neutral but on condition that the future status of Germany should be settled only in agreement with him. So he declared in a letter to Drouyn de Lhuys that was read before the Legislative Body. He felt sure of Prussia in view of Bismarck's repeated overtures. As for Austria he had in his pocket a treaty of June 12th that conformed to Metternich's proposal. Italy's interests were safe. Whatever the outcome of the campaign that was opening, he felt altogether certain that he would be the arbiter of the peace and one of its chief beneficiaries.

The Diet mobilized the Federal army on June 14th. As had been foreseen South Germany took sides with Austria. Prussia at once occupied Hanover, Hesse and Saxony, capturing the little Hanoverian army at Langesalza. "Trusting in the loyalty of France" and leaving not a single division on the Rhine, Prussia then flung all her forces upon Bohemia.

Italy meantime also took the field, with an army 130,000 strong under King Victor Emmanuel and another of 80,000 under Cialdini. The Austrians, only 70,000 strong but operating on interior lines, were commanded by the Archduke Albert, son of the Archduke Charles who had fought Napoleon at Essling and Wagram. The Italians were crossing the Mincio (June 24th) when Albert made a sortie from Verona and fell on them at Custozza, a battle-field that had been fatal to the Piedmontese on a previous occasion in 1848. The first Italian army fought courageously enough, but the king was a wretched strategist and threw everything into disorder by haphazard commands. Though losses were about equal, seven to eight thousand men on each side, the Italians were so thoroughly routed that Victor Emmanuel completely lost his head. Indeed, had the Archduke marched straight on Turin he could have taken that capital without firing a shot.

The Prussian command assumed that Austria was now secure on her Italian front and might even bring up reinforcements from that quarter. It therefore rushed its three armies southward at all speed. Commanded respectively by King William, by the Prince Royal and by Prince Friedrich Karl, they dashed into Bohemia, brushed the Imperials aside in a series of outpost skirmishes, and on July 3rd took up a position beyond the Bistritz, in the hilly, wooded region of Sadowa.

Opposite them they found Benedek, the man whom Napoleon III had beaten at Solferino. The Austrian general seemed to be over-whelmed by the heavy responsibilities that now rested on his shoulders. For days he had seemed to be going about in a sort of stupor. One element in his state of mind may have been the desertion of the Bavarian army which had prudently refused to leave its barracks. For that matter the other states of the south were certain of an Austrian victory and did not want it to be too complete. They also refrained from sending up the reenforcements they had promised. At any rate, having no confidence whatever as to the outcome of the battle, Benedek implored the Emperor Francis Joseph on July 1st to make peace at any price. Now he found himself obliged to accept the encounter. He was superior to the Prussians in artillery, but William's infantry was equipped with a needle-gun, brand new and excellent. Benedek, moreover, had chosen his terrain badly. He found himself backed up against the Elbe in a position that would prove very awkward if things went against him.

The battle opened at dawn with 200,000 men on a side. It was stubbornly contested all the morning. The Austrian cannon inflicted heavy losses on Friedrich Karl's infantry and by noon the Prussian lines seemed shaky. Had Benedek attacked energetically he would have won the day. Later on, in 1867, Bismarck was to say to

Canrobert that at that moment Moltke had handed him a cigar, and that as he lighted it he had sworn to himself that if the army of the Prince Royal had not come up by the time he finished it he would blow his brains out. The cigar butt was still smoking when the Prince's guns were first heard. The rescuing battalions carried the centre at Chlum and hurled the Austrians back towards the Elbe. Benedek hastily ordered a retreat upon Königgratz, and the retirement soon turned to a rout. Not until the next day did the Austrians manage to rally behind the river, but with 20,000 of their men dead or wounded on the battlefield and an equal number in the hands of the Prussians as prisoners. The Prussians had lost not more than 10,000. The road to Vienna lay open and the Hapsburg monarchy was at the mercy of Prussia.

Europe was stunned at the collapse of the imperial army. Everyone had expected an Austrian success. Opinion in France was divided. The parties of the Left rejoiced. *Le Monde* of August 7th said:

"Our efforts have been crowned with success. Austria, the Catholic head of Germany, is no more. Prussia, Protestant, nationalist, progressive, has today taken over leadership in Germany."

And *Le Siècle* of the 8th echoed:

"A clerical ultramontane power has succumbed. The spirit of free intelligence has triumphed."

That state of mind is all the more noteworthy in that it was to reappear in 1918 in the men who broke up Austria in the Versailles treaty, without realizing the full significance of the rôle she played in the balance of power in Europe.

La Valette, Minister of the Interior, asked Drouyn de Lhuys whether he should have public buildings put into lights. Drouyn told him to make no move, but Paris, without any nudge from above, broke into lights and flags.[1] Napoleon III was taken aback by so sweeping a victory on the part of Prussia. However, for a few hours, he seemed satisfied.

"It's a rout, it's a rout," he said to Canrobert, wearily, his eyes closed.

One part of Napoleon III's plan at least was working out: The Austrian disaster would give Venetia to Italy.

Surely enough, on that very 4th, Metternich appeared with an

[1] Ch. Bocher, *Mémoires*, II, 530 f.

offer of Venetia and a request for Napoleon III's mediation. The Emperor immediately set to work. He telegraphed King William and Victor Emmanuel asking them to conclude a general armistice; and on the following day, July 5th, he summoned his chief ministers to Saint-Cloud to decide on the attitude that France should take in view of the Prussian victory. By that time he had lost all illusions as to Sadowa's being a triumph for French diplomacy. He could feel the breath of a chill wind that was dispelling the fogs before his eyes.

For that matter he was a sick man, much run down by a recurrence of his bladder trouble. Dr. Larrey had diagnosed gravel in July, 1865. The diagnosis was kept from the Emperor and the malady grew worse through neglect. He traversed the crises of July, 1866, suffering those terrible gripes of pain that destroy the noblest courage and dull the keenest mind. As E. Denis says: [1]

"During weeks when the future of the world was hanging in the balance France was without a government."

When the Emperor appeared before the Council he looked more like a corpse than a man. Drouyn de Lhuys was for curbing Bismarck. He proposed massing a number of divisions in Alsace, asking the Chamber for war credits and informing Berlin that France would not permit any changes in Germany without her consent. Usually so ill-advised, the Empress saw clearly at this juncture. She was wholly in accord with Drouyn. On a question from her, Marshal Randon declared that 80,000 men could be concentrated at Strasbourg at once and 250,000 within about three weeks. "Forty thousand is enough," interjected Drouyn de Lhuys. It was, he explained, less a question of numbers of troops than of a resolute demeanor, of moral prestige. Victorious though Prussia might be, she was still off balance, he thought, with all her forces in Bohemia, not a regiment on the Rhine and South Germany ready to rise against her. If a French army appeared on the scene Bismarck would have to come around to concessions and France would win at least the frontier of 1814.

Drouyn de Lhuys was right. That is plain enough today. Bismarck himself was later on to admit as much.

"If the redbags had appeared on the Rhine, I would have lost

---

[1] *La Fondation de l'Empire allemand*, 320.

the game. I could not even say that we would have been able to protect Berlin."

And he declared openly before the Reichstag, January 16, 1874:

"A small force of French troops would have been enough to make up a very respectable army, added to the many corps in South Germany. Such an army would have forced us at the first move to defend Berlin and so lose the benefit of all our successes in Austria."

Rouher was then at the height of his influence and decided everything. He came out emphatically against Drouyn de Lhuys. He wanted peace and was afraid that any such demonstration might end in war. It was then the turn of La Valette, a man about town whom Rouher had forced into the Ministry, who had no great brains in diplomacy to begin with and who, at the most, was interested chiefly in hanging on to his job. He pronounced forcefully against the idea of an armed mediation. The Emperor had urged Prussia and Italy to join forces. He would be reversing himself in trying to separate them. The greatest advantages would come from peaceful negotiation. France was not ready to fight. Mexico had swallowed up her best troops. The arsenals were empty. La Valette ended by flatly accusing Drouyn de Lhuys of endangering France out of sympathy for Austria.

The Council adjourned, then met again. The Empress pressed her point with her usual eloquent ardor, which this time was prophetic:

"The fate of France is at stake! We must act, and at once. The moment the Prussian troops are free to leave Bohemia and can be turned against us, Bismarck will not care a fig for our protests!"

And she mentioned what had happened in 1859, when Prussia had halted the Emperor after Solferino. Why should he hesitate to halt Prussia after Sadowa? Napoleon III sat slumped in his chair, but his mind was clear. He said nothing. He did not trust the judgment of Drouyn de Lhuys, nor the Empress's. He knew that they were both too Austrian in sympathies. If he followed their advice would he not be setting the house of Hapsburg on its feet again— the historic enemy of his dynasty? Would he not be disappointing the oppressed peoples, after all the encouragement he had lavished on them? But eventually Drouyn de Lhuys and Randon returned to the attack. He roused himself from his prostration and announced his decision. Fifty thousand troops would be gathered on the Rhine. Berlin would receive the note of warning suggested by the Minister of Foreign Affairs. The Chambers would be convened by a notice in the *Moniteur* of July 6th.

But on July 6th the *Moniteur* was silent. It merely announced the ceding of Venetia to France and Napoleon III's proposal of an armistice to the belligerents.

During the night the Emperor had received a visit from his cousin, Prince Napoleon. The latter emphasized all the dangers into which he was running unarmed. Was the Emperor going to risk the fate of the country, of the Empire, on a throw of the dice? Would he yield to the Empress's baneful influence to the point of catastrophe? Was not the Mexican mistake enough? Coached by his hatred for Eugénie and his violent partisanship for Italy and Prussia, the Prince insisted, he threatened. The Emperor had no will of his own left. He reversed his decisions of the afternoon, succumbing to an attitude of fatalism that had been growing on him with the years. Drouyn de Lhuys told M. de Courcelle,[1] who vouches for the fact, that he went to see the Emperor after the Council meeting was over and again implored him to block Prussia for the sake of his dynasty if for nothing else. Napoleon III, he said, stopped pacing the floor in his study, where he was giving the audience, raised his arms above his head and snapped his fingers in a sort of rhythm, as though to say that the dynasty would have to accept the fate that awaited it.

This sense of fatalism had served the first Napoleon badly in his day. It was to lead Napoleon III to sheer ruin. In politics fatalism is an absurdity. Things may seem possible, difficult, impossible, but time, circumstances, people, the men involved, change everything, so that the impossible becomes possible, the difficult easy, and the reverse. To trust to luck is not the part of a leader.

Vainly the Empress stood her ground and continued the battle for intervention. Napoleon III had given up the idea entirely. He refused to send French troops to Venetia at Metternich's request and advised him to treat with Berlin at the earliest possible moment. Russia was suggesting an agreement among the neutral powers to prevent Prussia from settling affairs in Germany entirely as she saw fit. Napoleon III rejected cooperation, as though he still thought himself the man to force his arbitration all by himself.

---

[1] I owe this detail to Count Charles de Chambrun, the French Ambassador.

King William and Bismarck read the Emperor's proposal of an armistice with mingled alarm and anger. They accepted in principle but piled up conditions for the purpose of gaining time. As for Victor Emmanuel he felt insulted at having to receive Venetia as a gift from France, especially since he had been beaten. His prime minister, the gloomy, stiff-necked Ricasoli, addressed Malaret, the French minister in Florence, in a tone that was almost insolent. The Italian press was not stopping at Venice any longer. It was asking for the Trentino, for Istria, Trieste, Dalmatia. With Italian public opinion behind him Victor Emmanuel threw Cialdini forward against a Venetia now unarmed.

Checked on either hand Napoleon III ordered Benedetti from Berlin to Zwittau for a talk with Bismarck, in which he was directed to urge the Prussian chancellor to conclude the armistice. Bismarck "held his breath" on seeing Benedetti enter his study, in deadly fear lest he had come to announce armed intervention by France. On learning Benedetti's real errand Bismarck heaved a deep sigh of relief, beamed all over as he listened to the Emperor's anodine suggestion and then went on from his regained composure to climb the high horse. Of course he could do nothing about the truce without consulting Italy. What he wanted was Napoleon III's express approval of an outright annexation of Saxony, Hesse and Hanover, and then of a Federation of North Germany under the presidency of Prussia. Of course France would receive compensations—she could rely on Berlin's good will. As to what the compensations were to be he was as vague as he had been definite in the matter of his demands.

That could have left Napoleon III no doubt whatever as to the menace from Prussia One burst of energy and the day could still have been saved. The Austrian army had been disorganized but not destroyed. Let the French army make a move to join it and the Emperor of the French could still have dictated terms. "Caught between concessions and catastrophe" Prussia could not have hesitated. She would have yielded. But the Emperor was physically a broken man. Mentally he was caught in a confusion of conflicting emotions. He ended by drifting aimlessly along on the tide of events. He confessed plaintively to Von der Goltz that he had not had time to think things out—that he had miscalculated. Francis Joseph sent Beust to him—the Beust who was shortly to become Austrian chancellor—to request "the dispatch of an observation corps to the frontier." He replied in a sort of daze:

"I am not ready for war!"

Not ready for war! That was what he had said to Clarendon away back in April, 1864! And the fact in truth was that now, in 1866, he was even less ready for war. The French army had become a skeleton of itself and was wretchedly equipped to boot. The Mexican expedition was not responsible for that condition in the ordinary sense of the term. Mexico had not cost any great number of men—1,627 killed in action, 4,735 deaths from disease, 292 missing.[1] There had never been more than 38,000 French regulars on Mexican soil. What that senseless enterprise had done was to have wasted funds, caused reductions in active service lists and emptied the arsenals. In fear of Parliament and of public opinion the War Ministry had refrained from asking for the credits required for keeping the army on a normal footing. Large numbers of soldiers had either been sent home or not called to the colors. The Emperor knew all that and he also knew that he was partly responsible for the disorganization.[2]

But it was not a question of going to war. A simple show of force would suffice. Beust insisted:

"You have a hundred thousand men at Châlons. Well, shift them to the frontier. The Prussian line of operations is already strung out too thin. They will be obliged to halt. Vienna, Munich, Stuttgart, will take heart again and Germany will accept you gratefully as a mediator. If you don't do as I say, you will probably have Prussia on your hands yourself, and in that case I promise you that all Germany will march against you."[3]

Prophetic words—but Napoleon III did not listen to them! He thought it was too late. He was mistaken. It was on that day, July 12th, that he lost his last opportunity—throwing away the game, to use Talleyrand's phrase, with all the cards in his hand. He had the correct advice in plenty. At just that time, through Baron d'André, the French minister at The Hague, he received an urgent warning from Queen Sophie of Holland, a sincere and perspicacious friend.

[1] Franchet d'Esperey: *Histoire militaire, du Directoire à la Guerre de 1914.*
[2] Bapst, *op. cit.*, IV, 20, quoting Canrobert: "Under pressure from his ministers and from all the governmental deputies in the Legislative Body, the Emperor agreed to reductions in service lists and did not press Marshal Randon to keep fortresses in order or to restock the empty magazines."
[3] Beust, *Mémoires*, II, 13.

"Your prestige," she said, "has suffered more during these past two weeks than during the whole course of your reign. . . . I am sorry you did not see the deadly danger of a strong Germany and a strong Italy. Your dynasty is what is threatened and your dynasty will suffer the consequences. . . . Once Venetia had been given to you, you should have rushed to the aid of Austria, marched on the Rhine and dictated your terms. To allow Austria to be butchered was worse than a crime. It was a blunder" (July 8, 1866).[1]

Actually Napoleon III made no objection to Bismarck's demands. On July 19th Goltz called on Drouyn de Lhuys and explained that under pressure from the army and from public opinion Prussia would have to ask for a war indemnification through annexations, limited to 300,000 souls, to be carried out at the expense of Hesse, Saxony and Hanover. Drouyn replied in no very good-natured tone that he would take the matter up with the Emperor. Goltz at once set out for Saint-Cloud and was received by Napoleon III. Without the slightest difficulty he obtained the Emperor's consent to annexations infinitely more extensive—they totaled a figure of 4,850,000 souls. Bismarck had mentioned a maximum and a minimum to Goltz. With the minister wincing at a bold revelation of the minimum, the Emperor gratuitously accepted the maximum. Of the little states in the North which Prussia was proposing to gobble up he put in a word for none except Saxony. He sacrificed Hanover, the electorate of Hesse, the duchy of Nassau, the free city of Frankfurt. He even went so far as to advise Goltz to annex a portion of Hesse-Darmstadt, the Grand Duke to receive compensation on the left bank of the Rhine. The first great step towards German unification was made by the Emperor of the French! The very least that the Prussian ambassador could say to Bismarck after that was that France would keep hands off and never move.

The German Chancellor was much relieved. Really he was having perplexities not a few. The Austrian army had reorganized while the Prussian army was weakening through a breakdown in the food supply and from a cholera epidemic. Finally, on July 20th, Admiral Tegethof took out an Austrian fleet of old wooden vessels and destroyed Victor Emmanuel's new Italian navy at Lissa. But it was too late now for anything of that sort to matter. Prussia had her hands free. She was in a position to dictate peace, and peace she dictated

[1] Beaumont-Vassy, *Histoire intime du Second Empire.*

at Nikolsburg on July 26th, along the lines that Napoleon III and Goltz had agreed upon in principle in Paris. Austria was eliminated from Germany once and for all, and—the supreme stroke of genius of a man who saw far into the future—though she would cede her rights in the Danish duchies, no sacrifices in territory would be inflicted upon her as regarded her own domain. Gorged with five million new subjects Prussia did not need to be over-grasping. Saxony was spared, but, like Bavaria and the other states of the South, she was obliged to accept an alliance with Prussia and pledge herself to come to Prussia's aid in case of war. So it was nothing less than the whole of Germany that Prussia had succeeded in gathering around her. Neither Europe nor Napoleon III realized the fact as yet. It was to be brought to their notice very shortly.

The preliminary acceptance of Nikolsburg represented a stunning defeat for France. Mistaken for a moment French opinion suddenly awoke and reacted: The nation's pride flouted! The country in danger! All the enemies of the regime, legitimists and republicans alike, raised one cry of disaster. Thiers sent word to Jules Ferry:

"This mediation business is the most ridiculous fizzle that can be imagined. We have achieved the result which was inevitable and which I had only too accurately predicted: that France has dropped to the rank of a second-rate power."

The "disgrace of Sadowa" was to become the war-horse of the enemies of the Empire.[1] Louis Blanc wrote from London (July 7, 1866):

"Prussia's triumph has thrown everyone in England who is jealous of France into transports of joy, all those who have been afraid of her, all those who were angered in their patriotic pride at the spectacle of France posing as the arbiter of Europe."

But even friends joined in the chorus. Napoleon III got echoes of the public indignation and anxiety through several of his ministers. Magne, frank as always, wrote to him (July 20, 1866):

"Patriotic feelings would be deeply hurt if it should prove that when all is said and done, all that France has gained from her intervention is to have tied two dangerous neighbors to her flanks."

Rouher himself insisted that the Emperor should demand the

---

[1] Renan, writing disappointedly in the *Revue des Deux Mondes*, September 15, 1870: "The opposition was interested only in winning a false popularity and talked incessantly of 'the disgrace of Sadowa' and of the need of getting even."

frontiers of 1814 at the very least, as bond for something better. "That would give public opinion something to live on," he said.

The Empress, for her part, wanted "to ask for a great deal or for nothing at all." She had just suggested to Napoleon III that he abdicate, leaving her to exercise a regency in the name of their son. Metternich was in touch with the plan and eagerly seconded it. He wrote at the time to Mensdorff:

"I have never seen the Emperor counting for so little, nor the Empress siding with our interests with such extravagant enthusiasm and zeal."

Napoleon III was deeply hurt at seeing the woman who owed everything to him disposed at such a critical moment to strip him of his crown. He refused with a vehemence of which she had long thought him incapable.

Napoleon III set out for Vichy, ordering Drouyn de Lhuys to join him there. He was a very sick man. Canrobert saw him at Saint-Cloud just before his departure. He found him in a state that was "heart-breaking to look upon. He could hardly rise from his chair, and his drawn features betrayed both mental anguish and physical pain." [1]

During the weeks just past the opinion of the Emperor's Minister of Foreign Affairs had counted for exactly nothing, but Drouyn de Lhuys was now bent on evening the score. He suggested that Benedetti ask Bismarck to cede the whole left bank of the Rhine to France. Napoleon III acquiesced. But how could the Emperor and his minister ever have dreamed that the Prussians would consider such a proposal? Where could their wits have gone? The dispatch was sent off none the less, and to that precise effect. Benedetti well realized the folly of it. As early as June 4, 1866, he had told Drouyn on his own authority that King William would never cede an inch of Prussian territory. Bismarck had said to him that if "France were to claim Cologne, Bonn and even Mainz, he would much rather retire from public life than consent to such a thing." [2]

However, Benedetti presented the demand to Bismarck. Bismarck refused bluntly, and on two separate occasions.

"If you persist in these demands," he said, "we shall concentrate all our forces on the Rhine."

[1] Bapst, *op. cit.*, IV, 46.
[2] Benedetti, *Ma Mission en Prusse*, 165.

And without a moment's delay, in order to arouse public opinion not only in Germany but in all Europe against France, he informed Vilbort, the correspondent of the *Siècle,* of the Emperor's move. Vilbort's manager, Havin, published the item on August 11th, disregarding possible consequences.

The next day the whole world saw in Napoleon III the greedy expansionist who had been using the principle of nationalities as a pretext and a decoy. After two years of intriguing he had now come out and asked for his tip, his *Trinkgeld,* as Bismarck called it. The little moral prestige that Napoleon III had left was now completely gone. On August 14th the Berlin correspondent of the *Temps* wrote: "A report of alleged demands by the French government has aroused the greatest excitement all over Germany. It is important to note that the report emanates from M. de Bismarck himself." And he added: "At the first threat of intervention from abroad, all Germany would unite and rally to the Prussian flag. There can be no slightest doubt of that."

Russia had seemed to be moving in a French direction. She now drew back, the Czar assuring William that he would never ally with France against Germany. England, chaste as always, waxed indignant, and within a few days Württemberg, Baden and Bavaria, enlightened at last as to the seamy side of Napoleonic policy, signed secret agreements which had been drawn up by Bismarck and which bound them closely to Prussia. So Germany achieved military unity far in advance of political unity.

In an effort to save his face Napoleon III disavowed Drouyn de Lhuys. His minister, he declared, had acted without his knowledge. Drouyn resigned in utter disgust. Rouher and La Valette had fought Drouyn all along. They now hailed his retirement as a personal triumph for themselves. Private feelings and resentments exerted a baneful influence all through this crisis for France.

Drouyn was replaced by the Marquis de Moustier, the ambassador at Constantinople. Rouher took advantage of his opponent's withdrawal to involve the Emperor in a new manoeuvre. Evidently the men in power in France had lost their heads completely. After the fiasco that had just occurred any further dickering was sheer folly. On orders from Rouher Benedetti called on Bismarck on August 20th and proposed a treaty of offensive and defensive alliance, asking as a matter of form, for Landau, Sarrelouis and Sarre-

brück, which had been lost to France in 1814, and Prussia's assent
to the annexation of Luxembourg. Bismarck declined to give up
the towns in the Sarre, whereupon, still following instructions,
Benedetti fell back on Belgium, drawing up in his own handwriting a plan whereby France would recognize, along with Prussia's
recent annexations, her preeminence in the federation of all the
German states. In return, "in case the Emperor should be brought
by circumstances to marching his troops into Belgium or to conquering that country," Prussia would lend her full aid to France.

Bismarck despised Benedetti to begin with, but with his usual
farsighted and systematic treachery he tucked this document carefully away for future reference as supplying irrefragable proof of
Napoleon III's duplicity. He said he would consult King William
and reply in due course. The reply came a few days later and it was
noncommittal. A few days later still it was flatly negative; and well
armed now, the Prussian chancellor felt that he was in a position
to talk to Lefevbre de Behaine, the French chargé d'affaires, in
language which he was at no pains to soften and which expressed
the greatest contempt for France. He had, in fact, dismissed the
matter of the proposed treaty from his mind, except in so far as,
later on, it might serve to rouse the Belgians and the English against
the French!

Benedetti had merely been imprudent in leaving such a scandalous document in Bismarck's hands; but what can be said for the
prime minister and the Emperor who had instigated his intrigue
and who directed his movements from behind? What must one
think of their notion of finding compensation for the expansion of
Prussian power at the expense of Belgium, a small country, neutral
and friendly? Bismarck had devised the trap first at Biarritz. He
set it at Berlin. The French should not have fallen into it. Of all
reprehensible things for which Napoleon III may be justly blamed
this, without any doubt, is the worst. There can be no question as
to his actual responsibility, a responsibility, of course, that Rouher
and La Valette, in all justice, must share with him.

"There is no such thing as Belgian neutrality," he declared,[1] in
a dictation to Conti.

This disgraceful blunder was to cost France dearly. It was to
arouse in the people and in the governors of Belgium a suspicion

[1] *Papiers des Tuileries*, I, 16-17.

of French policy that was to endure for half a century, if not longer.

Italy did not get around to negotiating with Austria until October 3rd. Garibaldi had begun an invasion of the Tyrol and Italy had been obliged to recall him on an ultimatum from Vienna. Victor Emmanuel was anxious to receive Venetia directly from Austria. Napoleon III made it a point of honor to have the province a present from himself.

"It is the only thing I have gotten out of this war," he said to Nigra.

Another blunder! After moving heaven and earth to win the gratitude of the Italians he now proceeded to an act that wounded Italian susceptibilities deeply! General Le Boeuf was in Venice as French Commissioner. He barely escaped insult from the patriots and was obliged virtually to hide in order to effect the transfer of powers. In spite of Nigra's intelligent efforts the year of 1866 closed with the relations between the Paris and Florentine cabinets cold and constrained.

France issued from the Sadowa crisis isolated and with ruined prestige. That crisis Napoleon III should have prevented, following the advice of Thiers. Actually he provoked it by his ambiguous manoeuvres. In it he might have intervened to good purpose and with head high. Actually he used it to bargain to no purpose and with head low. La Valette might well issue on September 16th a fatuous circular in which he had the face to vaunt the Emperor's wisdom and pretend to express rejoicing over the new set-up in Europe.

"The Emperor," he declared, "does not believe that the greatness of a country depends on the weakness of the peoples about it. He can conceive of a real equilibrium in Europe only when the aspirations of the European nations shall have been satisfied. . . . The horizon now seems to him clear of any menacing prospects. . . . Whithersoever she turns her gaze France sees nothing that is calculated to halt her progress or to disturb her prosperity."

The sad truth was that Napoleon III had ceased to be the great sovereign to whom the peoples had been turning for fifteen years as to their natural protector. He had wantonly and fruitlessly spoiled a situation which many serious mistakes had still left unparalleled and which it had been quite within his power to turn to permanent advantage.

CHAPTER XXVI

The Desertion of Maximilian

ON AUGUST 9TH, AT THE MOST AGONIZING MOMENT OF THE SADOWA crisis, Napoleon III returned from Vichy to Paris as sick in soul as he was in body. Waiting for him he found the Empress Charlotte of Mexico who had suddenly appeared from nowhere, and, finding no one to receive her, had driven to the Grand Hotel. She had come home to Europe to beg the Emperor's consent to new efforts on the part of France to save Maximilian's crown.

The artificial empire that France had set up on the dangerous soil of Mexico had not, in fact, taken root. The very structure of the country from a social point of view was against any such thing. A small ruling class that was rich and jealous of its prerogatives; masses that were wretchedly poor; a grasping clergy; banditry on all hands, in the public offices as well as on the highroads! A deal of genius on Maximilian's part would have been required to fuse such heterogeneous elements into a nation. Let alone genius, he was not blessed even with character. He was just an Austrian Archduke, trained to the sheltered, cotton-wool life of European palaces. He was willing enough. He had big-hearted ideas and a sense of his duties; but he was too responsive to influences and too often inclined to set business second to pleasures. He had surrounded himself with Austrians and Belgians, who hated the country, despised the natives and quarreled fiercely among themselves. With their eyes ever on Europe this court clique built up a cardboard government, along the lines of the bureaucracies of the Old World: a Council of State, ministries, provincial governments—all good enough in theory but in no sense adapted to political realities in Mexico or to the manners of the country. There was nothing sound or vital about it.

The distrust that had featured relations between the Mexican

397

Emperor and the Commander-in-chief of the French troops during the first days ripened very soon into a virtually constant antagonism. Bazaine was actual master in a country where the fire had not been extinguished, but was smouldering underground. He maintained a semblance of obedience only by dint of endlessly furrowing the soil with marching columns and counter-guerilla raids. His officers abused the Mexican officials, and then in turn created all sorts of difficulties for their foreign superiors. Maximilian did not approve of certain military ventures and tried to interfere with expenditures which he considered unwise. As for political corruption, he wrote to Napoleon III (May 26, 1865):

"Many contracts here are so subtly fraudulent that one cannot get to the bottom of them without a more than careful investigation."

In his dispatches to Paris, on the other hand, Bazaine emphasized the new sovereign's inexperience. To Randon, for instance, the Minister of War, he wrote:

"One must face the fact that the Empire is far less popular today than it was in the beginning. . . . The masses are in extreme distress. How else could they be in view of the breakdown in public administration and the lack of any certainty as regards the future." [1]

The fact was that Bazaine had married a pretty Mexican girl much younger than himself and had gone on to cherish personal ambitions. He was judging himself much better qualified than Maximilian to bring happiness to the Mexicans. Maximilian was eager to have him recalled, but he was enough of the Austrian prince to keep putting things off and so avoid distressing scenes.

The major difficulty for him as well as for the Tuileries was the attitude of the United States. The Civil War had long prevented any important American interference in Mexico, but that war had ended with Lee's surrender (April 9, 1865), and meantime Napoleon III had lost American sympathies by the help he had given to the South. Now the great republic was making ready in any way possible to destroy the Mexican monarchy. Even at the height of its embarrassments the Federal government in Washington had contemptuously refused to recognize Maximilian's government. On the 18th of October, 1865, Drouyn de Lhuys suggested withdrawing the French army in exchange for an assurance that Washington

[1] Report, May 10, 1865.

THE EXECUTION OF EMPEROR MAXIMILIAN OF MEXICO

After a contemporary woodcut

would not seek to "hinder the consolidation of the state of affairs that had been set up in Mexico." The Union's refusal was as blunt as it was categorical:

"The presence of a French army in Mexico at this moment is a threat to the existence of a native republican government which was established by the Mexican people and for which the United States has always entertained the keenest sympathies."

Not only did Washington have a diplomatic representative at Juarez's headquarters, Juarez's troops were kept supplied with money, provisions, munitions and volunteers. When France insisted that Washington should keep to plain neutrality at least, that neutrality had already been violated by the American authorities and with an altogether democratic straightforwardness. By the end of 1865 the matter of peace or war between France and the United States was at the mercy of the most trivial incident.

Napoleon III was well aware that at such a distance, in such a country, he would not be able to uphold the Mexican empire for any length of time in the face of the insurmountable disapproval of the United States. The Empress cherished her personal illusions for a much longer time, the charitable souls about her doing their best to keep up an atmosphere of factitious optimism. Her stubbornness sometimes found expression in most undiplomatic outbursts. On one occasion she exclaimed to the minister from the United States:

"If my son were not just a child I would send him to take command of the French army, which is writing one of the most beautiful pages of its history in Mexico."

To which the diplomat replied, gravely:

"Madame, you ought to thank God that the Prince Imperial is still just a child."

It had been possible to conquer Mexico. That had required a certain number of men, and a certain amount of money. But to hold Mexico without some backing in public feeling in the country was impossible. The Legislative Body had voiced its regret or its bad temper at every opportunity, and on every pretext, whether a vote on the budget or on a request for a new credit. As a result the Legislative Body was consulted as rarely as possible and every effort was made to misinform it by every sort of juggling known to public finance. Sooner or later, of course, the tricks would be discovered and the lies brought to light. Sooner or later the losses and the huge expenditures in Mexico would become known. The newspapers of virtually all parties kept demanding the recall of the army from the New World.

Rouher himself understood that "the biggest idea of the reign" was threatening to end in a disaster. The Emperor warned Bazaine to hold his troops ready for a withdrawal, as early as January, 1866. On February 16th he was even more explicit.

"My intentions," he wrote, "may be summed up as follows: to evacuate as soon as possible but to do everything within our power to keep what we have started out there from collapsing on our departure."

He announced this policy at the opening of the legislative session. At the time when Maximilian was apprised of it, the military situation had taken a sudden turn for the worse. Mexico had caught fire again, in the south and in the west. Encouraged by the United States and financed by them, a new war was opening. The guerillas had reorganized everywhere and were turning every rock, every mountain pass, every cactus thicket, into a deadly trap. The French veterans—men who had seen service in Algeria, in the Crimea, in Italy, the finest soldiers, perhaps, that France has ever known—began to fall in large numbers. Bazaine's temper soured. Maximilian began to lose heart, taking to drink and spending altogether too much time with the attractive Mexican girls whom he had gathered about him in his summer residence at Cuernavaca. In all his indolence, however, he had spurts of courage and pride. Informed of the change of front in France he answered haughtily that if Napoleon III went back on his pledges, he, Maximilian, would manage to get along somehow just the same.

"I shall try," he wrote on February 18th, "to come to an understanding with my countrymen."

And by countrymen Maximilian meant the Mexicans!

The letter, for that matter, was a noble one:

"I am too much a friend of yours to be willing to be the cause, direct or indirect, of any danger to Your Majesty or to your dynasty. I suggest, therefore, with a cordiality equal to your own, that you withdraw your troops immediately from the American continent.

. . . On my part, with honor as my guide, I place my soul and my life at the service of my new country."

Maximilian's idea was to build up a national army about a skeleton of European units; but for that he needed time and he needed money. Napoleon III was entirely occupied and preoccupied with the complications that were to have their issue at Sadowa. He was determined to liquidate the whole ruinous expedition at the earliest possible moment and at the least possible expense. On April 5th he announced in the *Moniteur* that the evacuation would begin in the fall of '66 and be completed a year later. The Washington government was still in a disquieting frame of mind. The document was officially communicated to it.

General Almonte appeared in Paris. He had come to plead Maximilian's cause. He was greeted as an unwelcome bore, his requests were refused and he was even threatened with an immediate withdrawal of the French troops if the advances in money that France had made were not covered by a mortgage on import duties (May 31st). What the Tuileries really wanted now was Maximilian's abdication and his return to Europe. Napoleon III was afraid he might come to some terrible end if he stayed on in Mexico, and the Emperor was concerned to avoid any responsibility for any such catastrophe.

Maximilian had virtually broken with Bazaine, whose loyalty he mistrusted and not without reason. That left him with no support at all. With the Juarists gaining on every hand, he should, had he been sensible, have made up his mind to leave Mexico. But having once sat on a throne he could not see himself living without one; and there besides was his wife, the haughty Charlotte, who urged him to hold his ground and fight on. She resolved to make a trip to Paris herself. What Almonte had not been able to obtain from the French sovereigns, she could obtain, she thought, by meeting them on equal terms and reminding them to their faces of all their promises and encouragements. She made a sudden dash for the coast, found a ship waiting, and embarked for France, expecting to return in three months. She was never to see Mexico again nor Maximilian either.

Napoleon III and Eugénie received her at Saint-Cloud. She begged them, implored them, to put off the withdrawal of the French army, to recall Bazaine and give the young empire the help they had solemnly promised. Napoleon III was affectionate but unmoved. He was well aware that he could not, he must not, yield to the woman's entreaties. Eugénie's chivalrous nature was too deeply stirred. She could not control herself. She joined Charlotte in her pleading. Alas! Before Sadowa it would have been merely unwise to stay on in Mexico! After Sadowa it would be sheer madness. "Not a soul! Not a man!" The very words that Napoleon III wrote to Maximilian the morning after the heart-rending interview, August 29th:

"From now on I shall be unable to find one pound or one man for Mexico!"

France would need every one of her soldiers, the very next day perhaps!

"Well," exclaimed Charlotte, "if that's the way things stand, we'll abdicate."

"That's it," the Emperor answered. "Abdicate!"

That in truth was what he wanted and all he wanted. But Charlotte went off into a wild tantrum, shouting rebukes, nay insults, into his face:

"How could I ever have forgotten who I am—and who you are!"

Finally she fell over backwards, shrieking, moaning, her features twisting in convulsions as she writhed on the floor. It was a ghastly scene, a fore-warning of the madness that was about to settle upon the mind of the Empress of Mexico. Napoleon III was overwhelmed by it.

During the days following Charlotte seemed to recover her self-control. She called on Rouher and the other ministers, trying to win them to her views but receiving only respectful but categorical refusals. In utter despair the poor woman suddenly fled from that stingy, inhuman France and did not stop until she was in Rome. The Pope granted her an audience but she suffered a second attack in his presence. The curtain this time was to drop upon her mind for always. Only at rare intervals, thereafter, was she to have any lucid moments. With her soul cut off from happenings in the world about her, she was to survive Maximilian by fifty years.

Following orders from home Bazaine began to draw in his outposts. As the French retreated the Juarists occupied Monterey, Chihuahua, Durango and Tampico. Maximilian vehemently protested these evacuations to the commanding general and, returning to Chapultepec, frantically sought to get some order into his wretched army and his chaotic finances. In order to delay his desertion by France he signed the agreement that pledged away half the customs receipts at the seaports. He had lost all hope of winning the Liberals to his cause and therefore felt free to make Lares, a conservative and a clerical, his prime minister. His shoddy empire was shrinking thinner and thinner each day. Juarez was gaining headway in the South. Tuxpan, on the Pacific coast, fell into his hands. The Belgian legion was beaten at Ixmiquilpan, sixty miles from Mexico City.

Maximilian had known for some time of Charlotte's failure in Europe.

"It's all useless," the poor woman had telegraphed.

Since that telegram he had had no news. He learned of her mental breakdown in October, and from then on seemed to lose all energy. Suffering from a fever and worn out by his drink he was thereafter to have only occasional flashes of initiative.

Napoleon III had allowed a period of eighteen months for the total evacuation. Now he was impatient to be through with it. He mistrusted Bazaine, who was showing no great eagerness to get away. Letters of General Douay to his brother and of Colonel de Galliffet to Pietri were handed on to the Emperor (copies of them were found in the Tuileries after 1870). They must have had considerable influence on his state of mind. Douay hated Bazaine beyond all words and accused him of the most heinous crimes:

"He is sacrificing the country's honor and the safety of his troops by disgraceful acts of corruption. You have no idea of the discredit into which the Marshal has fallen. . . . This Mexican business is going to turn into a real catastrophe. The government has every interest in keeping things dark and saying nothing. Marshal Bazaine may, for that reason, very possibly escape the punishment he deserves. He will not escape the infamy of it."

That, very certainly, was going too far. Bazaine may have made mistakes in Mexico, and he may have conceived personal ambitions. It is known beyond question, today, that he did not amass any great amount of wealth in the country.

The Emperor, at any rate, ruled flatly that the whole expeditionary army should be away from Vera Cruz by the spring of 1867; and to ensure the execution of his orders, he sent his aide-de-camp, General Castelnau, to Mexico, equipping him with full powers.

"All French authorities," the Emperor wrote, "whether military, diplomatic, or civil, must, on written demand by General Castelnau, obey the instructions which he will issue in our name as implicitly as if they emanated directly from our person."

That was investing a plain brigadier-general with a sort of dictatorship. Napoleon III had not lost the habit of *missi dominici!*

Castelnau came up against Bazaine's disconcerting procedures and Maximilian's inertia the moment he arrived. While Napoleon III's envoy was urging Maximilian to abdicate, Bazaine, who had of late come a little closer to the poor sovereign, advised him to hold out and play for time. The Marshal was enamoured of his wife to the point of dancing *habañeras* in public in order to please her. She did not want to leave Mexico. She dreamed of becoming queen there, and the Marshal's ambition fitted in with this whim on her part. He saw himself at least a military dictator and perhaps an occupant of a throne in Mexico. He was in touch with one of Juarez's lieutenants, Porfirio Diaz. Diaz, later on, was to declare that Bazaine even suggested handing Maximilian over to him. That is hardly credible, but the mere fact of intrigues between the commander-in-chief of the French troops and an insurgent general was in itself disquieting. Bazaine, at any rate, cajoled the liberals and made promises to the conservatives; but he was undoubtedly well aware that the pear had to be thoroughly ripe before it could fall into his hand. Maximilian ought not to leave too soon, and much less the French army! With the help, therefore, of his factotum, the very shady Colonel Boyer, he did his best to block Castelnau, and with all the less considerateness in that Castelnau, strong in his *carte blanche,* had several times placed him in embarrassing predicaments. Then, in the end, sensing all the dangers that lurked in a half-treasonable attitude of which Castelnau, altogether honest and very strict, kept the Emperor informed, Bazaine reversed his game and resigned himself to leaving for France.

His plan was to draw in his troops towards the center, designating Querétaro as the point of concentration. The Juarists proceeded to reoccupy Oaxaca, San Luís de Potosí and Guadalajara. Maximilian had at first been reconciled to abdication. He left Mexico City for Orizaba in the wake of the French troops. Unfortunately the Belgian and Austrian members of his court disliked throwing up the sponge; and his generals, Miramon, Marquez, Mejía, implored him on their knees not to leave them to certain death. Finally he received a letter from his mother, the Archduchess Sophie, informing him that "he would be the laughing stock of Austria and find himself in a very humiliating situation." [1] Partly out of weakness, partly out of chivalry, Maximilian yielded to all these pressures. On November 30th, he issued a proclamation declaring that he would retain the crown; and slowly his pitiable little cortège "made up of four small carriages" and guarded by a squad of Austrian hussars, turned back along the road to Mexico City.

This time he took up residence not at Chapultepec but at the Hacienda de la Teja. Bazaine called on him there and now urged him to abdicate, since "his resources would be inadequate for dealing with the dangerous situation in which he would be placed after the departure of the French troops."

As a matter of fact everything about Maximilian was collapsing. In order to oblige him to come home Napoleon III had ordered the Foreign Legion and the Austrian and Belgian volunteers to embark with the regulars. That would leave Maximilian with not more than a thousand European soldiers to depend on. He burst into a rage. A number of minor matters came up to embitter relations between the Prince and the Marshal again. At the end of January they had ceased all conversation with each other.

Bazaine evacuated Mexico City on February 5, 1867, after destroying most of his war materials and equipment. The retreat was carried out in good order and there were no surprises from guerillas. Just before putting to sea, the Marshal had, one may imagine, a last twinge of remorse, for he sent a message to Maximilian urging him for the last time to return to Europe with the army. The appeal did not arrive in time. Maximilian would probably not have heeded it in any case. He had set out for Querétaro and was already in the clutches of his destiny.

Bazaine was not welcomed with military honors as he entered the port of Toulon in France, and he was virtually ostracized for some time. It was whispered about court, in the official world and

---

[1] Beust, *Mémoires*, II.

in the public at large that the Mexican expedition had failed only because of Bazaine's incompetence or treachery. Finally the opposition picked him up and made a hero of him. Thiers never spoke of Mexico without reference to "our glorious Bazaine"; and the republicans chimed in in chorus.

CHAPTER XXVII

The Liberal Reform of 1867

BISMARCK LOST NO TIME IN GATHERING THE NEW GERMANY AROUND Prussia, as he had been authorized to do by the Treaty of Prague. He set up a federal system with two chambers, the Bundesrath or Federal Council, and the Reichstag, a parliament conceived along very modern lines, which would be elected by universal suffrage and enjoy full freedom in law-making—a veritable German House of Commons. Only the northern states were actual members of the Federation, but the treaties of alliance that were signed by the states of South Germany brought these also under the control of Berlin. Gramont, the French ambassador in Vienna, could well write, as early as February, 1867:

"The ministers in charge in Baden, Württemberg and Munich are deporting themselves to all intents and purposes like Prussian officials."

On seeing this formidable instrument of power take shape, Napoleon III began looking around Europe for supports which, he was now aware, he sorely needed. Italy, first of all: Italy owed him so much, he thought, that there would be no great difficulty in bringing her back into the French orbit. He sent Fleury, his Grand Equerry and a man of his trust, to Florence to feel out Victor Emmanuel in the direction of a closer cooperation. He was ready to make an early withdrawal of French troops from Rome, but he wanted the Italian government to use its influence on its liberal party and forestall any uprising against Pius IX the moment the French had departed. He also thought the Pope should be reimbursed for the debts of the provinces Italy had annexed. Fleury was flexible, adroit and well liked by the Italians. He got assurances of good will in plenty, but no public renunciation of "Rome as the capital." In his speech from the throne Victor Emmanuel declared that he would "respect Papal territories" but that he owed it to

407

public opinion in Italy to note "a stirring of national aspirations in Rome itself."

There was a chance also that something might be done with Russia. Crete had risen in insurrection and declared for union with Greece. The Czar was eager to foster the Hellenic movement and French support would be very helpful in that regard. Moustier, the new chief at the French Foreign Office, was a shrewd diplomat, courteous and hard-headed, though his energies were somewhat impaired by a heart ailment that was soon to carry him off. He suggested aiding Greece to annex not only the Grecian mainland but Thessaly and Epirus, Turkey getting a big loan as a reward for her acquiescence. What Moustier wanted in exchange was the "sympathetic support" of St. Petersburg in the West. Well and good, answered Gortchakov, but what did France want—in the West? Moustier made vague allusions to frontier rectifications, and that was all. Conversations ended with no progress towards an understanding. The Sultan proceeded to put down the rebellion in Crete and bring the island under his rule again.

Moustier had shown his hand to some slight extent in the course of this bootless manoeuvre; and in spite of earlier fiascos Rouher too had not given up the idea of obtaining something in the Northeast which would satisfy French public opinion and make up in part at least for the phenomenal spurt in Prussian influence. That was a strange obsession indeed! There sat the Prussian army on the Rhine again with Bismarck ruling all Germany. Could anyone hope to find in him now a good will that he had signally failed to manifest at the time of Sadowa when the success of his whole policy depended on what Napoleon III should decide to do? Moustier felt, as Benedetti had felt, that the French were venturing out upon very thin ice. "But," as Rothan soundly remarks, "the French diplomats were working under a higher will, the will of the Emperor; and he also thought that he was yielding to a pressure of public opinion, whereas, really, Fate was leading him out to expiate mistakes resulting from his lack of foresight." [1]

This time the Emperor was not thinking of any Rhineland or any Belgium. His expectations had shrunk to wee little Luxembourg!

The grandduchy of Luxembourg was a dependency of the crown

[1] *Op. cit.*, 117.

of Holland, but it was part of the German system in virtue of a custom's union. As a hang-over from the Federation of 1815, Prussia still kept a small garrison in the fortress of the city of Luxembourg.

Moustier sounded out the cabinet at The Hague as to the prospects of an eventual purchase of the duchy. The King of Holland was under pressure from private influences which Paris had managed to interest in the matter, and his mouth watered, moreover, at the thought of four or five millions in cold cash. He consented out of hand, with the sole proviso that Prussia would have to agree and that the people in Luxembourg should be consulted.

Bismarck raised no serious objections at first. France had only to come to an agreement with the Low Countries and set the accomplished fact before him. He "would grumble a bit" in deference to German public opinion, and then acquiesce. To Benedetti he said:

"I don't care a hang about Luxembourg! If this will settle all accounts between us and lead to your approval of everything we have been doing, I am quite ready to say to you: 'Take Luxembourg! Make your terms with the King of Holland. We shall not stand in the way.'" [1]

But secrecy is indispensable in such manoeuvres, and there was too much talking about the Luxembourg affair—too much talking in Paris, in The Hague, at Vienna and everywhere else. The newspapers in Germany came into possession of very definite information and to their discoveries the Prussian chancellery could not have been entirely alien. They opened a violent campaign against the annexation. Bismarck was questioned by Benningsen in the Reichstag and refused to make a categorical answer, so deliberately shrouding himself with an air of mystery and caution; but he made haste to remind the Dutch cabinet of his responsibilities. The King of Holland took fright and called the whole deal off. France could only abandon hope of Luxembourg. Again she had been roundly tricked in the face of all Europe.

Napoleon III was angered at the checkmate.

"I have been made a fool of," he said to Sybel, the German historian, who had come to Paris to consult French records. "Now the Emperor of the French cannot be made a fool of with impunity!"

But what could he possibly do in the face of the German bloc, with no alliances and with an army which had not been reorgan-

[1] E. Ollivier, *op. cit.*, IX, 171.

ized as yet? Moustier deftly sidestepped the conflict, which seemed
about to come to a head in public opinion and in the parliaments
in both countries. He toned down in the negotiations, dropped the
question of annexing the grandduchy and asked merely that the
Prussian garrison evacuate the fortress at Luxembourg, whence it
seemed to constitute a needless threat at the French frontier.

Baron von Beust, a Saxon by birth, had now become Chancellor
in Austria. He was ambitious to play an important rôle in Europe
and restore the prestige of the Hapsburg monarchy. Actually he
was a fatuous chatterbox and a troublemaker. Bismarck said of him:

"Squeeze the vanity out of von Beust and you have nothing at
all left."

Von Beust lent France his good offices in this latest dicker. He
rejected a proposal for an Austro-Prussian alliance, which the minister from Bavaria brought to Vienna, on the ground that in such
an arrangement Austria could figure only as a brilliant second.
Then he applied every available pressure at Berlin to secure a
peaceful settlement of the Luxembourg question. Queen Victoria,
from London, did her best too, writing King William a letter in
which she appealed to all his humaner sentiments. Finally, after
some hesitation, Gortchakov, the Russian chancellor, put in a word.
He suggested referring the Luxembourg dispute to a conference of
the great Powers. Bismarck hemmed and hawed, let himself be
coaxed, then finally consented. The conference met in London,
May 7, 1867.

In the course of four sessions an agreement was reached on the
terms foreseen by Moustier. The grandduchy of Luxembourg was
declared neutral under a European guarantee. The city of Luxembourg became an open city and by that fact the occupation of its
citadel by Prussia came to an end.

So, without any great amount of damage, the Luxembourg question found its answer, a question that had been inconsiderately
opened and recklessly pressed, and which might easily have backed
France into a disaster. Thanks to Moustier's cool-headedness and
diplomatic talent France had pulled her own chestnut out of the
fire; but nobody in the imperial government could have had any
illusions left as to the extreme frailty of peace. From that moment
war with Germany became a certainty. The King of Prussia personally may not have wanted such a war. Bismarck and the German

General Staff not only wanted it. They were actively preparing for it.

"The Luxembourg question will probably not lead to hostilities," Moltke wrote regretfully just before the London conference. "For our part we should like nothing better than a war which, in any case, cannot be long avoided."

And Bismarck confesses in his memoirs:

"I always assumed that a war with France would follow inevitably on a war with Austria."

Napoleon III understood the drift of things at last, and began making efforts both at home and abroad to put the government and the country in a state of defense. He had had years and years of incredible successes. Now the time had come when nothing seemed to come out right, no matter what one did. Luck had all along been with him. Now it was turning. Fate had given him everything. Now it was knocking at his door and calling for its due. Only a man who was strong both in body and in mind could have dealt with such a situation. Napoleon III was worn out, as were the institutions of his Empire. The personnel which managed them was worn out, since he had been either unable or unwilling to replenish it. The Empire still offered an imposing front, but a discerning eye could thus early have seen broad cracks in the edifice. Those cracks were to widen and deepen with the passage of time and in spite of all efforts to patch them up.

The opposition in the Legislative Body, the republicans and the Third Party alike, kept incessantly demanding a return to freedom. Uneasiness in the country was deep and widespread.

"We are not being governed," Mérimée wrote. "The prefects are not receiving any guidance. Some are playing Capucin because they think that's the best way for them to get on in their careers. Others are manifesting an extravagant liberalism because they imagine the future lies in that direction. The majority are lying low in order to stand well with everybody. Really there should be either an energetic reaction or else a few timely and helpful concessions to liberalism. As things stand, everybody is waiting and doing nothing."

Rouher, in particular, held doggedly stubborn. The deputies were granted a few minor advantages. Their salaries were raised and their right to make amendments was expanded; but any thoroughgoing constitutional reform still seemed to be out of question.

The year 1866 had brought frightful disappointments—the break-

down in Mexico, insolent treatment by Prussia, the compensations
fiasco. Along with all those things the Emperor's health was becoming increasingly untrustworthy. Now, therefore, he was feeling more
and more inclined to enlarge the bases of his political system, to
seek help from new quarters, to mass the whole nation close about
him, in a word.[1]

A jest had gone the rounds in Paris to the effect that "the Emperor
had proved his affection for the Legislative Body by choosing so
many children of love to act as its presidents." The allusion was to
Walewski whom he had named to the post formerly held by Morny.
The nomination had been forced upon Rouher, who wrote in comment to Thouvenel:

"The man [Walewski] thinks himself immensely popular and
imagines he is acclaimed by Chamber and country alike. But everything will fall naturally into its proper place. One thing about these
prominent positions is that they leave no illusions in anyone." [2]

Walewski had, with the proper reductions in scale, inherited
Morny's ideas, just as he had inherited Morny's presidency of the
Chamber; and he now urged Napoleon III to loosen the reins of
authoritarian government and work it gradually over into constitutional channels. In that way, as that undistinguished but honest man
foresaw with his usual sound common sense, Napoleon III could be
kept from rushing into impulsive and disconnected enterprises.
With a normal parliament and more flexible institutions that would
satisfy a great majority in the country, peace abroad could be more
easily maintained. Then if a change in the form of government
were to be made in a near future, it could be brought about with
fewer shocks and less serious risks.

The Emperor listened to Walewski at great length during the
autumn of '66 at Compiègne. He seemed convinced. At Walewski's
suggestion he offered the portfolio of Education to Emile Ollivier.
The leader of the Third Party did not exactly relish service in a
ministry that kept time to Rouher's bâton. He hesitated, meantime
specifying three conditions for his acceptance: the dropping of the
government's bill on military reorganization; the passage of a con-

[1] In his researches into the imperial policy from Sadowa on, the author has had
the good fortune to have access to the files of M. Fernand Engerand, sometime deputy
from Calvados, who has made a collection of French and foreign documents bearing
on this whole period that is as notable for its conscientiousness as for its richness. The
author wishes at this point to express his deepest appreciation to M. Engerand.
[2] Thouvenel, *Mémoires*, 436.

stitutional amendment permitting ministers to remain deputies; finally a relaxation in the government's arbitrary interference with the press.

At last, on January 6, 1867, after thinking things over for five days, Ollivier decided "to hold himself on reserve." But he made a secret visit to the Tuileries and had a long talk with Napoleon III, insisting with all his persuasive eloquence on a whole series of reforms in a liberal direction. The Emperor was still doubtful. He was afraid that any concessions he might make just then would be attributed to his recent setbacks. The Empress got wind of what was going on and made vigorous objection. Wriggling free of her pressure, and in the face of Rouher's manoeuvres, Napoleon III made up his mind and had another talk with Ollivier.

He had not gotten over his liking for sudden and dramatic moves. On January 19, 1867, he called for the resignations of his ministers, who were almost all hostile to his project, and sent to the *Moniteur,* in the form of a letter to Rouher, an announcement of a number of constitutional changes.

"The time has come," he wrote, "when I believe it is possible, without prejudice to the powers with which the nation has invested me, to give the institutions of the Empire the full development of which they are susceptible and to grant new extensions of public liberties."

He went on to very precise specifications of the nature and extent of the changes he contemplated. They were not what Walewski had hoped they would be, nor what Ollivier had a right to suppose they would be. The "crowning," as Napoleon III called it, of the imperial edifice came down to a very limited, in fact a fairly wretched, series of reforms. The Address was done away with and replaced with a "wisely regulated" right of "interpellation," or questioning from the floor. The ministers would thenceforward appear in the Chambers, but in their proper turns only and when matters connected with their several departments were up for debate. They were still not "responsible" and still not responsible as a body. Newly framed laws would define the right of public assembly and give freer play to the press, which would no longer be punished for offenses by merely administrative process.

These innovations were modest enough, but they raised a storm of disapproval in the Emperor's environment. The Empress raged.

Rouher showed an inclination to retire from public life altogether. Vaillant predicted catastrophe. Was Napoleon III intimidated by the uproar? Or was he, rather, still attracted to power and disposed to take back with one hand what he let slip from the other? He renamed most of the old ministers, keeping Rouher and Baroche, La Valette and Duruy, and even giving Rouher, in addition to the Ministry of State, the portfolio of Finance of which he relieved Fould. In the Ministry of War Marshal Randon was replaced by Niel.

Whittled down to these proportions the "liberal" reform turned out to be not so very liberal after all. Thiers exclaimed:

"It's just a hoax!"

Prince Napoleon made himself the mouthpiece of the general disappointment when he wrote to the Emperor:

"The publication of your liberal program produced an effect of satisfaction at first. . . . The naming of your new ministry has modified that attitude and now all one hears is that 'There is nothing to it!' "

Napoleon III replied:

"I am the responsible party; there is no impropriety, therefore, in my ministers' changing policy along with me. . . . I have absolute confidence in Ollivier, but I am not putting him in the Interior just yet. The time has not come for that."

He had agreed to one step forward, an experimental step, so to say. Rouher pared the apple down still thinner when he issued the decree of January 19th relating to interpellation, the Senate further receiving a right of temporary veto on bills passed by the Legislative Body.

The Emperor made a speech at the opening of the session on February 14th. He meant it to be reassuring. Actually it rang false.

"The unification of Germany offers no occasion for alarm to a country like ours. . . . It was moreover foreseen by Napoleon I." He, Napoleon III, had a "firm conviction that peace would not be disturbed, but, conditions of war having greatly changed, France should so organize as to be invulnerable." In very imprudent language, used as a sop to public opinion to which he was becoming more and more sensitive, he declared that "without moving up one regiment the voice of France had been influential enough to halt the conquerors."

Such braggadocio was altogether out of place in view of the recent routs that France had suffered in the diplomatic field. Bismarck and his King could only regard it as a sort of challenge to them. The effects were discernible in a speech which King William delivered a few days later at the opening of the parliament of the Federation of the North, and which rang like a trumpet-call through all Germany. The King loftily avowed "Prussia's intention to extend her preponderance over Germany as a whole and to demand leadership of the common destinies for the Prussian government, the most powerful of the governments in the federation." [1]

The Legislative Body itself received the Emperor's speech coldly. There was hardly any applause. In fact, Jules Favre rose and without reference to the Emperor proceeded to question Rouher on the changes in the Constitution which he, Favre, could only consider ridiculous.

On March 14th foreign affairs came before the Chamber and Thiers mounted the tribune. The tribune had just been reestablished, on Walewski's initiative. It was a tall spindly structure. Thiers did not like the change. In speaking from his seat on the floor he had been in the habit of resting his back against the desk directly behind him. He protested the new arrangements to Walewski with such vehemence that the latter, to humor him, had the Speaker's desk cut down to suit his height. "Men of medium stature," as Ollivier relates, "could scarcely use it."

Thiers drew a comprehensive picture of the mistakes in imperial foreign policy. For four hours, with unfailing felicity of phrase, he blamed the government for the war in Italy, for the war in Mexico, for the aberrations that led to Sadowa. He emphasized "the danger that came from a Prussia that had suddenly expanded in deference to a fatal, chimerical and fatuous principle of nationalities." France had no allies left in Europe. Austria had been crushed, Italy was looking for adventure, Russia was biding her time, Spain had drawn apart. England was refusing to have anything more to do with the continent. Thiers ended with an appeal for a radical change in policy. He advocated the formation of a conservative party that would be Europe-wide. Basing on the English alliance, its principal aim would be to protect small countries. In his faint, squeaking but

[1] Rohan, *op. cit.*, 143.

clear voice he uttered one devastating sentence that was to be repeated throughout the world:

"There is no mistake left for us to make."

Rouher retorted clumsily:

"No mistake has been made." He heaped grandiloquent praise
on the French policy of mediation which had brought a war to such
an early end. Germany, he said, was more divided than she had
been before Sadowa. In fact, there was nothing left that could be
called Germany. There were just three "stumps": Austria, the Prussian Federation, the states of the South. He pretended to know
nothing of the military agreements which bound the states of the
South very closely to Berlin. For Rouher's benefit, probably, Bismarck was again to proclaim them, and in no uncertain language,
three days later.

Rouher's speech made a very bad impression on the deputies. The
Third Party voted against the government, though Ollivier and his
friend Darimon followed the majority. Ollivier had made a very op-
timistic speech on the unification of Germany.

"The only wise, the only shrewd, the only dignified thing for us
to do," he said, "is to accept an achievement which, I am convinced,
is not aimed at France. And we must accept it without weakness of
heart and without anxiety."

This debate, and those immediately following, were to be the
end of Walewski. In them he lost all prestige as chairman of the
Assembly. Probably he was embarrassed by his sympathies for the
liberals. At any rate both Rouher and the opposition ragged him
unmercifully. Thiers and others on the Left kept interrupting
Rouher during the latter's speech. Finally Rouher shouted brutally
at Walewski:

"For G—'s sake, why don't you preside, if you're going to be
chairman? Or else get up on the platform there and defend the
government, if you've got the brains to do so!"

Paling under the insult Walewski said to Thiers:

"Monsieur Thiers, I am obliged to call you to order."

"Call and be damned!" squeaked the little old statesman.

After that Walewski could only resign, and he resigned publicly.
Rallying to Rouher the majority sat silent and overtly hostile. The
Opposition members, instead, pressed around Walewski and shook

hands with him in appreciation of his liberalism and his conciliatory spirit.

Napoleon III replaced Walewski with Eugène Schneider, the
great manufacturer, founder and managing director of the Creusot
enterprises, the largest factories in France. Schneider was an independent, affiliating with none of the parties; but he was cool, adroit,
disinterested and devoted to the Emperor. He proved able to exert
a real influence. "His hair," Ollivier relates,[1] "was altogether white,
framing a very ruddy face. On that account his colleagues called him
'the white rabbit'; but they respected his judgment all the same and
usually followed his advice."

With Rouher's weight on the end of the lever, the majority pried
the Constitution back towards the Right somewhat by passing a
municipalities' bill that placed town administration as a whole in
the hands of the mayors and prefects. Ollivier had all along been
nursing a grudge against Rouher for blocking his advancement. He
attacked the Minister of State on July, 1867, during the debate on
the budget. What Rouher had called "a step towards wise and orderly progress," he, Ollivier, called mere "marking time," and, his
insolence getting the better of his usual courtesy, he bluntly asked
what Rouher's status in the government really was, now that he had
lost the monopoly of speaking for the government from the speaker's platform.

"Is he a grand vizier, perhaps, or the major-domo of a do-nothing
king?"

"No," he answered for himself, while the Chamber listened open-
mouthed, "he is Vice-Emperor without responsibility."

Vice-Emperor! The expression was to stick to Rouher. As for the
responsibility it may well have been that Rouher had no responsibility before the legislative assemblies of his day. But another sort
of responsibility he has, and it is a heavy one for him to bear—his
responsibility before the history of his country!

The World's Fair of 1867 opened just then. It was much more
comprehensive than the Exposition of '55. Overflowing the Industries Building it moved to the Champ de Mars, where an iron and
brick structure had been erected to receive it, a low, squatty affair,
extremely ugly, covering all of thirty acres.

The various stalls and booths showed the latest improvements in

[1] Ollivier, *op. cit.*, IX, 413.

science and the technical arts. There were machines of every description, from the newest locomotives, and fifty ton guns from the Krupp works in Germany, down to the latest high-powered microscopes. The textile industries showed new silks, woolens and cottons. Exhibits of house furnishings covered everything from the sumptuous salon of the millionaire to the plain room in the workingman's tenement. Chemistry boasted a new miracle-fuel—gasoline, and a new metal—aluminum. Specially interesting to the public was a museum of modern art.

In the park surrounding the actual Exposition, and separated from one another by hedges of shrubbery or by lawns and flower-beds, stretched endless rows of pavilions, porticoes, kiosks, domes, minarets, habitations of all countries, ages and climes; and about them swarmed Cossacks, Turks, Arabs, Egyptians, Chinamen, Hindus, Mexicans. It was one huge bazaar, one prodigious country fair, dazzling in color, bewildering in movement and noise. Here were conservatories, hot-houses, aquaria, aviaries; there side-shows with giants towering beside dwarfs. Next to a captive balloon was an auditorium with a concert. People ate, drank and danced to Viennese waltzes. A thousand games were available, not a few of them games of chance. An atmosphere of sensuous gaiety suffused a motley cosmopolitan throng that had gathered from the four corners of the earth to forget fears or troubles and make the most of a few moments of pure joy.

All Europe was in Paris, rushing back and forth between the Champ de Mars and the boulevards, cramming the cafés and the theatres, packing in herds to receptions both official and private. Napoleon III and Eugénie had invited every last crowned head in Europe. First to appear was the young King of Greece; then, in his wake, came Leopold II and the Queen of the Belgians, and Friedrich, the Prince Royal of Prussia, and his Princess. Mme. de Metternich gave a dazzling ball in their honor.

Napoleon III was concerned to prevent a meeting in Paris between the Czar and King William of Prussia. The uncle and nephew, on the other hand, were determined to see each other and the Emperor was literally forced to entertain them jointly.

The Czar arrived early, attended by his two sons and Gortchakov. Very tall, very cold, very bored—very imperial in a word, but with an interested, almost furtive expression about his eyes, he was escorted to the Elysée which Napoleon III had put at his disposal. Paris had counted on this visit to strengthen ties with Russia, and Gortchakov, in fact, showed himself exceedingly well disposed. To General Le Boeuf, who had gone to the border to welcome the Czar's party, he said:

"I have come with a whole regiment of secretaries. We are ready to do business!"

He went on to reproach the French government for its attitude at the time of the Polish insurrection but hinted that close relations could be restored if France would only second Russian policy in the Near East. Gortchakov was soon to become discouraged—and Paris too! Acts of bad taste, insults, finally an attempt at assassination, followed one on another in rapid succession to hurt the autocrat's feelings and alienate his sympathies. He attended the Grand Prix, sat in state at the Opera, visited the Exposition, the museums, the public buildings, and saw the sights in Paris. As he was entering the Sainte-Chapelle a voice coming from a group of betogaed lawyers smote him like a slap in the face:

"Long live Poland, *monsieur!*"

The Czar turned and stared haughtily at the group of insolent rogues.

To be sure the Polish cause was still dear to French hearts, but the young lawyer who was guilty of that breach of etiquette was not considerate enough of the interests of his country. Who was the culprit? Floquet always accused Gambetta, and Gambetta would answer, laughing:

"Even if you brought a hundred witnesses, Floquet, you could not gainsay what everybody knows. Your 'hurrah for Poland' made your political reputation! You should never be sorry for having shouldered authorship of it!"

The King of Prussia landed in France that same day. He was a red-faced, good-natured old gentleman, completely dwarfed by Bismarck. The latter had buttoned himself into the quite unusual and not a little symbolic uniform of the White Cuirassiers. There had been some fear of a hostile demonstration as the two Germans drove along. Lefebvre de Behaine wrote:

"We shall consider ourselves fortunate if police precautions prove adequate to save them from being booed."

As things turned out the crowds evinced nothing but the keenest curiosity in their regard.

On June 6th a great military review was held at the Longchamps race-course. It had been announced that 60,000 troops would take part. Half that number, under the command of Canrobert, proved quite satisfactory in the end. Napoleon III presided over the glittering spectacle, with one of the visiting sovereigns on his right, the other on his left. More theatrical than military in atmosphere the show ended with a great cavalry charge, the helmeted horsemen thundering down upon the grandstands, stopping short in their tracks with sabres raised, and cheering:

"Long live the Emperor!"

In congratulating Canrobert the King of Prussia said:

"I am a soldier. When I saw those magnificent troops I could only thrill with joy—a boundless joy."

A soldier above all else he was in fact. He had been at Buttes-Chaumont on March 30th, 1814, during the battle for Paris. Those memories of a day fifty years remote were still very much alive in his mind. He alluded to them tactlessly, just as, with the same tactlessness, he alluded to the dinner at Malmaison where his father, Frederick-William, and the Emperor Alexander forced themselves as uninvited guests upon Josephine's hospitality.

On the way back from the review the Czar rode in Napoleon III's carriage. Just past the Cascades in the Bois de Boulogne a shot rang out. Nobody was hurt except that the horse of Rainbeaux, the equerry, got two buckshot in its neck. The would-be assassin was caught on the spot. He proved to be a young Polish workingman, Berezowski by name.

"There we are—brothers-at-arms!" cried Napoleon III to the Czar. "We have been under fire together!"

"Our days are in the hands of Providence!" answered Alexander grimly.

Back at the Elysée he was so annoyed that he thought of leaving Paris that very evening. But on learning of the attempt on his life the Empress Eugénie ran in upon him, flung herself into his arms and, really hysterical, sobbed and sobbed, silently, without a word. Recovering after some minutes she took her leave.

The Czar seemed to be touched as a man, but the autocrat stiffened. He may have been doubtful in his own mind at first. The attempt on his life, following so directly on the insult at the Sainte-Chapelle, turned him definitely towards Prussia. Interviews between him, King William and Bismarck began almost at once. Shortly before the Czar's departure Napoleon III tried to start a conversation. Unluckily the thoughtless Eugénie burst into the study, began prattling of irrelevant matters and so prevented any resumption of important talk.

On his arrival home in St. Petersburg Alexander notified Gortchakov of his shift in policy. He would recognize the territorial changes that Prussia had forced upon Germany and which he had continually protested. Berezowski's trial, in Paris, was not calculated to appease the Czar's bitterness. Emmanuel Arago, the demagogue of '48, represented the Pole. Ignoring his client, he went out of his way to rail at Russian tyranny and the autocrat who impersonated it. The jury granted Berezowski extenuating circumstances and he was let off with life imprisonment. Alexander was to lay that up to the charge of France and Napoleon III.

Bismarck was as happy as a lark to be back in Paris again. He went to all the parties, dropping easily back into his style as "the goodnatured ogre." At the Variétés he saw the *Grande-Duchesse,* a caricature of German court life. He laughed uproariously.

"The very way it is!" he cried. "The very way it is!"

On every pretext, and often on no pretext at all, he would deliver himself brutally of the most cruel truths. In diplomacy, he said, "one might as well tell the truth. Your antagonist never believes you anyway." With Rouher, Persigny, Canrobert and La Tour d'Auvergne he had long conversations in which he made no bones of criticizing Napoleon III's conduct before Sadowa. France should have allied herself with Prussia at that time, he said.

"Your Emperor did not make the best of his position in 1866. He should have invaded Belgium, and England could not have peeped."

In treacherous intent he kept harping on the matter of Belgium. It was desirable, he said, that France should annex that country, and she could easily do so.

Between a dinner at the Tuileries and a ball at the Hôtel de Ville, he boasted of having staved off, two months earlier, the war with France which the Prussian military party was bent on having. At times he would drop a sentence that cast a harsh light forward upon the future. He said to Mme. de Pourtalès, an Alsatian, that

"Alsace was part of the great German fatherland" and urged her to come to Berlin. She was, in fact, to go to Berlin towards the end of the year 1868. There Schleinitz, the minister, remarked to her chivalrously:

"My dear Countess, within a year and a half your Alsace will have come back to Germany, and when we call on you at the Rohertsau to pay our respects we shall have the satisfaction of being quite at home."

On her return to Paris Mme. de Pourtalès made haste to report the remark to the Emperor and the Empress.

Bismarck at last went home with his king, but other sovereigns came on in procession. Among these was Francis of Assisi, the sickly consort of Spain, for whom the Empress, magnificent in a cloth-of-silver robe, gave a reception at Versailles worthy of the most gorgeous entertainments of Louis XIV. Ismail-Pasha, the Khedive of Egypt, came. He had given his friend, Ferdinand de Lesseps, the concession for the canal at Suez, which was almost completed at that moment. Others included Abdul Aziz, the Sultan of Turkey, a huge, bushy fellow, who sat silent and expressionless through a whole maze of entertainments that were devised to keep him amused. The King and Queen of Portugal, the King of Sweden, Queen Sophie of Holland, were already well-known figures in Paris.

The Emperor and Empress were scheduled to preside on July 1st at the distribution of prizes in the Central Palace at the Exposition. On the evening of June 30th they received a telegram at the Tuileries. It was a telegram of which a sense of their duty to the state compelled them to feign ignorance, except that Eugénie was seen to drive off alone to the Church of Saint-Roch and spend a long time there kneeling in silent prayer.

The next day the Imperial couple and the Prince Imperial, the Sultan, the other sovereigns, took their appointed places on a flag-decked dias in the Central Palace while the bands blared joyously in their honor. An aide-de-camp hurried to the Emperor's side and handed him another telegram. Napoleon III took the envelope and scratched a few words on it for Prince Metternich, who was attending the ceremonies in company with the whole diplomatic corps. Prince Metternich rose from his seat and left quietly, followed by the Princess.

The terrible news leaked out, nevertheless, and a pall fell upon

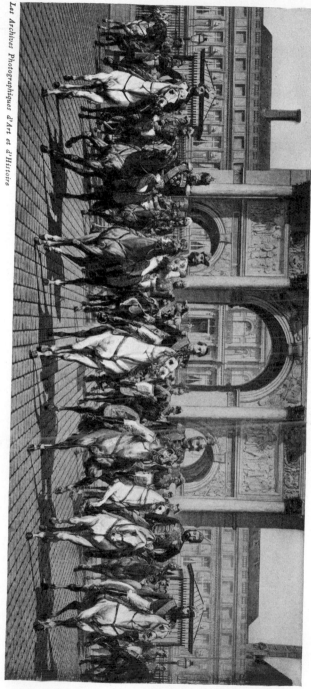

THE SOVEREIGNS GOING TO THE EXPOSITION OF 1867

From the Painting by Porion

the festivities. The Emperor Maximilian had been shot in Mexico.

After the departure of the French army the weak and unlucky Emperor had taken refuge at Querétaro. That town lay in the center of a mountainous region which his troops could easily defend. He still had ten thousand men, more or less, with him. They were commanded by Generals Mejia, Miramon, Marquez and Mendez. A colonel, Lopez, was regarded with suspicion by many, but he was in high favor with the sovereign. All Mexico, except Mexico City, was already in control of republican columns. Miramon was for taking the offensive and dealing with each army separately. That advice was not taken and the republicans were allowed to mass about Querétaro.

The siege lasted two months. The imperial forces put up a brave defense. They were short of food and ammunition. Many of them were ill. Maximilian himself fell sick of dysentery. In just those days, however, he gave his best exhibition of character. Danger made a man of the spineless Archduke. He got his troops ready for a sortie, then, at the last moment, he sent Lopez to open pourparlers with the enemy. It was to avoid any useless shedding of blood, he said.

Querétaro was surrendered to General Escobedo on May 15, 1867, at three o'clock in the morning. Beyond any doubt Maximilian could still have made his escape; but in an access of supreme lassitude he surrendered his sword and was incarcerated in the Capucin monastery.

Juarez established headquarters at San Luís de Potosí and ordered Maximilian and the imperial generals brought to trial. He wanted them executed as a reprisal for the shooting of so many republicans. The unfortunate Hapsburg cherished illusions about his adversary down to the very last. He asked for a personal interview. Juarez refused. Maximilian then chose attorneys and appealed for help to Magnus, the minister from Prussia. A Prussian, he thought, would be less unpopular than a French or an Austrian diplomat. Magnus's arguments and pleadings were not listened to. The United States might still have saved Maximilian. As a matter of fact the American government did make a try in response to a request by the governments of France, England and Austria. Francis Joseph hastily restored Maximilian to his rights to the throne of Austria, as a token of his final renunciation of the Mexican crown. Unfortunately

Campbell, the American agent, had halted at New Orleans and in spite of orders from Washington refused to budge, choosing to resign rather than appear before Juarez.

The trial of Maximilian, Miramon and Mejia began on June 13th. Maximilian was very ill and declined to appear before the court martial, leaving his defense to his lawyers. They took the line of excusing the Archduke by accusing France. The court martial replied by condemning the three defendants to death. Calm, dignified, Maximilian of Hapsburg faced the firing squad on the morning of June 19th with Miramon and Mejia standing to either side. The volley was discharged at such short range that his clothing caught fire from the burning powder. After some delay his remains were delivered to Admiral Tegethof, Austria's greatest sailor. Three years before the frigate *Novara* had brought Maximilian to Mexico as Emperor. The same frigate bore his coffin back to Europe.

This blood-chilling drama filled Napoleon III and Eugénie with deepest gloom. What folly it seemed to them now to have driven the unlucky Austrian couple, the one to death, the other to madness, at the cost of so many French sacrifices and so much French blood! The Empress may have felt more responsible than anybody else. At any rate, hysterically, she laid the blame for Maximilian's death upon Bazaine and bitterly reproached the Marshal. Then, before long, and again for the misfortune of France, she reversed herself and restored Bazaine to full trust and high favor.

The Tuileries went into deep mourning. All festivities connected with the Exposition were cancelled. On July 9th Thiers drew the moral of the Mexican disaster in the Legislative Body. If, said he, the Emperor had accepted control from a parliament any such catastrophe would have been avoided. Rouher had the face to answer. Twisting, turning, splitting hairs, he ended unctuously and half-wittedly:

"It was not God's will that we should restore a nation torn by civil war and anarchy to itself. Let us bow to His judgment."

The Exposition was such a brilliant success, and the sovereigns had presided over it so attractively, that France was for a moment dazzled and forgot the perils that were gathering about her. But while she stood bowing like a prima donna to world acclaim, her situation in Europe grew more and more desperate.

Napoleon III asked Prussia to restore northern Schleswig to Denmark. He got a curt refusal. Bismarck's personal position had been recently strengthened by his promotion to the title of "Federal Chancellor." He was angered at this new case of gratuitous French meddling in the Schleswig business and wrote to Kendell:

"Luxembourg about exhausted our good humor. If peace is not secure after our going as far as that, it really means that peace is out of the question."

Prussia, meantime, had just remoulded her loose economic union with the states of the South into a customs union that had a customs parliament. By that device complete unification of Germany under one government was brought one step nearer.

There were those in France, as notably Prince Napoleon, Emile Ollivier or Jules Favre, who were for accepting this development in Germany as having no ulterior significance. They thought that acceptance was the only way to keep Bismarck quiet and make sure of peace. Most of the out-and-out Imperialists, along with many opponents of the Empire, preferred the opposite policy, which insisted on limiting the implications of Sadowa, by force if necessary. The army generals, most of the ministers, Thiers himself, then Gambetta, all thought that sooner or later the issue would have to be fairly and squarely joined. The Emperor was afraid of war, but he was no less afraid of a peace that would gradually erode his personal prestige and the prestige of France. He was in a position where every move he made made history. He realized that and fearfully mistrusted every step he took.

One thing was clear and of prime necessity. If he was to meet the threat from Germany he had to strengthen his diplomatic and military situation. He had to have alliances and he had to have soldiers.

Alliances then? There was nothing in sight in the direction of Russia. That left Austria and Italy. The Empress and the Conservatives leaned warmly towards Austria. They wanted the close alliance with Vienna for which von Beust seemed to be preparing the ground. Beust was just bubbling over with plans. He thought he was a second Metternich and dreamed of making short shrift of Bismarck. Beust was a great talker. He was never energetic in action.

At any rate, an all-around confabulation was arranged for in Salzburg. Napoleon III and Eugénie arrived there on August 18th (1867) and met Francis Joseph and the Empress Elisabeth. Gloomy thoughts of Mexico, once the first conventional allusions were over, cast no pall over the conversations. Francis Joseph was a thorough-going egoist. His mourning for his brother was strictly formal.

Beust and Gramont had come on from Vienna. They joined the two emperors in walks and talks on romantic ground that lay under the shadow of the Kapuzinerberg and was redolent with memories of Mozart.

The views that were exchanged at no point went beyond a peaceful cooperation that would second Austrian policies towards Germany and in the Near East. If the Czar crossed the Pruth, Austria would occupy Wallachia with France at her side. As for Germany, the Treaty of Prague supplied a good working basis. Vienna would simply try to keep on good terms with south Germany. There was no talk of a military alliance. The net result of the meeting was therefore anodine.

All the same the press in Germany spat fire, and Bismarck sent a circular to his agents abroad protesting in advance against any "foreign meddling" in German affairs. Napoleon III delivered a mournful speech at Lille on his return.

"Black specks have suddenly appeared on our horizon. Well, good fortune never went to my head. So momentary disappointments will not discourage me."

His peroration appealed for the full trust of the country.

The World's Fair closed on this anxious note. Francis Joseph came to see it late in October, but his stay in Paris did not result in any negotiations. The two emperors separated friends but not allies.

So Italy then? Italy, alas, had never been a very good bet. Now a miserable affair at Rome had placed her in violent antagonism to France.

In conformity with his promises at the time of Fleury's mission, Napoleon III brought the French troops home from Rome in December, 1866. Only one regiment of volunteers was left behind— it was known as the "Antibes Legion." Six months passed, uneventful. The young Kingdom of Italy was engrossed with a number of difficulties—rivalries between the provinces, which had not been wholly amalgamated with the nation, crop-failures, epidemics, above all else, financial chaos.

The rough-handed Ricasoli lost his political life in the quest for a domestic readjustment in Italy. Ratazzi, his successor, was a pliant and shrewd statesman. On taking power he protested his respect for undertakings already assumed, but not long afterwards he made bold to advise the Romans in a speech in open parliament:

"Free yourselves! Do something in your own behalf and you will soon see that every Italian knows where his duty lies!"

The speech could only be interpreted as an encouragement to Garibaldi, whose committees began displaying revived activity. On his way home from Geneva, where he had hurled bitter diatribes at the peace conference, the adventurer slipped on towards Rome with a company of hot-heads. Alarmed at the protests from France Ratazzi had Garibaldi arrested and then escorted to Capraia. Shortly afterwards new bands of revolutionaries invaded the Papal State, which now consisted of Rome and the immediate environs of Rome. This time they were in Ratazzi's pay.

The Emperor was at Biarritz at that moment. Nigra called on him there and tried to influence him by emphasizing the danger of a republican revolution in Rome. Napoleon III showed him the door and notified Victor Emmanuel peremptorily that "the agreement of the 15th of September was being evaded."

"If this thing goes on," he added, "I shall be obliged, in spite of myself, to send an armed force to Rome."

He really could sacrifice the Pope no farther. Such a course would have been fatal to his hold on power in France. Moustier and Niel understood that and approved his policy. Prince Napoleon, La Valette and Rouher, on the other hand, were against intervention. Prince Napoleon's following was disposed to favor Italy at whatever cost. The Prince kept telling Victor Emmanuel and Ratazzi that they had "to force the Emperor's hand." Rouher, and men like Rouher, were afraid of throwing Victor Emmanuel into Bismarck's arms for good and all.

A French force was assembled at Toulon. Ratazzi, for his part, was in favor of a break with France and he informed Paris bluntly through Nigra that if France intervened, he would anticipate the move by occupying the Pope's territory himself.[1]

Ratazzi, however, did not feel strongly enough supported by his king and resigned. Disturbances broke out in Rome. Garibaldi

[1] "Eh bien, si vous intervenez, nous devancerons votre intervention et nous occuperons le territoire pontifical."

escaped from Capraia and appeared on the Roman frontier with a handful of patriots.

At a council held at Saint-Cloud on October 11th, the Empress, Rouher, Moustier and Niel declared very emphatically for an immediate reoccupation of Rome. Baroche, Duruy and La Valette were more far-sighted. They remonstrated that such a move would mean the final loss of Italy. The Emperor followed the former group. On October 28th a French fleet under Admiral Gueydon put a number of regiments ashore at Civita-Vecchia and the French were again in the Eternal City on October 30th.

News of the French landing roused all Italy to fury. Losing his head completely Victor Emmanuel ordered his troops to advance into Papal territory and for some days there was grave danger of a clash between the French and Italian forces. Niel sent word to Mac-Mahon, who was governor of Algeria, that he would command the army in Italy if war broke out and that he should have two regiments ready to embark at a moment's notice.

Ratazzi and the advanced parties in Italy called for an alliance with Prussia out of hand. Bismarck refused to intervene on two separate occasions. At the time he was in touch with Mazzini, and the latter assured him that Victor Emmanuel had struck an alliance with France in a secret agreement aimed at Prussia. He asked Bismarck for a million pounds and two thousand German "needle guns." That equipment, he thought, would be enough to enable him to overthrow the Italian government. Bismarck stopped right there and insisted on seeing proofs that the secret Franco-Italian alliance existed. Mazzini could not furnish the proofs, for a very good reason; whereupon Bismarck broke off negotiations with him.

Fortunately Victor Emmanuel and Napoleon III both came to their senses on the brink of the catastrophe and began shouting in whispers. The King of Italy made the first gesture and called his army off. Fortunately again, Garibaldi did not have time to mobilize the Roman patriots. The combined French and pontifical armies attacked him at Mentana on November 3 (1867). The action was short and decisive. The poorly armed Red Shirts could not hold on under the rapid fire of the new long-ranged "chassepots" of the French. They retreated across the frontier.

Once again the Pope had been saved. The Empress and her conservatives could not contain their delight, but all Italy raged against

France, especially after the *Moniteur* had published the communiqué of General Failly, who had commanded the French expeditionary force at Mentana.

"Our chassepots did wonders," he said among other things.

Napoleon III had ordered the deletion of the odious sentence, but Niel overrode him. It was picked up indignantly in Italy, but quite as vociferously in France, where the parties of the Left raised a terrible din.

"Dear Garibaldi," wrote Edgar Quinet, "you must forgive us! We have ceased to be ourselves."

And Victor Hugo chimed in:

> *"France, on te deshonore, on te traine, on te lie,*
> *Et l'on te force à mettre au bagne l'Italie."* [1]

To escape from his embarrassment Napoleon III thought of his usual panacea, a European Conference. The plan fell through before it was even formulated. A debate that should have been avoided at all costs opened in the Legislative Body and echoes of it were to reach Italian hearts that had already been bruised. Jules Favre attacked the government and inveighed against the Syllabus. Thiers then rushed into the fray and once more shifted the terrain of the debate.

"After failing in your mistaken policy of nationalities," he shouted in the Emperor's direction, "you have no policy whatever left. You have committed the irreparable blunder of allowing two national unities to come into being on your flanks and now they are joining hands across the Alps."

And he went on to demand that France cease beating about the bush.

"Why don't you declare frankly that we shall not desert the Pope under any circumstances?"

Rouher liked Thiers' last remark and rushed to the speaker's platform. Thinking to make a great personal coup, he burned all his bridges behind him and declaimed with Olympian pompousness:

"We make the declaration in the name of the French government: Italy will never get possession of Rome—never!"

Rouher's speech, in fact, roused a storm of applause and the Chamber italicized the word "never" by a vote of 237 to 17. Napo-

[1] "France, you are being dishonored, dragged in the mud, put in chains! You are forced to act as jailor to Italy."

leon III had a sounder perception of his minister's imprudence.

"In politics," he observed quietly to Rouher, "the word 'never' should never be used."

Nigra, in fact, promptly lodged his protest, while Victor Emmanuel grumbled under his wide-sweeping mustache:

"We'll show him about his *never!*"

So the world had gone around! For Italy France had fought a war. Italy then she had disappointed and embarrassed. Italy, finally, now rose before her as almost an enemy in arms! What a situation for France in that cold December of 1867! She stood alone among a family of bewildered or else hostile nations, none of whom feared her, none of whom believed in her, all of whom accused her of greed and duplicity. France was in that mood of undefinable distress which, for nations as for individuals, marks those moments when happiness is no more but when misfortune has not yet come—moments that are a sort of dead center in the movement of life and history: the tide has ebbed far out; one must wait till a new tide starts in again. Ten years had followed the Paris Conference and they had been wondeful years—years of material prosperity, of spiritual prestige, of a splendor that had its vulgar aspects but which was splendor all the same. Then had come one bad year, a year packed full of blunders and quailings. That year had been enough. French hegemony in Europe was a thing of the past. It had yielded the European stage to the hegemony of Prussia, a heavier, far more burdensome primacy that would last a far longer time!

CHAPTER XXVIII

The Effort for an Army

IT IS A STRANGE THING THAT NAPOLEON III SHOULD HAVE WAITED so long before starting a general reorganization of the French military establishment, which was the premise and the external evidence of his power at home as well as abroad. He should have gone about it after the Crimean War when the incompetence of the commissary and the inferiority of French equipment had come strikingly to the fore. He should have gone about it after the war in Italy when, with his own eyes, he had seen just what, in terms of suffering and death, the same incompetence meant to the French soldier.

The fact probably was that he had always been successful, and his successes had often looked like actual glory. He had lived on them, and many of the people about him had lived on them, in a sort of enchantment which the Mexican disaster had scarcely disturbed and which the crashing thunderbolt of Sadowa had alone been able to dispel. Sadowa had really opened Napoleon III's eyes. He saw the danger. He knew what the remedy had to be. When it came to applying the remedy he found unending obstacles in his path; and no longer possessing the physical and mental energy that was required to surmount them, he was to draw back in a mood of despondent fatalism.

To tell the truth, he had interested himself quite consistently in the nation's armament just before Magenta. He had forced the first rifled 4's and 12's on the army—guns that used the new cylindro-conical shells. By 1867, of course, that gun was considerably inferior, in respect of range and accuracy of aim, to the new Prussian breechloaders. He had diverted moneys from the privy purse to experiments designed to work out an artillery as good as the Prussian. Nothing definite had come of them as yet, though a few machine-guns had been manufactured. They were still being kept a closely

431

guarded secret and the soldiers did not know how to operate them. The French musket had made real progress under Napoleon III. His personal interest had enabled a model presented by Chassepot, a plain workingman in the Saint Thomas Aquinas factories, to overcome the ill-will of the war office routineers. The weapon was tried out at Magenta and Solferino. The Artillery Commission then declared it "unfit for service." The Emperor stubbornly stood out for it. Later on Randon, the Minister of War, objected to its manufacture. Not till 1866, and then at the Emperor's express command, were the first orders approved. By 1870 about a million were on hand.

The question that Napoleon III judged most urgent at that moment (1867) was the number of soldiers actually available for war. In September, 1866, the French army consisted of some 288,000 men, a third of whom at least were being used in Mexico, Algeria and Rome. Only a recasting of the recruiting system from the bottom up, and the adoption of conscription to begin with, could, the Emperor thought, supply an army capable of matching Germany's. In the event of war Germany could throw 1,100,000 experienced soldiers, including reserves, into the field.

The French press was almost unanimous in calling for an increase in the defensive equipment of the country. Forcade, in the *Revue des Deux Mondes,* wanted a million men available for service in wartime. Forcade was an apostle of universal conscription. In September, 1867, the *Temps* opened a campaign for army reorganization. Nefftzer and Henri Brisson emphasized at every opportunity the need of a great national effort to meet the Prussian menace. In taking this attitude Nefftzer had the courage to come to an open break with Charles Dollfuss, his chief financial backer.

Emile de Girardin in *Liberté* struck the one discordant note.

"There is just one system," he wrote, "that France should and must adopt: in case of war, voluntary enlistment carried to the limit; and if voluntary enlistment proves inadequate, the mass call to arms, the armed nation." [1]

The prevailing system of raising manpower dated, with the slight modifications introduced in 1855, from as far back as 1832. It was based, for a double injustice, on drawings by lot plus exemptions or substitutions purchaseable by money. The system had yielded a

[1] F. Engerand, "Le projet Niel et l'opposition," *Correspondance,* March 25, 1913.

fine army of professional soldiers, but too small an army for present needs.

The Emperor held a series of conferences during the months of November and December, 1866, first at Saint-Cloud, then at Compiègne. They were attended by Rouher and a number of ministers, by the marshals, then by Generals Fleury, Trochu, Frossard, Palikao, Bourbaki and Lebrun. A number of plans were laid before these meetings. The Emperor proposed universal conscription with short service terms and recruiting by districts. Niel was in favor of a strong standing army, to be doubled in time of war by a mobile national guard of 400,000 men. Vaillant thought the existing system would be sufficient if the annual drawings were enlarged.

Napoleon III held out for the need of a million men on a war footing, to match Prussian manpower. Vaillant answered that the Chamber would never give him that much money, and all the ministers agreed. Randon was quite satisfied with the army as it was. He merely wanted the enlistment period lengthened from seven to nine years. Trochu was strongly opposed to forced conscription, "a theory that could never be applied in practice." Vuitry, the chairman of the Council of State, even declared it unconstitutional, and Rouher and Fould nodded assent.

To offset all this opposition the only support the Emperor could find came from Prince Napoleon. Brilliantly and forcefully the Prince pleaded for general and obligatory military service for a three-year period. But positions had been taken and he convinced nobody. Napoleon III was vigorously pressed by his ministers, particularly by La Valette, who emphasized the alarm that the prefects would manifest and the certainty that the country would resist any such reform as the Emperor proposed. The latter ended by compromising on Niel's suggestion. In a note which appeared in the *Moniteur* under date of December 11th and which he had written himself, Napoleon III served warning on the nation that new sacrifices were to be required of it: an army of 824,000 men, half in active service, half on reserve; six years of military service to be required of all young men in the given drawing; a mobile militia of 400,000 men to be used for services within the borders of France.

The Emperor seemed resolved at that moment to override any opposition and force the reform through the assemblies. In the same conversation of January, 1867, in which he seemed so ready to abandon unlimited power and give a little free run to the nation, he again said to Ollivier, who did not think there was going to be a war:

"Numbers are going to be the decisive thing this time. We must absolutely make sure of them." And he added with apparent determination: "I know the plan is unpopular. One has to be strong enough to face unpopularity in order to do one's duty."

He removed Randon from the War Ministry and replaced him with Niel. Niel had the confidence of the army and of the country. He had been the Emperor's chief military adviser ever since the Crimea. Intelligent, well educated, perhaps a little too fond of talking, he often gave an impression of stubbornness and inflexibility. Actually when the occasion required, he could unbend and adapt himself.

Vigorous opposition to the plan announced in the *Moniteur* developed in all classes and all circles. It seemed as though, in spite of the many signs visible in the heavens, French public opinion had been taken by surprise. The economists predicted a shortage of labor. Army officers, enmired in routine, believed that nothing counted in war except individual courage. The middle classes mourned the loss of their time-honored exemption from military service. The masses foresaw that the heaviest burdens would as usual fall upon their children. At just that moment, moreover, the enthusiasm of the press cooled. Governmental papers joined the opposition papers in attacking the Emperor's bill. The *Constitutionnel* was about the only one to stand by its former position. Henri Brisson went back on himself, came out against large standing armies and asked for a "national militia." Petitions against the bill came in from many different departments. Two by-elections that were held in the Pas-de-Calais and the Isère showed doubled or tripled polls for opposition candidates.[1]

Trochu came out at this juncture with a pamphlet called "The French Army in 1867." It contained a biting criticism of the whole French military establishment—routine in the high command, lax discipline in the rank-and-file, incomplete military education, an unfair system of promotions, a scattering of troops in tiny garrisons where they went to sleep, incompetence in the commissary and in

[1] Engerand, *op. cit.*

the mobilization machine. Trochu suggested a system entirely different from the one that had resulted from the talks at Compiègne. He preferred keeping the law of 1832 and was satisfied with an annual drawing of 100,000 men on a basis of five years in active service and four in the reserve. That would bring the first line army to something like 500,000 men.

The success that Trochu's pamphlet enjoyed seems to have impressed the Council of State, which had the Niel plan under consideration. At any rate, it proceeded to emasculate the Emperor's bill. Napoleon III attended a number of sessions and vainly strove to guide things from the chair. He did not assert himself forcibly enough. Those vote manipulators could not find the courage to breast the tide of public opinion. The situation was much worse in the Legislative Body itself. Niel had to battle tooth and nail with the Committee on Armament. Thinking only of votes and elections the Committee rejected a fixed size for the army, claimed for parliament the right to vote the size each year, restored money substitutions, and made a social club of the mobile guard, which Niel wanted to subject to a thorough military education and drill.

"Of course we shall be obliged to pass this bill," said West, a majority deputy cynically, "but we shall fix it up in such a way that it will never work."

Napoleon III had such an exact perception of this state of mind that for a flash he considered dissolving the Chamber. Rouher objected on the ground that any new election would be fought with the army bill as an issue, that the country did not like the bill and would return a huge majority in favor of defeating it. Niel himself did not relish taking such a leap in the dark. He suggested concessions. Let the Legislative Body vote the size of the army as usual each year!

Public debate on the bill opened in the Chamber on December 19th. The text of the bill was already hardly recognizable. It was to be manhandled still further. Niel was being fought underground by Rouher and the latter's henchmen. He nevertheless waged a courageous fight against critics in all parties.

The republicans in particular seemed deaf, dumb and blind. Jules Simon exclaimed:

"I do not like standing armies. We ask you to arm the nation."

And the next year in a volume called *Radical Policy,* he was to write:

"The soldier is useless at home as regards the maintenance of public order. He is not necessary even on the frontiers."

Simon proposed reducing military service to three months. Carnot suggested one year, Glais-Bizoin, two years. Garnier-Pagès broke out into a glorification of defeat.

"A government," he cried, "loses its head after a victory. If we had been beaten at Solferino, if we had lost the war in Italy, we should have had complete freedom in France."

Jules Favre declaimed:

"We are told that France must be armed as heavily as her neighbors, that her security depends on the thickness of her bastions and armour and on the piles of powder and grape that are stored in her magazines. . . . I believe that the strongest nation is the nation that comes closest to total disarmament."

And as the heckling warmed up he was careless enough to ask of Niel:

"What is your idea? To turn the country into a barracks?"

"Look out!" Niel answered huskily. "You may be turning it into a cemetery."

The exchange was deleted from the stenographic record of the session.

Emile Ollivier seemed to have lost his head completely.

"I have always thought the French armies too large," he said. "Now they are to be increased to extravagant figures. Why, I ask? What need is there? Where is the danger? Who is threatening us?"

The wise, the cautious, the farsighted Thiers stood by the law of 1832. He was against the mobile guard.

"Our army is large enough to halt an invasion. Under its protection the country will have time to catch its breath and organize its reserve at leisure. Volunteers will come forward in plenty. You have too poor an opinion of your country, gentlemen!"

At bottom Thiers stood with the older soldiers. He did not like changing things. He wanted just a strengthening of the regular army.

In the end the bill passed the Legislative Body (Jan. 14, 1868); and it passed the Senate by a virtually unanimous vote—one dissenter, the economist, Michel Chevalier. Worn out by the long fight, Niel finally accepted the Committee's wording for the bill. So what did the whole fracas amount to? The old military system was continued, with its drawings by lot and its substitutions. The mobile guard was left as mere blueprint. For one important change, the service term was reduced from seven to five years. So the Emperor's army reform actually resulted in a reduction in the army!

People in France, or indeed in Europe, might have been misled by all the noise. Such a mistake was the more easy in that Niel himself pretended to be satisfied.

"I have the greatest confidence in our army," he trumpeted. "I am certain that man for man we have by far the best army in Europe." And he thought he could lay hands on 500,000 first line men—"the largest army we have ever seen in France." [1]

While the debate on the bill was still in progress, Napoleon III grew uneasy at the great disparity in size between the Prussian army and the French. He sent for Niel and asked him to organize twelve army corps in advance, without informing the Chambers. The Marshal did not think there was any immediate danger and the idea fell through.

The Emperor made as good a face as possible at his defeat and in his speech from the throne in 1868 he declared that "the military establishment of France was at the altitude of the nation's high destinies." But Bismarck was not deceived. He had been much interested in Trochu's pamphlet and had its allegations checked by his secret agents. He knew that they were well founded. There was nothing, therefore, to prevent him from going ahead with his plans.

This time it was to be the end. The Second Empire had never had the army that its foreign policy called for. But now it was no longer a question of foreign policy, of prestige, of conquests. The issue was simply life or death. While he still held possession of unlimited power, the Emperor should have used his dictatorship to force upon ministers who had rotted in routine, upon deputies who thought only of their wretched political interests, upon a public opinion that was utterly uninformed, an army reorganization that would have saved the country from disaster. Fate had still left him four years in which to prepare for a duel with Germany that all

[1] Minutes of the Legislative Body and of the Senate, Dec. 23 and 31, 1867, and Jan. 28, 1868.

thoughtful people now judged inevitable. The fact that in all that time he did not force through measures which he so clearly saw were necessary is his final and unappealable condemnation. The failure of the army reform bill of 1867 sounded the death knell of the Second Empire.

CHAPTER XXIX

The Liberal Empire

IN HIS LETTER OF JANUARY 19, 1867, ADDRESSED TO ROUHER, THE
Emperor had promised two bills, the one abolishing arbitrary governmental regulation of the press and the other broadening the
right of assembly. He kept his word. As soon as the army bill was
out of the way, the Legislative Body opened debate on the press
bill (January, 1868).

There had been some changes in the ministry, in which Rouher
was still the outstanding influence. Fould's death had made a big
hole, for his long experience in administration had been invaluable. Magne took Fould's place in Finance. La Valette had not been
able to swallow intervention in Italy and had resigned. In spite of
Rouher's manoeuvres Napoleon III replaced him with Pinard, a
former magistrate who had made his way into the Council of State.
Pinard was a tried and tested Catholic and stood high in the esteem
of the Empress.

Rouher was bitterly opposed to any weakening of the government's repressive agencies, but he had not been able to influence
Napoleon III as regarded the new press law. He therefore fell back
on his usual tactic of lobby politics and covert whispering to ruin
the bill either in whole or in part. The new wording abolished
advanced authorizations and ministerial admonitions (which for
that matter had fallen into virtual disuse). Offenses by the press
were left subject to ordinary judicial process. The stamp tax was
lightened to some extent.

The opposition declared the bill inadequate in the form in which
it had been proposed, and with good reason. Granier de Cassagnac,
a deputy from Gers, and editor of an ultra-Bonapartist paper, *Le
Pays,* attacked it brilliantly. He preferred keeping to the system of
1852.

"That system," he said, "has served France well for sixteen years. It will continue to do so."

His speech was hailed so enthusiastically by the majority that Napoleon III called meetings of the Council of Ministers and the Privy Council that very evening. Rouher suggested putting off the matter of press reform and dissolving the Legislative Body. The Empress backed him in this attitude and so, for once, did Persigny. Persigny even used the word *"coup d'état."*

"It's easier to talk of a *coup d'état* than to make one," La Valette remarked. "The only feasible thing is to complete these liberal measures, not withdraw them."

The Emperor was impressed by this attitude and refused either to withdraw the bill or to dissolve the Chamber. Rouher straightway presented his resignation. But honest as he may have been, he was extravagantly fond of power. Napoleon III had no difficulty in persuading him to stick to his post and support the bill. Rouher, indeed, reversed himself with a certain lavish broadmindedness.

"Let us not get too far apart," he said to the majority. "Let us make this law together, and together keep to a liberal course. . . . The election lists are the basis of our constitutional law. On them you will find the names of four million men who have registered since 1852. They have neither the background that you have nor your experience. Their hearts are stirring with new enthusiasms. Let us not exacerbate them. Let us not try to dampen them. Let us go along with them and do our best to guide and moderate them."

This was one of the rare occasions in Rouher's career when he talked and acted like a statesman. The majority voted the press law, but with no enthusiasm. In fact, none of the parties was satisfied with it.

The public assembly bill met the same sort of resistance. The bill did not go very far since it still required authorization in advance for meetings of a political character, and meetings of any sort could be forbidden or dissolved if the government saw fit.

"At the very most," wrote Prévost-Paradol, "it was a regularization of the right to confer in public."

The Legislative Body was inclined to defeat the bill outright. In reporting on it Peyrusse had no hesitation in declaring:

"France will have no more of free assembly."

The Chamber majority followed the official eloquence of Rouher and Pinard, in the end. When the two bills came before the higher house they got a very bad reception. The Senate did not regard them as either useful or timely. Maupas, the sometime minister of the 2nd of December, who had been stowed away in the registry office, seized the opportunity to take the lime-light again and weaken the position of Rouher. The Minister of State was put to it to save first the one and then the other reform.

The sullen obedience in parliament was a sort of echo to the discomfort and dissatisfaction that prevailed in the public at large. The World's Fair had been followed, according to rule, by a rise in the cost of living, and that had caused grumbling in the middle classes. The wheat crop was exceptionally poor, business slowed up, capital ran to cover, the stock exchange went dead. The reports which Pietri, the police prefect, sent to the Emperor personally speak for themselves. For September 22, 1867:

"The dissatisfaction caused by the rise in the price of bread is not dying down. A real uneasiness prevails among the working classes. We keep finding seditious posters stuck up in the tenement districts and they are directed against the Emperor himself."

For November 24th, of that same year:

"The active portion of society, the portion that takes the greatest interest in politics . . . is accentuating its attitude of opposition. The Emperor has probably retained his popularity among the masses; but there can be no doubt that a war as bitter as it is short-sighted is being waged against him in the ruling classes. Respect for authority is waning. Everything is the subject of slander."

Figures presented by the press supervisor in a report of September 15, 1867, show that the circulations of the opposition newspapers were constantly rising. In 1858 the governmental papers as a whole issued 67,000 copies, opposition papers, 75,000. In 1867 the governmental press had dropped to 42,000. The opposition press had risen to 128,000.

The labor movement was gaining headway. The year 1867 was a year of strikes. A strike of brass-workers in the Barbedienne factories was openly supported by the First International and the Company was obliged to capitulate. The International was winning recruits in increasing numbers. It had 250,000 members in France, 90,000 in Paris alone. The Brussels Congress of September, 1868, passed resolutions against private property, against the imperial government, against the army, against the Church.

After long hesitation the government decided (March, 1867) to prosecute the International, not as a secret society but on a charge of unauthorized association. Such socialists as were arrested were fined 100 francs. This absurd policy only called attention to the weakness of the central power.

Catholicism, meantime, was the butt of a large-scale offensive on the part of republicans and anti-clericals—these latter were becoming more and more active. The Solidarians pledged themselves to abstain from religious funerals and last rites. An Education League kept successful watch over lay education, especially in the larger towns. Free Masonry had for a time gone saccharine, but it still retained considerable power. In its higher reaches it was frankly atheistic. When the Catholics tried to bar Voltaire, Rousseau, Michelet and Renan from public reading rooms, which were more especially frequented by the lower middle classes, the students at the Ecole Normale, a very conservative institution, made anti-Catholic demonstrations in the streets. When the bishops attacked higher education Sainte-Beuve entered the lists in its defense, though with a voice that was faint from a progressive malady.

"The time has come," he said, "when we must proclaim absolute freedom of thought. . . . It is not too soon for that. It is not seven nor even ten o'clock in the morning. It is high noon."

Words that struck a sorrowful note and were far too charitable! High noon? Where then was the sun? The light was fading. It was almost sunset, though, as happens in countries of the north, the twilight might deceive by its long duration, and meantime the sky was a blaze of gorgeous color! The twilight of an era and perhaps of a nation! Fatigue, bad humor, mistrust were everywhere in the air. Interests were clashing one with the other. Social ties were strained and breaking. Absolutism was losing its nerve. Persigny wrote to Napoleon III (September 15, 1867) in a bitterly prophetic mood:

"The Empire seems to be crumbling in all directions. The relentless implacable struggle is being waged against us by men who have sworn our destruction in a pretended hope of restoring the parliamentary system. . . . As we flounder about between what has ceased to be the Empire and what has not yet become the parliamentary system, is it any wonder that thinking should be muddled and the public dismayed?"

In the south-west mobs protested registrations for the mobile guard and enforcement of the army law was abandoned. In a by-election in the Jura, Jules Grévy, a republican, was elected by an 11,000 majority. Every day brought incidents that manifested abiding political hatreds and also the growing unpopularity of the government, especially in Paris. At a distribution of prizes for the best final examinations in the National Competition, young Cavaignac, the son of the dictator of '48, refused to receive his chaplet from the hands of the Prince Imperial, and his schoolmates applauded.

When Napoleon III was informed of the incident he shrugged his shoulders and said:

"Well, sooner or later Louis will have to learn what public opinion is."

The Empress, for her part, choked with rage and humiliation.

"Now they are beginning to spare us nothing!" she muttered, over and over again.

Yes, they were being spared nothing! After the many happy years hard times were coming. Taking advantage of the new assembly law, all sorts of speakers rushed, during the spring of 1868, to reserve public halls for "lectures" on all sorts of subjects, literary, philosophical, economic, social. Such talks always had a tone of opposition to the government and "lectures" soon turned into political clubs where one met to sing the *Marseillaise,* lampoon the priests, rag too timid liberals and insult the "Badinguets." So a tidal wave of demagoguery made up and broke over Paris. After an absence of twenty years the disorders, the hatreds, the scandalous witticisms of '48 were back on the scene again. The government looked on patiently for a time. Then it ordered prosecutions. Some of the more violent orators were given a few months in jail. That kept them quiet for the time being, but once they were out it became apparent that the months in jail had merely ripened them into expert breeders of civil war.

As Persigny and Rouher had foreseen, the passage of the press bill at once resulted in a general onslaught by the opposition papers upon imperial administration. A cloud of new journals seemed to come buzzing from nowhere, like a swarm of June-bugs emerging noisily from a lawn in summer. In Paris one notes *L'electeur libre*

of Ernest Picard; *La Tribune* of Eugène Pelletan; *Le Réveil* of
Delescluze; later on *La Réforme,* and *Le Rappel* which were in-
spired by Victor Hugo. Lyons had its new *Discussion,* Marseilles its
Peuple, Toulouse an *Emancipation.*

Henri Rochefort, a reporter on *Figaro* and a writer of vaudeville
farces, started a little weekly in a red cover—*La Lanterne.* The publication had an immense success. It amused Paris, it delighted the
publics abroad, it worried the Tuileries. Rochefort set out to demolish the government by waggish jests often not over-clever.

" 'France,' says the Imperial Almanach, 'has thirty-six million
subjects, not counting subjects of dissatisfaction.' "

"As a Bonapartist I prefer Napoleon II. In my eyes he was the
ideal sovereign. What a reign, friends, what a reign! No taxes, no
wars, no privy purse!"

"Dialogue in a café: 'Waiter, bring me *France!*' 'Yes, sir, as soon
as it's free.' 'Well, perhaps I had better not wait!' "

Rochefort made direct allusions to the sovereigns, to the ministers
and to other public figures. He expressed frequent doubts about the
marital fidelity of Queen Hortense, made fun of the Ashes of Napoleon I, humorously foretold the fall of the dynasty. He was probably
going too far when he turned a great royal misfortune to rather
far-fetched jest:

"According to correspondence from Belgium the madness of Princess Charlotte, Maximilian's widow, has taken a very special turn.
Whenever she has an attack she cries out every minute or so: 'Lord,
how dirty everything is! Come, clean up here at once!' I am not an
alienist, but if you ask me I should say that the Princess Charlotte
has the clearest head in Europe."

The *Lanterne* sold between eighty and a hundred thousand
copies each Thursday. In Paris, at least, this slender collection of
jokes did more harm to the Empire, more surely cut the ground
from under it, than a whole series of riots would have done. Its success led a host of imitators into the same field and there was a rain
of comic weeklies, many of them filthy beyond words. After three
months (June, July, August, 1868) the government decided to con-
fiscate the *Lanterne* and prosecute Rochefort. The latter made good
his escape to Belgium, whence he continued to amuse and excite
Paris with a bootlegged *Lanterne.*

An effort was made to intimidate the opposition papers by very numerous prosecutions. Jules Favre figured in April, 1869, that "during the preceding thirteen months there had been 118 press actions with sentences totalling nineteen years in prison and 135,000 francs in fines." The flood had risen too high to be dammed, however. Hostile sheets would be suppressed only to reappear under new names and the numbers of the copies they circulated continued to grow.

Periodicals were far from being the only thing. There were books. Increasing throngs of readers consumed a veritable avalanche of anti-Napoleonic literature. In their *Story of a Conscript of 1813*, in their *Blockade*, in their *Story of a Farm Boy of Alsace*, Erckmann and Chatrian, inseparable collaborators, pictured with treacherous good humor the seamy side of the heroic age, contrasting the gentle attractiveness of life on Alsatian farms with the harshness and cruelty of life in the army in wartime.

"When they talk about Austerlitz or Jena or Wagram," says an old Jew in *Blockade*, "they say a lot about Napoleon but never a word about Johnny Doe or Dickey Roe, for they, poor devils, did nothing but lose their lives."

Pierre Lanfrey's *History of Napoleon I* neglected the military genius to berate the despot. In spite of its wretched execution Lanfrey's work, as it appeared in rapidly succeeding volumes, made its way deep down into the middle classes and had even greater influence in rural France than in Paris.

Napoleon III followed written opinion closely and was eager to answer such attacks. He outlined articles for Clément Duvernois, a republican deserter who had retired on an imperial pension, trying to defend his cause by emphasizing his personal popularity.

"Who really represents the people? The man who is supported by the votes of 8,000,000 Frenchmen! The man who impersonates order, good government, progress! . . . The Emperor is as popular today as he was fifteen years ago. The government may not be. . . . Instead of imitating the great benevolence of the Head of the State, his modesty, his unassuming ways, the instruments of his power have often lost their heads. The prefects think of themselves as so many pashas and try to force their will upon the people they rule."

A pitiable line of argument for an autocrat to take! If such a prince is dissatisfied with his servants, he reprimands or dismisses them—he does not parade his grievances in public.

Among other things the Emperor outlined the plot of a novel that was designed to appear serially in a large circulation daily, thought it was never written.[1] Benoît has been running a grocery store in the rue de la Lune. He emigrates to America in 1847, returning to France in 1868. Exiles had told him in America that France was groaning under despotic rule; but instead of finding the country "humiliated and impoverished," he finds it happy and prosperous, "rejoicing in universal suffrage and a maze of social betterments." Commercial treaties have made the necessaries of life much cheaper. There are no riots, no political prisoners, no exiles. And the Emperor went on to list all the achievements of his reign. It was a long list, especially in the field of public benefactions.

The trouble was, his adversaries were not admitting any such achievements. Never, not even in the days following the 2nd of December, had partisan spirit been more pronounced or more aggressive. One might suppose that the memory of the *coup d'état* would have faded with the years. Actually the wounds that that episode had opened had never healed. The blood it shed was still there, as red as ever. The republicans bent over, wet their fingers in it and then flipped them in the bruised face of the Empire. In July, 1868, a reporter on the *Siècle*, Ténot, wrote a wretched account of "Paris in December, 1851." Tiresome, flat, styleless, the article nevertheless made a public sensation. The opulent, haughty, glamorous era was forgotten. What people were shown was the act of violence from which the Empire had issued, the plot of a gang of desperados who had deceived the army and laid hold on France; the relentless repression that Morny had carried out; the bodies of innocent citizens littering the boulevards; Baudin wrapping the flag of France about him and falling at his barricade in defense of law and liberty.

The republicans took advantage of the emotion that Ténot's pamphlet aroused and intensified and prolonged it. Delescluze was an old hand at agitation—he was, in fact, a veteran of the first proscription. He had been a follower of Blanqui and like Blanqui he set fire to everything his fingers touched. In his *Réveil* he exhorted the people "to honor the men who had sacrificed their lives and bequeathed inspiring examples to posterity."

On All Souls' Day a large crowd assembled around Baudin's grave

[1] The autographs of this plot, as well as the outlines for Duvernois's articles, were found in the Tuileries in 1870 after the Empress's departure: *Papiers et correspondance de la famille impériale*, I, 218-219.

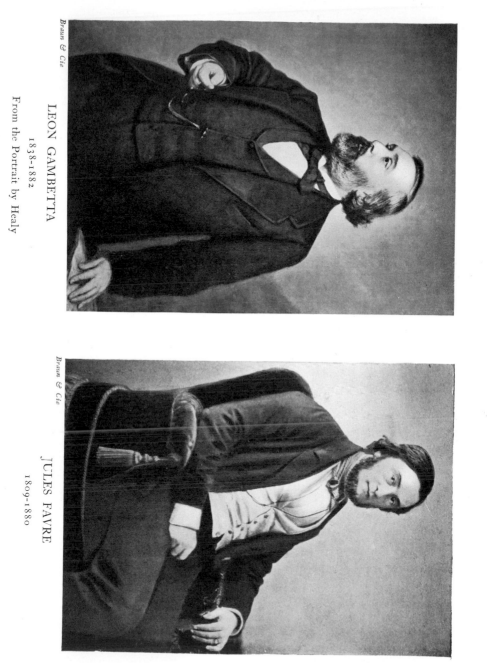

LEON GAMBETTA

1838-1882

From the Portrait by Healy

JULES FAVRE

1809-1880

in the Montmartre cemetery—a moss-flecked slab on which the rain and snow had all but obliterated the inscription: "Down with the Empire! Long live the Republic!" And the next day Delescluze opened a subscription in the *Réveil* to erect a suitable monument to Baudin.

Other republican papers, the *Siècle,* the *Temps,* the *Tribune,* the *Avenir national,* and Challemel-Lacour's *Revue politique,* a monthly, took up the idea. The lists of subscribers were not very long, but they contained many significant or glorious names from many different parties: Victor Hugo, Louis Blanc, Quinet, Odilon Barrot. Berryer was dying, at the time, of an abdominal cancer. The subscription from that aged and eminent royalist made a tremendous sensation. Still nothing would have come of the agitation had the government kept quiet; but Pinard lost his temper and demanded action. Rouher tried to call him off and so did Baroche. Pinard had his way. Delescluze, Challemel-Lacour and a few minor figures were haled into court on charges deriving from the general safety law that had been passed just after Orsini's bombs, a law of odious memory which everybody supposed had lapsed.

The defendants chose as their attorneys two old war-horses of '48, Emmanuel Arago and Crémieux, and then two newcomers, Laurier and Gambetta.

Léon Gambetta was the son of an Italian from Genoa and a mother from the French southwest. After a brilliant course in the grammar school at Cahors he went to Paris to study law. He was a huge, dark-complexioned fellow, with a great shag of whiskers. He had lost one eye. Gambetta had no end of imagination. He was master of a flood of audacious language which, implemented by iron-clad vocal cords, often soared to the loftiest eloquence. He was a strange mixture of vulgarity and polish. Gay, talkative, unconventional, he also had a firm resolve to succeed in life. He was an habitué of the Café Procope and the Café Voltaire in the Latin Quarter, where he won a far-flung popularity for scintillating diatribes against the imperial government. Moving about the lawcourts as Crémieux's secretary, he made his way into the society of the republican leaders; but he made special efforts to be noticed by celebrities in general—Garibaldi and Thiers, Morny and the Duc d'Aumale. Dugué de la Fauconnerie and Clément Duvernois called the Emperor's attention to Gambetta as an ambition that might profitably be courted, a talent that had better be guided into proper channels. Rouher replied contemptuously:

"Gambetta? Your Gambetta is just a bar-room Demosthenes, a speakeasy Solon."

Was Gambetta anything more than that? He did not work very hard or very well, though he had spurts of eager application. He hardly ever wrote anything. He was not what the French call the "homme de cabinet"—the respectable, inside manipulator. He was the "man of the forum," the born public leader, at his best before a crowd, where spontaneity, the off-hand inspiration, the striking gesture, more especially count. He applied some discipline to his vocal gifts. He learned the orations of Demosthenes, Cicero, Bossuet and the men of the Revolution by heart. He followed debates in the Chamber very closely and listened to all the important preachers at Notre Dame. For that matter he refined his style, corrected his bellow and acquired glibness more or less automatically. He had a remarkable memory. On one occasion, after he got to be a deputy in the Legislative Body, he gave an interview on the budget to a newspaper man, dictating the expenditures of each ministry table by table and never missing a figure, though he talked without notes. Jules Favre took him up. His friends on the *Temps,* chief among them Adrien Hébrard, predicted a great future for him. By the time he was thirty Gambetta was one of the hopes of the republican party.

Delescluze had only a slight acquaintance with Gambetta and no affection or respect for him. The fact, therefore, that Delescluze chose him for one of his counsel filled Gambetta with surprised delight. He saw in the windfall a stroke of luck that might bring him into nation-wide prominence.

Arguments opened on November 6th before a restless audience. Pleas were glowing, especially Laurier's. But when Gambetta's turn came it was thunder and lightning. He delivered less a defense, in fact no defense at all, of the insignificant Delescluze than an arraignment of the imperial system as a whole and of the *coup d'état* in particular. Napoleon III and his henchmen—they were the real defendants! They might well try to smile and snicker, away off there in the Tuileries, the Legislative Body, the Senate, the ministries— all places that they controlled. But the avenging cyclops, the lawyer with his one eye, his strangely resonant voice, his stevedore's gestures, took them by the collar, turned them around to face the music and then lashed them and hammered them to pulp.

"The Second of December! . . . You know what that date means in terms of blood and tears and anguish. . . . But what must be stressed here is the sequence of events, the consequences—all the harm that was done to France, the mischief that was wrought in the public conscience, by that brutal act. . . . The Second of December! Around a pretender gathered a group of men whom France did not know, men without talent or honor, without rank or profession—the sort of men that have been the accomplices of violent over-turns in all periods of history. Laws and institutions have been stabbed and sabred by people of that kind for centuries and centuries."

Over against those brazen rogues Gambetta set the Cavaignacs, the Thiers, the Lamoricières, the Berryers, the Michel de Bourges, the Charras—law-abiding men, defenders of legal society, men who were put into prison or exiled that the Republic might be the better strangled and Paris the more thoroughly subdued. "Subdued? Paris was murdered! Subdued? Paris was shot down with musketry and grapel"

It was a speech the like of which had never been heard in a French courtroom. It had a certain ferocious grandeur, a certain ravishing exaltation. The presiding justice, the state's attorney, the spectators, listened with bated breath while the orator's voice, now bellowing, now thundering, now acquiring a sort of rending shrill-ness from a throat infection, made its way through the courtroom walls, filled the city, swept out afar over the country like one of those sudden gusts of wind from a lowering sky that forewarn of the hurricane.

Gambetta's peroration was a direct and overwhelming assault of unheard-of violence.

"For seventeen years now you have been absolute masters in France. . . . We need not ask what use you have made of its treasures, its blood, its honor and glory. . . . What passes the soundest judgment upon you, as the testimony of your own remorse, is the fact that you have never dared make the Second of December a national holiday. Well, since you will have nothing of that anniversary, we will take it for ourselves. Each year that day will be the memorial day of our dead until such time as the country shall become master of itself again and force expiation upon you."

As might have been foreseen, Delescluze and his comrades at the bar were found guilty; but it was a costly victory for the Empire. Not Paris only but all France began to sit in judgment on the Emperor and his court, and henceforward the republicans would have a leader—Gambetta.

The evening after the trial the Empress protested plaintively to one of the judges:

"But after all—what harm have we ever done to that young man?"

No harm, in truth! The fact was that in that speech Gambetta had suddenly found within him the whole soul of a party that had long been gagged by the Empire but which in his person had torn the gag from its mouth and would thenceforward fight, fight fearlessly, recklessly, untiringly, with any available means and in fair weather and foul, until the Empire lay stretched on the ground.

The Emperor personally did not seem greatly affected by the episode. He had seen so many, so many such episodes in his life! Having had a vast experience of men he knew a man when he saw one.

"You were right," he remarked regretfully to Dugué de la Fauconnerie. "That Gambetta really is a great talent. Couldn't one find some way to tone him down?"

Alas! The time for that had passed. Gambetta might once have succumbed, like Mirabeau of yore, to the charm of court life. Had he been given a chance to, history might have been different. Now it was too late. All France knew his name and success had bound him inseparably to the Republic.

A government cannot live on prosecutions alone. In trying to do just that the Empire betrayed its basic weakness. But it was a weakness less of institutions—the institutions of the Empire were still sound—than of men, the men responsible for the functioning of the institutions. While opponents were increasing in numbers and aggressiveness, the higher personnel of the Empire was dying, quarreling, wearing itself down. Twenty years in power and still the same men in the key positions! In that lay the essential inadequacy of the absolutist system. Napoleon III did not apply himself soon enough to the task of preparing successors for his instruments of governing.

"There is no replacement material in sight," Prince Napoleon remarked.

As Conti, the Emperor's private secretary, put it:

"We've got to find political seedlings at the earliest possible moment."

Billault and Morny had been dead a long time. Thouvenel and Fould had vanished from the scene. Soon it would be the turn of Walewski, who had become the hope of the liberal imperialists; of Moustier, a deft negotiator; of Troplong, the president of the Senate, a pompous utility-man who was all for sticking to the Constitution. Niel was also to die before very long.

The Emperor's immediate circle was shot to pieces by rivalries and personal hatreds. Pinard, the Minister of the Interior, was at outs with Rouher. Rouher was in the stronger position and succeeded in ruining him after the Baudin subscription affair, which Pinard, in fact, had handled very unskilfully. Rouher got him replaced with a henchman of his own, Forcade la Roquette. Rouher himself was at outs with Fleury, whom Napoleon III was inclined to listen to in military matters and whose influence on the whole was beneficent.

"There are two Ministers of War," exclaimed Rouher to the Emperor, "one who works and gets things done—that's Niel; and one who finds fault and keeps things in confusion—that's Fleury."

Ever since his fall from favor Persigny had stubbornly fought the Minister of State. He was too bitter in attack and he attacked in and out of season, but there was no question of his courage. He fought just as hard against the more and more marked intrusion of the Empress upon processes of government. Among the grumbling letters which he sent from time to time to the Emperor, there was one that Eugénie intercepted and opened. It was a formal and thoroughgoing indictment of her personality and her policies. The fact, Persigny declared, that her attendance at Council meetings had become regular since 1865 and that she had allowed a faction to form about her, was seriously impairing the Emperor's prestige and curtailing his influence. The state now had two heads and that duality stimulated intrigue, paralyzed action, falsified supervision and encouraged opposition. The Emperor owed it to himself and to the country to take the business of governing back into his own hands and to order the Empress to keep to her proper function, which was to look pretty and shine at court festivities.

Persigny's letter was dated November 11, 1867. The Empress answered it herself and with a blistering fury. She was hurt to the quick all the same and declared that she would never set foot in the Council again. That would have been a rare chance to seize. But partly out of kindness of heart, partly in fear of the scenes she could make, the Emperor confirmed the Empress in her prerogatives and disavowed his friend of the old days. Persigny was less and less often seen at the Tuileries after that. But his straight talking had not been altogether without effect. Eugénie became less assiduous in her attendance at the Council and during the year 1869 appeared there hardly at all.

Had Napoleon's will power been at the old level he could easily have ended such bickering and restored wholehearted cooperation. Everything began and ended with him. He was still absolute master. But he had declined physically and mentally. He was definitely slowing up. His eyes had lost their glitter, his cheeks were bloodless and flabby. At the age of sixty-one he looked, on certain days, like an infirm octogenarian. Bladder attacks were becoming exceedingly frequent now and each left him a wreck for a longer and longer period. His mind was perfectly clear. He was keenly attentive to public affairs. In personal disinterestedness he was certainly superior to most of the people about him. But his recent failures had destroyed his self-confidence completely. He was just drifting now on the tide of events. Ludovic Halévy, a keen observer of people, noted on July 21, 1869:

"The thing that is going to destroy the Empire is not its bad policy but its lack of a policy. There has been, strictly speaking, no government in France for some years past. There is a man on the throne, and not a bad man at all, a man with the best of intentions. But at just this moment the man is out of luck and things have been going badly for quite some time. He is aging. He has certainly lost much of the confidence he once had in himself, and recent events have not contributed at all to restoring it." [1]

How retimber, how rejuvenate, the cohort of the faithful which age and mortality had so grievously dismantled? There were those —Giraudeau, for instance—who thought that some of the young lib-

[1] *Carnets*, II, 7.

erals or moderate republicans might be called upon. Clément Duvernois had come over to the Empire. Others might. Power had its
glamor even for honest men! To begin with, there was Emile
Ollivier. Napoleon III had never given up the idea of some day
offering the premiership to that promising liberal. But such a nomination would be a very serious step. It would mean dispensing with
Rouher and with most of the old standbys. Before taking it the
Emperor thought he ought to see what would come of the elections
of 1869.

CHAPTER XXX

The End of the Vice-Emperor

THEY WERE SCHEDULED FOR THE MONTH OF MAY. THE THIRD CON-sultation of public opinion since the advent of the Empire, they were looked forward to by imperialists and anti-imperialists alike as something fateful and decisive.

The final session of the Legislative Body had been a sort of preface to them. Napoleon III delivered a speech, half congratulatory, half scolding. Thiers and the republicans came back with an attack on the capricious management of Haussmann, the Prefect of the Seine.

There was no question of Haussmann's personal integrity. He had, however, surrounded himself with sharpers. He was always overdrawing on appropriations and then getting out of his predicament by engineering enormous loans by methods that could easily be called high-handed. Jules Ferry had just written a witty pamphlet on "Haussmann's Ingenious Book-keeping." It set all Paris laughing and virtually ended the availability of the grand old town-wrecker. The loan that the government wanted authorized, in order to wipe out Haussmann's latest deficit, was passed by a very slender majority.

The opposition was on solid ground in finding fault with the financial policy of the Empire. The state was now addressing the national savings directly, a thing the older regimes had never ventured to do. Each time, therefore, the better to attract investments in government debt bonds, the interest rate had to be raised, with the net result that the public debt of France had climbed by more than four billions. It was being paid off in absurdly low and very irregular amortizations, so that debt bonds were being quoted lower and lower each year. French 4½'s stood at 107 in 1852. They had dropped to 87 in 1859. A very costly operation converted them into 3's in October, 1862, but that had not halted the decline. Standing at 72 at that moment they had dropped to 62.45 by July, 1866.[1]

---

[1] They were to be quoted at 60.60 when war broke out in 1870.

Governmental expenditures had been increasing constantly. The budget of 1852 had called for 1,513 millions. The figure was 2,287 millions for the year 1863 and the rise was continuing. Budgets had been normally balanced in the years 1855, 1858, 1865, 1868 and 1869. The other twelve years had shown deficits. The bookkeeping was never clear. Some request for a supplementary credit was always before the Chamber.

One point, in all justice, had to be made, however. National wealth in France had increased very considerably under the Empire and, therefore, in spite of its growing demands, the imperial government had never forced any burdensome sacrifices upon the public. The tax rate and the tax system had remained virtually what they had been under the First Empire and during the Restoration. Taxpayers had been neither crushed nor harassed. There had been no prying to complain of, either, on the government's part. The tax load had been so well distributed and balanced that small incomes had paid small taxes, while the fiscal responsibilities of the wealthy and moderately wealthy were nothing that they could not easily meet.

With the financial debate ending in a drawn battle Thiers shifted once more to the inadequacy of civic liberties. Only a parliamentary check, he declared, could prevent the government from making some new blunder in foreign relations.

"Liberty means this," he said; "that France shall not wake up some morning to the surprise of finding that her sons have been called to some frontier to shed their blood."

At the last session Jules Favre and Ernest Picard vainly protested against official candidacies; but during the election campaign that now opened the old abuses continued unabated, especially in the large towns. Election districts were gerrymandered in ways most disconcerting to the opposition. The prefects kneaded the masses by most brazen methods. The departments were flooded with posters, pamphlets and newspapers that glorified the social achievements of the Empire, the portion of its work, in truth, that was least subject to controversy.

In the face of this steamroller, democrats, Catholics and royalists failed as usual to fuse. They wasted much of their energies in sniping at each other. There was division and discord in all parties. The Liberal Union was primarily Orleanist. It was bitterly combatted by the legitimists. So the socialists and the republicans were at each other's throats. The republicans were divided among themselves. The "old guard," men like Garnier-Pagès, Jules Favre or Carnot, were fought by newcomers such as Gambetta, Jules Ferry, Rochefort, and one "ghost" stalking out from the dead past— Raspail. For that matter there was a split in the government party itself. There "authoritarians" were booed and hooted by "reformists."

Platforms and tendencies were so numerous that the public mind was in utter confusion. Gambetta ran against Carnot in the Belleville quarter. He declared himself "irreconcilable" and asked those who were to vote for him to draw up, for his information, "notebooks" or individual platforms. These documents he digested and summarized in a platform that was to be known as the "Belleville Program." It really laid the foundations of what, under the Third Republic, was to be called the Radical party:

"Strict application of universal suffrage; election districts to be delimited according to actual numbers of voters; responsibility to parliament of public officials of all grades; complete freedom for the press; complete freedom of assembly; separation of Church and state; primary education to be free, compulsory and secular; all public offices to be elective; abolition of the standing army."

Strangely enough, almost all candidates in the elections of 1869 had this last item in their platforms, regardless of the party or party faction to which they belonged. So the lesson of 1866 had gone for nothing! The threat from Prussia was entirely ignored.

Returns came in on the evening of May 24th. The government polled 4,438,000 votes, the opposition 3,355,000. That meant that the republicans had registered tremendous gains. Paris, Lyons, Marseilles, Bordeaux, Rouen, Reims, Strasbourg, gave them landslide majorities. The split-ballots count, which was very large, was to increase their power still further.

The Orleanists were swamped, polling comparatively no vote at all. The rural vote saved the Empire, though the word "saved" was hardly appropriate for a dictatorship that had held the country strangled under the threat of administrative reprisals and yet had received a majority of a bare million, had carried no important city and had been swamped in its own capital. Nobody failed to see the significance of what had happened, nobody, either in the government or in the gutter.

When the results became definitely known a spirit of unruliness swept over Paris. A mob of "white blouses" of suspicious origin moved out from the tenement districts into the boulevards, cheering for Rochefort and the Republic and singing the *Marseillaise*. At the Ricamarie mine a mob of miners who were on strike rushed the soldiers on guard. The soldiers fired. Thirteen dead!

Napoleon III seems at first to have been dazed by the outcome of the elections. It had far exceeded his worst fears. During those evenings of early summer the sovereigns had arranged to entertain the Queen of Holland and the Grand Duchess Marie of Russia at the Tuileries. The gaiety was smothered as under a pall of catastrophe. The gilded halls were virtually deserted. Whenever the orchestra ended a tune cries could be heard from without, where the police were dispersing mobs.

"Everybody is alarmed without knowing just why," Mérimée wrote. "There is a general atmosphere of uneasiness. People's nerves are on edge. It's something like the way one feels in Mozart's *Don Juan* when the Commander is about to appear."

Rouher and the Empress begged the Emperor not to weaken, to rally all faithful elements about him—they were still numerous and strong—and offer a vigorous resistance to the democratic onrush. Quite in the other direction, two veterans of December Second emphatically advised him to drop unlimited power at once—it stood incarnate in their eyes in a common enemy, Rouher. Maupas declared openly that a new day was dawning in France. Persigny was much more specific. He wrote Emile Ollivier a letter that was published in the *Constitutionnel:*

"The Emperor has only to persevere unswervingly in the liberal direction which he has recently taken. He must gather about him a whole new generation that is young, strong, intelligent and, especially, courageous and fired by a living faith. . . . As for the men of December Second, of whom I am one myself, their day has passed."

Persigny was to say almost the same thing on the 3rd of June, 1869, and this time to the Emperor directly:

"The situation must be accepted just as it is. Liberal principles must be upheld and without hesitation. . . . Unlimited power has been too seriously shaken. . . . The whole trouble with the government right now is the presence in it of those two men [Rouher and Baroche] who personify its unpopularity in the eyes of a large part of the public."

Hurt, undoubtedly, by such blunt and such sound admonitions, Napoleon III had *Le Peuple* publish a letter which he had written to one of the new deputies, Baron de Mackau:

"A self-respecting government should not yield either to pressure, or to hysteria or to mob violence."

For the time being, at least, and more out of vanity than conviction, he had elected to stand firm. He appointed Jérôme David, a personal friend of Rouher, vice-chairman of the Legislative Body. He was aware that he would have to make some concessions to the Chamber, but he intended to make them in his own good time.

The moment the deputies got together, however, the Third Party, whose exact make-up had not been as yet determined, tried to force the Emperor's hand by an interpellation on the need of constitutional reform. The query was framed in unusually peremptory language.

"The deputies undersigned . . . are in agreement in demanding, in foreign relations, peace; in domestic affairs, the repeal of the general safety law; the prohibition of cumulations in high salaries; an election reform that will safeguard the freedom of the ballot; jury trials for political offenses committed through the press."

The document bore 116 signatures, among them the name of the Duc de Mouchy, a relative of the imperial family. Thiers and the republicans did not join in the move, but they were with "the 116" in spirit. That gave the insurrection a majority and the majority commissioned Schneider, the president of the Legislative Body, to inform the Emperor that it would not accept any government that contained Rouher.

Napoleon III tried at first to stifle the interpellation.

"It's unconstitutional!" he remarked to Buffet jovially on the evening of July 8th at Saint-Cloud. "You are trying to cut the old lion's claws and draw his teeth, leaving him only his handsome mane."

And to Clément Duvernois he complained:

"Why, they're backing me against the wall!"

No more and no less! But he could see that if he refused to

budge, he would find a general uproar on his hands. He gave in, accordingly, and proposed by way of compromise that he deliver a message which would pledge a whole body of reforms. Schneider answered that nothing could be done as long as Rouher were around. Regretfully the Emperor gave in again. He would sacrifice Rouher.

On July 12th the man Rouher mounted the speaker's platform for the last time as a minister. He read a message from the Sovereign. It enumerated the changes that were to be made. They would be enacted in the form of a resolution by the Senate. The Chamber would thenceforth elect its own officers and it would have the rights of initiative, amendment and interpellation. The budget would be voted table by table. Tariff laws would be passed by parliament. Deputies could be named ministers and remain deputies. Ministers would be responsible to the Emperor as in the past and take orders from him alone. The Senate would acquire prerogatives corresponding.

In accord with the pact that had been struck privately, the Third Party withdrew its interpellation. The Legislative Body at once adjourned and the ministry handed in its resignations (July 13, 1869).

In setting up the Liberal Empire—for that was the meaning of what had just taken place—Napoleon III should have organized a new team made up in large part of deputies. Saving the one detail of ministerial responsibility he had become a limited, parliamentary monarch. Unfortunately he was still loath to begin playing the rôle that events were inexorably thrusting upon him. He was tired of power, but he could not get used to the idea of being without it. He asked Forcade la Roquette to form a provisional cabinet. Niel stayed in War, Magne in Finance, Chasseloup-Laubat took the presidency of the Council of State. Duruy was hated by the Catholics and dropped. (On learning that he had a large family and no fortune the Emperor appointed him to the Senate.) The Ministry of State was abolished.

As Napoleon III had promised, Rouher left the government for good and all. A few days later, for a magnificent compensation, he was called to the presidency of the Senate, which was vacant through the death of Troplong. In that decorative position he was to stay on till the end of the reign as the upright counsellor, too often heeded and as often ill-inspired, of the Emperor and the Empress. His direct influence, however, his rôle as administrative head of the government, where he had functioned despotically for so many years, came to an end then and there. His fall, for it was indeed a fall, was loudly enough hailed by the opposition for the country to be left with no doubt as to the reality of the new outlook.

Unfortunately Rouher's political demise had come too late. He was a second-rate man at the very best. If he rendered long service, the effect of it had been to hold Napoleon III to absolutist policies for far too long a time. Rouher's influence in foreign relations—Italy and Germany—had been pestiferous. His opposition to the army reform bill had no excuse whatsoever. The Vice-Emperor should have been pushed out of sight immediately after Sadowa.

The centennial of Napoleon I fell on August 15, 1869. The celebration was listless and cold. Napoleon III declared a general amnesty and nobody was in the least grateful for it. The public was still in a mood of defiance. The agitators were still agitating, one strike following on another. For a replica of the Ricamarie catastrophe, a police squad fired on striking miners at Aubin in the Aveyron. This time fourteen dead! The First International adopted the social revolution at its Basel Congress. It was so sure the Empire was going to fall that it designated Paris as its next meeting place—and *September 5, 1870,* as its next meeting date! New newspapers of a more violent opposition sprouted: the *Marseillaise* of Rochefort; the *Rappel* of Victor Hugo and his friends; Vermorel's *La Reforme,* then two organs of militant socialism, *La Voix du Peuple* and *Le Travail.*

Sainte-Beuve died on the 13th of October (1869). He had been deeply affected by the elections and the disturbances that followed. Shortly before the end he wrote to a friend:

"Things are falling to pieces, dissolving. Soon everything will be at the mercy of the first incident. Don't wag your head! Don't smile! Don't, especially, play the optimist! All the regimes that have fallen in France have done just as this one is doing down to the day before the disaster, not to say down to the very last morning. Believe me, the Empire is very, very ill!"

Marshal Niel also died—after two years of overwork. His torturing gravel prevented his mounting a horse during the last weeks. Nelaton operated, as a desperate resort. The patient succumbed to the infection that followed. Niel thought the war was certain to come and was anxious to prepare for it. He did his utmost to put the French army on a new footing. Unfortunately he died without having accomplished anything. The Emperor gave him too feeble support. He had to battle endlessly with his colleagues in the ministry, with parliament and with his own subordinates. Yet he never lost courage. The bill of 1868 did not grant the forces which he and the Emperor demanded. He tried then to do the best he could in the field of equipment. He kept posted on what the Prussian army was doing and on German resources. He studied French railroads from the standpoint of mobilization and tried—unsuccessfully —to reorganize the French general staff. After scattering appropriations to left and right in other regards, the Legislative Body manifested a strange parsimony towards Niel. It seemed to enjoy blocking his reforms the moment they required money. It reduced the mobile guard appropriation to practically nothing. The funds absolutely necessary for rehabilitating fortresses and manufacturing artillery were pitilessly whittled down. Carrying niggardliness beyond all bounds the deputies forced the Ministry of War to lengthen furloughs for the rank and file. That reduced the active army by at least a third.

A Gascon and an optimist, Marshal Niel tried to make the best of everything. Undoubtedly he grew weary and despondent at times, as he glimpsed the catastrophe that he could not have failed to see in the offing. Ordinarily, however, he was hopeful, trustful. Nothing that he ever said betrayed the real dearth of men and the defects in the army's organization. Not content with assuring the Emperor in the open Council that France had "the best army in the world," he declared in July, 1868, from the speaker's platform in the Legislative Body:

"If need should arise there is not a soldier who would not re-enlist within a fortnight."

And again in April, 1869, he further said:

"Whether we have peace or war is a matter of complete indifference to the War Ministry. We are always ready."

In a summary report that he published at this time in the *Journal Officiel* he estimated that he had 750,000 men "available for war purposes."

Was that sheer irresponsibility on Niel's part, or just an expression of army loyalty for public consumption? Aware as we now are of what was to follow, such over-statement on the part of a key officer can only look like a distinct blemish on Niel's historical figure. He was certainly a man of energy and a patriot, but he can hardly be cleared of responsibility for contributing to the maintenance of most dangerous misapprehensions in the sovereign and in the country.

Niel's passing was a hard blow to Napoleon III. He was himself suffering tortures at just that moment from a kidney complaint, the most serious attack that he had so far had. Kelius hurried to Saint-Cloud from Heidelberg and prescribed opium. The Emperor dropped off into a coma that filled all the court circle with gravest alarm. Paris heard rumors that he was dying, and to quiet public opinion the Empress had him wheeled in a chair to the September 7th meeting of the Council of Ministers. He seemed more dead than alive, but the *Journal Officiel* could truthfully report that he had presided over the meeting. Shortly afterwards the attack of pain began tapering off. On the 11th Eugénie forced him to appear in public on the Champs Elysées during a rainstorm. Alas, he did not receive a single cheer!

Napoleon III chose General Le Boeuf to fill Niel's place. That was a bad mistake though it seems that Niel, feeling his own end near, recommended the appointment. Le Boeuf, round-faced, jovial, was a good soldier. He had worked hard on artillery reorganization —artillery was his specialty. He was not without intelligence nor without dash. But he was utterly devoted to the Emperor and too servile in his relations to him. He would lie to Napoleon III rather than tell him a painful truth. The Emperor grew personally fond of him as he had of Niel and Vaillant, and listening only to his feelings would never afterwards let the General go.

According to the strict letter of the Constitution the Legislative Body should have met again by October 26th at the very latest. The Emperor doggedly refused to convoke the session till late November. Following a suggestion of Kératry and Gambetta the republicans decided to gather in the Place de la Concorde and smash their way through the gates of the Palais-Bourbon. They gave up the idea on reflecting that such a procedure might give the government a pretext it was perhaps looking for. Supplementary elections in Paris, meantime, had sent four more deputies to reenforce the extreme Left: Emmanuel Arago, Crémieux, Glais-Bizoin and—Rochefort!

The pamphleteer of the *Lanterne* in parliament! The capital had given the Emperor another slap in the face!

CHAPTER XXXI

The Suez Canal

IN THOSE DAYS THAT WERE SO GLOOMY FOR THE EMPIRE, A BURST OF glory suddenly tinged the gables of the ancient Tuileries. The Suez Canal opened on the 16th of November, 1869.

The Canal had been a difficult enterprise and it was pushed to completion only through the constant encouragement of Napoleon III, and in advance of him, really, of the Empress. The effects were to be incalculable. The cutting of the Isthmus of Suez was to transform world economy, change the map of the whole globe, and stand in history as one of the major events of the nineteenth century.

In the heyday of ancient Egypt Rameses II had dug a canal connecting the Mediterranean and the Red Sea. The Arab invasion wiped it out. A thousand years rolled by. Then Leibnitz suggested to Louis XIV that he restore the cut. The Great King had all his eyes on Europe and did not listen. Bonaparte was in Egypt in 1799 and at that time returned to the idea. In company with Monge and Berthollet he visited such traces of the old canal as were still visible near Suez. Lepère, the engineer, even drew up plans, which the General's sudden return to France relegated to a dusty oblivion.

In 1833 a number of Saint-Simonians made a timid effort. They had just gone bankrupt when young Ferdinand de Lesseps arrived in Cairo as consul for France. Lesseps was a Frenchman of the South, cousin to Señora de Montijo and the future Empress. He was adroit, agile of mind and body, full of life, gaiety, imagination. A great dancer, he was also an accomplished horseman. His deeds of prowess dazzled the Arabs. Let a pestilence break out in Egypt and there he would be, racing from one pest-house to another and organizing a sanitary campaign. Mehemet-Ali, the Khedive, and his son, Saïd, thought of Lesseps as an intimate friend and righthand man.

464

Lesseps was eventually transferred to Spain and then to Rome. Placed, finally, on the reserve list, he retired to his old home in the country at La Chesnaye. There, for five years, roaming about or lounging under the trees, the heavy, restless Lesseps, with his dull complexion, his soft moist eyes, never once took his thoughts off the Near East. He considered at length and in every detail a scheme that had engrossed his attention during his stay in Egypt: to take up Lepère's plans again and dig a real ship canal across the isthmus that barred the road to Asia.

Saïd unexpectedly succeeded his father in 1854. Lesseps went to see him at once in a firm intent of making sure of his opportunity. Adroitly he obtained a concession for the canal. The concession was just an authorization signed by the Khedive. Lesseps still had to finance the project, begin work and keep it going in the face of hostility from the Sultan, who had rights as a suzerain, of jealousy from the English, of indifference from the viceroy, of fussiness and graft among the Egyptian ministers, of suspicions and fears on the part of his stock-holders at home. In dealing with all those difficulties Lesseps carried a giant's load, but he carried it good humoredly, with truly French graciousness and without ever losing heart.

As a matter of fact Lesseps would probably have stumbled at more than one point in the course of the long years that the building of the canal required, had he not had the enthusiastic and efficient support of the Empress and Napoleon III. The Emperor had sized Lesseps up exactly. He knew of what stuff dreams were made—he had had dreams of practically the same sort in his time. During the days at Ham he had worked out a scheme for a Nicaraguan canal. He backed Lesseps with money and in other ways. He subscribed personally for 177,000 shares in the Lesseps company. He induced England and the Porte to tone down their opposition. The Empress never once lost sight of her cousin's interests and when critical moments came, she took an active hand, defended the work that was being done and never allowed the Emperor's mind to drift away to other things. She could be as enthusiastic, obstinate and ardent as a friend as she could be as an enemy. She was well aware, besides, of all the prestige that would redound to France and the Empire if the herculean enterprise turned out successfully. She was truly its fairy godmother, its watchful and beneficent genius.

The work began in '59 and was not complete till ten years later.

The canal started at Port Saïd, ran first to Lake Timsah, then to the Salt Lakes so-called, and finally reached the Red Sea at Suez— some 115 miles in all. Seventy-five million cubic metres of earth had to be moved and terraced into embankments. There was no ledge to cut, but once the trench was dug it had to be kept from refilling with sand. There was a shortage of fresh water. Lesseps brought it from the Nile by a second canal, which could be used afterwards for navigation up the river. Labor problems were tremendous. Eighteen thousand workingmen were gathered from all parts of Europe and distributed to the appropriate sections. They had to be housed in the open desert and then fed and protected from cholera and typhus. Lesseps found ways to solve all such problems. Money was always giving out. Instead of an estimated 200 million francs, the canal cost 432 millions exclusive of interest payments. In such emergencies Lesseps would rush to Paris and obtain permission to float new issues of stocks. His unflagging enthusiasm swept one obstacle after another away. In the fall of 1869 the last barrier was pierced and the waters of the Red Sea ran through into the Salt Lakes and at last into the Mediterranean.

An achievement so portentous required a very formal inauguration. The world expected a great show. The Khedive, with Lesseps as co-host, very properly addressed the first invitation to the Empress of the French. After her all the crowned heads in the world were invited.

Eugénie assembled a little court and proceeded to Venice, where Victor Emmanuel offered her a reception. Boarding the yacht *Aigle,* she sailed first to Athens and then to Constantinople, the Sultan entertaining her at Yldiz-Kiosk with truly oriental magnificence and sumptuousness. But that was nothing, especially in point of ingenious attentions as compared with what the viceroy of Egypt— no longer Saïd but Ismaïl—had waiting for the Empress when the *Aigle* reached Alexandria. The Palace of Guezireh in Cairo was set aside for her use. Chancing one evening to allude to the fragrance of the orange blossoms in far away Granada, her homeland, she awoke in the morning to find that the Khedive had planted a blossoming orange grove with golden fruit under her windows during the night. While waiting for the formal opening, she ascended the Nile in a boat as far as Assuan, stopping off for visits at Luxor and Thebes.

FERDINAND DE LESSEPS

1805-1894

From the Portrait by Bonnat

Eight thousand persons, meantime, had flocked from all parts of Europe to Alexandria and Port Saïd. The hotels proving altogether inadequate, special barracks were built and five hundred chefs and a thousand waiters were imported.

November 16th was a day of perfect weather, cloudless, supremely bright. The *Aigle,* with the Empress aboard, entered the harbor at Port Saïd at eleven in the morning. Forty-eight warships of all nations, with their flags raised and their crews in white uniforms lining the yards, fired regal salutes as she sailed by, the Egyptian batteries on shore responding. It was one boundless acclamation in honor of France, in honor of Lesseps. Leaning on the rail of her yacht Eugénie could not restrain tears of emotion.

The *Aigle* came to anchor. The first to appear on board was Lesseps, the builder of the canal. He was followed by the Khedive, then by Francis Joseph of Austria, the Prince Royal of Prussia, the Prince and Princess of Holland, the heroic Emir, Abd-el-Kader, a sparkling procession of princes, ministers, ambassadors. To either hand of the sovereign in the reception line stood representative talents of France—writers, newspapermen, painters, scientists: Théophile Gautier, Eugène Fromentin, Tournemine, Bréguet, Quatrefages, Pelletan.

At three in the afternoon Ismaïl's guests attended religious services. On the seashore in front of a grandstand, and with a view out over the sea, an altar for a Catholic mass and a platform for a Mohammedan rite had been erected. Ulemas offered Mussulman prayers, the Bishop of Alexandria Christian prayers. Finally Monsignor Bauer, the Empress's almoner, pronounced a Roman blessing on the Canal.

In the evening all ships were outlined in lights, fireworks played from barges, the harbor rang with music from threescore naval bands. On the morning of the 17th the *Aigle* entered the Canal at the head of a fleet of vessels. It steamed slowly along between the two embankments that stretched away across the desert. Lesseps, who had passed his sixtieth year, became utterly exhausted by the emotions of his great day, and fell asleep. The Empress came and awakened him herself as the yacht reached Ismaïlia on Lake Timsah.

There, within a few weeks' time, a new town had sprung like a mirage from the desert. The Khedive had had a palace built, large enough and well appointed enough to offer his army of guests a luxurious hospitality. Delegations from all the races in Egypt had assembled and pitched their tents at Ismaïlia. It was a nomad city, ablaze with color. Through the streets marched long lines of dromedaries, their necks moving slowly up and down in cadence with their stride. A bazaar had been organized. Among the features were trained animal shows and exhibitions by spinning dervishes. The Khedive had arranged a dazzling ballet performance as a surprise entertainment for his big party. Then came a luncheon. In the evening, in the grand ballroom of the palace, which had mirrors on the walls to multiply the myriad lights, came a ball with twenty-five hundred couples.

On the 18th the fleet reached and crossed the Salt Lakes. On the 19th it was in the harbor at Suez on the Red Sea. So the miracle had been accomplished. The Mediterranean and the Indian Ocean were tied together as by a watery thread, along which, thenceforward, all the commerce between Europe and the Far East would pass. The forced rounding of the Cape was no more. The South Atlantic, for four hundred years a busy thoroughfare, was to become the most lonely of oceans.

The "great Frenchman" experienced at that moment an apotheosis, a world adoration, which neither Pasteur nor Victor Hugo were to equal after him. The Empress handed him the Grand Cross of the Légion d'honneur. Decorations poured in from all the sovereigns of the world. The Spanish Cortes resolved that "Ferdinand de Lesseps had deserved well of humanity." England chivalrously laid aside her reserve and hailed his "persevering genius." The glory of Lesseps was to be dimmed for a moment in years to come. But all that was to be remembered in the end was the unparalleled significance of his achievement at Suez.

Next in order of merit after Lesseps, it is only fair to place the two sovereigns of France. Their personal share in the accomplishment of the miracle was far from small.

CHAPTER XXXII

The Ministry of January 2nd

FRANCO-PRUSSIAN TENSION DID NOT EASE OFF AFTER THE COLLAPSE of compensations and the London Conference. A number of incidents supervened to keep feelings at a high pitch.

Bismarck was relentlessly pushing his drive for the unification of all Germany around Prussia, and this required that the states of the south should become members of the northern Federation. Now the states of the south did not want that. They were already tied to Berlin by the customs' union and by military agreements. They did not care to go farther and become mere vassals of Prussia. Covertly encouraged by Austria and France they held off.

This attitude became apparent at the Customs Parliament that met at Berlin in 1868. The delegates from Bavaria and Württemberg evinced hostility to the Prussian plan. Bismarck was furious but for the moment there was nothing much that he could do.

Meantime he was dogging and blocking French diplomatic moves everywhere in Europe, doing his best to destroy such prestige as France still retained.

He secretly supported the revolution in Spain that drove Isabella II, a friend of Napoleon III and Eugénie, from the throne and placed Marshal Prim in power. From that time on Prim and Bismarck were to work together hand and glove.

In a speech in the Reichstag in November, 1868, the Prussian Chancellor came forward as a champion of the independence of nationalities, so stealing a thunder that down to that time Napoleon III had considered his own. Carol of Roumania, in other words, Karl of Hohenzollern, owed his crown to France. He now forgot that obligation and turned towards Germany. He wrote to Bismarck, January 27, 1868:

"Prussia will at all times find in me a zealous representative of her interests in the Near East."

And to his father, Prince Anton von Hohenzollern, he wrote in a tone of satisfaction:

"France has been losing ground here rapidly of late, and all that France loses Prussia gains."

Carol's chief adviser was the Prussian consul at Bucharest, Kayserling. At the express request of Bismarck he dismissed his prime minister, Bratianu, who was too much of a Francophile to suit Berlin.

The troubles in Crete had degenerated into an open conflict between Greece and the Sultan. Napoleon III was unwilling to intervene for fear of hurting Russia's feelings. There again Bismarck stole the limelight and called a conference of the powers in Paris. The conference ruled in favor of the Sublime Porte and ordered Greece to sever all connections with the Cretan rebels.

A worse defeat still for France was the matter of the Belgian railways. Two lines in the Belgian system, the Liège-Limbourg and the great Luxembourg, were leased to a French company, the Railways of the East. Did Napoleon III actually see in that contract a roundabout way of bringing France and Belgium closer together, as a preparation of the ground for at least a customs' union? That was the belief in Belgium, and King Leopold and Frère-Orlan, the prime minister, objected to the arrangement. The French press burst into angry protest. Ordinarily quite self-contained in emergencies, the Emperor this time lost his temper too. In a letter to Niel (February 19, 1869) he declared:

"A government, like an individual, is obliged to accept a challenge when the provocation is gross and deliberate. . . . Belgium is acting thus arrogantly only because Prussia is standing behind her. In such circumstances, to try to be accommodating or to defer to an insulting procedure is to forfeit any legitimate influence we may have in the eyes of Europe. Is war to come of this disagreement? I do not know. I do know that we ought to act as though war were to come of it."

Niel was for emphatic action and repeated that he was ready. But Bismarck was not the only one standing behind Belgium. Clarendon was there too, speaking for England. However, Clarendon was not looking for trouble. He politely interposed, deftly smoothing ruffled furs on both sides. Napoleon III thought things over and finally gave in. However, he thought he ought to try at least to drag Frère-Orlans, who had come to Paris to negotiate, into an offensive-

defensive alliance. There too he failed. Belgium had been neutralized by the Treaty of 1832. She refused to be enticed into the orbit
of French power politics, and both London and Berlin congratulated
her officially on her stand.

An alliance! An alliance with somebody, somewhere! That was
the besetting thought of Napoleon III, who had no slightest doubt
that sooner or later the showdown with Bismarck would have to
come. The later it came the better! He was anxious to gain time
in order to separate the states of South Germany from Prussia and
to enable Austria to make good her losses in the last war. Gramont,
the French ambassador in Vienna, and Metternich the Austrian ambassador in Paris, were both actively promoting a formal treaty of
alliance. The Emperor of Austria himself dropped a significant remark. In Strasbourg on his way to Paris to visit the World's Fair,
he said to General Ducrot:

"I hope, General, that some day we shall find ourselves marching
side by side."

But, really, that was polite prattle! Von Beust, Francis Joseph's
prime minister, wanted just a defensive alliance—for the time being
at least. He was afraid that France might get him into hot water
before the Austrian army was reorganized. He was also afraid that
any close accord between Vienna and Paris might be met by a still
closer accord between Berlin and St. Petersburg.

If Italy would only behave! A combination uniting Italy, Austria
and France would make everything easy in Europe—both the Tuileries and the Hofburg agreed on that. As a matter of fact, Victor
Emmanuel seemed inclined to consider such a thing—only the presence of the French troops in Rome was holding him back. His aide-
de-camp, General Türr, came to Paris and then went on to Vienna
"to stake out the ground." Türr was a Hungarian patriot. On being
condemned to death in Hungary he had gone to Italy and seen
service under Garibaldi. He was intelligent, daring and very friendly
to France. Francis Joseph had given him a pardon for the three
death sentences he had received in Budapest.

A long and complicated series of negotiations ensued, occupying
almost the whole of the year 1869. Not much is known about them
since they were conducted by the sovereigns and their prime ministers in private, the ambassadors and the foreign offices being entirely
left out. What is certain is that the Roman Question again spoiled

everything. Napoleon III felt that his private honor had been pledged to Pius IX personally, and that he would be unable to withdraw from Rome as long as Piux IX lived. The three sovereigns got no farther than a general understanding. They exchanged autograph letters in which they declared that "the idea of an alliance between France, Austria and Italy appealed to them, since such a union would erect a powerful barrier against unjust pretensions from any quarter and contribute to establishing peace in Europe on a sounder basis."

The three signatories took it for granted that talks would be resumed as soon as the Pope died, since his death, which was believed to be close at hand, would make it possible to get the Roman Question out of the way.

All this was not, of course, an alliance. It was the rough draft of an alliance. The only thing needed was to give it final and binding form. Napoleon III could have done that with one word. That word he could not bring himself to utter, partly because of a point of honor that has its touch of nobleness; but partly too because he was afraid of rousing a storm among his Catholics—to say nothing of the scenes his wife would make at home.

So then—military precautions? What was going on in that direction? General Le Boeuf was anxious above all else to please. He loosened the screws that Niel had been assiduously clamping down. He could see no reason to worry. Like most of the French generals he had great confidence in the dash of the army's rank-and-file, taking little stock in the intensive training of staff-officers which Prussia was developing to a high finish. He was inclined to defer, also, to public opinion, which was growing more and more markedly pacific. The average Frenchman did not think there were going to be any more wars. He refused to consider such an odious possibility. An "International League for Peace" had been founded by Frédéric Passy. It held two conventions in Paris, one in 1868 and the other in 1869, and voted resolutions of protest against the unbearable burdens of standing armies. Preachers, literary men, editorial writers, vied with one another in predicting an era of peace and brotherly love. Lines that Michelet wrote in 1868 [1] are typical of the general trend in French thinking at that moment:

"France is delighted to see a united Italy and a united Germany

[1] *Histoire de la Révolution française*, preface, 4.

as new neighbors. She extends her hand to them in hearty greeting. The important thing to note is that on both sides of the Rhine people who are worth while despise war, well knowing that war is not a matter of personal worth or courage, but a competition in mechanics between a Chassepot and a Delvigne."

No war now! Never another war! Such the dream that ingenuous souls dream in every generation—only to find that the violence of men always upsets it!

To be sure there were far-seeing minds that did not share the general illusion. Prévost-Paradol, a dazzling writer and thinker, wrote a book at just this time called *France nouvelle* in which he declared that war was certain, predestined.

"The more one thinks of the matter the more one is forced to the conclusion that love of peace, calm reflection, any amount of good will on the part of those in power, cannot prevent a clash between a Prussia that is expanding and a France that is shrinking within her ancient boundaries and has lost all hope." Considering the chance for disaster he added: "Victory may desert us . . . and defeat would be the tomb of French greatness." Since the country was losing its moral and material stamina, it was "facing the most formidable test that had ever confronted it."

The Emperor and his chief advisers were not as despondent as that; but they had adequate data for gauging the reality and extent of the peril in reports which Benedetti, the French ambassador, and Stoffel, the French military attaché, kept sending home from Berlin.

Benedetti could not be accused of any unreasoning attachment to the old order in Europe. He had expressed positive approval of the recent territorial changes. But he saw things clearly and could only denounce Prussia's greed for power and the means she intended to employ in order to force her will upon all peoples of Germanic language.

Colonel Stoffel was an accurate, perspicacious observer, and he had been more and more on the alert since Sadowa. He cautioned and he warned. The Prussian military machine was, he said, something altogether new and incredibly powerful, something perfectly adjusted to modern conditions of warfare. No army in Europe could be compared with it in numbers of men, in training, in equipment, in excellence of command.

"People in France," he wrote, July 22, 1868, "are densely ignorant of everything pertaining to Prussia." And he went on to describe the motive power and inner workings of Germany's mighty instrument of war. "Watch that Prussian General Staff!" he repeatedly urged.

He repeated himself so often that people in the war office in Paris grew tired of his always crying wolf. The Emperor kept sending him questionnaires to fill out and several times called him home for long conversations. But the Colonel passed in Paris for an alarmist and his sound and far-seeing reports were allowed to pile up, unutilized, unconsulted, in the files of the War ministry.

All Prussia, by that time, had been remoulded, so to say, into a military pyramid that had the King for its peak. William I was seventy-one years old. He was truly nothing but a soldier, setting his military duties before everything else. He was part and parcel of the army. Everything human vanished from before his eyes the moment Prussian glory was concerned. Then he turned into a visionary and a mystic who could think of the Frenchman only as the born enemy of the German race.

The Queen of Prussia disapproved of war, and her son Friedrich, the Prince Royal, actually loathed the idea of war. Neither of them had the slightest influence. Bismarck and Moltke were the only ones for whom the King had any ears.

Moltke, the chief of staff, often carried the day over Bismarck. Smooth-skinned, as lean as a mummy, Moltke was absorbed in one sinister, devouring passion—work, work for the army. After his triumph over Austria in 1866 he had focussed all his thought, time and energy on the coming struggle with France. In April, 1868, he visited Lorraine to inspect the frontier area as likely to provide battlegrounds in the future, and he said to a man from Baden—as Ducrot reported to Frossard in October in Strasbourg:

"When we are free to do as we see fit with Alsace, and we shall be before long, we can make one fine province out of all this country between the Vosges and the Black Forest." [1]

Through a minutely diligent espionage service which he personally directed the German chief of staff possessed cruelly accurate information on the weaknesses of the French army. He had no doubt whatever that he could beat it the moment the signal was given. There was no trace of vanity or boastfulness in such self-

[1] *Papiers des Tuileries*, I, 225.

PRINCE OTTO VON BISMARCK

1815-1898

confidence. It was based on his knowledge of the excellence of the weapon that he had forged, with the help of Roon, the Minister of War, and which he was bringing closer and closer to perfection every day. Moltke was more of the scientist than the general proper. He never liked to gamble on circumstances.

"When you have made all arrangements carefully," he said, "things cannot fail to work out as you propose."

By 1869 he had fixed on his plan of campaign down to the last detail. He knew that when Bismarck, or the King, gave the word for war, he would merely touch a button and the gigantic machine that he had constructed would start in motion with irresistible precision and power.

The greatness of a country seems to depend at certain periods in history on a felicitous combination of superior talents. Bismarck worked in the diplomatic sphere with the same methodical thoroughness that Moltke displayed in the military sphere. He bent every effort towards isolating France in Europe. He did not think there was any chance of her finding an ally in Italy. The Roman Question would always be there to prevent that. All the same, to make quite sure, he spent a good deal of money on Italian newspapermen. He balmed Francis Joseph's hurt feelings in every way possible and effected a surface reconciliation, at least, both with the Austrian Emperor and with Baron von Beust. He strove to make the accord between Russia and Prussia stronger. The two countries had many common interests, especially in Poland. There was nothing to divide them in the Near East. England was more and more losing interest in the Continent. The outlook in that direction could not be better. Disraeli had a personal liking for Bismarck.

So Europe would be either friendly or neutral. South Germany would present no difficulties once the call was sounded. The submission of the country to Prussian leadership was progressing every day. Hesse and Baden had already joined the Federation of the North. Bavaria and Württemberg were, to be sure, still holding off. These were Catholic districts and very self-centered. They did not like militarization, and much less the tax burden that militarization required. But *once France had declared war* they would have to march with Prussia—they were bound to do so by the defensive alliance they had signed after Sadowa. France had to be the aggressor—that was a capital point. In the opposite case the pledge of Bavaria and Württemberg would not come into force.

Bismarck was going to bear all that in mind, in July, 1870!

The tottering cabinet that had been patched together after the elections was at once attacked by an aggressive opposition, and it could not decide offhand just what its attitude towards the republicans was to be. A number of the ministers, Forcade for instance, were for energetic action, in other words, for repression, with all the risks that a repressive policy might entail. Others, such as Magne or Chasseloup-Laubat, were for conciliation.

These latter thought that the government might be stronger if Emile Ollivier were a member of it—he was on a tour, at the moment, in the south. Ollivier, however, declined this offer as he had the earlier one. He did not want a mere portfolio. What he wanted was power. His dream was to be the artisan of a new policy that would rejuvenate the decrepit Empire and allow the dynasty to take root.

Clément Duvernois had been the go-between in the negotiations. Ollivier wrote to him from St. Tropez:

"If the Emperor thinks he ought to use me, he should do so in the way that would be most profitable to himself. He should insert a note in the *Journal Officiel* ordering me to make up a ministry." And he ended on a note of characteristic cocksureness: "I am ready to come to grips with the revolution." [1]

He had been ready for a long time. The hesitation had been all on Napoleon III's side. The Emperor liked Ollivier and the essential lines in his thinking. He appreciated his talents as an orator. What he was afraid of was Ollivier's inexperience in public affairs. He felt, however, that if he were ever going to take the advice that Morny had given him of yore and try, with any chance of succeeding, to work the dictatorial Empire over into a constitutional Empire, there was now no time to lose.

He sent for Clément Duvernois, who was acting as his semi-official factotum. Suppose Duvernois were to drop down into Provence and have a talk with Ollivier!

On October 31 Ollivier, in half-disguise, called on the Emperor at Compiègne. It was a long interview. In the course of it the two threshed out all their views. Napoleon III was for keeping most of

1 *Papiers des Tuileries*, I, 257 (October 2, 1869).

the ministers then in office. He had gotten used to working with them. He trusted them. Ollivier wanted a brand new outfit.

They had not come to an agreement by the time they separated, but the dickering went on, with Duvernois shuttling back and forth between them. Just what sort of men did Ollivier have in mind for the new cabinet?

"Young ones!" answered Ollivier. "It will take men of the rising generation to save Your Majesty's son. The old timers you now have about you are hopelessly self-centered. They can think only of themselves."

Unfortunately, as was apparent now, Ollivier was more or less of a lone wolf. There was no particular group on which he could rely. He would have to turn to the big men in the Third Party, Orleanists yesterday, Orleanists tomorrow, Buffet, say, or Daru—Daru, the relentless critic of the *coup d'état!*

Napoleon III all but lost his temper.

"Those men? I will have nothing to do with men who do not love the masses! Besides, I made that mistake once before. I began with the old rue de Poitiers. I am not going to end with the young rue de Poitiers!"

So really then—the thought struck the Emperor at the moment, though everything had long been pointing in that direction: Emile Ollivier was not the man he should entrust with power. The man was Thiers! That old warhorse would build him a cabinet that would be twice as strong and have greater prestige both at home and abroad. Thiers, moreover, would be more than ready to make the compromises required for bringing the imperialists and liberals together. There was only one drawback. Napoleon III could not endure Thiers as a person. He had always thought of him as his private and particular enemy.

Thiers, for his part, was in favor of falling back on Ollivier, whom he found not at all unattractive. He said of the young liberal leader:

"Ollivier? Well, Ollivier is young. He has charm, he has endowments. What he will never acquire is age and character."

Which was a way of saying that Thiers was really thinking of serving as Ollivier's coach and prompter. He wanted the power, but not the responsibility!

The Legislative Body met on November 29th (1869) as the Emperor finally had decreed, the deputies this time appearing without uniforms. The Emperor read them a speech that was rather pathetic and appealing—something very much in the tone of '48:

"France wants liberty but she also wants order. I can answer for the order. Help me, gentlemen, to give her liberty."

The assembly settled down, in the course of the early sessions, into four groups: first the Right, or Arcadians (so-called from the fact that they met habitually in rooms on the rue de l'Arcade; they were partisans of the absolutist Empire); second, the Right Center; third, the Left Center; finally the republican Left.

Emile Ollivier was continuing to reconnoitre the ground. He concluded that he could count on the Right Center and on some of the Arcadians. The Left Center, which contained Buffet and Daru, showed itself not a little condescending. Ollivier mistrusted that group—and the Emperor more than he did. After three weeks of head-scratching, acquiescing, wriggling, dickering, Napoleon III finally decided to entrust the tiller of his bark of state to Emile Ollivier.

"My ministers," he wrote Ollivier on the 27th of December (1869), "have now handed in their resignations. I therefore appeal to your patriotism and request you to name the individuals who will make up a homogeneous government around you and who will faithfully represent a majority in the Legislative Body."

Four days later the Emperor made the same announcement to the assembled organs of the state, whom he was entertaining at a general New Year's reception at the Tuileries:

"In sharing my responsibilities with the Legislative Body I shall feel more confidence in facing the difficulties which the future is to bring. When, after completing a large part of a long journey, a traveller lays aside a portion of the load he has been carrying, he does not feel any the weaker—he feels much stronger, much better able to go on."

Ollivier experienced the greatest difficulty in working out his combination. The Right Center insisted that Buffet and Daru be taken in. The Emperor was finally induced to swallow the pill, and the ministry was in shape on January 2nd. Ollivier took the Guardianship of the Seals, Daru Foreign Affairs, Buffet Finance. The Emperor had reserved the privilege of filling War, the Navy and the Imperial Household himself. He kept Le Boeuf, Admiral Régault de Grenouilly and Marshal Vaillant in those posts—Le Boeuf was to be named a marshal on March 24th (1870). Parieu became president of the Council of State.

So, after so many years of waiting, Emile Ollivier found himself at the helm of affairs in France, and he applied himself in all enthusiasm and self-confidence to the thankless task of crossing breeds between dictatorship and freedom.

"We will arrange a comfortable old age for the Emperor," he kept repeating.

And he meant it. He had eagerly aspired to power, but that ambition had undoubtedly had its disinterested side. He had wanted power not so much for power's sake as because he saw in it an opportunity to work out his idea of establishing a limited monarchy permanently in France. Ollivier was undoubtedly a well-educated man and a great worker. On the other hand, he attached too much importance to words. He was inclined to overestimate his own capacities. At bottom he was ingenious rather than profound, and naïve besides.

One can imagine the two of them—Napoleon III and his new minister, sitting together there at a fireside in the Tuileries in the cold January of The Terrible Year, swapping ideas like two old cronies, the aging Emperor reborn to hope, Ollivier, youthful, eager, eloquent, trying in all earnestness to work out a new order that would last, and bring happiness to France.

The "Ministry of Good Intentions," as it came to be called, began its work under excellent auspices. During the first days there was no doubt anywhere that it would be a success. Whenever Ollivier appeared in the Place Vendôme he attracted crowds of admirers in which long-standing republicans, such as Prévost-Paradol or J. J. Weiss, could be seen cheering along with leaders of old assemblies, such as Guizot or Odilon Barrot. At that time the fusion that Ollivier hoped to achieve seemed about to materialize. The business and professional classes, the Catholics, not a few republicans, approved of the ministry. The Orleanist salons stopped grumbling for a moment. During the last years the Academy had been toning down its opposition to the Empire, though its hostility was still overt enough. Many of the elections had been distasteful to the government—Dufaure, Prévost-Paradol, Jules Favre, A. Barbier, but relations with the Tuileries had always been the perfection of courtesy in outward forms. Now the Academy elected Emile Ollivier to the chair of Lamartine, and that choice was taken as the sign of a complete reconciliation. The Empire seemed to have taken on a new lease of life and the Emperor's power to have been strengthened rather than weakened by the limitations that had been thrust upon it.

The Emperor continued to preside over the Council. Of it Ollivier was just a member, though the leading one. The Councillors debated and voted freely in Napoleon III's presence. The Empress was no longer attending. She claimed to have "dropped politics for good." If anyone asked a favor of her, she would pout and answer bitterly:

"Go and see some minister! I have no influence any more!"

The first moves of the new ministry were good ones. Daru promised the Senate to answer any interpellations frankly and fully. A circular of Chevandier de Valdrôme, the Minister of the Interior, urged the prefects "to deal with honest men of all parties with equal impartiality." Haussmann's prodigious services had been blemished by office irregularities. He was removed and replaced, too summarily perhaps. Ollivier pleaded for the support of all groups in the Legislative Body. His majority seemed very sound. All the same, he had not entirely won the Arcadians, who wanted to keep the old dictatorship, nor the republicans, who still regarded him as a turncoat. Gambetta noisily rebuffed his advances (January 10, 1870): "If you are relying on our help to effect a fusion between liberty and the Empire, you need not expect to get it. Between the Republic of '48 and the Republic of the future, you are just a hyphen, and that hyphen we intend to ignore."

On that same day, January 10th, a lamentable incident occurred, restirring bitter hatreds and all but threatening the existence of the Empire by way of repercussion.

Lucien Bonaparte had a son, Prince Pierre Bonaparte, who was therefore own cousin to Napoleon III. The Emperor had kept the man on the outer margins of the imperial family in view of his tumultuous past and brutal temper, obstinately refusing to make use of him in any way. Pierre Bonaparte lived a half-savage life at Auteuil, subsisting on an income of 100,000 francs that the Tuileries had assigned him, plus special subsidies at irregular intervals. Through a paper called the *Avenir de la Corse* the Prince launched an attack, early in January, 1870, on the *Revanche,* a paper in which articles by Paschal Grousset, a friend and collaborator of Rochefort, often appeared. Prince Pierre used language so incredibly extreme that Grousset sent him his seconds. These were Ulrich de Fonvielle and a young twenty-year-old apprentice reporter, Victor Noir, short, thick-set, dark complexioned—"an Andalusian muleteer."

The Prince consented to see them. He had been expecting seconds from Rochefort. On learning that they came from Grousset he replied:

"I am fighting Rochefort. I am not going to fight his tools."

Whereupon he made a movement which Victor Noir interpreted as the start of a blow. Noir anticipated with a sound cuff on the Prince's ear. Pierre Bonaparte always went about armed. He whipped out a revolver and fired. The bullet entered Noir's chest and grazed his heart. He found strength to get out of the room and part way down the stairs, with Fonvielle following after. From the head of the stairs Bonaparte, in a raging fury, fired twice at Fonvielle without hitting him. Noir collapsed and lay dead on the bottom step.

The next day the *Marseillaise* appeared with its front page bordered in black, and in the inset Rochefort wrote:

"I was once so weak as to imagine that a Bonaparte could be something besides an assassin. . . .

"For eighteen years now France has been in the bloody hands of cut-throats who, not content with shooting republicans down in the streets with grape, now entice them into cowardly traps to murder them comfortably at home.

"Citizens of France, don't you really think you have had enough of it?"

The paper was confiscated, but already Paris was seething white hot. Rochefort rose in the Legislative Body and demanded judges for the murderer of Victor Noir.

"What I want to know," he cried, "is whether we are dealing with Bonapartes or Borgias."

Emile Ollivier answered with dignity and restraint:

"Let us not exaggerate the significance of what has happened. A murder has been committed by a person of high rank. He will be prosecuted. . . . As for the efforts that are being made to work up a popular disturbance, we view them with equanimity. We are the law, we are justice, we are moderation, we are liberty. If you push us that far, we can also be force."

The majority applauded but the extreme Left jeered and howled in angry disapprobation.

The revolutionaries tried, in fact, to take advantage of Victor Noir's funeral to "work up a day."

"Tomorrow," cried Flourens, "we must conquer or die. 1848 began with a corpse. Today we have Victor Noir's."

The government nipped the uprising in the bud. The burial was transferred from Père Lachaise to Neuilly. On the 12th of January more than a hundred thousand people marched past the unpretentious coffin as it lay in state. Flourens and his friends tried to get possession of the body and drag it to Paris in a wagon. Rochefort and Delescluze wisely discounseled that gesture. Troops in strong force held the Champs Elysée. Everything was ready for a merciless suppression. The Emperor spent the whole day at the Tuileries in his uniform ready to mount his horse at a moment's notice.

Pierre Bonaparte was arrested and remanded for trial to the High Court which had jurisdiction over crimes by princes. At the same time procedure against Rochefort was demanded in the Chamber. He was sentenced in contumacy to six months in prison for insulting the Emperor and fomenting civil war. He was not arrested till February 7th.

On that occasion Flourens again tried to start an uprising. Barricades were thrown up at Belleville and in the lower Temple. The police carried them, not without difficulty. The disturbances were prolonged and extended by the International, by the Blanquists, and by that swarm of agitators that seems to issue from the ground on every stormy day and set out joyously to explode bombs and apply the torch on every hand. There were parades almost daily along the boulevards. At banquets toasts were proposed "to the merciful bullet" that would rid France of Napoleon III. There were strikes in the Creusot factories, in the North and at Marseilles. In order not to be overridden Ollivier was obliged to order many arrests.

In spite of all the harassing from the Left in the Legislative Body, Ollivier tried to pour oil on the rough waters by a series of very liberal measures in which anybody in good faith could only have recognized the advent of a truly new era: repeal of the general safety law; repeal of press restrictions; appointments of commissions to reorganize municipal and provincial governments; to review higher education; to revise labor legislation; to study the question of a permanent system of government for Algeria.

Jules Favre none the less bitterly assailed the ministry:

"You are the outposts of the personal dictatorship. You are mounting guard over it to create an impression that we have a parliamentary system when really we have no such thing."

And cruelly he called attention to the hazy program of the ministry, its lack of cohesion, and therefore its impotence.

Jules Grévy proceeded to embarrass the ministry still further by pressing the question of official candidacies. Ollivier declared that the ministry intended to retain the right to designate its preferences but that it would not use official candidacies proper. It would remain strictly neutral in elections.

That brought the friends of Rouher and the Empress to their feet, men like Pinard and Jérôme David, who foresaw an early return to personal power. Clément Duvernois was as angry as a hornet at not receiving a portfolio. He joined in the outcry.

And yet, when it came to voting, all the Left, from Favre to Gambetta, supported the government. The fact that Ollivier had such men behind him brought an astonished frown from the Emperor. He also disapproved of dropping official candidacies. Ollivier called a cabinet meeting and talked of resigning. The Emperor yielded.

"But all the same," he remarked by way of admonition, "you had better not force my hand too often."

Daru had always lived in an ultra-Orleanist environment and he had never recovered from his mistrust of Napoleon III. With a round head, white hair, white mustache and beard, he had the stiff, erect carriage of a retired army officer. For that matter he was courtesy and geniality itself and people who got to know him found him an exceedingly good fellow. He was the archtype of the bourgeois parliamentarian, a trifle set in his ideas but of unimpeachable integrity.

On assuming his duties at the Quai d'Orsay he took the line of extreme caution.

"I want peace," he said, "and France wants peace. Great changes have occurred in Europe during these past twenty years. They are not changes of our making, but our policy should be to maintain the *status quo*. We must avoid stirring things up in Europe."

Cooperation with England if possible! If England was unwilling, then an understanding with Russia! Italy should be reassured, Austria deferred to—Austria was "our most dependable ally." Reserve towards Prussia! Under any and all circumstances avoid trouble or else nip it in the bud!

General Fleury, Napoleon III's closest confidant, was sent to St. Petersburg as ambassador. He soon became persona grata there. Verdière, one of Fleury's attachés, wrote (January 25, 1870):

"The Czar has conceived a great liking for Fleury. He is always taking him bear-hunting and crowds him in beside him on one hip in his single-seated sleigh. That is a real sign of imperial favor."

But Fleury's popularity did not prevent the Czar and the King of Prussia from being thicker than ever—letters, decorations, confidential messages, rained back and forth. However, a chance presented itself for offsetting the wiles of Bismarck and regaining Alexander's active friendship. Gortchakov suggested that France and Russia recast the Treaty of Paris, in other words, that Russia be given back her freedom of action in the Black Sea and the Straits.

Napoleon III would not agree to that, probably because he was afraid of angering England. The full weight of this mistake was soon to be felt by France.

Daru meantime was far too cautious. His order to Fleury was "inaction pure and simple."

"There are hardly any projects of any importance to be formulated," he wrote (March 1, 1870). "Your efforts should halt at coming to a general understanding by way of conversations."

He allowed the still pending question of Schleswig to drop, manifesting at every opportunity in Berlin the utmost eagerness for a reconciliation. Emile Ollivier shared this outlook. To a reporter for the *Gazette* of Cologne he declared:

"In our eyes there is no German question."

The better to emphasize the French resolve on peace for the benefit of European opinion, Daru took a very positive step. Lord Clarendon was back in the Foreign Office in London. He had all along expressed himself in favor of lightening military burdens all over Europe. Daru informed him that France was "willing to disarm." Though Napoleon III objected Daru went farther still. On the 13th of February he announced that the 1870 drawing of recruits would be reduced by 10,000 men. Lord Loftus, the British ambassador in Berlin, at once called on Bismarck. The Chancellor stopped him short. He refused even to consider the idea of limiting armaments. Military systems were too different in the different countries, he explained. There would be no adequate way of checking up on them.

Stoffel was to comment on this attitude in his report of February 28th:

"Prussia is not a country that possesses an army. Prussia is an army that possesses a country." There was no hope of anybody's following the example of France. Far from reducing her own forces France should "arm to the teeth."

Unfortunately Stoffel's opinion found no echo whatever in the ministry. Ollivier and Daru both went ahead on the assumption that no danger was in sight.

Napoleon III was now a constitutional sovereign, but he could not get over his habit of keeping his own counsel. Unbeknown to his ministers he resumed negotiations with the court of Austria. Archduke Albert, the victor of Custozza and a cousin to Francis Joseph, came to Paris incognito and the Emperor had a number of long talks with him in private. They came to an agreement on the general outlines of a plan of campaign for a hypothetical situation in which Austria and France would be fighting together against Prussia. On his departure the Archduke promised to use all his influence with Francis Joseph to persuade him to conclude the formal treaty of alliance that was still in abeyance. That was in April, 1870.

Following his policy of caution Daru had momentarily avoided any participation whatever in the deliberations of the Oecumenical Council that had opened in December at the Vatican. Discussions there had borne, for one thing, on the new dogma of the Pope's infallibility; and then on declarations by the Holy See that seemed to hint that the Church claimed authority over all acts pertaining to social life and was absolutely independent of secular governments. Daru was a Catholic, but a liberal one, in matters of dogma. He was a spiritual disciple of the Montalembert who was sitting up on his

deathbed at just that moment to protest against "the craven servility of the new ultramontanism in France." [1]

Daru now brought before the Council of Ministers a note of his
that voiced a mild protest against any ecclesiastical interference in
the affairs of secular governments. Cardinal Antonelli, the Pope's
prime minister, replied that the Holy See had merely been trying
to formulate principles that had come down from long-standing
tradition and involved no threat to any temporal authority. That
was a very correct way of tabling the whole question; and both the
Emperor and Ollivier were of opinion that the matter should be
allowed to lie on the table. But Daru was deeply interested in religious questions. He drew up a memorandum and had it approved
by all the Catholic powers. It requested the Pontiff to delete from
the texts that were to be submitted to the Oecumenical Council any
articles that "seemed to manifest an intent to subject civil society
to the control of the clergy."

Pius IX received the instrument graciously but held his ground,
declining to bring the memorandum before the Oecumenical
Council. Daru's departure from foreign affairs was soon to relieve
the Pope of any embarrassment, in case he had felt any. The French
government as a whole was not anxious to get involved just then
in any such dispute, and it was thereafter to confine itself to merely
watching the proceedings of the council in Rome.

The revolutionary agitation gradually died down. In March,
1870, the government seemed to be enjoying expectant and hopeful
support not only from the ruling classes but from the country at
large. The business world had started functioning again. The constitutional Empire had ceased to be debated. The Right opposition
had grown resigned to freedom.

The trial of Pierre Bonaparte opened before the High Court on
March 21st at Tours. The battle was a stirring one. The witnesses,
Paschal Grousset, Rochefort and Ulrich de Fonvielle, and the attorneys, Laurier and Floquet, far overstepped their respective rôles to
arraign imperial tyranny. The state's attorney, Grandparret, had no
difficulty in convincing the judges that Victor Noir had provoked
the deadly counter-attack by the prince. Pierre Bonaparte was acquitted of murder but sentenced to pay 25,000 francs damages and
interest to his victim's family. The republican press cried scandal

1 La Gorce, *Histoire du Second Empire*, VI, 68.

but the Emperor cut the uproar short by ordering his wretched cousin to go and live abroad for a good long time.

The return to a parliamentary system had made a change in the organization of the Senate indispensable. The prerogative of constitutional legislation still remained with the higher house, which was made up of notables nominated by the Emperor and had no tie whatever with the electing citizenry. To eliminate this anomaly the ministry suggested to the Emperor that the Senate be made a second legislative chamber while all constitutive powers should be restored to the people. The Emperor consented with the proviso that senators should continue to be appointed by him. His decision was made known through a letter to the Guardian of the Seals which commissioned Ollivier to prepare the appropriate text for action by the Senate.

In order to embarrass the ministry, Rouher and the rest of the senators declined to assume responsibility for such a far-reaching change and asked that the people be consulted, as had been done in 1852 when the Constitution as a whole had been adopted. They figured that a favorable plebiscite would give the Emperor a new prestige and tend to strengthen the dynasty.

Napoleon III himself was not in favor of the plebiscite at first. He thought it would lay too much emphasis on the evolution of the Empire in a constitutional direction. But Daru, unbeknown to Buffet, urged him vigorously to accept it. Ollivier took Daru's position and the Emperor gave in.

"Risk nothing and you gain nothing!" he said.

"Yes," answered Ollivier, "let's take a risk."

But was not the plebiscite, the appeal to the people, the very negation of the parliamentary system? The Legislative Body got excited and the Left, speaking through Grévy and Gambetta, underlined this indirect backward move towards despotism.

The Left Center disliked the plebiscite almost as much as the republicans. Buffet and Daru represented the group in the ministry. Having thought things over more maturely, they also became much alarmed. Buffet suggested an amendment which would make any change in the Constitution impossible without express authorization from the Chambers. He saw in this device a way to safeguard liberal institutions. The Emperor refused. Strictly, austerely scrupulous, Buffet at once handed in his resignation. Daru followed suit a few days later. Ollivier was all engrossed at the time with the debate on the resolution in the Senate. He did not realize at once just what his ministry was losing in terms of weight and prestige through the withdrawal of the two Orleanists.

Segris took the portfolio of Finance, Ollivier Foreign Affairs *ad interim*. He wanted to restore Education to Duruy, but his colleagues objected, in fear of angering the Catholics.

The new Constitution was passed by the Senate on the 20th of April, 1870. It is an interesting document in that it represents, after all the gropings and compromises, the final form that the imperial system was to assume in France. The Senate became a Chamber of Peers. The Council of State continued to prepare prospective legislation on governmental initiative, though the two assemblies retained their own right of initiative concurrently. Financial measures were to be voted first by the Legislative Body and then submitted to the Senate. The right to declare war and make treaties still resided with the Emperor. Ministers were still responsible to the Emperor, who was in turn "responsible to the French people, to whom he always had the right to appeal." The Constitutional power was to be exercised by plebiscite, the nation, however, having the right to answer only questions which were formulated by the Emperor.

This Constitution, evidently, was an amalgam of liberal traditions and dictatorial principles. It left the sovereign far too much power. As it was, however, it represented a very considerable progress, and had it remained in force it might have been perfected. Unfortunately it was to have a bare four months of life.

On the 8th of May, 1870, the voters were asked to accept or reject a plebiscite worded as follows:

"The people approves of the liberal reforms that have been introduced into the Constitution by the Emperor since 1860, with the concurrence of the great organs of the state, and ratifies the senatus-consultum of the 20th of April, 1870."

The question in that form was misleading in that an answer of a single "yes" or a single "no" was required to two separate and distinct questions: the question, first, as to whether past changes were acceptable, and the question, second, as to whether the imperial system were to be retained. The government hoped to benefit by the ambiguity.

The Emperor opened the campaign with a message that was posted in all towns and villages. He asked for an affirmative answer in order to "lay the spectre of revolution, to ground liberty and the public peace on solid foundations and to facilitate the transmission of the crown to my son."

After all, it was in order to save his son's throne that he had been making so many and such far-reaching sacrifices. But what he was really afraid of was lack of public interest. A small vote would be tantamount to a repudiation of the Empire. The government, therefore, bent all its energies towards obtaining mass results. The clergy, which was not all of one mind, was urged to rouse the indifferent. Office-holders, big and little, were mobilized.

"Remind all judges of the peace and all magistrates," Ollivier telegraphed on April 30th, "that I should be glad to see them serving on plebiscite committees."

He was backed by the members of the Right and Right Center in parliament. They organized a Central Committee under the chairmanship of the Duc d'Albufera, which comprised Jérôme David, Pinard, Chesnelong and Mackau. The committee had branch offices all over the country.

In the opposing camp forces were as usual divided. The Comte de Chambord requested faithful legitimists to "repudiate the plebiscite" by answering "no," or by keeping away from the polls. Many legitimists, however, were to vote "yes" under the influence of the clergy. The Left Centers also were to vote "yes" very generally in spite of the hostile attitude of Thiers and Dufaure, and friends of these latter.

The republicans were the only ones to organize an active campaign and the campaign they organized was active indeed.

"If you remember the lessons that events have taught," the manifesto read, "if you have not forgotten eighteen years of oppression, if you have not forgotten Mexico, or Sadowa, or a debt increased by five billions, or budgets in excess of two billions, or conscription, or heavy taxes, or big army drawings, you cannot vote 'yes.' "

They had committees everywhere. Everywhere they held meetings. These were not seldom so disorderly that they overreached their purposes, frightening many voters whose minds were not made up into the government's camp.

"I am told," Ollivier telegraphed to the state's attorney at Aix

(May 1, 1870), "that meetings in Marseilles have been intolerably violent. Do not hesitate to make examples, but strike preferably at the heads. Visit your wrath upon the lawyers, the so-called gentlemen, rather than upon poor folks from the masses."

The republicans tried to break down discipline in the army and navy. Soldiers and sailors also could vote, and they were showered with pamphlets, almanacs and packages of tobacco wrapped in obscene philippics. The International supported the republicans in all the large towns. Ollivier manifested not a few signs of hysteria. He ordered the arrest of all the International's leaders, telegraphing, for instance, to the state's attorney at Lyons (April 30, 1870):

"Arrest all individuals who are directing the International at once. We are prosecuting them in Paris. The situation is getting serious."

To his prosecuting officers in Paris he sent the order:

"Do not hesitate to prosecute any newspaper that to your knowledge contains an incitement to civil war or an insult to the Emperor. We cannot sit with our arms folded when the revolution is overstepping all bounds."

To rouse the lukewarm the *Journal Officiel* announced that a man named Beaury had come on from London to assassinate the Emperor, that he had been arrested and had confessed. A quantity of bombs and cartridges were found in the shop of a cabinetmaker, and an inquiry was instituted to get to the bottom of the "great plot." A trick known of old, but which never fails to find someone who will resort to it and many to be fooled by it!

The first returns to come in during the evening and night after the voting were from the large cities and towns. They were such as to dismay intimates of the Emperor who had gathered about him at the Tuileries. Napoleon III alone retained his composure.

"The Parisians have always been great fault-finders," he said, "though I believe I have treated them less stingily than Mazarin ever did. Well, they vote against me the way they sang songs in his face—and much he could do about it! It's a privilege they have!"

The Empress, for her part, was exasperation personified and she was heard to say:

"War is now the only thing that can save the Empire from the revolution."

The Seine, including Paris, returned a vote of 138,000 aye's,

184,000 no's with 83,000 not voting. No's were in a large majority at Lyons, Marseilles, Bordeaux and Toulon. The armed forces as a whole responded fairly well—218,614 aye's to 47,757 no's; but the Toulouse garrison was so emphatically anti-imperial that its commander, General de Lorencez, felt called upon to write a letter of apology to the Emperor, deploring the decline of esprit de corps in his men. But once again rural France came to the Emperor's rescue with better than a two to one support: 7,336,000 aye's, 1,560,000 no's, 1,894,000 not voting.

To grasp the full significance of this statistic one should compare it with the vote at the regular elections the year before. To be sure, adding abstentions to the no's one gets a 100,000 increase in the vote hostile to the Emperor; but the favorable vote had increased by a good three millions. The Emperor had a way of laying aside his emotions and seeing facts as they were. He was delighted. The morning after the count he took the Empress by the arm and entered the Prince Imperial's bedroom.

"My child," he said, "this plebiscite—it's your coronation!" And gathering the boy into his arms he cried joyously: "Long live our little Emperor!"

On May 21st he formally proclaimed the expression of the nation's will in a ceremony in the States' Room in the Louvre. The sovereigns sat on a dais on two identical thrones, he in military uniform, she in a street costume. The little prince stood at his mother's knee in the uniform of a second-lieutenant. Grand dignitaries, cardinals, ambassadors, marshals, magistrates, ladies, formed a glittering maze of ermines, scarlets, gold braid, silks, all about the room. The Emperor looked younger by many years and his speech rang confidence again.

"The enemies of our institutions forced the question: the revolution or the Empire. The country has answered." He gave assurance that his government would "never deviate from the liberal path upon which it had entered," and then he added with a joyous ring in his voice: "More than ever today may we gaze fearlessly forward into the future."

The applause was long protracted. He, to tell the truth, was not a little stunned by his victory, and with him, in fact more so than he, the partisans of the dictatorial Empire. They thought the victory was their victory and they declared that the Liberal Empire had been repudiated. Napoleon III, in any event, felt strengthened, and began talking down to the ministry in a tone of greater condescension. Clément Duvernois, who had been shoved aside, now came back into high favor at the Tuileries. The most aggressive of the leaders on the imperialist Right, Jérôme David, thought he ought to have the presidency of the Legislative Body.

The republicans were very much depressed.

"The Empire is stronger than it ever was," Gambetta mourned.

"It has taken a new lease on life," echoed Jules Favre.

Then they turned on one another. Ernest Picard, the most moderate of the republicans, declared, with sixteen of his friends, that they would have nothing more to do with revolution in any form. They moved away from the republican Left which had Grévy for a leader. The Left from that moment became an assembly of "lost causers" and "die-hards."

The ministry still had to find a permanent successor for Daru in Foreign Affairs. Ollivier was inclined to hang on to the post himself. But the Emperor, having recovered some of his old independence, insisted on having an experienced diplomat. Ollivier then proposed Gramont, the Ambassador in Vienna. Napoleon III agreed.

"Why, yes," he said. "Gramont might answer as well as anybody else. We are not going to do anything anyway."

Nothing for the time being, at least! The Emperor had grown resigned to that attitude. Later on things might be different. He had not abandoned the idea of striking some alliance that would be capable of checking Bismarck. Informing Le Boeuf only, he sent General Lebrun, his aide-de-camp, to Vienna to fix on a definite plan of campaign with the Archduke Albert. Albert was less expansive than he had been in Paris. It would take time for Austria to mobilize, he said. She could hardly start earlier than six weeks after France. The French army would advance into South Germany. Austria would concentrate in Bohemia. Meantime the Italians would be coming up through the Tyrol. But this outline was a purely academic disquisition. The Archduke did not make any promises. Francis Joseph, moreover, told Lebrun that he was resolved on peace.

"I would not make war unless I were actually compelled to."

He still regarded the alliance with France as primarily defensive. He did say, however:

"If the Emperor Napoleon found himself obliged to accept or declare war, and were to appear in southern Germany not as an enemy but as a liberator, I on my side would feel obliged to declare that I made common cause with him."

Lebrun reported on his mission on his return to Paris. Either he did not make himself understood or else Napoleon III read his report inattentively; for the Emperor was left in the persuasion that, in any case, however the war began, Austria would automatically place itself on the side of France. Metternich encouraged him, and the Empress too, in this mistaken sense of security.

Gramont shared the same illusion. Gramont was a nephew of the Comte d'Orsay, who had sent him as plenipotentiary to Cassel immediately after the *coup d'état*. That, along with the backing of Drouyn de Lhuys, had opened a brilliant diplomatic career for Gramont. At the time of his leaving Vienna von Beust had shown him the projected treaty and the autograph letters of the sovereigns—a negotiation of which he had had no previous knowledge. He saw in the documents the pledge of an alliance, though he well knew that everything had been left in abeyance. Gramont was a thoroughbred, a man of fine background, polished, chivalrous, sharp of wit. But he had no great vision, he was of a nervous disposition and he had a deal of pride, personal as well as patriotic. During his long years in Vienna he had been influenced, as anybody could hardly have helped being influenced, by the sheer charm of the place, by the Austrian atmosphere. He had been a good ambassador during the earlier part of his stay. Later on he came to see things from the standpoint of the Austrian chancellery—that is to say, he came to assume that Austrian interests were necessarily identical with French interests. In 1866 he had urged the Tuileries to enter the war and at that time he was right. He returned to the charge in 1868 and this time he was wrong. Like his old associates in Vienna he still thought of Prussia as a second-rate power. He took no stock in tales of her great military strength. He had nothing but contempt for Bismarck and, for a worse mistake, he thought von Beust a great man.

Neither Ollivier nor the other ministers were given an inkling of what was going on. Napoleon III was keeping his diplomatic secrets strictly to himself. For that matter, the ministry was finding the going rough. The desertion of the Left Center was making itself felt. The government was getting only patch-work majorities and in connection with the press bill Clément Duvernois managed even to put it in the minority. The Emperor gave Duvernois a dressing-down for his prank, but, there was no doubt about it, the good feeling of the ministry's first days had vanished. Ollivier was disappointing the Emperor. He did not seem to be working out very well in actual practice. Napoleon III's intimates in the Tuileries averred that, with his hand strengthened by his recent victory at the polls, he would soon be "throwing the Ollivier crowd out" and going back to his old staff.

CHAPTER XXXIII

Bismarck Springs His Trap

THE BILL RELATIVE TO THE YEAR'S DRAWING FOR THE ARMY CAME UP in the Legislative Body on the 30th of June (1870). The government still stuck to its intention of calling 90,000 instead of 100,000 men, in line with its idea of making a demonstration of pacific intentions for the benefit of Europe. This was deliberately overriding the Emperor's express opposition. Napoleon III felt so strongly on the matter that he went to the trouble of making the first draft of a circular, to be sent to each deputy, in which he begged that no reduction be made in the new contingent. Germany could put a million trained soldiers into the field, he declared:

"Consider the figure and then decide whether those who would reduce our national forces still farther are truly enlightened as to the real interests of the country."

He was reminded that such a circular would be unconstitutional. He therefore filed it away with his papers. There it was found three months later.

In the debate Thiers came out against the reduction, but Ollivier, sure of himself and of Europe, declared that of all countries France alone could afford to make such a gesture.

"At no time," said he, "has the maintenance of peace seemed better guaranteed."

That was June 30th.

On July 2nd the *Gazette de France* published the following item:

"The Spanish government has sent a delegation to Germany to offer the Spanish crown to Prince von Hohenzollern."

A giant fireraft that Bismarck had slyly set afloat! And it had drifted alongside a powder magazine—France!

Bismarck had worked the thing out with Marshal Prim, the dictator in Spain, away back in the fall of 1869 and in deepest secret.

Really it went even farther back, to the spring of that year. At that time a deputy in the Spanish Cortes, Salazar y Mazarrado, a man who was in Bismarck's pay, published a pamphlet advocating an offer of the Spanish throne to Leopold von Hohenzollern-Sigmaringen, brother to the Karl von Hohenzollern who had become King Carol of Roumania. The two princes sprang from the ancient line of the sovereigns of Prussia. They had remained Catholic. They had a Murat princess for one grandmother and a Beauharnais for the other. Napoleon III had favored the *coup d'état* of Karl von Hohenzollern in Bucharest. How then, it was figured, could he consistently object to the elevation of Prince Leopold in Spain? But of course Napoleon III could not help seeing that, if the intrigue succeeded, he would find a direct tool of King William of Prussia seated on a throne beyond the Pyrenees, and caught between two fires France would no longer be able to offer any serious resistance to Prussian expansion.

Catching wind of the Salazar manoeuvre Napoleon III had written to Benedetti in alarm, requesting him to ask Berlin what it was all about. He was told that "no such question had ever been broached." Later on Bismarck himself brought the matter up with Benedetti, describing it as "idle talk."

But there is no slightest doubt. Bismarck may not have foreseen all the potentialities of the manoeuvre in the beginning; but he had had it brewing in his mind for a long time. If he could, at any moment of his choosing, seat a German king on the Spanish throne he could confront France with the terrible choice between a submission which would leave her in a dangerous and humiliating position, and a declaration of war against a superior foe.

When Mercier de Lostende questioned Prim on the report in the *Gazette* on July 2nd, Prim shrugged his shoulders and said:

"I am not the one who invented this combination. I didn't even ask for it. It was tucked into my hand."

Sure of Prim to begin with Bismarck had now only to obtain the consent of Prince Leopold and the old Prince Anton, and he set about doing so. Leopold, however, was not over-keen. Prim returned to the charge in February, 1870. This time Bismarck thought it wise to take the matter up with his sovereign. King William did not know what to say and brought the question before a council. The council was a council of generals rather than of diplomats:

Roon, Moltke, and Bismarck, along with Leopold and Anton von Hohenzollern-Sigmaringen. They agreed unanimously on acceptance. It was now March 15th. But then, after reconsidering the matter for some days, Leopold changed his mind. He really didn't want to be a king, nor did his younger brother, Frederick, whom Bismarck was holding as his ace in the hole. King William did not care to use pressure on either of the young princes. The project looked dead.

But Bismarck was not the man to be checkmated by two boys. He knew that Anton von Hohenzollern had great ambitions for his sons. He told Prim to renew the offer, but this time directly, ignoring the Prussian court. That would make the proposal a strictly private matter.

Prim sent an agent—Salazar—to Sigmaringen. This time, under his father's browbeating, Leopold accepted and asked permission of his King. At Bismarck's suggestion William gave the authorization in his own handwriting, though with a trace of misgiving. It was now June 21st.

Prim knew all along but said nothing. He intended to take a trip to Vichy shortly and he was certain, for his presumption was great, that he could bring Napoleon III around to accepting the arrangement. Then his only remaining task would be to have it rubber-stamped by his Cortes. His calculations miscarried only in one respect. The editor of the *Epoca* in Madrid forgot himself and talked. The news spread like wildfire and was in Paris within the hour. Confronted by Lostende, Prim could only confess.

Napoleon III was at Saint-Cloud. He received the jolt with an exclamation of surprise. He noted the disloyalty of Prim and the Hohenzollerns and concluded that the situation looked grave. However, neither he nor Gramont lost their composure. Gramont requested information both of Madrid and Berlin. The replies were irritating. Prim had gone ahead and carried the Hohenzollern candidacy through his Council of Ministers and had fixed a date for a meeting of the Cortes. In Berlin Bismarck was not at home. His undersecretary of State, Thile, knew nothing and was otherwise evasive.

Paris opinion exploded like a powder magazine at the first break of the news. All parties declared that France had been placed under threat from Prussia and had to deal with the threat. The opposition leaders were the most violent. Jules Simon declared that France could not recognize the candidacy of Leopold von Hohenzollern without compromising her safety and her dignity. Jules Favre thought that a *casus belli* had arisen. Thiers found the German manoeuvre "intolerable." Gambetta besought "all Frenchmen to unite for a national war." The newspapers flared on high. Cassagnac wrote in the *Pays:* "A Prussian king is to be thrust upon us in Madrid? Not at all! We shall not permit such a thing!" And Edmond About in the *Soir:* "We are thirty-eight million prisoners— if this report is not false. . . . It will be false if we choose, but is the French government capable of choosing?" Pessard in the *Gaulois:* "If we are asked to choose between a shrunken, helpless country and war, we do not hesitate." Nefftzer in the *Temps:* "If a Prussian prince were to be set on the throne in Spain we would be thrown back to the time of Francis I." So the *Gazette de France,* legitimist, the *Français,* Orleanist, the *Siècle,* the *Rappel,* the *Avenir national,* republican. Francis Magnard could well conclude in *Figaro* on the 7th of July:

"We have rarely seen such general agreement in the organs of the different parties."

One might have noted the usual explosion of anti-imperial hatred in Delescluze's *Reveil:* "So there you are surrounded, my good people! Prussia across the Rhine, Prussia across the Alps, Prussia across the Pyrenees! If that is what 'vengeance for Sadowa' means you have it—with a vengeance!"

Altogether noteworthy and exceptional would be the thoughtful, cool-headed demeanor of John Lemoinne in the *Journal des Débats.* Lemoinne did not think dynastic questions could be very important in this day and age.

"France is all aflame," he said. "That is a mistaken attitude which we are not anxious to encourage."

Thiers, meantime, sent word to the Empress through the Duchesse de Mouchy that "if it proved that war could not be avoided, the Emperor could count on his patriotism. . . . He would loyally cooperate with all measures taken by the government."

Napoleon III received this offer of service coldly, interpreting it as a bid for a portfolio.

One more blunder, to reenforce all the others!

Napoleon III, Ollivier and Gramont were deeply impressed by

the unanimous outburst in the country. They felt they had a united nation behind them. Gramont had held himself in leash thus far. He now let go with an anger born of his innate haughtiness. To Lord Lyons, the British ambassador, he said:

"We cannot tolerate a deal which would compel us to keep an army corps on the Spanish frontier in case of a war with Prussia. We should consider no price too high, if paying it enabled us to thwart such a scheme." [1]

And to Metternich, whom he regarded as a friend, he said:

"This will not go through. We shall resist in every way possible, even if war with Prussia should come of it."

So the word "war" had been uttered officially and it was to be uttered again in a dispatch which Gramont sent to Fleury in St. Petersburg *by order of the Emperor:*

"If Prussia persists in pressing the candidacy of Prince Hohenzollern, it's war."

Now war is a word that no diplomat should allow to escape his lips till the passports have all been exchanged. Gramont had lost his wits completely. That same day, at five in the afternoon, he saw Werther, the Prussian ambassador. Werther was leaving Paris for Ems for a talk with King William, who was taking a cure there. Gramont said to Werther:

"France is not going to back down!"

On the morning of July 6th there was a Council meeting at Saint-Cloud. Ollivier asked of Le Boeuf, the Minister of War:

"Is the army ready?"

The marshal answered that if war was inevitable anyway this opportunity might be seized without misgiving:

"The army is wonderful. It is disciplined, it is in good practice, it is courageous. Our musket is far superior to the Prussian musket. Our artillery is in the hands of men who have been specially chosen for their competence. . . . Mobilization and concentration will be effected without a hitch."

He was in favor of an offensive strategy. He would have 300,000 men in a fortnight's time, not counting the mobile guard, which he estimated at 100,000 for the first call. [2]

The Marshal's figures were not questioned. No documents were

[1] Lyons to Granville, July 5, 1870—to Granville, because Clarendon had died on the 27th of June, when Granville had taken over the Foreign Office.
[2] Ollivier, *L'Empire libéral*, XIV, 100.

asked for. The Emperor had held staff conferences at Compiègne during the previous autumn. There the question of numbers had been thoroughly threshed out. He did not ask for detailed evidence, and what was good enough for him was good enough for the Council. As a matter of fact Le Boeuf did hand the Emperor, later on that day, a number of personal notes. One of them contained the historic boast:

"We are stronger than the Prussians on a peace footing. We are stronger than the Prussians on a war footing."

But was the man out of his senses? On the previous March 30th he had written:

"The German army today has 1,140,000 trained and disciplined men. We, in comparison, can throw not more than 510,000 men into our battle line."

All members of the Council, at any rate, took it for granted that a fine and powerful French army could at once cross the Rhine, whereupon South Germany would draw apart from Prussia and the alliances with Austria and Italy would come into play. The Emperor opened a drawer in his desk and produced letters which Francis Joseph and Victor Emmanuel had written him under dates in September, 1869. He read them aloud. "He had no doubt," writes Ollivier, "nor the Council either, that Italy and Austria would convert those letters into an offensive and defensive alliance *without being asked*. Our second basic assumption was that *we could count on those two allies*." [1]

A first and altogether inexcusable stupidity! It had not been possible to conclude those agreements after a year of arduous negotiation. The withdrawal of French troops from Rome was the prime requisite for their adoption. How then could those men—the Emperor, Ollivier, Gramont, to say nothing of the others—even imagine that binding treaties could now be obtained for the mere asking?

"I shall not make war unless my hands are full of alliances," Napoleon III was to reiterate time and time again during the days following.

But that was lying to himself. It was lying to the country. He had not one alliance in his hands, nor was he ever to get any.

In the Legislative Body that afternoon Gramont requested that an interpellation by Cochery, a deputy of the Left Center, be de-

[1] *L'Empire libéral*, XIV, 105-06.

ferred long enough for him to read a statement which had been passed on, and in fact strengthened, by the Council that forenoon.

But why a public declaration, which could only pour oil on the conflagration in public sentiment? Was it hoped that Prussia and Spain would be frightened? It meant taking a rashly dangerous position and burning one's bridges behind one. Why not have worked through diplomatic channels? Emile Ollivier was to answer that Prince Leopold's election was due at any moment. But he had to be elected by the Spanish Cortes and the Cortes had been convoked for July 20th. That left a full two weeks for negotiation.

One weakness in parliamentary government is that it has to run on words; and at that critical juncture, Ollivier, who was made of words to the marrow of his bones, did not sufficiently realize how dangerous words could be.

Gramont, from his place on the speaker's platform, read:

"We do not feel that the respect we owe to the rights of a neighbor people obliges us to suffer a foreign power to place one of its princes on the throne of Charles V and so upset the present balance of power in Europe to our detriment and imperil the interests and the honor of France. This, we firmly hope, will not come to pass. . . . To prevent it we count both on the wisdom of the German people and on the friendliness of the Spanish people. . . . But if the event proves to be different, strong in your support, gentlemen, and in the support of the nation, we shall be certain to do our duty without hesitation and without quailing."

A harsh document! Its trenchant tone brought instantaneous applause from the ultra-Bonapartists, and the majority came rippling in. There was some confusion on the Left. From the top row in the amphitheatre Garnier-Pagès, who had aged greatly, said something about the brotherhood of the peoples. Crémieux, lifting his dark monkey's face, cried out:

"That says war?"

And Ollivier came back forcefully:

"No!"

Thiers had just come in. He walked rapidly over to Ollivier and whispered to him, entreating him to say something or other that would calm the excitement in the Chamber. The Guardian of the Seals mounted the speaker's platform, therefore, and tried to soften the effects of the statement.

"The government desires peace," he said, "it desires peace passionately, but it wants peace with honor."

Ollivier's moderation was sincere. Later that day he expressed his alarm to the Emperor. "This first reaction," he said, "has overreached itself."

The press for the larger part approved of Gramont's position and said harsh things about Bismarck and Prussia. Newspapers in England were sympathetic. "This whole Spanish business," said the London *Times,* "bears every indication of being a vulgar and insolent diplomatic manoeuvre." "Humiliation today, danger tomorrow, that is what the accession of a Prussian Prince to the throne of Spain would mean for France." So the *Daily Telegraph.*

The Emperor's eyes were always on London. He scanned the implications of such attitudes carefully; but meantime his intimates were flocking around to express their delight at the statement.

"My warmest congratulations!" wrote Persigny. "All France will follow you. Enthusiasm is unanimous."

Marshal Vaillant strode into the Emperor's office.

"At last!" he exclaimed. "Now we've got Sadowa off our chest. It has been smothering us for four years. You could never find a prettier pretext. You should take advantage of it."

"Do you think they will back down?" asked the Emperor.

"No, sire, I don't. When I try to size up a situation I put myself in the other fellow's shoes! Well, would we back down? Anyhow, it doesn't matter. You have told them what your terms are. Now—on guard!"

That was the general atmosphere about the sovereigns, but they, for their part, did not share the enthusiasm. The Emperor was worried, the Empress dismayed. Whatever the papers were saying, war was a serious business. They hoped that Prussia would "knuckle under."

Napoleon III had no great hopes of that and he set out to achieve his purposes in indirect and secret ways. He sent a message to the Spanish regent, Serrano, appealing to his friendly feelings. Then, on the night of the 6th-7th, he talked with Olozaga, the Spanish ambassador, at Saint-Cloud. Olozaga brought Stratt with him—Stratt was the agent of Roumania in Paris. It was decided that Stratt, who was energetic, intelligent and in high favor with the Hohenzollerns, would go to Sigmaringen and try to call Prince Leopold off.

Ollivier and Gramont knew nothing about all this. In their eyes everything depended on what the King of Prussia would do, and they waited breathlessly for news from Benedetti.

Benedetti had been ordered to go to Ems and see King William. The King was entirely stranger to the intrigue that his minister had spun. He wanted an appeasement.

"Between ourselves," he wrote to the Queen on July 7th, "I would be glad if Leopold were not elected."

Gramont, in a personal letter, had directed Benedetti to ask the King to recall the authorization he had given to Leopold. The letter was absurdly urgent:

"We are in a great hurry because we want to get the start on them, in case of an unsatisfactory reply, and begin troop preparations by Saturday so as to be in the field within a fortnight."

The ambassador decided that his chief was on the wrong track in showing such great impetuousness. Ollivier, who did not like Benedetti, described him as "conscientious, hard-working, industrious, wide-awake, and apt at finding his way through the cracks in events." At the risk of incurring his superior's displeasure, Benedetti took it upon himself to tone down Gramont's language. And he did so— artfully, but to no great purpose. The aged king saw him but refused to interfere. Prussia, he said, was not concerned with the Hohenzollern question. The French government should take the matter up with Spain. He did say, however, that he had written to Prince Anton at Sigmaringen to ask him what his and his son's intentions were and to inform him of the excitement in France. The King was in excellent humor and asked his visitor to stay to dinner (July 9th).

Benedetti at once reported, in glowing language, and urged the people in Paris to keep cool. But Paris was hardly in a state of mind to grasp the meaning of such advice. What the Emperor and the government wanted was an answer! Gramont telegraphed or wrote Benedetti at least three times during the day of July 10th:

"We cannot wait any longer. . . . If the King refuses to advise Prince von Hohenzollern to decline—well, it's war and war at once! Within a few days he will find us on the Rhine. . . . You cannot imagine the extent to which public opinion is aroused here. It is out of our control and we are counting the minutes."

Hysteria was in fact mounting in Paris. The government was put to it to keep the Chambers in hand. The capital itself was in a state of acute nervous tension. Crowds surrounded the kiosks waiting for the latest issues of the newspapers. The papers had no great amount of news, but most of them carried editorials of incredible violence —the ministry, in fact, should not have allowed them to be printed. Said Cassagnac in the *Pays:* "Prussia stands between a threat and a disgrace. Let her take her choice. She must either fight or back down." Emile de Girardin in *Liberté:* "Prussia is a jackal nation. Let us treat her like a jackal nation. . . . Let us waste no time in looking for allies. We need be concerned only with keeping the war confined to France and Prussia. With a dose from the butts of our guns in her back she will soon be scooting across the Rhine. We will force her to clear out from the whole left bank."

Meantime Napoleon III was engaged in another manoeuvre with Vimercati, a semi-official agent of Victor Emmanuel. Vimercati was an Italian patriot. Going into exile from Italy he had enlisted with the Algerian Spahis, where he had known Fleury. After the foundation of the kingdom he had become a sort of secret ambassador for Victor Emmanuel. He was a shrewd negotiator and was the ordinary go-between in Napoleon III's secret dealings with the King of Italy. The Emperor sent Vimercati to inform Victor Emmanuel that "if he received a negative or inconclusive reply from Prussia the French army would at once march to the frontier," and that "he was counting on simultaneous intervention by Italy and Austria."

The Council met on the 11th to fix on military measures. Gramont read two telegrams from Benedetti. They warned that "war would become unavoidable if France began overt preparations." The Council went no farther than authorizing the organization of battalions of "minute men" in infantry regiments and recalling soldiers on furlough to their companies.

Europe had been following the march of events with the greatest anxiety. Gramont had asked for the good offices of St. Petersburg, London, Vienna and Florence as early as July 6th. The Czar bade Fleury be of good cheer and wrote two separate letters to King William, advising him to withdraw the Hohenzollern candidacy. England was cooler. Gladstone was in power just then and Gladstone did not like France. Queen Victoria had of late been hardly more than distantly polite to Napoleon III. Gladstone stopped at urging caution upon Berlin. Von Beust in Vienna talked a great deal but did nothing whatever. Visconti-Venosta, on the other hand, used energetic language in Madrid, but there was no sign of a major intervention from any quarter.

The King of Prussia consented to another talk with Benedetti. He evinced some irritation at France's arming but promised a definite answer as soon as he learned just how the Hohenzollerns felt about the matter. As warrant of his conciliatory intentions he ordered Werther, his ambassador, back to Paris (July 11th).

Actually King William was beginning to be bored with the whole business. Bismarck had dropped out of sight at Varzin on a pretext of illness. From there he kept bombarding the King with counsel that he talk rough and be tough. The King paid no attention. He really wanted peace. Naturally he was not going to be forced into a retraction that would ruin his prestige in Germany and in Europe. He did not order his young relative to refuse the Spanish crown, therefore. He merely advised him to decline it.

"I would be as happy as could be if Leopold would end the quarrel," King William wrote to the Queen. Later on he sent an army officer to call on the Prince and hurry things along.

As a matter of fact the Hohenzollern intrigue was to find its actual end in Spain through the protests lodged there by Italy and England. Prim took fright and beat a retreat. On the evening of the 10th the Madrid cabinet despatched General Lopez Dominguez to Sigmaringen to ask the Hohenzollerns to drop the plan.

That, of course, was not known in Paris. On the 11th Gramont appeared before the Legislative Body—to be booed by the Right, which was growing more and more bellicose. Scattering prudence to the wind, he telegraphed Benedetti to have a decisive answer by the following morning, saying:

"We shall consider silence or ambiguity a refusal."

Had Bismarck made that move himself he could not have done better.

In his hiding place in Pomerania the Chancellor felt certain that a mine so carefully laid could not fail to go off. But the greatest manipulators are often surprised at what actually occurs. They pile up the storm clouds, the lightning is about to crash, then suddenly, unexpectedly, the sky clears.

On the 11th, after three days of most painful discussion, Stratt persuaded Prince Anton that if he was concerned to save the throne of Roumania for his eldest son, he would be obliged to give up the idea of Spain for his younger son. It had been a most distressing negotiation. Nagged by his wife, Leopold now insisted that he wanted to be a king, and the old Prince had to threaten to shut him up in a lunatic asylum if he continued to disobey.[1]

Stratt telegraphed the news of what had happened to Olozaga on the evening of the 11th. The next morning, the morning of the 12th, the German news agencies received a communication from Prince Anton von Hohenzollern-Sigmaringen:

"The Prince heir-apparent of Hohenzollern-Sigmaringen desires to restore freedom of initiative to Spain. He therefore declines to be a candidate to the Spanish throne, in a firm resolve not to allow the possibility of a war to issue from a family matter that he regards as of secondary importance."

King William was satisfied. "There's one nuisance off my hands," he wrote to the Queen.

His good humor vanished as he found an emissary from Bismarck standing before him. The Chancellor was beside himself with rage. He was handing in his resignation.

For Bismarck, in truth, the fiasco was unbearable. A year's work gone for nothing! An insignificant prince had made a fool of him. His king had overruled him. He stood there vanquished and humiliated. His house of tricks had collapsed about his head. How Europe was going to laugh! The Emperor with the crazy ideas had won a victory over the rough-handed builder of a new Germany. The insolent France was getting her revenge for Sadowa, and the war that he had prepared for, the war that he needed, was going into the discard and with it his great plans for the future.

"He might have maintained his position for form's sake," writes the German historian Lenz, "but the game was up just the same. He had hoped to take France by surprise. Failing in that he would ever after find her blocking his path. The moment for a backdown had come. For the first time in his life the great statesman had suffered a defeat." [2]

The joy in Paris, however, was by no means as universal as has been imagined. Satisfaction was indeed the dominant note—French 3%'s rose three points. But army circles, the ultra-Bonapartists and

[1] Ollivier, op. cit., XIV, 212.
[2] Geschichte Bismarcks, 349-350.

not a few republicans were grievously disappointed. At a meeting
of "die-hards" at the Sourdière, Gambetta declared that the Hohenzollern affair was merely incidental, that advantage should be taken
of it to demand the application of the Treaty of Prague and the dis-
mantling of Prussian fortresses that constituted threats to the French
frontier.

Ollivier brought the official news to the Legislative Body before
the session opened. He was radiant. Thiers cautioned him to beware
of any imprudent remark, and he answered:

"Don't worry! Now that we have our hands on peace again we
shall not allow it to escape."

Bitter against Ollivier, Duvernois began the session by requesting
permission to interpellate the cabinet "as to the guaranties that it
had stipulated or intended to stipulate with a view to avoiding a
repetition of such complications with Prussia." The day for the debate was not agreed upon. It seemed that the majority was not very
well settled and the ministry looked insecure.

The Emperor sent word for Ollivier to come to the Tuileries.
The Guardian of the Seals found him saying to one of his officers:

"It's a great relief to me. I am very happy that things have turned
out this way. A war is always a great gamble."

At the same time he was worried as to what the country might be
thinking. Was there any real disappointment? He decided with his
minister that it was better "not to stir" before the Council met on
the morrow.

Nigra came in.

"It's a great moral victory for France," said the Italian ambassador. "I hope the Emperor is satisfied."

"Yes, it means peace," said Napoleon III. "The French public
wanted war, but I realize that the Prince's withdrawal was a satisfactory way out."

To his aide-de-camp, Bourbaki, he was to say later on in the afternoon:

"Suppose an island suddenly leaps from the sea somewhere between France and Spain. The two countries begin to dispute possession of it. Then just as suddenly the island disappears. Well—
what is there left to quarrel about?"

He was so convinced that there was nothing left to quarrel about that he directed Le Boeuf to cancel orders relating to preparations for war.

Then he set out for Saint-Cloud.

He found the Empress, the Prince Imperial and their intimates waiting for him at the door of the billiard room.

"Well," he announced. "It's peace!"

He was astounded to see the faces about him fall and to hear a chorus of voices:

"The country will not like it."

The Empress began to argue. She had 'been won over by the war party. The tone of the newspapers, the attitude in the Chamber, a thousand rumors that she exaggerated, had filled her with alarm. She thought that peace was contrary to feeling in the nation and that the Empire would suffer from it. When earlier that day she had read a telegram informing her of Prince Leopold's withdrawal she had crumpled it up and dashed it to the floor.[1] Later on she was to plead to Paleologue:

"We could not expose the Empire to a second Sadowa. The Empire could not have stood it." [2]

Not being able to consider calmly all aspects of such a complicated situation she saw her son losing his throne unless the Emperor seized this opportunity to redeem French prestige and fortify it on a very high level.

Losing her poise completely she cried:

"This is a disgrace. The Empire is simply putting on skirts!"

Bourbaki was bravery and honor itself, but he had a very fiery temper. He unbuckled his sabre and tossed it upon a billiard table.

"If that's the way it is, I refuse to serve any longer." [3]

Everybody was talking at once, as though the Emperor did not count. Voices rose in anger. The Duvernois interpellation was mentioned. Napoleon III disapproved of it. But those about him approved. Duvernois had used the word "guaranties." The word was being tossed freely about there in the billiard room at Saint-Cloud.

Just then Gramont came in. The Minister of Foreign Affairs was the living picture of disappointment. He had been counting on making an historic diplomatic coup. Now he had been robbed of it! Prince Anton had withdrawn by a telegram to Prim so that the King

[1] Bapst, *Canrobert*, IV, 19.
[2] M. Paléologue, *Entretiens de l'Impératrice Eugénie*, 146.
[3] Ollivier, *op. cit.*, XIV, 253.

of Prussia had been in no way involved. Even before coming to Saint-Cloud, Gramont, in Ollivier's presence, had suggested to Werther that the latter ask his master to write the Emperor a private letter associating himself with the Hohenzollern withdrawal. Gramont had so far lost his head that the text he proposed made the letter a veritable apology such as no sovereign would have consented to sign, even one less fastidious in point of pride than King William of Prussia.

"In authorizing Prince Leopold to accept the crown of Spain, the King of Prussia had no idea that he was offending the interests or the dignity of the French nation. His Majesty concurs in the Prince's withdrawal and expresses his hope that any cause of misunderstanding between his government and the government of the Emperor has been removed." [1]

Gramont now brought the matter of the letter before the Emperor. Napoleon III took him along with the Empress into his study and together they talked the situation over. Gramont declared that the satisfaction that had been given was altogether lame, that King William should be required to give "a guarantee that he would not again authorize the candidacy of Prince Hohenzollern to the throne of Spain."

The Empress agreed with Gramont. If such a statement could be obtained the effect in France and in all Europe would be so tremendous that the Empire could go back to the dictatorship and be rid of this liberalism which she despised and in which she could see nothing but embarrassment and weakness.

Napoleon III once again allowed himself to be swayed. He could not have underestimated the seriousness of the move. He may not have perceived all its possible implications. There he sat alone between a willful woman and a minister who was doubly stirred by patriotism and by wounded vanity. He had lost the capacity for quick and resolute decision, and he was all the more susceptible to influences because of his poor state of health. He finally gave in.[2]

With Napoleon III's authorization Gramont prepared a telegram directing Benedetti to procure a statement from King William of Prussia which would contain an explicit guarantee. None of the ministers were consulted on this step, which was to reopen the con-

---

[1] Ollivier, op. cit., XIV, 246.
[2] "He made no objection," said the Empress, later, to Paléologue. M. Paléologue, op. cit., 149.

flict and supply Bismarck with a new pretext for war. Napoleon III
believed he had a right to take it on his own initiative. Moreover,
he was swept down that fatal incline as it were by force of destiny.
That evening he saw Jérôme David and Cassagnac at Saint-Cloud.
They informed him that "the renunciation of father Anton" was
the joke of the day in Paris and that Gambetta had "a scorching
speech" in the making.

The Emperor turned and ordered Gramont to send off his telegram.

For this egregious stupidity, which probably has no parallel in
all history, Napoleon III must be held solely responsible. He was
not wrong in protesting against the Hohenzollern candidacy, though
he might have lodged his protest in a calmer frame of mind. But
once he had obtained Leopold's withdrawal he should have stopped
there. Instead, he had been tempted to turn a reasonable satisfaction into a resounding personal triumph. After dreading a humiliation for himself he now wanted to inflict one upon King William
of Prussia. Where the actual balance of military power lay Napoleon
III knew better than anybody else, for he had read and annotated
Stoffel's reports. To do as he was doing in the face of that knowledge
was sheer folly. No excuse can be offered for him.

That very evening the British ambassador, Lord Lyons, warned
Gramont as forcefully as diplomatic language permitted:

"If war comes now all Europe will say that France has brought it
on, that she has provoked a quarrel without any real justification,
as a matter of pride and resentment. To be sure at first blush some
people in parliament, or even in the country at large, may express
some disappointment at a peaceful solution; but the government
will be in a stronger position if it rests satisfied with its diplomatic
triumph than if it plunges the country into a war that has no valid
pretext." [1]

Had Ollivier been the truly parliamentary minister that he
boasted of being he would have resigned. He thought he had no
right to, he explains, because of the seriousness of the crisis. The
next morning, the morning of the 13th, at the Council meeting,
Parieu, who was in the chair, voiced his disapprobation, and two
ministers, Louvet and Plichon, agreed with him.

[1] Lyons to Granville, July 10, 1870.

"Very probably, almost certainly, this means war," said Plichon, "and who can guarantee victory?"

Gramont answered feebly that time was pressing. The Emperor said nothing. The matter went to a vote. The majority—for what else could it do?—ratified the instructions that had been sent to Benedetti.

The Council, however, was drifting towards moderation. It rejected Le Boeuf's request for an immediate calling of reserves to the colors. Le Boeuf was furious. As the Council was breaking up he was heard to exclaim:

"If it weren't for the Emperor I would not remain five minutes longer a member of this cabinet, which is compromising the whole future of the country by its brainlessness."

The Empress expressed similar sentiments. At the luncheon that followed she berated Ollivier and ended by turning her back on him.

After action on the Le Boeuf motion, the Council listened to a telegram from Lord Granville, which reminded the French government of the censure it would rightfully incur if it reopened the quarrel. The Council was impressed and voted not to force the demand for guarantees from the King of Prussia and to rest content, for lack of anything better, with the satisfaction already obtained.

In the Chamber, meantime, the Right, which Rouher was egging on underhandedly, was berating the ministers. Jérôme David had been playing a mischievous rôle as a troublemaker during all those days. He now asked permission to question the cabinet "on a conduct of affairs which was likely to reflect on the nation's dignity."

Debate on the interpellation was fixed for July 15th. Thiers now collared five of the ministers, took them into a room apart, and said:

"An effort is on foot to drag us into war. . . . Now the time for a war has not yet come. . . . You have no alliances." And he begged them to move cautiously.

But there was no room left for caution. The cogged machine that had been so madly set in motion had already ground out its deadly consequences.

Benedetti was meeting the King in the park at Ems at the very moment of Thiers' warning. The ambassador requested, in the proper diplomatic language, permission to announce that he, the

King, would forbid any further move by the Hohenzollerns to ascend the throne of Spain.

The King was first astonished, then nettled. He could not make any commitment in the regard suggested. "But this business," he said, "has been such a great nuisance that I really would like to have it out of the way." Benedetti, anxious to follow the letter of his instructions, may have pressed his point a little too far. The King lost his temper and ended the interview.

Then shortly he received the text of the letter which Gramont had suggested to Werther. His rage knew no bounds.

"Was such insolence ever heard of?" he wrote to the Queen. "I am asked to appear before the world in the rôle of the repentant sinner. They have made up their minds, those accomplished intriguers, to provoke us, whatever the costs, and the Emperor lets them lead him by the nose."

On Eulenburg's advice he declined to participate in any further direct negotiations. Benedetti would have to approach him by way of Berlin, in other words, by way of Bismarck. The French ambassador called twice, and twice the King refused to see him; but he sent his aide-de-camp, Radziwill, on three separate occasions—at two o'clock, at three o'clock, finally at half-past five—to get hold of Benedetti and tell him that he had received the text of Prince Leopold's withdrawal, that it had his unqualified endorsement, that he considered the matter closed and that he would not resume discussions as to a guarantee for the future.

All that was reasonable and courteous enough. The next morning, the morning of the 14th, the King started back for Berlin. Benedetti went to the station to see him off. The King bade him goodbye with his accustomed graciousness. So, by a singular chance, Benedetti's skill in clothing Gramont's demands in diplomatic language had left it still possible to save the situation. The King had endorsed Leopold's withdrawal. The Paris cabinet could desire nothing more. Peace was still within reach.

But Bismarck was on watch and succeeded by a boldly treacherous manoeuvre in upsetting things. His agent, Abeken, had informed him of Benedetti's advances and of the King's refusal. He had Moltke and Roon to dinner with him, and both were brimming with eagerness for news. He showed them Abeken's dispatch.[1] Then, turning to Moltke, he said:

[1] Bismarck, *Gedanken und Erinnerungen*, II, 108.

"Is there any reason why we should postpone things?"

"There is every reason to hurry," answered Moltke.

The Chancellor got up, went to a little table and began to write. Looking up, he read to his guests the text that he had composed:

"The ambassador of France asked His Majesty at Ems to authorize him to telegraph to Paris that His Majesty undertakes never to permit a renewal of the Hohenzollern candidacy. His Majesty the King has refused to see the Ambassador again and has informed him through his aide-de-camp that he has nothing further to communicate to him."

This condensed and accented account of the Ems incident was not a falsification of the literal facts. It was a falsification of their meaning. The manner in which the facts were combined made a travesty of their actual implications. The King's refusal, which in the circumstances was natural enough, was shaded into an insult to the Ambassador.

The idea of the ruse had been suggested to Bismarck by Abeken's dispatch, which had ended with the sentence: "His Majesty leaves it to Your Excellency to decide whether this new demand by Count Benedetti and the refusal which was given it should be communicated at once to our ministers abroad and to the press."

That authorized the Chancellor to publish the King's refusal to give his guarantee. It did not authorize him to say that the door had been shut in Benedetti's face.

Now all that Bismarck had to do was to publish the telegram he had composed and the imaginary insult to Benedetti would become an insult to France. Bismarck was a genius at instantaneous adaptation to circumstances. A wholly unexpected opportunity had arisen. He made haste to take full advantage of it. He absolutely needed the war. The war had slipped through his fingers. Now he had it back again.

He expounded the intricacies of his manoeuvre for the benefit of his two confederates.

"You see," he said, "it is essential that we be the ones who are attacked. . . . If I hand this telegram to the press and to our ambassadors, it will be known in Paris before midnight. It's not only what it says, but also the manner of its publication. It will act on the Gallic bull over there like a red rag."

He had to have France take the initiative in the war. Otherwise the treaties of 1866, which were strictly defensive treaties, would not come into force. Not only that: If France were the aggressor public opinion in Europe would side with Germany.

Moltke and Roon sat down at table again and drank a toast to Prussian victory. Beating his hollow chest with his fist Moltke cried joyously:

"If it is given me to live long enough to command our armies in such a war, the devil can have this old hulk of mine afterwards and welcome."

Bismarck's telegram was at once dispatched to the Prussian ambassadors abroad. It appeared that same evening in a special edition of the North German *Gazette*. This "extra" was distributed gratis to the public, and straightway from the throngs that were packing the streets in Berlin a mighty shout of rage and greed arose.

"Nach Paris!"

"The excitement was tremendous," writes Sybel, the German historian. "Men hugged and kissed each other with tears of joy streaming down their faces. The air shook with cheers for the King."

In Paris during the same hours, mobs of students and workingmen, their emotions whipped to a frenzy by the raging editorials in the papers, were parading the boulevards to the rhythm of a chant:

"On to Berlin!"

The *Pays* said: "The Emperor cannot leave us forever with our faces in the dust. For five days now France has been resolved to fight. This ministry is earning a name for itself: 'The Ministry of Shame.'" And the *Gazette de France:* "There is not going to be any war. Prussia is going to keep the dividends of Sadowa!" Many of the newspapers called the ministers "Prussians."

Rural France, on the other hand, seems not to have been at all bellicose. Only fifteen of the prefects reported any war sentiment in their districts. The others all declared that public opinion was fearful of war.

Early in the morning of the 14th Gramont burst into Ollivier's office.

"My dear fellow," he exclaimed, "you see before you a man who has received a box on the ears."

And he produced a copy of the extra of the North German *Gazette.*

"There's no use in deceiving oneself any longer," said Ollivier, aghast. "They want war."

A council meeting was hurriedly called for one o'clock, at the Tuileries. Napoleon III hurried on from Saint-Cloud to preside over it. On the way he drove through crowds that were almost hostile from impatience.

The meeting lasted six hours. There was a split among the ministers at first. A number of them, Plichon, Segris, Louvet, still argued for peace. Gramont and Le Boeuf were just as set on war. Ollivier vainly sought a compromise formula. Plichon said to the Emperor:

"Sire, your situation and the King of Prussia's are not at all the same. He can lose any number of battles. A defeat for you means revolution."

Napoleon III replied simply:

"Oh, Monsieur Plichon, you remind me of very sad truths, but I thank you for your honesty."

Le Boeuf announced that the Prussian army had started preparations. The *Landwehr* had been notified to be ready. Roon was buying horses in Belgium. Le Boeuf was almost violent in his demand that the reservists be called up. His request was put to an oral vote and was granted unanimously.

"Now," said the Marshal. "I don't care what else goes on in here."

And he strode from the room, on his way to headquarters to issue the appropriate orders.

Another telegram from Benedetti came in. It described the King's attitude as far less offensive than had been represented. The atmosphere in the Council changed. Yielding to this new current Gramont proposed calling a European conference, which would forbid all members of families then reigning to take over foreign thrones. The Emperor accepted enthusiastically.

"Just the thing, just the thing!" he cried, brushing tears of joy from his eyes.

Ollivier worded a declaration and the Council adopted it. Napoleon III thought it ought to be read to the Chamber at once. But the session had adjourned. Publication of the statement—another mistake—was put off to the following day.

Back at Saint-Cloud the Emperor explained to his intimates the device by which it was hoped to clarify the situation.

"I doubt whether that will correspond with sentiment in the Chamber and the country," observed the Empress dryly.

The group agreed with her, with plenty to spare. Le Boeuf came in. Eugénie asked him whether he approved of "that act of cowardice." And she added, drawing up to her full height in her wrath:

"Well, disgrace yourselves, if you choose. But don't disgrace the Emperor!"

Then she repented of the caustic remark, ran to the Marshal and kissed him.

Another Council meeting was called at Saint-Cloud. By a strange oversight, Louvet was not informed at all, Segris did not get his notice in time and Plichon came in very late.

In order more accurately to appraise the real significance of the Ems incident it would have been the part of wisdom to wait for Benedetti. He was on his way home from Germany and would be in by morning. Then the pit in the ground would have been discovered without falling into it and Bismarck's trick would have been unmasked. Unfortunately the pit was lined with loadstone.

Gramont brought a bundle of clippings from German papers. They were all menacing in tone. He also read dispatches from his agents. They revealed that the King's refusal to see the ambassador of France had been officially communicated by Prussia to all the foreign offices in Europe. The Empress had come to the Council without a word of explanation. She took the floor and declared that "war was inevitable if any consideration were to be given to the country's honor." [1] Marshal Le Boeuf agreed with her. The Emperor and Ollivier were the first to give way. The others followed. Parieu was the only one to hold out for peace till the end. The plan for a European conference was discarded. It was decided that a statement would be sent to the Chambers announcing war.

While these deliberations were in progress at Saint-Cloud, Paris was in a half festive, half riotous mood. Crowds in the streets were so dense that traffic came to a standstill. Throngs marching on the boulevards acclaimed the army and the Emperor. A huge parade headed by flags started at the Bastille and made its way to the Madeleine singing the *Marseillaise*.

[1] Lord Malmesbury, *Memoirs of an ex-Minister*, II, 415. Malmesbury had a description of the whole scene from Gramont.

In the great hymn of the Revolution, rising spontaneously from the silence in which the police had thought to dissolve it into dust in the course of twenty years, the figure of the country seemed to be rising with wide-opened arms. People looked at each other, their faces paled and their hearts stood still. Thousands of voices began to chant those stanzas and seemed to fuse in a sort of superhuman voice which was the voice of France in arms. The vagabonds of the outskirts understood that as clearly as did the "dandies" at the Jockey Club. Marie Sasse came out on the stage at the Opera in a tricolored costume and sang the song while the audience rose in awe with tear-filled eyes. The Prince Imperial and his young playmates had never been taught the song, but it must have been lurking in some fold of their memories; for there they were, parading the walks in the gardens at Saint-Cloud and singing it at the top of their voices under the stars of that summer evening.

La Liberté made bold to declare war before the ministers had finished their deliberations at Saint-Cloud.

"Paris has answered Bismarck's challenge. It has declared war on Prussia."

The government's statement, which had been drawn up by Ollivier and Gramont, was read to the Senate and to the Legislative Body at one o'clock on the 15th of July. It rehearsed all that had taken place since July 6th, the demand for guarantees, the Ems interview, King William's refusal, the insulting publicity that the Prussian Chancellery had given to the refusal.

"We have omitted no step to avoid war. We are going to prepare to carry on the war that is offered us, leaving to each the share of responsibility that belongs to him."

The declaration was greeted in the Senate by unanimous applause. In the Chamber the Right and Right Center approved. The Left Center was silent, the Left hostile. Thiers rose from his seat and, while the extreme Right booed and the republicans bravoed, besought the Legislative Body to think carefully before it committed itself.

"Is it true," he asked of the government, "that while your demands as to substance—as to the Hohenzollern candidacy, that is—have been granted, you are now breaking off relations on a point of susceptibility? Do you intend to validate the charge that you have decided to spill rivers of blood for a mere question of form?"

His words were drowned out. Insults rained upon him. The Marquis de Piré called out:

"You are the unpatriotic trumpet of disaster."

The little man in the white wiglet did not wince. He went on with his dismembered speech:

"I regard this war as sovereignly unwise. I am as anxious as anybody to repair the wrong of Sadowa, but I think the pretext has been abominably chosen."

There he laid his finger on the real sore: Sadowa! Had there been no Sadowa neither the government, nor the Assemblies, nor the Press, nor Paris, would have succumbed so readily to the hysteria. Their thought was to avenge Bismarck's premeditated insult, but they were also thinking of vengeance for Sadowa.

Thiers ended by demanding that all the dispatches be read to the House and by disclaiming for himself personally "any responsibility for a war that had so little justification."

Never had the old veteran of political combats displayed sounder vision. With a deep study of modern French history behind him, lifted above his personal vanities and his many smallnesses by love of his country, he had never been so thoroughly right. For a second a fresh breeze of truth seemed to charge the air in the Chamber. Then the fog of error closed in again, and the booing.

As the old man took his seat, Ollivier mounted the speaker's platform to reply. He testified at great length to the earnest struggle he had fought for peace. Then he said:

"If, with a wrench of our hearts, we resolve on this war to which Prussia has challenged us it is because this war is more necessary than any war ever was."

In spite of repeated demands by Gambetta he refused to communicate the dispatches to the Chamber, alleging diplomatic propriety. He did read significant excerpts. Then suddenly, soaring into rhetoric, he declared:

"On this day I and my colleagues assume a great responsibility. We assume it lightheartedly. . . ."

That was a slip. As "oh's" came from all directions, he corrected:

"We assume it, I mean, with hearts that feel no remorse, with hearts that are confident; because the war that we are about to fight is thrust upon us, because our cause is just and because it is entrusted to the French army."

But one might ask: Why should the excellent, the brilliant, the eloquent Ollivier have tried to interpret away a word that was to be branded upon his forehead for the rest of his life and then for all the duration of history—and very fairly, one must say. Lightheartedly! An unlucky word, but a significant, a revealing word, a word which soundly characterized those men so inadequate to the duties that events had laid upon them, and which soundly characterized the imperial system, its policies and its epoch! Those people lived lightheartedly, governed lightheartedly, lightheartedly involved their country in raids and adventures in which she lost both substance and prestige. Lightheartedly now without an adequate army, without an alliance, they were forward marching to the deaths of thousands of their countrymen, to the collapse of a political system that had but flimsy underpinnings, and to the ruin and abasement of France for many years to come. Alas! "Lightheartedly" would have been the proper motto for the Second Empire.

"On the evening of the 15th," writes Ludovic Halévy,[1] "Messrs. Thiers and Buffet were driving together in a closed carriage about the boulevards. Great crowds, great excitement! Bands everywhere playing the *Marseillaise!* 'Listen to me now,' said Monsieur Thiers to Monsieur Buffet. 'I know the military situation in France and I know the military situation in Germany. We haven't a chance.' "

The Committee that was appointed to study laws that would be required for the prosecution of the war questioned the ministers more in detail. Le Boeuf gave assurance that he was ready, that he even had a start on the enemy. Gramont asserted that France had not altered her demands on Prussia since the opening of the crisis. That was a lie. Benedetti had been in Paris since morning. His testimony would have cleared up the frightful misunderstanding and brought Bismarck's imposture into the clear light of day. No one thought of giving him a hearing. To a question about alliances, Gramont, hedging, said that he had just seen the ambassadors of Austria and Italy.

"I hope," he added, "that the committee will ask me no further questions on this point."

The Committee, in fact, completely blind, was satisfied with that vague language and handed in an inaccurate and complacent report.

The deputies were very tired. They were inclined to provision-

[1] *Carnets,* II, 224.

alize everything and get home. But Gambetta insisted on speaking and he did speak with a political insight that shows he had been making considerable progress of late as a statesman. He did not find fault with the war in itself—he was about to vote for it (whereas Jules Ferry, Ernest Picard and Jules Simon, Jules Favre and Grévy were to vote against it). What he did not like was the pretext for the war.

"You can count on sympathy from Europe and on approval in France only if your statement makes it clear that you have been actually and seriously insulted."

He again demanded that Bismarck's dispatch to the Prussian embassies be read in full. That was wasting his breath. The Chamber voted credits and the call of the reservists to the colors by unanimity minus eleven nays and five abstentions.

Rouher was more than eager to be in the limelight at a moment so historic. He moved a resolution which dragged the Senate off to Saint-Cloud. There, in a wordy speech predicting victory, Rouher dared to congratulate the Emperor on "having been so wise as to wait till the organization of his living forces had been brought to their full power."

That fatuous verbiage was to be advertised to all Europe as a confession that Napoleon III had long premeditated war.

The Emperor responded in a tone that betrayed an unconfessed dread:

"We are beginning a very hard struggle."

And a little later he said:

"It is going to be long and difficult. Great efforts will be required of us."

The Empress, in contrast, was confident, bubbling with energy, and she kept saying:

"We have all the chances that one can count on in human affairs. Things can only go well."

At the time when the French Chamber was voting the credits, King William of Prussia, who had hurried home from Coblentz to Berlin, was ordering mobilization. England offered her good offices. Both France and Prussia declined them. On July 19th, so shouldering all the blame for the conflict in the eyes of the world, France formally declared war. In making the announcement to the Reichstag, Bismarck's face was "radiant with joy, as though at that moment he had realized the ambition of his whole life." [1] Of the unity of his German fatherland he had had a glimpse for the first time the night after Sadowa. Now before his eyes blazed a dazzling vision of it.

"France," he declared, "has resolved to fight because she is jealous of our independence and of the prosperity we have attained."

He received a unanimous response. The imperial government had voluntarily assumed the rôle of the aggressor. That fact fused all Germany into one within the space of a few hours. The states of the south joined Prussia in one impulsive uprising and placed their armies under her command.

So the decisive battle, which had been so often predicted and so often deferred between the greatest military powers of the era and which was destined to change the whole face of Europe, was about to be joined.

[1] Robert Konio, quoted by Ollivier, XIV, 512.

CHAPTER XXXIV

From Wissenbourg to Forbach

IN ORDER TO HAVE ITS HANDS FREE THE GOVERNMENT CLOSED THE Chambers after a law had been passed prohibiting discussion of military operations by the press (July 24th). It was decided that the Empress would assume the regency while Napoleon III took command of the army.

He did not seem, really, to be in condition for the hardships of war, the attacks of recent months having quite exhausted him. The Empress teased him to cheer him up; then, repenting of her levities, buried him in endearments.

Again in June Conneau had become greatly alarmed at the Emperor's state of health; and at the physician's request a consultation of specialists was held at Saint-Cloud on the first of July—Drs. Nélaton, Ricord, Germain Sée, Fauvel and Corvisart participating. They diagnosed a condition of "purulent cystitis caused by a calculus in the bladder." Nélaton remarked to General de Montebello later on—July 8th:

"It is unallowable even to think of war. The Emperor is a sick man. He couldn't mount a horse. There has been a consultation, and it's serious."

The specialists were not in agreement as to procedure. The Emperor was himself afraid of the sort of operation that Nélaton had performed on Niel and which had carried the Marshal off. He sealed the report which Germain Sée made on the consultation and then handed it to Conneau, asking him to lock it up in a safe place.

His cousin Mathilde was frightened at the signs of illness she could see in his wasted features. She urged him to continue to head the government, leaving the hardships of the field to others. He replied that he felt that his honor had been pledged before the country.

"I have to," he said. "My name is Napoleon."

The Empress, really, was at the bottom of this attitude. She was interested strictly and exclusively in her son's future and she wanted the victory to belong to the Emperor. Then he could easily go back to the dictatorial empire. That had been her whole thought from the very beginning. She wanted the war as a means of burying constitutional government once and for all. She knew that her husband was ill—but not as ill as all that! The Prince Imperial would go with his father. That would give him, in the eyes of the French, the baptism of fire that befitted the heir of a line of soldiers.

Eugénie well realized that this time her regency was going to be something far more exacting than the short and perfunctory ascents of the throne that she had so far made. But she had a man's temperament. In the dark moments she could rise to real heroism. A hard task not so much frightened her as kindled her courage and stiffened her in her pride.

To her influence seems to have been due the abandonment of the original plan for beginning the campaign. Three armies had been foreseen, the first in Alsace under MacMahon, the second in Lorraine under Bazaine, the third in reserve at Châlons under Canrobert. The Emperor, meantime, would stay in Paris. That was a thoroughly sound plan. Suddenly everything changed. There would be—as for that matter Archduke Albert had himself advised—just one manoeuvring army divided into eight corps, one of which would be the Guard under the command, in the last instance, of the Emperor. Le Boeuf would hand over the Ministry of War for the time being to General Dejean and take a major-general's command himself. That was a ridiculous shuffle. Le Boeuf was an artillery man. He knew nothing whatever about staff work.

Official predictions notwithstanding, instead of the 300,000 or 350,000 line men that had been foreseen for the start, the army was to count 215,000 men on July 27th and 264,000 ten days later. The trouble lay in the slowness of mobilization, in a shortage of arms and equipment and in the confusion that developed in the military offices. The Germans, on their side, had sixteen army corps totalling 450,000 men,—and the number was to be doubled by the *Landwehr*, a reserve force made up of carefully trained veterans.

The French regulars, man for man, squadded around veterans of Algiers, Italy or Mexico, were probably superior in dash and endurance to the Prussian troops. But they knew nothing of war and took badly to discipline. They thought that "going at them" was all there was to a campaign. The reservists did not know how to handle the new musket. They were either young men, who had never seen service, or else discharged men who had thought they were done with military service for good and answered the call without any enthusiasm—many would have deserted had they not been closely watched. As for the mobile guard, it was just a collection of mobs entirely without training and in the worst possible frame of mind.

French armament was wretched. The French chassepot was a better weapon than the twenty-year-old Dreyes needle-gun. The Prussians had heavier field artillery and more of it. Their breech-loading cannon had a longer range than the old brass muzzle-loaders of the French—2,800 yards to 1,700—and they could be aimed more accurately. The German cavalry was well mounted but it was to be little used. The French was badly equipped and could only charge.

Such the tools of war. How were they to be used? The French command had never, probably, been worse. Except in special arms the lower officers came mostly from the ranks. They were just old privates decorated with stripes. Their superiors themselves knew little more than the rudiments of tactical or strategical science. There was no organization, no anticipation of needs. The General Staff itself did not get any maps till the 4th of August—that meant three weeks after the declaration of war—and in deciding what they were to do or where and how they were to go, the generals had to get along with rough sketches hastily made on the spot by hand. Most of the generals were too old. They were brave under fire, but when they were required to decide something, to order this or that, the responsibility overwhelmed them: they grew timid, then nervous, then irritable and sullen. They were terribly jealous of each other and were always ready to do each other bad turns. These rivalries and this shirking of responsibility were to put the French army on the defensive at the very start, a thing that was contrary to the national temperament and tended to discourage everybody.

The Prussian command possessed a highly advanced theoretical training. The General Staff, ready to move at a moment's notice, was imbued with the methods of Clausewitz—Clausewitz merely systematized the basic ideas of Napoleon I. The object of a war, the Germans taught, was not to occupy territory but to destroy enemy armies. The best way to do this was to throw superior masses upon the enemy's weaker points. Even when operating as separate units generals should "march towards the cannonade"—they should support each other. This doctrine of activity and movement had stood up well under test in the short campaign of '66. In the Franco-Prussian war it was easy to overpower an adversary who was inferior in numbers to begin with and then remained doggedly set on defending positions.

The government, the parliament, the press, in France, went to war in the firm persuasion that Austria and Italy would intervene on the French side. That was to know very little about those countries and the men who governed them.

Austria felt no obligation whatever to the man who had beaten her at Solferino and deserted her at Sadowa. She detested Bismarck but was mightily afraid of him. She was bound to be very chary of attacking Prussia before France had won some decisive advantage.

In Italy all memories of the old brotherhood in arms had been wiped out by Mentana. Victor Emmanuel was probably the only man in Italy who was sincerely anxious to support Napoleon III. The outstanding figure in his cabinet was Quintino Sella. Sella hated France. Leaders in parliament, such as Ratazzi, reflected public opinion in opposing any French alliance. Garibaldi wrote that "not one Italian would dirty his hands with service under The Scoundrel." Parades marched the streets of Florence shouting, "Long live Rome," "Long live Prussia," "Down with France."

Victor Emmanuel, however, tried to breast this tide. On July 17th he sent Napoleon III a first assurance of his good will.

"My friendship," he wrote, "will never fail you."

But he set two conditions: first the participation of Austria; then the evacuation of Rome. He sent Vimercati to Vienna to talk with von Beust. The latter always considered his own interests first. He could not and would not assume any undertakings. As early as July 11th he reminded Metternich that Austria, aside from not being ready, had given no pledges and preferred to retain her freedom of action. That perfect specimen of the diplomatic chameleon wrote:

"The contingency of war was, it is true, considered at the time of the conversations, but nothing was decided on. We always said that we would be glad to appear actively on the scene if Russia took the side of Prussia, but that if the latter alone were at war with France we would reserve the right to be neutral."

And he added:

"The Emperor Napoleon promised us to come to our aid if we were attacked by Prussia, but he could hardly feel himself obliged to fall into step with us if we took a whim to declare war on Prussia without his consent." [1]

Metternich, who was half a fool, half an intriguer, with a general varnishing of cowardice, did not inform Gramont of this attitude on von Beust's part. Gramont was taken in to such an extent that he wrote to Vienna to give the signal for the concentration of troops in Bohemia. Francis Joseph called a Council meeting and the Council declared for neutrality—July 20th.

Beust was under strain between his general hostility to Prussia and the caution enjoined upon him by his sovereign. On that same July 20th he sent another embarrassed dispatch to Metternich:

"Please reemphasize to the Emperor and his ministers that in the strict spirit of our undertakings we consider the cause of France our own and that we shall contribute as far as we possibly can to the success of her arms."

That might have been mistaken for a promise; but a qualification followed:

"We have got to keep the Russians guessing by a temporary neutrality. We say the word 'neutrality' with regret, but it is forced upon us by an imperious necessity. . . . This neutrality, however, is only a device, the only means we have of completing our preparations without opening ourselves to an attack from Prussia—or maybe Russia—before we are in a position to defend ourselves."

Gramont and the Emperor were disappointed by all this gabble, but they did not give up hope of eventually bringing Austria into the war on their side. Metternich, moreover, encouraged them in that illusion. He wrote to Gramont that "the war having caught Austria by surprise, she could not possibly take the field before early September."

That was July 24th. A little later he was to write to Le Boeuf:

"I shall never be happy till I have supplied you with a nice little reenforcement of 300,000 men." [2]

[1] Beust, *Mémoires*, II, 340 f.
[2] Ollivier, XV, 485; Beust, *Mémoires*, II, 366.

Napoleon III and his ministers were to cherish their illusions about Austria for a long time, too long a time.

To meet Italy halfway the Emperor decided to call the brigade stationed at Civita-Vecchia home; but he still clung to the famous Agreement of September 15th, which guaranteed the Pope's possession of his territory. A halfway measure, it has been said, and a mistaken measure! Prince Napoleon claimed that had the French handed Rome over at once, they would have had Austria with them from the start, and Italy too.

"The upholding of the temporal power," he wrote, "cost us Alsace and Lorraine."

That is a debatable theory. The Prince himself admitted that the two powers could not have intervened before the 15th of September. The first French defeats occurred on the 6th of August. Even had they been bound by a treaty, neither Francis Joseph nor Victor Emmanuel would have adhered to it under later circumstances.

Certainly it would have been a cowardly act on Napoleon III's part to deprive the pontiff, whom he had so long protected, of his last shreds of power, even under a need so pressing. He was now paying the price for the policy he had followed from the beginning. It had never led to anything except paralysis and confusion for France. The first mistake of Napoleon III's reign was now rising before him at a most critical juncture to smite him and destroy him.

Beust treacherously pressed for French consent to the immediate occupation of Rome by the Italians, as the indispensable condition for any aid from the two powers. Napoleon III and his ministers were indignant at the blackmail.

"France," said Gramont, "cannot defend her honor on the Rhine and sacrifice it on the Tiber."

The negotiations, however, continued between Vienna and Florence. They resulted finally in a tentative agreement that Austria and Italy would first declare armed neutrality and then intervene on the side of France *as soon as they should be ready*. But that intervention was dependent on the desertion of Rome by France. In the best possible case it was an exceedingly doubtful intervention. Bismarck, it seems, never had any serious worry that Italy might enter the war. He remarked to Prince Hohenlohe:

"Victor Emmanuel is capable of doing anything for money or

for women. He might sign a treaty of alliance. His people would never allow him to live up to it."

Italy would never have dreamed of going to war apart from Austria. Even if Austria had wanted to do something she would have been restrained by her fear of Russia. That was a well-grounded fear. Alexander promised William of Prussia to enter Galicia the moment Austria stirred. General Fleury expressed his concern on the point and the Czar answered ironically:

"Just a matter of form, my dear General! I can't quarrel with my own uncle, can I? But you are so certain to beat Prussia that any promise I might make would hardly matter."

He had not been very fond of France since his trip to Paris. What he hoped was that her "fly-by-night sovereign" would take a thrashing.

Napoleon III had foreseen the dispatch of a fleet to the Baltic on the very first day of the war for an attack, with Danish support, on German harbors. Prince Napoleon was to command landing forces. If this project, which was a sound one, were to succeed, it was important to appear before Copenhagen without a moment's delay. The expedition was slow in outfitting. Prussia got wind of it and massed 80,000 men on the Danish frontier, ready to strike. With no help in sight Denmark could only defer to Prussian threats and Russian counsel and declare her neutrality. That meant a good opportunity lost. The French navy was far superior to the Prussian. It could have destroyed the latter and created a very helpful diversion along the German coast. Having no adequate bases available after the loss of Denmark the French navy was to remain virtually inactive throughout the course of the war.

There was no hope of sympathy from England. On July 25th, in an amusedly cynical frame of mind, Bismarck sent the London *Times* a transcript of the French plan for the annexation of Belgium that Benedetti had thoughtlessly left in his hands in 1866. That ruined France in British opinion for the time being and for a long time to come.

The British government demanded of the two belligerents a pledge that they would respect Belgian neutrality. Following so closely on Bismarck's revelations the move could only be regarded as an evidence of hostility to France.

Queen Victoria entered in her Diary:

"Dr. MacLeod preached on war today. Without his mentioning France one could see what he meant when he showed how God always punishes wickedness, vanity and sensuality." [1]

Queen Victoria showed herself otherwise hostile to France at the opening of the conflict. On July 20th she wrote to the King of Prussia:

"No one here conceals the opinion as to the *extreme iniquity* of the war, and the unjustifiable conduct of the French! Still *more, publicly,* we cannot say; but the feeling of the people and country here *is all* with you, which it was not *before*."

To Queen Augusta she wrote the same day:

"May God protect our beloved Germany."

Later on, in another letter to Augusta (August 29th), she rejoiced over German victories.

As the campaign developed her sense of pity came to the fore, and she tried on two occasions to stop the war. On December 18, 1870, she appealed to King William's "generosity and Christian feelings"—vainly, as is well known.[2]

Bismarck had counted on Prim to send at least one Spanish army corps to the Pyrenees. Spain, however, held off and declared her neutrality. Carol of Roumania was bitter against Napoleon III for the latter's stand against his brother Leopold, but he did not dare show his feelings too emphatically. In case Russia entered the war, Roumania would have to fight on the side of Austria and France. Like a good German patriot, however, Carol hoped that "within two months Napoleon III would be beaten and his power destroyed."

The little countries were indignant on the publication of Benedetti's plan, and three of them, Belgium, Holland and Switzerland, turned away from France. Sweden and Turkey, instead, were warmly sympathetic. The Sultan telegraphed the Emperor:

"I ask Your Majesty to tell me where I am to send my army."

The chivalrous offer was declined for fear of complications in Russia's direction.

Napoleon III planned to direct operations from General Staff Headquarters at Metz. On July 28th at a Council meeting at Saint-Cloud, over which he presided, he announced nominations of

[1] Retranslated.
[2] Kurt Jagow, *La reine Victoria, lettres.*

eighteen new senators, the more notable among them, Pasteur, Emile Augier, Maxime de Camp, Emile de Girardin and Pietri. Then at a reception he bade adieu to the ministers, the grand dignitaries and the circle of court familiars. He tried to appear in high spirits, but chance remarks were always betraying his deeper mistrust. Somebody said:

"In a fortnight Your Majesty will be in Berlin."

He shook his head:

"No, there's no hope of that, even if things go well."

Those last days had formed one chain of disappointments—evasions by prospective allies, repudiation by Europe, mistakes and miscalculations in mobilization. It all filled him with gloomy forebodings. For a flash he even thought of writing to King William and calling everything off. At times, probably, he realized that his doom was sealed. He was just drifting along with the forces that had him in their clutch. The sirens of disaster were calling? Well—he would go out and follow them, eyes closed. He was sixty and more. If he had to end, better end in a flicker of glory.

He started away with his son—with all that he really loved. The boy seemed very tiny in his second-lieutenant's uniform. The two took leave of Eugénie at the Saint-Cloud station. She had worries in plenty too, but she smiled bravely.

"Goodbye, Louis. Do your duty!"

"We are all going to do our duty," the father answered.

"Vive l'Empereur!" cried the group of courtiers.

As the locomotive began to puff, Napoleon III leaned out of the compartment window and waved his army cap. The train headed East. So—over there lay Paris, a jumbled and fearful agglomeration of buildings and men!

The Emperor gazed at the skyline. There he had been monarch for a score of years! There he had been host to Europe! There Fortune had smiled on him perhaps more than he had deserved. Paris! Paris he would never see again!

He was ill when he got to Metz. The jostling of the train had opened the abscess in his bladder again. He pulled himself together and called a council of war.

The situation was far worse than anything he had imagined. Instead of mobilizing first and concentrating afterwards, Le Boeuf had been anxious to save time and take the offensive before the Germans got under way. He therefore tried to combine the two operations. The disorder resulting was indescribable. Regiments had been hurried forward with their slender peace-time effectives, and were now waiting for their complements of reservists. These the recruiting stations were arming with great difficulty and then sending out according to old routine. So a Zouave from Alsace would be sent to Marseilles, then on to Algeria, then finally to Strasbourg. As a result the railways were in a jam and whole days would pass without a train's moving.

Le Boeuf's irresponsible braggadocio as a mere courtier now stood out in a lamentable light. He had declared before the Chamber:

"If the war were to last two years even, our soldiers would still lack for nothing."

Instead everything was lacking. There was no hardtack and in the frontier fortresses in the East no provisions. In one of its waves of pacifism the Chamber had refused the credits required for restocking them. The then existing supplies had been distributed at the end of legal terms of serviceability and had not been replaced.

There was a shortage in war materials, and such as were available were scattered about here and there, untraceable and therefore unusable. Generals did not know where their regiments were.

Le Boeuf himself—a major general!—telegraphed on July 27th: "Where are my divisions?"

Debauched, drunk, singing obscene songs, the mobile guard was shoved on from Paris to Châlons. There the men were put into barracks to spend days, without guns or equipment, idle, carousing in lack of anything better to do, disorderly. Canrobert tried to hold a review. The men booed and jeered him and beat up officers who tried to restrain them. But how expect anything else from that wretched, uncomfortable mob? If those men could have been properly squadded and trained they could have been turned into a good fighting force. They were finally told off into companies and used to garrison the various forts about Châlons. The government very wisely declined to have any of them back in Paris.

Napoleon III planned to cross the Rhine above Strasbourg and make a rapid offensive into Baden. That would give the reserves time to organize, drive a wedge between south and north Germany and encourage Austria and Italy to come in.

The plan had to be abandoned at the first survey. The troops actually ready were not numerous enough and there were no shells for the artillery. Bazaine, moreover, was strongly opposed to the idea. He was for staying on the defensive, and, without as yet admitting as much, for the war of positions.

Field-Marshal Moltke had been expecting a French drive into the Palatinate. On the 19th of July he wrote to King William:

"We shall have to deal with a small army of between 130,000 and 150,000 men, but it is well organized and well supplied with artillery and cavalry."

He was astounded at the inactivity of the French. Did it hide some deep design? As the days went by he grew more and more apprehensive. What were all those Frenchmen doing, massed like that on the frontier? Not till later on did he grasp the multiple causes of French inertia. Public opinion in France was alarmed however, Europe was astonished and German morale soared.

Self-confidence seems not to have been greatly shaken in the French command by the wretched failure that had been made of mobilization. Twenty years of victory lay behind them. The officers were proud of leading the finest soldiers in the world. Defeat seemed to be out of the question. But already it was becoming apparent that, as the Emperor had said too frankly in his proclamation to the army, the struggle was going to be "long and fatiguing." He was estimating the adversary at the latter's true worth; and Mac-Mahon said to Du Barail:

"Don't make any mistake: that German army has to be reckoned with. The German soldier has sound qualities. He hasn't the individual courage ours has, perhaps, but he is disciplined and patient and he obeys his officers literally."

MacMahon did not underestimate the German army but he had no remotest conception, as yet, of its actual power. He was to find himself facing forces that were twice or three times as large as he had foreseen, and they were led by generals who were not astounding geniuses, with the exception perhaps of Moltke, but who had dash and decision, who knew their business thoroughly and would be able to take full advantage of French mistakes.

Colonel Stoffel, the French military attaché in Berlin, was famous for his pessimism, but he said himself to Bourbaki on July 16th:

"I have no doubt at all that France will finally win; but, you must understand, it is not going to be easy. Prussia is exceedingly well prepared." [1]

Moltke had drawn his plan of campaign in 1868. First the Germans would be mobilized in their recruiting camps. Regiments would be filled up to full strength there and then marched or transported to the various concentration points on the frontier. By the end of July he would have three armies ready. The first, on the right, would come up by the Moselle under the command of old Marshal von Steinmetz. It comprised the VIIth and VIIIth army corps—in other words, 60,000 men. The second, in the center, commanded by Prince Friedrich Karl of Prussia, would come up by way of Mainz. It was the largest of the German armies, comprising the Royal Guard and the IIIrd, IVth, IXth, Xth and XIIth army corps—190,000 men. The third, on the left, would advance by way of Landau upon northern Alsace under the Prince Royal of Prussia. It contained the Vth and XIth army corps of Prussia, two Bavarian army corps, and one corps each from Württemberg and Baden—130,000 men. Three army corps would be held in reserve to reenforce anybody who got into difficulties.

As against these compact and well-defined masses the French army was strung out in a long ribbon from Thionville to Belfort. Napoleon III saw the danger fairly soon and drew the Lorraine corps in a little closer. The French troops were in position by early August. MacMahon had been brought on from Algeria. To protect Alsace he had the Ist and the VIIth army corps, 63,000 men, deployed behind the Rhine opposite the Prince Royal. In the center, facing the main German army, were Frossard's corps, the IInd; Bazaine's, the IIIrd; Failly's the Vth; then Bourbaki with the Guard, and Canrobert with a corps in reserve—140,000 men, also in widely scattered formation. To deal with the first Prussian army General Ladmirault had only one army corps, the IVth, of 27,000 men.

Paris was impatient at the lack of any important action. Ollivier wrote to Le Boeuf on August 1st:

"Why don't you do something? Make up your minds, please! I appeal to your patriotism and your common sense. We are astounded that you have done nothing so far."

To meet the political need at home and impress Europe Napoleon III decided to attack Sarrebrücken, a little open town some

---

[1] General Faverot de Kerbrech, *La Guerre contre l'Allemagne*, 15-16.

miles from the frontier and held by a small German force. The idea had been Frossard's and he had charge of the action of the 2nd of August. He used absurdly large forces—three army corps. The town was easily occupied and railroads, bridges, even telegraph lines, were found intact. Had Frossard exploited his success, marched straight on and beaten Steinmetz, who was in the neighborhood with smaller forces badly deployed, the whole story might have been different. Unfortunately Frossard had received no further orders. Sarrebrücken remained a mere skirmish with the French deriving no profit from it. It was none the less trumpeted as a victory in the communiqués. The Prince Imperial had watched the battle. He displayed considerable coolness. Napoleon III sent the Empress a telegram, which, at Ollivier's direction, she made the mistake of publishing. Paris was already ill-disposed and laughed aloud.

"Louis picked up a bullet that fell near him and he has kept it. There were men who wept at seeing him so calm."

Replying to an urgent request from the Empress he ended the telegram:

"I will find the appropriate language to answer Vimercati with."

The allusion was to talks that had been continuing with Victor Emmanuel's agent. Vimercati came to Metz with the rough draft of a treaty that had been worked out at Vienna. It called for the abandonment of Rome without any definite undertaking on the part of Italy and Austria to enter the war. Napoleon III did not yield in spite of Prince Napoleon's vehement urging. He changed the wording in such a way as to require immediate intervention and then countered by making no reference to the Roman Question.

Vimercati left for Florence. His mission had failed. Now only a great victory for France could bring in the two elusive allies. Did the Emperor understand that? Apparently not, for on the 3rd of August he wrote to Ollivier:

"We have every interest in prolonging the war since we cannot end it by a lightning drive."

So he started nothing at all. He seemed to be afraid of making the least move. The decision that he dreaded to make was now to be forced upon him by the enemy.

The action at Sarrebrücken led Moltke to imagine that a mass attack might be coming in the Sarre region. He resolved to upset it by an immediate offensive. The King had arrived at German headquarters at Mainz. With his master's permission Moltke ordered the Prince Royal to advance with the Third Army into Alsace.

That gave MacMahon the task of meeting the first shock from the invader. MacMahon was sixty-two years old. Tall, solidly timbered, with grey eyes and a mustache now white, he had the army's full confidence. He was a brave man, ready to sacrifice anything to his duty. He was also a fine dashing soldier. Unfortunately he needed someone to direct him. When he was left to his own devices, which were of very narrow range, his limitations began to manifest themselves. MacMahon was a good tactician. He was a wretched strategist. He had no mental poise. He could not take in a battle or a campaign as a whole. He feared responsibility and rather than make a decision himself he would follow an order from someone else which he knew was bad.

MacMahon was informed of a great German concentration to the north of the Lauter by Hepp, the under-prefect at Wissenbourg. He took no great stock in the report, but did order Abel Douay, one of his division commanders, to go up the river from Haguenau towards Wissenbourg and look things over. On the morning of August 4th, through inadequate scouting, Douay was caught with 42,000 men between a Bavarian division and two Prussian corps— 60,000 men—under the Prince Royal. Douay, with his Turcos, fought courageously on the Lauter till he was killed by a shell fragment. General Pellé, who took his place, hung on in hopes that Ducrot's division, twelve miles away, would come to his rescue. That help not materializing, he finally ordered a retreat. A stubborn defense of the château at Geisberg enabled the division to fall back with heavy losses—2,000 men, but the victory cost the Germans almost as dearly.

On learning of the fall of Wissenbourg, MacMahon concentrated all troops within reach in a good position on the mountainous escarpment at Froeschwiller, with the Sauer in front of him. The Emperor heard of MacMahon's inferiority in numbers and thought he could remedy it by placing Failly, with the Vth corps, under the Marshal's orders. Failly had deported himself brilliantly in the Crimea. With age he had grown irritable of temper and inert. He sent MacMahon only one division and that one came up too late.

On the 6th the whole of the German Third Army was encamped

on the Sauer. Ducrot proposed to MacMahon to side-step in the direction of the Vosges. They were not given time. One of the generals of the Vth Prussian corps misunderstood his orders and attacked, the Bavarians coming in after him. Ducrot repulsed them. Then fourteen German batteries opened in front of the village of Woerth. The French artillery was completely crushed. The Prussians crossed the Sauer. However Raoult stopped them short and the Prince Royal ordered a retreat. Nobody listened. After another artillery storm the enemy returned to the assault on the French positions. They carried Morsbronn on the French right, but only in the face of a hot defense.

With his infantry thus uncovered General de Lartigue ordered the Michel brigade of cuirassiers and two squadrons of the lancers to charge troops of the Prussian XIth that were moving out from Morsbronn. For some unexplained reason this heroic cavalry charge is known to history as the "Charge of Reichshoffen." The French horsemen dashed out into rough ground broken by ravines and honeycombed with vineyards and high hop-fences. Most of the cuirassiers were killed or forced to surrender inside the village of Morsbronn. It was a fruitless sacrifice. The French right was turned all the same. The Zouaves clung desperately to the Niederwald, south of Froeschwiller. Finally the Prussians overran such of them as had not fallen. Lartigue's division, "having had enough," made a quick retirement behind the Eberbach.

MacMahon had been directing the battle from the top of a knoll near Elsasshausen. He now ordered a vigorous counterattack. Had any reserves been available he might have won the day. But the Prussian artillery had too many guns, the Prussian infantry too many muskets. After a two hours' fight the French army found itself surrounded on three sides. Elsasshausen was carried, creating a threat to Froeschwiller.

To cover a retreat which could no longer be deferred MacMahon ordered his cuirassiers to charge again.

"Forward!" he cried to General de Bonnemains. "You've got to, to save the army. Stop those guns for a bare twenty minutes."

The magnificent heavy cavalry dashed forward, to be cut to pieces by the German artillery. A colonel had his head carried away by a shell, but his body galloped on for some distance before falling from the horse. The dead lay about in frightful heaps. Catch-

THE CHARGE OF THE CUIRASSIERS AT REICHSHOFFEN

From the Painting by Yvon

ing the mad fury of the combat the Turcos charged with the bayonet and carried Elsasshausen and the slopes of the Niederwald
again. But then the oncoming German masses overwhelmed them,
swallowed them up. Froeschwiller was on fire from bursting shells.
It was as though engulfed under a great wave of Prussians. General
Raoult was killed. Fragments of the French army reached Reichshoffen and Niederbronn in great disorder. There they came upon
Failly's division, which had been coming along at its leisure. Instead of falling back on Bitche towards the Army of Lorraine, Mac-
Mahon retreated on Saverne (Zabern).

The battle of Froeschwiller, which the Germans call the battle of
Woerth, cost the French twenty-seven guns and 20,000 men in
killed, wounded and prisoners. It gave Alsace to the Germans. Over-
running the plain of the Ill they were before Strasbourg the next
morning.

To make the 6th of August a doubly catastrophic day, Frossard
was beaten at Forbach. The defeat, this time, was not due to the
enemy's superior numbers. Incompetence in the French command
can only be held responsible. Frossard was an unusually talented
engineer. Actually his chief experience had been as governor to
the Prince Imperial. But he had had no contacts whatever with war
strategy. He was not a fighter—he was a scholar. The soldiers did
not like him—they called him "the schoolmaster." Skinny, weasel-
like of face as well as of brain, he was harsh towards inferiors and
could neither obey conscientiously nor command with decision. He
might have been in his place at the head of a corps of engineers.
The Emperor was always weak before those who stood up to him.
He could never bring himself to putting Frossard in his proper
place.

On the 5th of August the Emperor shuffled things about a little
to improve cooperation between units. He placed the Ist, Vth and
VIIth army corps under MacMahon's orders, the IInd, IIIrd and
IVth under Bazaine's. Frossard commanded the IInd and was therefore now under Bazaine. After failing to develop his advantage at
Sarrebrücken on the 2nd, Frossard halted his 28,000 men on the
hills to the south of the little town which commanded the whole region. On the 5th, seeing German cavalry advancing to the frontier
and fearing he might be outflanked, Frossard drew in closer to Forbach. There the commissary and the artillery had—taking undue

risks—accumulated large stocks of provisions and ammunition. Frossard's right was at Spickeren, his left at Stiring.

Perceiving Frossard's movement and thinking the French were in retreat, Kameke, one of Steinmetz's generals, decided to start in pursuit. He occupied Sarrebrücken and then the heights that Frossard had abandoned the day before, moving up his artillery.

Frossard informed Bazaine of these changes but did not ask for help. His position was very strong and he himself declared it impregnable. The Prussians attacked him on the flanks but made only slight gains at costly sacrifices. Frossard was stronger than his adversary. He could have counterattacked and driven Kameke into the Sarre. Instead he idled at Forbach without even riding out to look over the battlefield. Meantime reenforcements from the Second Army reached the Prussians. This time they carried the approaches to Stiring and Spickeren. In spite of partial successes energetic counterattacks did not succeed in dislodging them. With the enemy receiving fresh troops all the while, the battle was turning against the French.

Frossard now hastily called for help from the IIIrd corps and then he called again. Bazaine did not know what it was all about. He sent the Metman and Castigny divisions, then the Montaudon, but in no great hurry and without orders. He was at Saint-Avold himself only twenty minutes distant by train. It did not occur to him to go to the scene of the fighting. The Germans by now had 50,000 men in action and a powerful artillery which beat the Forbacherberg unmercifully and compelled the abandonment of that crucial position, the key to the whole French line. On the extreme left the Germans reached Stiring after a furious battle. Just then still another Prussian division appeared in the French rear. It had marched down the Sarre and then up a tributary of the Sarre—the Rosselle. Frossard up to that moment had been merely puzzled. He now took fright. His regiments had been shot to pieces. No help was in sight. He ordered a retreat. A few hundred men, mostly reservists, hung doggedly to a hill in front of Forbach and held off a whole Prussian division. The town was not occupied till the following morning. During the night Frossard's army reached Sarreguemines and Puttelange. Four thousand men failed to answer roll-call. They were either dead or prisoners. The Germans lost more.

Bazaine's three divisions appeared in the region of Forbach about an hour after the action was over. The Marshal's inattention had fitted in perfectly with the incompetence of his three generals. Each of them had been thinking of himself—of his own personal credit and security. Had even one of them moved towards the cannonade, Frossard would have been saved and the outcome of the battle reversed.

So by flagrant incompetence in the command, the day that saw the loss of Alsace saw serious inroads upon Lorraine. But the defeat in the field was as nothing compared with the moral defeat. The two reverses completely destroyed French prestige in Europe and Napoleon III's prestige in the country dropped to a low level from which it was never to rise again.

As he looked on at the action at Sarrebrücken the Emperor had not been able to keep to his horse and he had walked to a carriage leaning on the arm of General Lebrun, his aide-de-camp.

"The Emperor does not look very well," said the General.

"I am in terrible pain," Napoleon III answered.

Nélaton had come to Metz on the 2nd of August and on returning to Paris had left one of his pupils, Dr. Augier, to look after the Emperor and give him the necessary care in case of a new attack. Now, on the 6th, Napoleon III's kidney trouble was aggravated by a cold that completely clouded his mind. He received news of the twin defeats in a sort of daze. Though they were defeats and nothing more, he thought all was lost. The only definite idea he seemed to have was to defend Paris. On the evening of the 6th, in a four-cornered talk between himself, Prince Napoleon, Le Boeuf and Castelnau, he outlined a plan for drawing most of the army together and retreating on Châlons. There, strengthened by the recruits which had been pouring in from all France, he might be able to halt the enemy's advance.

Le Boeuf protested. To fall back into the Champagne would be to confess a disaster which had not been suffered at all. And that was true. The Prussian armies had more or less lost contact with each other by their rapid advance and would have been in no position to deal with a determined and unexpected counterthrust. Napoleon III argued. Jérôme David came in just then and managed with difficulty to persuade him. The Emperor was to leave at four in the morning for Saint-Avold, to organize the counter-offensive. A telegram came in to inform him that "no one knew where

Frossard was." He seized on that as a pretext to give up the idea of the attack. Le Boeuf handed in his resignation, offering himself as the scapegoat. The Emperor agreed that it might be well to replace him in the Ministry of War, but insisted on keeping him as a major-general.

Prince Napoleon and Pietri, the Emperor's private secretary, were fully aware of the Emperor's physical and moral deterioration. They thought he ought to return to Paris at once. General Castelnau courageously took the lead in broaching the painful subject to the Emperor. Napoleon III shook his head; then, setting the Prince Imperial on his knee, he asked the boy what he thought about it.

"Go home before we've fought a battle?" cried the little fellow. "That would be dishonorable!"

General Lebrun took a hand. Napoleon III answered:

"I think it impossible to desert my soldiers."

Pietri none the less sent word to the Empress. He thought the place for the Emperor was not with the army now but at the head of the government. He suggested giving the command-in-chief to Bazaine.

Eugénie did not see things that way. She telegraphed back to her husband at Metz:

"Have you considered all the consequences that would follow your return to Paris under the shadow of two reverses?"

Napoleon III decided to keep the command. Bazaine, for a moment, talked like a great soldier. He proposed concentrating the army between Frouard and Nancy on the impregnable plateau of Les Hayes and holding the enemy back from there.

"That would mean uncovering Paris," replied the Emperor.

When he should have been thinking of Lorraine and Alsace he could not get his mind off Paris! Bazaine shrugged his sturdy shoulders.

"Perhaps!" he said.

It was decided that the Ist and Vth corps would proceed to Châlons to form the nucleus for a new army—to be commanded by MacMahon (there, but later on, on the 16th of August, they would be joined by the VIIth corps which had been headed for Belfort but was ordered, at that time, to return to Châlons). All the other troops would be sent to Metz, where they would camp in the shelter of the advanced forts with Bazaine in command. In spite of the incompetence he had demonstrated at Forbach, Bazaine retained the confidence of the army and high favor in public opinion at home.

On August 9th Napoleon III received a call from General Changarnier at the prefecture in Metz. After eighteen years of solitude and silence his adversary of far away Second Republic days had come to offer his services. The Emperor embraced him. The old general was wearing a mixed, outlandish uniform. To Du Barail, who gazed at him in astonishment, Changarnier said:

"France is in trouble. Those who love her must stand together. I have brought my sword to the Emperor. I have forgotten everything. He has too!"

This ghost from the battlefields of Africa was strong for the offensive. Nobody listened to him, just as nobody listened to Le Boeuf. Changarnier was not offered any command.

CHAPTER XXXV

The End of Ollivier

FREED OF THE EMBARRASSMENT OF PARLIAMENT EMILE OLLIVIER had been governing, ever since the Emperor's departure, under the authority of the Empress-Regent who had applied herself energetically to affairs. Public opinion in Paris was uneasy. The revolutionaries and even the republicans were agitating. They wanted Napoleon III defeated, without realizing, one may hope, that that also meant defeat for France.

M. Lagrange testified later on at an inquiry into the causes of the insurrection of the 18th of March:

"At the time [August, 1870] when misfortunes began for France, the members of the secret societies were all hoping that we would be beaten. It was noted that at every meeting of the socialist committees there were speeches expressing eagerness that France should be 'beaten flat.' It was an enthusiastic desire on their part. They argued that if France were defeated, a revolution would be unavoidable and they would climb into the saddle."

"Oh, if we could only be beaten!" was an exclamation that Jules Simon heard on the lips of any number of Leftists, and his testimony could not be considered biased. The *Rappel* of Victor Hugo's sons even dared to say:

"The most serious danger is the danger of victory. The Empire is playing dead. Let the Prussians be beaten and it will come to life."

In his *Réveil* Delescluze paid his respects to "cardboard-and-tin generals who have never been good for anything except squandering the lives of their soldiers."

There were partial demonstrations against the government in a number of cities. The country, at bottom, was still loyal. The crowds in Paris were violently patriotic.

The Wissenbourg disaster was made doubly cruel for the capital.

542

On August 6th an exchange manipulator posted a counterfeit dispatch on a pillar in the Bourse:

"MacMahon wins great victory. 25,000 prisoners, among them the Prince Royal of Prussia."

The city thrilled and burst out into flags. The *Marseillaise* was heard everywhere. Then came the crash. Confirmation of the dispatch was sought at the ministry. It issued a denial, whereupon mobs began tearing down the flags. Newspapermen crowded the Ministry of the Interior.

"It's going to be hot tonight," said Pietri, the prefect of police.

He was mistaken. The evening was to be quite calm. But towards midnight a telegram from the army was delivered at Saint-Cloud. It read:

"MacMahon has lost a battle. Frossard retreating. Everything can be remedied. You must declare martial law and make ready to defend the capital."

The Empress set out at once for the Tuileries, escorted by Metternich. There she summoned the ministers.

They had all appeared by three o'clock in the morning. The members of the Privy Council and the presidents of the two Chambers were also present, along with General Trochu. Trochu was enjoying high esteem among liberals and republicans for his pamphlet on the army, which had won him semi-ostracism at court. Had he agreed to become Minister of War in Le Boeuf's place he might have strengthened the government. Instead he adopted a quarrelsome, bitter attitude and discouraged every proposal that was put forward. It was decided to proclaim martial law and call all men of military age to the colors. On a motion by the Empress, which drew expressions of alarm from Ollivier, the Chambers were convoked for the 11th. Then the date was changed to the 9th.

A proclamation was posted on walls about the city, making public the harsh news. Paris was dumbfounded. The army had been called so strong, and the leaders without equals! Yet they had not managed to take the offensive and they had given ground before the first assaults by the enemy! Was the Empire going to end, then, in the bloody disaster that had been foretold by its opponents? There were demonstrations along the boulevards. They called for a national uprising. The republicans were in ecstasy. Jules Ferry met young Déroulède and shouted in his face:

"The Emperor's armies are beaten!"

Jules Favre and sixteen of his colleagues on the Left went to the Ministry of the Interior and demanded arms for all citizens.

A hundred or more deputies belonging to the dynastic groups and manipulated by Clément Duvernois and Jérôme David sent a delegation to the Empress to demand the dismissal of the Ollivier ministry and the appointment of Trochu to the Ministry of War. Eugénie had aged during those days. There were rings around her eyes. Her cheeks were pale. She answered with an archness and loftiness that she had never displayed even in her best days. She had never liked the Ollivier ministry and the ministry, for its part, was chafing overtly under her regency. She defended it nevertheless. A change of governments in the face of the enemy would be perilous, she said. She would not assume responsibility for any such move. As for Trochu, she had sounded him out. If he was going to retail in public all the mistakes that had been made since 1866, she would not have anything to do with him.

In accord with Chevandier de Valdrôme, the Minister of the Interior, Ollivier had devised a scheme for depriving the republicans of their leaders, overawing the revolutionaries and perhaps forcing his bitterest enemies, the ultra-imperialists, to silence. It was what he called a *"coup de justice"* and what was called ordinarily a *coup d'état.*[1]

The idea was to arrest the principal agitators, among whom Ollivier deliberately classed Gambetta, Arago, Jules Favre, Jules Ferry, Pelletan, Dorian and Kératry. Pietri, the prefect of police, warned the Empress of what was going on. She thought the idea frankly crazy and said that she would resist it with all her might.[2]

Ollivier, however, thought he ought to postpone the execution of his plan until the Emperor was back in Paris, in other words, till the Regency had come to an end. Eugénie being as unpopular as she was, his coup, he felt, might involve too great risks.

Chevandier and Ollivier went to the Tuileries to browbeat the Empress into informing the Emperor by telegraph that his presence in Paris was absolutely necessary.

The scene, in which the talking was without gloves, was a dramatic one.

[1] Ollivier, *op. cit.*, XVI, 368 f.
[2] M. Paléologue, *Entretiens*, 204.

Eugénie refused to send any such message.

"If he came home he would look like a deserter. The only place for the Emperor is with the army. He can come back only after a victory."

"Madame," answered Ollivier, "there won't be any victory if the Emperor stays with the army. He stands in the way of victory. He does not know how to command an army and he prevents those who do know how from commanding."

The Empress, bursting into sobs, replied with almost the very words that her son had used:

"Come home before he's won a victory? That would be dishonorable!"

"No, Madame. It would mean saving the country and the dynasty."

She looked him straight in the eye and said:

"I don't care about the dynasty. I care only about the country."

Ollivier pressed his point without dwelling on words which were as noble as they were, in that flash, sincere.

"At least leave my son with the army!"

"What could he do—with the army?"

Eugénie was beside herself. With her excitement lending radiance to her face, she cried:

"He could be killed in battle! Yes, let him be killed in battle!"

Chevandier and Pietri, who were present at the interview, were in tears, but the former now tried in his turn to influence this woman who towered before him like a Roman matron.

Finally Eugénie gave in. She went and wrote out a dispatch.

But when she read it before the Council, Persigny objected flatly to sending it. The army, he said, was going to win out. Its defeats had been due simply to the egregious strategical error of stringing it out in little units over a front of a hundred and sixty miles. The Emperor should participate in that recovery and retemper his prestige in it.

Rouher and Baroche agreed with Persigny and the Council adopted that partisan point of view. Repudiated by the Regent and already discredited in public opinion, Ollivier had now only to appear before the Legislative Body to receive the finishing blow.

The streets along the river and the Place de la Concorde were filled with milling crowds. The Palais Bourbon was closely guarded by troops under the personal command of the governor of Paris, Baraguay d'Hilliers. The head of the government read a brief statement to the deputies:

"We have had some setbacks, but the larger part of the army has not been defeated nor even engaged. None of our defenses are in the hands of the enemy. Our immense resources are untouched." And he went on to enumerate the steps that had been taken to put the country in a state of defense. The class of 1870 had been called up. The mobile guards had been increased and had been made a part of the regular army.

While the Left peppered him with sarcastic interruptions, Ollivier found himself deserted by the Right. Then, seeing his grave open before him, he thought of a handsome gesture:

"Please think only of the country, gentlemen. Dismiss us all if you wish and at once; for what is needed above all is not a peroration by me but action by others."

He came down from the speaker's platform with a mortal silence impending like a hammer above his head.

A motion from the Left Center demanded the retirement of the Ministry and a transference of power to Trochu.

Jules Favre, pale, tense, his lips curling, demanded in the name of the republicans that the Emperor relinquish the command of the army, and that the Chamber elect a commission of fifteen members to have full powers till the enemy should be driven from the country.

The Right protested clamorously. Jérôme David blistered the cabinet with one trenchant sentence:

"Prussia was ready. We were not."

Clément Duvernois, now certain of his vengeance, thought of enjoying it by a resolution that meant the opposite of what it said:

"Resolving to support a cabinet that has shown its capacity to provide for the defense of the country. . . ."

Ollivier was on his feet, protesting. The Chamber rejected the resolution with the all but unanimous vote that Duvernois desired (August 9th).

An inglorious end for the first and last parliamentary government under the Empire, a government that had had excellent ideas and only one fault, but a fatal one: the fault of not paying close enough attention to foreign affairs and to the army, leaving these to be play-things of the absolute power.

It was at once replaced with a Palikao ministry. Even while Olliv-ier was squirming before the Chamber, General Palikao had been summoned by the Empress. On her pledge that he would be made a marshal he agreed to form a "strong" government.

That was a difficult undertaking. The ministry, however it might be constituted, would come into being in the midst of a stew of bit-terness, fear and cowardice—all the mud that the end of a tottering regime stirs up. Many advances, many pleadings were needed be-fore ministers could be found. Béhic and Talhouët declined. Chev-reau accepted on a personal plea by the Empress. Jérôme David, long hungry for power, was the only one to enter the formation with any satisfaction. The Prince de la Tour d'Auvergne, who was then ambassador at Vienna, was named Minister of Foreign Affairs without being consulted. Magne declined, but was placed in Finance just the same.

The Regent did not have the right to appoint ministers. That prerogative belonged to the Emperor alone. She boldly usurped it.

"Your Majesty is making a *coup d'état,*" cautioned Augustin Filon.

"What else can I do?" she cried. "My conscience tells me that I must sign these appointments. I will explain to the Emperor when the time comes."

With Napoleon III far away and shrinking smaller and smaller in defeat his wife could hardly perceive him as anything more than a wraith from the past. Instinctively she was stepping into his shoes, laying hold on all authority within reach in order to govern in his stead, save France and—if that were still possible—her son's crown.

Taking it as it was, the Palikao ministry, directed by a man sev-enty-four years old, was not at all bad. It had intelligence and it had courage. It was to succeed in mobilizing all the still scattered re-sources of the nation with a view to the country's defense. It was to create new armies, fortify Paris, stock the city with food, fodder and cattle, get the great works of art into safe places and ease the cur-rency stress by making bank notes legal tender and raising a loan of a billion francs. Not only that: in a country that had been shaken to its foundations it kept order. There were attempts, not very seri-ous attempts, to start riots in Marseilles, in Lyons, in Paris even. It put them down. With more good faith than political wisdom it kept the Chambers in permanent session. Parliament, for its part, created no great embarrassment for the government. In fact, as the Emperor's dispatch had said, everything could still be set in order again if Bazaine would only win a victory. And the country looked forward expectantly to that victory, with its eyes glued upon Metz, a city now girt about with the awe-inspiring thunder of heavy guns.

CHAPTER XXXVI

Gravelotte—Mars-la-Tour—Saint-Privat

THE RETREAT OF THE ARMY OF THE RHINE UPON METZ WAS EXE-
cuted after a fashion on the 9th and 10th of August under a driz-
zling rain and in a maze of orders and counter-orders. Many soldiers lost their knapsacks and camp equipment, some even their
muskets. They had nothing but mildewed bread to eat. They
grumbled whenever an officer was within earshot, but they were still
in good spirits, ready for action.

By the 11th, accordingly, the IInd, IIIrd and IVth army corps
and the Guard were massed in front of the fortresses of Queulen
and Saint-Julien. The VIth, under Canrobert, would soon be coming up. Bazaine had his headquarters at Borny. He was commanding the army though still under the higher authority of the Emperor and Le Boeuf.

Le Boeuf, however, was a major-general only in name. His resignation having failed of acceptance, he was filling his post only out
of a sense of duty. The chatterbox, at bottom, had his dose of character! In Paris, meantime, public opinion, the Chambers, the
ministry, were clamoring for his head. Napoleon III held out, on a
point of honor, as a matter of loyalty and friendship. At the Empress's request, Conti finally telegraphed that it was "unwise longer
to resist the pressure of public opinion, however unfair it might
be." Palikao was hard and he was harsh. He threatened to remove
Le Boeuf. The Marshal thereupon retired—with very good grace.
As he still was anxious to remain in active service he was eventually
placed in command of Decaen's corps when Decaen was killed.

"Only Bazaine inspires my confidence," the Empress reiterated
nervously. "Work with Bazaine in every move you make."

What she wanted was not just the elimination of Le Boeuf! She
wanted the military abdication of Napoleon III also! The Emperor

was well aware of that and did not try to offer any resistance. He was too conscious of the complete paralysis into which he had fallen. He stepped into the background of his own accord.

"We have both been fired," he said to Le Boeuf.

On the evening of the 12th he handed the command-in-chief over to Bazaine. The Marshal's relatives and friends had intrigued energetically for him. He accepted without any pleasure. Perhaps he realized that things had gone too far wrong. But he could not help himself. The army and the country were turning to him in a panic of trust. Thiers and Gambetta were lauding him to the skies in the Legislative Body. His nomination was acclaimed.

Rarely in history has a nation more emphatically misplaced its trust. MacMahon and Canrobert may have been as inadequate as one please. They would have been better than Bazaine. The stocky little man with the shifting eye may once have been a sparkling soldier. Now, since his marriage and his adventures in Mexico, he had greatly changed. At fifty-nine he was as apathetic as a dotard. With no trace of conscientiousness he had no thought save of himself. His first concern was to shirk responsibility. He was interested neither in the country nor in the Empire, but only in the narrowing future that his advancing years still left him. For that matter he had never been the man for the task now laid upon him. He had never had so large an army under his orders. He had had no military education. He was just a "colonial" fighter, a guerilla, an ambusher. He knew nothing about strategy and was lost in a daze the moment great masses of men began to move. He had never outgrown the lieutenant, the major, at the very most, the colonel. And here he was, now, generalissimo, the man who was asked to guarantee, under specially difficult circumstances, the lives, the safety, the success of 160,000 men and the fate of a dynasty and a country! It was all a case of mass hallucination and the results were to be so disastrously disappointing that the French public could explain them only as treason.

In spite of Bazaine, who wanted a free hand, the Emperor stayed on four more days in Metz, issuing no further orders but expressing hopes or desires that looked like orders. His bladder pains held him in acute physical depression—he was undergoing two catheter operations a day. His mental torture was even greater. On Ollivier's fall from power he had not even been consulted in the choice of new ministers. Civil dispossession after military failure! He moved in an atmosphere of reproachfulness, disregard, even insult. Commander Duperré, of the navy, brought a message from Eugénie to Metz. He told the Emperor to his face that if he "ever returned to Paris something worse than mud would be thrown in his face." All that was more torturing than the cruelest punishment. If expiation be considered his due, Napoleon III certainly expiated. There was no one about him on whom he could lean. His son was a mere child happily dreaming. Prince Napoleon was rage and bitterness personified. The Empress was gradually stripping him of power. History offers few examples of such utter loneliness.

The Germans were astounded at the French retreat. Steinmetz and Prince Friedrich Karl, with the first two German armies, followed Bazaine, but slowly, circumspectly, making no effort to keep in contact. They seemed to be afraid of a sudden spring by the French. King William moved his headquarters forward to Sarrebrücken. The Third German Army under the Prince Royal followed on after MacMahon across Lorraine. Moltke now was planning to hold the French with the First Army while the Second, slipping off to the southwest, would cross the Meuse at Pont-à-Mousson, move quietly upstream on the left bank, then suddenly appear in the French rear on a line with Metz. That would catch Bazaine as in a net.

Napoleon III and Bazaine saw through the manoeuvre and, to escape being cut off from Paris, decided to cross the Meuse and make Verdun. Thence the army could form a junction with the troops at Châlons.

That was going back to the Emperor's former plan. But Bazaine was loath to quit the defenses of Metz and did not stir for two days, sheltering himself behind the dead authority of the Emperor, never issuing an order, not even blowing up the bridges across the Moselle in front of the town, over which eventually the enemy was to pass. He was on bad terms with Jarras, his chief-of-staff, a man far too outspoken. He gave Jarras no instructions, refused to see him, and took full personal charge of the difficult task of moving an army of twenty-two divisions along the one road through Gravelotte and Mars-la-Tour.

At half-past one, on August 14th, Napoleon III climbed feebly into a carriage, took his son in beside him and set out from Metz, escorted by the Hundred Guards.

Shortly afterwards the army followed in a disorderly mob, greatly impeded by the wide-spreading camions that all but blocked the road. By four o'clock the IInd and VIth corps, and part of the IVth, had left their positions to the east of the city and crossed to the left bank.

Suddenly the cannon began to boom at Borny. Von der Goltz, one of Steinmetz's generals, had perceived the French movement and, acting on his own responsibility, had ordered an attack upon the IIIrd corps, which was breaking camp at the village of Colombey. Just such an unforeseen initiative had won the battles at Froeschwiller and Forbach. Ladmirault dashed to the rescue with the divisions of Cissey, Lorencez and Grénier. The French counterattack was furious, enthusiastic. The men were eager to avenge their two defeats. As the bugles sounded the infantry rushed forward, shouting: *"Vive l'Empereur!"*

Von der Goltz carried Colombey, but when he tried to debouch from the village the French halted him before Borny. Steinmetz thought his general had dangerously exposed himself and ordered him to fall back. Von der Goltz refused to obey and forced Steinmetz to come to his support. The battle raged furiously on the slopes of the plateau of Borny, at Colombey and at Ney.

Bazaine came on the scene at last, angry that a battle had started without his permission. He did not see the opportunity that lay before him. It was a fine one. He had 50,000 men, the enemy 30,000. He had more artillery. He might have won. Unfortunately, nothing of the sort occurred to him. He ordered everybody to keep on the defensive and refused to throw new units forward.

"I don't want any advance, not even by an inch!" he shouted.

The Prussians were now reenforced. They intensified their attack. Bazaine had gone in among the men and was touched by a bullet. Decaen, commanding the IIIrd army corps, was killed. Possession of a hill road between Colombey and Pellecroix was long disputed. The French were holding their positions. The enemy was making no headway in the direction of Borny. Grénier's division first lost and then rewon the forest at Ney. Night fell with the guns still booming. Bazaine ordered the retreat to continue.

So the French had their first day of successes during the war.

They had lost 3,500 men, the Prussians 5,000. But the French had not won the real victory that the valor and devotion of the troops deserved. Instead of giving Steinmetz a thorough trouncing they were now in retreat. The Prussians assumed that they had won a victory since the ground was being left in their hands.

The Emperor had halted in alarm at Longueville on hearing the cannonade. Bazaine joined him late that night.

"Well," said the Emperor, who was in bed, "you have broken the spell."

The officers about him began to take heart again.

On the 15th, Prince Friedrich Karl, ascending the Moselle on the right bank, continued his enveloping movement. By evening on that day it had almost closed in on the Verdun highway. Napoleon III was still on the road. With the main artery choked by masses of soldiers, who were staggering on half asleep, he mounted a horse and by side roads reached Gravelotte, where, against Bazaine's advice, he stopped at the Hotel Plaisant. It was as though a deep-seated fear were keeping him from leaving the army.

On this roundabout ride he halted to rest, for a moment, at the Point-du-Jour farm. Seeing a little knoll nearby he started for it and then sat down on a tumbled-down stone wall that commanded a distant view over the countryside. Not far away stood some farm-hands gazing at him sadly, reverently. He asked one of them the names of the farms and hamlets which were sprinkled over the circle of rounded hilltops, each plateau sloping off into deep wooded ravines.

"Sire, before you lies *Moscow,* behind you, *Leipzig.* Straight ahead, the way you were going, lies *La Folie.*"

The Emperor quivered as though he had been struck with a lash. A deathly pallor overspread his face under the rouge which he was now using in order not to discourage the people and soldiers about him with the signs of wastage from his disease. Finally he rose and mounted his horse again.

Canrobert and Frossard were sure there was going to be an attack the next day. Bazaine, however, took no precautions. At dawn on the 16th he called on the Emperor to bid him goodbye. The Emperor, this time, would surely make Verdun.

Napoleon III said that they would meet again at Châlons.

"Start as soon as you can in that direction. . . . Austria may even yet come in. Don't do anything irremediable."

As he shook hands he said:

"I am entrusting you with the last army that France has. Think of the Prince Imperial."

Then he drove off, slumping back in the carriage, with his tunic unbuttoned in front. He looked like a corpse.

At Verdun that same day he took a train for the camp at Châlons. Only a third-class carriage was available in the station. Cushions were laid on the hard wooden seats and he stretched out upon them. He reached Châlons without knowing that the greatest battle of the war had just been fought.

Instead of hurrying the labored march of his soldiers along the tree-bordered road that crossed the highlands past Gravelotte, Rezonville and Mars-la-Tour, Bazaine halted all the forenoon of the 15th in order to give the IIIrd and IVth corps a chance to catch up. They were still far behind and he wanted to have the whole army within reach.

At nine o'clock on the 16th the Vth Prussian cavalry, picking its way through the wooded ravines, stumbled upon the Murat brigade of French dragoons at Vionville where they were resting.

As the Germans charged the civilians driving the wagons stampeded in panic and the French line was thrown into confusion for a moment. But it re-formed very soon. Frossard with the IInd corps repulsed the Prussian cavalry and recovered Vionville. But then General Alvensleben, commanding the IIIrd Prussian corps, very active, very bold, came on the scene in his turn. In a first attack he was thrown back with heavy losses on the wooded slopes to the south of Rezonville. Had Bazaine been good for anything, he would have taken the offensive at that moment, and with the Guard and the troops of Frossard and Canrobert, which were at Gravelotte, he could have crushed Alvensleben. His one thought, instead, was to maintain communication with Metz, so he piled up his reserves on his left, where they could be of no possible use.

The Prussians by now had brought up artillery. They attacked again before Rezonville, but were held. Farther west Bataille's division lost Vionville again, and Flavigny and the IInd corps had to give ground. That uncovered the French flank at Rezonville. The Cuirassiers of the Guard charged. It was in vain. Bazaine himself was caught while busy figuring out the position for a battery. Sword in hand he leapt on a horse and galloped and fenced about like a second-lieutenant. He was all but captured—and that might have meant a change in the fortunes of the war for the French. Unfortunately he was rescued by the return of his escort.

The Grenadiers of the Guard managed to halt the rout of the IInd corps. Canrobert came in and delivered a vicious thrust at the German left. It gave ground. To gain time for help to arrive Alvensleben threw in his cavalry—for the historic *Todtenritt*, or "Death Ride of Rezonville." His cuirassiers and uhlans charged magnificently, to be mowed down with terrific slaughter.

Again Bazaine failed to follow up his advantage.

The battle so far had gone through two phases. Frossard had failed on the defensive. Canrobert had halted the enemy onrush. The issue was still uncertain.

At this juncture Ladmirault appeared on the field—he had heard the cannonade at Sainte-Marie-aux-Chênes and had hurried up. Deploying on the extreme right of the French in front of the forest of Tronville, he decided to try to turn the Prussian left. Changarnier was with him and advised the move.

"There they are, in there, quite close," stammered the aged general. "Don't we clean them out?" [1]

Ladmirault's infantry had carried the wood by four o'clock and his cavalry had reached Mars-la-Tour. The Germans were giving way. Ladmirault, however, was not strong enough to make it a rout. For that he had to wait for Cissey's division, which had lost its way at Saint-Privat. That was due to lack of maps for Lorraine. The French often marched more or less at random. They had more maps than they could use, however, for the Rhineland and Germany.

The enemy reenforcements got there first—the whole Xth army corps called in from the west by Prince Friedrich Karl. Ladmirault had to fall back. Cissey came up at last—at five o'clock. He crushed Wedel's Westphalians in a ravine called the "Washtub"—the Fond de Cuve—to the north of Mars-la-Tour. The German cavalry then collided with the French horse—a magnificent, brutal mêlée in which six thousand men, lancers, hussars, African chasseurs, the Empress's dragoons, fought tooth and nail under the setting sun. The Frenchmen were lighter, man for man, than the Germans and

[1] *Revue d'histoire*, February, 1904.

not so tall. They had the worst of it. They drew off and rode away towards the north.

Ladmirault could still have won the day had he acted boldly. His regiments were intact, while the German line was in great disarray. But Le Boeuf had sent him only Clérambault's division. He had no news of Bazaine. He decided to draw back upon Arcourt, with the further thought that his men would then be fresh for the battle which he foresaw for the next day.

The fighting lasted around Rezonville for some time still. The Maison Blanche farm was bitterly disputed. It finally remained with the French. Prince Friedrich Karl vainly cannonaded their positions. Finally he tried a cavalry charge. It brought no decision. The battle of Gravelotte-Rezonville-Mars-la-Tour ended at dark in a draw.

And yet it should have been a great victory for the French. They had excellent positions and an advantage of 136,000 men to 91,000, 364 guns to 222. Unfortunately their generals did not know how to use them. They fought the whole battle against superior forces at every point. Gravelotte was a battle of incoherences, delays and wasted heroism. Even so, it was by no means a defeat. The French lost 14,500 men, the Germans more than 16,000 and one flag.

The next day, as Ladmirault had assumed, the battle could have been resumed and made decisive. There was not going to be any next day, nor any victory. Bazaine did not want a battle. He had decided to leave the field and return to Metz. The fortress pulled at him like a magnet. He had been dragged from it in the first place only by sheer force. He had given a lip-promise to the Emperor to meet him in Châlons. He had never intended to go there. At Châlons he would have been something less than master and too close to MacMahon. Bazaine hated MacMahon. He had hated him ever since Algeria, when MacMahon had refused to endorse a request which Bazaine was sending to the Ministry in connection with his first marriage. In Metz he would not be called upon to manoeuvre in the open country. He would be his own master and could use his troops as his own interests or the course of events seemed to require.

He forgot that a victory at just that moment might have changed the whole physiognomy of the war, that it might have halted the Empire in its dizzy slide to destruction. As was later urged against him with very proper force, thinking only of himself he forgot his country. His defenders were to argue that General Coffinières de Nordeck, the governor of Metz, had not sent him the dispatches from the observation units, that he thought himself beaten. That was a lame excuse. At ten o'clock that night he himself sent a letter to Coffinières requesting ammunition. In it he said:

"We have fought a battle that is all in our favor."

His subordinates were congratulating him and they supposed that on the following day he would drive the Germans into the Moselle.

At eleven o'clock he decided to accept defeat. He informed the Emperor not that he was retreating upon Metz but that he was going to try to make Châlons by way of Briey. In dictating the order of retreat to Jarras, he alleged, altogether falsely, a shortage of munitions and food. As his officers stood aghast he said, looking up:

"If anybody can think of anything better to do, let him speak up."

No one spoke up, and the Marshal added:

"Besides, we've got to save the army. To do that we must go back to Metz."[1]

At that same moment Prince Friedrich Karl was issuing the order for the next day to his troops. It read:

"Hold your present positions."

He could have been more aggressive than that. The victory, which he quite reasonably doubted he had won, was being handed to him by Bazaine on a silver platter.

The corps generals began executing the retirement at early dawn. Prince Friedrich Karl was at Flavigny. He could not believe his eyes as he saw the French army folding back towards Gravelotte and Verneville. He at once hurried the news to Moltke and ordered his own men to follow the French in a vast turning movement. Steinmetz now crossed the Moselle also, and served as the Prince's pivot. From that time on superior numbers were to be on the side of the Prussians.

At eight o'clock on the evening of the 17th the French army was settled on a line ten miles long, stretching along a chain of plateaux between Bozérieulles and Roncourt. With the forts of Metz in the rear that was a good position. Frossard's corps, on the extreme left, had a firm hold on the Verdun road and the approaches to the Moselle. Le Boeuf and Ladmirault were in the center. On the right

1 Bapst, *Canrobert*, IV, 161.

Canrobert was settled at Saint-Privat. The Guard was in reserve at Plappeville with Bazaine.

Prince Friedrich Karl and Steinmetz had completed their rather delicate evolution, which was open at many points to surprises, by noon on the 18th. They now approached the French 160,000 strong. Moltke had urged caution. Bazaine ordered his subordinates to keep on the defensive. The two orders laid the foundations for a quiet day. But Manstein, the Commander of the IXth Prussian corps, grew impatient and advanced, attacking Ladmirault who, he thought, was in a weak position. He failed. His artillery was out-shot by the French artillery, while the chassepots wrecked his infantry. The Prussian batteries were raked by machine-gun fire from Lorencez's division and lost most of their gunners. Two of Manstein's cannon were captured.

Manstein had quite lost contact with the rest of the German army and he would have been the victim of his own rashness had Bazaine given the order to overwhelm him, as he could easily have done. Sitting comfortably in his headquarters at Plappeville Bazaine did not move.

"It's nothing important," he said.

Meantime, Friedrich Karl, coming up from Habowiller, saw the peril that Manstein was in and sent in the IIIrd Prussian corps to support him. The French artillery was now the inferior and had to draw back. At half-past four the Prussian infantry advanced courageously upon the French center and the latter had great difficulty in holding on. At the same time the battle opened on the wings. On the French right Steinmetz, advancing under the eyes of Moltke and King William, attacked Frossard and Le Boeuf. In crossing the Moscow farm his columns met such a withering fire that they fell back in disorder. King William went back to Gravelotte, disappointed, and Moltke made ready for a retreat by the bridges across the Moselle.

The Germans, however, succeeded in occupying the Saint-Hubert farm. They could not get beyond the deep ravine called "the Mance." Their stubbornness under shell and solid shot from the French artillery cost them dearly. Steinmetz had thought the battle won. At five o'clock he found himself not only halted but in danger. Had Bazaine thrown in his reserve Steinmetz's line would have been shattered.

Unfortunately things were not going so well for the French on their right. Canrobert had only 23,000 men and no artillery. In the intent of turning the whole French line the Royal Guard under Prince Augustus of Württemberg and the Saxon corps under the Crown Prince of Saxony attacked the village of Sainte-Marie-aux-Chênes, a mile and a half from Saint-Privat. One French regiment defended the village heroically, but it could not stand the fire of ninety-six guns followed by an attack by fifteen battalions. Having lost half its numbers it fell back upon Roncourt.

The encircling movement of the Germans was now clearly defined. Canrobert saw his flank in danger and asked Bazaine for help. The commander-in-chief answered that he would send one division from the Guard, and ammunition. He did nothing of the kind. Bourbaki, with his grenadiers and riflemen, stood marking time. They received no orders. The Prince of Württemberg now threw in the best regiments of the Prussian Guard to take the village of Saint-Privat. Under a cool, methodical fire from the French they were shot to pieces. Eight thousand German dead covered the field in heaps.

That, unmistakably, was the critical point of the battle—and of the whole war. Bazaine held everything in his hands. He let everything slip. He was stationed on top of Fort Saint-Quentin. From there he could see only part of the battle. He stood deaf to Canrobert's desperate appeals for help.

"It's only an outpost affair. It can't last," he kept repeating.

Bourbaki was a brave man. To save the day he might have gone in on his own initiative or, if necessary, against the orders of his chief. He did not dare. Having advanced part way, he lost confidence and fell back.

Canrobert was now holding on at Saint-Privat under the fire of 210 guns, with the Saxons threatening to turn his flank. From Sainte-Marie-aux-Chênes he could see the blue-uniformed Prussian Guard advancing towards him wave on wave. The Marshal dismounted and, on foot, bareheaded, ran along his lines encouraging the troops. Tears of rage were running down his ruddy face. It was seven o'clock. Saint-Privat was burning. The Germans came on with sounding fifes and beating drums, the Saxons from the northeast, the Guard from the south. As they entered the town the lines broke and soldiers and officers mingled in one general confusion. The

French fought back with cold steel, under the walls of the church, in each house. The last outwork of the French defense, the little cemetery of Saint-Privat, was piled high with dead and wounded.

Canrobert could only order a retreat. The VIth corps fell back through the woods towards Metz, in good order, protected by the artillery of the Guard. Seeing his flank uncovered Ladmirault was obliged to do the same shortly afterwards. He too had vainly called for help. Le Boeuf might have reenforced him. He did not move.

Just as Saint-Privat was falling Steinmetz gave way before Frossard. But with Canrobert and Ladmirault in retreat the whole French line collapsed. Bazaine received the news quite calmly. Even when the battle was over he seemed not to have grasped what had taken place. At 8.20 that evening he telegraphed the Emperor:

"I am just back from the plateau. The attack was pretty hot. Fire has ceased this minute. Our troops have held firmly to their positions."

"Don't be downcast!" he said to his officers.

Captain de la Tour d'Auvergne declared in his presence:

"The battle is not lost. It will begin again tomorrow."

Bazaine replied dryly:

"It's not a case of a battle. You were to be called back tomorrow anyway. The only difference is that you are falling back this evening."

The French lost 12,500 men killed and wounded, the Germans 20,000. This defeat at Saint-Privat, which was so costly to the enemy, could have been altered by Bazaine into a splendid victory. In his report he called it, hypocritically, "the defense of the Armanvillers line." By denying that there had been such a battle the idiot imagined he was erasing it from history. But more emphatically than any of his failures it was to rise afterwards to confound and condemn him.

During those heartbreaking days of the 14th, 16th and 18th of August, 1870, the army of the Second Empire really perished. That unskilled, but wide-awake, proud, heroic army, the army that had conquered Algeria, carried the Malakoff bastion and the Solferino tower and then tore its uniforms on the cactuses of Mexico, had really deserved a better fate. It had fought so bravely that in spite of its miserable generals and its wretched equipment it had been able all but to snatch victory from a better trained, a better equipped, a better commanded foe. From history in its company vanished picturesque warfare, the warfare that knew breath-taking charges, lusty sabre thrusts and handsome gestures. Thereafter all that the world was to know would be a tiresome, mechanical, scientific warfare conducted by engineers according to preconceived plans.

Moltke was afraid of a new attack. He was cured of his fears by the next day. The French had withdrawn under the forts of Metz. All he had to do now was cut communications between that fortress and the rest of France. It really was the end. Bazaine's hour had come and gone. Had he displayed the most elementary sense of his duties as a commander-in-chief, those three days, which he spent on the brink of victory, would have crowned him with undying glory. But he proved incapable of conceiving a plan to take the place of the one that he had promised to execute. Sly and shrewd in detailed actions he was inept in grasping a battle, much less a campaign, as a whole. He had been given six or seven certain opportunities to beat his adversary. He had lost them by sheer inertia and lack of character. Now by his deceitfulness and stupidity he was to entice his country into still more complete disaster.

On the 19th of August, from his headquarters in Ban-Saint-Martin, a suburb of Metz, the Marshal assured the Emperor that he had merely ordered "a change of front to thwart a turning movement." He was "counting still on moving north to Sedan, or even Mézières, to end up finally at Châlons." [1] So, deliberately, he was deceiving his master and benefactor. By persuading the Emperor that he was still making an effort to join him, he was to lead him to ruin. The word "Sedan" stood written in Bazaine's dispatch from Metz. His lie was to be the bait that would entice Napoleon III into the last trap, the trap into which he was to disappear from history.

Moltke seemed by now to have taken Bazaine's exact measure. In order to keep the French army shut up he did not think it necessary to waste the armies of Steinmetz and Friedrich Karl in front of the terraces of Metz. Counting reserves which had come up they numbered 280,000 men. Of the best of them, the Royal Guard and the IVth and XIIth corps, he made a new army, the Army of the Meuse, which would be commanded by the Crown Prince of Sax-

[1] *Papiers des Tuileries*, I, 46.

ony and would join the Prince Royal on the road to Paris. In case of need it could stop any forces that might be sent to the relief of Metz. Seven corps, in other words more than 200,000 men, would camp on the heights that surrounded the fortress, and maintain a blockade till it saw fit to surrender.

CHAPTER XXXVII

Napoleon and Eugénie

SHORTLY AFTER THE EMPEROR REACHED THE CAMP AT CHÂLONS MacMahon came in, following troops of the Ist corps whose retreat he had personally commanded. Unfortunately he had not taken care to destroy the tunnels and railways in the Vosges. That was to make the Prince Royal's pursuit much easier.

On MacMahon's right, the Vth corps under the fatuous Failly had also fallen back into Lorraine, marching in a driving rain. The soldiers were without changes of clothing and often without food. They travelled in bands of repulsive vagabonds of whom the country people were afraid.

"It's the retreat from Moscow without the snow," someone said of them.

Almost all their officers, commissioned and non-commissioned, were dead. Discipline and morale had dissolved completely. Finally, on August 14th, it proved possible to transport MacMahon's men by rail from Neufchâteau to Mourmelon, and on the 17th Failly's from Chaumont.

That made the camp at Châlons one immense dumping ground for the refuse of the war. The barracks there contained a mixture of thugs from Paris disguised as mobile guards, laggards ready to lag again, raw recruits discouraged in advance, veterans still dismayed at having run so long and so far.

General Trochu came on from Paris under orders from the government to organize a new corps, the XIIth. At the station he saw Zouaves dancing entirely naked on the roofs of cars, brandishing bottles in their hands and shouting obscenities. Schmitz, his chief of staff, had already proposed to Palikao that the Châlons camp be given up for good.

Prince Napoleon had not left his cousin since the departure from

Metz. He judged him a terrible handicap to an army of which he was no longer in command. Mobile guards and soldiers hooted at him and insulted him whenever he went by in front of their wretched huts. Speaking of the additional responsibility which his presence laid upon the general in command the Prince said:

"You might as well ask a general to go into battle balancing a full soup tureen on his head with the stipulation that he must not spill a drop."

On the morning of the 17th the Emperor assembled a council in his camp-tent—Prince Napoleon, MacMahon, Trochu, Schmitz and General Berthaut, commander of the mobile guards of the Seine. The Prince had talked to Schmitz and the latter brought up the burning question: Would it not be better for the Emperor to go back to Paris? His position among the troops was becoming untenable.

"That's true," commented Napoleon III. "I look as though I had abdicated."

Doubtless by prearrangement with Trochu Schmitz next proposed that Trochu be made military governor of Paris. The Emperor could then return under cover of the great popularity of the general.

Prince Napoleon agreed, with his usual eloquent brutality:

"You don't command the army any more. You are not governing the country any more. What are you doing here? Are you anything more than a correspondent for the London *Times?* . . . If we've got to fall, at least let's fall like men."

That rough-handed language was not without its political motivation. The Prince was figuring that the Emperor's return to Paris would mean the end of the Empress's regency and the suppression of her party. He claimed that Trochu had been badly used so far.

"Name him governor of Paris. He will issue a proclamation saying that you are to follow him within a few hours. Everything will come out all right—you'll see!"

The Emperor drew MacMahon to one side and asked his advice. He suspected that Trochu was an Orleanist. He had voted "no" in the plebiscite after the *coup d'état*. He, the Emperor, had always thought the man a lopsided fellow.

The Marshal reassured him. Trochu was a man who could be trusted.

Napoleon III came back and approached the general.

"General," he asked. "Would you accept this appointment?"

Trochu did not hesitate:

"I am at Your Majesty's service."

He had foreseen the moment. It was his revenge. He had been waiting for it for a long time. As MacMahon had said, Trochu was an honest man. Not only that: He was devoutly religious and, in certain departments of life, thoroughly unselfish. He had adopted his brother's orphan children and had refused an endowment which the Emperor had offered for their education. That lean Breton with the feverish eye of a bird had enough in him to make two talents. But his qualities were at war with each other. He was full of ideas but too much of an analyst. That paralyzed him as a man of action. He was eloquent but he often dropped into mere grandiloquence. He was a devoted patriot, but personal worries always cramped his expansiveness. No one was more susceptible than Trochu, no one more bitter, more suspicious, more discouraging about other men and about the future. He had a clearer vision of mistakes that had been made than of the ways and means of correcting them. Trochu had talents that would have enabled him to play a great rôle during those dark days; but his grudges, his ambitions, his unbalanced judgment, were to prevent him from serving the Empire, which really he did not like, at all high-mindedly, and also from serving the country for which he would gladly have given his life.

As almost always happened when he had made a decision, the Emperor at once began to regret it. He was afraid of the Empress. He thought he ought to consult her and the ministers.

Prince Napoleon exploded:

"What, aren't you the sovereign any more?"

"I am a constitutional sovereign," the Emperor answered quietly. "My decrees have to be countersigned."

"Nothing simpler!" countered the Prince. "The Emperor signs the papers. General Trochu is going back right away. He will have them ratified in Paris."

Convinced or not convinced Napoleon III had not the strength to argue any longer. On two pieces of soiled paper the Prince had drawn up two acts, the one appointing MacMahon commander of all the forces at Châlons under the higher command of Bazaine; the other appointing Trochu military governor of Paris.

Napoleon III signed them.

Before the Council broke up it decided, on a motion by Berthaut, that the mobile guards of the Seine, which were useless at Châlons, and dangerous, should be sent back to Paris. The camp would then be evacuated and the troops drawn in close to the capital, serving to cover it from the army of the Prince Royal—the latter was already being reported in the valley of the Marne. They would also keep any insurrectionary movement from breaking out within the city. With MacMahon posted under the walls, the government would not have to worry about enemies at home. It could devote all its attention to fighting the Prussians.

Somewhat later Prince Napoleon came back to his cousin's tent. The imperial agnate of the long-smothered ambitions thought that he, no less than Trochu, had come to the high point in his life. He explained to the Emperor just what the latter should do. The Emperor should get back to Saint-Cloud under cover of the night, escorted by a regiment that he could trust. He would at once ask the Legislative Body for dictatorial powers. In case of a refusal he would abdicate in favor of his son.

The Prince did not add that, in this latter case, he thought he would be the man to exercise the regency in the name of the young sovereign.

The Emperor seemed to agree. He was tired of everything and of everybody—he was tired of himself. He sent Duperré to apprise Eugénie of the decrees that had just been issued. Almost immediately afterwards Trochu, with the documents in his pocket, took the train for Paris.

Instead of following him the Emperor delayed his departure. He had better wait for news from Bazaine. In the course of the afternoon he got word of Gravelotte and then of the retreat on Metz. In the evening a telegram came from Palikao in answer to the message delivered by Duperré:

"The Empress communicates to me a letter in which the Emperor announces his intention of bringing the Army of Châlons in upon Paris. I implore the Emperor to give up that idea, which would seem like a desertion of the Army of Metz."

Almost immediately afterwards an angry, quivering message came from Eugénie:

"Don't dream of coming back unless you intend to unchain a

most frightful revolution. . . . They would say here that you are leaving the army because you are afraid of danger."

The Emperor's head drooped. Then, turning to Prince Napoleon, he said:

"I can't go back to Paris. The Empress answers that my situation would be untenable."

He was silent a moment; then he looked up again with tears in his eyes.

"The truth is," he said, "they are throwing me out. They don't want me in the army. They don't want me in Paris." [1]

Well, what could he do? Trochu had not reached Paris yet. Perhaps Trochu would force the hand of the Regent and the cabinet. He fell silent, putting off any decision till the morrow.

Trochu got to Paris at midnight. He at once called on Chevreau, the Minister of the Interior. The latter, after some argument, went with him to the Tuileries. The Empress consented to see them, but in the presence of Admiral Jurien de la Gravière and Pietri, whom she sent for.

She had been living on her nerve ever since Forbach. Courageously, in spite of a number of breakdowns in private, she had faced all the dangers, visible or unknown, that lurked about her. She had eaten hardly at all. What sleep she had had came from doses of chloral. Trochu's arrival she feared was a threat to her powers as Regent. She scarcely acknowledged his bow.

Trochu, overawed, informed her of his appointment, then handed her the decrees and the rough draft of a proclamation that he had written out in pencil, using his knees as a table, on the train.

The Empress broke him off harshly:

"The Emperor must not come back! He will not come back!"

She began talking excitedly. After a flood of words she cried:

"He would never arrive here alive! . . . Those who gave him that advice are his enemies."

She felt a need for saying something insulting.

"General, don't you think the best thing we could do, in view of the danger we are in, would be to call the Princes of Orleans back to France?"

That was a scathing allusion to the General's supposed Orleanism.

[1] Ollivier, *op. cit.*, XVII, 269.

He was dumbfounded at the Empress's attitude and only by degrees did her meaning dawn upon him. Jurien de la Gravière had been friends with him since boyhood. The Admiral ran to him and almost pushed him into the Empress's arms.

"Madame," he said, "give your full trust to the General. He deserves it. You are just the people to understand each other. Embrace him! He is a good man!"

Eugénie pretended not to hear, then softened a little. Trochu protested his devotion, in grandiloquent language. The Regent finally compromised. She accepted Trochu as military governor but with an emphatic scratch of a pencil cancelled from the proclamation the announcement of the Emperor's return to Paris.

She did not want the Emperor back. He had handed power over to her. Could he take it back again—a sick man, in disgrace? She thought herself better able than he to exercise power. She was less afraid of a military disaster than of an insurrection. For Napoleon III to return to Paris a beaten man would be to rouse too much anger, too many hatreds.

"Then," she said, "one of two things would happen: Either the army would side with him, and that would be civil war; or else it would turn against him, and that would be the mob and a general massacre. In either case who would win? The Prussians!"

She refused to have him back! She was his wife, yes, and she owed him everything. But she was a mother too—and she would sacrifice everything for her son. An Emperor—an Emperor was a victorious leader! He disappeared from the scene the moment he was beaten. Otherwise—the word had no meaning, it was nonsense! She had thought the dynasty lost after the first defeats. Now she was willing to do the impossible to save it. With all the warm faith of a Spanish woman she hoped for a turn in fortune. Like so many others she was still counting on Bazaine. He would break Moltke's clutch—or else MacMahon, the hero of Italy, would halt the enemy before he could appear before Paris. Then she would make peace—peace with honor and not too many losses. Then having restored peace to the country and made sure of the "little Prince's" throne, she would go to the fallen Emperor, if he were still alive, and grow old and die with him.

Dreams, fancies, a frenzied raving of dread!

Trochu went on to the Ministry of War. Palikao received him even less cordially than the Regent.

"If I were not afraid of starting a revolution I would resign," he said.

He criticized the shunting of the mobile guards off on Paris and declared his absolute opposition to the return of the Châlons army. MacMahon should get his troops together and head for Metz, with the Emperor, to join Bazaine.

Trochu had displayed praiseworthy self-control all that night. He let Palikao have his say. With manifest unwillingness Palikao countersigned Trochu's decree and it was taken at once to the office of the *Journal Officiel*. The Minister was none the less brazenly to declare before the Legislative Body that afternoon that he had himself called on Trochu, in order to have the arming of the capital in good hands.

From the camp in Châlons MacMahon asked instructions of Bazaine, his superior in command (August 19th, 3.25 A.M.):

"I cannot see at this distance from you how I can get away to help you without uncovering Paris. If you have a different idea, let me know."

Bazaine could not let him know because the telegraph and railroad lines were already cut.

The Prince Royal's advanced regiments were already being reported on a line between Ornain and Vitry. The camp at Châlons had no defensive organization. It would soon be in danger. MacMahon saw himself forced, very unwillingly, to make a decision. He finally ordered the camp evacuated, heading the troops for Reims.

"If Bazaine breaks out to the north I will be better able to support him," MacMahon explained to Palikao by telegraph (August 20th, 4:45 A.M.).

A provisory disposition, therefore. He still hoped to be able to do something for Bazaine.

On the 21st the army started its march for Reims across the gloomy, chalky plain. The Emperor settled in the château of Courcelles, a mile or more outside the town. There almost immediately Rouher called on him.

Since Ollivier's fall the sometime Minister of State had become the Empress's chief adviser again. Eugénie had sent him to persuade the army to effect a junction with Bazaine. In his talk with Napoleon III Rouher stressed the weight that his long experiences in public affairs ought to give to his opinions.[1] The Châlons army should quickly unite with the Army of Lorraine, and then both should fall upon the Prince Royal and destroy him. MacMahon very sensibly observed that Bazaine's silence showed that he was cut off.

"He hasn't enough food and no ammunition at all. He will be obliged to capitulate. We can't get there in time."

Very wisely he preferred to keep near Paris.

Rouher had never been obstinate except when he felt himself the strongest. He had no knowledge of strategy. He bowed. He himself drew up a decree placing MacMahon in command of the troops in Paris, and a rough draft of a statement that the Marshal would sign. Then he took the train back to the capital.

His reception at the Tuileries on the 23rd was not very enthusiastic. Palikao stormed in the Council of Ministers. Backed by his colleagues and the Regent he telegraphed Napoleon III:

"Not to rescue Bazaine would have the most deplorable consequences in Paris. In the face of such a disaster there would be every reason to fear that the capital would make no defense."

That was talk. The defense that Paris would put up was shortly to be seen. But before the telegram got to Reims MacMahon and Napoleon III had changed their plans. They had just received the message that Bazaine had sent out the day after Saint-Privat. A forest guard had got it through to Verdun. The dispatch was the one that concealed Bazaine's defeat and talked of a movement north towards Montmédy. A somewhat later dispatch that Bazaine sent off on August 19th never reached MacMahon for reasons that have never been entirely made clear—was it lost, or suppressed? In it Bazaine showed himself much less positive. He said he would "send further word if he thought he could get out to the north." Had MacMahon received this second message his conduct would doubtless have been different.

As things were, and without trying to find out whether Bazaine had really gone north, MacMahon, in a true spirit of military brotherhood, big-hearted and imprudent at once, gave up the idea of falling back on Paris and decided to answer Bazaine's call. The Emperor approved and telegraphed Palikao:

"We are leaving tomorrow for Montmédy."

[1] Parliamentary Investigation, September 4, testimony of MacMahon and Rouher.

On the 23rd, in fact, the whole Châlons army started off to the northeast. MacMahon thought it was going to Montmédy. It was going to Sedan.

Prince Napoleon did not accompany the Emperor this time. He had left on the 19th for Florence, to make one last appeal to the King of Italy.

Austria had abruptly changed her attitude after Forbach. Beust dropped France to begin making eyes at Russia. Victor Emmanuel was a man of a quite different stamp.

"Poor Napoleon!" he cried, in real sorrow. But then he added, thinking of the danger he had himself been in:

"All the same—it was a pretty close call for me!"

Gramont was about to fall with Ollivier. Unable to cherish any further hopes in Austria's direction he still thought something might be done with Italy. Discreetly, almost humbly, the French minister Malaret asked Italy to send 60,000 men into France by way of the Mont Cénis. Both statesmen and generals in Florence cried aloud against any such move.

"As a statesman and a general," said La Marmora, "I declare that we can do nothing whatever for the French."

Public opinion in Italy was still hostile to any intervention. The *re galantuomo* vainly sought a way to demonstrate his good will. Mobilization would take a month. By that time the game would surely be up and to the advantage of Prussia. The opening of the campaign had revealed to everybody in Europe the inferiority of the French in numbers and the utter incompetence of their command.

The Italian ministers, moreover, soon found, with England's help, a satisfactory offset to any new requests from Napoleon III. Working with Florence and St. Petersburg Lord Granville hurriedly organized a "League of Neutrals," the member nations pledging themselves not to take any part in the conflict. Any mediation, for that matter, seemed to be out of the question. Prussia had appointed a governor for Alsace and Lorraine as though to give a foretaste of what her peace conditions would be. The French did not care to negotiate till after they had won a battle. Gramont's successor, La Tour d'Auvergne, speaking of the League of Neutrals to Lord Lyons on the 6th of August, said:

"We could treat only on the twin bases of territorial integrity and the maintenance of the dynasty." [1]

He was thinking of a "blank peace" to be followed by limited armaments. London shrugged its shoulders without going to any pains to conceal its contempt.

La Tour d'Auvergne was not consulted on the matter of Prince Napoleon's trip to Italy. He would doubtless have advised against it as a hopeless gesture. Nevertheless Victor Emmanuel received his son-in-law cordially. The Prince got scant courtesy everywhere else. He seemed to have some hopes at first, as witness a strange telegram which he sent to Trochu, inquiring whether the troops from Italy were to be sent towards Belfort or Munich! He soon caught the drift of the wind, however. On the 25th he telegraphed:

"Italy will not do anything by herself. If our army were to have some successes, things might change."

He said he was coming home. The Emperor was already in the Ardennes. He asked him to stay where he was.

The only step that Italy was to take was to suggest to Lord Granville that the neutrals intervene jointly to halt the war. Granville took the proposal coldly.

"The time has not come for that," he said.

Alas, yes—the time had not come for that!

There was nothing to hope for in the direction of Russia. The Czar was still disposed to attack Austria if she gave the slightest indication of stirring. Shifty, quick-tempered, he twitted Fleury on Poland and Denmark. The French defeats, however, gave him food for thought. He hoped the war would soon be over, just as later on he hoped that Prussia would be moderate in her demands. What he saw, meantime, was a good chance to have the Treaty of 1866 revised.

Only one crowned head frankly offered mediation, and that one was the weakest and the most big-hearted of them all. Pius IX forgot his disagreements with France but not her services to the Papacy. The King of Prussia, of course, politely showed him the door. With the French expeditionary force called home from Rome not a month was to pass before the Italian army entered the Eternal City through the breach in Porta Pia. Victor Emmanuel settled in the Quirinal.

---

[1] Lyons to Granville, August 16th in *Further Correspondence Respecting the War between France and Germany*, 1871.

Pius IX shut himself up in the Vatican. Papacy and Kingdom were not to be on speaking terms for sixty years—till the reconciliation under Pius XI.

Those days did not pass without deep stirrings in the various classes of the population in Paris. Disappointment was cruel but people still hoped. The Regent and the ministry were displaying real energy and that impressed the public favorably. The "fourth" or independent battalions were organized into enough regiments of minute-men to make up the XIIIth and XIVth army corps. The Champ de Mars became a camp. Paris was crowded with volunteers, riflemen, ambulance workers. There was a concentration of pack-mules in the Grenelle forest. The Bois de Boulogne became a pasture for cattle and sheep. Trees were felled in front of the ramparts to make chevaux-de-frise. The people were courageous and in good humor.

The republicans in the Chamber could see their hour approaching and they were disposed to hurry it along. The majority did not second their manoeuvres. In fear of a revolution it was loath to rise against the Emperor. On August 16th it refused to vote the permanent session as the Left demanded. Old Palikao, however, angered the most long-suffering by reading absurd news dispatches from the speaker's platform:

"White cuirassiers of Bismarck shot down." "A Prussian army corps destroyed at Jaumont Roads." "Heavy Prussian losses before Phalsbourg."

The aged General rapidly lost prestige and opposition voices began to grumble and threaten. Thiers said:

"Our war preparation was inadequate and our leadership lamentably incompetent."

And Gambetta:

"We ought to decide whether we have made our choice between the safety of the country and the safety of a dynasty."

The Empress sent Mérimée to ask advice of Thiers, reminding him of the offer of service that he had made to Napoleon III just before the war and which had been ignored. With the exquisite gracefulness which only he could display, the author of Colomba—his legs swollen from the malady that was to carry him off within a few weeks—tried his best to move the old standard-bearer of liberalism who had now become the oracle of the Chambers.

Thiers had never been a generous soul. He now held off, saying: "If I were to give any advice no one would regard it as sincere."

On the 17th of August the government appointed a Committee of Defense with Trochu as chairman, though he was completely at odds with Palikao. On the 22nd Kératry proposed that nine deputies be added to the Committee and, in mistrust of the ministry, the Chamber made the motion an emergency issue. The cabinet, thereupon, threatened to resign. Finally a compromise was effected. The Committee would take on five parliamentarians—two senators and three deputies, one of the latter to be Thiers.

Thiers at once became the outstanding figure in the defense of Paris. As the historian of Napoleon I he thought himself a good deal of a military strategist, and in fact he could take in a complicated situation at a glance. He was practical, active. He inspected the Paris forts, advocated an army for the Left Bank to prevent a complete investment of the city and opposed sending any reenforcements to MacMahon who had set out to effect a junction with Bazaine.

"You have one marshal trapped," he said. "Before long you will have two."

CHAPTER XXXVIII

Sedan

THE ARMY OF CHÂLONS, WHICH, IN THE POPULAR MIND, HAD BECOME the "Army of Rescue," comprised four army corps at the time of its departure from Reims. The Ist had suffered severely at Froeschwiller. It had to be filled out with reservists and raw recruits. It was commanded by a good general, Ducrot, a rough outspoken fellow, altogether a man. The Vth was still in charge of Failly—a man uncertain of himself and discouraged. The VIIth had hardly been in action. It was under Félix Douay, a very brave man but gloomy, discouraging, foreseeing only disaster. The XIIth was a new formation. It was made up of marines—"porpoises"—and remnants from other units. Its commander, Lebrun, formerly aide-de-camp to the Emperor, was a brilliant but muddle-headed person. The Bonnemains and Margueritte cavalry divisions brought the whole army up to 130,000 men, but it had no cohesive personality, no soul. It was just a mob of beaten soldiers whom no one had had time to whip into shape.

The Emperor followed MacMahon, the army regarding him as nothing but the most useless of its duffel. He stuffed himself with morphine to keep down his pain and had to make an effort whenever he was required to open his eyes or say a few words. His mental state was anguish itself. Not only fortune had played him false, but the nearest and dearest he had among human beings. His repudiation by the Empress had opened a wound that would not heal.

"If I could only die," he would say at times.

The Prince Imperial was still with him, Eugénie judging the boy safer with the army than anywhere else. Napoleon III out of sheer affection was to send him away when the army entered the Ardennes. There he entrusted him to Captain Du Perré, who took him to Avesnes.

MacMahon thought he could get to the Meuse before the Germans. He calculated on being at Montmédy after a five days' march. There, following the Palikao plan, which he was executing to the letter, he would fall upon the Prince of Saxony, beat him with his superior numbers, then join Bazaine and overwhelm the Prince Royal, who had ventured too far out into the Champagne.

The plan was not the absurdity that it has been described as being; but it was really a surprise move and everything depended on rapid execution. Actually, the army was delayed by its wagon trains. The weather was rainy and stifling hot. Sluggish, slow-moving, MacMahon was at Vouziers on the 26th—thirty miles in three days.

Furthermore, in order to be effective, the march had to be kept a perfect secret. A dispatch from the Havas agency appeared in the London *Times* on the 23rd:

"MacMahon's army is marching north to lend a hand to Bazaine."

This treasonable revelation emanated from someone in the office of Palikao!

The Prince Royal was on the lower Ornain on the 23rd. His cavalry was at Vitry. He was waiting in that neighborhood for the Prince of Saxony to come along and then they would march together on Paris. News that MacMahon was heading for the Meuse reached the Prince Royal on the evening of the 25th. Moltke at once changed plans. The Third and Fourth Armies would turn about and make for the Meuse by forced marches.

This movement was executed like a flash of lightning. The Prince of Saxony reached the Meuse at Stenay within forty-eight hours; the Prince Royal was at Buzancy at the very same time. On the 27th MacMahon learned of the changed direction of the German armies at Le-Chesne-Populeux. He foresaw that they would try to cut him off from Paris. He also learned that Bazaine had not stirred from Metz. He was inclined to leave him to his fate, but did not dare take the responsibility for such a serious decision. In his anxiety he asked the Emperor's opinion. When the Emperor was not semiconscious he saw as clearly as the generals and reasoned even more soundly. He advised a quick retreat to the northwest to save the army.

MacMahon prepared the appropriate orders and informed Palikao (August 27, 1870, 8.30 A.M.):

"I have had no news of Bazaine since the 9th. If I go forward to meet him, I shall be attacked in front by part of the First and Second Armies. At the same time I shall be attacked by the army of the Prince Royal of Prussia and my retreat will be cut off. Tomorrow, therefore, I shall draw in to Mézières, whence I shall continue my retreat, according to circumstance, towards the west."

The Minister did not take time to consult his colleagues. At eleven o'clock, with the Empress's approval, he telegraphed back, adding a deal of misinformation for good measure:

"If you desert Bazaine Paris will revolt and you will yourself be attacked by all the enemy's forces. Perceiving the danger to which your turning movement is exposing his army the Prince Royal is said to have changed direction and to be marching north. You have a start of at least thirty-six hours on him, perhaps forty-eight. In front of you you have only a portion of the army that is blocking Metz."

The Marshal did not underestimate the risks he would be running if he obeyed Palikao.

"They want us to go and kill ourselves down there," he said. "Well—let's go!"

The unhappy Emperor vainly advised caution. MacMahon held on. The demoralized army got laboriously into motion and, in indescribable confusion and under a driving rain, started for Montmédy.

During the afternoon a new and very peremptory injunction came in from Palikao:

"On behalf of the Council of Ministers and the Privy Council I order you to assist Bazaine, taking advantage of the thirty hours' start you have over the Prince Royal of Prussia."

MacMahon, after all, felt better. That took a load of responsibility off his shoulders.

On the way out from Le-Chesne-Populeux the Emperor had a narrow escape from death. In a field some twenty-five yards off the road lay a corps of riflemen commanded by Mocquard, the son of the Emperor's first office chief. Napoleon III was riding slowly by on horseback, his face blank, his shoulders bent forward under his dripping waterproof. Suddenly a lieutenant spied one of his men crouching behind a bush and taking careful aim at the Emperor. He leaped upon the soldier, kicking his rifle aside as it went off.

"I was going to down that swine," the man said. "He's the cause of all our trouble."

The assassin was a veteran of the Crimea. He had come on evil days in Paris but had volunteered for the war. The young lieutenant, out of pity, did not report the incident, and the would-be murderer fell in action before Sedan.

The morale of the troops had by this time wholly collapsed. Worn out by these unending marches who could say whither or why, half-starved, wet to the skin, covered with mud, they had no confidence in their leaders and no respect for them.

At Raucourt some farmhands called to the Zouaves and asked where they were going. Cursing, jeering, the marching soldiers chanted back:

"To the slaughter house! To the slaughter house!"

The Emperor looked out through a window in a humble farmer's cot where he was resting. He saw them. He heard what they said. He pressed a hand over his two eyes and groaned.

MacMahon elected to cross the Meuse at Remilly and Mouzon, intending then to strike down to the Briey road. Moltke knew exactly where the French army was, what it was doing, what it intended to do. He thought he would halt it before it reached the river. He ordered the Prince of Saxony to attack near Beaumont-en-Argonne—the Prince Royal would support him if any help were needed.

Failly let himself be caught by surprise, in a bad position, without sentinels and while his men were resting at noon. Alvensleben had stolen upon him with the XIVth Prussian army corps, advancing unobserved through some woods. The French were soon in line and their hot fire stopped the Germans, but within minutes German reenforcements were upon them in overwhelming numbers. At an advantage of four to one they carried Beaumont, taking prisoners. No help came from the Vth and VIIth corps which were nearby and heard the cannon plainly. Ducrot continued his march on Carignan. Félix Douay was afraid of involving his men in the defeat. Lebrun, who was already across the Meuse, was the only one to try to help Failly. MacMahon, however, attached no importance to the action at Beaumont and he was anxious to make Montmédy. He called Lebrun off. Failly was quite unable to fight against such odds. He ordered a retreat on Mouzon and the retirement soon be-

MARSHAL MacMAHON

1808-1893

came a rout. Under heavy fire from the German artillery the French barely managed to get across the Meuse. Failly bravely dashed in at the head of a regiment and halted the German pursuit. But it was a bad day for him: 5,000 men gone and most of his artillery.

The Marshal now saw his mistake in underestimating the action at Beaumont. Though he still thought he had the little army of the Crown Prince of Saxony on his heels, he decided to seek shelter some miles down the river at Sedan. He sent word to the Emperor through Ducrot to meet him there.

Napoleon III was astonished and protested feebly. Ducrot insisted. He gave in. He took a train at Carignan. On board he was informed that the line was clear as far as Mézières, if he cared to go that far.

"No," he repeated a number of times. "I refuse to have any other fate than the army's."

He reached Sedan late at night and took a room at the Prefecture.

Sedan lies almost in the center of a pocket that is shut in by two converging chains of hills between which the Meuse twists and winds like a silver serpent. The gloomy little town had been fortified under the old regime by Vauban. In 1870 the forts had no artillery and no provisions of any sort; but the surrounding bastions and the citadel made it look like a fortress. MacMahon had judged it a good place to rally and reorganize his troops before retiring on Mézières—he thought the roads were still open that far. Actually he was walking into the most perfect trap imaginable for catching an army. Let the enemy get possession of the commanding hills and not a man would escape.

The four French army corps marched down the two banks of the Meuse helter-skelter, with no pretense at order. On the morning of the 31st the Vth corps settled in "the Old Camp" to the northeast, the VIIth a little farther along on the Butte de l'Algérie, the XIIth some three miles south of Bazeilles. Ducrot had not come along yet.

King William was at German General Headquarters at Bazancy. There Moltke issued his orders. The Crown Prince of Saxony, on the right bank of the Meuse, would block the road to the east. The Prince Royal would cut off the roads to the south and west. That would leave MacMahon nowhere to go except northeast into Belgium. So France would be without an army and Bazaine could only capitulate!

Gradually Sedan filled up with stragglers and men who had lost their companies. They had no knapsacks, no food. There was no way of giving them any—the supply trains had been misdirected to Mézières! MacMahon was terribly tired. He nevertheless consented to receive General Wimpffen, who had been sent on by Palikao to replace Failly. The ministry had judged the latter not good enough for a situation so important. Wimpffen did not present another commission which he had in his pocket. It appointed him to the command-in-chief in case anything should happen to MacMahon.

It was not long before MacMahon discovered the deadly trap into which he had deliberately marched himself. Residents of the neighborhood came running in in full flight, reporting that the Germans were closing in from three directions. The army would have to move on—and right away—to the north, the only aperture still open. MacMahon may have figured on some protection from the Meuse. At any rate he rested for hours doing nothing. He did so literally nothing that not one of the bridges across the river was destroyed. At least he might have occupied the hills overlooking the loop in the river at Iges. That would have protected the next lap in his retreat. He neglected that elementary precaution. As a result no obstacle whatever lay in the way of executing the German blockading movement.

So the day passed fruitlessly. The coming night would have been MacMahon's last chance. Moltke, in fact, was afraid that his prey might elude him in the dark, since the choke of the net had as yet not been drawn as tight as might be. Moltke really should not have worried. MacMahon had everything waiting for him at daybreak.

The exhausted French troops, with empty stomachs and despairing hearts, got hardly any sleep on the wet, chilly ground. The generals could feel that the end was drawing near. Douay said to one of them:

"Well, all we can do is do our best before we fall."

Ducrot was ragingly angry at his discomforts. He ended by lying down on the ground near a fire, among his Zouaves.

The light of dawn had not yet freed itself from the autumn fog when the Ist corps of the Bavarians attacked Bazeilles. Bazeilles was a big village lying along the Givonne brook and solidly held by the French marines. The enemy forced its way into the town, but there it was met by a murderous fire. The inhabitants of Bazeilles, the women as well as the men, joined the defenders. The Germans had to send for reinforcements. The sun came up and with it the Bavarian artillery. Shells began to fall on the village.

While the attention of the French was fixed on this diversion the enemy armies were scaling the heights that formed the sides of the gigantic funnel. King William himself went up to the Forest of La Mariée, whence he could see the whole countryside as on a beautiful map in relief. The Prince Royal took up a position on the hill in front of Donchéry.

At five o'clock MacMahon rode out to inspect his troops, first at Bazeilles. He galloped up beyond the Givonne and mounted a hillock to examine the enemy position through his field glass. A shell exploded near him and a fragment struck him in the groin. He fainted and fell from his horse. He was carried back to Sedan.

Learning that MacMahon had been hurt, Napoleon III came riding out to meet him. His doctor, Augier, examined the Marshal and declared that he would live. Without consulting the Emperor, MacMahon designated Ducrot as his successor. Ducrot was a good choice. A man capable of bold resorts he was the only one of the generals who might perhaps have saved the army.

Ducrot had consistently advised a retreat on Mézières. He ordered it now, and in a hurry. A number of the officers about him began to grumble.

"It's the one way to save the army," he returned hotly.

He had some difficulty in convincing Lebrun. If not a moment were lost, the army could just get through the Falizette gap and reach Vrigne-aux-Bois.

The XIIth corps had just begun to wheel when Wimpffen informed Ducrot that in virtue of his commission from the ministry, which he now produced, he claimed command-in-chief of the army. He halted the retreat and ordered battle. Ducrot ran to him, pleaded with him.

"For a month now," he protested in his rough, intense voice, "I have been dealing with these Prussians. I know them. Their aim is to encircle us. . . . I beg you to continue the retreat."

Wimpffen paid no attention. He had eyes only for the local advantage that had been won at Bazeille. He thought he could extend it.

"What the country needs is a victory," he declared, self-sufficiently.

Ducrot turned away, hopeless.

"We are lost," he said, as he rejoined his staff.

Wimpffen was a brave but conceited individual. He thought he could overrun the Germans to the south and reach Carignan. He encountered the Emperor as the latter was wandering from place to place in the battle area, attended by a slender escort.

"Your Majesty need not worry," he said. "Within two hours I shall have those Germans in the Meuse."

He was sure of it. Unfortunately he had no plan and could not even understand one. As a general-in-chief he foresaw detailed actions here and there. For the moment his mind was on Bazeilles.

The Germans by this time had tripled in numbers and they were throwing a fresh attack upon the village. The defense was admirable. The French marines, interspersed with raw recruits from the Lacretelle division, fought like demons. In the end they were obliged to yield to sheer numbers. Bazeilles was evacuated with the exception of the Bourgeries house—the "House of the Last Cartridge" now old in story. In that house, which stands on the edge of the village on the side towards Sedan, three French officers and fifty men stood off a whole German regiment for more than an hour. The Bavarians were furious at their heavy losses. They dishonored their final victory. They shot all civilians whom they found bearing arms and a number of French officers who were their prisoners.

After this hard trial the XIIth intrenched a mile or more to the north in front of the village of Balan. The IInd Bavarian corps, after a long struggle, obliged it to fall back.

The main battle, however, was to be fought to the northeast of Sedan. The Vth and XIth Prussian corps rounded the loop in the Meuse and settled on ground commanding the positions of Douay, while the Saxons and the Prussian Guard got possession of all the villages in the Givonne valley, threatening Ducrot. So the two German armies had come together: the jaws of the nut-cracker were closing. Five hundred and forty pieces of artillery were concentrated on the French positions.

Wimpffen's incompetence was by now evident enough and, as it were by Wimpffen's default, Ducrot took actual charge and directed the remainder of the battle. The Ilby plateau with its cemetery was the keystone in the whole arch of the French defense. If the Prussians captured that hill the French army would be lost. Ducrot massed all available artillery upon it. Caught in a cross fire the guns were silenced almost immediately. Douay's infantry was already badly shot up. He led it into the cemetery. There it was immediately scattered by a deluge of shells, the General vainly trying to persuade his men to hold on.

Ducrot then ordered Margueritte's light cavalry to stop some German columns that were marching on Floing. General Margueritte had been severely wounded. General de Galiffet was in command of his squadrons of hussars and African chasseurs. A familiar figure at balls in the Tuileries, a great flaunter of frivolous adventures of the heart but a dazzling soldier nevertheless, Galiffet was the man born for the cavalry charge of the story books. His trumpets sounded. Five regiments of horse dashed down over the terraces that cut the side of the hill. They reached the first Prussian line, broke through and exterminated the gunners of a battery behind. Facing a line of muskets at point blank range his regiment lost a third of its numbers. To charge again the men had to reform in the full midst of the Prussians. The mêlée was something fantastic— clouds of dust, steel blades flashing in the sunlight, men and horses churning like a whirlwind of smoky wraiths, bullets spattering on the ground like a hail of lead! The horsemen fell by hundreds. Galiffet rallied the survivors and dashed back up the hill again. Ducrot, livid, galloped out to meet him and shouted in between the salvos of heavy guns:

"One more effort, my little Galiffet—just for the honor of the army!"

"As many as you wish, General, as long as one of us is left!"

Again the cavalry charged. Ducrot intended to throw his infantry in behind it.

"Forward, boys! Give them the bayonet!"

He was not followed. Not a soldier stirred. The cavalry reached the Prussian line alone. But this time the enemy had stiffened. The horse did not break through. They sabred desperately to right and left, in front and behind, but they were beaten. Sadly their general led them back to the top of the hill. In sheer admiration the Prussians suspended fire and their officers saluted with their swords. On the top of La Mariée King William turned to Moltke and Bismarck, who were watching the development of the battle, and exclaimed like the soldier he was:

"Oh, what brave men!"

A sheer waste of heroism, a costly gallantry! The point has been made by not a few historians. They may well be right. As it stands Galiffet's charge illumined that dark day for France with its one bright flicker of glory. As Ducrot had said, it did save the honor of the army. After it was over there was just a rout. A few companies under the cemetery at Ilby, Liébert's division on the outskirts of Cazal—they continued fighting. All the rest, irrespective of units and arms, stampeded up the valley towards the bastions of Sedan in one vast and horrible panic. The Prussian infantry followed in close pursuit already taking thousands of prisoners. By two o'clock the battle had ended—and the Empire too!

Napoleon III had sought death all that day. Like the uncle at Waterloo the nephew at Sedan, who knew it was his Waterloo, deliberately exposed himself on ground that was beaten by shot and shell. On Phoebus, his handsome chestnut, he paid a first visit to the "porpoises," who were defending Bazeilles and Balan, dismounting every so often because of his intense pain and going to lean against a tree. Ordering his escort to crouch behind a wall for shelter he would stride out into the open where the bullets were flying. At Bazeille, Haudecourt, his orderly, who was riding beside him, was killed.

Next he went to a battery that was in a very exposed position and stayed with it for an hour. In the cemetery at Balan he worked a machine-gun himself and was a long time in the open. He rode down into the Givonne valley, then uphill again to the Garenne Wood. The sky was filled with bursting shells. Two officers were killed at his side. He continued to go about now most often on foot, his face black with dust and burned powder.

Dr. Augier, Nélaton's assistant in caring for the Emperor, relates in his *Notes of Wartime:*

"I did not leave the Emperor once between eight o'clock and noon. Cannonballs were whistling past our ears incessantly and shells were bursting almost under our feet. . . . At one moment the Emperor dismounted behind a little hedge. A shell burst about ten yards away. If the man did not stop just there for the purpose of being killed I cannot imagine what other reason he could have had. I did not see him give an order in the whole course of the forenoon."

But vainly he sought the jagged shred of steel that would kill him and save his name. Vainly he turned his pain-racked face towards a final deliverance. Fate which had often been so lavish of favors to him withheld from him the privilege of dying the death of a military sovereign. He had to drain the bitter cup to the dregs.

He returned to Sedan at eleven o'clock. Shells were already falling upon the town. He talked for a second with Colonel Stoffel, then rode out on the bridge over the Meuse. A shell coming from La Mariée burst directly in front of him. The horse reared and two men in his escort were thrown from theirs. He did not bat an eyelash. Turning to Stoffel he said reproachfully:

"Colonel, you spoiled everything. You prevented me from being killed."

His one thought now was to save the lives of his soldiers. It was at his order that a white flag was run up on the citadel. No one saw it apparently, for the battle continued. Finally General Faure spied it and ordered it shot down.

Still dreaming on, still understanding nothing, Wimpffen sent a note to the Emperor:

"I have decided to break through the line in front of Generals Lebrun and Ducrot rather than allow ourselves to be made prisoners in the square at Sedan. If Your Majesty will come and place yourself in the center of your troops, they will be honored to cut a path for you."

Napoleon III refused. He would not escape by deserting the army. Those men had sacrificed themselves for him. He would sacrifice himself for them, and again he ordered the white flag raised. The cannonade and the musket fire continued.

"Why does it still go on?" he asked in a tone of agony.

General Margueritte was brought to the Prefecture, dying. The Emperor stooped over the litter and shook his hand. Margueritte's tongue had been shot away by a bullet. He could not speak. He motioned for a pencil and wrote:

"Me, it's nothing: But France?"

Douay and then Ducrot came in, swept back by the stampede of their troops into the town.

Napoleon III said to Ducrot:

"I want to see the King of Prussia. I hope I can get advantageous terms."

Ducrot answered that he did not believe in the enemy's generosity. He was going to wait till dark and try a sortie.

"No," Napoleon III answered. "We have no chance left."

Every time a shell burst now he would start nervously. Finally he said:

"This firing absolutely must end. General, sit down there and write!"

And he dictated.

"The flag of truce having been raised, negotiations will be opened with the enemy. Firing must cease all along the line."

"Now, General, sign that!" he ordered.

Ducrot refused. Wimpffen had to sign, he said, as commander-in-chief, or else Faure, as head of the General Staff.

Finally, with no little difficulty, Wimpffen and Faure were found and brought in together. They also refused to sign. Whatever fault may be found with Wimpffen he had really resolved to try his break through then and there. With four or five thousand men from the XIIth corps, "porpoises," zouaves, regulars, he dashed upon Balan and swept the place clean of Bavarians. He was not able to debouch from the village, however. Lebrun dashed in to support him and still they failed. They were obliged to fall back to Sedan.

The town was now jammed with unarmed, famished soldiers, raving from fatigue and anger and shouting treason. Shells were falling into the crowded mobs, opening frightful clearings in them. The bombardment of Sedan was growing hotter.

At four o'clock the Prussians sent two officers under a flag of truce to summon the fortress to surrender. Napoleon III asked them to escort General Reille to King William. Reille would be the bearer of a letter, which he sat down and wrote—in his small close-packed handwriting. The note read:

"Monsieur mon frère:
"Having failed to die at the head of my army, I can do nothing more than deliver my sword into the hands of Your Majesty.
"I am, of Your Majesty,
              "Le bon frère,
                          "NAPOLÉON."

The King of Prussia had come down from La Mariée and gone to Frénois. He and the people about him supposed that Napoleon III had long since left Sedan. When he learned the contrary he stood as in a daze, exclaiming:

"What? The Emperor—in there!?"

Braun & Cie

LOUIS ADOLPHE THIERS

1797-1877

The news spread like wildfire about German Headquarters. The officers started to cheer, but the Prince Royal hushed them.

Reille came in, bareheaded. He presented the Emperor's letter to the King. In line behind His Majesty stood Moltke, Roon, Bismarck, a number of princes.

King William answered with a message that was courteous, but demanded the surrender pure and simple of the army.

When Reille was back at the Prefecture the question arose: Who of the generals would negotiate with the Prussian plenipotentiaries? All of them refused. Napoleon III finally thrust the painful duty upon Wimpffen. It was a most unpleasant scene. Wimpffen accused the generals of disobeying him, and Ducrot replied fiercely:

"You alone are responsible. . . . Since there has been a defeat and a surrender you must bear the disgrace of it."

Wimpffen went to Donchéry that same evening to meet Moltke and Bismarck. Castelnau accompanied him as Napoleon III's personal representative. The statesman and the Field-Marshal were in full previous agreement. France had been defeated and would not be allowed to stagger to her feet. The two victors stood inexorable. Moltke read off the conditions: the whole army, prisoners of war; officers could keep their swords in view of the bravery with which they had fought.

Wimpffen argued fruitlessly. Bismarck talked of peace in an offhand sort of way, hinting at the terms that he would later "dictate": Alsace, four billions. . . . Wimpffen stiffened and talked of fighting on. Moltke snickered boorishly:

"You have 80,000 men, very few supplies, no ammunition at all. We have 230,000 men. Our artillery can destroy you within two hours."

General Castelnau at this point remarked that if the Emperor had placed himself at the King's mercy, it was because he hoped that the latter would be generous and grant the army terms worthy of its courage.

"Which sword has been delivered here?" asked Bismarck. "Is it the sword of France or the Emperor's? If it is the sword of France your message has a much more serious import."

Castelnau was frightened.

"In question here is the sword of the Emperor."

"If that's the case," said Moltke flatly, "nothing can be changed."

When Wimpffen reported back to the Prefecture Napoleon III resolved to take a supreme step. King William and Bismarck had been his personal friends and his guests. He could not believe they would refuse him some attenuation at least. He was ready to pay for it with his personal humiliation.

On September 2nd at six in the morning, in a general's undress uniform, in company with the Prince de la Moscowa, Reille and two other generals, he left Sedan in a carriage and drove to Donchéry. There he thought he would find the King. Actually he found no one but Bismarck.

Bismarck dressed in great haste, fussily apologizing. The fact was, he had shooed his sovereign away to prevent Napoleon III from meeting him. He knew that the King of Prussia was quite capable of a chivalrous weakening.

The Emperor and the Chancellor drove out along the road to a cottage of a weaver that stood a quarter of a mile beyond the outskirts of the village of Donchéry. They went in and sat down in two straw chairs. What Napoleon III wanted was that the army should be paroled home to France, or at the worst to Algeria.

Bismarck replied that that was a purely military question. It concerned Moltke only. He would be glad to communicate the request to him. As for himself, he said, he was ready to begin real peace negotiations.

Bismarck, differing on the point with Moltke and Roon, really wanted peace. Peace would mean finishing off the campaign by an unexpectedly rapid and brilliant triumph. He thought he could force on the unhappy Emperor, whose despondency he could take for granted, a treaty that would definitely transfer leadership in Europe from France to Germany. If one had to go on with the war and lay siege to Paris, who could foresee what counterthrust might come from a nation that was so haughty and after all so rich in resources? If a revolution swept the Empire away, who would there be to treat? An angry, excited and dangerous Republic might promise and then not fulfill.

Napoleon III sidestepped the trap:

"What am I? Just a prisoner of war!"

Bismarck's face fell. He asked who did have authority to treat.

"The present government," answered the Emperor. "The Empress Regent and her ministers."

"In that case," said the Chancellor, "we cannot get anywhere. In order not to endanger our victory, we need a bond—the army."

In those few sentences Napoleon III voluntarily laid aside his crown. Had he accepted Bismarck's conditions the troops both in Sedan and Metz would have been restored to his command. He would have been mutilating France but he could have strangled Paris and staved off the revolution.

Moltke came in. The Emperor pressed his request that the army might be interned in Belgium. To avoid a direct refusal the Field-Marshal answered that he would refer the matter to the King, but his leaden face gave no ray of hope. Before leaving Napoleon III, Bismarck invited him to go to the little château at Bellevue, near Frénois. There the King would call on him, once the surrender had been signed.

Alone, the unlucky monarch paced up and down in the kitchen garden that girt the little weaver's cottage. Then he sat down again and smoked cigarette after cigarette, oblivious to the crowds of German soldiers and foreign newspaper correspondents who were watching him from across the road.

At half-past nine a squadron of White Cuirassiers appeared. The commander, sabre in hand, placed himself behind the Emperor's carriage, which was driven to Bellevue.

Wimpffen was already there to sign the terms of the surrender. They had been drawn up by the Prussian General Staff. No attenuating modifications had been introduced into the text. The remnants of the army would be interned in Germany till peace was made!

Napoleon III sent off a laconic dispatch to the Empress:

"The army has been defeated and captured. As for myself, I am a prisoner."

The King of Prussia called on him later in the day—a painful meeting between two men who, just a few weeks before, could have talked as friends and equals.

"The chances of war have decided between us," said the King, "but I am distressed to see Your Majesty in this painful situation."

Napoleon III's face bore all the signs of his mental anguish and physical pain, but he tried to preserve a correct demeanor. The King placed at his disposal, for the duration of his captivity, the castle at Wilhelmshöhe in Westphalia, which had been the residence, of yore, of his uncle Jerome Bonaparte. There he had spent some time as a child. The King also read the list of the officers and attendants who would accompany him thither. As the Emperer escorted King William to the door his composure failed him. He had to brush the tears from his eyes with his glove.

After a time the Emperor began a letter to his wife.

"My dear Eugénie:
"I cannot tell you how I have suffered and am still suffering. Our march was something contrary to every principle and to all common sense. It could only end in catastrophe and the catastrophe is in fact complete. I should much rather have died than witness such a disastrous capitulation, but in the existing circumstances it was the only way to avoid a slaughter of sixty thousand men. If only my worries were all here! I am thinking of you, of our son, of our unhappy country! May God keep you! What will happen in Paris?!"

That evening the German soldiers lighted bonfires and their regimental bands played war tunes, bits from the *Tannhäuser* that Paris had hissed, gay movements from *La Belle Hélène* which all Europe had been humming three years earlier in front of gorgeous opera backgrounds.

The following morning, September 3rd, Napoleon III set out for Cassel escorted by a platoon of the Death's Head Hussars. He was in chills and had a fever. He hid his face inside the upturned collar of a cavalryman's overcoat. The last French soldiers he saw along the road shook their fists at him.

The captured troops reached a total of 106,000 men: 83,000 were surrendered in the capitulation, 23,000 had been taken prisoner in the fighting around Sedan, 3,000 French soldiers had been killed, 14,000 wounded, 3,000 men made their way across the Belgian frontier and were interned. For the two or three weeks before trains could be made available to transport them to Germany, the men were camped on the soggy intervale in the loop of the Meuse to the north of Sedan. They were left destitute of almost everything. They had no shelter and very little food. Thinking only of himself Wimpffen set out for Stuttgart as soon as he could. With a finer sense of their duties Ducrot and Lebrun shared the lot of their men.

The French officers had burned their flags on September 2nd, but huge quantities of war materials, which it would have required months to replace, fell into the enemy's hands. France was now

open to the invaders. They needed only a few days' march to appear
before Paris.

Nothing could be expected of Bazaine. Sticking tight to his quarters in the Ban-Saint-Martin, he took little interest if any in the
173,000 men whom it was his duty to feed, drill and keep busy.
Knowing that MacMahon was trying to relieve him, he did nothing
to enlighten him as to his peril. He even kept the news from the
members of his staff. There was a faint gesture towards a sortie on
the 26th, when Bourbaki wanted to try a break towards Château-
Salins. It was called off by a council of war. More serious efforts
were made on the 31st and on September 1st. Le Boeuf drove the
Germans out of Servigny but then lost the position again. The
slaughter had been heavy with no gains. Bazaine ordered the fighting stopped, though with better management and carried farther the
action at Servigny might have come to something. The battle at
Sedan was fought that same day. The fact was, Bazaine was thinking of something else and he wanted his army whole for it. Just what
was the shady political rôle that he thought of playing? Negotiations
with Germany! For reestablishing the ruined Empire? For a pronun-
ciamento of his own? Nobody knows or perhaps even cares. Thiers'
"glorious Bazaine" had ended as a miserable intriguer.

CHAPTER XXXIX

The Republican Revenge

PALIKAO RECEIVED A DISPATCH FROM GENERAL VINOY, WHOM HE had sent to Mézières with the XIIIth army corps, during the afternoon of September 1st. It reported that MacMahon's army was surrounded at Sedan. The Minister of War said nothing. Rumors of a very favorable character were in circulation, arousing false hopes in the public. At six o'clock on the 2nd, Jérôme David received a private message from Brussels.

"Great disaster. MacMahon killed. The Emperor a prisoner."

He made haste to inform the Empress. She only half believed him. He went on to the room where the Committee of Defense was sitting. Thiers was making a forceful plea for MacMahon's return to the neighborhood of Paris. Jérôme David whispered to him:

"Don't go on—I have something to tell you."

Thiers followed him out of the room and Jérôme David imparted his news. They walked the hundred yards across the Solferino bridge in silence. Those two men so opposite in political beliefs were as one in the same anguish.

David pleaded with Thiers:

"You can render great services to the country in this crisis. You must!"

"I can do nothing," answered Thiers. "There is no remedy for such a catastrophe. Where will we be a week from now?"

Rumors of the defeat reached Paris generally through travellers coming from Brussels. It spread like wildfire, gaining headway as it progressed. Official circles knew no more than anybody else, but they foresaw the worst. At the Legislative Body the republican leaders, Jules Favre, Garnier-Pagès, Jules Simon, Ernest Picard, Jules Ferry, Gambetta, dragged Thiers into an office. A revolution, they said, could not be avoided. They intended to move the deposition of the Emperor. Thiers should take the lead! They pleaded, they threatened, Thiers evaded. His shrewdness, as well as his keen sense of his own interests, told him that his moment had not yet come.

Quite independently of anybody else, it would seem, Mérimée dragged himself to Thiers's house and besought him:

"You care nothing about the dynasty. Your sole interest is in France. The Emperor is a prisoner. All that is left is a woman and a child. What a moment to establish the representative system once and for all!"

A dying man pleading for a dying house! Thiers rebuffed him.

"After disasters such as we have been through there is nothing that anybody can do." And he pronounced a blunt word: Abdication! Mérimée drew his dropsical frame together and departed, shivering.

The session in the Chamber opened at three o'clock. Palikao mucked about in a new slough of inventions. His stammering, his utter dejection, confessed a catastrophe that his words belied.

Jules Favre stood erect on the speaker's platform.

"The government," he cried, "has de facto ceased to exist." He suggested, without mentioning any names, that power be entrusted to Trochu. "His presence will lay this phantom government which has brought France to the place where she now is."

Schneider, the president, declared the session adjourned before any decision was reached. It had been Bazaine. It was now Trochu. The Left had to have its saviour. Such hallucinations of "siege fever" were many times to rise during the months that followed—wraiths that stalked forth to mislead, and then vanished.

The Emperor's brief dispatch, announcing the capitulation, reached the Tuileries at that moment. Chevreau, the Minister of the Interior, took it to the Empress. Though she had long since lost hope, the full extent and depth of the disaster had never come over her till then. A sort of frenzied hysteria laid hold on her. All the sufferings and angers of the weeks preceding, all the cowardice she had seen about her, all the humiliations she had experienced, seemed to rush to her head and carry away her reason.

"No," she cried. "The Emperor has not surrendered! A Napoleon does not surrender! He dies!"

Tearing her hair down with her clutching fingers, her eyes flashing, she shouted:

"Why did he not get himself killed—bury himself under the walls of Sedan? Didn't he see that he was disgracing himself? What sort of a name will he leave his son?"

Then her strength gave way. She collapsed, sobbing. Asking the Emperor to forgive all the harsh things she had just been saying, she went off into a faint.

Before long she sat up and was herself again. The ministers were admitted. They were all too small for the situation before them. They talked of moving the government to Tours, of treating with the enemy, of dividing power with the Chamber. . . . Clément Duvernois drew up a proclamation that would officially report the disaster to the public. Schneider, who was also present, suggested that the Empress delegate all her authority to the Legislative Body. That was the view of the imperialist majority. Eugénie did not state her attitude. With no very definite outlook she was trying to gain time.

In response to a clamor from all groups Schneider called a session of the Chamber on his own authority. It met at midnight. At the Tuileries the ministers had said they would not attend. They attended all the same, but with no two in agreement on anything, with nothing precise in view—fagged out nags ready for the knacker's hammer!

Palikao could evade no longer. He read the Sedan dispatches and then asked that all debate be postponed till morning. Gambetta was more and more coming into the spotlight. He objected. Jules Favre rose. Speaking for the twenty-seven deputies of the Left, and in a pin-fall silence, he read a trenchant motion for deposition:

"Louis Napoleon Bonaparte and his dynasty are declared relieved of the powers conferred upon them by the Constitution: The Legislative Body will appoint a Commission invested with all the powers of the government. It will have the specific task of resisting the invasion to the last limit and of driving the enemy from French soil. General Trochu is retained as Governor of Paris."

The stunned majority sat silent. Finally one of its members, the former minister Pinard, arose to protest.

"We are empowered by the Constitution to adopt temporary

measures," he said. "We are not empowered to depose the sovereign."

Nobody listened. The assembly adjourned, having voted to resume the debate at noon.

A number of the deputies went to police headquarters to make sure that the government was not preparing a *coup d'état*. The high officials of the Empire were hardly dreaming of such a thing. Rouher himself was letting go. To Ferdinand Barrot he said:

"There's nothing that can be done now. Revolution tomorrow!"

The Empress was entirely alone in a deserted palace. From the windows of the Tuileries she looked down on the crowds that were parading along the rue de Rivoli by torchlight carrying flags draped in mourning, shouting:

"Down with the Empire! Long live the Republic!"

The windows rattled from the violence of the uproar.

It ceased as the night wore on. Paris tired under its fury and fell asleep. But she, the Empress, stayed awake till dawn, burning papers, churning the most fanciful schemes about in her head, sincerely prepared for the supreme sacrifice should her life be the price for anything constructive.

The 4th of September was a Sunday. It dawned hot under a cloudless sky. All Paris was in the streets, snatching up the latest extras, reading the official posters with the dispatches from Sedan. A great crowd filled the Place de la Concorde, pressing close about detachments of the National Guard that stood in squares with fixed bayonets. The mob milled threateningly in front of the iron gates of the Chamber. Behind them, speaking from a chair, Gambetta could be seen. He was urging calm upon the citizenry.

Inside, in the offices and lobbies, the leaders of the Left and a few outstanding figures of the other groups—Thiers, Buffet, the Duc de Broglie—were in eager conference. They were trying to devise some formula that would transfer leadership in the country to new hands without too serious a political convulsion.

Thiers thought it sufficient to declare the seat of power vacant. Buffet wanted the Regent to hand power over to the Legislative Body. The Left wanted to abolish the Empire.

The republicans had their revenge within reach. They did not intend to let it slip from their hands. For eighteen years they had been waiting. The abhorred imperial system had been built at the cost of their liberties and of the blood of people dear to them. At each of its mistakes, at each defeat in the descending curve that had ended in the ruin of France, they had thrilled with hope. An aversion so long-standing and so bitter could not reason. They could not tell themselves that to stab the Empire in the back when it was grappling with the enemy was an ignoble act and a political blunder. For the purpose of fighting the war and making peace the Regency would have been far more serviceable than a haphazard government, unstable as yet, with no recognized leaders and inspiring no confidence in the other countries in Europe.

But in very truth the Empire had made too many mistakes. To have thrown the country into a war, finally, and then to have been unable to fight it—that was indeed the unpardonable sin. One could expect no historical perspective of men who were partisan by background and by experience, who had been reared on hatred and who now found a terrible justification in the country's dire misfortune. The Empire had declared itself guilty by its own doings. The republicans stood ready to act as its pitiless executioners.

At the Tuileries on that Sunday morning the Regent attended Mass and visited the hospital that had been established in the palace. Then she went to the Council meeting over which she was to preside. That an insurrection was brewing there could be no doubt. What could be done about it?

Trochu gabbled and prattled:

"The great hour of peril is upon us. We will do all that we ought."

A few days earlier he had told the Empress that he would die for her, delivering in a dramatic pose on that occasion a line that became famous:

"Remember: I am a Catholic, a Breton and a soldier!"

Trochu was nervous and the ministry thought him actually hostile. Palikao had blasted him the evening before by issuing orders for dealing with the mobs to Trochu's subordinates over his head.

There was a report that the Republic had already been proclaimed at Lyons. Clément Duvernois proposed that martial law be declared as a way of strangling the revolution. The motion was voted down.

Should the government move to some place in the country? It was too late for that. Besides, it would mean losing Paris.

The Empress finally said, in a very matter of fact tone:

"We must fall, that's all, and in such a way as not to make the defense of the country any harder."

A message was brought to Palikao. His son had fallen in battle with the enemy.

He sat there motionless, mute, as though he had been hit on the head with a hammer.

The ministers finally decided to send to the Chamber the draft of a bill creating a Council of Regency which the Chamber would itself nominate, Palikao continuing to function as Lieutenant-General. That was an attempt at a national defense government. Nobody had a hope in the world that the bill would pass.

In terms of force the government had at its disposal, in addition to the National Guard which was more than unreliable, two squadrons of mounted police, two battalions of police infantry, a thousand Paris policemen, two battalions of regular infantry made up of raw recruits. These troops were all massed in the vicinity of the Palais Bourbon under the command of the aged General Caussade. Trochu, in a sulk, shut himself up in the Louvre and refused to come out.

Standing at a window the Empress watched the mob in the Place de la Concorde through her opera glasses. She was told that it was preparing to storm the Tuileries—a false report at just that moment. She sent for General Mellinet, commander of the palace guards.

"General, can this building be defended?" she asked.

"I am afraid not, Madame!" he replied.

"There must be no shooting, General, on any pretext. I refuse to have one drop of blood shed for me or for mine."

In the lobbies of the Legislative Body the deputies were discussing a motion by Thiers.

"In view of the vacancy of the Throne the Chamber nominates a Commission of Government and National Defense, a Constituent session to be convoked as soon as circumstances permit."

"Deposition without the word," was the comment of many deputies.

To meet that objection the formula was finally softened: "In view of the circumstance at present prevailing."

Buffet was commissioned to present the bill to the Empress and obtain her assent. He reached the Tuileries about noon in company with Daru and a number of other deputies. The Regent received them at once. Buffet, reverent, asked her consent to the transfer of power to the assembly in order to avoid any appearance of a revolution and keep the future open.

The Empress thought a moment. Then she said:

"If it is felt that I am of any hindrance, let the deposition be voted. I shall not complain. But I shall not desert my post. . . . The only conduct on the part of the representatives that would be really sensible and patriotic would be to unite around me and concentrate all efforts on repelling the invasion. I will follow the Legislative Body wherever it may choose to organize resistance. If resistance becomes impossible I could still be useful for obtaining less unfavorable conditions of peace."

Buffet was conscious of the wisdom that lay in her words. With tears in his eyes he answered:

"There is of course no doubt that the maintenance of the Regency would be the best solution, but in the present state of mind in the country that procedure cannot possibly be followed. . . . By yielding at the right time Your Majesty will be keeping everything that can be kept of the present order and so saving the country from a revolution."

Not at all convinced she saw that further resistance would be useless.

"See my ministers!" she said. "If they agree I will agree."

She rose, still the sovereign. Each of the deputies, whether friendly or unfriendly, bowed before her. At the door she held out her hand to them and they all kissed it.

When they got back to the Chamber it was too late for conferences. The session had opened, the galleries were packed. The excitement was intense. Palikao, speaking for the government, presented the bill for the Council of National Defense to be made up of deputies from the Legislative Body. Favre again demanded deposition. Thiers argued for his own motion—a compromise. The session adjourned temporarily to permit office study.

The Government and the Chamber had not moved fast enough. The insurrection boiled over. The National Guard had sided with the mob and the mob had burst through the fences and brushed aside the doormen. It entered the auditorium with deafening shouts:

"Deposition! Deposition!"

White blouses, workingmen, students, piled into the seats of the deputies. A number of republican representatives, Glais-Bizoin, Crémieux, Gambetta, strove to quiet the tumult. They had no success. It was three o'clock. Gambetta strode up to the speaker's platform and drowning out the uproar with his mighty bellowing voice delivered the last fatal thrust at the dying Empire:

"Whereas the country is in danger; whereas all necessary time has been given to the representatives of the nation to pronounce deposition; whereas we are and constitute the regular power emanating from universal suffrage; we declare that Louis Napoleon Bonaparte and his dynasty have forever ceased to reign over France."

Thunderous applause answered his words.

"Proclaim the Republic! Proclaim the Republic!" voices shouted amid the din.

The Leftist leaders were afraid extremist elements might sweep them off their feet. Besides, it was an old tradition in Paris: the Republic was always proclaimed not in the Palais Bourbon but from the Hôtel de Ville. Jules Favre ran up beside Gambetta on the speaker's platform and managed to make the mob understand.

"Do you want civil war or do you not?" he asked.

The mob answered with a thunderous "No!"

As the din was beginning again he continued:

"We must set up a provisional government at once. That government will take charge in France. It will fight the foreigner to the end. It will be on your side and each member of it will take an oath in advance to die rather than surrender."

A mighty shout was his answer:

"To the Hôtel de Ville!" "To the Hôtel de Ville!"

"Let us go all together!" Favre shouted back.

He hurried down from the speaker's platform and out of the building. Behind him and Jules Ferry a long procession formed, hedged in on the sides by National Guards. It crossed the Concorde bridge like a boiling river and headed for the Place de Grève down the right bank. Another procession, headed by Gambetta, followed down the left bank.

At the Solferino bridge Favre met Trochu on horseback, but not in uniform. He told him of the deposition and asked him to turn around and accompany him to the Hôtel de Ville—a most valuable recruit for the insurrection. Another struggle between his interests and his duty! He evaded and rode back to the Louvre.

It was four o'clock when the two processions reached the Place de Grève. There was no resistance from the officers on guard. The great auditorium in the historic home of the City of Paris was full in an instant. Jules Favre got up on a bench and called for order. He made a short speech enjoining the keeping of the peace and confidence in victory and in the Republic.

At the word "Republic" a mighty shout arose, gradually falling off into the *Marseillaise*. The new government was set up at once in the offices of the prefect. Quite sure now that the Empire was defunct, Trochu reappeared. He consented to participate in the new regime if he were made president of it. Favre stepped aside in his favor. Thiers refused to serve on the ministry. The latter comprised, along with Trochu and Favre, Jules Ferry, Pelletan, Garnier-Pagès, Rochefort, Crémieux, Glais-Bizoin, Arago, Gambetta and Ernest Picard. They drew up a proclamation that would be posted on the walls of Paris.

The Tuileries meantime became an empty building. After protracted refusals the Empress finally consented to depart.

"I am not afraid," she kept saying. "How could I go away?"

Raised as a child amid guerilla bands, reaching the throne by a most singular chance, she watched the whole incredible fairyland dissolve before her eyes with a sort of indifferent wonder.

Three of her ministers, Busson-Billault, Chevreau and Jérôme David, hurried to her from the Legislative Body. They assured her that the Tuileries was going to be stormed from one moment to the next. The Empress simply had to get away.

"No! No!" she answered, stamping her foot. "I was placed here by the Emperor. Here I shall stay!"

The mob was beating at the gates and cries of "Death to the Spaniard!" could be made out in the din.

The people about her besought her to flee the palace. Still she refused.

Finally two ambassadors came in, intimate friends, Metternich and Nigra.

"Madame," said Nigra, "for you to stay here longer will mean death for all your friends."

That argument persuaded her. Calmly she put on a hat, then a veil, then she slipped on a coat. Followed by a few friends who were faithful to the end, she walked along the Grand Gallery in the Louvre, crossed the Square Room and the Gallery of Apollo. In the Hall with the Seven Fireplaces she stopped, with her back to the *Raft of the Méduse*. There she bade her last farewells.

With her reader, Mme. Lebreton, and the two ambassadors, she stepped out upon the vaulted sidewalk of the Colonnade. Insurgents were streaming past her in a raging flood:

"Down with Badinguet! Down with the Spaniard!"

She showed no emotion. She walked along to the Place Saint-Germain l'Auxerrois. There were no carriages in sight, but a ramshackle cab was ambling slowly across the Square. Nigra dashed out and stopped it, then literally thrust the two women into it.

A street gamin recognized Eugénie and cried out at the top of his voice for the fun of it:

"Aha—the Empress-s-s!"

Nigra caught him, silenced him. The cab rolled slowly down the rue de Rivoli.

Eugénie drove from door to door among houses of her friends. Not one was at home. Finally she ended at the apartment of her American dentist, Dr. Evans. He sheltered her for the night. The next day he drove her out of the city in a carriage. Finally they took a train for Deauville. The sea was calm and a little yacht was found to make the crossing to England. Two days later, at Hastings, the Prince Imperial was in her arms. Duperré had brought him on from Belgium.

At the Tuileries the mob was stopped on the very threshold by a smooth, lean young man, Victorien Sardou. Adroitly he diverted the attention of the rioters and prevented the looting of the palace. The crowned N's and eagles were hammered off the gates. The imperial banner was lowered and carried off amid a gigantic ovation. No other harm was done.

So that beautiful autumn day marked the end of the Second Empire, which less than four months before had won the vote of the country. It had had no deep roots and such roots as it had were more a matter of habit than of sentiment. Its artificial and bril-

liant display, its lofty façade of power, vanished as it were within
hours, as though a regime that had filled French life, nay, the life
of Europe, for eighteen years were a mere piece of painted stage-
setting that someone had left out in the rain. No revolution in
France was ever easier or more simple. Like the fall of the First Empire the fall of the Second caused no looting and no killing. The
Third Republic was born unstained.

The evening of September 4th ended in joy and hope. Many
thought that the war had been declared by the Emperor and would
end with his fall. Alas! Bismarck and his King, already in Reims,
had other plans. The revolution that had taken place weakened
France, they thought. Furthermore it relieved them of certain restraints which they might have felt, under the pressure of European
opinion, in dealing with the Regent and the Emperor, who were
now receiving much personal sympathy in their hour of trouble.
For the republicans they had nothing but contempt and aversion,
as they were soon to make clear. So the 4th of September did not
bring peace any nearer. In fact it made the return to peace more
distant, more difficult, more onerous.

The Government of National Defense was aware of its weakness
and tried to treat at once; but Bismarck, with his heavy touch and
roughhanded manner, quite dismayed Jules Favre at Ferrières—
Favre's head was still very much in the clouds. As prerequisites to
an armistice the Chancellor demanded possession of one of the
forts of Strasbourg and one of the forts at Paris. Favre and his colleagues preferred to continue the war. It was a heroic mistake. At
that moment, probably, peace would have cost France no more than
Alsace.

The IIIrd and IVth German armies appeared before Paris. The
government did its best to struggle on. It reorganized remnants of
the old armies. It levied and armed new troops. Delighted to have
an official voice again, Thiers took to the unpleasant road about
Europe, begging assistance here, intervention there, and everywhere obtaining polite refusals. Everywhere—except in Italy! Garibaldi had fought imperial France. He came to the help of republican France. Paris bravely sustained a siege of 130 days under the
sybilline and stupid leadership of Trochu. Armies raised out in the
country won some few successes. Bazaine, after a series of shady
negotiations with Bismarck and a beginning of an intrigue with the

Empress, which she rebuffed, capitulated, surrendering even his flags. To the astonishment of the Prussians the war lasted five months. Coulmiers, Patay, Villersexel and Bapaume were almost French victories. However, the unexpected resistance in France drew the German princes closer together. King William of Prussia was proclaimed Emperor of Germany at Versailles on January 18, 1871. The Defense Government, against the wishes of Gambetta, whose patriotism had made a greater man of him and who wanted to continue the struggle, finally asked for an armistice and surrendered Paris. France sent to Bordeaux an assembly that was great by the quality of its membership and by the integrity of its convictions. Despairingly it voted to accept the peace which Thiers, "head of the executive branch of the French Republic," negotiated. Alsace, a third of Lorraine, Strasbourg, Metz, five billions of francs, were the price demanded by the Prussian Shylock. The Germans, victorious, marched down the Champs Elysées.

Having suffered too much, being too sorely bruised, Paris rose in insurrection and Thiers had to reduce it by a second siege. The Commune tried to perish in a flaming brasier. The old Hôtel de Ville, which had survived the city's storms over centuries, succumbed along with the Tuileries—the Tuileries of the old monarchy and the two Napoleons, the Tuileries that more than any other building impersonated the imperial era.

Eighteen months later, on the 7th of January, 1873, Napoleon III died at Chiselhurst in England of the disease that had given him so much anguish before and during the war. He was thinking at the time of a new return from Elba and in order to be able to ride a horse into Paris he insisted on an operation for his calculus. His poor physical condition made him unable to survive it. He died in his sleep after whispering his last words to his old friend, Dr. Conneau:

"Henri—you were at Sedan?"

With that life, one of the most romantic and variedly eventful known to history, the Second Empire also descended to the tomb, with all its somewhat vulgar glories, its frivolities, its terrible mistakes and the prosperous living which it incarnated. It was to know no resurrection. While hardly yet of a man's age, the Prince Imperial, charming and melancholy, the "little Prince" so beloved of Paris, was to get himself killed on an absurd raid into Zululand.

CHAPTER XL

Conclusion

As long as the consequences of the catastrophe of 1870 weighed in all their enormity upon France, it was hardly possible for any Frenchman to consider the period of the Second Empire and its major actors with any of the dispassionateness that scientific history requires. A half century had to go by, the Treaty of Versailles had to erase the Treaty of Frankfort, before even a little restraint could influence a thinking that had all along been distorted by too much rancour. The World War, with its bleeding, dripping hands, finally thrust the War of 1870 into history and removed it from the clash of partisan opinion. Then at last it became possible to view Napoleon III and his reign with the detachment which alone enables the historian to see the true meaning of things that are no more.

The Second Empire was a most extraordinary experiment in revival and imitation. Napoleon III was a more or less genuine nephew of the Corsican. But he was closer to the first Napoleon in spirit than he was in family relationship. As a disciple smitten with admiring wonder, Napoleon III tried, during all the ascending period of his curve, to make that curve coincide exactly with the orbit followed by the victor of Austerlitz. The 2nd of December was, or could be supposed to be, the 18th of Brumaire. The Presidency tried to suggest the Consulate. Napoleon III also had his war with Italy. But at this point the parallelism which he had sought so deliberately got control of him and strangled him. The war in Mexico was the war in Spain, the war with Prussia was the war with Russia. Sedan was Waterloo. Contemporaries could hardly perceive such relationships in the beginning. Napoleon III and Persigny were the only ones to be more or less instinctively conscious of it. Changed times and exteriors, changed people, timbered the Second

604

Empire with sentiments, interests, theories, facts, which were original and which the First had not known.

Louis Napoleon had in his favor the same extraordinary luck that did so much for Napoleon Bonaparte. He went as far as the latter went. Then his luck changed. Nothing any longer seemed to work—which was a way of saying that the mistakes that had been committed during the early period of the reign combined into one mass of influences to overwhelm it in its latter days.

When he set out to restore the Empire the son of Hortense was thinking not merely of finding a crown for himself and good places in life for the hungry and eager camarilla about him. He also wanted to wipe out the defeat that revolutionary and imperial France had suffered at Waterloo. He wanted to rebuild Europe according to the desires or interests of the peoples, not according to the desires or interests of the kings. That was no mean outlook. It had scope and it had its nobility. It was in accord with the general drift of feeling in France. Napoleon III had some success at first. If he failed in the end it was for a complex of reasons that are not all attributable to him, that depend partly on circumstances and partly on the qualities of the people with whom he had to deal. His basic mistake comes down to the fact that he was not able to make the right choices of assistants at the right times in either his domestic or his foreign policy.

Bonaparte issued from the 18th of Brumaire with his hands unsoiled. Napoleon III won his dictatorship by a bloody act of force. This was less his fault than the fault of Morny, but he had to bear the responsibility for it. After such a *coup d'état* no way was left open except arbitrary rule. In a country like France, situated in a modern world, a system so dictatorial had little chance of lasting. Sooner or later the turn towards liberty had to be taken. Memories of the 2nd of December and the whole chain of people and habits that the 2nd of December dragged along in its wake prevented the Empire from taking that turn at the right moment, the moment, that is, when the imperial system was still strong and brilliant and when concessions that it wanted to make and eventually had to make could be made without seeming to be conquests wrenched from a tottering dynasty.

In the regard of Europe, however set the Emperor may have been on his principle of nationalities, he showed backslidings in plenty

towards the traditional policy of France—a wise and sound policy—
of maintaining a balance of power in Europe and of protecting the
independence of small states. Each of the two policies had plenty in
its favor. Napoleon III should have adopted the one or the other
frankly. The attempt to combine them gave rise to an altogether
incoherent, an altogether chaotic diplomacy. Prosecuted in the deepest dark with sudden, startling emergencies, Napoleon III's hybrid
policy aroused mistrust and hostility in other countries and brought
France to a humiliation that had had no parallel since the Hundred
Years' War.

Too many ideas were stirring around in the head of the second
Emperor. They were noble, broadminded ideas most often, but the
attempt to reconcile them the one with the other raised unsolvable
problems. How could France, how could the other countries, long
retain faith in this juggler of antimonies? He called himself a child
of the Revolution but also a child of the Church. He wanted peace
but he also wanted France to have her "natural" frontiers. He stood
forth as the mandatory of the people but he insisted on keeping
absolute authority. He was well aware of these incompatibilities.
Since he could not harmonize them, he disguised them, compromised, played for time.

From the point of view of politics pure and simple, the reign of
Napoleon III could only look like a reign of uncertainty and compromise. It was based on principles that sooner or later it had to
repudiate or else ignore: peace, the Church, the alliance with England, the army. He abandoned all these foundations one after the
other, fighting a series of needless wars, sacrificing the Papacy to
Italian unity, flouting English good will, letting his military establishment go to rack and ruin. What wonder then that he was un-
steady on his legs and finally fell? Governments can have no ethical
principles that are very definite. They must have practical principles and they must adhere to them on peril of their lives.

There were fields in which Napoleon III's ideas were clearer and
more coherent and in which they yielded indisputably happy results—the economic and social fields, for instance. Napoleon III was
an out-and-out urbanist. He rioted in public works, demolishing
and rebuilding cities and towns to adapt them to modern needs. He
invented credit in its modern form and therefore made wealth more
flexible and increased it. He tried to increase production by increas-

ing mechanization, meantime lowering the cost of living by free trade. Much of his thought was devoted to the poorer classes. He favored raises in wages and better laboring conditions. He increased as far as he could the numbers of institutions relating to relief and involving group activities.

This phase of his life makes him a great prince, one of the most constructive that have ruled in Europe. In very truth he was the first modern monarch, applying his power to progress. One may safely say that France has never known such contented years. At its high point, around 1860, the Second Empire took the form of a nationalism that had a social outlook, without bearing any resemblance to what is commonly known today as a totalitarian system. Private property was solidly established. Taxes were low. Power favored concentrations of capital but always kept a practical and intelligent eye on the interests of the world of labor.

These are not the only merits of the Second Empire. It rescued the country from the disorderly demagogueries of 1848. It established peace in the field of religion, restoring the Church to a prestige which it had never enjoyed since the heyday of the old monarchy. During the Second Empire France again, over a period of ten years, held leadership in Europe. From the treaty of Paris down to Sadowa France was the preponderant influence in European affairs.

This enviable and in fact envied position Napoleon III owed to the alliance with England and the Crimean War. The latter was too costly an enterprise, but in the light of its consequences it could be justified. The real mistakes came afterwards. The war in Italy upset French policy and drove it out of the world of realities into the world of ideologies. It seems, to be sure, that considering Napoleon III's past and the balance of the various currents of opinion in France, the Italian war was really unavoidable; but in that case it could have been better utilized by adopting a clear-cut attitude at the very beginning and by foreseeing the consequences and accepting them. By conspiring with Cavour, by making promises he could not keep, by allowing the Roman Question to develop into an incurable cancer, the Emperor lost the Italians, the Pope and his Catholics to boot. To be sure he got Nice and Savoy, but that very fact tended to intensify his dependence on his interests in Italy, which thereafter was to become one of his main preoccupations and in almost every crisis to cloud his judgment.

Mexico was a deplorable adventure from first to last. Even had it proved successful it could have ended in no real or considerable profit to France. Possibly too much stress has been laid upon the Mexican blunder. The expedition, taken in its accurate proportions, was very small business. Its worst effects lay in its weakening of the Empire's prestige in public opinion at home. Whatever may have been said on the point, Mexico had nothing to do with the Empire's fatal inactivity during the Austro-Prussian War of 1866.

His policy towards that conflict was the capital and fatal mistake of Napoleon III. He had two courses open to him: either he could have allowed Germany to achieve her national unity around a nucleus, Prussia—and this would have been wholly in line with the nationality principle of which he was the outstanding promoter; or he could have resisted German unification and sided with Austria in order not to have too powerful a rival on his Rhine flank. Once again he proved unable to make his choice. Bismarck stood ready to talk business. Instead of talking business Napoleon III ran off and hid in the clouds, so allowing a crisis to develop for which he had not in the least prepared the country. Physically ill, his mental energy greatly impaired, he allowed himself to drift along on the surface of events. He looked on while Bismarck crushed Austria. Then when the Chancellor no longer feared him, he pressed annoying demands for compensations at the expense of small and friendly countries. Very little was left to French prestige after that.

With the danger from Prussia growing Napoleon III really tried to reorganize his army; but even when he still had the power to do so, he failed to force his will upon an inferior parliament. Then when he had a disorganized army, no generals and no allies at all, he joined in the public clamor instead of moderating it and so walked blindly into the trap that Bismarck had set for him.

When he was conquered, overwhelmed by a frightful disaster, he did his country one last bad turn and the worst, the one that was most damaging to the country's future. When he handed his sword to the King of Prussia at Sedan he could have made peace. Bismarck offered him peace, and the terms he would have insisted on would have been much less onerous than the terms that were to be forced five months later upon the Government of National Defense.

At that moment Napoleon III should have sacrificed his name

and his dynastic pride to his country's interests. He preferred to step down before the Regency, knowing well that the Regency could not last a week. Having led France into the quagmire, he should have tried to extricate her at the least possible cost. He would certainly have been overthrown afterwards, but France would not have been so badly cut up—she would not have borne him such a bitter grudge for so long a time.

That Napoleon III had his faults cannot therefore be denied. They are many and great. To be sure he was a man of his time and many errors, many blind-spots, that most people of his time had he was bound to have. He simply threw them into relief by his acts, giving them force and conspicuous expression.

His worst stroke of bad luck, if we except the too early collapse of his physical health, was the fact that in his counsel as well as in the army he happened to encounter few if any exceptional abilities, men who were capable of really working with him and preventing him from adopting the unwise course when he was headed in a wrong direction. He was able to work out his counterfeit of the other Empire only on a very secondary plane in this respect. Genius there was none and even talent was scarce. Brains were small, characters very ordinary. Morny was the best of them all, but he could hardly be compared with his grandfather, Talleyrand. Rouher was an efficient administrator, but what was he beside a Cambacérès? Who was Napoleon III's Fouché? Certainly not Maupas, certainly not Pietri. Consider Bonaparte's marshals—Murat, Ney, Lannes, Davout, Masséna, Berthier; and then balance them against the captains of the Second Empire—the best that can be found: Saint-Arnaud, Canrobert, Niel, MacMahon! The only real general that Napoleon III met was probably Pélissier—and Pélissier vanished from the scene in 1864.

The most interesting, at bottom, of all the men of the period, the man who seems really superior in spite of weaknesses and deficiencies, is always Napoleon III himself. Where others saw the big adventure he saw the mission, and he had a blind faith in the mission, in the need of it, in the good it would do. That lifts him at the outset somewhat above the mere political gambler who plays a risky game with his eye strictly on the stakes. He none the less staked his throne too far and trusted too much in his star. He can be condemned since he did not win—success is the one criterion for judging a statesman. But his distinctiveness as a "reform sovereign" cannot be disputed. The liberal Empire, the last product of his system, was an experiment that is worthy of the closest attention and respect. This death-bed marriage of dictatorship and liberty might have proved satisfactory to France over a long period of time. It might have proved more satisfactory, perhaps, than the limited monarchy of Louis Philippe, though this last was certainly preferable on a number of other grounds, on the grounds, namely, that it had a principle and a tradition and was basically pacific and did not like adventures. The liberal Empire, as Napoleon III finally worked it out, was well suited to a people that has its liking for strong government but at the same time wants a certain amount of elbow-room—the room required, for instance, for talking, which in France is a real need though no one pays any great attention to what is said. The liberal Empire would have been not a military dictatorship but a people's rights monarchy, pretty to look at and possessing flexible institutions that could readily have been improved.

From a broader point of view one can only be impressed with the important rôle that Napoleon III played in rearing the structure of modern Europe. Whether or not his policies were wholly to the interests of France, he contributed very substantially to the rise of two of the great modern nations—Germany and Italy. He favored the one, he actively helped the other. He dreamed of freeing Poland and had his reign lasted a little longer he would probably some day have gone to war in her behalf. Italy owes Napoleon III quite as much as she owes Victor Emmanuel or Cavour. She has done her best to forget the debt, but had it not been for the second Emperor Italy would have had to suffer a much longer time before winning her rightful place in our present-day world.

Rarely were Napoleon III's ideas selfish or narrowminded, and the fact is probably due to his early life and education. Quite as often as not he reasoned less like the head of a particular state than like a citizen of a larger Europe.

"In this whole business," grumbled Thiers in 1866, "I can see that now we are Italians and now we are Germans. I cannot see that we are ever Frenchmen."

The rebuke was not without foundation. Napoleon III was deeply concerned with the interests of the French nation, but he thought they could be reconciled with the broader interests of the

Continent. He thought the day would come when a higher court of reference would pass on differences between peoples and end wars. To hasten the advent of that rational era he tried to instill Europe with the habit of going into conference.

As the years roll by this particular significance of the career of Napoleon III will be better and better appreciated. It is within the range of possibility that, when the day of a truly impartial history dawns, he may be ranked higher, much higher, than his contemporary, Bismarck. Bismarck was just a great German. He succeeded on a national plane but by brutally destroying the European spirit.

"There's no Europe left now," said Beust after Sedan.

Beust was more than right. Europe, Europe, that is, as a complex of common ways of feeling, thinking and doing, of mutual goodwill and understanding, of friendship in a word, came to an end in 1870. The sense of oneness among the European countries had been latent but effective. After Bismarck those countries were to shut themselves up inside aggressive nationalisms that were to lead to the murderous follies of 1914. From them one may wonder whether Western civilization is ever to rise again.

Now through mistakes of his own, now through bad luck, the bearing of which upon his career should never be minimized, Napoleon III may not have brought his strictly French task to full completion—though even in this regard he can claim very considerable merits. He never ceased to be a great European. History will recognize this fact, the history, that is, which recovers the lines that endure from the flux of varying fact. History undoubtedly will look at Napoleon III as one of the forerunners, one of those forerunners whom fate betrays in their attempt to realize great conceptions.

Bibliography

ADAM (Mme J.): *Le roman de mon enfance et de ma jeunesse.*
—— *Mes souvenirs et nos idées avant 70.*
ALLISON: *Monsieur Thiers.*
AMBÈS (Baron d'): *Mémoires.*
AMIGUÈS (J.): *L'homme de Sedan et les hommes de Septembre.*
ANDLAU (Colonel d'): *Metz.*
ANDLER (Ch.): *Le prince de Bismarck.*
AUGER (Docteur): *Notes de guerre.*
ANTIOCHE (Comte d'): *Vie du général Changarnier.*
ARAGO (E.): *L'Hôtel de Ville au 4 septembre et pendant le siège.*
Archives diplomatiques relatives à la guerre de 1870.
ARGYLL (Duke of): *Autobiography and Memoirs.*
ARISTE (P. d'): *La vie et le monde du Boulevard (1830-1870).*
ARMAILLÉ (Comtesse d'): *Quand on savait vivre heureux (1830-1868).*
ARNAUD (René): *La Deuxième République et le Second Empire.*
ASHLEY (E.): *The Life of Viscount Palmerston.*
AURIANT: *Les lionnes du Second Empire.*
AZEGLIO (Massimo d'): *Lettere inedite.*

BABAUD-LARIBIÈRE: *Histoire de l'Assemblée nationale constituante.*
BAC (Ferdinand): *Intimités du Second Empire.*
BAINVILLE (J.): *Histoire de trois générations.*
BAMBERG: *Geschichte des Zweiten Kaiserreichs.*
BAPST (G.): *Le maréchal Canrobert.*
BARAIL: See Du Barail.
BARANTE (P. de): *Souvenirs.*
BAROCHE (Mme J.): *Le Second Empire. Notes et souvenirs.*
BARRAL (Comte E. de): *Les Zouaves pontificaux (1860-1870).*
BARTHEZ (E.): *La Famille impériale à Saint-Cloud et à Biarritz.*
BASTIDE (J.): *La République française et l'Italie.*
BAUNARD (Mgr.): *Vie du Cardinal Pie.*
BAZAINE (Maréchal): *L'armée du Rhin.*
BAZANCOURT (Baron de): *Campagne d'Italie.*
BEAUMONT-VASSY: *Histoire intime du Second Empire.*
BELLESSORT (A.): *La Société française sous Napoléon III.*
BENEDETTI: *Ma mission en Prusse.*
—— *Essais diplomatiques . . . Ma mission à Ems.*
BERKELEY: *On the French and Prussian War.*

BERNSTORFF (Von): *Bernstorff Papers.*
BERSEZIO: *Il regno di Vittorio-Emmanuele.*
BERTAUT (J.): *Les belles nuits de Paris.*
—— *1848 et la Seconde République.*
BLED (V. du): *La Société française depuis cent ans.*
—— *Quelques salons du Second Empire.*
BEUST (Comte de): *Mémoires.*
BEYENS (Baron): *Le Second Empire.*
BIANCHI (N.): *La politique du comte de Cavour de 1852 à 1861.*
BICKNELL (Miss A. L.): *Life in the Tuileries.*
BIGOT (L.): *Jules Favre, avocat et homme politique.*
BISMARCK: *Correspondance.*
—— *Mémoires et entretiens.*
—— *Lettres à sa femme pendant la guerre de 1870.*
BLANC ET CERTON: *Œuvre parlementaire du comte de Cavour.*
BLANC (Louis): *Histoire de dix ans.*
—— *Histoire de la révolution de 1848.*
BOCHER (Ch.): *Lettres de Crimée.*
BONAPARTE (Prince Jérôme-Napoléon): *Les alliances de l'Empire en 1869-1870.*
BORDEAUX (Henry): *Le cœur de la reine Hortense.*
BOSQUET (Maréchal): *Correspondance.*
BOSCHOT (A.): *Berlioz.*
BOULENGER (M.): *Le duc de Morny.*
BOURGEOIS (E.): *Manuel historique de politique étrangère.*
BROGLIE (Duc de): *Souvenirs—1781-1870.*
BULLE (G.): *Geschichte des Zweiten Kaiserreichs.*

CAMP (M. du): *Souvenirs littéraires.*
CARRETTE (Mme): *Souvenirs intimes de la cour des Tuileries.*
CASSAGNAC (Granier de): *Souvenirs du Second Empire.*
CASTELLANE (Maréchal de): *Journal.*
CASTELNAU (Général): *Journal.*
CASTILLE (H.): *Histoire de la Révolution de 1848.*
—— *Portraits politiques et historiques.*
CAUSSIDIÈRE: *Mémoires.*
CAVOUR (Comte de): *Lettere edite et inedite.*
CHAMBRIER (J. de): *La cour et la société du Second Empire.*
CHARLES-ROUX (F.): *Alexandre II, Gortchakoff et Napoléon III.*
CHARLETY (S.): *Histoire du Saint-Simonisme.*
CHESNELONG (Ch.): *Les derniers jours de l'Empire et le gouvernement de M. Thiers.*
CIRCOURT (A. de): *Souvenirs d'une mission à Berlin.*
CLARETIE (J.): *Histoire de la révolution de 1870.*
CLERMONT ET BOURGEOIS: *Rome et Napoléon III.*
CORTI (Comte): *Maximilien and Charlotte in Mexico.*

DARIMON: *Histoire d'un parti. Les Cinq sous l'Empire.*
—— *L'opposition libérale sous l'Empire.*
DAUDET (A.): *Le Nabab.*
—— *Trente ans de Paris.*
DAUDET (Lucien A.): *L'Inconnue (L'Impératrice Eugénie).*
DEBIDOUR (A.): *Histoire diplomatique de l'Europe.*
—— *L'Eglise et l'Etat en France depuis 1789.*
DELBRÜCK (H.): *Der Ursprung des Krieges.*
DELESCLUZE: *Souvenirs de soixante années.*
DELORD (T.): *Histoire du Second Empire.*
DENIS (E.): *La fondation de l'Empire allemand 1852-1871.*
DENIS (S.): *Histoire Contemporaine. La chute de l'Empire, le gouverne-
    ment de la Défense nationale. . . .*
DÉROULÈDE (P.): *Feuilles de route.*
DOUDAN: *Correspondance.*
DREYFUS (Robert): *M. Thiers contre l'Empire.*
DU BARAIL (Général): *Mes Souvenirs.*
DU CASSE (Baron): *Les dessous du coup d'Etat.*
DUCHATEL (A.): *La guerre de 1870-1871. Causes et responsabilités.*
DUCROT (Général): *Vie et correspondance.*
—— *La journée de Sedan.*
DUGUÉ DE LA FAUCONNERIE: *Souvenirs d'un vieil homme.*
DUMAS (Alexandre): *Mémoires.*
DUNHAM (A. L.): *The Anglo-French Treaty of Commerce.*
DURRIEU (X.): *Le coup d'Etat de Louis Bonaparte.*
DURUY (Victor): *Souvenirs.*

EBELING (Ad.): *Napoléon III. und sein Hof.*
EMERIT (Marcel): *Lettres de Napoléon III à Madame Cornu.*
Enquête parlementaire sur les événements de 1870.
Enquête parlementaire sur les causes de l'insurrection du 18 mars.
EVANS (Docteur T. W.): *Memoirs.*

FALLOUX (Comte de): *Mémoires.*
FAUCHER (L.): *Correspondance.*
FAVEROT DE KERBRECH (Général): *La guerre contre l'Allemagne.*
FAVRE (J.): *Discours.*
FAY (C. A.): *Souvenirs de la guerre de Crimée.*
—— *Journal de l'armée du Rhin.*
FEUILLET (Octave): *Correspondance.*
FEUILLET (Mme O.): *Souvenirs.*
FILON (Augustin): *Souvenirs sur l'impératrice Eugénie.*
—— *Le Prince impérial.*
—— *Mérimée et ses amis.*
FLAUBERT (G.): *Correspondance.*
FLEURY (Comte): *Souvenirs.*
FLEURY ET SONOLET: *La Société du Second Empire.*

FRASER (Sir W. A.): *My Recollections.*
FREYCINET (Ch. de): *Souvenirs.*

GABRIAC (Marquis de): *Souvenirs diplomatiques de Russie et d'Alle-magne.*
GAMBETTA (Léon): *Discours.*
GARIBALDI: *Autobiographie.*
GAULOT (Paul): *La vérité sur l'expédition du Mexique.*
GHEUSI (P. B.): *Gambetta par Gambetta (Correspondance de famille).*
GIRARD (Georges): *Vie et souvenirs du général Castelnau.*
GIRARDIN (E. de): *Questions de mon temps.*
GIRAUDEAU (F.): *Napoléon III intime.*
GONCOURT (E. & J. de): *Journal.*
GOURDON (E.): *Histoire du Congrès de Paris.*
GOYAU (Georges): *L'idée de patrie et l'humanitarisme.*
GRABINSKI: *Le comte Arese, un ami de Napoléon III.*
GRAMONT (Duc de): *La France et la Prusse avant 1870.*
GREARD (O.): *Prévost-Paradol.*
GREVILLE (H.): *Memoirs.*
GUEDALLA (P.): *Le Second Empire.*
GUERIOT (P.): *Napoléon III.*
GUIZOT: *Lettres à sa famille et à ses amis.*

HALÉVY (Daniel): *La fin des Notables.*
HALÉVY (Ludovic): *Carnets.*
HAMEL (Ernest): *Histoire de la IIᵉ République.*
HANOTAUX (Gabriel): *Histoire de la France contemporaine.*
HARCOURT (R. d'): *Les quatre ministères de M. Drouyn de Lhuys.*
HAUSSMANN (Baron): *Mémoires.*
HAUTERIVE (Ernest d'): *Correspondance inédite de Napoléon III et du prince Napoléon.*
HAUTPOUL (A. d'): *Mémoires.*
HÉRISSON (D'): *Journal d'un officier d'ordonnance.*
—— *Le Prince impérial.*
HOUSSAYE (A.): *Souvenirs de jeunesse.*
HÜBNER (Comte): *Neuf ans de souvenirs.*
HUGO (Victor): *Choses Vues.*
—— *Histoire d'un crime.*
—— *Napoléon le Petit.*
—— *Pendant l'exil.*

IDEVILLE (H. d'): *Journal d'un diplomate en Italie (1859-1862).*
IMPÉRATRICE FREDERIC: *Lettres.*

JÉROME (Roi): *Mémoires.*
JERROLD (Blanchard): *Life of Napoleon III.*
JOLLIVET (G.): *Souvenirs de la vie de plaisir sous le Second Empire.*

KERRY (Earl of): *The Secret of the Coup d'Etat.*

KING (Bolton): *Mazzini.*

KINGLAKE (A. W.): *The Invasion of the Crimea.*

KOSSUTH: *Souvenirs et écrits de mon exil.*

LA CHAPELLE (Comte de): *Le livre de l'Empereur.*
—— *Œuvres posthumes de Napoléon III.*

LA FERRONAYS (Marquis de): *Mémoires.*

LAGRANGE (F.): *Vie de Mgr Dupanloup.*

LA GORCE (P. de): *Histoire de la Deuxième République française.*
—— *Histoire du Second Empire.*
—— *Napoléon III et sa politique.*
—— *Au temps du Second Empire.*

LA MARMORA (Général): *Un peu plus de lumière sur les événements de 1866.*

LAMORICIÈRE (Général de): *Mémoires.*

LA MOSKOWA (Général prince de): *Notes intimes sur la guerre de 1870.*

LA MOTTEROUGE (Général de): *Souvenirs et campagnes.*

LA RIVE (W. de): *Le comte de Cavour—Récits et souvenirs.*

LARONZE (G.): *Le Baron Haussmann.*

LEBEY (André): *Louis-Napoléon Bonaparte et le ministère Odilon Barrot.*

LEBRUN (Général): *Souvenirs militaires (1866-1870). Mes missions à Vienne et en Belgique.*

LECANUET (R. P.): *Montalembert, d'après son journal et sa correspondance.*

LEDRU-ROLLIN: *Discours politiques et écrits divers.*

LEFEVRE: *L'intervention française au Mexique.*

LEGGE: *Empress Eugénie.*

LENZ (M.): *Geschichte Bismarcks.*

LEONARDON (H.): *Prim et la candidature Hohenzollern.*

LEROY (A.): *George Sand et ses amis.*

LESSEPS (F. de): *Souvenirs de quarante ans.*

LEVASSEUR: *La population française.*

LITTRÉ: *Politique et positivisme.*

LOCKROY (Ed.): *Au hasard de la vie.*

LOFTUS (Lord): *Diplomatic Reminiscences.*

LOLIÉE (F.): *Femmes du Second Empire.*

LUDWIG (Emil): *Bismarck.*

MACMAHON (Maréchal de): *Mémoires.*

MAGEN (H.): *Histoire de la Terreur bonapartiste.*
—— *Histoire du Second Empire (1848-1870).*

MALAKOFF (Duchesse de): *Lettres inédites.*

MALMESBURY (Earl of): *Memoirs of an ex-Minister.*

MALO (Henri): *Thiers.*

MARCKS (E.): *Kaiser Wilhelm I.*

MARX (Karl): *Der Burgerkrieg in Frankreich.*

MARX (Karl): *Die Klassenkämpfe in Frankreich.*
MARTIMPREY (Général de): *Correspondance inédite.*
MARTIN (Th.): *The Life of the Prince Corsort.*
MASSA (Marquis de): *Souvenirs et impressions.*
MASSARI: *Vita di Vittorio-Emmanuele.*
—— *Il conte Cavour.*
MASUYER (Valérie): *Mémoires.*
MATTER (P.): *Bismarck et son temps.*
MAUDUIT (Capitaine de): *La révolution militaire du 2 décembre.*
MAUPAS (Comte de): *Mémoires.*
MAYER (P.): *Histoire du Deux Décembre.*
MAZADE (Ch. de): *Portraits d'histoire morale et politique du temps.*
MAXWELL (Sir Herbert): *Life of the 4th Earl of Clarendon.*
MELUN (Comte A. de): *Correspondance inédite.*
MÉRIMÉE (Prosper): *Lettres à Panizzi.*
—— *Lettres à une inconnue.*
—— *Lettres à la comtesse de Montijo.*
METTERNICH (Prince de): *Mémoires et papiers.*
METTERNICH (Princesse de): *Souvenirs (1859-1871).*
MEYER (Arthur): *Ce que je peux dire.*
—— *Ce que mes yeux ont vu.*
MONTS (Général von): *La captivité de Napoléon III en Allemagne.*
MORAIN (J.): *La politique ecclésiastique du Second Empire.*
—— *Baroche.*
MORNY (Duc de): *Mon ambassade en Russie.*
MOUY (Comte Ch. de): *Souvenirs, causeries d'un diplomate.*
MURET (P.): *Ollivier et le duc de Gramont.*

NADAR: *Quand j'étais photographe.*
NAPOLÉON III: *Œuvres.*
NIGRA (Comte): *Souvenirs diplomatiques.*
NORMANBY (Marquis of): *Une année de révolution.*

OLLIVIER (Emile): *L'Empire libéral.*
ONCKEN (W.): *Die Rheinpolitik des Kaisers Napoleon III.*
Origines diplomatiques de la guerre de 1870-71. Documents publiés par le ministère des Affaires étrangères.

PALAT (Général): *Bazaine et nos désastres.*
PAILLERON (Mme M. L.): *Ecrivains du Second Empire.*
PALÉOLOGUE (Maurice): *Un grand réaliste: Cavour.*
—— *Entretiens avec l'impératrice Eugénie.*
PALIKAO (Général Montauban-): *Un ministère de la guerre de 24 jours.*
Papiers et correspondance de la Famille impériale.
PELLETAN (C.): *L'opinion républicaine à la fin de l'Empire.*
PERSIGNY (Duc de): *Mémoires.*
PICARD (Colonel): *Sedan.*

PINARD: *Mon Journal.*
PINGAUD (A.): *Un projet d'alliance Franco-Russe.*
POUJADE (E.): *La diplomatie du Second Empire et celle du 4 septembre.*
POUMIÈS DE LA SIBOUTIE: *Souvenirs d'un Parisien (1789-1863).*
PRAVIEL (A.): *L'impératrice Charlotte.*
PRÉVOST-PARADOL: *Les élections de 1863-1864.*
PROUDHON: *Correspondance.*

QUENTIN-BAUCHART: *Etudes et Souvenirs sur la IIe République et le Second Empire.*
QUINET (Edgar): *Lettres d'exil.*

RAMBAUD: *Histoire de la Russie.*
RANC (A.): *Souvenirs: correspondance (1831-1908).*
RANDON (Maréchal): *Mémoires.*
RATAZZI: *Ratazzi et son temps.*
RECLUS (Maurice): *Jules Favre.*
—— *Monsieur Thiers.*
—— *Ernest Picard.*
—— *Emile de Girardin.*
REINACH-FOUSSEMAGNE (Comtesse de): *Charlotte de Belgique, impératrice du Mexique.*
REISET (Vicomte de): *Mes souvenirs.*
RICARD (Général de): *Autour des Bonaparte.*
RICASOLI: *Lettere e documenti del barone Ricasoli.*
ROCHEFORT (Henri): *Les aventures de ma vie.*
—— *La Lanterne.*
ROON (Général von): *Mémoires.*
ROTHAN: *L'Europe et l'avènement du Second Empire.*
—— *Napoléon III et l'Italie.*
—— *La politique française en 1866.*
—— *L'Allemagne et l'Italie.*
—— *Souvenirs diplomatiques de 1870.*
ROUSSET (C.): *La guerre de Crimée.*

SAINT-AMAND (I. de): *Louis-Napoléon et Mlle de Montijo.*
—— *Napoléon III et sa cour.*
SAINT-ARNAUD (Maréchal de): *Correspondance.*
SALOMON (H.): *L'ambassade du prince de Metternich.*
—— *L'incident Hohenzollern.*
SCHOELCHER: *Le Gouvernement de Décembre.*
SCHEURER-KESTNER: *Souvenirs de jeunesse.*
SCHOLL (A.): *L'esprit du boulevard.*
SCHULTZE (W.): *Die Thronkandidatur Hohenzollern.*
SEIGNOBOS (Ch.): *La révolution de 1848 et le Second Empire.*
—— *La Révolution de 1848.*
—— *Le Second Empire.*
—— *Le déclin de l'Empire et l'établissement de la Troisième République.*

SOREL (Albert): *Lectures historiques.*
—— *Essais d'histoire et de critique.*
—— *Histoire diplomatique de la guerre de 1870.*
SPULLER (E.): *Histoire parlementaire de la Seconde République.*
STANLEY: *Twenty Years at Court 1842-1862.*
STEED (Wickham): *Mémoires.*
STEEFEL (L. D.): *The Schleswig Holstein Question.*
STEFANE-POL: *La jeunesse de Napoléon III.*
STEIN (L. von): *Geschichte der Socialen Bewegung in Frankreich.*
STODDART: *Life of Empress Eugénie.*
SYBEL (Von): *Die Begründung des deutschen Reichs.*

TARGÉ (A.): *Souvenirs d'avant 1870.*
TASCHER DE LA PAGERIE (Comtesse): *Mon séjour aux Tuileries.*
TCHERNOFF (J.): *Le parti républicain au coup d'Etat et sous le Second Empire.*
—— *Histoire des associations et des sociétés secrètes sous la IIᵉ République.*
TENOT (E.): *La province en décembre 1851.*
—— *Paris, en décembre 1851.*
THAYER (W. R.): *Three Peace Congresses of the 19th Century.*
THIEBAUT (Marcel): *Edmond About.*
THIERS (A.): *Notes et Souvenirs.*
—— *Discours parlementaires.*
THIRRIA (H.): *Napoléon III avant l'Empire.*
THOMAS (A.): *Le Second Empire.*
THOUVENEL (L.): *Nicolas Iᵉʳ et Napoléon III (1852-1854).*
—— *Le secret de l'Empereur.*
TOCQUEVILLE (A. de): *Nouvelle correspondance.*
TODLEBEN (Général): *Défense de Sébastopol.*
TROCHU (Général): *L'armée française en 1867.*
—— *Mémoires.*

VANDAM: *Undercurrents of the Second Empire.*
VANEL (G.): *Le Second Empire.*
VERLY (A.): *Les étapes douloureuses.*
VERMOREL: *Les hommes de 1851.*
VERON (Docteur): *Mémoires d'un bourgeois de Paris.*
—— *Nouveaux mémoires d'un bourgeois de Paris.*
VEUILLOT (L.): *Correspondance.*
—— *Les odeurs de Paris.*
VICTORIA (Reine): *Journal—Lettres.*
VIEL-CASTEL (Comte H. de): *Mémoires sur le règne de Napoléon III.*
VILBORT (J.): *L'œuvre de M. de Bismarck.*
VILLEMESSANT: *Mémoires d'un journaliste.*
VITU (Aug.): *Les réunions électorales de Paris, mai 1869.*
VITZTHUM: *St Petersburg und London.*

WALPOLE (Sir Spencer): *The Life of Lord John Russell.*
WEILL (G.): *Histoire du mouvement social en France (1852-1924).*
—— *Histoire du parti républicain en France (1814-1870).*
WELLESLEY: *The Paris Embassy.*
WELSCHINGER (H.): *La guerre de 1870, causes et responsabilités.*
WEST (Sir A.): *Recollections (1832-1886).*
WIMPFFEN (Général): *Souvenirs et campagnes.*
—— *Sedan.*

Index